D1336534

READER'S DIGEST

Microwave
Cookbook

READER'S DIGEST

Microwave Cookbook

![DK]

DORLING KINDERSLEY · LONDON

A DORLING KINDERSLEY BOOK

Managing Editor	Jeni Wright
Art Editors	Sally Powell Sue Storey
Designer	Sally Hibbard
Editors	Norma MacMillan Felicity Jackson
Photographers	Clive Streeter Karl Adamson
Home Economists	Lyn Rutherford Elizabeth Wolf-Cohen
Recipe Development	Joyce Kenneally Rebecca Marshall
Editorial Director	Amy Carroll
Art Director	Denise Brown

First published in Great Britain in 1990 by Dorling Kindersley Limited, 9 Henrietta Street, Covent Garden, London WC2E 8PS.

Copyright © 1990 by Dorling Kindersley Limited and The Hearst Corporation

All rights reserved. No part of this book may be reproduced, stored in a retrieval system, or transmitted in any form or by any means, electronic, electrostatic, magnetic tape, mechanical, photocopying, recording or otherwise without prior permission in writing from Dorling Kindersley Limited.

® READER'S DIGEST is a registered trade mark of The Reader's Digest Association Incorporated of Pleasantville, New York, NY, USA.

British Library Cataloguing-in-Publication Data

Reader's digest microwave cookbook.
1. Food: Dishes prepared using
microwave ovens – Recipes

I. Title
641.5882

ISBN 0-86318-482-0

Typeset by Tradespools Ltd, Frome, Somerset
Reproduced by Colourscan, Singapore
Printed in Great Britain
by Jarrolds, Norwich

Foreword

A new kind of cooking has taken us by storm. In busy households all across the country, and in many other parts of the world as well, the microwave oven is becoming the cooking appliance of choice. That's what this book is all about. Whether you are a novice microwave cook or an experienced one, The READER'S DIGEST Microwave Cookbook is the book you can turn to for everything you'll need to know. It's full of delicious step-by-step recipes, cooking tips, techniques and useful charts, plus a wealth of easy-to-understand information about microwave ovens and cooking methods, all to guarantee perfect food every time you cook.

A beautiful full-colour 'picture book' index of all the recipes is found at the beginning of the book, organised according to the time required for preparation and cooking. This makes recipe selection and meal planning even easier, because you can see exactly how the food will look and how long it will take before you make your selection.

Next, we show you step-by-step how to prepare the recipes. We illustrate the cooking techniques you will use, list the equipment needed and tell you exactly how long the recipe will take from start to finish.

We know you are interested in good nutrition and healthy-eating facts, so each recipe includes not only the calorie count, but a thorough nutritional analysis as well.

Menus are included to show how to combine recipes for everyday and special occasion meals, and a plan of action is included with each menu so you will know exactly what to prepare and when, and how much time will be needed.

All of the recipes in this book were developed and thoroughly tested in a wide variety of 600-, 650-, and 700-watt microwave ovens. Because time is of the essence, they have been made as simple as possible, and cookware has been kept to a minimum. We hope, through the pages of this colour-packed new cookbook, that you will discover what fun microwave cooking is — and that it is possible to produce almost everything a conventional oven does — only faster and better.

Contents

How to Use the Book

The **Reader's Digest Microwave Cookbook** contains everything today's cook needs to know to make eye-catching and delicious meals in the microwave for everyday and special occasions. The book is divided into three major sections – *Microwave Know-How, The Colour Index*, and *The Recipes* – with problem-solving *Questions and Answers* and an *Index* at the back. The recipe section also contains tips on preparing ingredients and ideas for serving and presentation, plus full-colour menus for entertaining.

Even if you are an experienced microwave cook, it is a good idea to read through *Microwave Know-How* first, as the information in this section clearly illustrates tried-and-tested microwave cooking techniques. Then browse through *The Colour Index* to choose those dishes that suit your schedule and meal plans. Finally, turn to the listed page in the appropriate chapter of *The Recipes* and follow step-by-step instructions and colour photographs for culinary success.

MICROWAVE KNOW-HOW
This introductory chapter illustrates the cookware and cooking techniques you need to turn out attractive and well-prepared food. Also included are cook's tips for using the microwave in conjunction with conventional cooking appliances, and for entertaining, as well as advice on taking care of your microwave.

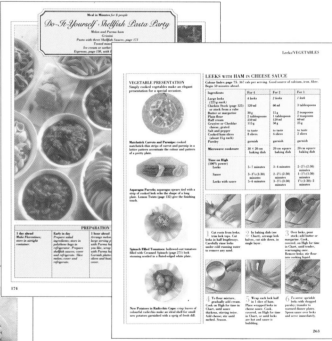

THE COLOUR INDEX
In this section you will find photographs of over 500 specially created recipes in menu order, organised according to the time required for preparation and cooking – under 30 minutes, 30–60 minutes, and over 1 hour. Captions describe the dishes in detail, inform you how many servings they make, and direct you to the pages where the recipes appear in the book.

THE RECIPES
Among over 600 triple-tested recipes are more than 170 key recipes and 1,100 step-by-step pictures. Where applicable, step-by-step recipes are written for 4, 2, and 1 servings. Every recipe is accompanied by a calorie count, and nutritional information based on criteria printed at the back of the book. You will also find explanations and illustrations throughout for preparation and serving techniques, including handling ingredients, types of equipment and garnishes. There is also a wide selection of menus for such special occasions as dinners, buffets and parties, each photographed in colour and accompanied by a preparation timetable.

Microwave Know-How

All About Microwave Ovens and Microwaving

Microwave ovens offer many choices, so you will be certain to find one just right for you. *Free-standing ovens* that sit on the worktop are the most popular. To save space, some models can be installed under a wall cupboard or built into a base unit. An *over-the-hob microwave oven* with built-in ventilation and light takes the place of a cooker hood. Another option, a built-in *double oven*, is an all-in-one unit that features an eye-level microwave oven above a gas or electric oven. A *combination microwave oven* can be used as a convection oven, a microwave oven, or with the two methods together. It's like having three ovens in one, and some even have a grill as well. Convection ovens are conventional thermal ovens, some of which have fans to circulate the hot air so they cook more quickly. Fan-assisted ovens also brown and crisp foods more quickly, when baking, roasting and grilling.

Microwave ovens are available in a variety of sizes. *Full-size ovens* (21–31 litres) are ideal for families or anyone who entertains a lot because they are roomy enough for large cookware and bulky foods. *Compact ovens* (20 litres or less) are perfect for cooking for one or two, or to use as a second or 'back-up' oven. *Combination ovens* are a space-saving type of worktop or built-in oven. They perform the functions of several appliances – a microwave oven, a conventional oven and often a grill, all in one.

MICROWAVE WATTAGE AND POWER

It is essential to know the wattage output of your oven. Oven wattages range from 500–780 watts. Higher wattage ovens (600–780) cook faster than lower wattage ovens (500–550 watts). The most popular oven wattage is 650, and all the recipes in this book have been developed for cooking in 600- to 700-watt ovens. With a lower wattage oven, food takes longer to cook and you need to increase cooking times.

Variable power levels let you adjust the cooking power to get better, more even results. This is accomplished by cycling the microwave power on and off at various intervals to achieve different percentages of full power. Models are available with High power only or with up to 10 power levels. Four or five levels are adequate to cook most foods.

All microwave ovens have automatic defrost, but a Defrost setting is useful as you may get a better result using manual defrost with some types of food.

MICROWAVE FEATURES

Microwaves are distributed in the oven in a variety of ways. An oven may have a wave stirrer, rotating antenna or turntable, all designed for even cooking of food. Some ovens have both a wave stirrer and a turntable; others feature a turntable that can be switched off or removed (portable spring-operated turntables are also available).

Electronic touch controls are more accurate than mechanical dial-type controls and are easier to use.

Automatic programmes eliminate guesswork and are particularly helpful to cooks new to microwaving. All that is necessary is to enter the food category, desired doneness and weight or amount. The oven then automatically selects the correct time and power levels to cook, defrost or reheat. Some models have sensors to monitor humidity, vapour or heat given off by food, and the oven uses this information to calculate precise cooking times.

'Push-button magic' can include pads marked with standard food items, an 'automatic cook' key and reheat sensors labelled 'fresh', 'frozen' or 'chilled' for no-guess warming up (although it is still essential to test food to see if it is piping hot before being served).

A temperature probe is another feature on some ovens; it works like a thermometer. The probe is inserted into the food and the desired temperature is set. When that temperature is reached, the oven turns off automatically.

MICROWAVE FOOD SAFETY

All microwave ovens are manufactured to the highest possible standards, and all food cooked or heated in them will be safe if manufacturers' instructions are followed. Food in a microwave can reach a temperature of up to 100°C and hold that temperature long enough to destroy food contaminant.

Microwave ovens have 'hot' and 'cold' spots; when instructions are given for stirring, turning, rotating, rearranging or otherwise moving food, and for standing, it is important to follow these instructions – to ensure that food is cooked. When reheating ready-prepared 'cook-chill' foods, these techniques should also be applied, and it is also essential to know the wattage output of your oven. If your oven has a low wattage output, food will take longer to reach its required temperature than in one with a higher wattage.

Some microwave ovens have turntables that help ensure even cooking of food

Temperature probe turns oven off when desired temperature is reached

HOW MICROWAVE OVENS WORK

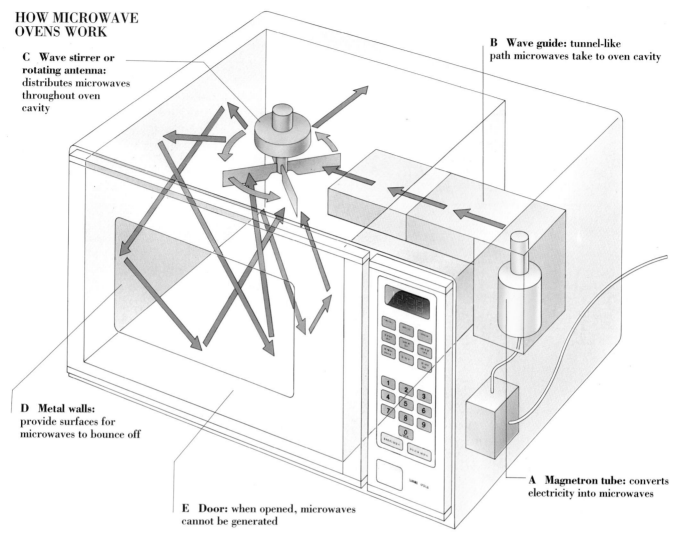

C Wave stirrer or rotating antenna: distributes microwaves throughout oven cavity

B Wave guide: tunnel-like path microwaves take to oven cavity

D Metal walls: provide surfaces for microwaves to bounce off

A Magnetron tube: converts electricity into microwaves

E Door: when opened, microwaves cannot be generated

Microwaves are high-frequency, electro-magnetic waves, similar to radio waves. When a microwave oven is turned on, microwaves are generated by the magnetron tube (A), which converts household electricity into microwaves. It's a little like having a miniature broadcasting station in your oven.

Microwaves travel from the magnetron through a tunnel-like wave guide (B) and enter the oven cavity through one or two openings at the top, bottom or sides. A wave stirrer or rotating antenna (C) distributes microwaves throughout the oven's cavity. Never operate an empty microwave; if food isn't present to absorb the microwaves, the oven may be damaged.

Because microwaves cannot penetrate metal, they bounce off the oven's metal walls (D) and penetrate the food from all directions to a depth of up to 4 cm. They do not cause any structural or chemical change in food molecules; they simply cause water, fat and sugar molecules in food to vibrate about $2\frac{1}{2}$ billion times per second, producing heat from friction. The centre of the food is cooked by transference of heat (conduction), as in conventional cooking.

When the oven is turned off, or the door (E) is opened, microwaves cannot be generated and none remain inside, just as when you turn off your radio the sound stops.

MICROWAVE TIMINGS

Most of the recipes in this book give a range of microwave cooking times, for instance '3–4 minutes', because of the variations in microwave wattage, cookware and density of food. To avoid overcooking, choose the shorter time, then check to see if food is done (page 26). Continue cooking for the longer cooking time, if necessary, then check again. Food should be thoroughly cooked through and piping hot right to the centre; stirring, turning and rotating are often necessary for food to be cooked properly – see Cooking Techniques on pages 24–25.

POWER LEVELS

High	100% power
Medium-High	70% power
Medium	50% power
Medium-Low	30% power
Low	10% power

Among manufacturers there is no standard language for power levels. The recipes in this book, however, all use the scale on the left.

If your microwave has different power settings, i.e. 100%, 80%, 60%, 40%, 20%, you will have to experiment.

Cookware and Utensils

Cookware and utensils specifically designed for use in the microwave oven are widely available. For the most part, this special equipment is made from materials that allow microwave energy to pass through their surfaces to heat the food within. Remember that the density of cookware affects the cooking time (eg plastic cooks faster than glass and porcelain), and that although the microwaves pass through the cookware, it can still become hot if the food gives off heat.

Browning dishes are designed to make the finished

appearance of microwaved food resemble conventionally cooked food. They are only for microwave use.

Many everyday kitchen items can be used in the microwave, including casseroles, bowls and dishes made of heatproof glass, glass-ceramic, china and pottery free of metal. Plastic containers marked 'Microwave-safe' or 'Suitable for the microwave' are useful. Paper goods can be used for short-term heating. Do not use recycled paper as it may contain metal fragments.

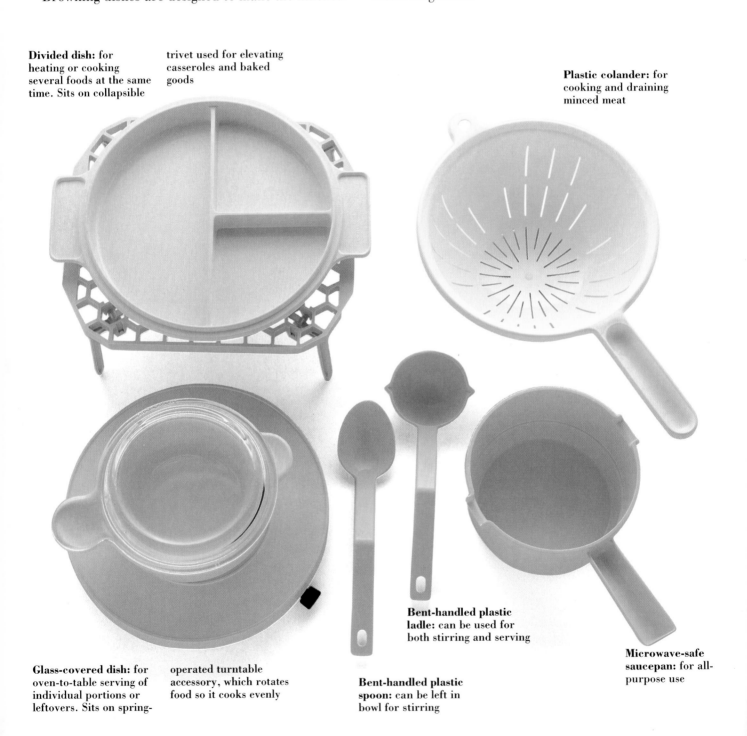

Divided dish: for heating or cooking several foods at the same time. Sits on collapsible trivet used for elevating casseroles and baked goods

Plastic colander: for cooking and draining minced meat

Bent-handled plastic ladle: can be used for both stirring and serving

Microwave-safe saucepan: for all-purpose use

Glass-covered dish: for oven-to-table serving of individual portions or leftovers. Sits on spring-operated turntable accessory, which rotates food so it cooks evenly

Bent-handled plastic spoon: can be left in bowl for stirring

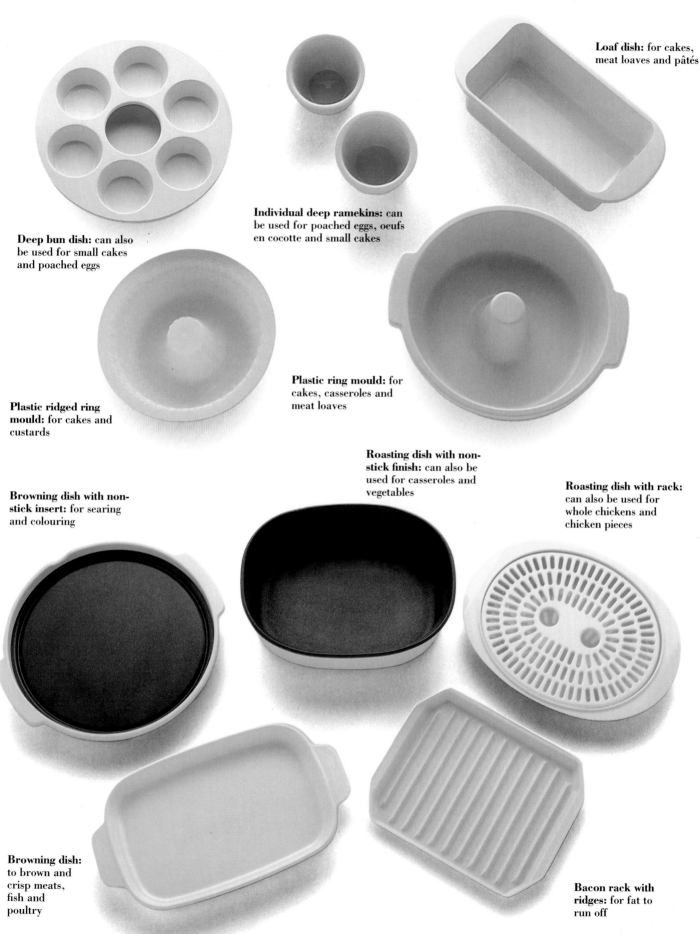

Deep bun dish: can also be used for small cakes and poached eggs

Individual deep ramekins: can be used for poached eggs, oeufs en cocotte and small cakes

Loaf dish: for cakes, meat loaves and pâtés

Plastic ridged ring mould: for cakes and custards

Plastic ring mould: for cakes, casseroles and meat loaves

Roasting dish with non-stick finish: can also be used for casseroles and vegetables

Browning dish with non-stick insert: for searing and colouring

Roasting dish with rack: can also be used for whole chickens and chicken pieces

Browning dish: to brown and crisp meats, fish and poultry

Bacon rack with ridges: for fat to run off

13

Suitable Kitchenware

Testing for microwave safety: to determine the suitability of a piece of cookware, pour cold water into a 250 ml glass bowl or jug and place in the microwave next to the dish or utensil to be tested. Heat on High (100% power) for 1 minute. The water should be warm, the dish or utensil cool. If the dish is warm, do not use it in the microwave – it may overheat and break.

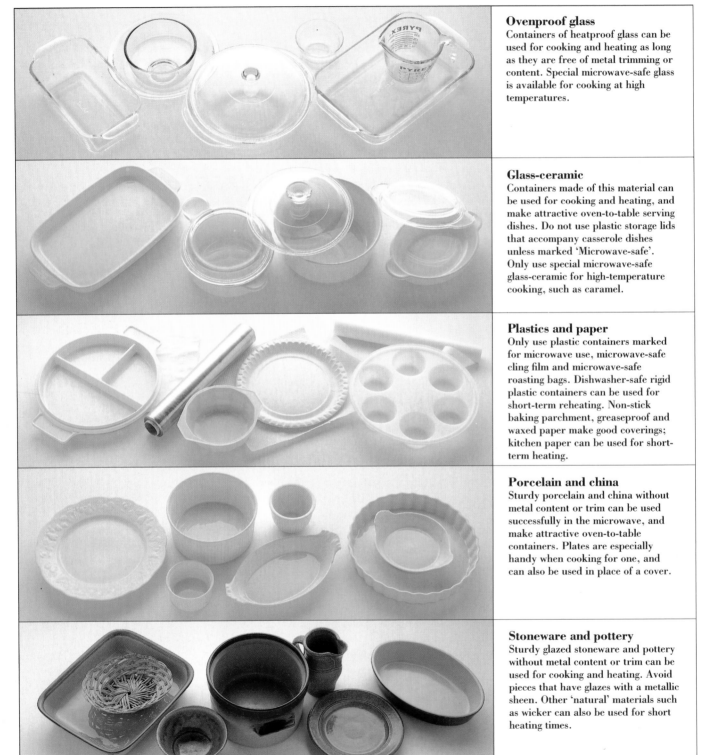

Ovenproof glass
Containers of heatproof glass can be used for cooking and heating as long as they are free of metal trimming or content. Special microwave-safe glass is available for cooking at high temperatures.

Glass-ceramic
Containers made of this material can be used for cooking and heating, and make attractive oven-to-table serving dishes. Do not use plastic storage lids that accompany casserole dishes unless marked 'Microwave-safe'. Only use special microwave-safe glass-ceramic for high-temperature cooking, such as caramel.

Plastics and paper
Only use plastic containers marked for microwave use, microwave-safe cling film and microwave-safe roasting bags. Dishwasher-safe rigid plastic containers can be used for short-term reheating. Non-stick baking parchment, greaseproof and waxed paper make good coverings; kitchen paper can be used for short-term heating.

Porcelain and china
Sturdy porcelain and china without metal content or trim can be used successfully in the microwave, and make attractive oven-to-table containers. Plates are especially handy when cooking for one, and can also be used in place of a cover.

Stoneware and pottery
Sturdy glazed stoneware and pottery without metal content or trim can be used for cooking and heating. Avoid pieces that have glazes with a metallic sheen. Other 'natural' materials such as wicker can also be used for short heating times.

Unsuitable Equipment

While much equipment normally found in the kitchen can be used in your microwave oven, certain items should definitely be avoided; not only will they interfere with the normal microwave cooking processes, but they may also cause damage to your oven. The main materials to avoid are metal – it can cause arcing (blue sparks), which can pit oven walls or cause fires – unglazed pottery, certain plastics (see below) and recycled paper. If in doubt, carry out the simple suitability test shown on the opposite page.

Metals and foils

Do not use any metal item unless it is marked 'Microwave-safe', or your microwave instruction booklet gives guidelines for its use. Avoid metal or part-metal pots, pans, thermometers, skewers, baking trays and utensils. Make sure containers do not have metal in their handles or around their rims, or any metal screws. Do not use paper bags and boxes, large sheets of foil, or metal ties for roasting bags. Small, smooth pieces of foil used for shielding food should not come into contact with the oven's walls; keep at least 2.5 cm away. Carefully follow recipe instructions, and any other guidelines on using foil in the microwave.

Melamine and polystyrene

Some hard and soft plastics like Melamine dinnerware and polystyrene cups and boxes, may overheat and break or melt if used for microwaving. Foods high in fat or sugar can also cause plastic containers to distort or melt.

Decorated china and glass

Many dinner sets contain gold or silver decorative trims. These pieces are not suitable for the microwave – they can cause arcing, and a broken dish or damaged oven can result. Do not use lead crystal or any glass and china that have been repaired with glue.

Unglazed pottery

Do not use pottery or earthenware, either handmade or commercially produced, if it is not covered with a glaze on the outside as well as inside; it may absorb moisture and become hot. Pottery with a metallic glaze is also unacceptable for use in the microwave.

Food Facts

Microwave energy cooks food quickly but not always evenly. Microwaves penetrate food up to a depth of about 4 cm, and heat is conducted from the outer edges towards the centre (much as it is in conventional cooking); it is therefore possible to overcook or burn the outside edges of foods while the centres remain underdone. Special techniques have been developed to ensure that food is cooked evenly throughout; these are shown on the following pages. But the composition of the foods themselves can also affect the way they react to microwaves. Size, shape, density, thickness, temperature, water, fat and bone content of food

together with the presence of a membrane, casing or hard skin, all affect the cooking process and the final result.

Knowing how and why food reacts the way it does will mean there will be fewer surprises when it is cooked, and will make clear why recipes recommend that you cook food in a particular way. Moreover, the 'starting' temperature of foods can make a big difference in cooking results. Recipes in this book assume that meat, fish, poultry, eggs and most vegetables will be at refrigerator temperature, and canned and dry goods at room temperature.

THE COMPOSITION OF FOOD

Water attracts microwaves, so food high in water like tomatoes as well as food low in moisture like popcorn, can be microwaved without added liquid or fat.

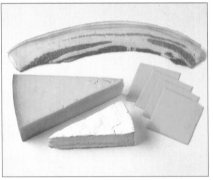

Fat attracts microwaves, too. Cheese cooks quickly but does not brown. Bacon cooks and browns quickly. Large joints of meat brown only with prolonged cooking.

Sugar also attracts microwaves. The sugary fillings of foods such as pastries and pies reach a high temperature faster than the outsides.

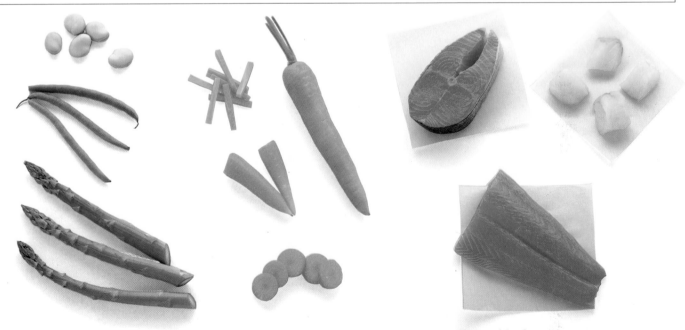

Moisture content of food
Foods that have a high moisture content cook better and more quickly in the microwave oven than those with a low moisture content.

Size of food
Large, bulky pieces take longer to cook than smaller or thinner pieces. The more exposed the surface area, the faster the item will cook. Here, the sliced and matchstick-thin strips will cook more quickly than the larger pieces and whole carrot.

Shape of food
The thinner parts of unevenly shaped food will cook more quickly than the thicker parts. Here, the salmon steak and monkfish pieces will cook more evenly than the fillet; thinner edges should be placed in the centre of the dish or folded under.

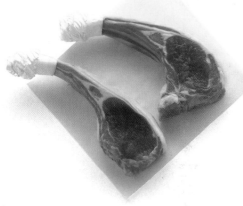

Bone content
Bones conduct heat, so cuts that contain bone, or the part of the meat that does, will cook more quickly than the boneless parts.

Fat content
Since fat attracts microwaves, meat high in fat will cook more quickly than lean meat. Lean, boneless meat cuts cook more slowly but more evenly than those with a higher fat and bone content. Both bone and fat attract microwaves, resulting in quicker, less even cooking.

Membranes
Egg yolks, oysters and chicken livers have membranes that need piercing to stop steam from building up and causing bursting.

Casings
Sausages and other foods with casings should also be pierced to prevent steam from building up and causing bursting.

Outer skins
Vegetables such as potatoes, peppers and tomatoes should be pierced before microwaving to prevent steam build-up.

Density of food
Dense, heavy foods like potatoes take longer to cook than porous, airy ones like breads and cakes.

Temperature of foods
Recipe timings are influenced by the 'starting' temperature of foods used; microwave cooking is so fast that this can make a big difference. Room-temperature foods, whether fresh, packaged or canned, normally cook faster than chilled or frozen foods.

Height of food in oven
Areas closest to the source of energy cook fastest. The breast of a whole chicken, which is closer to the top of the oven and receives more energy in some microwave ovens, is therefore likely to be cooked before the centre part. Chicken pieces in a casserole, however, are more likely to cook evenly.

Arranging Food for Better Cooking

For an even result throughout, food should be cooked in dishes of the appropriate shape and size. Ring-shaped dishes are best as microwave energy penetrates the food from the centre, sides and bottom. Round dishes also permit fairly even cooking. With square and oblong dishes, corners cook faster than the centres. When cooking more than two dishes at a time, arrange them in a circle if possible.

The centre of a dish heats more slowly than its edges, so place foods that take longer to cook towards outer edges of dish, quicker-cooking ones towards centre. If possible, arrange pieces of food in a circle, and leave space between the pieces. This allows microwave energy to penetrate the food quickly and evenly. Smaller amounts of food cook more quickly than larger ones, and so do the thin ends of meat, fish and poultry, and meat near the bone. These must be shielded – covered with smooth strips of foil to prevent overcooking. If the strips of foil are applied at the beginning of cooking time, be sure to remove them in time to allow the shielded portions to cook thoroughly.

Always be sure to use the exact size and shape of dish specified in the recipe, or the timing and the finished results may be different from those expected.

Unequal food composition
Delicate, quicker cooking parts should be placed towards the centre, more fibrous, less tender parts closer to edges.

Unevenly shaped foods
Alternate ends of foods such as corn-on-the-cob, then rearrange halfway through cooking to produce an overall uniformity in finished dish.

Foods of uniform size
Place food in circle with space between pieces. This enables microwave energy to reach all sides of food so it cooks evenly.

Foods of different densities
Place denser, slower cooking ingredients near edge of dish, more delicate, quicker cooking ones in centre to ensure even cooking.

Pieces, slices and whole items
Pieces or slices cook more quickly than whole items. Thinner parts should be placed towards centre of dish while thicker ends should face outwards.

Large or small quantities
Small amounts cook faster than large ones. Cooking time in the microwave is always directly related to the amount of food and increases with the quantity: the more food, the longer the cooking time. Individual portions cook faster than large casseroles or joints of meat.

Individual portions
Placing small dishes or ramekins in a circle with space in between dishes will result in more even cooking, particularly in ovens without turntables. However, individual dishes may need to be rearranged during cooking due to uneven heat patterns in oven.

Shielding vulnerable parts of food
Shield thin ends of meat, bone tips, meat near the bone and the cut edges of meat joints and poultry with smooth strips of foil to prevent them from overcooking.

ARRANGING FOOD FOR REHEATING

Platefuls of leftovers can be reheated easily in the microwave oven. Make certain all the food is of the same temperature, either chilled or at room temperature. Arrange thick and dense pieces of food such as chicken pieces on the outside of the plate, with quicker-to-heat foods such as rice on the inside. If possible, arrange foods in a ring shape, and spread them so they are low and even in the dish. You can do this with mashed potato, for instance, by making a depression in the centre. Delicate foods like stuffing should be placed underneath denser meat slices to prevent overcooking. Cover plates with microwave-safe cling film and microwave until all the food is piping hot, rotating plate as often as possible.

Covering Techniques

By covering food to be cooked in the microwave oven, moisture is retained and steam is produced. Steam heat, added to the molecule-vibrating action of microwaves, results in a faster cooking time, and more even cooking of certain foods. Steam also tenderises foods. Those that especially benefit from covering are vegetables, casseroles, less tender cuts of meat, thicker pieces of fish and soups.

Microwave-safe casserole lids, roasting bags and cling film are all equally effective in retaining heat and moisture. However, when cooking foods that require frequent stirring, rearranging and/or checking such as custards, sauces, stews and casseroles, it is easiest to use a lid. Use greaseproof paper to hold in some steam and to prevent spatters with food that does not need much steam to tenderise, such as a joint of meat. Greaseproof paper is often blown off the food by the action of the microwave's fan: crumpling the paper slightly helps keep it in place.

Microwave-safe kitchen paper is good for short-term heating and reheating, and for foods that can be cooked uncovered but tend to spatter, such as bacon and butter or margarine. It is also useful in absorbing extra fat or moisture and for keeping bread surfaces dry. For more information on the type of kitchen paper to use in the microwave, see pages 14 and 220.

Lids and covers
Casserole and dish lids made of microwave-safe material are perfectly adequate as coverings, if recipe does not specify any other.

Microwave-safe cling film
Use microwave-safe cling film (non-PVC) to cover dishes without lids. Steam can cause splitting, so vent when using (see opposite).

Greaseproof
This forms a looser covering than cling film, and is particularly good for preventing spatters. Use it with foods that might become soggy if tightly covered.

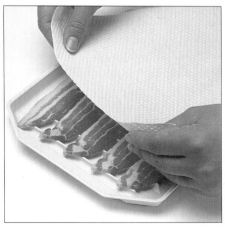

Kitchen paper
When used as a covering, white microwave-safe kitchen paper allows steam to escape and prevents spatters. It can also be used on oven floor, to help absorb moisture.

Plates as covers
If no other suitable cover is available, a plain, untrimmed and undecorated plate can be used. Select one large enough to cover the cooking bowl completely.

Venting cling film
Cover casserole or dish with cling film, then turn back corner to form narrow vent: this allows excess steam to escape.

Removing cling film
Carefully peel back film away from you to avoid any escaping steam, which can cause burns.

Removing lids
Use oven glove or pad to lift the cover as it will be hot from rising steam, and open it away from you to avoid escaping steam.

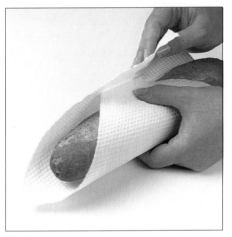

Kitchen paper
Wrap it around food or place it underneath to soak up excess moisture and prevent certain foods from becoming soggy.

Plastic freezer bags and roasting bags
These handy kitchen items can be used to reheat leftovers or to steam and tenderise food. If cooking large items, which take longer and reach a high temperature, use a roasting bag loosely fastened with string or plastic ties. Pierce if instructed in recipe, or according to manufacturer's instructions.

LINING DISHES

Microwave-safe cling film
This can be used under meat loaves, pâtés and terrines to prevent sticking, and in order to remove them easily.

Kitchen paper and non-stick baking parchment
Cut to fit, these can be used to line cake moulds and dishes for baking; they will prevent contents from sticking when removed. The paper is not affected by microwaves and can be easily peeled off bottom of cake after standing time.

Browning Techniques

Most food cooked in the microwave is done so quickly that fat rarely has a chance to rise to the surface and brown. This is why microwaved meat, for instance, usually looks different from meat that has been cooked conventionally. Some foods such as bacon, joints with a good fat covering, whole chickens and turkey breasts, will brown because they have a high fat content. Except for bacon, however, they will not crisp.

Specially designed cooking equipment, called browning dishes, sear and brown foods the way a conventional frying pan does. They are made from, or coated with, a special material that absorbs microwave energy and reaches temperatures of 220°C–280°C. They have feet or ridges to keep work surfaces safe from scorching. (Even so, be careful not to place them directly on surfaces that are not heat-resistant.) Browning dishes and grills should be preheated according to manufacturer's instructions.

For foods that cannot be cooked on a browning dish, there is also a wide variety of readily available sauces and coatings that are brushed or sprinkled on, or rubbed into the food to produce a more attractive finished appearance. Some even add extra flavour and texture to the meat.

Browning dish
This dish contains a special substance that causes it to become extremely hot. Often there is a well to catch drippings, and feet to protect work surfaces.

Using a browning dish
Preheat dish according to manufacturer's instructions. Add meat, pressing down so that it is seared on the hot surface, then return to oven. Do not cover dish. Turn meat over to brown other side – if possible, on an unused part of dish. If food is cooked in batches, dish may need to be reheated. Always follow manufacturer's instructions.

Using a browning agent
Chicken cooked in the microwave without a browning agent is pale, such as the leg above. However, it if is coated with gravy browning, as on the whole bird (right), it looks brown and crisp.

BROWNING AGENTS

Soy, teriyaki and browning sauces and diluted **gravy browning** are highly seasoned coatings for meat and poultry.

Barbecue sauce can be brushed on meat and poultry occasionally during cooking to add flavour and colour.

Fruity brown or Worcestershire sauces can be brushed on to beef, pork or lamb cuts, or hamburgers.

Paprika is a delicious coating for poultry. Brush on some melted butter first, then sprinkle paprika on surface.

Breadcrumbs, seasoned or unseasoned, can be used on top of uncovered foods or casseroles before microwaving.

Herb and spice mixes, if added to poultry pieces and hamburgers before cooking, enhance appearance and taste.

Microwave browning should be sprinkled on meat and poultry before cooking as an appearance enhancer.

Dry onion soup or gravy powder can be sprinkled on hamburgers and other beef or lamb cuts before cooking.

Brown sugar can be sprinkled on cakes and tea breads before, during or after cooking.

Marmalade or jam can be brushed on ham after microwaving, and on poultry halfway through cooking.

Cinnamon sugar or toasted coconut can be sprinkled on cakes and tea breads before, during or after cooking.

Toasted chopped nuts make an attractive topping for cakes and tea breads. Sprinkle on before cooking.

Brushing on gravy browning before cooking gives meat and poultry a darker, richer colour.

Rubbing soy or barbecue sauce on poultry skin before cooking can improve its normally light appearance.

Glazing with marmalade or specially prepared fruit glaze improves both appearance and flavour of gammon steaks.

Sprinkling on microwave browning or other seasoning can make hamburgers look more tempting.

Cooking Techniques

Because microwaves penetrate food only to a certain depth, it is often necessary to stir, turn over, rearrange or rotate food to guarantee thorough and even cooking. Various techniques have evolved to enable microwaves to reach every part of the food.

Some microwave ovens have areas with a concentration of microwaves ('hot spots'), where food cooks more quickly. To identify these spots, place some water-filled microwave-safe dishes in the oven and heat on High (100% power); check to see which one or ones start to bubble first. Food in these areas will cook most quickly.

As a reminder to stir or rotate foods according to recipe instructions, set the oven to that time, rather than to the total cooking time in the recipe, then reset as necessary.

Identifying 'hot spots'
Place water-filled dishes on oven floor and heat on High (100% power). Food will cook faster in areas where water bubbles first.

Stirring foods
Casseroles, soups and stews should be stirred from outer edges (where food cooks first) towards centre; cooler food at centre should be pushed towards edge of dish.

Whisking sauces
During the cooking process, whisking keeps sauces smooth and ensures more even cooking. Microwave-safe whisk has bent handle so that it can be left in bowl while microwave is in operation.

Turning foods
Dense pieces such as fish cakes should be turned over as should food cooked in liquid. Hot liquid in bottom of dish can transfer additional heat to one side of food and result in uneven cooking.

ROTATING A DISH IN THE MICROWAVE

Casseroles or baked dishes may need to be rotated for even cooking. Make certain to rotate dish in one direction only.

For a quarter turn, rotate casserole or dish so that side that faced back of oven faces side of oven.

For a half turn, rotate casserole or dish until side facing back of oven is to the front.

ELEVATING FOODS

Raise foods like crumbles, cakes and quiches off oven floor to allow microwave energy to cook centre bottom. Special microwave-safe racks or trivets can be used underneath dishes: meat racks in roasting dishes keep joints from stewing in own juices.

Elevate loaf dish, bowl or casserole on inverted microwave-safe plate or ramekin, if you do not have special microwave-safe rack or trivet.

Rearranging dishes
For individual portions to cook evenly, it may be necessary to rearrange them at least once during cooking. Turn each dish so that outside edges move to inside.

Rearranging delicate foods
With delicate foods that can be damaged through handling, such as baked apples, you can rearrange food by turning entire dish.

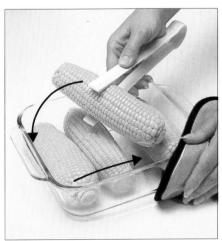

Rearranging pieces of food
Pieces of food such as corn-on-the cob have to be turned over or rotated during microwaving. Take pieces from centre of dish and move to outside, and vice versa.

Testing for 'Doneness'

When removed from the oven, microwave-cooked food may look different from conventionally cooked food, so there are a number of tests to tell if it is done.

In assessing the 'doneness' of food, you must take into account the standing time, if this is indicated in a recipe. Standing time is part of the cooking process – the food is removed from the oven and allowed to stand, covered, for several minutes while it finishes cooking. This is why it can look underdone when it is first removed from the oven, but will be done after standing for the time given in the recipe. For this reason, many tests for 'doneness' are carried out after standing time. Most of the recipes in this book give a range of cooking times for 600- to 700-watt microwave ovens, but it is also important to recognise that your microwave has a 'personality' and cooking pattern of its own, which you should get to know, that can also influence cooking time. To avoid overcooking, choose the lesser amount of time, check to see if food is done, then cook longer if necessary. Always undercook rather than overcook, and allow the food to stand exactly as instructed in the recipe; if it is underdone, it can be cooked further. When cooking individual portions, test each one separately.

THERMOMETERS

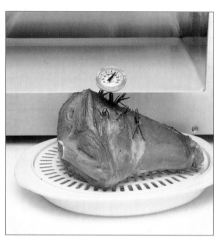

Microwave-safe thermometers: for meats such as lamb and pork, the most reliable test is a thermometer. This can be used inside a microwave oven.

Probe: certain ovens contain probes that monitor food temperatures throughout the cooking process and turn off the oven when the pre-set temperature is reached.

Instant-read thermometer: this is used to test food outside the microwave. It should be inserted in food immediately after it has been taken out of oven.

Testing reheated food
Feel centre of bottom of dish with your hand; if it is hot, food is heated through; if it is cool, so is food.

Testing cakes
After standing time in recipe, moist spots on top of cake will have dried out and cake will begin to pull away from side of mould. Cake is done when cocktail stick or skewer inserted in centre comes out clean.

Testing custards
These are done when knife inserted halfway between centre and edge comes out clean. Centre will look soft, but it will set during the standing time.

Testing fish
Fish is cooked when flesh is opaque; it should flake easily when tested with fork.

Testing meat
Meat reaches its final desired temperature outside oven. Small pieces or cubes are done when fork easily penetrates surface through to bottom.

Testing whole chicken
Chicken is done if thickest part of leg feels soft when pressed with fingers and juices run clear if this part is pierced.

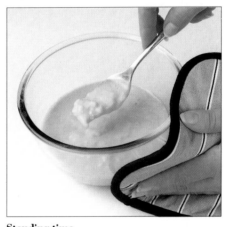

Standing time
Microwaved foods continue to cook by internal heat after they are removed from oven. For instance, eggs should be just past the runny stage when removed from oven. After standing for 1–2 minutes, they will be set, and will look similar to conventionally cooked eggs.

TENTING
Standing time is important for meat joints. The internal temperature of the joint rises significantly during standing time, and this extra time is necessary for it to reach the final, desired temperature. Letting joints stand also allows their juices to settle and meat to firm up – this makes carving much easier. Most joints should be left to stand covered with a loose tent of foil and checked with a thermometer to see if they have reached the final temperature specified in recipe.

Cook's Tips

Use your microwave oven for a variety of cooking techniques. Soften cream cheese or butter for cakes and biscuits, melt chocolate without fuss, and toast seeds or nuts for many dishes. You can even make caramel in the microwave: follow recipe instructions, watching carefully since caramel continues to cook and darken when removed from oven. Do not stir unless instructed in recipe.

Melt chocolate
In small microwave-safe bowl, place 25 g chocolate. Heat on High (100% power) for 1–2 minutes, just until shiny. Stir until melted and smooth.

Soften butter
On microwave-safe plate, place butter in non-foil wrapper. Heat on Medium-Low (30% power) for 30–40 seconds for 115 g, until spreadable.

Soften cream cheese
On microwave-safe plate, place 225 g cream cheese. Heat on Medium-Low (30% power) for 1½ (1:30)–2 minutes, until spreadable.

Toast coconut
On microwave-safe plate, place 200 g desiccated coconut. Heat on High (100% power) for 5–6 minutes, until toasted, stirring occasionally.

Toast sesame seeds
In shallow microwave-safe pie dish, place 75 g sesame seeds. Heat on High (100% power) for 3–5 minutes, until golden, stirring occasionally.

Toast nuts
In shallow microwave-safe pie dish, place 60 g shelled nuts. Heat on High (100% power) for 2½ (2:30)–4 minutes, until lightly browned, stirring occasionally.

Scald milk
Into 500 ml microwave-safe measuring jug, pour 250 ml milk. Heat on High (100% power) for 2–2¾ (2:45) minutes, until bubbles form round edge.

Caramelise sugar
In 1 litre microwave-safe glass measuring jug, place 200 g sugar; add 3 tablespoons water. Cook on High (100% power) for 5–7 minutes, without stirring, until golden.

Clarify butter
In 500 ml microwave-safe glass measuring jug, place 115 g butter, cubed. Heat on High (100% power) for 1½ (1:30)–2 minutes, until melted. Skim foam from top.

Soften peanut butter
Remove lid from jar of peanut butter. Heat on High (100% power) for 1½ (1:30) minutes per 225 g. If softening more than 225 g, stir halfway through.

Soften crystallised honey
Remove lid from jar of hardened and crystallised honey. Heat on High (100% power) for 30 seconds; stir until honey loses its granular texture and is smooth. Repeat if necessary.

Soften brown sugar
Place brown sugar in microwave-safe glass dish. Add 1 apple wedge or 1 slice white bread. Heat, covered, on High (100% power) for 30–40 seconds. Allow to stand for 30 seconds; remove apple and stir sugar once.

Prove yeast bread dough
In microwave-safe bowl alongside 1 litre microwave-safe measuring jug containing 750 ml very hot tap water, place dough. Heat, covered with kitchen paper, on Low (10% power) for 20–25 minutes.

Flavour candied and glacé fruit
Into small microwave-safe bowl, pour 60 ml liqueur. Heat on High (100% power) for 30 seconds. Add 150 g candied and glacé fruit; stir to mix. Heat on High for 2 minutes. Allow fruit to stand until liquid is absorbed.

Blanch almonds
In 1 litre microwave-safe bowl, heat 250 ml water on High (100% power) for 3–4 minutes, until boiling. Add 140 g whole shelled almonds. Heat on High for 1 minute; drain. Cool, slip off skins; pat dry.

Dissolve gelatine
In small microwave-safe bowl, sprinkle gelatine over measured liquid. Allow to stand for 1 minute. Heat on High (100% power) for 1–2 minutes, stirring until dissolved.

Soften dried fruit
In 1 litre microwave-safe measuring jug, place 125 g dried fruit and 60 ml water. Heat, covered, on High (100% power) for 45 seconds. Allow to stand for 1 minute.

Shell nuts
In medium microwave-safe bowl, place 150 g nuts and 60 ml water. Heat, covered, on High (100% power) for 2–3 minutes, until boiling. Stand for 1 minute. Drain; shell.

Cook's Tips

Your microwave oven can be used to prepare fruit and vegetables. It can ripen avocados, take the chill off refrigerated fruit, and have crisp- or soft-skinned baked potatoes ready for filling or eating plain in a matter of minutes. It can also make it easier to squeeze lemons, limes and oranges, and substantially reduce the time involved in peeling tomatoes and garlic cloves – and onions without tears!

Take chill off refrigerated foods
To bring out flavour of fruit that has been stored in refrigerator, place it on microwave-safe plate and heat on High (100% power) for 1–2 minutes.

Soften underripe avocado
On oven floor, place unpeeled avocado. Heat on High (100% power) for 1 minute, or until slightly softened. Cool completely, peel, then slice or mash.

Tear-free onions
Trim ends of large onion. Place on kitchen paper on oven floor. Heat on High (100% power) for 1 minute. Remove skin, then slice or chop as desired.

Squeeze citrus fruit more easily
On oven floor, place 1 orange, lemon or lime. Heat on High (100% power) for 30 seconds, or just until warm. Cut in half and squeeze to get fresh juice.

Bake potatoes
With fork, pierce skin of one 225 g potato in several places. Place on kitchen paper. Cook on High (100% power) for 4–6 minutes, until tender, turning over once.

Crisp- or soft-skinned baked potatoes
After removal from oven, wrap baked potato in kitchen paper for crisp skin; for soft skin, wrap in foil. Allow to stand for 5 minutes.

Peel tomatoes
To 500 ml boiling water in microwave-safe glass jug, add 2 tomatoes. Heat on High (100% power) for 45–60 seconds, until skins split. Put into cold water; peel.

Peel small onions
In small microwave-safe glass bowl, place 75 g small trimmed onions. Heat on High (100% power) for 45 seconds. Squeeze stalk end until onions pop out of skins.

Peel garlic
On oven floor, place 3 garlic cloves. Heat on High (100% power) for 15–30 seconds, just until warm. Squeeze at one end until clove pops out of skin.

Use your microwave to get foods ready just before you bring them to the table. It's easier to spread jams, scoop out ice creams and pour syrups if they are heated for a short time. Crackers and crisps can be refreshed; pies and biscuits can be warmed for a freshly baked taste; cheese can be brought to room temperature; poppadoms can be heated until beautifully crisp.

Soften jams
Remove lid from jar of jam that has become difficult to spread. Heat on High (100% power) for 1½ (1:30)−2 minutes per 225 g.

Heat maple or golden syrup
Remove lid from syrup bottle or transfer to microwave-safe serving jug. Heat on High (100% power) for 1½ (1:30)−2 minutes per 250−500 ml syrup, until warm.

Refresh potato crisps
On kitchen paper laid on microwave-safe plate, place 50−60 g potato crisps in thin layer. Heat on High (100% power) for 15−60 seconds. Stand for 5 minutes.

Soften ice cream
On oven floor, place 500 ml carton ice cream. Heat on Medium-Low (30% power) for 15−20 seconds, until slightly softened. Scoop ice cream straight from carton.

Heat taco shells
On kitchen paper, place 8−10 precooked, crisp taco shells. Heat on High (100% power) for 1−3 minutes, until warm. Spoon in filling of your choice.

Warm biscuits
In kitchen paper, wrap 2−4 biscuits. Heat on High (100% power) for 30−40 seconds, until biscuits are warm.

Bring cheese to room temperature
On microwave-safe plate, place 225 g unwrapped cheese. Just before serving, heat on Medium (50% power) for 45 seconds−1 minute.

Warm individual serving of pie
Place 1 serving of pie on microwave-safe plate. Heat on High (100% power) for 30−45 seconds, until warm.

Crisp poppadoms
Brush poppadoms lightly with oil. Place on kitchen paper on oven floor. Heat on High (100% power) for 1 minute, or until crisp, turning once.

How to cook your favourite dishes in the microwave

You may not always find your favourite recipe in this or any other microwave cookbook, so it helps to know how to take a recipe normally cooked on the stove or in a conventional oven and 'convert' it to microwave cooking – it will save time and energy!

As examples, on this and the opposite page, we've taken three different recipes and shown you how simple it is to change them for microwave cooking.

GUIDELINES FOR CONVERTING 'CONVENTIONAL' RECIPES TO MICROWAVE COOKING

1 Smaller quantities cook fastest in the microwave, so keep to a maximum of 8 servings at any one time.

2 Reduce or omit fats, liquids and seasonings (see Ⓐ, Ⓒ, Ⓓ, Ⓔ).

3 Use microwave-safe cookware and suitable utensils (see Ⓕ).

4 Cut back cooking time to between a quarter and a half of conventional recipe time, depending on size, shape, density and composition of food (see Food Facts, page 16). Test to see if food is cooked after minimum time.

To microwave:

Ⓐ Reduce to 1 tablespoon

Ⓑ Reduce to 1 clove

Ⓒ Omit

Ⓓ Reduce slightly

Ⓔ Omit

Ⓕ Use microwave-safe baking dish

Ⓖ Cook vegetables, covered, on High (100% power) for 6 minutes, or until soft, stirring twice.

Ⓗ In microwave-safe colander set over microwave-safe pie dish, cook minced beef on High for 1 minute, or until no longer pink, stirring twice; discard dripping. Add meat to vegetables with remaining ingredients.

Ⓘ Cook sauce, covered, on High for 10 minutes, or until thickened, stirring twice.

Example 1: MEAT SAUCE FOR PASTA

8 servings

3 tablespoons olive oil Ⓐ	*2 × 400 g cans tomatoes*
1 carrot, finely chopped	
1 celery stick, finely chopped	*80 ml water* Ⓒ
1 onion, finely chopped	*60 ml dry red wine*
2 garlic cloves, finely chopped Ⓑ	*1½ teaspoons dried oregano* Ⓓ
450 g minced beef	*1 teaspoon salt* Ⓔ
175 g tomato purée	

1. In 4 litre saucepan Ⓕ over medium-high heat, Ⓖ in hot oil, cook carrot, celery, onion and garlic for about 15 minutes, until tender.
2. Add beef. Ⓗ Cook until well browned, stirring frequently. Add remaining ingredients; heat to boiling.
3. Reduce heat to low; cover and simmer Ⓘ for 30 minutes or until sauce thickens.

If all vegetables are chopped to equal size, they will cook quickly and evenly.

Replace saucepans with microwave-safe cookware that can be used for serving; this saves on washing-up.

Stir from outer edge towards centre, pushing cooler food to edge. Re-cover after stirring.

Cooking minced meat in microwave-safe colander greatly reduces fat content of finished dish.

FAVOURITE RECIPES IN THE MICROWAVE

Here are two more recipes ideal for converting to microwave cooking: potatoes cook faster; tea breads take less time and are moist and light when cooked in the microwave. Underneath the conventional recipes, instructions are given for successful microwaving.

Example 2: TWICE-BAKED POTATOES

6 servings

6 medium baking potatoes, scrubbed and unpeeled	80 ml milk
	Toppings:
45 g butter or margarine	Finely chopped onion, chopped chives, diced
1 teaspoon salt	Cheddar cheese,
Pinch white pepper	crumbled crisp bacon

1. Preheat conventional oven to 230°C (450°F, gas mark 8). Pierce potatoes in several places, then put potatoes in oven and bake for 45 minutes or until fork-tender.
2. With sharp knife, and holding potato with clean oven glove, slice each potato lengthways, to remove top quarter.
3. With spoon, carefully scoop out potatoes to form 6 shells. Scrape potato from top quarters; discard tops.
4. In large bowl with mixer at low speed, beat scooped-out potato, butter or margarine, salt and pepper until well combined and fluffy.
5. Slowly add milk, beating constantly until smooth. With spoon, pile mashed potato mixture back into reserved potato shells.
6. Sprinkle generously with topping of your choice (above). Place filled potatoes on baking sheet; return to oven and bake for 10 minutes or until tops are golden.

To microwave: pierce potatoes in several places; place on kitchen paper on oven floor. Cook on High (100% power) for 16–20 minutes, turning potatoes over and rearranging halfway through cooking. Prepare potato mixture as above. After filling, reheat for 5–7 minutes, until hot. *Saves about 30 minutes.*

Example 3: BANANA AND PECAN TEA BREAD

Makes 1 loaf

370 g plain flour	115 g butter or margarine
140 g caster sugar	2 very ripe medium bananas, mashed
1 teaspoon ground cinnamon	1 teaspoon grated lemon zest
1 teaspoon baking powder	
1/4 teaspoon bicarbonate of soda	2 eggs, beaten
1/2 teaspoon salt	60 g shelled pecan nuts, chopped

1. Preheat conventional oven to 180°C (350°F, gas mark 4). Grease 22.5 × 12.5 cm loaf tin.
2. In bowl, combine flour and next 5 ingredients. With fingertips or 2 knives used scissors fashion, cut in butter or margarine until mixture resembles coarse crumbs. Stir in bananas, lemon zest, eggs and pecans, reserving 1 1/2 tablespoons, just until flour is moistened. Spoon into prepared loaf tin, smoothing surface. Sprinkle over reserved pecans.
3. Bake for 55 minutes or until skewer inserted in centre of bread comes out clean. Cool bread in tin on rack for 10 minutes; remove from tin and finish cooling on rack.

To microwave: line 22.5 × 12.5 cm microwave-safe loaf dish with kitchen paper. Omit salt. Spoon mixture into prepared loaf dish and top with reserved nuts. Cook, covered loosely with greaseproof paper, on Medium (50% power) for 15 minutes, or until top of bread is moist and springs back when lightly touched, rotating a quarter turn every 2 minutes. Allow to stand in dish for 10 minutes. Invert on to rack; remove kitchen paper; cool. *Saves about 40 minutes.*

Caring For Your Microwave

Microwave ovens are simple to care for and easy to clean. Because they stay cool, spills do not cook on. It is best to wipe spills off while they are still warm, however, because if they are left in the oven, they can absorb microwave energy during cooking. Don't worry if some moisture forms on oven walls or door; it is normal for foods to give off moisture and steam during cooking. Just wipe moisture away after cooking.

CLEANING THE OVEN

It is easy to wipe the inside of a microwave after every use, so cleaning is not hard work at all. To clean the touch-control panel, be sure to open the door first to prevent the oven from starting accidentally.

For combination ovens, follow the manufacturer's recommended cleaning methods in the instruction booklet. If your oven has a removable turntable, check the instructions to see if it can be put in the dishwasher.

1. Use a clean cloth or sponge dipped in a mild all-purpose cleaner or a solution of washing-up liquid dissolved in warm water. Rinse well with clear, warm water and dry with a soft cloth or kitchen paper.

2. Pay special attention to cleaning the area around the door seal thoroughly; this is where small pieces of food often get trapped.

3. If there are areas of cooked-on food, clean them by rubbing gently with a plastic scrubbing pad. An alternative method of removing stubborn food is to soften it with steam by boiling some water in the oven. Do not use steel-wool scrubbing pads.

CLEANING MICROWAVE DISHES

To clean plastic microwave-safe dishes stained by tomatoes, blackberries or other foods, make a solution of 1 tablespoon household bleach per 250 ml water. Soak dishes for about 1 hour, then wash, rinse and dry. For everyday cleaning, use a mild washing-up liquid. Rub gently with a plastic scrubbing pad to remove stuck-on food.

DEODORISING THE OVEN

Your microwave oven may pick up odours from cooking. Air the oven occasionally by leaving the door ajar, and wipe the inside with bicarbonate of soda dissolved in warm water. From time to time, use this 'magic' deodorising formula: in 1 litre microwave-safe measuring jug, combine **250 ml warm water** and **a few thyme sprigs** or **2 lemon slices** or **2 teaspoons mixed spice**. Heat on High (100% power) for 3 minutes, or until boiling. As a bonus, your whole kitchen as well as the inside of your oven will smell fresh.

BEFORE YOU RING FOR SERVICE

Are you using your microwave oven correctly? Before you ring for service, make the following checks:

Oven not turning on?
Make sure that the oven door is securely closed. The oven will not switch on if it is not closed properly; this is a safety measure built into microwave ovens. Check that your oven is properly plugged in, that no circuit breakers are open, and that the fuse in the plug has not blown.

Food isn't cooking?
Check that the oven is not set on 'timer' or 'hold'.

In recipes where food is microwaved in its own packaging, such as store-bought frozen vegetables, be sure the packaging is not foil, through which microwaves cannot pass. Check that your cookware is microwave-safe (page 12); some materials, such as glazed pottery, block microwave energy.

Food cooking too slowly?
Your oven may not be operating at full power if it is sharing a circuit with another appliance. Also your microwave may be a lower wattage than the microwave used in the recipe you are following: all recipes in this book are developed in 600- to 700-watt ovens, but if your oven has a lower wattage, cooking is slower.

Check to see if power level is set correctly.

Also, make sure food is at the correct temperature. Meat, fish, poultry and most vegetables should be at refrigerator temperature, and canned and dry goods at room temperature.

If standing time is included in the recipe, make sure you let the dish stand for the full time specified. The standing time is needed to equalise the temperature through the food, and to complete the cooking process, and should not be ignored. Also, be sure food is left covered or tented during standing, if instructed in recipe. You should always check that the food has been cut to the size specified in the recipe; you may have cut it too large.

Food cooking too quickly?
The starting temperature of food going into the microwave oven affects cooking time. Microwave recipes assume that foods used in the recipe have been stored correctly. Refrigerated food should be cold, not brought to room temperature before use, or it will cook too quickly.

You may have a single-setting oven which cooks certain foods like eggs and cheese too quickly. If this is the case, pour 500 ml water into a microwave-safe measuring jug and place in the oven while cooking these foods. The water attracts microwave energy and 'slows' down the oven.

Check that the power level is set correctly, and that food is cut to the specified size and not smaller.

Check the wattage of your oven. The higher the wattage, the faster food will cook.

Food cooking unevenly?
Make sure the air vent in your microwave oven is not blocked, and that there is nothing heavy placed on top of the oven.

There are also several techniques to prevent uneven cooking in the microwave, such as elevating the dish on a trivet or rack, or on inverted ramekins; this exposes areas at the bottom of the dish to the microwaves. Other techniques include arranging food with thicker parts towards edges of dish and stirring and rotating during cooking.

In recipes calling for food to be cut into pieces, check that the pieces are of uniform size.

Some microwave ovens have 'hot spots' where there is a concentration of microwaves. Fans inside the ovens help to distribute the microwaves more evenly, but it is still necessary to use techniques such as rotating the dish and rearranging food.

Blue sparks (arcing)?
Be sure any foil you use to shield food, or to cover food you do not want to cook, is smooth and at least 2.5 cm away from oven walls. Check that the cookware is microwave-safe (even metal rims on dishes can cause arcing), and that any ties used to seal roasting bags are made of nylon or string, not metal.

MICROWAVE SAFETY

Microwave ovens are made in compliance with strict safety standards: a seal round the oven door keeps the microwaves inside, and a special system stops the generation of micro-waves the instant the door is opened. You should, however, examine a new oven for any signs of shipping damage.

Never operate the oven if the door does not close pro-perly, or if the door, its latch, hinge or sealing surfaces have been damaged in any way. Never block the vents of your oven because they keep the microwave-producing mag-netron tube cool and cut down on moisture build-up, en-abling you to get the best results from your oven.

Microwave ovens are cooking appliances, designed to defrost, heat and cook food. You may have heard of other uses for the oven – don't try them; they can be dangerous,

possibly lead to a fire and, at the very least, damage your oven. Use the microwave oven only as intended. Always use microwave-safe cookware and utensils (page 12), and do not turn the oven on when the cavity is empty. If you have young children, it is a good idea to leave a bowl of water in your microwave when the oven is not in use. This way, if the oven is accidentally turned on, the water attracts the micro-waves and prevents damage to the oven.

If you are concerned about the safety of your oven, have it tested by a qualified service engineer – do not try using 'leakage detectors' which are inaccurate and unreliable.

Meal Planning With Your Microwave

Your microwave oven can be a great boon when planning meals for yourself or the whole family and when entertaining. It can help save on preparation and washing-up time, and it preserves the nutrients in the food as well. To plan meals to be cooked in your microwave, keep in mind the following points.

BASIC PRINCIPLES

1. The more food in the oven, the longer it takes to cook. It is best to keep the number of servings down to eight to take advantage of the oven's ability to cook quickly. If serving meat and potatoes to feed 12, for example, cook the joint in the microwave oven, but plan to bake the potatoes in your conventional oven.

2. You can switch power settings in the time it takes to push a button. This means that after you have cooked the joint on a lower power setting, you can cook the vegetables on High (100% power) without waiting for the oven to warm up, as you would when cooking conventionally. There is no need to cool the microwave down either, when going from a higher to a lower power setting.

3. Dense foods such as joints, whole birds and casseroles usually require standing time to complete the cooking process, and they retain heat well after being removed from the oven. While they finish cooking outside the oven, you have time to cook the vegetables and reheat soups and sauces, rolls and bread, etc.

4. Use microwave-safe dishes, serving platters and casseroles so you can heat up food between courses and bring it to the table piping hot. Pretty china and serving pieces for use in the microwave are widely available.

COMBINATION COOKING

A microwave used in combination with one or more other appliances is often the most efficient way to prepare a meal. For example, you can cook pasta just as quickly on top of the stove, leaving your microwave oven free for making your favourite sauce to be ready at the same time as the pasta.

After cooking a casserole in the microwave, you can place it under the grill for a browned topping, while using the microwave to cook accompanying vegetables. Or you can brown meat on top of the stove before you begin cooking it in the microwave. Look for cookware that can be used on top of the stove and in the microwave as well as in a conventional oven.

FREEZER-TO-TABLE COOKING

It is easy to cook food in advance, freeze it, then pop it in the microwave oven so that when guests arrive it is ready in a matter of minutes. For example, the Savoury Sausage Parcels and Crab-Filled Mushrooms in the Snacks and Starters chapter can be frozen up to 1 month ahead, then cooked from frozen in the microwave just before you are ready to serve.

Holiday pies and tarts can be made ahead of time; favourites such as mince pies defrost well in the microwave. A 22.5 cm tart takes only 6–8 minutes on High to defrost completely and evenly.

THE QUICK WAY TO COOK INGREDIENTS

It saves time to cook poultry, vegetables and fruit in the microwave before using in salads, casseroles and other dishes. Chicken is tender and juicy when cooked on Medium (50% power) for 7–9 minutes per 450 g. Four medium potatoes (about 175 g each), peeled and cut into 2.5 cm chunks, for example, cook on High (100% power) in 10–12 minutes. See also the vegetable charts (pages 237–251) and fruit charts (pages 313–315).

CUT DOWN ON OUTDOOR COOKING TIME

Use your microwave to precook vegetables before you finish them on the barbecue: the time can be reduced to 2–5 minutes if you cook your vegetables first in a small amount of water until almost tender (see vegetable charts on pages 237–251). Meat and poultry can be partially cooked so the barbecuing time is cut in half. Avoid spoilage by barbecuing immediately after precooking in the microwave – never leave precooked food out at room temperature. Barbecue sauces can also be prepared in double-quick time using your microwave.

ENTERTAINING MADE EASY

Throughout the *Reader's Digest Microwave Cookbook* there are suggestions for serving and garnishing the recipes to make them perfect for that special occasion. Also included are special *Meal in Minutes* menus, complete with preparation timetables and serving suggestions to cover most of your entertaining needs. Not all the dishes and ingredients in these menus are prepared in the microwave; many can be bought commercially prepared, and some are conventionally cooked. In each menu, however, the microwave is used as much as possible, to make entertaining easier. The preparation timetables also give advice for advance preparation, so there should be no last-minute panics, and you can enjoy the meal as much as your guests.

The Colour Index

HOT PRAWN DIP WITH DILL
*Prawns, garlic, spring onion and celery
blended with a peppery sauce. Served with
tortelloni on wooden skewers.*
Makes 500 ml. Page 112

BACON AND HORSERADISH DIP
*Cream cheese dip in Pepper Bowl,
garnished here with chives. Served with
celery, grissini and Bagel Chips.*
Makes 500 ml. Page 111

CURRIED CRAB DIP
*Crabmeat combined with pimientos, curry
powder and cream cheese. Served with a
selection of vegetables.*
Makes 500 ml. Page 111

BAKED STUFFED TOMATOES
*Scooped-out tomatoes filled with a mixture of Parmesan cheese,
breadcrumbs and garlic, quickly cooked, then served with uncooked
tomato tops and a decorative garnish of parsley sprigs.*
4 tomatoes. Page 119

ANGELS ON HORSEBACK
*Oysters flavoured with Worcestershire
sauce and mustard, wrapped in bacon and
garnished with lemon and parsley.*
24, 12, 6 oysters. Page 113

BOMBAY MIXED NUTS *(left) Mixed nuts cooked in spices and left to cool.* Makes 350 g.
Page 294. **MEXICAN DIP** *(centre) Cream cheese mixed with taco sauce and spring onion.*
Makes 250 ml. Page 112. **MEDITERRANEAN AUBERGINE DIP** *Cooked aubergine mixed
with red onion, green pepper and tomato. Served with pitta bread.* Makes 750 ml. Page 111

SPICY CHICKEN WINGS
Chicken wings cooked in a tomato and fruity brown sauce, served with celery and a blue cheese dip or dressing.
12 pieces. Page 114

NACHO BAKE
Alternate layers of tortilla chips and a spicy mixture of melted cheese, chillies, onion, coriander and black olives.
6 servings. Page 114

CHEESE STICKS
Grissini spread with a cream cheese mixture, rolled in poppy and sesame seeds, chives and paprika; with a chive garnish.
16 sticks. Page 113

OYSTERS ROCKEFELLER
Oysters topped with a spinach mixture and diced bacon, here shown on half shells; garnished with lemon.
12 large oysters. Page 122

CREAMED MUSHROOMS ON TOAST
Quartered mushrooms cooked in a sherried cream sauce. Garnished with spring onion and served with toast.
4 servings. Page 120

TARTLETS: ASPARAGUS AND BRIE; MUSHROOM; TOMATO AND BASIL; AND RED AND BLACK BEAN FILLINGS *Homemade or bought tartlet shells with a choice of tasty fillings and complementary garnishes; served hot.*
Each filling is enough for 16–20 tartlets. Page 117

**POTATO SKINS WITH CHEDDAR
CHEESE** *Wedges of scooped-out baked
potatoes, topped with a cheese mixture.
Served with soured cream or yogurt.*
16, 8, 4 pieces. Page 114

CHEESE AND CHILLI CHAPATIS
*Chapati 'sandwiches' with a chilli-cheese
filling, here served with relish, yogurt,
radish, Chilli Flower and lettuce.*
16 wedges. Page 116

STUFFED ARTICHOKE BOTTOMS
*Bacon with sultanas, onion and
breadcrumbs, served in artichoke bottoms
with salad and lemon garnish.*
4, 2, 1 servings. Page 118

MIDDLE EASTERN MEATBALLS
*Spicy minced beef mixture shaped into
bite-sized meatballs. Served on skewers,
with a lemon and mint garnish.*
About 26 meatballs. Page 113

POACHED APPLES WITH PARMA HAM
*Apples cooked in spiced white wine, filled with soured cream and blue
cheese, served with salad leaves, capers and thin slices of Parma ham.
Accompanied by creamy scrambled eggs with chives.*
6 servings. Page 119

**ARTICHOKES WITH LEMON AND
GARLIC** *Artichokes with slices of lemon
and garlic between their leaves, cooked
with wine and served with clarified butter.*
4, 2, 1 servings. Page 120

OVER 1 HOUR

CRAB-FILLED MUSHROOMS
Mushroom caps filled with a zesty mixture of crabmeat and mayonnaise. Garnished here with Lemon Twists and parsley.
12 mushrooms. Page 118

COUNTRY-STYLE PORK PÂTÉ
Minced pork and beef combined with diced ham, minced chicken livers, herbs and spices, set into bacon-lined dish to cook. Served chilled with garnish of gherkins, salad leaves and olives.
16 servings. Page 115

ELEGANT SHELLFISH SALAD
Chilled cooked prawns, scallops and mussels, served on salad leaves, with Lemon-Basil Sauce and chilli sauce.
6 servings. Page 122

SEAFOOD PÂTÉ
Prawns and scallops blended with fresh tarragon, tomato and cream. Served chilled with tarragon and tomato garnish.
16 servings. Page 115

CHICKEN LIVER PÂTÉ
Chicken liver, onion and garlic mixture, served on Radish Flowers, Pear Slices and savoury biscuits; with garnishes.
Makes 250 ml. Page 116

CASINO CLAMS
Chopped clam, bacon and breadcrumb mixture cooked in clam shells. Garnished with lemon slices and red pepper strips.
12 clams. Page 122

SAVOURY SAUSAGE PARCELS
Spicy Italian sausage, onion, cheese and breadcrumb mixture wrapped in vine leaves and 'tied' with pimiento strips.
12 parcels. Page 118

CELEBRATION PRAWNS
King prawns stuffed with savoury cheese and pepper mixture; here garnished with lamb's lettuce and peach slices.
4, 2, 1 servings. Page 119

SOUPS

FRESH TOMATO SOUP
*Tomatoes and vegetables blended until
smooth, then cooked in seasoned stock,
garnished with soured cream and chives.*
Makes 1.5 litres. Page 127

**LIGHT AND CREAMY ASPARAGUS
SOUP** *Blended asparagus, onion and
stock with half cream. Served hot or
chilled with yogurt or cream and chervil.*
Makes 1 litre. Page 128

VEGETABLE STOCK
*Leek, onion, celery, carrots, tomatoes and
mushrooms cooked with tomato juice,
seasonings and water; strained.*
Makes 750 ml. Page 125

CHICKEN STOCK
*Chicken bones cooked in water with herbs,
peppercorns, leek, carrot and celery;
strained.*
Makes 750 ml. Page 125

CARROT SOUP WITH ORANGE
*Thinly sliced carrots cooked with onion and grated orange zest in
butter and stock, then blended until smooth and reheated. Served
with a decorative garnish of feathered cream and parsley.*
Makes 1 litre. Page 128

FISH STOCK
*White fish bones cooked in dry white wine
and water with leek, carrot, celery, thyme
and peppercorns; strained.*
Makes 750 ml. Page 125

FOUR BEAN SOUP
Black, red and white kidney and borlotti beans cooked with vegetables and bacon in stock. Garnished with celery leaves.
Makes 1.7 litres. Page 129

FRENCH ONION SOUP
Sliced onions simmered in condensed beef consommé flavoured with sherry or Madeira and tomato purée. Served piping hot with classic topping of toasted French bread covered with melted Gruyère cheese.
Makes 1.5 litres. Page 131

WINTER VEGETABLE SOUP
Carrot, turnip, celery, cabbage, swede and onion cut into delicate pieces and cooked in seasoned stock.
Makes 1.5 litres. Page 128

CURRIED PARSNIP SOUP
Parsnips blended with onion, apple, curry powder and stock. Garnished with almonds and coriander.
Makes 1.5 litres. Page 129

SWEETCORN CHOWDER
Frozen sweetcorn kernels cooked in creamy potato, celery and onion mixture; garnished with parsley.
Makes 1.5 litres. Page 133

WEST COUNTRY CLAM CHOWDER
A filling, substantial soup made with diced clams, pork rashers, celery, onions, milk and diced potatoes. Here garnished with clam shells and chopped fresh parsley.
Makes 1.5 litres. Page 133

VEGETABLE CHOWDER
Onion, carrots, celery, parsnip, potato and herbs are cooked with butter beans and tomatoes in this hearty soup.
Makes 1.5 litres. Page 133

CREAM OF SPINACH SOUP *(left) Blended spinach, potatoes and stock enriched with half cream. Here garnished with cream. Makes 1 litre.*
VICHYSSOISE *Classic creamy leek and potato soup, served chilled with apple and parsley for garnish. Makes 2 litres. Page 127*

CHICKEN NOODLE SOUP
Tender pieces of chicken and vegetables in Chicken Stock with fine egg noodles added. Serve with crackers if you like. Makes 1 litre. Page 131

MINESTRONE
Fresh vegetables cooked with Parma ham, beans, pasta and tomatoes; topped with grated Parmesan cheese. Makes 2 litres. Page 130

BEEF STOCK
Beef bones, onion and tomato roasted in conventional oven, then cooked with water, leek, herbs and peppercorns; strained. Makes 750 ml. Page 125

SPLIT PEA AND HAM SOUP
Ham bone cooked in Chicken Stock with split peas and vegetables. Garnished with parsley and served with French bread. Makes 2 litres. Page 129

LOUISIANA GUMBO
Prawns, oysters and okra in a thick, spicy tomato base with celery, onions and garlic. Served here with Hot Cooked Rice. Makes 2 litres. Page 132

PEACH SOUP *(left) Fresh or canned peaches cooked with dry white wine and chopped ginger root; garnished with yogurt and mint and served chilled. Makes 750 ml.* **RED PLUM SOUP** *Red plums cooked in spiced red wine, chilled and topped with soured cream or yogurt. Makes 750 ml. Page 134*

EGGS BAKED IN HAM NESTS
Thinly sliced ham, spring onions and egg baked in individual dishes; here served with toast triangles.
4, 2, 1 servings. Page 137

POACHED EGGS
Eggs simply cooked in water and vinegar; here served on toast with herb-flavoured sausage patties and a parsley garnish.
4, 2, 1 servings. Page 138

SCRAMBLED EGGS
Seasoned eggs cooked until light and fluffy; here served with toast triangles, cherry tomatoes and a parsley garnish.
4, 2, 1 servings. Page 139

PIPÉRADE
Red peppers and chopped onion, cooked, then mixed with eggs and scrambled. Here served with French bread and basil garnish.
6 servings. Page 139

EGGS AND BACON
Crisply 'fried' bacon rashers and an egg; here served with a warm bread roll and a tomato half sprinkled with chives.
4 servings. Page 140

EGGS IN BRIOCHES
Hollowed-out individual brioches lined with Gruyère cheese are used as cases for baking eggs. Served here with smoked salmon, fresh asparagus with Hollandaise Sauce and a chive garnish.
6 servings. Page 137

WELSH RAREBIT
Well-seasoned thick cheese topping, here served on toast and garnished with gherkins, olives, onions and parsley.
6 servings. Page 142

SWISS CHEESE FONDUE
Microwave version of traditional cheese and wine mixture; served with bread cubes, tomatoes and green pepper for dipping. 4 servings. Page 142

POACHED EGGS FLORENTINE
Classic combination of eggs and spinach on muffin halves. Served with asparagus and Hollandaise Sauce.
4 servings. Page 138

PEPPER AND TOMATO OMELETTE *(left) Onion, green pepper and tomato fill this savoury omelette. 2 servings.* **FRENCH DESSERT OMELETTE** *Moist omelette with filling of strawberries, decorated here with icing sugar and a whole strawberry. 2 servings.*
Page 141

MACARONI CHEESE
Elbow macaroni, covered in a thick, onion-flavoured cheese sauce, with crunchy breadcrumb topping and parsley garnish.
4 servings. Page 142

CAMEMBERT IN VINE LEAVES
Camembert with a layer of apple slices, wrapped in vine leaves. Served with apple wedges and garnished here with parsley.
2 servings. Page 144

SOUFFLÉED CHEESE OMELETTE
Egg yolks folded into whisked egg whites give a light, fluffy omelette. Garnished with cucumber, tomato and parsley.
2 servings. Page 141

MEXICAN CHEESE AND TOMATO BAKE
Creamy onion and tomato mixture layered with tortilla chips and cheese.
6 servings. Page 143

TOMATOES WITH GOAT CHEESE AND BASIL SOUFFLÉ
Hollowed-out tomatoes filled with goat cheese soufflé; served here with salad and garnished with basil. 8 servings. Page 145

SMOKED SALMON AND CHIVE ROULADE *(top) A light soufflé roll with filling of smoked salmon and cream cheese. 4 servings.*
MUSHROOM AND CHEESE ROULADE *Rolled soufflé filled with onion, tomatoes and mushrooms cooked in wine, and Gruyère cheese.*
4 servings. Page 146

CHEESE SOUFFLÉ
Grated Gruyère and Parmesan cheeses in a white sauce form the basis of this microwave version of an old favourite.
6 servings. Page 145

ASPARAGUS TIMBALES
Asparagus, onion, eggs and cheese cooked in ramekins, served with smoked salmon; garnished with asparagus and lemon.
4 servings. Page 143

CRUSTLESS BROCCOLI AND GRUYÈRE CHEESE QUICHE *(left)*
Lightly cooked broccoli and onion in creamy egg and cheese mixture.
6 servings. **BACON AND POTATO QUICHE** *Potato cubes, peas, spring onions and crisp bacon in a mixture of Cheddar cheese and eggs.*
8 servings. Page 144

47

FISH AND SHELLFISH

SAVOURY SALMON STEAKS
Salmon steaks topped with spring onion and mayonnaise, and garnished with Radish Flowers, spring onions and cucumber. 2 servings. Page 152

PLAICE FILLETS WITH SAVOURY SAUCE *(left) Plaice fillets in crumb coating; here served with two sauces.* 4 servings. Page 157.
ROLLED PLAICE WITH CUCUMBER, TOMATO AND BASIL SAUCE *Plaice fillets with cucumber stuffing, served with a cucumber, tomato, basil and wine sauce.* 4 servings. Page 156

SOLE WITH GRAPES
Sole fillets flavoured with tarragon and lemon juice are served with a creamy white wine sauce and grapes.
4, 2, 1 servings. Page 155

SWORDFISH STEAKS AMANDINE
Tender swordfish steaks served with a buttery toasted almond and parsley sauce. Garnished with parsley.
4 servings. Page 155

FISH STEAKS WITH SALSA
Salmon, cod or halibut steaks with chilli-flavoured mayonnaise; served with tomatoes, green pepper, onions and olives.
4 servings. Page 151

SEA BASS WITH RIBBON VEGETABLES
Whole sea bass brushed with butter, sherry and lime juice before cooking; served with a colourful assortment of carrot and courgette ribbons. Garnished here with endive, lemon and lime.
6 servings. Page 161

FISH FILLETS FLORENTINE
Fish fillets filled with spinach, mushrooms, bread cubes and grated cheese. Served with cooked tomato wedges.
4 servings. Page 157

SOLE AND ASPARAGUS WITH CHEESE SAUCE *Tender sole fillets wrapped around asparagus spears in a creamy cheese sauce.*
4 servings. Page 159

TUNA STIR-FRY *(left) Fresh tuna strips cooked with Chinese-style flavourings; served with mange-touts, shiitake mushrooms, onions, tomatoes and baby sweetcorn.* 4 servings. Page 155. **MONKFISH SATAY WITH CHUNKY PEANUT SAUCE** *Skewered monkfish, red pepper and spring onions served with oriental-style sauce.* 4 servings. Page 154

CHINESE RED SNAPPER
Whole fish cooked with matchstick-thin vegetables in Chinese-style sauce of sherry, soy sauce, garlic and ginger; here garnished with kiwi fruit and toasted almonds.
4 servings. Page 161

SCALLOPS IN CHIVE CREAM
Scallops cooked in blend of Chicken Stock, cream and wine flavoured with chives. Here served in scallop shells.
4 servings. Page 168

SALMON WITH LETTUCE AND RED PEPPER
Salmon steaks cooked on bed of lettuce and sliced red pepper.
2 servings. Page 152

SPICY PRAWN SAUCE *(left) Tomato-based sauce, served here with tagliatelle.* 4 servings. **RED CLAM SAUCE** *(centre) Bacon and clam sauce, served here with paglia e fieno.* 4 servings. **TUNA AND TOMATO SAUCE** *Rich tuna sauce, served here with pasta bows.* 4 servings.
Page 173

PIQUANT PRAWNS *(left) Raw prawns tossed in herbs and cooked in lager with a dash of Worcestershire sauce; garnished here with lime.* 4, 2, 1 servings. Page 164. **CREOLE PRAWNS** *Fiery mixture of prawns, green pepper, onions and tomatoes served on rice. Here with thyme garnish.* 4 servings. Page 165

SCALLOPS WITH BACON AND BASIL *Scallops, bacon and mushrooms in cream sauce flavoured with fresh basil. Here garnished with basil.* 2 servings. Page 169

CURRIED SCALLOPS *Queen scallops cooked in a curry-flavoured mixture with onion, celery and carrots; garnished here with coriander.* 4 servings. Page 169

MUSSELS IN CREAM AND GARLIC *Fresh mussels steamed open in the microwave, then served in half shells with sauce of onion, garlic, cream, mussel liquid and chopped parsley.* 4 servings. Page 168

CREAMED OYSTERS IN PUFF PASTRY *Fresh oysters cooked in a creamy onion and celery mixture, served in vol-au-vents. Here garnished with Lemon Twists and parsley.* 4 servings. Page 169

CRAB CAKES *(top) Tasty patties, here garnished with lemon and coriander.* 12 Crab Cakes. **DEVILLED CRAB** *Crabmeat in piquant cream-based sauce.* 4 servings. Page 170

CHILLI CRAB *Fresh crab in shell, cut into pieces and cooked in a spicy sauce; here garnished with Spring Onion Tassels and served with rice and cucumber.* 2 servings. Page 170

TUNA AND SPINACH LOAF
Satisfying dish of chopped spinach and flaked tuna mixed with bread, soured cream and eggs, flavoured with lemon juice and Tabasco sauce. Garnished with lemon and parsley.
6 servings. Page 162

MEDITERRANEAN COD
Cod steaks flavoured with oregano and served with a rich tomato and vegetable sauce; garnished here with oregano.
2 servings. Page 153

PEPPERY COD STEAKS
Chilli-flavoured red pepper sauce spooned over lightly cooked cod steaks; served here with French beans.
6 servings. Page 153

TUNA FISH CAKES FLORENTINE
Flaked tuna and spinach patties, here served with tomato and cucumber salad and garnished with lemon wedges and parsley. 6 servings. Page 163

STUFFED TROUT *(top) Trout stuffed with a well-seasoned mixture of onion, carrot, celery and walnuts. 4, 2, 1 servings.* **CAJUN TROUT**
Whole trout coated in cornmeal and herb mixture; served with a flavoursome sauce of onion, green pepper, tomatoes and herbs.
2 servings. Page 160

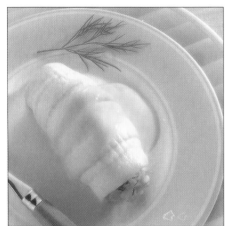

PRAWN-STUFFED SOLE
Sole fillets with a prawn, vegetable and breadcrumb stuffing; served with Hollandaise Sauce and garnished with dill.
4, 2, 1 servings. Page 156

SAVOURY FISH KEBABS
Chunks of monkfish, green pepper, mushrooms and tomatoes marinated in mixture of spring onions, curry powder, marmalade and Worcestershire sauce; cooked on skewers and served on herbed rice.
4, 2, 1 servings. Page 154

PLAICE IN PAPER PARCELS
Plaice fillets cooked in baking parchment with orange-flavoured vegetables, garnished with orange and basil.
4, 2, 1 servings. Page 157

MOULES MARINIÈRE
Mussels cooked with tomatoes, white wine, onion, garlic and basil. Traditionally served with French bread.
4, 2, 1 servings. Page 168

LOBSTER AND PRAWN STEW WITH CHICKEN *Rich, tasty stew of lobster, prawns and chicken with sweetcorn, onion and tomatoes. Here with chive-topped potatoes.* 4 servings. Page 173

COUNTRY-STYLE SEA BASS AND POTATOES
Hearty dish of whole sea bass cooked on bed of browned, chopped bacon, thickly sliced onions and potato chunks. Here delicately garnished with a thyme sprig.
6 servings. Page 161

ITALIAN SHELLFISH STEW
A hearty dish of clams, prawns, scallops and crab in a tomato and red wine broth; served with French bread.
8 servings. Page 173

'STIR-FRIED' PRAWNS AND BROCCOLI
Prawns tossed with broccoli, red pepper and mushrooms; here served with rice.
4, 2, 1 servings. Page 166

STUFFED PRAWNS SUPREME
Prawns with courgette and red pepper stuffing, cooked in a sherry and lemon sauce; served with nut-coated goat cheese.
4 servings. Page 165

LOBSTER THERMIDOR *(top) Chunks of lobster meat in creamy mushroom and sherry sauce, served in the shell.* 4, 2, 1 servings.
SZECHUAN LOBSTER *Lobster meat served with tender vegetables cooked in blend of garlic, cashews, soy sauce and sesame oil.*
4 servings. Page 167

PRAWN AND RED PEPPER RISOTTO
Prawns, mange-touts and red pepper mixed into Italian arborio rice that has been cooked in Fish Stock and white wine with chopped vegetables and garlic; garnished with fresh basil.
6 servings. Page 166

PRAWNS IN SAFFRON CREAM
Prawns tossed in a creamy saffron-flavoured sauce, served with tender-crisp mange-touts and matchstick-thin carrots.
6 servings. Page 164

ORIENTAL FISH IN LETTUCE LEAVES
*Plaice fillets wrapped in lettuce leaves,
served with vegetables in Chicken Stock,
and garnished with coriander.*
4, 2, 1 servings. Page 158

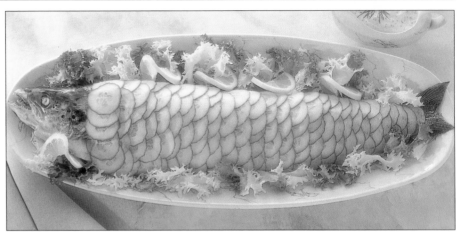

PARTY POACHED SALMON
*Whole salmon poached with fresh herbs and white wine; when cool,
fish is skinned and covered with thin cucumber slices to resemble
scales. Served with Green Mayonnaise Dressing.*
10 servings. Page 162

CALIFORNIAN SALMON STEAKS
*Salmon marinated in jalapeño chillies,
lime juice, oil and honey before cooking,
then served with lime and parsley.*
4, 2, 1 servings. Page 152

DELUXE OCEAN PIE
*Scallops, prawns, mussels and crab sticks in thyme-flavoured onion
sauce with mushrooms and peas; cooked in gratin dish with
potato topping. Here browned under conventional grill.*
4 servings. Page 172

**SALMON STEAKS WITH MARINATED
CUCUMBER** *Salmon steaks served with
sliced cucumber in vinegar, sugar and
onion, and Green Mayonnaise Dressing.*
4, 2, 1 servings. Page 151

PAELLA
*Classic party dish of shellfish, sausage,
chicken, green pepper and tomatoes
cooked with rice. Garnished with parsley.*
8 servings. Page 171

BOUILLABAISSE
*Well-seasoned Mediterranean fish stew of
mussels, lobster, sea bass and cod, served
with French bread.*
8 servings. Page 172

SPICY CRUMBED CHICKEN
Chicken joints with coating of mustard, honey, breadcrumbs and spices. Garnished with salad, cucumber and lime.
4 servings. Page 183

CREAMY CHICKEN BREASTS
Chicken breasts in curried asparagus, spring onion and cream sauce. Here served with rice garnished with spring onion. 4 servings. Page 187

CHICKEN À LA KING
Warmed vol-au-vents with colourful filling of chicken, onion, mushrooms, green pepper and pimiento in a rich sauce.
4 servings. Page 189

DEVILLED CHICKEN
Chicken drumsticks and thighs coated in mustard mayonnaise and breadcrumb mixture. Garnished with lemon and parsley. 4 servings. Page 188

CHICKEN LIVERS WITH TOMATO SAUCE *Livers in tomato sauce flavoured with fruity brown sauce, oregano and thyme; here served with rice.*
4 servings. Page 189

'BARBECUED' CHICKEN *(bottom) Chicken thighs cooked until tender in piquant onion and green pepper sauce. 4 servings. Page 188.* HONEY-SOY CHICKEN *Chicken joints with oriental-style glaze, served with medley of mange-touts, carrot and mushrooms. Here accompanied by rice with spring onion garnish. 4 servings. Page 184*

COQ AU VIN
Microwave version of classic French dish of chicken portions cooked in red wine sauce with carrots, mushrooms, onions and tomatoes. Flavoured with thyme and garnished with chopped parsley.
4, 2, 1 servings. Page 182

CHICKEN PAPRIKASH
Warming dish of chicken cooked in tomato sauce flavoured with paprika; served here with soured cream and chive garnish.
4 servings. Page 182

LEMON CHICKEN
Chicken joints in piquant lemon and pimiento sauce, topped with crumbs and garnished with Lemon Twists and parsley.
4 servings. Page 182

CHICKEN CACCIATORE
Chicken joints in pasta sauce with olives, green pepper, pesto sauce and onions. Served with spaghetti and a basil garnish.
4 servings. Page 183

CHICKEN MARENGO
Classic dish of chicken pieces, prawns, onions and mushrooms in a tomato sauce with wine and rosemary.
4 servings. Page 183

QUICK CHICKEN STEW
Hearty stew of chicken pieces, potatoes, carrots, green beans and onions cooked in stock. Garnished here with chopped thyme.
4 servings. Page 184

CHICKEN KIEV
Boned, skinned chicken breasts rolled round butter filling, dipped in egg yolk mixture and garlic and breadcrumb coating. Garnished with lemon and parsley and served here with green salad.
4 servings. Page 186

CHICKEN FRICASSÉE
Chunks of boneless chicken breasts with peas, carrots and green beans in a rich sauce; served here with tagliatelle.
4 servings. Page 185

BROCCOLI-STUFFED CHICKEN BREASTS *Crumb-coated chicken breasts stuffed with ham, broccoli and cheese; served with cheese sauce.*
6 servings. Page 186

POACHED CHICKEN WITH VEGETABLES *Chicken breasts, leeks, mushrooms and artichoke hearts. Served here with basil garnish.*
4, 2, 1 servings. Page 185

CHICKEN BREASTS PARMESAN
Crumb and cheese-coated chicken breasts with zesty olive, basil and tomato sauce. Accompanied by tagliatelle.
4 servings. Page 187

MEXICAN PANCAKES
Turkey, onion, green pepper, tomato and sweetcorn filling rolled up in crêpes; topped with tomato sauce and cheese.
4 servings. Page 194

WHOLE STUFFED POUSSINS *(left) Poussins with savoury stuffing of mushrooms, courgettes, cheese and rice, coated with dry stuffing mix.* 2 servings. **POUSSIN HALVES WITH HERB STUFFING** *Split poussins with garlic and herb stuffing; garnished with cherry tomatoes and basil.*
4, 2, 1 servings. Page 191

CHICKEN CRÊPES FLORENTINE
*Crêpes with chicken and spinach filling,
topped with Parmesan-flavoured Basic
White Sauce, garnished with chives.*
4, 2, 1 servings. Page 190

CHICKEN RATATOUILLE
*Hearty mixture of chicken, green pepper,
courgettes, tomatoes and herbs, topped
with melted mozzarella cheese.*
4 servings. Page 190

**HERB AND CHEESE CHICKEN
BREASTS** *Crumb-coated chicken breasts
with herby cheese filling; served with
asparagus and cherry tomatoes.*
8 servings. Page 185

DUCK BREASTS WITH APPLE AND GREEN PEPPERCORNS (top)
*Sliced boneless duck breasts and apple served with green peppercorn-
flavoured sauce. 4 servings. Page 193.* **CHICKEN WITH
CRANBERRIES AND WALNUTS** *Chicken breasts with honey and
walnut coating, served with cranberry sauce. 6 servings. Page 187*

**TURKEY ROLLS WITH CHEESE
FILLING** *Crumbed turkey breast fillets
filled with cheeses, herbs and sun-dried
tomatoes; here sliced, with basil and salad
garnish. 4, 2, 1 servings. Page 196*

TURKEY AND NOODLE BAKE
*Chunks of turkey breast, peas and noodles
in creamy sauce, topped with Melba toast
crumbs. Here garnished with parsley.*
4 servings. Page 196

TURKEY BREAST WITH CHESTNUT STUFFING *Quickly cooked turkey breast joint, served with stuffing of whole chestnuts, celery and sultanas.*
8 servings. Page 195

CURRIED CHICKEN THIGHS
Marinated chicken thighs coated in crumbs before cooking; served with curried yogurt sauce.
4 servings. Page 189

DUCKLING WITH ORANGE SAUCE
Tender duckling quarters in rich orange sauce flavoured with brandy and fine orange zest; served here with mange-touts and garnish of orange slices and parsley.
4 servings. Page 192

APRICOT GLAZED DUCKLING
Duckling quarters with glaze of mustard, apricot jam, soy sauce and ginger; served with sliced carrots and courgettes.
4 servings. Page 192

DUCKLING WITH CHERRY SAUCE
Tender duckling quarters served with rich cherry and red wine sauce; garnished with watercress.
4 servings. Page 193

DUCKLING WITH OLIVES AND ALMONDS *Duckling quarters served in seasoned sauce of almond-stuffed olives, onions and dry sherry.*
4 servings. Page 193

STEAK AU POIVRE
Succulent beef fillet steaks with crushed peppercorn coating; served with tasty brandy and cream sauce and accompanied here with sautéed julienned leeks.
4, 2, 1 servings. Page 204

BEEF STROGANOFF
Tender beef and mushrooms in creamy sauce; here garnished with parsley and served with tagliatelle.
4 servings. Page 206

STEAK FORESTIÈRE
Juicy fillet steaks with Madeira, mushroom and tomato sauce. Garnished here with watercress and served with beans.
4 servings. Page 204

STEAK WITH MUSHROOMS AND ARTICHOKES *Medium-rare steaks, sprinkled with mixed herbs and served with vegetables in a red wine sauce.*
4 servings. Page 204

BEST-EVER BURGERS
Medium-rare beefburgers topped with onion rings in a wine sauce. Accompanied with carrot and courgette ribbons.
2 servings. Page 210

SURPRISE BURGERS
Pimiento, olive and chilli sauce-filled burgers; here served with baby sweetcorn, salad leaves and sliced tomato.
4, 2, 1 servings. Page 209

CHEESEBURGERS
Minced beef and grated cheese patties in a seasoned coating topped with a lightly spiced mixture of onion rings and sliced mushrooms. Here served with toast triangles and garnished with parsley.
4 servings. Page 209

KEEMA CURRY
Minced beef, tomatoes, peas and green pepper with garlic, ginger and spices. Here with coriander garnish and rice.
4 servings. Page 210

CHILLI CON CARNE
Classic, spicy chilli topped with soured cream, grated cheese and coriander. Here with tortilla chips and bowl of taco sauce.
6 servings. Page 211

QUICK AND EASY CHILLI
Spiced minced beef with red kidney beans, courgette, sweetcorn and onions. Here served with long-grain rice.
8 servings. Page 211

INDIVIDUAL MEAT LOAVES
Seasoned beef and cucumber loaves filled and topped with cheese; garnished with salad and parsley.
4, 2, 1 servings. Page 211

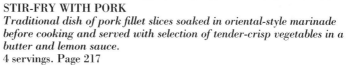

SMOKED PORK AND BEAN BAKE
Smoked boneless pork loin slices and beans cooked in sweet and sour sauce; garnished with parsley sprig.
6 servings. Page 220

STIR-FRY WITH PORK
Traditional dish of pork fillet slices soaked in oriental-style marinade before cooking and served with selection of tender-crisp vegetables in a butter and lemon sauce.
4 servings. Page 217

PORK WITH VEGETABLES
Juicy pork loin slices cooked until tender in stock and arranged with lightly cooked asparagus, baby carrots and chicory. Spring onion sauce, flavoured with mustard, is spooned over.
4 servings. Page 217

HAM AND BEAN CASSEROLE
Substantial casserole of smoked ham cubes, white kidney beans and vegetables cooked in herby chicken stock.
6 servings. Page 221

VEAL MARSALA
Veal escalopes dipped in Marsala butter and coated with crumbs; sprinkled with parsley and served with asparagus.
4, 2, 1 servings. Page 224

VEAL WITH SPINACH
Veal escalopes in a seasoned crumb coating; served with lemon-flavoured spinach and cherry tomatoes.
4 servings. Page 224

HASH BROWN PORK AND POTATOES
Cubes of cooked roast pork combined with onion, potatoes, eggs and cream. Served with thyme-sprinkled carrots.
4 servings. Page 216

LAMB NOISETTES WITH ORANGE
Boneless lamb chops on parsleyed toast with orange and herby mayonnaise. Served with mange-touts and rosemary garnish. 8 servings. Page 229

BACON-WRAPPED LAMB CHOPS
Juicy boneless lamb loin chops with fruity bread filling, wrapped in bacon and cooked. Here accompanied with French beans, new potatoes sprinkled with chopped chives, and Redcurrant and Orange Sauce.
4 servings. Page 228

FRANKFURTER AND VEGETABLE MEDLEY *Ratatouille-style casserole with aubergine, courgette, yellow pepper, frankfurters and chick peas.*
6 servings. Page 234

CONTINENTAL MEAT LOAF
Sauerkraut and Gruyère cheese in meat loaf topped with Thousand Island dressing. Garnished with Radish Flowers and parsley. 6 servings. Page 212

MEAT LOAF MILANESE
Meat loaf with red potatoes and beans, and a tomato and basil sauce. Garnished here with parsley and Lemon Julienne.
6 servings. Page 212

FRANKFURTER AND RED CABBAGE CASSEROLE
Frankfurters, apples and red cabbage. Here with watercress garnish.
4 servings. Page 232

CUMBERLAND SAUSAGES WITH GLAZED ONIONS
Sausages and onions cooked with herbs. Served with potatoes and courgettes.
4 servings. Page 232

ROAST FILLET OF BEEF WITH HERBS
Tender fillet of beef joint coated with herby mustard, black pepper and breadcrumb mixture and cooked medium-rare. Cut into thin slices and garnished with whole radishes and basil leaves.
10 servings. Page 202

BEEF AND MANGE-TOUTS IN BLACK BEAN SAUCE *(left) Chinese dish of tender beef and mange-touts in spicy chilli and ginger sauce. 4 servings.* **STIR-FRIED BEEF IN OYSTER SAUCE** *Strips of rump or fillet steak with red pepper and spring onions, flavoured with ginger, soy and oyster sauces; garnished with coriander. 4 servings. Page 203*

SWEDISH MEATBALLS *Balls of minced meat, onion, cream and dill in soured cream sauce garnished with dill. Served with rice and carrots. 6 servings. Page 219*

SAVOURY SPARERIB CHOPS *Pork sparerib chops cooked in tangy tomato sauce with sauerkraut and green pepper. Here with salad garnish. 4 servings. Page 220*

PORK LOIN WITH GARLIC SAUCE *Pork loin joint cooked in stock with 20 garlic cloves. Served thinly sliced and garnished with sprigs of watercress. 10 servings. Page 216*

GAMMON STEAKS WITH ORANGE-HONEY GLAZE *Gammon steaks with spicy glaze; garnished with orange segments and parsley. Served here with new potatoes. 2 servings. Page 221*

SHEPHERD'S PIE *Popular supper dish of minced lamb, tomatoes and mushrooms topped with mashed potato. With parsley garnish. 6 servings. Page 231*

ZESTY LEG OF LAMB *Leg of lamb brushed with flavoursome glaze of chutney, mustard, garlic, vinegar and Worcestershire sauce during cooking. Here served with new potatoes and peas, and garnished with sprig of mint. 8 servings. Page 227*

APRICOT-GLAZED RACK OF LAMB
Delicious glaze of apricot jam, lemon juice and mustard gives this best end of neck of lamb its beautiful colour. Garnished with watercress sprigs and accompanied here with glazed carrots.
4 servings. Page 227

STUFFED CABBAGE
Traditional dish of cabbage leaves with beef, rice and raisin filling. Served with delicately spiced tomato sauce.
4 servings. Page 213

SALT BEEF AND CABBAGE
Traditional, hearty dish of spiced salted beef and cabbage with sliced carrot, onions and celery.
6 servings. Page 208

SAUSAGE AND PEPPERS
Colourful combination of spicy pork sausages, onions, and green, yellow and red peppers, in fennel-flavoured tomato sauce. 6 servings. Page 234

KNACKWURST AND POTATO SUPPER
Sausages and potatoes in piquant onion sauce on bed of endive; sprinkled with bacon. Here with beetroot garnish.
4 servings. Page 232

'BARBECUED' BRISKET
Lean beef brisket cooked in tangy barbecue sauce. Served here with dill-topped potatoes and salad garnish.
6 servings. Page 208

PASTA POT
Pasta shells and chopped vegetables in hearty meat sauce. Here sprinkled with Parmesan and garnished with parsley.
6 servings. Page 213

STEAK AND MUSHROOM PIE
Hearty pie filled with tender beef, mushrooms and onions cooked in wine sauce; topped with conventionally cooked golden pastry crust. Here accompanied with lightly cooked carrots.
8 servings. Page 205

BEEF BOURGUIGNON
Beef chunks with mushrooms, baby onions, carrots and celery in red wine sauce; garnished with sprig of parsley.
4 servings. Page 206

ROAST RIB OF BEEF
Traditional succulent beef wing rib joint seasoned with spices and herbs and cooked to medium-rare. Here accompanied with steamed broccoli florets, carrots and roast potatoes.
6 servings. Page 202

STEAK AND KIDNEY PUDDING
Filling of rump steak, lamb kidneys and mushrooms in rich gravy, cooked in suet pastry case.
4 servings. Page 205

BEEF CARBONNADE
Casserole of beef, bacon and onions cooked in beer. Here served with potatoes sprinkled with chopped parsley.
8 servings. Page 207

OLD-FASHIONED BEEF STEW
Traditional dish of vegetables and beef cooked in tomato-flavoured Beef Stock with thyme and bay leaf.
6 servings. Page 207

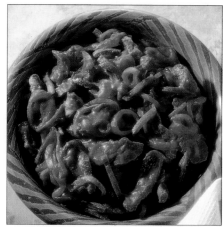

BEEF GOULASH
Hearty blend of beef, onions and green peppers in tomato and paprika sauce. Delicious alone or with buttered noodles.
6 servings. Page 206

PARTY BURGERS
Medium-rare sirloin steak burgers arranged on herb-dipped toast rounds with variety of decorative party toppings.
12 servings. Page 210

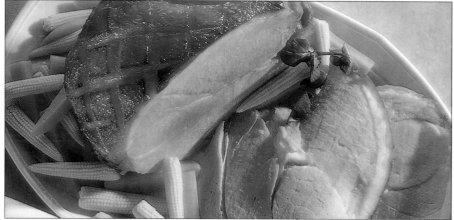

GLAZED HAM
Joint of fully cooked honey roast ham coated with zesty apple sauce and mustard glaze. Here served with thin carrot strips and baby sweetcorn and garnished with sprig of watercress.
8 servings. Page 221

LOIN OF PORK WITH APRICOT STUFFING
Boneless pork loin seasoned with pepper to taste and cooked until tender. Cut into thin slices and complemented with fruity stuffing of apricots, apple, onion and celery.
12 servings. Page 216

PORK JAMBALAYA
Hearty casserole of pork cubes, rice and medley of vegetables cooked in Beef Stock with Creole flavourings.
6 servings. Page 219

SPICY PORK TURNOVERS
Spicy pork filling in cheesy cornmeal pastry parcels; here with tomato chutney and soured cream.
4 servings. Page 218

ROAST LOIN OF VEAL WITH PURÉE OF SWEDE *Tender veal roast with garlicky swede purée. Here garnished with watercress and served with courgettes.*
8 servings. Page 223

HOLIDAY VEAL ROAST *(top) Lean veal breast stuffed with spinach, cheeses and canned pimientos. Here served with Sweet Pepper Medley.* 12 servings. Page 222. **STUFFED SHOULDER OF VEAL** *Veal shoulder with stuffing of spinach-filled ravioli, ham and cheese; cooked in dry white wine and stock.* 10 servings. Page 223

OSSO BUCO
Veal knuckle, vegetables and arborio rice in tomato and wine sauce with dried mushrooms and herbs; with parsley garnish. 4 servings. Page 224

VEAL STEW PROVENÇALE
Seasoned veal, onions, green and red peppers and olives in herby sauce; here with pasta bow ties tossed with parsley.
4 servings. Page 226

VEAL RAGOÛT
Veal chunks, baby onions, mushrooms, celery and carrot in cream sauce; served with herbed rice and parsley garnish.
4 servings. Page 226

LAMB CURRY
Indian-style dish of tender lamb chunks cooked in spicy fruit and vegetable sauce, with traditional garnish of toasted almonds and coriander leaves. Accompanied with rice and mango chutney.
4 servings. Page 230

MOROCCAN LAMB WITH COUSCOUS
Savoury couscous topped with mixture of lamb chunks and selected vegetables cooked in richly spiced tomato sauce.
6 servings. Page 230

LAMB STEW WITH FETA
Traditional mixture of lamb, courgettes and olives cooked in tomatoes and wine served over cheesy macaroni with dill.
6 servings. Page 231

MARINATED LAMB CUTLETS WITH HERBED PEAS *Lamb marinated in mustard, mint, and mint and apple jelly; served with minty peas and mint garnish.*
4, 2, 1 servings. Page 228

LAMB PILAF
Vegetables, rice and cubes of roast lamb cooked in curried stock. Served with cooling yogurt sauce and mint garnish.
8 servings. Page 227

MOUSSAKA
Greek dish of aubergines, herby minced lamb, tomato and feta cheese; topped with cheesy sauce and coriander garnish.
6 servings. Page 231

LEMON AND LIME THAI KEBABS
Chunks of lamb soaked in spicy lemon and lime marinade, cooked with chunks of papaya and green pepper on wooden skewers. Served on bed of Hot Cooked Rice.
4 servings. Page 229

UNDER 30 MINUTES

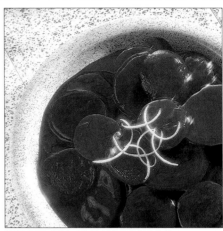

SWEET AND SOUR BEETROOT
Easy dish of canned sliced beetroot in tangy sweet and sour sauce, garnished with Orange Julienne.
4, 2, 1 servings. Page 255

ASPARAGUS WITH CELERY AND WALNUTS *(top) Tender-crisp asparagus and celery tossed with toasted walnuts. 4 servings.*
ASPARAGUS BUNDLES *Asparagus spears with spring onion tie in buttery pimiento and spring onion sauce. 4, 2, 1 servings. Page 252*

NEAPOLITAN BROCCOLI
Broccoli cooked with mixture of red pepper, black olives, capers, garlic and spring onions. Garnished with almonds.
4 servings. Page 256

CREAMED SWEETCORN WITH PEPPERS *Sweetcorn with green pepper, onions and tomato in creamy sauce flavoured with oregano.*
4 servings. Page 273

BROAD BEANS WITH BUTTERED BREADCRUMBS *Quick-and-easy dish of broad beans with added Parmesan cheese, sprinkled with crispy breadcrumbs.*
4, 2, 1 servings. Page 254

PETITS POIS À LA FRANÇAISE
Frozen peas cooked with diced bacon, lettuce and onion; garnished with chopped parsley.
6 servings. Page 267

PARTY BRUSSELS SPROUTS
Baby onions and Brussels sprouts flavoured with thyme and cooked until tender-crisp, served tossed with crispy bacon pieces. 6 servings. Page 257

FRENCH BEANS WITH PEANUT SAUCE *French beans cooked until tender-crisp, tossed in spicy oriental-style sauce with peanut butter and red pepper.*
4, 2, 1 servings. Page 254

GINGER-ORANGE CARROTS
Ginger, orange and spring onion mixture combined with matchsticks of carrot; here garnished with Orange Julienne.
4 servings. Page 259

GLAZED CARROTS
Sliced carrots cooked in stock and sugar until tender-crisp, then glazed with butter and garnished with parsley.
4 servings. Page 259

THREE PEPPER BUTTER *(top) Green pepper, black peppercorns and cayenne in melted butter.* **FRESH HERB BUTTER** *(centre) Chopped fresh herbs in melted butter and lemon juice.* **GOLDEN SPICED BUTTER** *Curry powder and Dijon mustard in melted butter.*
Each enough for 4 ears of corn. Page 273

CAULIFLOWER WITH MINTY HOT SPINACH SAUCE *(left)*
Cauliflower florets cooked in spiced spinach mixture with yogurt added.
6 servings. Page 260. **CAULIFLOWER WITH LEMON AND DILL**
SAUCE *Whole cauliflower served with creamy sauce delicately flavoured*
with lemon and dill. 8 servings. Page 260

SWEETCORN PUDDING
Delicious combination of sweetcorn,
breadcrumbs, eggs and cream cooked until
set; sprinkled with paprika.
4 servings. Page 273

OKRA, HAM AND TOMATOES
Diced ham and onion with whole okra
cooked in spicy tomato sauce. Here served
over rice and garnished with lemon slices.
4 main course servings. Page 265

SZECHUAN AUBERGINE
Oriental-style dish of strips of aubergine in spicy-hot soy and ginger
sauce with sliced spring onion added; garnished with Spring Onion
Tassel.
4 servings. Page 252

MUSHROOMS À LA GRECQUE *Whole*
button mushrooms with herbed vinegar,
tomatoes, garlic and onions. Here with
chopped parsley garnish.
6 servings. Page 264

CREAMED ONIONS
Baby onions cooked in onion and nutmeg
flavoured white sauce; here garnished with
chives.
8 servings. Page 266

PEAS WITH BACON AND ONIONS *Peas*
and baby onions cooked in bacon fat for
extra flavour, then sprinkled with diced
bacon.
4 servings. Page 267

LEMON PEAS
Simple dish of tender peas lightly cooked with grated lemon zest and butter, then garnished with lemon and mint.
4, 2, 1 servings. Page 267

MASHED POTATOES
Fluffy potatoes beaten with butter and cream then topped with chives. Here shown with Almost Instant Gravy.
4 servings. Page 269

SPRING VEGETABLES WITH LEMON AND CHIVE BUTTER *(left)*
Zesty butter is spooned over this seasonal selection of tender-crisp vegetables. 6 servings. Page 275. **NEW POTATOES WITH BUTTER AND CHIVES** *Elegant dish of new potatoes with chive butter; garnished here with chives.* 4, 2, 1 servings. Page 268

BROCCOLI WITH SESAME SAUCE
Tender-crisp broccoli served cold with sauce of toasted sesame seeds, spring onions, garlic and soy sauce.
4 servings. Page 257

HOME STYLE POTATOES WITH BACON AND ONIONS *Diced potatoes cooked with sliced onion, with diced bacon added. Garnished here with parsley.*
4 servings. Page 269

CURRIED POTATOES WITH PEAS
Potato chunks and peas cooked in tomato sauce spiced with ginger, chilli and coriander; garnished here with Chilli Flower. 6 servings. Page 270

73

BABY AUBERGINE BROCHETTES WITH SATAY SAUCE *Baby aubergines on skewers brushed with garlic-flavoured oil and served with spicy peanut sauce.* 4 servings. Page 253

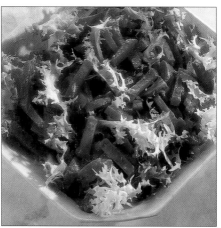

FRESH BEETROOT WITH ENDIVE *Endive with tender strips of beetroot coated in a tangy dressing of olive oil, red wine vinegar, mustard and oregano.* 6 servings. Page 255

BROCCOLI MORNAY *Tender-crisp broccoli coated in cheese sauce with hint of mustard, sprinkled with onion and crumb topping.* 4 servings. Page 256

CHICORY WITH CHEESE SAUCE *(top) Halved chicory with rich cheese sauce.* 4 servings. **BRAISED CHICORY** *(bottom) Chicory cooked until tender in herby stock.* 4, 2, 1 servings. Page 261. **CARROT AND POTATO PANCAKES** *Variation of a homely recipe; here served with apple sauce and soured cream.* 4 servings. Page 259

CREAMY CABBAGE *Shredded cabbage and sliced onions cooked with cream until tender, then topped with breadcrumbs; here with dill garnish.* 8 servings. Page 258

SWEET-AND-SOUR SHREDDED RED CABBAGE *Brown sugar and red wine vinegar give shredded red cabbage a distinctive flavour.* 8 servings. Page 258

CELERIAC PURÉE
Puréed cooked celeriac and potato mixture with butter, cream and seasonings; garnished here with parsley.
6 servings. Page 261

STUFFED ONIONS
Cooked, hollowed-out onions filled with celery, red pepper, onion and breadcrumbs; here with parsley garnish.
4, 2, 1 servings. Page 266

SWEET AND SOUR ONIONS
Sliced onions cooked in stock, red wine and vinegar until glazed. Here garnished with parsley.
8 servings. Page 266

LEEKS WITH HAM IN CHEESE SAUCE
Leeks cooked in stock, then wrapped with ham and served in cheese sauce. Here with parsley and endive garnish.
4, 2, 1 servings. Page 263

BRUSSELS SPROUTS WITH CHESTNUTS *Hearty side dish of tender Brussels sprouts cooked in stock with butter and whole chestnuts.*
4, 2, 1 servings. Page 257

POTATOES AU GRATIN
Classic dish of sliced potatoes topped with melted cheese, onion and seasoned breadcrumbs; here with parsley garnish.
8 servings. Page 268

STUFFED POTATOES ORIENTALE *(left) Baked potatoes with Chinese-style filling. Garnished here with Spring Onion Tassels. 4, 2, 1 servings. Page 269.* **ORIENTAL MUSHROOMS** *Marinated pork with mushrooms, mange-touts and tomato strips in ginger and soy sauce.*
4 main course servings. Page 264

CREAMED SPINACH
Cooked spinach in seasoned white sauce. Here shown drizzled with sauce and garnished with lemon.
4 servings. Page 271

ACORN SQUASH WITH ORANGE AND HONEY GLAZE *(top) Squash halves with sweet glaze.* **MAPLE BUTTERNUT SQUASH** *(centre) Tender squash with apple, onion and syrup.* **SPAGHETTI SQUASH WITH MEAT SAUCE** *Pork sausagemeat sauce tops tender squash strands.* 4 servings. Page 272

MASHED HARVEST VEGETABLES
Mashed butternut squash and swede are combined with orange-flavour liqueur, orange zest and cinnamon.
8 servings. Page 274

RATATOUILLE
Traditional French vegetable mixture of red pepper, aubergine, courgettes and tomatoes; garnished with basil.
8 servings. Page 275

GARDEN VEGETABLE MEDLEY
Colourful combination of courgettes, red peppers, aubergines, potatoes, onions and tomato, garnished here with basil.
6 servings. Page 274

SPECIAL MIXED VEGETABLES
Attractive selection of sliced carrots, broccoli and button mushrooms cooked until tender and combined with strips of red pepper and soy and spring onion sauce.
8 servings. Page 274

TWICE-BAKED SWEET POTATOES
Mixture of cooked sweet potato, yogurt and chilli powder served hot in sweet potato shells; garnished here with parsley.
4, 2, 1 servings. Page 270

SWEET POTATO BAKE
Sweet potatoes mashed with cream, mixed spice, brown sugar and vanilla, then cooked with walnut and crumb topping.
10 servings. Page 270

MARINATED OKRA
Lightly cooked okra marinated in mixture of oil, vinegar, mustard, sugar, thyme and hot red pepper flakes.
4 servings. Page 265

COURGETTE LINGUINE WITH SUN-DRIED TOMATOES AND PINE NUTS
Imaginative dish of courgette strips cooked with pine nuts and sun-dried tomatoes.
4 servings. Page 262

STUFFED COURGETTES
Hollowed-out courgettes filled with diced courgette, red pepper, tomato, breadcrumbs and Parmesan cheese.
2 servings. Page 262

AUBERGINES WITH TABBOULEH STUFFING *(top) Aubergine halves filled with refreshing minted bulgur mixture.* 4 main course servings. Page 253. **SPINACH GNOCCHI WITH BUTTER AND PARMESAN** *Italian dish of spinach and ricotta ovals with melted butter and Parmesan; here garnished with parsley.* 8 servings. Page 271

SALADS

SPINACH SALAD WITH HOT BACON DRESSING *Unusual salad of spinach and sliced red onion tossed in tangy mustard dressing and sprinkled with diced bacon.* 4, 2, 1 servings. Page 278

WARM SALAD OF ROCKET, SWEETCORN, BLACK BEANS AND AVOCADO *Wilted rocket with sweetcorn, black beans and onion.* 8 servings. Page 279

OLD-FASHIONED CHICKEN SALAD *Chicken breast chunks in mayonnaise dressing with celery, onion and pimiento. Here garnished with oak leaf lettuce.* 4, 2, 1 main course servings. Page 276

ANTIPASTO SALAD *(top) Vegetables, salami and cheese in Vinaigrette Dressing.* 6 main course servings. Page 277. **PEPPER SALAD** *(bottom) Peppers, onion and olives with feta and dressing.* 6 servings. Page 279. **CLASSIC POTATO SALAD** *Potatoes, celery and egg in mayonnaise; here with parsley garnish.* 6 servings. Page 281

CHICKEN CLUB SALAD *Thyme-flavoured chicken breasts sliced and served with crisp bacon, tomato slices, lettuce and toast triangles.* 2 main course servings. Page 276

DELICATESSEN SALAD *Potatoes, bacon, celery and onion in tangy dressing served with salad leaves, delicatessen meats and cheese strips.* 6 main course servings. Page 277

78

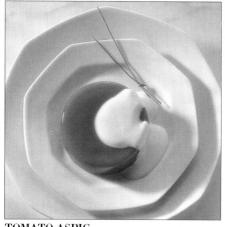

**WARM SALAD OF ARTICHOKE
HEARTS AND CHERRY TOMATOES**
*Artichoke hearts and tomatoes in buttery
onion, tarragon and wine sauce.*
6 servings. Page 279

THAI-STYLE BEEF AND NOODLE SALAD *(left) Imaginative dish of
beef with red pepper, noodles and cashews in Thai-style dressing. 4 main
course servings.* Page 277. **PRAWN SALAD WITH MANGE-TOUTS**
*Large prawns, mange-touts, spring onions, red pepper and baby
sweetcorn cooked in wine. 4 servings.* Page 282

**GARDEN VEGETABLE AND PASTA
SALAD** *A hearty combination of fresh
vegetables, cheese cubes and bow tie pasta
in a flavourful dressing.*
6 main course servings. Page 280

TOMATO ASPIC
*A simple, chilled tomato aspic spiced with
Tabasco sauce and garnished with plain
low-fat yogurt and chives.*
4, 2, 1 servings. Page 281

**CHICKEN AND POTATO SALAD WITH
ZESTY DRESSING** *Chicken, potatoes, red
onion, yellow pepper and olives in
dressing. Here with basil garnish.*
6 main course servings. Page 276

PRAWN SALAD SUPREME
*Prawns, new potatoes, French beans,
chick peas, red pepper and olives tossed
with Zesty Mayonnaise Dressing.*
6 servings. Page 282

HIGH-FIBRE SALAD *(left) Colourful dish of pulses in a French
dressing. 8 servings.* Page 280. **LENTILS VINAIGRETTE** *(centre)
Lentils and vegetables in fresh herb dressing. 8 servings.* Page 280. **WILD
RICE SALAD** *Wild rice and long-grain rice with spring onions, apple,
celery, pine nuts and raisins. 8 servings.* Page 281

SPAGHETTI BOLOGNESE
Tomato-based meat sauce with herbs and chopped vegetables served over cooked spaghetti in this ever-popular dish.
4, 2, 1 servings. Page 286

PENNE WITH CHEESE, RED PEPPER AND OLIVE SAUCE *Onions, red peppers and olives with mozzarella and Fontina cheeses, basil and penne.*
4 servings. Page 286

CHEESE TORTELLONI WITH BROCCOLI AND PINE NUTS
Hearty dish of cheese-filled tortelloni and broccoli cooked with hot red pepper flakes, garlic and pine nuts for added flavour; tossed with Parmesan cheese before serving.
8 servings. Page 287

TAGLIATELLE WITH BACON, MUSHROOMS AND PEAS *Pasta tossed with creamy spring onion, mushroom and pea sauce, sprinkled with Parmesan and bacon.* 4 servings. Page 286

MADE-IN-MINUTES BOLOGNESE SAUCE *(left) Pasta sauce of beef, mushrooms, tomatoes and herbs; here with basil garnish. Makes 1.5 litres. Page 289.* **CREAMY TOMATO SAUCE** *Pasta sauce with tomatoes, cream, herbs and garlic; here with parsley garnish.*
Makes 500 ml. Page 288

CHEESE-FILLED JUMBO SHELLS
Jumbo pasta shells filled with three cheeses, egg and parsley cooked in pasta sauce; garnished with chopped parsley and grated cheese.
4 servings. Page 289

CHICKEN AND VEGETABLE PASTA
Farfalle combined with strips of chicken breast and vegetables cooked in an oriental-style sauce.
4 servings. Page 287

SAVOURY RICE
Rice cooked in Chicken Stock with onion and green pepper, combined with Cheddar or Fontina cheese and soured cream.
4, 2, 1 servings. Page 291

MILANESE-STYLE RISOTTO
Arborio rice, garlic and onion cooked in saffron-flavoured stock, then mixed with peas and grated Parmesan cheese.
4 servings. Page 291

FETTUCCINE PRIMAVERA
Colourful combination of springtime vegetables – leeks, broccoli, mushrooms, courgettes, peppers, carrots and tomatoes – mixed with a creamy white sauce, Fontina or Cheddar cheese and fettuccine.
4 servings. Page 287

RED BEANS AND RICE
*Filling dish of rice topped with red kidney
beans, celery and onion in spicy sauce;
sprinkled with crisp diced bacon.*
4 servings. Page 291

CHINESE-STYLE RICE WITH PORK
*Cubes of tender boneless pork loin cutlets cooked with onion, celery, red
pepper and rice, then flavoured with soy and ginger oriental-style sauce;
here accompanied with soy sauce.*
4 servings. Page 290

ARROZ CON POLLO
*Chicken pieces coated in flour and browned in olive oil, cooked with
turmeric-flavoured rice, smoked ham, onion, celery and green pepper.
Garnished with canned pimiento and parsley.*
4, 2, 1 servings. Page 290

INDIAN PILAF
*Authentic dish of spiced rice, chopped
coriander or parsley and raisins, topped
with golden-brown flaked almonds.*
4 servings. Page 292

BULGUR PILAF WITH PEPPERS
*Cracked wheat softened in stock, then
mixed with peppers, mushrooms, garlic
and basil; here with basil garnish.*
8 servings. Page 293

BARLEY WITH WILD MUSHROOMS
Savoury combination of pearl barley and wild mushroom pieces cooked until tender in Beef Stock; garnished with parsley.
4 servings. Page 293

SAUSAGE, RICE AND BEANS
Hearty dish of pork sausages, cooked rice, kidney beans, onion and tomatoes, with oregano and garlic.
4 servings. Page 290

CANNELLONI MILANESE *(top) Meat with herbs, currants and nuts in cannelloni tubes; here with white sauce and Parmesan. 4 servings. Page 289.* **WILD RICE AND MUSHROOM PILAF** *Wild rice cooked in chicken stock, then combined with onion, mushrooms and seasoning. Garnished here with coriander. 4 servings. Page 292*

POLENTA WITH MEAT SAUCE
Decorative dish of seasoned cornmeal (polenta) and mozzarella, cooked with Made-in-Minutes Bolognese Sauce.
4 servings. Page 293

LASAGNE
Layers of rich meat sauce, pasta and cheese, finished with mozzarella and Parmesan. Here accompanied with salad.
10 servings. Page 288

CANNELLONI WITH SPINACH AND MUSHROOMS *Cannelloni with cheese, spinach and mushroom filling; here with Creamy Tomato Sauce.*
4 servings. Page 288

**CARROT AND PINEAPPLE TEA
BREAD** *Moist and munchy, this
delicious bread is good served
with tea.*
12 servings. Page 298

SAVOURY SCONES
*Poppy, sesame and caraway seed toppings
add interest to these traditional
teatime scones.*
Makes 14. Page 299

PORK BARBECUE SANDWICHES
*Breadcrumbed pork loin topped with
barbecue sauce and coleslaw in hamburger
bun; here with watercress garnish.*
4 servings. Page 301

WARM VEGETABLE SALAD WITH CHEESE IN PITTA *(top) Crisp
vegetables with melted cheese in pitta breads; garnished with parsley.*
4, 2, 1 servings. **PITTA POCKETS WITH SOUVLAKI** *Sliced lamb with
piquant vegetables and feta cheese in toasted pitta breads. 4 servings.*
Page 305

**SMOKED TURKEY AND GRUYÈRE ON
CROISSANTS** *Croissants with mustard,
smoked turkey, tomato and Gruyère;
garnished here with salad leaves.*
4 servings. Page 300

ROAST BEEF AND BRIE SIZZLER
*Tarragon and mustard flavoured butter on
French bread with hot roast beef and Brie;
here with cherry tomatoes and tarragon.*
4 servings. Page 301

CHILLI IN A BUN
Minced beef, onion, green pepper and celery with ketchup and chilli sauce in hamburger buns; here with celery garnish.
4 servings. Page 303

DESIGNER BAGELS *Warmed bagel halves topped with: Orange Julienne with Orange Butter; black olives, sun-dried tomatoes and basil with ricotta cheese; red-pepper strips with Smoked Salmon and Chive Spread.*
Makes 12 bagel halves. Page 309

EASY BEEF TORTILLAS
Minced beef with onion and garlic in spicy tomato sauce on tortillas; here served with Mexican accompaniments.
4 servings. Page 302

MUFFINS WITH MELTED CHEESE AND TUNA *Tuna in piquant cream cheese mixture in toasted muffins with melted cheese. Here accompanied with salad leaves.* 4 servings. Page 308

REUBEN SANDWICHES
Salt beef, sauerkraut and Emmenthal on rye with Thousand Island dressing. Here with pickled cucumbers and parsley.
4, 2, 1 servings. Page 303

HOT TURKEY OPEN SANDWICHES WITH GRAVY *Thinly sliced cooked turkey on wholemeal toast with piping hot gravy. Garnished here with parsley.*
2 servings. Page 300

SAVOURY BREADSTICKS *(left) Bacon rashers wrapped round breadsticks make an irresistible canapé, served here with decorative tomato and chive garnish. Makes 12. Page 306.* **MOZZARELLA GARLIC BREAD** *Popular accompaniment to Italian food with added mozzarella cheese; served here with salad. 6 pieces. Page 308*

MOZZARELLA FRENCH BREAD
Hollowed-out French bread filled with cheese, pimiento-stuffed green olives, spring onions and Parma ham.
8 servings. Page 309

NUTTY GOAT CHEESE TOASTS
Walnut coated goat cheese on toasted French bread with sun-dried tomatoes and olive oil. Accompanied with salad leaves.
Makes 15. Page 306

PIZZA TARTLETS
Warmed tartlet shells filled with Italian pasta sauce, mozzarella, anchovies and olives. Garnished with basil.
Makes 16. Page 306

CRANBERRY AND NUT BREAD
Digestive biscuit crumbs add texture to this tea bread with cranberries, walnuts and orange. Here served with butter pats.
12 servings. Page 297

DATE AND WALNUT BREAD
Traditional teatime favourite made in microwave; here served sliced with dainty butter curls.
12 servings. Page 297

COURGETTE TEA BREAD
Walnuts, poppy seeds and lemon zest are combined with grated courgettes in this unusual tea bread. Served here with Orange Butter. 12 servings. Page 297

GINGERBREAD
Soured cream and black treacle make this traditional bread deliciously moist; here with cream cheese and apple.
12 servings. Page 298

STEAK SANDWICHES
Thin slices of sirloin steak topped with green pepper and red onion mixture in toasted French bread spread with Dijon mustard; sprinkled with grated cheese and microwaved until melted.
4, 2, 1 servings. Page 301

CHICKEN CLUB SANDWICHES
Filling sandwich of chicken coated with stuffing mix, bacon and tomatoes in wholemeal toast.
4 servings. Page 300

CALZONE
Italian-style folded pizzas with hearty fillings of your choice; here with radicchio leaf and parsley garnish.
2 servings. Page 310

MEATBALL 'SUBMARINES'
Mushroom and garlic flavoured meatballs in Italian pasta sauce; served in individual French loaves. Here with parsley garnish.
4 servings. Page 303

FOUR SEASONS PIZZA
Artichoke hearts, Parma ham, tomatoes and canned pimientos top pesto sauce or basil on pizza base.
4 servings. Page 310

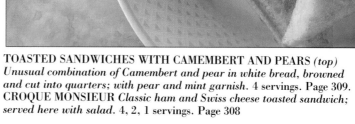

MEDITERRANEAN PIZZA
Sliced red onion and assorted herbs with tangy crumbled goat cheese or feta create an original pizza topping.
4 servings. Page 310

TOASTED SANDWICHES WITH CAMEMBERT AND PEARS *(top)*
Unusual combination of Camembert and pear in white bread, browned and cut into quarters; with pear and mint garnish. 4 servings. Page 309.
CROQUE MONSIEUR *Classic ham and Swiss cheese toasted sandwich; served here with salad. 4, 2, 1 servings. Page 308*

FRUIT AND DESSERTS

SPICED APPLE SLICES
Fluted apple rings gently poached in apple juice with brown sugar, spices and lemon zest. Decorated here with mint.
4 servings. Page 317

GLAZED BANANAS WITH ORANGE
Bananas and oranges in cinnamon-flavoured brown sugar and butter glaze with pecan nuts and Orange Julienne.
4 servings. Page 319

CHERRIES IN RED WINE
Fresh cherries cooked in wine sauce with redcurrant jelly and cinnamon; here served with ice cream and mint.
6 servings. Page 319

CRÈME PÂTISSIÈRE
Tartlet shells with variety of flavoured Crème Pâtissière fillings and complementary toppings: Almond and Mocha Fillings (left); plain Crème Pâtissière (top); Orange Filling (right).
Makes 750 ml. Page 324

RED FRUIT COMPOTE
Colourful dish of mixed berries and cherries in sauce flavoured with orange-flavour liqueur; decorated with kiwi fruit.
8 servings. Page 323

SPICED PINEAPPLE
Ground ginger or cinnamon flavour these sugar-glazed pineapple slices; decorated with Lime Julienne and mint leaves.
4 servings. Page 321

APPLE CARAMEL DESSERT
Lightly spiced pastry base topped with decoratively arranged apple slices in rich caramel sauce.
6 servings. Page 318

DELUXE BAKED APPLES
Seedless raisins, chopped walnuts and ground cinnamon mixed with butter or margarine fill hollowed-out dessert apples that are then cooked and basted with apple juice and golden syrup.
4, 2, 1 servings. Page 317

APPLE SPICED PUDDING
Spicy, apple-flavoured wholemeal pudding, enriched with cream; served here with cream and orange.
6 servings. Page 318

APPLE AND WALNUT CRUMBLE
Spiced walnut, flour and sugar topping over apple slices; served here with whipped cream, apple slices and mint.
8 servings. Page 318

DRIED FRUIT COMPOTE
Dried apricots, prunes and figs with glacé cherries in spiced syrup, decorated with Orange Julienne.
8 servings. Page 323

CARAMEL PEARS IN STRAWBERRY SAUCE
Poached whole pears served on individual dessert dishes with smooth strawberry purée; creamy caramel sauce is spooned over just before serving. Here topped with mint.
4, 2, 1 servings. Page 321

POACHED PEARS WITH CHOCOLATE SAUCE *Poached pear 'fans' served with rich chocolate sauce, here feathered with extra cream and decorated with mint.*
4 servings. Page 321

ZABAGLIONE WITH CHERRIES
*Rich Italian-style dessert of egg yolks
beaten with sugar and kirsch or Marsala,
served over fresh or canned cherries.*
4 servings. Page 319

PLUM KUCHEN
*Stoned plum quarters arranged in baking dish on pizza-base dough and
topped with crumbly mixture of brown sugar and Melba Toast Crumbs.*
6 servings. Page 322

WHITE CHOCOLATE MOUSSE
*Rich, chilled dessert made with melted
white chocolate, beaten eggs, vanilla
essence and softly whipped cream.*
8 servings. Page 329

CHOCOLATE-DIPPED FRUIT
*Selection of fruit dipped in melted plain
and white chocolate makes an impressive
end to any meal.*
14–30 pieces. Page 327

**CHOCOLATE AND COCONUT
DESSERT CUPS** *Ice cream served in
chocolate and coconut cups; here served
with Chocolate-Dipped Fruit and mint.*
6 cups. Page 331

CREAMY RICE PUDDING
*Filling family favourite made with cream,
vanilla, ground spices and raisins. Can be
served warm or chilled.*
6 servings. Page 334

**OLD-FASHIONED BREAD AND
BUTTER PUDDING** *Cinnamon, nutmeg,
cloves and vanilla add flavour to this
microwave version of classic pudding.*
10 servings. Page 334

**CHOCOLATE AND CINNAMON BREAD
PUDDING** *Cinnamon-flavoured raisin loaf
combined with cream, eggs, sugar and
chocolate for a new twist to an old
favourite.* 10 servings. Page 335

CHOCOLATE PUDDING
Warm dessert made from chewy chocolate cake mixture sprinkled with chopped walnut and brown sugar topping.
8 servings. Page 330

STRAWBERRIES 'NOUVELLES'
Here, strawberries are cut in half and attractively arranged on chilled orange- and chocolate-flavoured custard sauces.
6 servings. Page 322

RASPBERRY POACHED PEARS WITH CHOCOLATE AND RASPBERRY SAUCE
Elegant dessert with sumptuous sauce; here feathered with whipped cream.
6 servings. Page 320

SYRUP SPONGE PUDDING
Classic sponge pudding flavoured with vanilla and lemon. Here with extra warmed golden syrup poured over.
4 servings. Page 334

RICH NOODLE PUDDING
Conventionally cooked egg noodles with cottage cheese, soured cream, apricots, sultanas and browned breadcrumbs.
8 servings. Page 335

LIGHT CHEESE RING WITH FRUIT (top) *Moulded cottage cheese and soft cheese mixture; served with selection of sliced fresh fruit.* 8 servings. Page 323. **STRAWBERRY CHARLOTTE** *Rich mousse encircled with sponge fingers, decorated with cream and strawberries and tied with ribbon.* 12 servings. Page 324

FRUIT AND DESSERTS

CHOCOLATE MOUSSE TORTE
Creamy chocolate mousse with crunchy chocolate-nut base; decorated with cream, chopped nuts and Chocolate Rounds.
16 servings. Page 328

ELEGANT POACHED PEACHES
Peaches cut in half and cooked in grenadine-based syrup, then filled with moistened amaretti-biscuit crumbs; served on puréed raspberry sauce flavoured with almond essence.
4 servings. Page 320

CRÈME CARAMEL
Velvety smooth set custard flavoured with vanilla; served chilled with rich, golden-brown caramel sauce.
4 servings. Page 325

RASPBERRY CREAM PARFAITS (top) *Layers of luscious raspberry mousse and whipped cream; here decorated with Chocolate Curls.*
6 servings. **ICED LEMON SOUFFLÉS** *Deliciously flavoured lemon custard with cream and egg whites; served frozen.* 8 servings. Page 326

CRÈME BRÛLÉE
Melted brown sugar forms crisp topping over chilled, rich custard base; decorated here with Strawberry Fan.
4 servings. Page 325

RHUBARB RICE CREAM
Two favourite family desserts combined in one, made richer with topping of whipped cream. Decorated here with mint leaf.
8 servings. Page 326

CHOCOLATE AND CHESTNUT CREAM
Chestnut purée and chocolate set with gelatine in this soufflé-like dessert. Here decorated with cream and Chocolate Curls. 12 servings. Page 327

NUTTY CHOCOLATE DELIGHT
Chopped nuts add crunch to this rich pudding topped with whipped cream and sprinkled with cinnamon.
6 servings. Page 330

RICH CHOCOLATE MOUSSE
Simple mousse of plain chocolate and eggs, flavoured with vanilla and topped here with whipped cream.
4 servings. Page 328

TINY CHOCOLATE CONES
Chocolate and cream mixture piped into colourful foil cones and sprinkled with finely chopped macadamia nuts.
Makes 25 cones. Page 329

TIRAMISÚ
Layers of almond-flavoured cake, mascarpone cheese, coffee and liqueur, lightly dusted with cocoa and served chilled. 16 servings. Page 327

CHOCOLATE CREAM LOAF
Finely chopped pistachio nuts top this chilled dessert 'loaf' of plain chocolate and whipped cream; here shown sliced and served with raspberry sauce and Chocolate Leaves.
16 servings. Page 328

CHOCOLATE ALMOND DESSERT
Raisins plumped in almond-flavour liqueur combined with crushed amaretti biscuits in chocolate-covered, cake-like dessert.
8 servings. Page 329

INDIVIDUAL RASPBERRY CHEESECAKES *Puréed raspberries in cream cheese mixture on digestive-crumb base, decorated with raspberries and mint.* 8 servings. Page 336

CREAMY CHEESECAKE *Classic lemon- and vanilla-flavoured cheesecake in crumb crust. Here decorated with strawberries, raspberries and mint.* 12 servings. Page 335

CHOCOLATE AND AMARETTI CHEESECAKE *(top) Chocolate mousse-like cake with amaretti crust, decorated with cream and Chocolate Curls.* 12 servings. Page 336. **CHOCOLATE PROFITEROLES** *Choux pastry puffs filled with Crème Pâtissière, drizzled with Chocolate Glaze and here dusted with icing sugar.* 12 profiteroles. Page 331

VANILLA ICE CREAM *Classic vanilla-flavoured ice cream, served here with sliced orange, strawberries and kiwi fruit and decorative mint sprig.* 8 servings. Page 332

MANGO SORBET *Mango, lime juice and dark rum puréed together and frozen to make this exotic dessert.* 4 servings. Page 332

KIWI FRUIT SORBET *Frozen tangy purée of kiwi fruit and lemon juice, served here with kiwi fruit slices and mint leaves.* 4 servings. Page 332

ORANGE CHIFFON PIE
Orange zest and orange and lemon juice make refreshing additions to this classic pie, here decorated with Orange Julienne.
10 servings. Page 346

BANANA COCONUT PIE
Sliced banana covered with creamy vanilla flavoured filling in Pastry Shell; topped with toasted coconut.
10 servings. Page 344

MINTY CHOCOLATE TART
The filling in this Chocolate Wafer Crust is a luscious combination of creamy custard, coffee and crème de menthe liqueur. Chocolate Curls add a sophisticated finishing touch.
10 servings. Page 345

DIGESTIVE BISCUIT CRUST
This versatile biscuit crust is shown here with a creamy chiffon filling, decorated with piped cream and mandarins.
Makes 21.5 cm crust. Page 339

PASTRY SHELL
Conventionally baked, classic shortcrust shell for tarts of all types; here filled with fresh strawberries and glazed.
Makes 22.5–25 cm shell. Page 339

PASTRY CRUST
Traditionally baked pastry crust with Fork-Scalloped Edge; here shown filled with custard and topped with gooseberries.
Makes 21.5 cm crust. Page 339

LEMON MERINGUE PIE
*Classic, all-time favourite of lemon-flavoured custard in Pastry Crust
with attractively swirled meringue topping; conventionally baked until
golden.*
10 servings. Page 343

DELUXE APPLE PIE
*Old-fashioned pie filled with lightly spiced
apples. Oat-based crumble provides a
crunchy topping.*
10 servings. Page 341

LIGHT LEMON AND ALMOND TART
*Creamy lemon and almond filling in
conventionally baked Pastry Shell, topped
with cream, almond and Lemon Julienne.*
10 servings. Page 348

PEACHES AND CREAM PIE
*Crème Pâtissière combined with peach jam
in a biscuit crust, topped with cooked
peach slices.*
10 servings. Page 343

SUMMER FRUIT TART
*Creamy custard in a sweet biscuit crust
here topped with glazed strawberries,
raspberries, blueberries and kiwi fruit.*
10 servings. Page 342

STICKY WALNUT TART
*Syrup, sugar and walnuts combine with
eggs and butter to make toffee-like filling
in Pastry Crust; here decorated with
cream.* 10 servings. Page 349

BLACK BOTTOM PIE
*These slices elegantly reveal a Ginger Biscuit Crust filled with layers of
rich chocolate custard and delicate rum-flavoured custard. Here
decorated with piped whipped cream.*
10 servings. Page 345

MINCEMEAT AND APPLE TARTLETS
Mincemeat filling with added diced apple, chopped walnuts, brown sugar and lemon juice in tartlet shells. Here topped with pastry holly leaves and berries, hearts and stars.
10 tartlets. Page 349

AMARETTO PIE
Amaretto-flavoured chiffon filling in amaretti biscuit crust; here topped with piped cream and flaked almonds.
10 servings. Page 348

CHOCOLATE WALNUT PIE
Chocolate and walnut filling cooked until lightly set in Pastry Crust; with cream and walnut decoration.
10 servings. Page 343

PECAN PIE
Traditional favourite for Thanksgiving day in America; here in Pastry Crust with Plaited Edge.
10 servings. Page 349

STRAWBERRY CHIFFON PIE
Attractively arranged strawberry slices top light and creamy mousse-like mixture set in Digestive Biscuit Crust. Topped with whole strawberry, glazed, and served chilled.
10 servings. Page 346

COCONUT CREAM PIE
Toasted coconut crust holds chiffon filling flavoured with coconut and almond; cream and coconut make attractive edge.
10 servings. Page 347

APPLE, PEAR AND CRANBERRY TART *Popular combination of fruits in shortcrust pastry shell, topped with decorative pastry shapes glazed with egg yolk.* 10 servings. Page 341

HIGHLAND CREAM PIE
Rich vanilla filling with whipped cream and egg whites in Pastry Crust, here with Leaf Edge.
10 servings. Page 347

RASPBERRY CUSTARD TART
Fresh raspberries top Crème Pâtissière in Pastry Crust, here shown with attractive Plaited Edge.
10 servings. Page 342

CHOCOLATE CREAM PIE
Generous layer of cream tops luscious chocolate filling in Vanilla Wafer Crust; with piped cream edging.
10 servings. Page 344

QUICK FRENCH APRICOT TART
Bought tart shell filled with canned apricot halves lightly set in almond-flavoured creamy custard; sprinkled with toasted flaked almonds after cooking in microwave.
10 servings. Page 342

WHITE CHOCOLATE AND STRAW-BERRY GÂTEAU *Sumptuous cake layered with strawberries and White Chocolate Mousse.*
12 servings. Page 356

SUNNY ORANGE LAYER CAKE *Mandarin orange segments top this cake filled with Lemon Curd Filling and covered with Orange Whipped Cream.*
10 servings. Page 354

BLACK FOREST GÂTEAU *Kirsch flavours this extra-rich cake made from devil's food cake mix and decorated with cream, cherries and chocolate.*
12 servings. Page 357

CHOCOLATE CREAM SANDWICH *Crème Pâtissière sandwiched between cake layers, topped with Chocolate Glaze and feathered Glacé Icing.*
12 servings. Page 358

BÛCHE DE NOËL *Traditional French Christmas 'log' of chocolate Swiss roll with chocolate mousse filling, generously covered with Chocolate Cream Icing and marked to resemble bark; here dusted with icing sugar and decorated with holly sprig.* 14 servings. Page 359

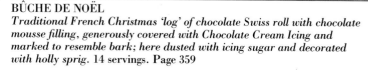

STRAWBERRY CREAM LAYER CAKE *Whipped cream flavoured with vanilla is combined with cut-up strawberries to fill luscious three-layer cake.*
8 servings. Page 356

PINEAPPLE UPSIDE-DOWN CAKE
Canned pineapple rings and maraschino cherries in sugar-butter glaze top this simple, vanilla-flavoured sponge. Can be served warm or chilled.
8 servings. Page 353

PEANUT BUTTER FAIRY CAKES
Creamy Peanut Butter and Chocolate Icing tops these light fairy cakes made with yellow cake mix and peanut butter.
12 cakes. Page 354

TWO-TONED LAYER CAKE
Chocolate mousse is spread between four cake layers, the whole cake then lavishly iced with Chocolate Cream Icing.
12 servings. Page 355

VICTORIA SANDWICH CAKE
Basic sponge cake baked in microwave; here shown filled with cream and jam and dusted with icing sugar.
12 servings. Page 353

CARROT CAKE
Ground cinnamon, ginger, allspice and nutmeg are combined with sunflower oil, sultanas, walnuts and grated carrots in this all-time American favourite.
10 servings. Page 355

APRICOT CREAM ROULADE
Light-as-a-feather Swiss roll filled with apricot jam and coated with almond-flavoured whipped cream.
14 servings. Page 360

MARBLED CHOCOLATE RING
Devil's food cake mix with surprise filling of sweetened cream cheese; drizzled with Chocolate Glaze.
16 servings. Page 361

CHOCOLATE MOUSSE BOMBE
Rich chocolate bombe cake lavishly filled with chocolate mousse and beautifully decorated with piped whipped cream rosettes and dusting of cocoa.
10 servings. Page 361

RICH NUT-TOPPED BROWNIES
Moist brownies enriched with eggs and topped with extra chocolate and chopped walnuts; chilled after cooking until firm.
24 brownies. Page 362

BUTTERSCOTCH SQUARES
Pecans, desiccated coconut and plain chocolate chips are added to these flavour-packed cookies.
24 cookies. Page 362

NO-BAKE MINT CHOCOLATE SQUARES
Crushed digestive biscuits combine with chocolate and chopped walnuts in these quick and easy cookies.
24 cookies. Page 362

OVER 1 HOUR

CREAM CHEESE BROWNIES *(left) Almond-flavoured softened cream cheese creates marbled design in fudge brownie mix. 16 brownies.*
CHOCOLATE AND MARSHMALLOW TRIANGLES *Miniature marshmallows, chocolate chips and walnuts top fudge brownie mix.*
16 triangles. Page 363

ALMOND SHORTBREAD
Vanilla and almond essences flavour this classic shortbread which is attractively topped with toasted flaked almonds.
8 wedges. Page 363

COCONUT ROUNDS
Delicate toasted coconut biscuits flavoured with orange zest and attractively decorated with melted chocolate.
30 biscuits. Page 364

LEMON TUILES
Light-as-a-feather biscuits flavoured with lemon zest and almond essence and sprinkled liberally with flaked almonds.
30 tuiles. Page 364

FRUIT AND NUT BARS
Dried apricots, raisins, prunes, almonds and walnuts covered with plain chocolate topping.
16 bars. Page 368

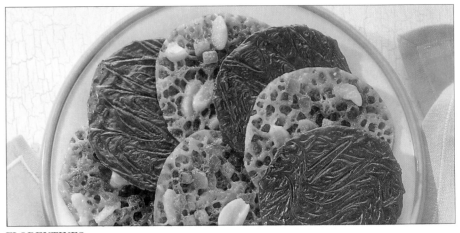

MEXICAN WEDDING BISCUITS
Novelty crescent-shaped walnut biscuits dusted with thick layer of icing sugar until completely coated.
24 biscuits. Page 365

FLORENTINES
Authentic thin, chewy biscuits made from sugar, cream, honey, butter or margarine, diced candied peel and flaked almonds. Coated on one side with plain melted chocolate.
24 pieces. Page 365

MAPLE SNAPS
Buttery walnut biscuits flavoured with maple and golden syrups, cooked in microwave until golden.
24 biscuits. Page 365

CHOCOLATE CHIP CRISPIES
Sweetened and lightly spiced ground walnut biscuits topped with chopped walnuts and chocolate chips.
30 biscuits. Page 368

VIENNESE MELTAWAYS *(top) Melt-in-the-mouth almond biscuits, here dusted with both icing sugar and cocoa. Makes 36. Page 364.* **CARAMEL PECAN BARS** *Biscuit base topped with pecans and creamy caramel, drizzled with melted chocolate.* 24 biscuits. Page 368

CHOCOLATE MALLOW FUDGE
Squares of fudge created from two types of chocolate, chopped walnuts and melted marshmallows.
36 pieces. Page 371

MINT IMPERIALS
White, green and pink mints here shown half-dipped into melted plain chocolate for added interest.
36 pieces. Page 369

PEANUT BRITTLE
Classic combination of roasted peanuts and caramel made from golden syrup, sugar and butter or margarine.
Makes 450 g. Page 370

VANILLA-WALNUT DROPS
Sweets based on the delicious combination of walnut and vanilla, sweetened with brown sugar.
42 pieces. Page 369

PISTACHIO BITES
Vanilla and pistachio flavour layers of creamy white chocolate in these melt-in-the-mouth sweets.
32 pieces. Page 372

CHOCOLATE AND CHERRY FUDGE SLICES
Plump maraschino cherries in chocolate fudge roll, coated with melted caramel and chopped walnuts. 36 slices. Page 371

BUTTER CARAMELS
Individually wrapped chewy sweets made from cream, sugar, golden syrup, butter and vanilla essence.
64 caramels. Page 370

CHOCOLATE CHERRY CUPS (top) *Tiny chocolate cups with orange filling, each one topped with maraschino cherry. 36 cups. Page 370.*
SUPER-EASY TRUFFLES *Melted plain chocolate with added butter, cream and almond essence; attractively piped into gold foil cups.*
30 truffles. Page 371

COCONUT HAYSTACKS
Lightly toasted coconut mixed with melted chocolate and shaped to resemble haystacks.
Makes 20. Page 372

PEACH SAUCE
Simple and elegant purée of peaches, flavoured with almond essence and nutmeg; served here with raspberries and mint. Makes 250 ml. Page 382

BRANDIED STRAWBERRY SAUCE
Strawberries and brandy added to melted redcurrant jelly; here served chilled over ice cream and decorated with mint. Makes 600 ml. Page 382

FUDGE SAUCE
Luscious sauce of cocoa and sugar with added cream; here poured over sautéed bananas and sprinkled with almonds. Makes 300 ml. Page 383

CUSTARD SAUCE
Popular dessert sauce of half cream, sugar, egg yolks and vanilla; here served poured over colourful sliced fruits. Makes about 300 ml. Page 382

ORANGE SAUCE
Orange-flavour liqueur and grated orange zest in sugar syrup; served here with orange slices and whole strawberries. Makes 600 ml. Page 383

MELBA SAUCE
Sieved, thickened sauce of raspberries and redcurrant jelly; here with poached pear halves and mint decoration. Makes 250 ml. Page 383

CHOCOLATE SAUCE
Plain chocolate melted with sugar, cream and butter, flavoured with vanilla; here poured over banana split. Makes about 750 ml. Page 382

HOT FRUIT SAUCE
Chopped nectarines and plums cooked with sugar and orange juice; served here with ice cream and mint decoration. Makes 1 litre. Page 382

BLACKCURRANT SAUCE
Delicately spiced blackcurrants with sugar, lemon juice and lemon zest; here with poached whole peach decorated with mint. Makes about 250 ml. Page 383

BUTTERSCOTCH SAUCE
*Warm sauce of brown sugar, half cream,
golden syrup and butter; served here
poured over ice cream.*
Makes 250 ml. Page 382

CHERRY SAUCE
*Sweet cherries cooked with sugar and
water, flavoured with almond essence and
served warm; here poured over crêpes.*
Makes 500 ml. Page 383

BRANDY BUTTER
*Butter-based sauce with icing sugar and
vanilla; here served with warm Mincemeat
and Apple Tartlets.*
Makes about 150 ml. Page 383

BÉARNAISE SAUCE
*White wine vinegar, spring onion,
tarragon and parsley in classic French
sauce; served here with steak and salad.*
Makes about 250 ml. Page 381

HOLLANDAISE SAUCE
*Seasoned sauce of egg yolks, lemon juice
and melted butter, served here with
asparagus; with herb garnish.*
Makes about 250 ml. Page 381

BARBECUE SAUCE
*Onion, garlic, chilli and ketchup mixture
shown here with cooked chicken,
parsleyed potatoes and salad.*
Makes about 250 ml. Page 379

BROWN GRAVY
*Traditional gravy made from vegetables
and stock; here shown with lamb chops
and vegetable accompaniments.*
Makes about 500 ml. Page 380

SATAY SAUCE
*Peanut butter sauce with garlic, diced red pepper, ginger, vinegar
and soy. Here shown with chicken kebabs, garnished with lemon,
radish and coriander.*
Makes about 80 ml. Page 379

CRANBERRY SAUCE *Classic accompaniment to turkey, given extra zest with orange juice and port. Makes 425 ml. Page 379.*
GIBLET GRAVY *Thickened strained chicken and vegetable stock with added giblet meat. Makes 1 litre. Page 380. Both shown here with roast turkey, potatoes, carrots and chive garnish.*

SWEETCORN RELISH
A spicy mixture of corn, green and red peppers, tomato, onion, and vinegar; served here with glazed chicken.
Makes about 1 litre. Page 377

MINT JELLY
A set jelly of mint, apple juice and vinegar; served here with lamb chops, new potatoes and green beans.
Makes 1 litre. Page 376

TOMATO SAUCE
Thickened, strained sauce flavoured with spring onion, garlic, parsley and basil; shown here with jumbo prawns.
Makes about 600 ml. Page 380

APRICOT/PINEAPPLE BUTTER
Delicious spread of dried apricots and crushed pineapple; here on toasted muffin half with butter curls.
Makes about 500 ml. Page 375

TOMATO KETCHUP
Piquant relish flavoured with vinegar and mixed spices; here shown with hamburger and French fries.
Makes 750 ml. Page 377

OVER 1 HOUR

CURRIED MELON CHUTNEY
Curried mixture of melon, tomatoes, onions and sultanas; served here with samosas and lime and coriander garnish.
Makes about 1 litre. Page 378

HOT PEPPER JELLY
Sweetened set mixture of red pepper juice and white vinegar; here served with ham, tomato and mixed salad.
Makes 500 ml. Page 376

CRANBERRY CHESTNUT RELISH
Spicy mixture of cranberries, marrons, sultanas and onions; here with cold roast turkey and mixed salad.
Makes 1 litre. Page 377

APPLE AND ONION CHUTNEY
Apples, onions, pepper and prunes spiced with ginger and mustard; here with ploughman's lunch.
Makes about 1 litre. Page 378

GREEN TOMATO CHUTNEY
Spiced green tomatoes, peppers and onion; here served with cheese, crackers and salad garnish.
Makes 1 litre. Page 378

BLACKBERRY SPREAD *(left) Zesty blackberry and apple mixture.* Makes 1 litre. Page 376. **FRESH STRAWBERRY JAM** *(centre) Crushed fresh strawberries, sugar and lemon juice.* Makes about 1 litre. Page 375. **PEACH PRESERVE** *Peaches in sugar and lemon syrup.* Makes 1 litre. Page 375. *All shown with croissants, rolls and butter.*

Snacks
and Starters

DIPS · NIBBLES · PÂTÉS · FILLED STARTERS
VEGETABLE STARTERS · SHELLFISH STARTERS

Snacks and Starters

A microwave makes entertaining easier and far less time consuming. Many of the starters in this chapter can be made and frozen 1 month before serving; instructions are given in individual recipes. When you are ready to serve, they can be popped into the microwave to be ready in moments. If you arrange hors d'oeuvre on microwave-safe trays when cooking, they can be served straight from the microwave, saving on extra washing up. Also, they can be quickly popped back into the microwave for reheating during the course of the occasion. You can even add cocktail sticks before cooking: wooden or plastic sticks, including those with frills, may be used in the microwave, as can bamboo skewers. Do not use coloured sticks, however, as these may leave dye on your food.

When unexpected guests drop in, you can have something hot and delicious to welcome them with in only a few minutes. Variously shaped tartlet shells can be kept in the freezer and, when needed, defrosted in the microwave oven and quickly filled.

In addition to the delicious assortment of snacks and starters included here, many of the sandwiches in the Breads and Sandwiches chapter (pages 295–310) can be adapted for buffets and other special occasions. Your microwave oven can also be used for a wide variety of commercially available packaged and frozen starters: just follow the microwave instructions provided with the product.

The microwave can be used to soften cheeses for use in dips or for making into cheese balls, and it is wonderful for bringing hard cheese from the refrigerator to eating temperature. Place 225 g unwrapped hard cheese in the microwave and heat on Medium (50% power) for 30–45 seconds, until chill is gone. To bring chilled dips to room temperature, heat 500 ml dip on Medium for 1–2 minutes just before serving. Use your microwave as well to refresh stale snacks such as popcorn and potato crisps. Heat them in 100 g batches on High (100% power) for 15–60 seconds.

QUICK AND EASY STARTERS

When unexpected guests drop in, use the microwave as an extra helper in the kitchen to create quick and easy starters from ingredients on hand. In a matter of minutes, you'll have an attractive dish that looks like it took a great deal of time and effort to prepare.

Sliced tomato and avocado (left) *drizzled with Italian salad dressing and sprinkled with microwave-crisp bacon. Garnished with basil leaves.*

Well-drained canned pineapple rings (right) *topped with cream cheese and chives, sprinkled with paprika. Garnished with celery leaves, chives and Lime Twists* (page 132).

Dips

CURRIED CRAB DIP

Colour Index page 38. Makes 500 ml. 37 cals per tablespoon. Low in sodium.
Begin 15 minutes ahead.

15 g butter or margarine
2 teaspoons curry powder
1 onion, finely chopped
1 celery stick, finely chopped
25 g canned pimientos, drained and diced

225 g cream cheese
1 tablespoon milk
1 teaspoon lemon juice
225 g white crabmeat
2 tablespoons chopped fresh parsley
Crudités

1. In medium microwave-safe bowl, place butter or margarine, curry powder, onion, celery and pimientos. Cook on High (100% power) for 2½ (2:30) minutes, or until soft, stirring twice.
2. To mixture, add cream cheese. Cook on High for 1 minute, until softened. Stir until well mixed.
3. Into cream cheese mixture, gently stir milk, lemon juice, crab and parsley.
4. Spoon dip into serving bowl. Serve with crudités.

BACON AND HORSERADISH DIP

Colour Index page 38. Makes 500 ml. 38 cals per tablespoon. Low in sodium.
Begin 25 minutes ahead.

4 rashers rindless streaky bacon, diced
225 g cream cheese
120 ml soured cream
2 tablespoons prepared horseradish
¼ teaspoon pepper

Pepper Bowl (below, optional)
Celery sticks, potato crisps, grissini (breadsticks) and Bagel Chips (page 112)

1. In 30 × 20 cm microwave-safe baking dish, place diced bacon. Cook on High (100% power) for 4 minutes, or until browned, stirring occasionally. Remove bacon to kitchen paper to drain.
2. Discard all but 1 teaspoon bacon fat. Add cheese to dish. Cook on High for 1 minute.
3. Into mixture, stir soured cream, horseradish and pepper. Crumble bacon; add to dip. Cover and refrigerate for at least 15 minutes.
4. Spoon dip into dish or Pepper Bowl; serve with celery, crisps, grissini and Bagel Chips.

Making the Pepper Bowl

With sharp knife, cut off top of pepper and thin slice from bottom so pepper sits flat.

From top of pepper (stalk end), scrape out seeds and white membrane; discard.

Dips are popular because they are so quick and easy to prepare and can be served at any time: here is a selection of different flavours that will suit all occasions. Freshly cut raw vegetables, or crudités, are low-calorie accompaniments, while potato crisps and corn chips are more substantial.

MEDITERRANEAN AUBERGINE DIP

Colour Index page 38. 16 cals per tablespoon. Low in cholesterol, fat, sodium.
Begin 25 minutes ahead.

Ingredients for 750 ml		Microwave cookware
1 medium aubergine 1 small red onion 1 green pepper 4 garlic cloves 2 celery sticks with leaves 4 tablespoons olive oil 1 tomato, chopped 2 tablespoons red wine vinegar 1 tablespoon caster sugar	1 teaspoon dried oregano ½ teaspoon dried thyme 6 green olives, chopped 1 tablespoon capers, drained Pepper to taste Parsley sprigs to garnish Pitta bread, toasted and cut into triangles	30 × 20 cm baking dish Medium bowl

1 Pierce aubergine in several places. Line baking dish with kitchen paper. Place aubergine on paper. Cook on High (100% power) for 7 minutes, or until softened, turning over halfway through cooking.

2 Meanwhile, chop red onion, green pepper, garlic and celery.

3 In bowl, mix chopped vegetables, oil, tomato, vinegar, sugar, oregano and thyme. Cook, covered, on High for 3 minutes, until vegetables soften, stirring once; set aside.

4 Cut aubergine in half lengthways. With spoon, scoop out flesh. In food processor with knife blade attached or in blender, process flesh until smooth. Spoon into bowl with vegetable mixture.

5 Stir vegetable mixture and puréed aubergine together. Add olives, capers and pepper.

6 Spoon dip on individual plates or into serving bowl and garnish with parsley. Serve with toasted pitta triangles.

Fast Light Lunch

Artichokes with Lemon and Garlic, page 120
Pipérade, page 139, with
Heart Shaped Croûtons (below)
Fresh fruit

PREPARATION TIMETABLE

1¹/₂ **hours ahead**	*Prepare a selection of fresh seasonal fruit. Sprinkle cut fruit with lemon juice to prevent discoloration: cover and refrigerate.*
1 **hour ahead**	*Prepare and cook Artichokes with Lemon and Garlic: do not garnish. Set on serving plates and keep warm. Make Croûtons. Prepare Pipérade up to end of step 2.*
Just before serving	*For artichokes, reheat butter in microwave; garnish. Continue with Pipérade from beginning of step 3. Garnish with Croûtons and basil.*

HEART SHAPED CROÛTONS

1 Remove crusts from **4 *slices bread.*** Cut bread diagonally into quarters.

2 Round off top 2 corners of each triangle; cut a 'V' from top centre to form heart shape. Bake conventionally as for Croûtons (page 127).

3 Dip tops of croûtons into **2 tablespoons melted butter**, then into **4 tablespoons chopped parsley**.

Dips

MEXICAN DIP

Colour Index page 38. Makes 250 ml. 45 cals per tablespoon. Low in sodium.
Begin 15 minutes ahead.

1 spring onion, finely chopped	*1–2 tablespoons milk*
15 g butter or margarine	*Chopped spring onion to garnish*
175 g cream cheese	
4 tablespoons bottled taco sauce (or to taste)	

1. In medium microwave-safe bowl, place spring onion and butter or margarine. Cook on High (100% power) for 1 minute, or until onion softens.
2. To spring onion mixture, add cream cheese. Heat on Medium (50% power) for 1–1¹/₂ (1:30) minutes, until softened. Stir until smooth.
3. Into cream cheese mixture, stir taco sauce; add milk to thin dip to desired consistency.
4. Spoon dip into serving bowl and garnish with spring onion.

HOT PRAWN DIP WITH DILL

Colour Index page 38. Makes 500 ml. 25 cals per tablespoon. Low in fat, sodium.
Begin 20 minutes ahead.

2 tablespoons olive or vegetable oil	*3 tablespoons plain flour*
3 garlic cloves	*300 ml milk*
1 spring onion, thinly sliced	*1¹/₂ teaspoons tomato purée*
1 celery stick, cut into 5 cm pieces	*Good pinch cayenne pepper (or to taste)*
225 g medium raw prawns, shelled and deveined	*2 teaspoons lemon juice*
	Fresh dill to garnish
	Cooked tortelloni

1. In medium microwave-safe bowl, combine oil, garlic, spring onion, celery and prawns. Cook, covered, on High (100% power) for 3 minutes, until softened, stirring halfway through cooking.
2. With slotted spoon, remove prawn mixture from bowl, reserving liquid. In food processor with knife blade attached or on chopping board, finely chop prawn mixture; set aside.
3. To liquid remaining in bowl, add flour; stir until blended and smooth. Cook on High for 1 minute. Remove from microwave.
4. Into flour mixture, gradually stir milk and tomato purée; add cayenne pepper. Cook on High for 4 minutes, or until thickened, stirring twice.
5. Into mixture, stir lemon juice and reserved prawn mixture. Cook on High for 2 minutes, or until hot.
6. Spoon dip into serving bowl and garnish with dill. Serve immediately, with tortelloni on sticks.

BAGEL CHIPS: thinly slice bagels (egg-enriched Jewish bread rolls), brush with oil, then toast under grill for 1 minute. Turn bagels over, brush with more oil and grill for 1 further minute. Use to accompany dips.

Nibbles

MIDDLE EASTERN MEATBALLS

**Colour Index page 40. Makes about 26. 33 cals each. Low in cholesterol, sodium.
Begin 35 minutes ahead.**

1 egg	*1/2 teaspoon pepper*
350 g minced beef	*1/4 teaspoon ground*
1 onion, grated	*cloves*
3 garlic cloves, crushed	*1/4 teaspoon grated*
2 tablespoons raisins,	*nutmeg*
finely chopped	*Lemon slices and mint*
2 tablespoons chopped	*leaves to garnish*
fresh mint leaves	
1 tablespoon lemon juice	
2 teaspoons ground	
cumin	
1/2 teaspoon ground	
cinnamon	

1. In medium bowl, beat egg. Add minced beef, onion, garlic, raisins, mint, lemon juice, cumin, cinnamon, pepper, cloves and nutmeg; mix until well combined.
2. Shape mixture into 2.5 cm meatballs. Place on microwave-safe rack set in 30 × 20 cm microwave-safe baking dish.
3. Cook meatballs on High (100% power) for 4–5 minutes, rearranging meatballs halfway through cooking. Allow to stand, covered with kitchen paper, for 3 minutes before serving.
4. Thread each meatball on long wooden skewer; arrange on individual plates. Garnish with lemon slices and mint leaves.

CHEESE STICKS

**Colour Index page 39. Makes 16. 90 cals each. Low in sodium. Good source of vitamin A.
Begin 20 minutes ahead.**

115 g cream cheese	*16 grissini (breadsticks)*
30 g butter or margarine	*4 tablespoons each:*
2 tablespoons grated	*poppy seeds; chopped*
Parmesan cheese	*chives; sesame seeds;*
1/2 teaspoon Dijon	*paprika*
mustard	
4 drops Tabasco sauce	

1. In medium microwave-safe bowl, place cream cheese and butter or margarine. Heat on High (100% power) for 1 1/2 (1:30) minutes. Stir until smooth.
2. Into cream cheese mixture, stir Parmesan, mustard and Tabasco sauce; mix well.
3. With knife, spread equal amount of cheese mixture on to half of each grissini.
4. Place the poppy seeds, chives, sesame seeds and paprika on separate pieces of greaseproof paper. Lightly roll 4 grissini in each coating. Serve immediately.

All of these nibbles can be prepared in advance. For an alternative to Angels on Horseback (below), make Devils on Horseback by substituting stoned prunes for oysters.

ANGELS ON HORSEBACK

**Colour Index page 38. 29 cals per oyster. Low in fat, sodium.
Begin 25 minutes ahead.**

Ingredients	For 24 oysters	For 12 oysters	For 6 oysters
Streaky bacon rashers	*12 rashers*	*6 rashers*	*3 rashers*
Worcestershire sauce	*4 teaspoons*	*2 teaspoons*	*1 teaspoon*
Dijon mustard	*1 teaspoon*	*1/2 teaspoon*	*1/4 teaspoon*
Fresh oysters	*24 oysters*	*12 oysters*	*6 oysters*
Lemon slices and			
parsley sprigs	*garnish*	*garnish*	*garnish*
Microwave cookware	32.5 × 22.5 cm baking dish	30 × 20 cm baking dish	30 × 20 cm baking dish
Time on High (100% power) Bacon	4 minutes	2 minutes	1 1/2 (1:30) minutes
Oysters	3 minutes	1 1/2 (1:30) minutes	1 minute
Standing time	2 minutes	1–2 minutes	1 minute

1 With sharp knife, remove any rinds from bacon; cut each rasher in half crossways.

2 Line baking dish with double thickness of kitchen paper. Arrange bacon on paper, in batches if necessary; cover with kitchen paper. Cook on High for time in Chart. Transfer bacon to kitchen paper to drain.

3 Meanwhile, in bowl, combine Worcestershire sauce, mustard and oysters; stir until oysters are coated in sauce mixture.

4 Wrap each oyster with 1 bacon rasher, securing with wooden cocktail stick.

5 In dish used for bacon, place oysters. Cook, covered with kitchen paper, on High for time in Chart, turning oysters once. Allow to stand for time in Chart.

6 Transfer oysters to serving platter; garnish. Serve hot.

Nibbles

POTATO SKINS WITH CHEDDAR CHEESE

Colour Index page 40. 72 cals per piece (without dip). Low in sodium.
Begin 40 minutes ahead.

Ingredients	For 16 pieces	For 8 pieces	For 4 pieces
Baking potatoes, washed and dried	4 medium	2 medium	1 medium
Cheddar cheese, grated	175 g	75 g	25 g
Spring onions, chopped	2 spring onions	1 spring onion	1/2 spring onion
Salt	1/2 teaspoon	1/4 teaspoon	to taste
Pepper	to taste	to taste	to taste
Spring onions	garnish	garnish	garnish
Soured cream or yogurt	dip	dip	dip
Microwave cookware	30 cm plate	30 cm plate	20 cm plate
Time on High (100% power)			
Potatoes	16–18 minutes	10–12 minutes	6–7 minutes
With cheese topping	4–5 minutes	2–3 minutes	1 minute
Standing time			
Potatoes	5 minutes	5 minutes	5 minutes
With cheese topping	2 minutes	1–2 minutes	1 minute

1 Pierce each potato 3 times. Place on kitchen paper.

2 Cook potatoes on High for time in Chart, turning over once.

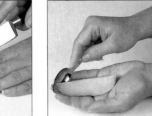

3 Wrap potatoes in tea towel. Allow to stand for time in Chart.

4 Meanwhile, in bowl, combine cheese and chopped spring onions.

5 Cut each potato into quarters lengthways.

6 Scoop out potatoes, leaving 5 mm potato flesh on skins.

7 On plate (see Chart), arrange skins spoke-fashion.

8 Sprinkle skins with salt, pepper and cheese mixture.

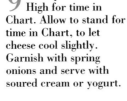

9 Cook potato skins on High for time in Chart. Allow to stand for time in Chart, to let cheese cool slightly. Garnish with spring onions and serve with soured cream or yogurt.

NACHO BAKE

Colour Index page 39. 6 servings. 256 cals per serving. Good source of vitamin A, calcium.
Begin 15 minutes ahead.

115 g Double Gloucester cheese, grated
115 g Cheddar cheese, grated
1/2 red onion, diced
2–4 tablespoons diced canned jalapeños (pickled green chillies)
50 g stoned black olives, sliced
4 tablespoons chopped fresh coriander leaves
200 g corn tortilla chips
Soured cream and bottled taco sauce

1. In medium bowl, mix cheeses, onion, jalapeños, olives and coriander; set aside.
2. On 30 cm round microwave-safe plate, arrange one-third of tortilla chips in single layer. Top with one-third of cheese mixture. Continue alternating tortilla chips and cheese mixture, making 2 more layers and finishing with cheese.
3. Cook on High (100% power) for 2–3 minutes, until cheese melts and bubbles.
4. Serve immediately accompanied with soured cream and taco sauce.

SPICY CHICKEN WINGS

Colour Index page 39. Makes 12. 190 cals each.
Begin 25 minutes ahead.

6 chicken wings
1 small onion, finely chopped
4 tablespoons tomato ketchup
30 g butter or margarine
2 tablespoons fruity brown sauce
2 tablespoons light brown sugar
2 tablespoons orange juice
1/4–1/2 teaspoon Tabasco sauce
3 celery sticks, cut into fingers
250 ml creamy blue cheese dip or salad dressing

1. With sharp knife, remove small tips from each chicken wing. Cut wings in half at joint, making 12 pieces.
2. In medium microwave-safe bowl, combine onion, ketchup, butter or margarine, brown sauce, brown sugar, orange juice and Tabasco sauce. Cook on High (100% power) for 4 minutes, or until onion softens and flavours blend, stirring halfway through cooking.
3. In 30 × 20 cm microwave-safe baking dish, arrange chicken pieces in single layer; spoon over half of sauce. Cook chicken pieces on High for 6 minutes.
4. Turn wings over and coat with remaining sauce. Cook on High for 6 minutes, or until chicken is fork-tender and juices run clear.
5. Transfer chicken pieces to warmed serving dish. Garnish with prepared celery fingers. Serve with blue cheese dip or salad dressing.

Pâtés

COUNTRY-STYLE PORK PÂTÉ

Colour Index page 41. 16 servings. 198 cals per serving. Good source of vitamin A, iron. Begin 1 day ahead.

12 rashers rindless streaky bacon	¹/₂ teaspoon grated nutmeg
225 g cooked ham, diced	350 g minced pork
225 g chicken livers, minced	350 g minced beef
1 onion, finely chopped	¹/₂ teaspoon pepper
4 garlic cloves, crushed	Sliced gherkins, salad leaves and stuffed olives to garnish
4 tablespoons brandy	
1 teaspoon dried thyme	
1 teaspoon dried oregano	
¹/₂ teaspoon ground cloves	

1. With sharp knife, dice 4 bacon rashers. In large bowl, combine diced bacon, ham, chicken livers, onion, garlic, brandy, thyme, oregano, cloves and nutmeg; cover and set aside.
2. Line 22.5 × 12.5 cm microwave-safe loaf dish with remaining 8 bacon rashers, allowing rashers to hang over edges of dish; set aside.
3. To ham mixture, add minced pork, beef and pepper; stir until well mixed. Spoon pâté mixture into bacon-lined dish, smoothing top with back of spoon. On level surface, tap corner of dish several times to disperse any air bubbles. Fold bacon over top of pâté mixture.
4. Elevate loaf dish on microwave-safe trivet or rack, or on ramekin turned upside down. Cook, covered loosely with greaseproof paper, on High (100% power) for 20 minutes. Pour off excess fat.
5. Allow pâté to stand for 30 minutes to cool. Cover loaf dish with clean greaseproof paper or cling film, then foil-wrapped cardboard and foil-wrapped weight (below). Refrigerate pâté overnight.
6. Remove weight, cardboard and greaseproof paper or cling film. Place plate or chopping board upside down on loaf dish and invert to unmould. With knife, scrape off any coagulated cooking juices and excess fat.
7. Transfer pâté to serving platter and garnish. Serve cut into thin slices.

Wrapping and Weighting the Pâte

Cut piece of cardboard to size of top of loaf dish and wrap completely in foil. Place over pâté mixture.

Wrap brick in foil or use several cans to weight pâté. Place weight on foil-wrapped cardboard.

Pâtés make elegant starters that cook quickly in the microwave but need to be chilled to be at their best. In Seafood Pâté (below), microwave-safe cling film is used to line loaf dish for easier removal, and the dish is elevated to ensure even cooking.

SEAFOOD PÂTÉ

Colour Index page 41. 128 cals per serving. Begin early in day.

Ingredients for 16 servings		Microwave cookware
225 g raw prawns, shelled and deveined	350 ml double or whipping cream, chilled	22.5 × 12.5 cm loaf dish
1 shallot, chopped	1 egg	Small bowl
15 g butter or margarine	¹/₄ teaspoon salt	Trivet, rack or ramekin
1 tomato, seeded and chopped	Good pinch white pepper	
3 tablespoons chopped fresh tarragon	Tarragon leaves and chopped tomato to garnish	
450 g scallops	Mayonnaise (optional)	

1 Line loaf dish with microwave cling film, allowing film to extend 5 cm beyond edges of dish.

2 With sharp knife, chop prawns. In small bowl, mix prawns, shallot and butter or margarine. Cook on High (100% power) for 1 minute, stirring once. Add tomato and tarragon; stir and set aside.

3 In food processor with knife blade attached or in blender, process scallops until smooth. Gradually pour in cream until well mixed; blend in egg, salt and pepper. Transfer to mixing bowl; fold in reserved prawn mixture.

4 Into loaf dish, gently spoon pâté mixture; smooth with back of spoon. On level surface, tap corner of dish several times to disperse any air bubbles. Fold edges of cling film over pâté mixture.

5 Elevate dish on trivet or rack, or on ramekin turned upside down. Cook on Medium (50% power) for 10 minutes, or until pâté is set. Cover dish with baking sheet or tray to flatten surface of pâté. Allow to stand for 20 minutes. Refrigerate for at least 3 hours.

6 To serve: unfold edges of cling film. Place chilled serving platter upside down on loaf dish and invert to unmould; remove cling film. Garnish pâté with tarragon and tomato. If you like, serve with mayonnaise.

Pâté and Filled Starters

CHICKEN LIVER PÂTÉ

Colour Index page 410. Makes 250 ml. 46 cals per tablespoon. Low in sodium. Good source of vitamin A. Begin early in day.

60 g butter or margarine
1 spring onion, chopped
1 garlic clove, chopped
225 g chicken livers
1 tablespoon brandy
½ teaspoon dried
  thyme
½ teaspoon pepper
Assorted savoury
  biscuits
Radish Flowers and
  Pear Slices (below)

1. In 1 litre microwave-safe casserole, place butter or margarine, spring onion and garlic. Cook on High (100% power) for 3–4 minutes, until onion softens, stirring halfway through cooking.
2. Pierce chicken livers with fork; add to butter mixture. Cook, covered loosely with greaseproof paper, on High for 3–5 minutes, just until livers are no longer pink, stirring halfway through cooking. Allow to stand for 2 minutes.
3. In food processor with knife blade attached or in blender, process chicken liver mixture, brandy, thyme and pepper until well blended and smooth, stopping occasionally and scraping sides with rubber spatula.
4. Spoon chicken liver mixture into freezer-to-microwave container; cover and freeze.
5. About 15 minutes before serving, thaw pâté. Remove container cover. Cook, covered loosely with greaseproof paper, on Medium (50% power) for 4–6 minutes, just until thawed but not warm, stirring twice to break up frozen mixture. Serve pâté on biscuits, Radish Flowers and Pear Slices.

Making the Radish Flowers

With small sharp knife, about 5 mm from stalk end, cut zig-zag pattern through radish.

Twist top from bottom of radish, leaving flower-shaped cup (which can be filled).

Making the Pear Slices

Cut pear into quarters lengthways. Core centres, then cut pear into thin slices.

Rub each pear slice with cut lemon to prevent flesh discolouring.

CHEESE and CHILLI CHAPATIS

Colour Index page 40. 111 cals per wedge. Good source of calcium. Begin 35 minutes ahead.

Ingredients for 16 wedges		Microwave cookware

5 fresh green chillies
175 g Cheddar cheese
4 tablespoons chopped
  fresh coriander
  leaves
2 spring onions, sliced
1 × 195 g can
  sweetcorn, drained
	8 chapatis (bought)
	Salad leaves and
	  radishes to garnish
	Chutney or relish
	Natural yogurt
		Browning dish

1 Make Chilli Flowers: with sharp knife, slit 4 chillies several times, about 1 cm from stems. (If you like, wear rubber gloves for protection.)

2 Place cut chillies in iced water to separate petals: set aside for garnish. Preheat browning dish according to manufacturer's instructions.

3 Meanwhile, into shallow pie dish, grate cheese. Finely chop remaining chilli; add to cheese with coriander, spring onions and sweetcorn.

4 Spoon equal amount of cheese and chilli mixture on to each of 4 chapatis.

5 Cover each chapati with 1 of the 4 remaining chapatis to make a sandwich.

6 On preheated browning dish, place 1 chapati sandwich. Cook on High (100% power) for 1½ (1:30) minutes, or until hot, turning sandwich over after 1 minute.

7 Remove sandwich from dish; let stand 2 minutes. Meanwhile, repeat with remaining chapatis. Reheat browning dish as necessary and keep cooked chapati sandwiches warm.

8 Cut chapatis into wedges. Arrange wedges on plates.

9 Garnish and, if you like, serve with chutney or relish and yogurt.

Filled tartlets make attractive starters. Buy the shells or make
them yourself and keep them in the freezer. They can be
quickly heated in the microwave then filled with these delicious hot fillings.
Each filling is enough for sixteen to twenty 5 cm tartlets.

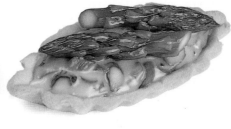

ASPARAGUS AND BRIE FILLING

Colour Index page 39. Fills 16 tartlets. 28 cals per serving of
filling. Low in cholesterol, fat, sodium.
Begin 15 minutes ahead.

*450 g very thin
(sprue) asparagus
spears
115 g Brie cheese
2 spring onions,
thinly sliced
1 teaspoon dried
tarragon
1 tablespoon water*

1. Hold base of each asparagus
spear firmly and bend; end will
break off where spear becomes too
tough to eat. Discard tough ends.
2. Trim asparagus tips to 5 cm
pieces; set aside for garnish. Thinly
slice remaining asparagus.
3. Cut Brie into 1 cm cubes. In
medium microwave-safe bowl, combine sliced asparagus, Brie, onions
and tarragon. Cook, covered, on
High (100% power) for 2½ (2:30)
minutes. Stir until cheese is melted.
Spoon filling into tartlets.
4. On small microwave-safe plate,
place reserved asparagus tips and
water. Cook, covered, on High for 1
minute. Use for garnish.

MUSHROOM FILLING

Colour Index page 39. Fills 20 tartlets. 21 cals per serving of
filling. Low in fat, sodium.
Begin 25 minutes ahead.

*225 g mushrooms
4 spring onions,
finely chopped
3 garlic cloves,
crushed
45 g butter or
margarine
4 tablespoons
chopped fresh
parsley
3 tablespoons dry
sherry
Pepper to taste
Parsley to garnish*

1. In food processor with knife
blade attached or on chopping
board, finely chop mushrooms.
2. In medium microwave-safe bowl,
place mushrooms, spring onions,
garlic and butter or margarine.
Cook on High (100% power) for 6
minutes, stirring occasionally.
3. Into mixture, stir chopped
parsley, sherry and pepper. Cook
on High for 6 minutes, or until liquid
evaporates, stirring halfway through
cooking. Spoon filling into tartlets;
garnish with parsley.

TOMATO AND BASIL FILLING

Colour Index page 39. Fills 16 tartlets. 8 cals per serving of
filling. Low in cholesterol, fat, sodium.
Begin 10 minutes ahead.

*2 tomatoes
2 garlic cloves,
crushed
1 celery stick, finely
chopped
1 tablespoon grated
Parmesan cheese
2 teaspoons bottled
pesto sauce
¼ teaspoon salt
Cayenne pepper to
taste
Small basil leaves to
garnish*

1. Seed and chop tomatoes. In
medium microwave-safe bowl, combine tomatoes, garlic and celery.
Cook on High (100% power) for 4
minutes, or until vegetables soften,
stirring halfway through cooking.
2. Into tomato mixture, stir Parmesan, pesto sauce, salt and cayenne
pepper. Spoon filling into tartlets;
garnish with basil leaves.

RED AND BLACK BEAN FILLING

Colour Index page 39. Fills 20 tartlets. 47 cals per serving of
filling. Low in cholesterol.
Begin 15 minutes ahead.

*½ small red onion,
finely chopped
½ small red pepper,
finely chopped
3 garlic cloves,
crushed
2 tablespoons
vegetable oil
2 teaspoons chilli
powder
1 teaspoon dried
oregano
1 × 213 g can red
kidney beans,
drained and rinsed
2 tablespoons bottled
black bean sauce
1½ teaspoons cider
vinegar
Pepper to taste
Soured cream to
garnish*

1. In medium microwave-safe bowl,
combine onion, red pepper, garlic,
oil, chilli powder and oregano. Cook
on High (100% power) for 3 minutes, or until vegetables soften, stirring halfway through cooking.
2. Into onion mixture, stir beans,
black bean sauce, vinegar and pepper. Cook on High for 3 minutes,
stirring halfway through cooking.
Spoon filling into tartlets; garnish
with soured cream.

Filled Starters

STUFFED ARTICHOKE BOTTOMS

Colour Index page 40. 125 cals per artichoke. Low in cholesterol. Begin 55 minutes ahead.

Ingredients	For 4	For 2	For 1
Globe artichokes, rinsed	4 medium	2 medium	1 medium
Water	120 ml	4 tablespoons	2 tablespoons
Rindless streaky bacon, diced	4 rashers	2 rashers	1 rasher
Red onion, diced	1 small	½ small	¼ small
Dried breadcrumbs	45 g	4 tablespoons	2 tablespoons
Sultanas	2 tablespoons	1 tablespoon	1½ teaspoons
Dried rosemary	1½ teaspoons	¾ teaspoon	to taste
Pepper	to taste	to taste	to taste
Microwave cookware	3 litre casserole	2 litre casserole	2 × 21.5 cm
	Shallow 25 cm pie dish	Shallow 25 cm pie dish	shallow pie dishes
Time on High (100% power)			
Artichokes	22–24 minutes	14–16 minutes	7–9 minutes
Bacon	4–5 minutes	2–3 minutes	1½ (1:30)–2 minutes
Stuffed artichokes	2 minutes	1 minute	15 seconds

1 With serrated knife, cut off artichoke stalks and 2.5 cm straight across tops. Pull off any small, loose or discoloured leaves.

2 With kitchen shears, carefully trim off thorny tips of artichoke leaves. In casserole or pie dish (see Chart), place artichokes, base down.

3 Over artichoke, pour water. Cook, covered, on High for time in Chart, until leaf can be pulled out easily, rotating once.

4 In pie dish (see Chart), place bacon. Cook, covered with kitchen paper, on High for time in Chart, until browned, stirring twice. Transfer to clean kitchen paper to drain. In bowl, combine bacon and next 5 ingredients. Pull off all artichoke leaves.

5 In pie dish used for bacon, place artichoke bottoms. With spoon, scrape out and discard fuzzy centres (chokes). Trim base and edges of each artichoke bottom.

6 Fill each artichoke bottom with about 2 tablespoons stuffing. Cook on High for time in Chart. Transfer artichokes to individual plates and serve immediately.

SAVOURY SAUSAGE PARCELS

Colour Index page 41. Makes 12. 60 cals each. Low in cholesterol, sodium. Begin early in day.

500 ml water
2 tablespoons lemon juice
12 medium vine leaves, fresh or in brine (rinsed and drained)
115 g fresh Italian or other spicy pork sausages
½ small onion, finely chopped
115 g canned pimientos, drained
25 g mozzarella cheese, shredded
2 tablespoons dried breadcrumbs
Vegetable oil

1. In medium microwave-safe bowl, place water and lemon juice. Heat on High (100% power) for 5–6 minutes, until boiling. To water, add vine leaves. Cook, covered, on High for 10 minutes. Drain; cover leaves with cold water.
2. Remove skins from sausages. Crumble sausage into 1 litre microwave-safe casserole; stir in onion. Cook on High for 2–3 minutes, until sausage loses its pink colour, stirring twice to break up meat. Drain well.
3. From pimientos, cut 24 matchstick-thin 5 cm strips; set aside. Chop remaining pimiento; add to sausage with cheese and breadcrumbs.
4. Pat vine leaves dry. Place 1 tablespoon sausage mixture in centre of each leaf; fold sides over, then roll up. Decorate parcels, seam side down, with pimiento strips. Line baking sheet with greaseproof paper. Place parcels on paper; freeze until firm. Place in freezer container; cover and return to freezer.
5. About 5 minutes before serving, place parcels, seam side down, on microwave-safe rack set in 30 × 20 cm baking dish; brush lightly with oil. Cook, covered, on High for 1½ (1:30)–2 minutes, until hot.

CRAB-FILLED MUSHROOMS

Colour Index page 41. Makes 12. 90 cals each. Begin early in day.

75 g white crabmeat, drained
80 ml mayonnaise
1 large celery stick, finely chopped
½ small onion, finely chopped
2 tablespoons dried breadcrumbs
1 tablespoon lemon juice
1 tablespoon dry sherry
Dash of Tabasco sauce
12 mushroom caps
2 tablespoons vegetable oil

1. In medium bowl, mix first 8 ingredients.
2. Brush mushrooms with oil. Spoon equal amount of crab mixture into each. Line baking sheet with greaseproof paper. Place mushrooms on paper; freeze until firm. Place in freezer container; cover and return to freezer.
3. About 10 minutes before serving, on microwave-safe rack set in 30 × 20 cm baking dish, place frozen mushrooms. Cook on High (100% power) for 5–6 minutes, until hot.

POACHED APPLES WITH PARMA HAM

Colour Index page 40. 6 servings. 236 cals per serving. Begin 40 minutes ahead.

6 small apples	3 tablespoons coarsely
250 ml dry white wine	crumbled blue cheese
1 teaspoon whole	4 eggs
allspice	3 tablespoons double
Salad leaves	cream
Capers	2 teaspoons chopped
175 g thinly sliced	chives
Parma ham or smoked	¼ teaspoon salt
salmon	Pepper to taste
80 ml soured cream	

1. Cut off top quarter of each apple; set aside. Core each apple without cutting through base.
2. In 2 litre microwave-safe casserole, arrange apples; replace tops. Add wine and allspice. Cook, covered, on High (100% power) for 5 minutes, until softened, rearranging halfway through cooking. Drain apples and tops on kitchen paper.
3. Arrange salad leaves on 6 plates; dot with capers. Place apples and Parma ham or salmon alongside.
4. In small bowl, combine soured cream and blue cheese. Spoon mixture into apples. Replace tops.
5. In 1 litre microwave-safe casserole, beat remaining ingredients. Cook on High for 1½ (1:30) minutes, or until softly set, stirring twice. Spoon on to plates. Allow to stand for 2–3 minutes before serving.

BAKED STUFFED TOMATOES

Colour Index page 38. Makes 4. 121 cals each. Low in cholesterol. Good source of vitamin A. Begin 20 minutes ahead.

4 tomatoes	1 tablespoon chopped
¼ teaspoon salt	fresh parsley
25 g Parmesan cheese,	1 teaspoon dried
grated	oregano
2 tablespoons dried	Pepper to taste
breadcrumbs	2 tablespoons olive or
2 garlic cloves, crushed	vegetable oil

1. Cut thin slice from base of each tomato so tomatoes sit flat. Cut slice from top of each tomato and reserve.
2. With spoon, scoop out flesh and seeds from tomatoes; discard. Sprinkle inside with salt.
3. In small bowl, combine Parmesan, breadcrumbs, garlic, parsley, oregano and pepper.
4. In 30 × 20 cm microwave-safe baking dish, arrange tomatoes about 2.5 cm apart. Spoon stuffing into tomatoes; pack in firmly. Drizzle oil over tomatoes. Cook on High (100% power) for 6 minutes, rearranging halfway through cooking.
5. Allow tomatoes to stand for 2 minutes. Transfer to serving platter; place reserved tomato slices on top of stuffing. Serve immediately.

CELEBRATION PRAWNS

Colour Index page 41. 113 cals per prawn. Good source of calcium. Begin early in day.

Ingredients	For 4	For 2	For 1
Raw king prawns, shelled and deveined	12 large	6 large	3 large
Lemon juice	1 tablespoon	2 teaspoons	1 teaspoon
Dry sherry	2 tablespoons	1 tablespoon	1½ teaspoons
Dried breadcrumbs	4 tablespoons	2 tablespoons	1 tablespoon
Gruyère or Edam cheese, grated	3 tablespoons	1½ tablespoons	2 teaspoons
Red, green or yellow pepper, finely chopped	3 tablespoons	1½ tablespoons	2 teaspoons
Parmesan cheese, grated	2 tablespoons	1 tablespoon	1½ teaspoons
Tabasco sauce	to taste	to taste	to taste
Peach slices and lamb's lettuce	garnish	garnish	garnish
Microwave cookware	27 cm flan dish	24 cm flan dish	Shallow 21.5 cm pie dish
Time on Medium-Low (30% power)	6–8 minutes	4–6 minutes	2–3 minutes

1 In bowl, combine prawns, lemon juice and half of sherry. Toss to coat; set aside. In another bowl, combine next 5 ingredients and remaining sherry.

2 With sharp knife, cut each prawn three-quarters of the way through along centre back; spread open. Pound prawns lightly to flatten.

3 Divide cheese mixture into same number of balls as prawns; roll into log shapes. Place 1 log along centre back of each prawn. Reshape prawn firmly round filling.

4 In freezer container, place prawns in single layer; cover and freeze until ready to use.

5 About 15 minutes before serving, in flan or pie dish (see Chart), arrange frozen prawns in circle, with tails pointing towards centre of dish.

6 Cook prawns, covered loosely with greaseproof paper, on Medium-Low for time in Chart, just until prawns turn pink. Turn each prawn over and rotate dish halfway through cooking. Garnish and serve immediately.

Vegetable Starters

ARTICHOKES WITH LEMON AND GARLIC

Colour Index page 40. 260 cals per artichoke. Good source of vitamin C, iron. Begin 55 minutes ahead.

Ingredients	For 4	For 2	For 1
Globe artichokes, rinsed	4 medium	2 medium	1 medium
Lemon, thinly sliced and cut into quarters	1 lemon	½ lemon	¼ lemon
Garlic cloves, thinly sliced	4 cloves	2 cloves	1 clove
Dry white wine	120 ml	4 tablespoons	2 tablespoons
Butter	115 g	60 g	30 g
Lemon and parsley	garnish	garnish	garnish
Microwave cookware	3 litre casserole	2 litre casserole	Shallow 21.5 cm pie dish
	Medium bowl	Medium bowl	Small bowl
Time on High (100% power) Artichokes Butter	22–24 minutes 1½ (1:30)–2 minutes	14–16 minutes 45 seconds–1 minute	7–9 minutes 45 seconds

1 With serrated knife, cut off artichoke stalks and 2.5 cm straight across tops. Pull off any small, loose or discoloured leaves from bases. With kitchen shears, carefully trim off thorny tips of artichoke leaves.

2 Push lemon quarters and garlic slices between artichoke leaves. In casserole or pie dish (see Chart), place artichokes, base down. Drizzle over wine.

3 Cook artichokes, covered, on High for time in Chart, until leaf can be pulled out easily, rotating casserole or dish halfway through cooking.

4 In bowl (see Chart), place butter. Heat, covered with kitchen paper, on High for time in Chart. Skim off white foam; discard. Pour clarified butter into ramekin or small bowl.

5 Gently push artichoke leaves out from centres; remove centre leaves to expose fuzzy centres (chokes). With spoon, scrape out and discard chokes.

6 Place artichokes on individual plates; drizzle over cooking liquid. Garnish with lemon and parsley. Serve with clarified butter for dipping.

CREAMED MUSHROOMS ON TOAST

Colour Index page 39. 4 servings. 245 cals per serving. Good source of riboflavin, niacin, iron. Begin 25 minutes ahead.

450 g mushrooms
30 g butter or margarine
4 spring onions, sliced
3 garlic cloves, crushed
175 ml Chicken Stock (page 125) or stock from a cube
2 tablespoons dry sherry
2 tablespoons double or whipping cream
¼ teaspoon salt
Pepper to taste
1 tablespoon cornflour dissolved in 2 tablespoons cold water
8 slices white bread, toasted and cut in half

1. Trim mushrooms and cut into quarters.
2. In 30 × 20 cm microwave-safe baking dish, place mushrooms and next 3 ingredients. Cook on High (100% power) for 5 minutes, stirring twice.
3. Into mushroom mixture, stir stock, sherry, cream, salt and pepper. Cook mixture on High for 3 minutes. Stir in dissolved cornflour. Cook on High for 3 minutes, or until slightly thickened, stirring halfway through cooking.
4. Arrange 4 pieces toast on each plate. Ladle mushroom mixture over toast.

MUSHROOMS

Nowadays, there are many kinds of mushrooms available, both homegrown and imported varieties. They are a delicious and low-calorie ingredient. Try mixing two or three types together in dishes like Creamed Mushrooms on Toast (above).

Shiitake Mushrooms

Oyster Mushrooms

Cultivated Mushrooms

Button Mushrooms

Cocktails For A Crowd

Cocktails with Bombay Mixed Nuts, page 294, olives and grissini
Bacon and Horseradish Dip, page 111 (double quantity), with crudités and Bagel Chips
Spicy Chicken Wings, page 114 (double quantity)
Celebration Prawns, page 119
Country-Style Pork Pâté, page 115, with gherkins and crackers
Cheese and fresh fruit

PREPARATION TIMETABLE

Up to 1 week ahead	**Up to 2 days ahead**	**1 day ahead**	**2 hours ahead**	**About 15 minutes ahead**
Prepare Celebration Prawns up to end of step 4. Prepare Bombay Mixed Nuts and store in airtight container.	*Make Country-Style Pork Pâté: wrap well and refrigerate without unmoulding. Check all bar supplies: spirits, wines, mixers, soft drinks and mineral water: buy or make ice and keep in plastic bags in freezer.*	*Prepare Spicy Chicken Wings: cover and refrigerate. Select cheeses and fruit; keep chilled. Make Bacon and Horseradish Dip; cover and refrigerate. Prepare vegetables for crudités; store in plastic bags in refrigerator.*	*Arrange crudités and Bagel Chips on platter. Spoon Bacon and Horseradish Dip into serving bowl. Unmould pâté and accompany with gherkins and crackers. Arrange cheese and fruit on board or tray; keep covered until guests arrive. Arrange seasonal fresh fruit in bowl.*	*Fill serving bowls with olives and Bombay Mixed Nuts. Arrange grissini for serving. Place glasses, cocktail ingredients and ice bucket on trays. Reheat chicken wings and cook prawns in microwave just before you are ready to serve.*

Shellfish Starters

ELEGANT SHELLFISH SALAD

Colour Index page 41. 214 cals per serving. Good source of iron.
Begin 2¼ hours ahead or early in day.

Ingredients for 6 servings		Microwave cookware
225 g medium raw prawns, shelled and deveined 225 g scallops, sliced 3 spring onions, sliced or cut into very thin strips 2 tablespoons lemon juice 1 tablespoon olive oil ½ teaspoon salt	12 mussels, cleaned Lemon-Basil Sauce (below) Salad leaves 120 ml bottled chilli sauce Green grapes, Pear Slices (page 116) and redcurrants to garnish	30 × 20 cm baking dish 24 cm flan dish

1 In baking dish, place prawns, scallops, spring onions, lemon juice, olive oil and salt. Cook, covered, on High (100% power) for 3–5 minutes, just until prawns turn pink and scallops are opaque.

2 Stir seafood mixture. Cover and refrigerate until chilled. Meanwhile, in flan dish or pie dish, arrange mussels. Discard any that are open.

3 Cook mussels, covered, on High for 2–2½ (2:30) minutes, just until shells open; discard any that remain closed. Remove mussels from shells; reserve 12 half-shells.

4 Make Lemon-Basil Sauce: in food processor with knife blade attached or in blender, place 45 g fresh basil leaves, 4 tablespoons olive oil, 2 tablespoons lemon juice, 1 garlic clove, 1 tablespoon water, ¼ teaspoon salt and ¼ teaspoon pepper; process.

5 Line 6 plates with salad leaves; arrange prawns, scallops and mussels on top. Fill 6 reserved mussel half-shells with Lemon-Basil Sauce and 6 with chilli sauce; arrange 1 of each on each plate.

6 To serve: garnish each plate with green grapes, Pear Slices and redcurrants.

OYSTERS ROCKEFELLER

Colour Index page 39. Makes 12. 51 cals each. Low in sodium. Good source of vitamin A, iron. Begin 25 minutes ahead.

2 rashers rindless streaky bacon, diced 150 g frozen chopped spinach, slightly thawed 2 spring onions, sliced 1 garlic clove, chopped 2 tablespoons chopped fresh parsley 30 g butter or margarine	2 tablespoons grated Parmesan cheese Good pinch cayenne pepper 2 tablespoons anise-flavoured liqueur 12 large oysters on the half shell Rock or coarse sea salt (optional)

1. In 21.5 cm microwave-safe shallow pie dish, place bacon. Cook, covered with kitchen paper, on High (100% power) for 2–3 minutes, until browned, stirring halfway through cooking. Transfer to kitchen paper to drain.
2. In medium microwave-safe bowl, combine spinach and next 4 ingredients. Cook on High for 4 minutes, stirring occasionally.
3. In food processor with knife blade attached or in blender, process spinach mixture until smooth. In bowl, mix spinach with Parmesan, cayenne pepper and liqueur; set aside.
4. Arrange oysters on 30 cm microwave-safe plate. (If you like, press oysters in shell into 5 mm deep layer of rock or coarse sea salt to keep from tipping over.) Spoon spinach mixture on to oysters; sprinkle with bacon. Cook oysters on High for 3–4 minutes, until hot.

CASINO CLAMS

Colour Index page 41. Makes 12. 55 cals each. Low in sodium. Good source of iron.
Begin early in day.

3 rashers rindless streaky bacon, diced 12 large clams, shelled, reserving 12 bottom shells 30 g fresh breadcrumbs (1 slice bread)	3 tablespoons grated Parmesan cheese ½ green pepper, finely chopped 1 garlic clove, crushed ½ teaspoon dried oregano

1. In 30 × 20 cm microwave-safe baking dish, place bacon. Cook, covered with kitchen paper, on High (100% power) for 4–5 minutes, until browned, stirring halfway through cooking. Transfer to kitchen paper to drain. Reserve 2 tablespoons bacon fat in dish.
2. Coarsely chop clams. To bacon fat, add clams and next 5 ingredients; mix well.
3. Spoon equal amount of clam mixture into each clam shell. Line baking sheet with greaseproof paper. Place clams on paper; freeze until firm. Place in freezer container; cover and return to freezer.
4. About 10 minutes before serving, place clams in 27 cm microwave-safe flan dish. Cook, covered loosely with greaseproof paper, on Medium (50% power) for 6–7 minutes.

Soups

STOCKS · QUICK AND EASY SOUPS · VEGETABLE SOUPS
HEARTY SOUPS · SOUP GARNISHES · CHOWDERS
FRUIT SOUPS · GARNISHES FOR FRUIT SOUPS

Soups

Recipes in this chapter range from simple basic stocks for use as soup bases, to more substantial soups such as Four Bean Soup (page 129) and Minestrone (page 130), that are main dishes. Some are warm and welcoming on a cold winter's day: others, like chilled Vichyssoise and Cream of Spinach Soup (page 127) and the fruit soups on page 134, are a refreshing treat on a warm day.

The microwave oven can be used to cook soups made from fresh ingredients that would take much longer if cooked conventionally. Other time-saving uses for the microwave include reconstituting dried soups, cooking ingredients from frozen, and heating canned soups (always remove soup from can first). Soups should be stirred during cooking in the microwave and especially just before serving, in order to equalise the temperature – the edges of the soup may bubble long before the centre becomes piping hot. The microwave can make stock – an essential base for soups and other recipes – in a fraction of the normal cooking time. On page 126 you will find how,

with only a few extra ingredients, stock can quickly be transformed into elegant and unusual soups.

Homemade stocks (page 125) are superior in flavour to commercial stock cubes or canned consommé, and they do not contain salt, but these products can be used in the recipes if you do not have time to make your own stock.

Most stocks and soups can be frozen and then defrosted and reheated in the microwave. Soups are best frozen in 250 or 500 ml quantities, but make sure containers are only two-thirds full, otherwise they may overflow when reheating. If you freeze soup in a non-microwave-safe container, remove it as a block by placing container under hot running water, then placing the block in a microwave-safe bowl or casserole to defrost in the microwave. Using a fork, break the block apart as it thaws to speed up the process. (For more information, see Chart page 130.) If you are going to freeze soup, season lightly when making, then adjust seasoning after reheating.

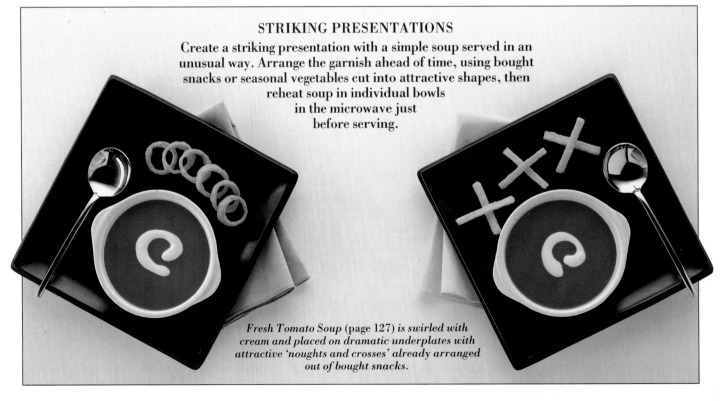

STRIKING PRESENTATIONS

Create a striking presentation with a simple soup served in an unusual way. Arrange the garnish ahead of time, using bought snacks or seasonal vegetables cut into attractive shapes, then reheat soup in individual bowls in the microwave just before serving.

Fresh Tomato Soup (page 127) is swirled with cream and placed on dramatic underplates with attractive 'noughts and crosses' already arranged out of bought snacks.

The microwave shortens the time for making stock at home, and an added advantage is that you can make a relatively small quantity quickly, as and when you need it. Alternatively, you can make a larger quantity and freeze it in 250 or 500 ml containers.

VEGETABLE STOCK

Colour Index page 42. Makes 750 ml. 37 cals per 250 ml. Low in cholesterol, fat, sodium. Good source of vitamin A. Begin 40 minutes ahead.

1 leek
1 onion with skin
3 carrots
2 tomatoes
1 garlic clove
6 mushrooms, cut in half
4 large celery sticks, cut into thirds
1 parsley sprig
1 bay leaf
6 whole peppercorns
120 ml tomato juice
850 ml water

1. Cut leek in half lengthways; carefully wash under cold running water until all sand is removed. Cut onion, carrots, tomatoes and garlic into quarters.
2. In deep 2 litre microwave-safe bowl, combine all ingredients. Cook, covered, on High (100% power) for 20 minutes, stirring occasionally. Allow to stand for 5 minutes.
3. Line strainer with double layer of muslin. Into medium bowl, strain liquid through muslin. Discard vegetables.

FISH STOCK

Colour Index page 42. Makes 750 ml. 41 cals per 250 ml. Low in cholesterol, fat. Begin 40 minutes ahead.

700 g white fish bones (not from oily fish)
¹/₂ leek
¹/₂ carrot
¹/₂ celery stick
6 whole peppercorns
¹/₂ teaspoon dried thyme
250 ml dry white wine
750 ml water

1. Under cold running water, wash fish bones to remove any blood or scales. With kitchen shears, cut into 10 cm pieces.
2. Cut leek in half lengthways; carefully wash under cold running water until all sand is removed.
3. In deep 2 litre microwave-safe bowl, combine all ingredients. Cook, covered, on High (100% power) for 15 minutes, stirring occasionally. Allow to stand for 5 minutes.
4. Line strainer with double layer of muslin. Into medium bowl, strain liquid through muslin. Discard bones and vegetables.

BEEF STOCK

Colour Index page 44. Makes 750 ml. 31 cals per 250 ml. Low in cholesterol, fat, sodium. Begin 1¹/₂ hours ahead.

1.4 kg beef or veal bones
1 onion with skin, cut into quarters
1 tomato, cut into quarters
1 small leek
2 garlic cloves, cut into quarters
1 bay leaf
1 parsley sprig
6 whole peppercorns
1 litre water

1. Preheat conventional oven to 230°C (450°F, gas mark 8). In foil-lined roasting tin, brown bones with onion and tomato for about 1 hour.
2. Cut leek in half lengthways; carefully wash under cold running water until all sand is removed.
3. In deep 2 litre microwave-safe bowl, combine all ingredients. Cook, covered, on High (100% power) for 20 minutes, stirring occasionally. Allow to stand for 5 minutes. Skim off any fat.
4. Line strainer with double layer of muslin. Into medium bowl, strain liquid through muslin. Discard bones and vegetables.

CHICKEN STOCK

Colour Index page 42. Makes 750 ml. 47 cals per 250 ml. Low in cholesterol, fat, sodium. Begin 40 minutes ahead.

700 g chicken bones
1 leek
1 carrot
1 celery stick
1 parsley sprig
1 thyme sprig or ¹/₂ teaspoon dried thyme
1 bay leaf
6 whole peppercorns
1 litre water

1. With kitchen shears, cut chicken bones into 10 cm pieces.
2. Cut leek in half lengthways; carefully wash under cold running water until all sand is removed.
3. In deep 2 litre microwave-safe bowl, combine all ingredients. Cook, covered, on High (100% power) for 20 minutes, stirring occasionally. Allow to stand for 5 minutes. Skim off any fat.
4. Line strainer with double layer of muslin. Into medium bowl, strain liquid through muslin. Discard bones and vegetables.

Quick & Easy Soups

Use the homemade stocks (page 125) as a base for these instant soups that are suitable for a first course, light meal, or after-school snack. Or create your own recipes by adding different combinations of ingredients according to personal taste.

Oriental Style Soup (*right*): to *500 ml Fish Stock*, add *50 g chopped, cooked prawns, 3 sliced spring onions*, and *¹/₂ teaspoon slivered peeled root ginger*. Cook, covered, on High (100% power) for 5 minutes, or until boiling. Garnish with *fresh coriander leaves*.

Double Vegetable Soup (*below*): to *500 ml Vegetable Stock*, add *25 g* each *thinly sliced celery, carrot* and *leek* and *25 g asparagus tips*. Cook, covered, on High (100% power) for 3 minutes. Add *15 g shredded spinach*. Cook, covered, on High for 2 minutes.

Beefy Italian Broth (*above*): to *500 ml Beef Stock*, add *25 g* each *sliced mushrooms, fennel* and *carrots*, and *1 tablespoon shredded basil leaves*. Cook, covered, on High (100% power) for 5 minutes, or until boiling. Add *25 g Gruyère or provolone cheese cubes*. Garnish with *fresh rosemary* and *basil leaves*.

Chicken and Pasta Soup (*left*): to *500 ml Chicken Stock*, add *25 g small pasta shapes* (animals and bow ties, etc) and *25 g diced carrots*. Cook, covered, on High (100% power) for 5 minutes, or until boiling. Add *35 g cooked, shredded chicken*. Cook on High for 2–3 minutes, until hot. Serve with *savoury biscuits*.

126

Vegetable Soups

VICHYSSOISE

Colour Index page 44. Makes 2 litres. 133 cals per 250 ml. Good source of vitamin C, fibre. Begin early in day.

350 g leeks	*1 small apple, peeled,*
450 g potatoes, sliced	*cored and sliced*
30 g butter or margarine	*250 ml half cream*
¼ teaspoon salt	
¼ teaspoon pepper	
250 ml water	
250 ml Vegetable Stock	
(page 125) or stock	
from a cube	

1. Cut off roots and green tops from leeks; discard. Cut white part of leeks into 2.5 cm pieces; wash carefully under cold running water until all sand is removed.
2. In deep 3 litre microwave-safe bowl, place leeks, potatoes, butter or margarine, salt and pepper. Cook, covered, on High (100% power) for 7 minutes, stirring halfway through cooking.
3. To vegetables, add water, stock and apple slices. Cook, covered, on High for 6–8 minutes, until potatoes are tender, stirring halfway through cooking.
4. In food processor with knife blade attached or in blender, process soup until smooth (in 2 batches if necessary). Return to bowl and stir in cream; cover and refrigerate. Serve chilled.

CREAM OF SPINACH SOUP

Colour Index page 44. Makes 1 litre. 174 cals per 250 ml. Good source of vitamin A, vitamin C, calcium, iron, fibre. Begin early in day.

30 g butter or margarine	*1 tablespoon cornflour*
1 onion, chopped	*dissolved in 2*
2 small potatoes, diced	*tablespoons water*
300 ml Vegetable Stock	*¼ teaspoon salt*
(page 125) or stock	*¼ teaspoon pepper*
from a cube	*Grated nutmeg to taste*
350 g spinach leaves,	
torn	
125 ml half cream or	
milk	

1. In deep 3 litre microwave-safe bowl, combine butter or margarine, onion, potatoes and 4 tablespoons stock. Cook, covered, on High (100% power) for 8 minutes, or until potatoes are tender, stirring twice.
2. To vegetable mixture, add spinach. Cook, covered, on High for 5 minutes. In food processor with knife blade attached or in blender, process soup until smooth; return to bowl.
3. To soup, add remaining stock, cream or milk, dissolved cornflour, salt, pepper and nutmeg; stir until smooth. Cook on High for 5 minutes, or until piping hot, stirring halfway through cooking. Cover and refrigerate until well chilled. Alternatively, serve hot.

FRESH TOMATO SOUP

Colour Index page 42. 55 cals per 250 ml. Low in cholesterol and fat. Good source of vitamin A, vitamin C, fibre. Begin 25 minutes ahead.

Ingredients for 1.5 litres		Microwave cookware
1.1 kg ripe tomatoes	*1 tablespoon tomato*	Deep 3 litre bowl
1 onion, chopped	*purée*	
1 celery stick, chopped	*¼ teaspoon pepper*	
2 garlic cloves,	*Tabasco sauce to taste*	
crushed	*Soured cream and*	
½ bay leaf	*chopped chives to*	
¼ teaspoon ground	*garnish*	
cloves		
250 ml Vegetable Stock		
(page 125) or stock		
from a cube		

1 With small sharp knife, remove stalk ends from tomatoes; cut tomatoes into small chunks.

2 In bowl, combine tomatoes and next 5 ingredients. Cook, covered, on High (100% power) for 15 minutes, or until soft, stirring often.

3 Discard bay leaf. In food processor with knife blade attached or in blender, process tomato mixture until smooth.

4 In same bowl, add remaining ingredients (except garnish). Cook, covered, on High for 5 minutes, stirring once.

5 Serve hot or chilled, garnished with soured cream and chives.

CROÛTONS

In baking dish, combine *1 tablespoon melted butter* and *2 tablespoons vegetable oil*. Add *4 slices bread* cut into small shapes; turn to coat. Bake in conventional oven at 230°C (450°F, gas mark 8) for 8–10 minutes, turning once.

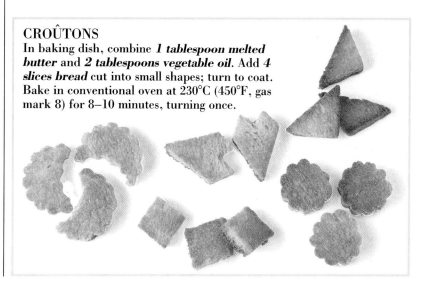

Vegetable and Hearty Soups

WINTER VEGETABLE SOUP

Colour Index page 43. 108 cals per 250 ml.
Good source of vitamin A, vitamin C, fibre. Begin 35 minutes ahead.

Traditionally, vegetable soups are thick, substantial dishes. This Winter Vegetable Soup is a lighter version which can be made in much less time than if cooked conventionally. If you like, vary the recipe by using other seasonal vegetables.

Ingredients for 1.5 litres		Microwave cookware
1 large carrot	*¼ teaspoon dried*	Deep 3 litre bowl
225 g turnips	*rosemary*	
1 large celery stick	*750 ml Vegetable Stock*	
1 onion	*(page 125) or stock*	
350 g white cabbage	*from a cube*	
225 g swede	*½ teaspoon salt*	
30 g butter or	*Pepper to taste*	
margarine		
½ teaspoon dried		
thyme		
1 bay leaf		

1 With sharp knife, cut carrot, turnips and celery into matchstick-thin strips. Thinly slice onion and white cabbage.

2 With sharp knife, peel swede; cut into dice-sized pieces.

3 In bowl, place butter or margarine. Heat, covered with kitchen paper, on High (100% power) for 45 seconds, or until melted.

4 To same bowl, add carrot, turnip, celery, onion, cabbage, swede, thyme, bay leaf and rosemary. Add 120 ml stock; mix well.

5 Cook mixture, covered, on High for 12 minutes, or until vegetables are tender, stirring occasionally.

6 Into soup mixture, pour remaining stock; add salt and pepper. Cook, covered, on High for 3 minutes, or until piping hot, stirring halfway through cooking. Discard bay leaf. Serve hot.

CARROT SOUP with ORANGE

Colour Index page 42. Makes 1 litre. 137 cals per 250 ml. Good source of vitamin A, fibre. Begin 25 minutes ahead.

30 g butter or	*600 ml Vegetable Stock*
margarine	*(page 125) or stock*
1 onion, chopped	*from a cube*
450 g carrots, thinly	*¼ teaspoon salt*
sliced	*Large pinch of pepper*
1 teaspoon grated	*Whipping cream and*
orange zest	*parsley to garnish*

1. In deep 2 litre microwave-safe bowl, place butter or margarine and onion. Cook on High (100% power) for 45 seconds, or until butter or margarine is melted.
2. To onion, add carrots, orange zest and 120 ml stock. Cook, covered, on High for 12 minutes, or until carrots are tender, stirring twice.
3. In food processor with knife blade attached or in blender, process carrot mixture until smooth.
4. Return carrot mixture to bowl. Stir in remaining stock, salt and pepper. Cook, covered, on High for 4 minutes or until piping hot, stirring halfway through cooking.
5. Serve hot, or cover and refrigerate to serve chilled later. Garnish with cream and parsley.

LIGHT and CREAMY ASPARAGUS SOUP

Colour Index page 42. Makes 1 litre. 157 cals per 250 ml. Good source of vitamin C, fibre. Begin 25 minutes ahead.

30 g butter or margarine	*1 vegetable stock cube*
1 onion, sliced	*250 ml half cream*
450 g asparagus,	*Plain yogurt or*
trimmed and cut into	*whipping cream and*
5 cm pieces	*chervil sprigs to*
250 ml water	*garnish*

1. In deep 2 litre microwave-safe bowl, place butter or margarine and onion. Cook on High (100% power) for 45 seconds, or until butter or margarine is melted.
2. To onion, add asparagus, water and stock cube. Cook, covered, on High for 10–12 minutes, until asparagus is tender, stirring twice.
3. In food processor with knife blade attached or in blender, process asparagus mixture until smooth. Return to bowl. Stir in cream. Cook on High for 2–3 minutes, until piping hot, stirring halfway through cooking.
4. Serve hot, or cover and refrigerate to serve chilled later. Garnish with swirl of yogurt or whipping cream and sprig of chervil.

CURRIED PARSNIP SOUP

Colour Index page 43. Makes 1.5 litres. 175 cals per 250 ml. Low in sodium. Good source of vitamins A and C, calcium, iron, fibre.
Begin 35 minutes ahead.

60 g butter or margarine	700 g parsnips
1 onion, chopped	750 ml Vegetable Stock
1 cooking apple (about	(page 125) or stock
175 g), peeled, cored	made from a cube
and sliced	200 ml milk
1 tablespoon curry	Toasted flaked almonds
powder	and chopped fresh
1/2 teaspoon turmeric	coriander leaves to
(optional)	garnish

1. In deep 3 litre microwave-safe bowl, combine butter or margarine, onion, apple, curry powder and turmeric. Cook, covered, on High (100% power) for 5 minutes, or until onion and apple soften, stirring twice.
2. Meanwhile, peel parsnips. Cut each in half lengthways and slice thinly. To onion and apple mixture, add parsnips and stock. Cook, covered, on High for 18–20 minutes, until parsnips are very soft, stirring twice.
3. In food processor with knife blade attached or in blender, process soup. Return to bowl and add milk. Cook on High for 2 minutes, or until piping hot, stirring halfway through cooking. Serve hot, garnished with almonds and coriander.

FOUR BEAN SOUP

Colour Index page 43. Makes 1.7 litres. 301 cals per 250 ml. Low in cholesterol. Good source of iron, fibre. Begin 35 minutes ahead.

3 rashers rindless	1 teaspoon dried
streaky bacon, diced	oregano
1 onion, chopped	1 × 400–450 g can each
1 celery stick, chopped	borlotti, white kidney,
2 garlic cloves, crushed	red kidney and black
1 1/2 teaspoons ground	kidney beans, drained
cumin	500 ml Vegetable Stock
1 teaspoon chilli	(page 125) or stock
powder	from a cube

1. In deep 3 litre microwave-safe bowl, place bacon. Cook, covered with kitchen paper, on High (100% power) for 4–5 minutes, until browned, stirring halfway through cooking.
2. To bacon, add onion, celery, garlic, cumin, chilli powder and oregano; mix well. Cook on High for 5 minutes, or until vegetables soften, stirring halfway through cooking.
3. To bacon mixture, add beans and stock; mix well. Cook on High for 10 minutes, or until all ingredients are very soft, stirring twice.
4. In food processor with knife blade attached or in blender, process 500 ml soup. Return to unblended soup; stir. Serve hot.

Small portions of these hearty soups can be served as first courses before light main dishes. Larger bowls of soup can make a filling informal lunch or supper, especially when accompanied with garlic bread or rolls warmed briefly in the microwave.

SPLIT PEA AND HAM SOUP

Colour Index page 44. 282 cals per 250 ml. Low in cholesterol. Good source of vitamin A, thiamine, iron, fibre. Begin 1 1/2 hours ahead.

Ingredients for 2 litres		Microwave cookware
450 g split peas	1 teaspoon dried thyme	Deep 3 litre bowl
1/2 smoked gammon	1/2 teaspoon dried	
knuckle, or 1 ham	rosemary	
bone with about 450 g	About 1 litre water	
meat left on	750 ml Chicken Stock	
1 onion, chopped	(page 125) or stock	
1 carrot, thinly	from a cube	
sliced	Pepper to taste	
1 large celery stick,	Chopped parsley to	
thinly sliced	garnish	
1 bay leaf		

1 In sieve under cold running water, rinse split peas.

2 In bowl, combine split peas, gammon knuckle or ham bone, onion, carrot, celery, bay leaf, thyme and rosemary. Add about 750 ml water, to cover ingredients in bowl.

3 Cook, covered, on High (100% power) for 20 minutes, stirring halfway through cooking. Add stock. Cook, covered, on High for 20 minutes longer, or until peas are soft, stirring halfway through cooking. Allow to stand on heatproof surface, covered, for 30 minutes. Discard bay leaf.

4 Remove gammon knuckle or ham bone from soup and, with sharp knife, cut off meat; discard bone. Cut meat into bite-sized pieces and return to soup, reserving some for garnish if you like.

5 In food processor with knife blade attached or in blender, process soup until smooth (in several batches if necessary). Return to bowl; if you like, adjust consistency by adding more water.

6 Stir any reserved meat into soup. Cook, covered, on High for 6 minutes, or until piping hot. Add pepper to taste. Serve hot, garnished with parsley.

Easy Italian Supper

Antipasto with grissini
Minestrone (right)
Creamy Cheesecake, page 335 (or bought cheesecake)
Espresso (below) with amaretti biscuits

PREPARATION TIMETABLE

1 day ahead	If making cheesecake, prepare, cover and refrigerate overnight.
2 hours ahead	Prepare antipasto: arrange Italian salami, ham and mortadella on a platter; garnish with wedges of melon wrapped in Parma ham, black olives, sliced fennel and strips of red and yellow pepper. Cover until ready to serve.
1½ hours ahead	Make Minestrone. Remove cheesecake from refrigerator: place on serving plate.
Just before serving	If necessary, reheat soup on High (100% power) until piping hot. Make Espresso.

ESPRESSO

Espresso is the perfect coffee to round off an Italian-style meal. Use a dark roast coffee, from Italian delicatessens and some supermarkets.

Brew **12 tablespoons espresso coffee** with **550 ml water** in an espresso pot. Serve in demitasse cups with **lemon zest**. Add **sugar** if you like. **Amaretti biscuits** are a traditional accompaniment.

Hearty Soups

MINESTRONE

Colour Index page 44. Makes 2 litres. 151 cals per 250 ml. Low in cholesterol. Good source of vitamins A and C, calcium, iron, fibre. Begin 1¼ hours ahead.

2 tablespoons olive or vegetable oil	½ small green cabbage, cut into 5 cm pieces
25 g Parma ham, thinly sliced, or cooked ham, diced	115 g green beans, cut into 2.5 cm pieces
1 onion, diced	2 × 400 g cans tomatoes
1 celery stick, diced	1 × 400 g can white kidney beans or cannellini beans, drained
1 carrot, diced	
2 garlic cloves, crushed	
½ teaspoon dried oregano	2 tablespoons torn basil leaves
500 ml water	Grated Parmesan cheese
50 g elbow macaroni	

1. Into deep 3 litre microwave-safe bowl, pour oil. Heat on High (100% power) for 3 minutes. Stir in Parma ham or cooked ham, onion, celery, carrot, garlic and oregano. Cook on High for 4 minutes, stirring twice.
2. To mixture, add water, macaroni, cabbage, green beans and tomatoes with their liquid. Cook, covered, on High for 10 minutes, stirring twice.
3. Add white kidney beans; cook, covered, on High for 10 minutes, until vegetables and macaroni are tender, stirring twice. Add basil and allow soup to stand, covered, for 5 minutes.
4. Ladle soup into warmed bowls and sprinkle with Parmesan. Serve hot.

REHEATING FROZEN SOUP

For 4	For 2	For 1
1 litre	500 ml	250 ml
Microwave cookware		
2 litre bowl	1 litre bowl	Deep bowl
Time on Medium-Low (30% power)		
12–15 minutes	6–8 minutes	3–4 minutes
Time on Medium-High (70% power)		
10–12 minutes	9–11 minutes	6–8 minutes

1. Defrost soup in microwave-safe bowl (see Chart) on Medium-Low for time in Chart, breaking soup apart with fork as it thaws.
2. Increase power level to Medium-High and heat soup for time in Chart, until piping hot, stirring twice.

FRENCH ONION SOUP

Colour Index page 43. Makes 1.5 litres. 221 cals per 250 ml. Good source of calcium.
Begin 45 minutes ahead.

45 g butter or margarine	1 tablespoon tomato
3 large onions, sliced	purée
1 × 300 g can condensed	1/2 French stick, cut into
beef consommé	6 slices and toasted
2 tablespoons dry sherry	175 g Gruyère cheese,
or Madeira	grated
500 ml water	

1. In deep 3 litre microwave-safe bowl, place butter or margarine. Heat, covered with kitchen paper, on High (100% power) for 45 seconds–1 minute, until melted. Add onions; stir to coat. Cook, covered, on High for 15 minutes, or until onions soften, stirring twice.
2. To onion mixture, add undiluted consommé, sherry or Madeira, water and tomato purée; stir until blended. Cook, covered, on High for 8 minutes, or until piping hot, stirring twice.
3. Ladle soup into 6 microwave-safe bowls or mugs. Place 1 slice toast in each bowl of soup and sprinkle generously with grated cheese.
4. Arrange soup bowls in a ring on a 30 cm round microwave-safe plate (in batches if necessary). Cook on High for 3 minutes, or until cheese melts. Serve hot.

Serving the soup

Top each serving with slice of toasted French bread. Sprinkle toast generously with grated Gruyère cheese.

Heat soup in microwave as in step 4 above, until cheese melts and begins to bubble.

Freezing the Soup

If you like, this soup can be frozen. At end of step 2, cover soup and refrigerate until cold, then ladle into freezer containers in 250 or 500 ml quantities. Seal, label and freeze.

For a complete meal, serve these hearty soups with a vegetable side dish or tossed salad and hot crusty bread. Quick and easy to prepare in the microwave, they also make substantial first courses.

CHICKEN NOODLE SOUP

Colour Index page 44. 202 cals per 250 ml. Low in sodium.
Good source of vitamin A, niacin, iron. Begin 1 1/4 hours ahead.

Ingredients for 1 litre		Microwave cookware
30 g butter or margarine	750 ml Chicken Stock (page 125) or stock from a cube	Deep 2 litre bowl
1 onion, thinly sliced	25 g fine egg noodles	
1 large celery stick, thinly sliced	Pepper to taste Chopped parsley to garnish	
1 large carrot, thinly sliced		
4 chicken legs or 450 g chicken pieces, skinned		

1 In bowl, place butter or margarine. Heat, covered with kitchen paper, on High (100% power) for 15 seconds, or until melted.

2 Into melted butter or margarine, stir onion, celery and carrot. Cook on High for 3 minutes, stirring halfway through cooking. Remove bowl from oven; stir in 250 ml stock.

3 On top of vegetables, place chicken. Cook, covered, on High for 10 minutes, or until chicken juices run clear, turning pieces over once during cooking. Transfer chicken to board.

4 To vegetable mixture, add remaining stock and noodles. Cook, covered, on High for 7 minutes, or until noodles are al dente, stirring halfway through cooking.

5 Meanwhile, remove chicken meat from bones; discard bones. Coarsely chop chicken meat, stir into soup. Allow to stand for 3–5 minutes.

6 With spoon, skim off any fat from surface of soup. Add pepper. Ladle soup into bowls and garnish with chopped parsley. Serve hot.

Hearty Soups

These hearty soups, containing vegetables combined with meat, chicken, fish or shellfish, make meals in themselves. To serve Louisiana Gumbo (below) in true Creole style it should be ladled over hot cooked rice in deep soup plates.

LOUISIANA GUMBO

Colour Index page 44. 157 cals per 250 ml. Good source of calcium, iron, fibre. Begin 1¼ hours ahead.

Ingredients for 2 litres		Microwave cookware
350 g large raw prawns	2 × 400 g cans tomatoes	Deep 3 litre bowl
30 g butter or margarine	250 ml freshly shelled	
3 tablespoons plain	oysters with their	
flour	liquid	
3 celery sticks with	275 g canned okra, cut	
leaves, sliced	crossways into 2.5 cm	
2 large onions,	pieces	
chopped	Salt and Tabasco sauce	
2 garlic cloves,	to taste	
crushed	Hot Cooked Rice (page	
1 tablespoon	293, optional)	
Worcestershire sauce		

1 Insert tip of kitchen shears under shell of each prawn and snip along back to expose vein. Peel back sides and lift prawn out, holding tail. Rinse under cold running water to remove vein. Cover and refrigerate until needed.

2 In bowl, place butter or margarine. Heat, covered with kitchen paper, on High (100% power) for 45 seconds, or until melted. Stir in flour until smooth.

3 Cook roux on High for 7 minutes, or until rich golden brown in colour, stirring often. Remove bowl from oven.

4 To roux, add celery, onions and garlic; stir. Cook on High for 4 minutes, stirring halfway through cooking. Add Worcestershire sauce and tomatoes. Cook, covered, on High for 5 minutes longer, stirring halfway through cooking.

5 To gumbo, add prawns, oysters and okra. Season with salt and Tabasco sauce.

6 Cook gumbo, covered, on High for 7 minutes, or just until prawns turn pink and oysters curl, stirring twice. If you like, serve with Hot Cooked Rice.

SOUP GARNISHES

Even the most simple soup can be made to look elegant by just adding a garnish. Some garnishes are a little time-consuming to prepare, but most can be ready in minutes.

Spring Onion Tassel: trim top of spring onion. Slit top down to bulb 3 or 4 times; place in bowl of iced water so top will curl.

Lemon/Lime Twist: cut thin slice from lemon or lime. Make 1 cut from centre to edge of slice; twist into spiral shape.

Carrot Curl: with swivel vegetable peeler, shave strips lengthways off carrot. Roll up and secure each strip with cocktail stick. Place in bowl of iced water for 1 hour. Drain; remove stick and use immediately.

Leek/Carrot Julienne: cut leek and carrot lengthways into matchstick-thin strips. Sprinkle on individual servings.

Turned Mushroom: holding blade of paring knife against mushroom cap and pressing gently, twist blade edge clockwise from centre to edge of mushroom. Repeat evenly around mushroom cap.

Fresh Herbs: chop fresh herbs with knife on cutting board, or use whole leaves or sprigs.

Chowders

VEGETABLE CHOWDER

Colour Index page 43. Makes 1.5 litres. 162 cals per 250 ml. Low in sodium. Good source of vitamin A, vitamin C, fibre. Begin 35 minutes ahead.

60 g butter or margarine	1/4 teaspoon dried thyme
2 large carrots, chopped	500 ml Vegetable Stock
2 large celery sticks,	(page 125) or stock
chopped	made from a cube
1 large onion, chopped	1 × 400 g can tomatoes
1 medium potato (about	1 × 220 g can butter or
175 g), peeled and	broad beans, drained
chopped	and rinsed
1 medium parsnip,	1/2 teaspoon pepper
peeled and chopped	Chopped parsley to
1 bay leaf	garnish

1. In deep 3 litre microwave-safe bowl, place butter or margarine. Cook, covered, with kitchen paper, on High (100% power) for 2 minutes, or until melted.
2. To melted butter or margarine, add vegetables and herbs; stir to combine. Cook, covered, on High for 7–9 minutes, until vegetables are tender-crisp, stirring twice.
3. To vegetable mixture, add stock, tomatoes with their liquid, beans and pepper; stir to break up tomatoes. Cook, covered, on High for 5 minutes, or until piping hot; discard bay leaf. Serve hot, garnished with parsley.

SWEETCORN CHOWDER

Colour Index page 43. Makes 1.5 litres. 220 cals per 250 ml. Good source of vitamin A, fibre. Begin 35 minutes ahead.

30 g butter or margarine	120 ml water
1 tablespoon plain flour	500 ml half cream
1 tablespoon paprika	275 g frozen sweetcorn
225 g potato, peeled and	kernels
chopped	Chopped parsley to
1 celery stick, finely	garnish
chopped	
1/2 onion, chopped	
1 chicken stock cube	

1. In deep 3 litre microwave-safe bowl, place butter or margarine. Heat, covered, with kitchen paper, on High (100% power) for 45 seconds, or until melted. Stir in flour and paprika; mix well. Add potato, celery, onion, stock cube and water. Cook, covered, on High for 10–12 minutes, until vegetables are tender, stirring twice.
2. To vegetable mixture, add cream and sweetcorn. Cook on High for 6–8 minutes, until sweetcorn is tender (do not boil), stirring twice.
3. *To serve:* ladle soup into warmed bowls and sprinkle with parsley. Serve hot.

Chowders are thick, substantial soups that make complete meals in themselves. Cooked in the microwave, they can be ready on the table in just over half an hour.

WEST COUNTRY CLAM CHOWDER

Colour Index page 43. 374 cals per 250 ml. Good source of calcium, iron, fibre. Begin 45 minutes ahead.

Ingredients for 1.5 litres		Microwave cookware
1 × 300 g jar or can baby clams in brine	500 ml milk	Large bowl
250 g thick streaky pork rashers or streaky bacon, diced	1 teaspoon chopped fresh thyme or 1/2 teaspoon dried	
1 large celery stick, finely chopped	1/4 teaspoon pepper	
1 large onion, chopped	Chopped fresh thyme or parsley to garnish	
450 g baking potatoes, peeled and diced		
3 tablespoons plain flour		

1 Drain clams; reserve liquid. Cut clams into dice-sized pieces; reserve. In bowl, place pork or bacon. Cook on High (100% power) for 4–5 minutes, until browned, stirring twice.

2 To pork or bacon, add celery and onion; stir to combine. Cook on High for 2 minutes, or until vegetables soften, stirring halfway through cooking.

3 To pork or bacon mixture, add potatoes; stir to combine. Cook, covered, on High for 7–9 minutes, just until potatoes are tender, stirring often. Into mixture, stir flour to coat potatoes. Cook on High for 3 minutes, stirring halfway through cooking.

4 Into mixture, gradually stir milk; add reserved clam juice and stir until smooth. Cook, covered, on High for 4–5 minutes, until slightly thickened, stirring twice.

5 To chowder, add diced clams, thyme and pepper. Cook on High for 5 minutes, or until piping hot, stirring twice.

6 *To serve:* ladle chowder into warmed soup bowls and sprinkle with thyme or parsley. Serve hot.

Fruit Soups

RED PLUM SOUP

Colour Index page 44. Makes 750 ml. 99 cals per 250 ml. Low in cholesterol, fat, sodium. Good source of fibre if soup is not sieved. Begin early in day.

700 g red plums	*1 × 7.5 cm cinnamon*
350 ml fruity red	*stick*
wine	*50 g sugar*
1 teaspoon vanilla	*Soured cream or plain*
essence	*yogurt to garnish*

1. Stone plums and cut into quarters. In deep 2.5 litre microwave-safe bowl, combine plums, wine, vanilla essence, cinnamon stick and sugar. Cook, covered, on High (100% power) for 8–10 minutes, until plums are tender, stirring twice. Discard cinnamon stick.
2. In food processor with knife blade attached or in blender, process plum mixture until smooth. If you like, sieve soup to remove plum skins.
3. Cover soup and refrigerate until chilled. Garnish each serving with soured cream or yogurt.

GARNISHES FOR FRUIT SOUPS
A pretty garnish can add greatly to the decorative appeal of a refreshing summer soup. Edible flowers make a particularly attractive garnish, as do any of the garnishes suggested here.

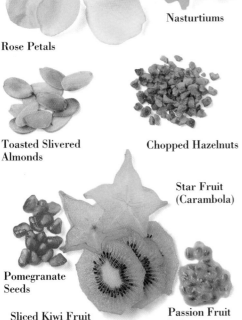

Rose Petals

Nasturtiums

Toasted Slivered Almonds

Chopped Hazelnuts

Star Fruit (Carambola)

Pomegranate Seeds

Sliced Kiwi Fruit

Passion Fruit Pulp

Fruit soup is best known as a dessert but can also make an unusual, refreshing first course, especially for a summer meal. It looks particularly attractive served in white china bowls or goblets. Most fruit soups are sweetened purées diluted with wine, fruit juice or water; they only take a few minutes to cook in the microwave. Once you have tried Red Plum Soup (left) and Peach Soup (below), experiment with other fruit such as cherries, blueberries, raspberries, strawberries and tropical fruits.

PEACH SOUP

Colour Index page 44. 77 cals per 250 ml. Low in cholesterol, fat, sodium. Good source of fibre. Begin early in day.

Ingredients for 750 ml		Microwave cookware
700 g ripe peaches or 2 cans peaches in natural juice, drained *250 ml dry white wine* *120 ml water* *50 g sugar*	*1 teaspoon finely chopped root ginger* *4 tablespoons plain yogurt* *Plain yogurt, mint leaves and cracked ice*	Deep 2.5 litre bowl

1 Cut peaches in half; twist apart. Remove stones. Cut peach halves into halves or quarters lengthways.

2 In bowl, combine peaches, wine, water and sugar. Cook, covered, on High (100% power) for 10 minutes, or until peaches soften, stirring twice.

3 In food processor with knife blade attached or in blender, process peach mixture until smooth.

4 Over bowl, set sieve. Work peach mixture through sieve to remove skins.

5 Into peach mixture, stir root ginger. Cook, covered with kitchen paper, on High for 5 minutes, or until flavours blend, stirring twice. Cover and refrigerate until chilled; stir in yogurt until evenly blended.

6 *To serve:* ladle soup into bowls. If you like, garnish with plain yogurt and mint leaves and surround bowl with cracked ice.

Eggs and Cheese

**BAKED EGGS · POACHED EGGS · SCRAMBLED EGGS
FRIED EGGS · OMELETTES · MELTED CHEESE
BAKED CHEESE · SOUFFLÉS · ROULADES**

Eggs and Cheese

Eggs and cheese are delicate ingredients that need careful handling when cooked in the microwave. Cooked conventionally, the white of an egg sets before the yolk, but the opposite is true in microwave cooking – because egg yolks contain a high proportion of fat, they attract more microwave energy. Recipes for eggs in this book therefore include standing times, in which the white sets without the yolk overcooking. Even when yolks and whites are mixed together, as in scrambled eggs, they still require standing time. Expect eggs to look very soft when removed from the microwave. Mixing in a little cream or milk before standing slows the cooking process, making the eggs creamier.

Most importantly, never put an egg in its shell into the microwave, whether to cook or reheat it: steam builds up in the shell and the egg will burst. Even out of the shell, you should pierce the yolk with the tip of a sharp knife or a cocktail stick before it is fried, baked or poached in the microwave; the yolk has an outer membrane and an unpierced egg yolk can burst. Cheese melted in the microwave makes a quick and easy topping for hamburgers, sandwiches and other snacks, and grated cheese melts very quickly when added to a hot mixture. Most cheeses melt rapidly because of their high fat content, but not all of them soften at the same rate. In general, hard, dry cheeses such as Cheddar, Double Gloucester, Parmesan and Gruyère take more time to soften than soft, moist ones such as cream cheese, Brie, Camembert and Bel Paese. However, cheese can quickly overcook and become stringy in the microwave, so that processed cheese often produces more acceptable results.

Soufflés can be cooked in the microwave, but be sure to follow instructions in individual recipes. Soufflés cook very rapidly in a microwave; they rise very high, but fall quickly when removed from the oven, and they do not form a crust.

Egg and cheese based quiches and casseroles reheat successfully in the microwave, but most other egg and cheese dishes tend to toughen.

CREATIVE CHEESE TOPPINGS

Decorate soft cheese – either slices of Brie or smaller whole cheeses – by marking patterns on top with a sharp knife, then adding flavourings of your choice.

Press nuts, seeds, spices and herbs on to surface of cheese. Refrigerate, then bring to room temperature on Medium (50% power) for 5 seconds at a time when ready to serve.

COOKING EGGS IN THE MICROWAVE

Here are a few guidelines for perfectly cooked eggs:

● Most egg recipes are cooked on Medium-High (70% power). When cooking whole eggs, the yolks cook before the whites because the fat content of the yolks attracts more microwave energy; cooking on High (100% power) therefore tends to make yolks overcook. Scrambled eggs and omelettes can be cooked on High, however, because yolks and whites are mixed together.

● Before cooking whole eggs broken from their shells, pierce yolks with a cocktail stick to allow excess steam to escape; this prevents yolks bursting.

● Eggs continue cooking after removal from oven, so always cook for minimum recommended time, then allow to stand for 1–2 minutes to complete cooking. If not done to your liking, return to oven for 15 seconds at a time.

EGGS IN BRIOCHES

Colour Index page 45. 6 servings. 311 cals per serving. Good source of calcium, iron. Begin 25 minutes ahead.

6 individual brioches
6 slices Gruyère cheese
6 eggs
Salt and pepper to taste
Smoked salmon

Fresh chives to garnish
Asparagus (page 237) with Hollandaise Sauce (page 381)

1. Cut top from each brioche; set aside. Hollow out each brioche, leaving a 5 mm thick shell.
2. Line each brioche with slice of cheese. On 30 cm round microwave-safe plate, arrange brioches in ring, 2.5 cm apart.
3. Break 1 egg into each brioche; with cocktail stick, pierce yolks. Cook, covered, on High (100% power) for 4–5 minutes, until almost set.
4. Allow brioches to stand, covered loosely with greaseproof paper, for 2–3 minutes, until whites are opaque. If eggs are not done to your liking, cook on High for 15 seconds at a time, until done. Season.
5. On serving plate, arrange each brioche with its top. Serve with smoked salmon garnished with chives, and Asparagus with Hollandaise Sauce.

Preparing the Brioches

Using spoon or small, serrated knife, hollow out inside of each brioche.

Line each brioche with slice of cheese, pushing cheese into hollow.

Baked Eggs

Timing is crucial when cooking eggs in the microwave. Do not return eggs to the oven without letting them stand for the time specified: this allows the whites to continue cooking until just set without overcooking the yolks. Eggs Baked in Ham Nests (below) makes a change from baking eggs in ramekins.

EGGS BAKED IN HAM NESTS

Colour Index page 45. 200 cals per serving. Good source of thiamine. Begin 15 minutes ahead.

Ingredients	For 4	For 2	For 1
Cooked ham	8 slices	4 slices	2 slices
Spring onions	2 spring onions	1 spring onion	½ spring onion
Butter or margarine, softened	2 teaspoons	1 teaspoon	½ teaspoon
Eggs	4 eggs	2 eggs	1 egg
Salt and pepper	to taste	to taste	to taste
Microwave cookware	4 × 12.5 cm baking dishes	2 × 12.5 cm baking dishes	1 × 12.5 cm baking dish
Time on Medium-High (70% power)	5–6½ (6:30) minutes	2½ (2:30)–3 minutes	1–1½ (1:30) minutes
Standing time	2 minutes	2 minutes	1 minute

1 Stack ham slices. Roll up or fold; slice thinly.

2 Slice spring onions thinly. Place in bowl with ham; toss

3 In baking dishes (see Chart), brush softened butter or margarine. For each serving, arrange ham and onion mixture round edge of dish.

4 One at a time, break eggs on to saucer and gently slip into centre of ham nests. With cocktail stick, pierce yolk of each egg to prevent bursting during cooking.

5 Cook eggs, covered, on Medium-High for time in Chart, until whites are opaque but not set.

6 Allow eggs to stand, loosely covered, for time in Chart. If eggs are not done to your liking after standing time, cook on Medium-High for 15 seconds at a time, until done. Sprinkle with salt and pepper before serving.

Poached Eggs

POACHED EGGS

Colour Index page 45. 80 cals per serving.
Begin 15 minutes ahead.

Ingredients	For 4	For 2	For 1
Water	120 ml	60 ml	2 tablespoons
White vinegar	2 teaspoons	1 teaspoon	½ teaspoon
Eggs	4 eggs	2 eggs	1 egg
Salt and pepper	to taste	to taste	to taste
Parsley sprigs	garnish	garnish	garnish
Microwave cookware	4 deep ramekins 250 ml jug	2 deep ramekins 250 ml jug	1 deep ramekin 250 ml jug
Time on High (100% power) Water and vinegar	3 minutes	1½ (1:30) minutes	45 seconds
Time on Medium (50% power) Eggs	3–3½ (3:30) minutes	1½ (1:30)–2 minutes	45 seconds–1 minute
Standing time	2–3 minutes	2 minutes	1 minute

1 Into each ramekin (see Chart), break 1 egg. In glass jug (see Chart), heat water and vinegar on High for time in Chart, or until boiling.

2 Meanwhile, with cocktail stick, pierce yolk of each egg to prevent bursting during cooking.

3 Over eggs, carefully pour water and vinegar. Cover each ramekin with microwave cling film. Place ramekins on oven floor.

4 Cook eggs, covered, on Medium for time in Chart, until whites are opaque but not set.

5 Allow eggs to stand, loosely covered, for time in Chart. If eggs are not done to your liking after standing time, cook on High for 15 seconds at a time, until done.

6 With slotted spoon, remove each egg from ramekin and drain over kitchen paper. Transfer to serving dish; sprinkle with salt and pepper. Garnish with parsley sprigs and serve immediately.

POACHED EGGS FLORENTINE

Colour Index page 46. 4 servings. 397 cals per serving. Good source of vitamin A, calcium, iron, fibre. Begin 40 minutes ahead.

Hollandaise Sauce (page 381)
120 ml water
2 teaspoons white vinegar
4 eggs
Grated nutmeg to taste
Salt and pepper to taste
275 g frozen spinach, thawed

2 muffins, split and toasted
225 g asparagus, cooked and drained (optional)
Fresh chives and crisply fried bacon to garnish

1. Make Hollandaise Sauce; cover and keep warm, stirring occasionally.
2. In 250 ml microwave-safe glass jug, heat water and vinegar on High (100% power) for 3 minutes, or until boiling. Meanwhile, break eggs into 4 deep ramekins. With cocktail stick, pierce yolk of each egg to prevent bursting during cooking.
3. Over eggs, carefully pour water and vinegar. On 30 cm microwave-safe plate, arrange ramekins. Cook eggs, covered, on Medium (50% power) for 3–3½ minutes, until whites are opaque but not set. Allow to stand, loosely covered, for 2–3 minutes. Season with nutmeg, salt and pepper.
4. Meanwhile, in 21.5 cm microwave-safe shallow pie dish, place thawed spinach. Cook on High for 3 minutes, until hot, stirring halfway through cooking.
5. *To serve:* place 1 toasted muffin half on each plate. Top with equal amounts of hot spinach. With slotted spoon, drain each egg over kitchen paper; place on spinach. If you like, accompany with cooked asparagus. Spoon over Hollandaise Sauce. Sprinkle with chives and crumbled bacon. Serve immediately.

Assembling the Poached Eggs Florentine

Using slotted spoon, carefully place each egg on spinach-topped toasted muffin half.

Spoon warm Hollandaise Sauce over each egg; garnish with chives and crumbled bacon.

Scrambled Eggs

PIPÉRADE

Colour Index page 45. 6 servings. 195 cals per serving. Good source of vitamin A, vitamin C, iron. Begin 20 minutes ahead.

2 tablespoons olive or vegetable oil	*6 eggs*
2 medium red or green peppers, cut into thin strips	*½ teaspoon dried basil*
	Salt and pepper to taste
1 onion, chopped	*Basil leaves to garnish*

1. Into 24 cm round microwave-safe flan dish, pour oil. Heat on High (100% power) for 3 minutes. Stir in pepper strips and onion. Cook on High for 4 minutes, or until softened, stirring twice.
2. In mixing bowl, with whisk or fork, beat eggs, basil, salt and pepper.
3. Over pepper and onion mixture, pour beaten eggs. Cook on High for 2½ (2:30) minutes, or until eggs are softly set but still very moist, beating with a fork several times during cooking.
4. Allow to stand, covered loosely with cling film, on heatproof surface for 2–3 minutes.
5. If eggs are not done to your liking after standing, remove cling film and cook on High for 15 seconds at a time, until done. Garnish with basil leaves. Serve immediately.

SCRAMBLED EGG AND BACON BREAKFAST
It is easy to cook scrambled eggs and bacon for 4 in a matter of minutes. Begin with steps 1 and 2 of the *Scrambled Eggs* recipe (right), then separate **8 rashers streaky bacon** and arrange on microwave-safe plate lined with kitchen paper. Cover with another sheet of paper and place on microwave oven shelf. Cook on High (100% power) for 2–3 minutes. Turn bacon rashers over and return to microwave. Continue with steps 3, 4 and 5 of Scrambled Eggs recipe, cooking eggs and bacon together on High for time in Chart, until eggs are softly set but still very moist, beating with fork several times, and bacon is browned. Transfer bacon to a clean sheet of paper to drain. Remove eggs from oven and allow to stand, covered loosely with cling film, on heatproof surface for time in Chart. If eggs are not done to your liking after standing, remove cling film and cook on High for 15 seconds at a time, until done.

To prevent overcooking, scrambled eggs should be removed from the microwave before they are completely cooked: they will set during standing time. If you like, mix a little milk or cream into scrambled eggs after they have been removed from the oven; this will slow down the cooking process and also make the eggs creamier.

SCRAMBLED EGGS

Colour Index page 45. 104 cals per serving. Begin 10 minutes ahead.

Ingredients	For 4	For 2	For 1
Butter or margarine	15 g	1½ teaspoons	1 teaspoon
Eggs	4 eggs	2 eggs	1 egg
Water	2 tablespoons	1 tablespoon	1½ teaspoons
Salt	to taste	to taste	to taste
Pepper	to taste	to taste	to taste
Microwave cookware	Medium bowl	Medium bowl	Small bowl
Time on High (100% power) Butter or margarine Eggs	30 seconds 1½(1:30)–2½ (2:30) minutes	15 seconds 1–1½ (1:30) minutes	10 seconds 45 seconds–1 minute
Standing time	2–3 minutes	2 minutes	1 minute

1 In bowl (see Chart), place butter or margarine. Heat, covered with kitchen paper, on High for time in Chart, or until melted.

2 In mixing bowl, with whisk or fork, beat eggs, water, salt and pepper; pour into melted butter or margarine.

3 Cook egg mixture on High for time in Chart, until softly set, beating with fork several times during cooking.

4 Remove eggs from oven. Eggs will still be very moist.

5 With cling film, loosely cover bowl. Allow eggs to stand on heatproof surface for time in Chart; eggs will finish cooking during standing.

6 If eggs are not done to your liking after standing, remove cling film and cook eggs on High for 15 seconds at a time, until done.

<table>
<tr><td>

Meal in Minutes *for 6 people*

Sunday Brunch

Buck's fizz
Citrus fruit salad
Eggs in Brioches, page 137, with extra smoked salmon
Asparagus, page 237, with Hollandaise Sauce, page 381
Chocolate-Dipped Fruit, page 327
Coffee with cakes and Danish pastries (bought)

</td></tr>
</table>

PREPARATION TIMETABLE

Early in day	*Make fruit salad of grapefruit, orange and tangerine segments; cover and refrigerate. Make Chocolate-Dipped Fruit, arrange on serving plate and loosely cover; store in cool, dry place (do not refrigerate). Chill orange juice and Champagne for Buck's fizz.*
2 hours ahead	*Make Hollandaise Sauce; keep warm, stirring occasionally. Prepare asparagus, but do not cook.*
30 minutes before serving	*Prepare Eggs in Brioches up to end of step 2. Cook asparagus according to instructions in Chart on page 237; arrange on warmed serving platter; pour over Hollandaise Sauce.*
Just before serving	*Complete Eggs in Brioches; arrange on platter with smoked salmon. Make Buck's fizz with orange juice and Champagne. Make coffee and arrange cakes and Danish pastries on serving plate.*

Fried Eggs

EGGS AND BACON

Colour Index page 45. 4 servings. 270 cals per serving. Begin 15 minutes ahead.

8 rashers streaky bacon	Chopped chives to
4 eggs	garnish
Salt and pepper to taste	Bread rolls (optional)
2 tomatoes, cut in half	

1. Preheat browning dish according to manufacturer's instructions. Arrange bacon rashers in single layer on browning dish. Cook on High (100% power) for 2 minutes. With tongs, turn bacon over. Cook on High for 2–3 minutes, until done to your liking. Transfer to kitchen paper to drain; set aside and keep warm. Discard half of bacon fat.

2. One at a time, break eggs on to saucer and gently slip on to browning dish, placing them evenly round dish. With cocktail stick, pierce yolk of each egg to prevent bursting during cooking.

3. Cook eggs on High for 1½–2 minutes, until done to your liking. Season with salt and pepper.

4. *To serve:* arrange eggs and bacon on warmed individual plates. Garnish with tomato halves sprinkled with chopped chives. If you like, accompany with warm bread rolls.

FRIED EGGS

Fried eggs are quick and easy to make in the microwave. Preheat browning dish according to manufacturer's instructions. For each *egg*, melt *15 g butter or margarine* in browning dish. Break egg on to saucer and gently slide on to browning dish. If frying only 1 egg, place in centre of dish; if frying more than 1 egg, space them evenly. With cocktail stick, pierce yolk(s). Cook on High (100% power) for 1½ (1:30)–2 minutes for 4 eggs; 45 seconds–1¼ (1:15) minutes for 2 eggs: 30 seconds–1 minute for 1 egg. If you like egg yolks cooked more than this, turn them over with fish slice after 1¼ (1:15) minutes for 4 eggs: 45 seconds for 2 eggs; 30 seconds for 1 egg.

Quick eggs and bacon for one: preheat browning dish according to manufacturer's instructions. Cut 2 bacon rashers in half crossways and arrange against edge of dish. Cook on High (100% power) for 45 seconds–1 minute; turn bacon over. Break 1 egg on to saucer, gently slide on to browning dish; pierce yolk with cocktail stick. Baste egg with bacon fat; cook on High for 45 seconds–1 minute. Allow to stand, covered, for 1 minute.

Omelettes

SOUFFLÉED CHEESE OMELETTE

Colour Index page 46. 2 servings. 261 cals per serving. Good source of vitamin A, calcium. Begin 15 minutes ahead.

3 eggs, separated	*30 g butter or margarine*
1 teaspoon milk	*Cheddar cheese, grated*
½ teaspoon dried	*Cucumber, tomato and*
tarragon	*parsley to garnish*
¼ teaspoon salt	
Good pinch of pepper	

1. In small mixing bowl, with fork, beat egg yolks with milk, tarragon, salt and pepper.
2. In large mixing bowl, whisk egg whites until stiff peaks form. With rubber spatula, gently fold egg yolk mixture into whisked egg whites.
3. In 21.5 cm microwave-safe shallow pie dish, place butter or margarine. Heat, covered with kitchen paper, on High (100% power) for 45 seconds, or until melted.
4. Into melted butter or margarine, spoon egg mixture. With spatula, smooth top. Cook on High for 1½ (1:30)–2½ (2:30) minutes, until top is almost dry.
5. With spatula, mark line through centre of omelette. Sprinkle cheese over half of omelette. With spatula, gently fold omelette over cheese.
6. Slide omelette on to warmed serving platter. Garnish with cucumber, tomato and parsley. Serve immediately.

USING LEFTOVER CHEESE: small pieces of one or more hard cheeses can be grated and used as an alternative filling.

FRENCH DESSERT OMELETTE

Colour Index page 46. 2 servings. 209 cals per serving. Good source of vitamin A, iron. Begin 15 minutes ahead.

75 g strawberries, sliced	*1 teaspoon milk*
½ teaspoon sugar	*Icing sugar*
2 teaspoons butter or	*Strawberry to decorate*
margarine	
4 eggs	

1. In small mixing bowl, combine strawberries and sugar. In 21.5 cm microwave-safe shallow pie dish, place butter or margarine. Heat on High (100% power) for 30 seconds, or until melted.
2. In another small mixing bowl, with fork, beat eggs and milk; pour into pie dish. Cook on High for 1 minute. With spoon or spatula, move cooked edge to centre of dish. Cook, covered with kitchen paper, on High for 1–1½ (1:30) minutes, until omelette is set but moist in centre.
3. Over half of omelette, spoon strawberries. With spatula, fold omelette over strawberries.
4. Slide omelette on to warmed serving platter; sift icing sugar over top. Decorate with whole strawberry. Serve immediately.

Omelettes should be cooked in shallow pie dishes in order to have smooth, neat edges. To ensure a flat surface, carefully move the cooked edge to the centre with a spoon or spatula so that the uncooked egg mixture flows under the omelette. A properly cooked omelette will be set throughout but the centre top will appear moist. If the omelette is too moist in the centre when checked with a knife, return to oven for 15 seconds at a time.

PEPPER AND TOMATO OMELETTE

Colour Index page 46. 253 cals per serving. Good source of vitamin A, vitamin C, iron. Begin 15 minutes ahead.

Ingredients for 2 servings		Microwave cookware
1 tablespoon olive or vegetable oil	*4 eggs*	Shallow 24 cm glass pie dish
1 medium onion, thinly sliced	*1 tablespoon milk*	
1 small green pepper, coarsely chopped	*Tabasco sauce to taste*	
1 small tomato, chopped	*Salt and pepper to taste*	
	Parsley to garnish	

1 In pie dish, place oil, onion, green pepper and tomato; stir to combine. Cook, covered, on High (100% power) for 4 minutes, or until softened, stirring twice.

2 Meanwhile, in mixing bowl, with fork, beat eggs, milk, Tabasco sauce, salt and pepper. With slotted spoon, remove vegetable mixture from pie dish; set vegetable mixture aside.

3 Into pie dish used for cooking vegetables, slowly pour egg mixture. Cook egg mixture on High for 1 minute.

4 With spoon or spatula, move cooked edge to centre of dish. Cook, covered with kitchen paper, on High for 1–1½ (1:30) minutes, until omelette is set but still moist in centre.

5 Over half of omelette, spoon vegetable mixture. With spatula, gently fold omelette over vegetables.

6 *To serve:* slide omelette on to warmed serving platter. Garnish with parsley and serve immediately.

Melted Cheese

Cheese is a delicate ingredient that needs careful handling in the microwave to avoid becoming tough and stringy. Recipes in this section call for grated cheese because in this form it will melt rapidly in a hot mixture. It is important to stir grated cheese after it has been added to any hot mixture, to make sure that it melts completely and blends evenly.

MACARONI CHEESE

Colour Index page 46. 581 cals per serving. Good source of riboflavin, thiamine, calcium, iron. Begin 35 minutes ahead.

Ingredients for 4 servings		Microwave cookware

225 g elbow macaroni
45 g butter or
  margarine
1 small onion, finely
  chopped
1 tablespoon plain flour
1/4 teaspoon salt
1/4 teaspoon dry
  mustard
	Good pinch of pepper
	350 ml milk
	225 g Cheddar cheese,
	  grated
	25 g dried wholemeal
	  breadcrumbs
	Extra grated cheese
	  (optional)
	Parsley to garnish
		2 litre soufflé dish or
		casserole

1 Cook macaroni conventionally according to instructions on packet; drain in colander.

2 Meanwhile, in soufflé dish or casserole, place butter or margarine. Heat, covered with kitchen paper, on High (100% power) for 45 seconds, or until melted. Add onion; stir to coat. Cook on High for 2 minutes, or until soft.

3 Into onion mixture, with whisk or spoon, stir flour, salt, mustard and pepper until smooth and blended. Cook on High for 1 minute, stirring halfway through cooking.

4 Into mixture, gradually stir milk. Cook on High for 3–4 minutes, until mixture thickens and is smooth, stirring twice. Remove from oven and add cheese. Stir sauce until cheese melts.

5 Into cheese sauce, stir drained macaroni. Cook on High for 5–7 minutes, until hot, rotating twice during cooking. Allow to stand on heatproof surface for 5 minutes.

6 On to macaroni mixture, sprinkle dried wholemeal breadcrumbs and, if you like, extra grated cheese. Cook on High for 30 seconds, or, if you like and dish is flameproof, brown under preheated grill. Garnish before serving.

WELSH RAREBIT

Colour Index page 46. 6 servings. 347 cals per serving. Good source of vitamin A. Begin 15 minutes ahead.

60 g butter or margarine
35 g plain flour
1/4 teaspoon dry mustard
Pinch of cayenne pepper
120 ml brown ale
350 ml milk
1 teaspoon
  Worcestershire sauce

225 g Cheddar cheese,
  grated
6 slices white or rye
  bread, toasted, or 6
  muffin halves

1. In 2 litre microwave-safe casserole, place butter or margarine. Heat, covered with kitchen paper, on High (100% power) for 45 seconds–1 minute, until melted.
2. Into melted butter or margarine, with whisk or spoon, stir flour, mustard and cayenne pepper until smooth and blended. Cook on High for 1 minute, stirring halfway through cooking.
3. Into mixture, gradually stir brown ale, milk and Worcestershire sauce until smooth. Cook on High for 5 minutes, or until mixture thickens and is smooth, stirring twice. Add grated cheese; stir until melted.
4. Spread hot cheese mixture on toast or muffin halves. Serve immediately.

SWISS CHEESE FONDUE

Colour Index page 46. 4 servings. 825 cals per serving. Good source of vitamin A, thiamine, iron. Begin 10 minutes ahead.

1 garlic clove, cut in
  half
350 ml dry white wine
450 g Gruyère cheese,
  grated
25 g plain flour
Pinch of pepper
Pinch of grated nutmeg

Paprika (optional)
1 French stick, about
  45 cm long, cut into
  2.5 cm cubes
16 cherry tomatoes
1 green pepper, cut into
  cubes

1. In 2 litre microwave-safe bowl, place garlic and wine. Cook on High (100% power) for 4 minutes, or until wine is boiling.
2. Meanwhile, in mixing bowl, toss grated Gruyère cheese with flour until evenly combined.
3. Remove garlic from wine; discard. To wine, add cheese mixture, a handful at a time, stirring constantly until cheese melts. Season with pepper and nutmeg. If you like, sprinkle with paprika.
4. *To serve:* place fondue in centre of table. With long-handled fondue forks or skewers, let each person spear chunks of French bread, cherry tomatoes and green pepper cubes to dip into the hot fondue.

ASPARAGUS TIMBALES

Colour Index page 47. Makes 4 timbales. 314 cals each. Good source of vitamin A, thiamine, vitamin C, iron. Begin 40 minutes ahead.

45 g butter or margarine	1/4 teaspoon grated
2 tablespoons dried	nutmeg
breadcrumbs	Pepper to taste
225 g asparagus	120 ml half cream
1 small onion, finely	175 g thinly sliced
chopped	smoked salmon or
4 egg yolks	Parma ham
25 g Parmesan cheese,	Lemon to garnish
grated	

1. In medium microwave-safe bowl, place butter or margarine. Heat, covered with kitchen paper, on High (100% power) for 45 seconds–1 minute, until melted. Brush inside of 4 × 120 ml ramekins with some melted butter or margarine. Coat inside of each ramekin with breadcrumbs.

2. Hold base of each asparagus spear firmly and bend; end will break off where spear becomes too tough to eat. Discard tough ends.

3. Trim 4 asparagus tips to 5 cm pieces; set aside for garnish. Coarsely chop remaining asparagus. In bowl with melted butter or margarine, combine chopped asparagus and onion. Cook, covered, on High for 4–5 minutes, until tender, stirring halfway through cooking.

4. On cutting board, finely chop asparagus mixture; return to bowl. With fork or whisk, beat in egg yolks, cheese, nutmeg and pepper.

5. Into 500 ml microwave-safe measuring jug, pour cream. Heat on Medium (50% power) for 1½ (1:30)–2 minutes, until small bubbles form around edge.

6. Into asparagus mixture, gradually stir cream. Ladle one-quarter of mixture into each ramekin. Arrange in 30 cm ring on microwave-safe plate. Elevate plate on microwave-safe trivet or rack, or on ramekins turned upside down. Cook on Medium for 5–7 minutes, until knife inserted 1 cm from centre comes out clean, rotating ramekins a quarter turn twice during cooking. Allow to stand, covered, on heatproof surface, for 5 minutes.

7. To serve: unmould timbales on to individual plates. Serve with smoked salmon or Parma ham. Garnish with reserved asparagus and lemon.

Preparing the Ramekins

Using pastry brush, brush ramekins with some melted butter.

Coat each ramekin with breadcrumbs; tilt to cover bottom and sides.

When microwaving cheese casserole or quiches, elevate the dish on a microwave-safe trivet or rack, or on a ramekin turned upside down, to ensure even cooking on the underside. Ramekins arranged in a ring should be rotated during cooking.

MEXICAN CHEESE AND TOMATO BAKE

Colour Index page 46. 390 cals per serving. Good source of vitamin A. Begin 45 minutes ahead.

Ingredients for 6 servings		Microwave cookware
1 tablespoon olive oil	Tabasco sauce to taste	30 × 20 cm
1 onion, chopped	115 g mild Cheddar	baking dish
2 spring onions, sliced	cheese, grated	Trivet, rack or
1 garlic clove, crushed	15 g fresh coriander	ramekins
1/2 teaspoon dried	leaves, chopped	
oregano	175 g tortilla chips	
1/2 teaspoon ground	Coriander leaves to	
cumin	garnish	
1 × 400 g can crushed		
tomatoes		
250 ml double or		
whipping cream		

1 In baking dish, place oil, onion, spring onions, garlic, oregano and cumin. Elevate dish on trivet or rack, or on ramekins turned upside down.

2 Cook onion mixture, covered, on High (100% power) for 3 minutes, or until onion softens slightly, stirring halfway through cooking.

3 To onion mixture, add tomatoes, cream and Tabasco. Cook on High for 7–8 minutes, until sauce thickens, stirring twice.

4 Meanwhile, in mixing bowl, toss grated cheese with coriander until well mixed. Remove tomato sauce from oven. Pour half of sauce into jug; reserve.

5 Cover remaining tomato sauce in baking dish with half of tortilla chips and half of cheese mixture; pour over reserved tomato sauce. Add another layer of tortilla chips and cheese mixture. Cook on High for 4–5 minutes, until cheese melts and tomato sauce is bubbling, rotating dish halfway through cooking.

6 On heatproof surface, allow dish to stand for 5 minutes. Garnish with coriander leaves before serving.

Baked Cheese

Traditional quiches cannot be cooked successfully in the microwave, but crustless varieties are delicious and have less calories. Medium power is necessary to prevent the delicate texture of cheese from becoming tough and rubbery. For a perfect quiche that is light and tender, preheat the liquid ingredients first, then combine with eggs. This way, the eggs will not overcook, as they might if heated with a cold liquid.

CRUSTLESS BROCCOLI AND GRUYÈRE CHEESE QUICHE

Colour Index page 47. 244 cals per serving. Good source of vitamin A, vitamin C, calcium, fibre. Begin 45 minutes ahead.

Ingredients for 6 servings		Microwave cookware
1 bunch broccoli (about 450 g), chopped 1 small onion, finely chopped 120 ml half cream 4 eggs	225 g Gruyère cheese, grated 1/4 teaspoon cayenne pepper Tomato Rose (page 236) and basil leaves to garnish	21.5 cm flan dish 500 ml measuring jug Trivet, rack or ramekin

1 In flan dish, place broccoli and onion. Cook, covered, on High (100% power) for 5 minutes, stirring halfway through cooking. Set aside, covered.

2 Into measuring jug, pour cream. Heat on Medium (50% power) for 1 1/2 (1:30)–2 minutes, until small bubbles form round edge.

3 In mixing bowl, beat cream and eggs until blended; stir in cheese and cayenne pepper. Pour mixture slowly over broccoli and onion.

4 With fork, stir mixture gently to distribute vegetables evenly. Elevate dish on trivet or rack, or on ramekin turned upside down.

5 Cook quiche on Medium for 12–14 minutes, until knife inserted in centre comes out clean, rotating dish a quarter turn twice during cooking. Allow to stand, covered, on heatproof surface for 10 minutes.

6 Garnish quiche with Tomato Rose and basil leaves. Serve warm.

BACON AND POTATO QUICHE

Colour Index page 47. 8 servings. 241 cals per serving. Good source of vitamin A. Begin 45 minutes ahead.

6 rashers rindless streaky bacon, cut into 5 cm pieces
225 g potatoes, cut into 2 cm cubes
225 g fresh peas, shelled
175 ml milk
6 eggs
175 g Cheddar cheese, cut into 1 cm cubes
2 spring onions, thinly sliced

1. In 25 cm microwave-safe flan dish, place bacon. Cook, covered with kitchen paper, on High (100% power) for 5–6 minutes, until browned, stirring halfway through cooking. Transfer to kitchen paper to drain. Discard all but 2 tablespoons bacon fat. Stir in potatoes and peas. Cook, covered, for 4–6 minutes, until tender, stirring halfway through cooking.
2. Into medium microwave-safe bowl, pour milk. Heat on High for 2–2 1/2 (2:30) minutes, until small bubbles form round edge. Add eggs; beat until blended. Add cheese, spring onions and bacon; mix well. Carefully pour mixture over vegetables in dish.
3. Elevate dish on microwave-safe trivet or rack, or on ramekin turned upside down. Cook on Medium (50% power) for 10–12 minutes, until egg mixture is slightly set but still moist, stirring cooked edge towards centre twice. Allow to stand, covered, on heatproof surface for 5 minutes before serving.

CAMEMBERT IN VINE LEAVES

Colour Index page 46. 2 servings. 250 cals per serving. Good source of vitamin A. Begin 20 minutes ahead.

1 red-skinned dessert apple
2 teaspoons brandy
1 × 125 g Camembert cheese
2 vine leaves, fresh or in brine (rinsed and drained), or fresh lettuce leaves

1. Core apple. Thinly slice one-quarter of apple; cut remainder into wedges. In small bowl, toss apple slices and wedges in brandy. Set aside.
2. Cut Camembert in half horizontally. Arrange apple slices on cut side of one-half of cheese; cover with remaining half of cheese, cut side down.
3. Place cheese in centre of 1 vine or lettuce leaf. Cover with remaining leaf. Fold edges of leaves round cheese to enclose it completely; secure with string. Place wrapped cheese in centre of small microwave-safe plate. Cook on Medium (50% power) for 2 minutes. Remove string.
4. To serve: cut wrapped cheese in half; place on individual plates with apple wedges.

Soufflés

TOMATOES WITH GOAT CHEESE AND BASIL SOUFFLE

Colour Index page 47. 8 servings. 106 cals per serving. Low in sodium. Good source of vitamin A. Begin 35 minutes ahead.

8 tomatoes	1 tablespoon finely
Salt and pepper to taste	chopped fresh basil
30 g butter or margarine	leaves
2 tablespoons plain flour	2 eggs, separated
120 ml milk	Basil leaves to garnish
50 g soft goat cheese	

1. Cut thin slice from base of each tomato so tomatoes sit flat. Cut slice from top of each tomato; discard. With spoon, scoop out flesh and seeds from tomatoes to leave 5 mm shell. On 30 cm microwave-safe plate, arrange tomato shells in ring. Season each tomato; set aside.
2. In medium microwave-safe bowl, place butter or margarine. Heat, covered with kitchen paper, on High (100% power) for 45 seconds, or until melted. With whisk or spoon, stir in flour until smooth and blended. Cook on High for 1 minute, stirring once. Into mixture, gradually whisk milk. Cook sauce on High for 2–3 minutes, until thick and smooth, whisking twice.
3. To sauce, add cheese; stir until cheese melts. Add basil, salt and pepper.
4. Into cheese sauce, whisk egg yolks. In large mixing bowl, whisk egg whites until stiff peaks form. With spatula, gently fold cheese mixture, one-third at a time, into whisked whites, just until blended.
5. Spoon equal amount of mixture into each tomato shell. Cook on Medium-Low (30% power) for 6 minutes. Increase power level to Medium (50% power) and cook for 5 minutes longer. Increase power level to High and cook for 2 minutes more, or just until set.
6. *To serve:* place each stuffed tomato on warmed dinner plate. Garnish with basil leaves.

COOKING WITH CHEESE

The quality of cheese used in cooking makes a great difference to the finished microwave recipes. Always add cheese towards the end of cooking so it does not overcook and become stringy or tough. For melted cheese dishes, well-aged, high-quality cheeses will result in smooth, tasty dishes. If a sauce separates or curdles, pour it into a blender or food processor and blend for 1–2 minutes. To reheat cheese sauces, heat on Medium (50% power) and stir frequently.

CHEESE SOUFFLÉ

Colour Index page 47. 335 cals per serving. Good source of calcium. Begin 35 minutes ahead.

Ingredients for 6 servings		Microwave cookware
60 g butter or margarine	225 g Gruyère cheese, grated	1 litre measuring jug
35 g plain flour	Pinch of grated nutmeg	2 litre soufflé dish
250 ml milk	Salt to taste	
5 eggs, separated	Tomato Sauce (page 380, optional)	
25 g Parmesan cheese, grated		

1 In measuring jug, place butter or margarine. Heat, covered with kitchen paper, on High (100% power) for 45 seconds–1 minute, until melted. With whisk or spoon, stir in flour until smooth and blended. Cook on High for 1 minute, stirring once. Into mixture, gradually whisk milk.

2 Cook sauce on High for 2–3 minutes, until very thick, whisking twice. In mixing bowl, lightly beat egg yolks. Whisk small amount of hot sauce into egg yolks.

3 Into remaining hot sauce in jug, slowly pour egg yolk mixture, whisking rapidly to prevent lumping. Whisk in Parmesan and 25 g Gruyère cheese; add nutmeg and salt.

4 In large mixing bowl, whisk egg whites until stiff peaks form.

5 With spatula, gently fold cheese mixture and remaining Gruyère cheese alternately, one third at a time, into whisked egg whites, just until blended. Pour mixture into ungreased soufflé dish. Gently smooth top. Cook on Medium-Low (30% power) for 8 minutes.

6 Increase power level to Medium (50% power) and cook for 7–9 minutes longer, until top is dry but soufflé still moves when dish is shaken gently (soufflé will rise and fall several times during cooking in microwave). If you like, serve with Tomato Sauce.

Roulades

Soufflé-based dishes like this Smoked Salmon and Chive Roulade and Mushroom and Cheese Roulade make pretty food for a buffet party. If you follow the instructions for rolling the roulades from a long rather than a narrow end, you will find they are easier to cut into neat, thin slices – just perfect for dainty presentation on a large serving plate or tray.

SMOKED SALMON AND CHIVE ROULADE

Colour Index page 47. 233 cals per serving. Good source of vitamin A. Begin 45 minutes ahead.

Ingredients for 4 servings		Microwave cookware

6 eggs
Pepper to taste
75 g thinly sliced
  smoked salmon or
  off-cuts
115 g cream cheese
  with chives, softened
	4 tablespoons chopped
	  fresh chives
	Chives to garnish
		32 × 26 cm baking tray
		Trivet, rack or
		  ramekins

1 Separate 4 eggs. In small mixing bowl, with fork or whisk, lightly beat egg yolks, 2 remaining whole eggs and pepper. Line baking tray with non-stick baking parchment.

2 In large mixing bowl, whisk egg whites until stiff peaks form. With rubber spatula or large metal spoon, gently fold egg yolk mixture into egg whites, just until blended. Pour into lined tray or dish.

3 With palette knife or spatula, smooth top of soufflé mixture. Elevate tray or dish on trivet or rack, or on ramekins turned upside down. Cook on High (100% power) for 3–4 minutes, until knife inserted in centre comes out clean.

4 Invert roulade on to clean tea towel lined with non-stick baking parchment. Peel parchment off top of roulade. Starting at 1 long end, roll roulade with parchment, Swiss roll fashion. Allow to stand, seam side down, for 5 minutes; carefully unroll.

5 Arrange smoked salmon on top of roulade, to within 5 cm of long edges. Spread cream cheese over salmon; sprinkle with chopped chives. Starting from same long end, roll up roulade without parchment.

6 To serve: lift roulade with palette knife on to serving platter. Refrigerate for 15 minutes. Cut into slices and garnish with chives.

MUSHROOM AND CHEESE ROULADE

Colour Index page 47. 4 servings. 242 cals per serving. Good source of vitamin A, riboflavin, iron. Begin 45 minutes ahead.

30 g butter or margarine
1 small onion, chopped
2 tomatoes, diced
225 g mushrooms,
  coarsely chopped
60 ml dry white wine
1 tablespoon chopped
  fresh basil leaves
50 g Gruyère cheese,
  grated
6 eggs
Salt and pepper to taste
Basil leaves to garnish

1. Line 32 × 26 cm microwave-safe baking tray with non-stick baking parchment; set aside.
2. In 20 cm square microwave-safe baking dish, place butter or margarine. Heat, covered with kitchen paper, on High (100% power) for 45 seconds, or until melted. Add onion, tomatoes and mushrooms. Cook on High for 5 minutes, or until vegetables soften, stirring twice.
3. To vegetable mixture, add wine. Cook on High for 5 minutes, or until most of wine has evaporated; add chopped basil. Strain liquid from vegetable mixture and discard; stir in cheese.
4. Separate 4 eggs. In small mixing bowl, with fork or whisk, lightly beat egg yolks and 2 remaining whole eggs. Season.
5. In large mixing bowl, whisk egg whites until stiff peaks form. With rubber spatula or large metal spoon, gently fold egg yolk mixture into egg whites, just until blended. Pour into lined tray or dish.
6. With palette knife or spatula, smooth top of soufflé mixture. Elevate tray or dish on microwave-safe trivet or rack, or on ramekins turned upside down. Cook on High for 3–4 minutes, until knife inserted in centre comes out clean.
7. Invert roulade on to clean tea towel lined with non-stick baking parchment. Peel parchment off top of roulade. Starting from 1 long end, roll roulade with parchment, Swiss roll fashion.
8. Allow to stand, seam side down, for 5 minutes; carefully unroll. Spread mushroom mixture over roulade to within 5 cm of long edges. Starting from same long end, roll up roulade without parchment.
9. To serve: lift roulade with palette knife on to serving platter. Refrigerate for 15 minutes. Cut into slices and garnish with basil leaves.

SPINACH AND RICOTTA CHEESE ROULADE: prepare as for roulade (above), substituting **275 g frozen chopped spinach, thawed and squeezed dry**, for mushrooms. Cook with tomatoes for 3 minutes only. Omit wine. Stir in **175 g ricotta cheese** with basil. If you like, serve with Tomato Sauce (page 380).

Fish and Shellfish

**DEFROSTING AND COOKING FISH AND SHELLFISH · FISH STEAKS
FISH FILLETS · WHOLE FISH
CANNED FISH · PRAWNS · LOBSTERS
MUSSELS · SCALLOPS · OYSTERS · CRAB
MIXED SHELLFISH DISHES**

Fish and Shellfish

The microwave is ideal for cooking both fish and shellfish, as they are naturally delicate foods and require minimal cooking to preserve their flavours and textures. Fish and shellfish cooked conventionally can easily dry out, toughen or break apart, so the quick, moist cooking of the microwave, combined with careful handling, can produce excellent results. Microwaved fish can be made to look grilled by cooking it in a browning dish or by brushing it with browning, teriyaki or soy sauces. Breaded fish, such as frozen fish fillets and fish fingers, can be cooked successfully in a browning dish, or on special microwave crisping and browning wrap.

If a fish is done, the outer edge of the flesh should be opaque; it should also flake easily when pierced with a fork. Fish that turns dark and dry when removed from the microwave has been overcooked. To prevent this, place thicker areas towards edge of dish and overlap thin ends of fillets (or tuck thin ends under). Cook the fish in the microwave for the minimum suggested time only, then test to see if fish is done. Shielding will prevent delicate or thin areas from overcooking. Recipes for large whole fish usually call for standing time, in which case, test to see if fish is done afterwards, as fish continues to cook during standing time. Shellfish cooks quickly in the microwave, so be careful not to let it overcook or it will become tough and rubbery. Prawns should be just pink, oysters should just curl at the edges; scallops should be opaque. Clams and mussels cooked in the shell should be removed from the microwave when shells have opened: any that remain closed should be discarded.

Thick fish steaks or pieces cooked in liquid should be carefully turned over halfway through cooking. To avoid uneven cooking, dishes in which whole fish and fish fillets are cooked should be rotated in the microwave; this prevents heat building up in any one part of the fish. To avoid unwanted cooking juices in bottom of dish, line it with kitchen paper or elevate fish on a microwave-safe trivet or rack in baking dish.

PARTY PRAWNS

Large prawns are always a popular choice for elegant appetisers and salads. Prawns can be made even more appetising by wrapping them in thin strips of bacon or vegetables, creating a pretty spiral effect.

Pre-cooked bacon strips wrap large prawns (left) and crisp while prawns cook. Serve with mixed salad leaves.

Quickly cooked strips of leek or spring onion wrap king prawns (right) and create an elegant look. Garnish with Spring Onion Tassel (page 132) and salad leaves.

Defrosting Fish and Shellfish

Frozen fish and shellfish defrost rapidly in the microwave, but care must be taken not to let them start cooking during the defrosting process. When defrosted, they should feel cold but pliable.

Most fish fillets and blocks of shellfish such as crabmeat and scallops, can be defrosted in their packets. If you carefully separate fish and shellfish pieces as soon as possible during defrosting and spread them in a single layer, they will defrost more quickly.

During defrosting time, some thin areas of whole fish may become warm and start to cook; protect these spots by shielding them with smooth pieces of foil.

Whole fish and large shellfish should be left to stand, covered, after defrosting in the microwave – to let the temperature equalise throughout the food. Whole fish must be completely defrosted before cooking. There should be no ice crystals in the cavity, so rinse whole fish under cold running water if cavity is still icy.

As with all frozen foods, it is best to cook fish and shellfish as soon as possible after defrosting, to prevent the growth of harmful bacteria in the defrosted food, as well as for maximum freshness and flavour. Many ovens have a special defrosting facility, in which case follow the manufacturer's instructions.

DEFROSTING A LARGE PACKET OF FISH FILLETS

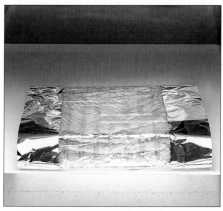

Heat fish in packet on Medium (50% power) 1½ (1:30) minutes. Turn packet over; shield ends with smooth pieces of foil.

Heat on Medium-Low (30% power) 1½ (1:30) minutes. Turn packet over and rotate a half turn. Heat on Medium-Low 1½ (1:30) minutes.

On heatproof surface, allow to stand for 10 minutes. Carefully separate fillets; rinse under cold running water if some areas are still icy or stiff.

DEFROSTING WHOLE FISH AND STEAKS

Place fish in microwave-safe dish and turn over halfway through defrosting time. Shield vulnerable areas with smooth pieces of foil after turning.

DEFROSTING SHELLFISH

Shellfish can be defrosted in packet, but large quantities are best defrosted in shallow microwave-safe dish. Separate pieces halfway through defrosting.

Cooking Fish and Shellfish

Quick cooking method
To 'steam' fish portions quickly and easily, place them in centre of lightly moistened kitchen paper. Bring all corners to centre and twist to close; place on microwave-safe plate. Cook 1 × 225 g fish steak on High (100% power) for 2–3 minutes, 2 × 225 g fish steaks on High for 3–4 minutes, rotating once.

Improving appearance
Microwaved fish can be made to look grilled by cooking in a browning dish (right) or by coating with browning, teriyaki or soy sauces.

Absorbing excess moisture Unwanted juices in bottom of dish can be absorbed by using kitchen paper as liners; separate ends of fish with microwave cling film. Alternatively, elevate fish on microwave-safe trivet or rack in dish.

Even cooking
Roll fillets Swiss roll fashion; secure with wooden cocktail sticks and arrange round edge of round dish. Leave space between each portion and leave centre open for even cooking.

Shielding
Cover delicate parts of a whole fish, like the tail or eyes, with smooth strips of foil.

ROTATING AND TURNING FISH AND SHELLFISH

Whole fish and fish fillet dishes should be rotated to avoid heat building up in any one spot during cooking.

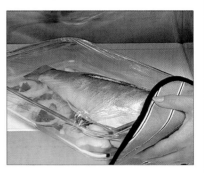

Prawns arranged in circle with tails pointing towards centre should be turned over with tongs and dish rotated halfway through cooking.

Thick fish pieces or steaks cooked in liquid should be turned over halfway through cooking to ensure even distribution of heat.

'Stir-frying' prawns
Because prawns cook rapidly, stir-frying in a browning dish is an ideal way to prepare them. The frequent turning and stirring ensures even distribution of heat.

Fish Steaks

FISH STEAKS WITH SALSA

Colour Index page 48. 4 servings. 503 cals per serving. Good source of vitamin A, vitamin C, iron, fibre. Begin 25 minutes ahead.

1 × 400 g can tomatoes	3 tablespoons lime or
1 green pepper, thinly	lemon juice
sliced	4 salmon, cod or halibut
1 onion, chopped	steaks (175 g each)
1/2 × 100 g can stoned	2 tablespoons dry sherry
black olives, drained	4 tablespoons
and cut in half	mayonnaise
3 tablespoons chopped	1 teaspoon cider vinegar
fresh coriander	1/2 teaspoon chilli
1 tablespoon vegetable	powder
oil	
1 garlic clove, crushed	

1. Prepare salsa: drain tomatoes, reserving 4 tablespoons tomato liquid. In medium microwave-safe bowl, combine tomatoes and reserved liquid, green pepper, onion, olives, coriander, oil, garlic and 1 tablespoon lime or lemon juice; stir to break up tomatoes. Cook on High (100% power) for 7–8 minutes, until green pepper is tender-crisp, stirring halfway through cooking. Cover and set aside.
2. Lightly moisten 4 sheets kitchen paper; place 1 fish steak on each. In small bowl, combine sherry and remaining lime or lemon juice; pour quarter of mixture over each steak.
3. Bring all corners of each paper sheet to centre and twist to close. Place fish steaks on microwave-safe platter. Cook on High for 4–5 minutes, just until outer edges of fish are opaque, rotating steaks halfway through cooking.
4. Meanwhile, in small mixing bowl, combine mayonnaise, vinegar and chilli powder.
5. *To serve:* transfer fish steaks to warmed dinner plates. Spoon over mayonnaise mixture and accompany with salsa.

Preparing the Salsa

In colander set over bowl, drain canned tomatoes. Reserve 4 tablespoons tomato liquid. Cook drained tomatoes on High for 7–8 minutes with reserved liquid, thinly sliced green pepper, chopped onion, halved black olives, chopped coriander, oil, garlic and lime or lemon juice.

SALMON STEAKS WITH MARINATED CUCUMBER

Colour Index page 54. 320 cals per serving (without dressing). Low in fat (without dressing). Good source of vitamin A, thiamine, riboflavin, niacin, iron. Begin early in day.

Ingredients	For 4	For 2	For 1
Salmon steaks (225 g each)	4 steaks	2 steaks	1 steak
Lemon juice	2 tablespoons	1 tablespoon	1 1/2 teaspoons
Cucumber, thinly sliced	350 g	175 g	75 g
Salt	1 teaspoon	1/2 teaspoon	1/4 teaspoon
White vinegar	80 ml	3 tablespoons	1 tablespoon
Sugar	1 tablespoon	2 teaspoons	1 teaspoon
Pepper	1/4 teaspoon	to taste	to taste
Onion, thinly sliced	1 small	1/2 small	1/4 small
Salad leaves and lemon wedges	garnish	garnish	garnish
Green Mayonnaise Dressing (page 159)	4 tablespoons	2 tablespoons	1 tablespoon
Microwave cookware	20 cm square baking dish	20 cm square baking dish	20 cm square baking dish
Time on High (100% power)	4–5 minutes	3–4 minutes	2–3 minutes

1 In baking dish (see Chart), arrange salmon steaks. Sprinkle with lemon juice.

2 Cook, covered, on High for time in Chart, just until outer edges of fish are opaque, rotating dish once.

3 Drain fish over kitchen paper. Place in same cleaned dish; cover and refrigerate. In mixing bowl, toss cucumber and salt; allow to stand for 30 minutes.

4 Over small bowl, set sieve. Place cucumber mixture in sieve. Press to extract excess liquid; discard liquid.

5 Return cucumber to mixing bowl. Add vinegar, sugar, pepper and onion; mix well. Cover and refrigerate for 3 hours, or until well chilled.

6 Place salmon steaks on individual plates with salad leaves, marinated cucumber and lemon wedges. Serve Green Mayonnaise Dressing separately.

Fish Steaks

For best results when microwaving, fish steaks should be arranged in dish so that thickest parts are at the edges. With delicate fish, it is best to rotate dish halfway through cooking rather than to turn fish over. Thicker fish steaks can be carefully turned over, however, to help prevent juices in bottom of dish transferring additional heat to only one side.

CALIFORNIAN SALMON STEAKS

Colour Index page 54. 292 cals per serving. Good source of vitamin A, riboflavin, niacin. Begin 2¼ hours ahead.

Ingredients	For 4	For 2	For 1
Canned whole green chillies (jalapeños), drained	2 medium, or to taste	1 medium, or to taste	1 small, or to taste
Lime juice	80 ml	3 tablespoons	1 tablespoon
Vegetable oil	2 tablespoons	1 tablespoon	1½ teaspoons
Honey	1 teaspoon	½ teaspoon	¼ teaspoon
Dried oregano	½ teaspoon	¼ teaspoon	pinch
Cayenne pepper	good pinch	pinch	pinch
Salmon steaks (175 g each)	4 steaks	2 steaks	1 steak
Lime wedges and parsley	garnish	garnish	garnish
Microwave cookware	Browning dish	Browning dish	Browning dish
Time on High (100% power)	3–4 minutes each batch	3–4 minutes	2–2½ (2:30) minutes

1 Wearing rubber glove for protection, slit chillies lengthways. With tip of sharp knife, remove seeds and discard. Finely chop chillies.

2 In baking dish, combine lime juice, oil, honey, oregano, cayenne pepper and chopped chillies.

3 To mixture, add salmon steaks. Cover and refrigerate for 2 hours, until flavours blend, turning steaks often.

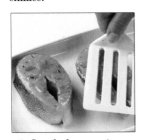

4 Just before serving, preheat browning dish according to manufacturer's instructions. On browning dish, place salmon steaks; press with fish slice to sear.

5 Cook on High for time in Chart, just until outer edges of fish are opaque, turning once. If cooking for 4, cook in 2 batches, reheating dish between batches.

6 To serve: arrange salmon steaks on warmed dinner plates. Garnish with lime wedges and parsley and serve immediately.

SAVOURY SALMON STEAKS

Colour Index page 48. 2 servings. 316 cals per serving. Good source of vitamin A, riboflavin, niacin. Begin 10 minutes ahead.

2 salmon, cod or halibut steaks (175 g each)
4½ teaspoons lemon juice
1 teaspoon made mustard
2 tablespoons mayonnaise

1 teaspoon finely chopped spring onion
Radish Flowers (page 116), spring onions and cucumber slices to garnish

1. In 30 × 20 cm microwave-safe baking dish, arrange salmon steaks. Sprinkle each steak with 2 teaspoons lemon juice. Cook, covered, on High (100% power) for 2 minutes.
2. Meanwhile, in small bowl, combine mustard, mayonnaise, spring onion and remaining lemon juice.
3. Turn steaks over in baking dish. On to each steak, spoon half of mayonnaise mixture. Cook on High for 30 seconds, or just until outer edges of fish are opaque.
4. To serve: place fish steaks on warmed serving platter. Garnish with Radish Flowers, spring onions and cucumber slices and serve immediately.

SALMON WITH LETTUCE AND RED PEPPER

Colour Index page 49. 2 servings. 361 cals per serving. Good source of vitamin A, thiamine, riboflavin, niacin, vitamin C, iron. Begin 15 minutes ahead

1 large red pepper, thinly sliced
30 g butter or margarine
1 small Cos lettuce or escarole (350 g), cut into 7.5 cm pieces
1 tablespoon soy sauce

¼ teaspoon crushed black peppercorns
2 salmon, cod or halibut steaks (175 g each)
1 tablespoon lemon or lime juice

1. In 30 × 20 cm microwave-safe baking dish, place red pepper, butter or margarine and lettuce. Cook, covered, on High (100% power) for 2–3 minutes, until lettuce is slightly wilted. Add soy sauce and crushed peppercorns; stir.
2. Arrange fish steaks on vegetables; sprinkle fish with lemon or lime juice. Cook, covered, on High for 2–3 minutes, just until outer edges of fish are opaque, rotating dish halfway through cooking.
3. To serve: place wilted lettuce and red pepper on warmed dinner plates; arrange fish steaks on top. Serve immediately.

MEDITERRANEAN COD

Colour Index page 51. 2 servings. 318 cals per serving. Good source of vitamin A, riboflavin, niacin, vitamin C, iron, fibre. Begin 35 minutes ahead.

1 small onion, chopped	2 tablespoons tomato
1 garlic clove, crushed	purée
1 tablespoon vegetable	75 g stoned black olives,
oil	cut in half
1 courgette	2 cod or halibut steaks
1 × 225 g can tomatoes	(175 g each)
115 g mushrooms,	½ teaspoon dried
sliced	oregano

1. In 1.5 litre microwave-safe casserole, place onion, garlic and oil. Cook, covered, on High (100% power) for 4–4½ (4:30) minutes, until onion is soft, stirring halfway through cooking.
2. Cut courgette into 5 mm thick slices. To onion mixture, add courgette, tomatoes with their liquid, mushrooms and tomato purée. Cook, covered, on High for 10 minutes, stirring halfway through cooking.
3. To vegetables, add olives. Cook, covered, on High for 5–7 minutes, until flavours blend, stirring halfway through cooking.
4. Lightly moisten 2 sheets kitchen paper; place 1 fish steak on each. Sprinkle with oregano. Bring all corners of each paper sheet to centre and twist to close. Place on microwave-safe platter. Cook on High for 3–4 minutes, just until outer edges of fish are opaque, rotating steaks once.
5. *To serve:* transfer fish steaks to warmed dinner plates; spoon vegetable mixture around.

PEPPERY COD STEAKS

Colour Index page 51. 6 servings. 163 cals per serving. Begin 35 minutes ahead.

1 small onion, chopped	¼ teaspoon hot red
1 small red pepper,	pepper flakes
chopped	¼ teaspoon garlic salt
1 celery stick, chopped	6 small cod steaks, each
120 ml bottled chilli	1 cm thick
sauce	Basil leaves to garnish
2 tablespoons vegetable	
oil	

1. In 1 litre microwave-safe bowl or casserole, combine onion, red pepper, celery, chilli sauce, oil, red pepper flakes and garlic salt. Cook, covered, on High (100% power) for 6–8 minutes, stirring occasionally. Reduce power level to Medium (50% power) and cook for 3 minutes longer, or until vegetables are tender.
2. In 32.5 × 22.5 cm microwave-safe baking dish, arrange cod steaks. Cook, covered, on Medium-High (70% power) for 9–10 minutes, just until outer edges of fish are opaque, rotating dish halfway through cooking.
3. *To serve:* place cod steaks on warmed dinner plates. Spoon sauce over and around cod. Garnish with basil leaves and serve immediately.

Meal in Minutes *for 4 people*
Elegant Summer Supper
Hot Peanut Dip (below) with crudités
Salmon Steaks with Marinated Cucumber, page 151
Fresh mangoes with strawberry sauce
feathered with cream

PREPARATION TIMETABLE

Early in day	*Cook salmon; cover and refrigerate. Prepare marinated cucumber and dressing; cover and refrigerate.*
30 minutes ahead	*Prepare crudités and arrange on small plates; cover. Prepare dip; spoon into small bowls. Slice mangoes; cover and refrigerate.*
10 minutes ahead	*Arrange salmon steaks on dinner plates with marinated cucumber and salad. Assemble mangoes and sauce on individual plates. Heat dip in small bowls; place on plates with crudités.*
Just before serving	*Feather strawberry sauce with cream and decorate with strawberries.*

HOT PEANUT DIP
Served with crisp vegetables, this dip makes a tasty appetiser.

In 1 litre measuring jug, combine **120 ml water, 60 ml soy sauce, 65 g sugar, 1 tablespoon chilli powder** and **1 crushed garlic clove.** Cook, covered, on High (100% power) for 3 minutes. Allow to stand for 5 minutes. Into chilli mixture, whisk **6 tablespoons smooth peanut butter** and **2 tablespoons lime juice.** Spoon into 4 small microwave-safe bowls. Heat on High for 1 minute, or until hot.

Fish Steaks and Fillets

SAVOURY FISH KEBABS

Colour Index page 52. 187 cals per serving. Low in cholesterol, fat, sodium. Good source of vitamin A, niacin, vitamin C. Begin 55 minutes ahead.

Ingredients	For 4	For 2	For 1
Vegetable oil	1 tablespoon	1½ teaspoons	1 teaspoon
Spring onions, sliced	6 spring onions	4 spring onions	2 spring onions
Mild curry powder	1 teaspoon	½ teaspoon	to taste
Marmalade	1 tablespoon	1½ teaspoons	1 teaspoon
Worcestershire sauce	1 tablespoon	2 teaspoons	1 teaspoon
Monkfish, filleted	450 g	225 g	115 g
Green pepper	1 pepper	½ pepper	¼ pepper
Mushrooms	4 mushrooms	2 mushrooms	1 mushroom
Cherry tomatoes	8 tomatoes	4 tomatoes	2 tomatoes
Hot Cooked Rice (page 293)	400 g	200 g	100 g
Chopped fresh herbs	to taste	to taste	to taste
Lemon slices and parsley sprigs	garnish	garnish	garnish
Microwave cookware	30 × 20 cm baking dish	30 × 20 cm baking dish	30 × 20 cm baking dish
Time on High (100% power)			
Onion mixture	2–3 minutes	2 minutes	1½ (1:30) minutes
Kebabs	2½ (2:30)– 3 minutes	1½ (1:30)– 2 minutes	1–1½ (1:30) minutes

1 In baking dish (see Chart), combine oil, spring onions and curry powder. Cook, covered, on High for time in Chart, or until onions are soft. Stir in marmalade and Worcestershire sauce.

2 With sharp knife, cut monkfish into 4 cm chunks. Cut green pepper into 4 cm pieces. Cut each mushroom in half.

3 Into spring onion mixture, stir fish, green pepper, mushrooms and tomatoes. Cover and allow to marinate for 30 minutes.

4 On to 25 cm wooden skewers, thread fish and vegetables, alternating different colours.

5 In dish used for marinating, place kebabs. Cook on High for time in Chart, just until fish is opaque, turning skewers over halfway through cooking.

6 *To serve:* fork hot rice and chopped fresh herbs together; spoon on to warmed serving platter. Arrange kebabs on top and garnish.

MONKFISH SATAY WITH CHUNKY PEANUT SAUCE

Colour Index page 49. 4 servings. 305 cals per serving. Low in cholesterol. Good source of vitamin A, vitamin C. Begin 25 minutes ahead.

1 red pepper
4 spring onions
3 tablespoons groundnut or vegetable oil
1 garlic clove, crushed
3 tablespoons soy sauce
1 tablespoon rice wine vinegar or cider vinegar
½ teaspoon ground ginger
1 tablespoon apricot jam
4 tablespoons crunchy peanut butter
3 tablespoons lemon juice
450 g monkfish, filleted
Lemon slices and Spring Onion Tassels (page 132) to garnish
Hot Cooked Rice (page 293, optional)

1. Finely dice one-quarter of red pepper; reserve. Cut remaining pepper into 4 cm chunks; set aside. Thinly slice 1 spring onion.

2. In 1.5 litre microwave-safe casserole, combine reserved diced red pepper, sliced spring onion, 1 tablespoon oil, garlic, 2 tablespoons soy sauce, vinegar and ginger. Cook on High (100% power) for 2 minutes, or until vegetables are softened.

3. Into vegetables, stir apricot jam, peanut butter and 1½ tablespoons lemon juice until blended. Set sauce aside.

4. In 500 ml microwave-safe measuring jug, combine remaining oil, soy sauce and lemon juice. Cook on High for 1 minute.

5. Cut fish into 4 cm cubes. Cut remaining 3 spring onions into 5 cm lengths. On four 25 cm wooden skewers, thread red pepper pieces, fish cubes and spring onion pieces. Brush with lemon and soy mixture. Arrange skewers in 30 × 20 cm baking dish. Cook on High for 2½ (2:30)–3½ (3:30) minutes, just until fish is opaque, turning skewers over halfway through cooking.

6. *To serve:* place skewers on individual plates with small bowls of peanut sauce, lemon slices and Spring Onion Tassels; if you like, serve with rice.

PREPARING KEBABS

Kebab recipes can be prepared quickly and easily in the microwave as the same microwave-safe baking dish, tray or plate can be used for marinating and arranging the kebabs on skewers, thus saving on washing up. Be sure to use wooden or other microwave-safe skewers, and leave a small space between each piece of food for even cooking, as shown above.

TUNA STIR-FRY

Colour Index page 49. 4 servings. 293 cals per serving. Good source of potassium, iron, fibre. Begin 25 minutes ahead.

450 g boneless fresh tuna, cut into 1 cm strips
2 tablespoons soy sauce
2 tablespoons dry sherry
1 tablespoon honey
2 tablespoons vegetable oil
¹/₂ teaspoon Chinese five-spice powder

115 g mange-touts
2 tablespoons water
115 g fresh shiitake mushrooms, sliced
2 spring onions, thinly sliced
175 g cherry tomatoes
1 × 425 g can baby sweetcorn, drained and rinsed

1. In mixing bowl, combine tuna, soy, sherry, honey, 1 tablespoon oil and five-spice powder.
2. Preheat browning dish according to manufacturer's instructions. Place tuna strips on browning dish in single layer. Cook on High (100% power) for 1 minute. With fish slice, turn tuna strips over. Cook on High for 30 seconds longer; set aside.
3. In 32.5 × 22.5 cm microwave-safe baking dish, place mange-touts and water. Cook on High for 3–3¹/₂ (3:30) minutes, until almost tender. Rinse under cold running water; drain.
4. In same dish, combine remaining oil, mushrooms and spring onions. Cook on High for 2 minutes, or until softened, stirring once.
5. To mixture, add mange-touts, tomatoes, baby sweetcorn and 1 tablespoon marinade from fish. Cook, covered, on High for 3–4 minutes, until vegetables are tender-crisp, stirring once.
6. Arrange vegetables on microwave-safe serving platter; place fish strips on top. Reheat on High for 1 minute. Serve immediately.

SWORDFISH STEAKS AMANDINE

Colour Index page 48. 4 servings. 220 cals per serving. Good source of vitamin A. Begin 20 minutes ahead.

30 g flaked almonds
30 g butter or margarine
¹/₄ teaspoon paprika
1 swordfish steak, 1 cm thick (450 g)

1 tablespoon dry white wine
1 tablespoon chopped parsley

1. In small microwave-safe bowl, combine almonds, butter or margarine and paprika. Cook on High (100% power) for 4–5 minutes, until almonds are golden brown, stirring after 2 minutes, then at 1 minute intervals; set aside.
2. In 20 cm square microwave-safe baking dish, place swordfish; sprinkle with wine. Cook, covered, on High for 4¹/₂ (4:30)–6¹/₂ (6:30) minutes, just until fish is opaque, rotating dish twice.
3. *To serve:* divide fish into 4 or 8 pieces; place on warmed dinner plates. Stir parsley into almond mixture; spoon over fish.

SOLE WITH GRAPES

Colour Index page 48. 282 cals per serving. Good source of vitamin A. Begin 25 minutes ahead.

Ingredients	For 4	For 2	For 1
Sole or plaice fillets (175 g each)	4 fillets	2 fillets	1 fillet
Lemon juice	1 tablespoon	1¹/₂ teaspoons	³/₄ teaspoon
Dried tarragon	¹/₂ teaspoon	¹/₄ teaspoon	good pinch
Salt and white pepper	to taste	to taste	to taste
Green or red seedless grapes	165 g	80 g	40 g
Dry white wine	3 tablespoons	2 tablespoons	1 tablespoon
Butter or margarine	30 g	15 g	1¹/₂ teaspoons
Plain flour	1 tablespoon	1¹/₂ teaspoons	³/₄ teaspoon
Half cream	120 ml	60 ml	2 tablespoons
Lemon slices, parsley sprigs and grapes	garnish	garnish	garnish
Microwave cookware	20 cm square baking dish	20 cm square baking dish	Shallow 21.5 cm pie dish
	Small bowl	500 ml jug	250 ml jug
Time on High (100% power)			
Butter mixture	1 minute	1 minute	45 seconds
With cream	3 minutes	2 minutes	1 minute
Fish	5–6 minutes	3–3¹/₂ (3:30) minutes	1¹/₂ (1:30)–2 minutes

1 Brush fish fillets with lemon juice. In small bowl, combine tarragon, salt and white pepper; sprinkle evenly over fillets.

2 Fold fish fillets into thirds. In baking or pie dish (see Chart), arrange fillets in single layer. Add grapes and sprinkle with one-third of wine. Cover dish with greaseproof paper; set aside while preparing sauce.

3 In bowl or jug (see Chart), place butter or margarine, flour, salt and pepper. Cook, covered, on High for time in Chart, or until butter or margarine has melted. With whisk, stir until smooth. Gradually stir in cream until blended. Cook on High for time in Chart, or until mixture thickens. Into sauce, stir remaining wine; cover and keep warm.

4 Cook fish, covered, on High for time in Chart, or just until flesh flakes easily. If cooking for 4, rotate dish after 4 minutes.

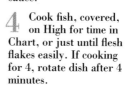

5 On warmed plates, arrange fish, sauce and grapes; garnish.

Fish Fillets

PRAWN-STUFFED SOLE

Colour Index page 52. 344 cals per serving. Good source of iron.
Begin 45 minutes ahead.

Ingredients	For 4	For 2	For 1
Hollandaise Sauce (page 381)	120 ml	60 ml	2 tablespoons
Vegetable oil	2 tablespoons	1 tablespoon	1½ teaspoons
Onion, finely chopped	1 small	½ small	¼ small
Garlic clove, crushed	1 clove	½ clove	to taste
Green pepper, diced	40 g	2 tablespoons	1 tablespoon
Raw prawns, shelled, deveined and diced	450 g	225 g	115 g
Dried breadcrumbs	4 tablespoons	2 tablespoons	1 tablespoon
Fresh dill, chopped	1 tablespoon	1½ teaspoons	¾ teaspoon
Salt and pepper	to taste	to taste	to taste
Sole or plaice fillets (175 g each)	4 fillets	2 fillets	1 fillet
Dill sprigs	garnish	garnish	garnish
Microwave cookware	2 litre casserole	1 litre casserole	Medium bowl
	30 × 20 cm baking dish	20 cm square baking dish	Shallow 22.5 cm dish
Time on High (100% power)			
Vegetables	2–2½ (2:30) minutes	1½ (1:30) minutes	1 minute
With prawns	3 minutes	2 minutes	1½ (1:30) minutes
Stuffed sole	5–6 minutes	3–3½ (3:30) minutes	1½ (1:30)–2 minutes

1 Make Hollandaise Sauce; keep warm. In casserole or bowl (see Chart), place oil, onion, garlic and green pepper. Cook on High for time in Chart.

2 To vegetable mixture, add prawns; stir to coat with oil. Cook on High for time in Chart, or just until pink, stirring halfway through cooking.

Into prawn mixture, stir breadcrumbs and chopped dill; mix well. Season with salt and pepper.

4 On cutting board, lay fillets, boned side down. Place equal amount of stuffing in centre of each fillet.

5 Starting at narrow end, roll up each fillet. In baking dish or pie dish, place fish bundles, seam side down.

6 Cook fish bundles on High for time in Chart, just until flesh flakes easily and stuffing is hot. If making for 4, rotate dish after 4 minutes. Place fish bundles on warmed dinner plates; pour over Hollandaise Sauce. Garnish with dill sprigs and serve immediately.

ROLLED PLAICE WITH CUCUMBER, TOMATO AND BASIL SAUCE

Colour Index page 48. 4 servings. 144 cals per serving. Good source of vitamin A.
Begin 25 minutes ahead.

15 g butter or margarine
2 spring onions, cut into matchstick-thin strips
2 teaspoons finely chopped fresh basil
175 g cucumber, cut into matchstick-thin strips
450 g plaice or sole fillets

¼ teaspoon salt
120 ml dry white wine
2 tomatoes, seeded and diced
1 teaspoon cornflour dissolved in 1 tablespoon cold water
Basil leaves to garnish

1. In 25 cm microwave-safe shallow pie dish, place butter or margarine. Heat on High (100% power) for 30–45 seconds, until melted.
2. Into melted butter or margarine, stir spring onions and half each of basil and cucumber. Cook on High for 2–2½ (2:30) minutes, until cucumber is slightly softened.
3. Cut each plaice fillet in half lengthways, removing all bones and any cartilage. On cutting board, lay fillet halves, boned side down; sprinkle with half of the salt. Arrange one-quarter of the cooked cucumber pieces at wide end of each piece of fish. Starting at wide end, roll up each fillet and secure with wooden cocktail stick.
4. In same pie dish, arrange fish bundles in a ring. Pour in white wine. Cook, covered, on High for 3–4 minutes, just until flesh flakes easily, rotating dish halfway through cooking. Meanwhile, dice remaining cucumber.
5. With fish slice, transfer fish bundles to platter. Into wine mixture, stir tomatoes, dissolved cornflour, remaining half of cucumber, basil and salt. Cook on High for 2–3 minutes, until sauce thickens, stirring twice. Add fish bundles. Cook on High for 1 minute longer.
6. *To serve:* place fish bundles on warmed dinner plates; spoon sauce around. Garnish with basil leaves. Serve immediately.

Rolling and Arranging the Fish Fillets

At wide end of fish fillet, place cucumber pieces. Roll up fillet Swiss roll fashion and secure with wooden cocktail stick.

Stand fish bundles filled with cucumber mixture upright in pie dish, leaving space between each one.

FISH FILLETS FLORENTINE

Colour Index page 48. 4 servings. 396 cals per serving. Good source of vitamin A, riboflavin, niacin, vitamin C, calcium, iron, fibre. Begin 25 minutes ahead.

2 tomatoes, each cut into 8 wedges	1 onion, chopped
¼ teaspoon salt	30 g fresh bread cubes
2 tablespoons vegetable oil	¼ teaspoon pepper
¾ teaspoon dried oregano	275 g frozen chopped spinach, thawed and drained
225 g mushrooms, sliced	115 g fontina or Gruyère cheese, grated
	4 fish fillets (175 g each)

1. In 1.5 litre microwave-safe casserole, place tomatoes, salt, 1 tablespoon oil and ¼ teaspoon oregano. Cook, covered, on High (100% power) for 2–3 minutes, until tomatoes are softened. Set aside.

2. In 30 × 20 cm microwave-safe baking dish, place mushrooms, onion and remaining oil. Cook, covered, on High for 5–6 minutes, stirring halfway through cooking. With slotted spoon, transfer half of mushroom mixture to small bowl; set aside. Into mushroom mixture remaining in baking dish, stir bread cubes, pepper, spinach, remaining oregano and 75 g cheese.

3. On to each fillet, spoon one-quarter of spinach mixture to cover half of fish. Fold over other half to cover mixture. Arrange fillets in same baking dish; sprinkle with remaining cheese and reserved mushroom mixture. Cook on High for 5–6 minutes, just until flesh flakes easily, rotating dish once. Reheat tomatoes on High for 30 seconds.

4. To serve: place fillets in warmed serving dish. Accompany with cooked tomato wedges.

PLAICE FILLETS WITH SAVOURY SAUCE

Colour Index page 48. 4 servings. 235 cals per serving (without sauce). Good source of vitamin A, thiamine, riboflavin, iron (without sauce). Begin 20 minutes ahead.

Spicy Cocktail Sauce or Zesty Cucumber Sauce (page 159)	1 teaspoon grated lemon zest
90 g golden dried breadcrumbs	¾ teaspoon paprika
2 tablespoons chopped parsley	4 plaice or sole fillets (115 g each)
	1 egg, lightly beaten

1. Prepare sauce of your choice.

2. On greaseproof paper, combine breadcrumbs, parsley, lemon zest and paprika. Dip fillets in beaten egg, then coat with crumb mixture.

3. On microwave-safe rack set in 32.5 × 22.5 cm microwave-safe baking dish, place fillets. Cook on High (100% power) for 5–6 minutes, just until flesh flakes easily, rotating dish halfway through cooking. Serve with sauce.

PLAICE IN PAPER PARCELS

Colour Index page 52. 51 cals per serving. Low in cholesterol, sodium. Good source of vitamin A, vitamin C. Begin 35 minutes ahead.

Ingredients	For 4	For 2	For 1
Green peppers, cut into thin strips	2 small peppers	1 small pepper	½ small pepper
Cherry tomatoes, cut into quarters	8 tomatoes	4 tomatoes	2 tomatoes
Spring onions, sliced	2 spring onions	1 spring onion	½ spring onion
Mushrooms, sliced	4 mushrooms	2 mushrooms	1 mushroom
Fresh basil leaves	8 leaves	4 leaves	2 leaves
Grated orange zest	1 tablespoon	2 teaspoons	1 teaspoon
Plaice or sole fillets (175–225 g each)	4 fillets	2 fillets	1 fillet
Salt	to taste	to taste	to taste
Butter or margarine	4 teaspoons	2 teaspoons	1 teaspoon
Orange slices and basil leaves	garnish	garnish	garnish
Microwave cookware	30 cm plate	30 cm plate	22.5 cm plate
Time on High (100% power)	3–3½ (3:30) minutes each batch	3–3½ (3:30) minutes	1½ (1:30)– 2 minutes

1 In small bowl, place green pepper strips, cherry tomatoes, spring onions, mushrooms, basil leaves and orange zest; toss to mix. For each fish fillet, fold 35 × 20 cm sheet of non-stick baking parchment in half lengthways. Cut a large heart shape.

2 On work surface, place open sheets of parchment. Using half of green pepper mixture, place even amount on right hand side of each heart, near fold line.

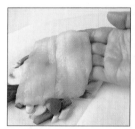

3 Place 1 fish fillet, with thin end folded under, on top of each layer of green pepper mixture. Season with salt. Place remaining mixture evenly over fillets. Dot with butter or margarine.

4 Fold left side of parchment over fish. Double fold edges to seal.

5 On plate (see Chart), place parcels with double-folded edges facing outwards. Cook on High for time in Chart, until parcels puff up, rotating plate once. If cooking for 4, cook in 2 batches.

6 To serve: place each parcel on plate. With small, sharp knife, cut cross in centre of each parcel to allow steam to escape. Fold back parcel edges; garnish and serve.

Fish Fillets

ORIENTAL FISH IN LETTUCE LEAVES

Colour Index page 54. 167 cals per serving.
Low in fat. Good source of vitamin A. Begin 1¼ hours ahead.

Ingredients	For 4	For 2	For 1
Plaice or sole fillets (115–175 g each), cut into 5 cm pieces	4 fillets	2 fillets	1 fillet
Soy sauce	1 tablespoon	1½ teaspoons	¾ teaspoon
Rice wine vinegar or cider vinegar	1 tablespoon	1½ teaspoons	¾ teaspoon
Garlic cloves, crushed	2 cloves	1 clove	½ clove
Peeled and finely chopped root ginger	½ teaspoon	¼ teaspoon	to taste
Chopped fresh coriander leaves	1 tablespoon	1½ teaspoons	¾ teaspoon
Lettuce leaves (round)	4 large	2 large	1 large
Carrots, cut into matchstick-thin strips	2 medium	1 medium	½ medium
Spring onions, thinly sliced	2 spring onions	1 spring onion	½ spring onion
Celery sticks, cut into matchstick-thin strips	1 stick	½ stick	1 × 5 cm piece
Chicken Stock (page 125) or stock from a cube	250 ml	120 ml	60 ml
Coriander leaves	garnish	garnish	garnish
Microwave cookware	32.5 × 22.5 cm baking dish 1 litre soufflé dish	32.5 × 22.5 cm baking dish Medium bowl	Soup plate Small bowl
Time on High (100% power) Lettuce leaves	1–1½ minutes	1 minute	30–45 seconds
Vegetables in stock	4–5 minutes	3–4 minutes	2–2½ (2:30) minutes
Fish bundles	3–5 minutes	2–3 minutes	1–2 minutes
Standing time	3 minutes	2 minutes	2 minutes

USING LEAVES TO MAKE PARCELS

Lettuce, cabbage, spinach and vine leaves make ideal wrappers. Stuffed Cabbage (page 213) and Camembert in Vine Leaves (page 144) also use leaves to protect their fillings and flavours.

On cutting board, place leaves, vein side up. With sharp knife, remove any tough ribs or stalks from leaves.

After cooking leaves, fold sides round fillings as if wrapping parcel, making sure fillings are completely enclosed.

1 In mixing bowl, combine fish, soy sauce, vinegar, garlic, root ginger and coriander; cover and leave to marinate for 45 minutes.

2 Meanwhile, in dish or soup plate (see Chart), place lettuce leaves. Cook, covered, on High for time in Chart, just until wilted. Uncover and allow to cool; leaves may darken on standing.

3 In soufflé dish or bowl (see Chart), combine carrots, spring onions, celery and stock. Cook, covered, on High for time in Chart, or until vegetables are tender-crisp.

4 On cutting board, place lettuce leaves. Place equal amount of fish in centre of each leaf; fold to enclose (see Using Leaves to Make Parcels, above right).

5 In baking dish or soup plate used for lettuce, carefully place fish bundles, seam side down, leaving 2.5 cm space between each.

6 Over fish bundles, ladle hot vegetable stock mixture. Cook, covered, on High for time in Chart, until fish feels tender when bundles are pierced with skewer. Allow to stand on heatproof surface for time in Chart.

7 *To serve:* transfer fish bundles to warmed soup plates. Ladle equal amounts of vegetables and stock over each bundle; garnish with coriander leaves and serve immediately.

SAUCES FOR FISH

Because fish and shellfish are usually delicate in flavour, they can be enhanced if served with a sauce. If making ahead, cover and refrigerate until ready to use.

Zesty Cucumber Sauce: finely shred *1 small cucumber;* pat dry with kitchen paper. Combine cucumber with *4 tablespoons mayonnaise, 1 teaspoon chopped parsley, 1 teaspoon cider vinegar* and *1 teaspoon made mustard.* Makes 120 ml. 53 cals per tablespoon.

Spicy Cocktail Sauce: combine *60 ml bottled chilli sauce, 3 tablespoons tomato ketchup, 1 tablespoon hamburger relish* and *1 teaspoon prepared horseradish.* Makes 120 ml. 19 cals per tablespoon.

Green Mayonnaise Dressing: in blender, process *500 ml mayonnaise, 6 tablespoons finely chopped parsley, 4 teaspoons tarragon vinegar, 1/2 teaspoon dried tarragon* and *2 chopped spring onions,* until smooth and evenly blended. Makes 500 ml. 93 cals per tablespoon.

SOLE AND ASPARAGUS WITH CHEESE SAUCE

Colour Index page 49. 249 cals per serving. Good source of calcium. Begin 25 minutes ahead.

Few things are tastier than the classic combination of cheese and wine sauce poured over delicate white fish, as in this recipe for Sole and Asparagus with Cheese Sauce. Dover or lemon sole can be used, although lemon sole is far less expensive. Plaice makes an inexpensive alternative, while asparagus gives the finished dish an extra special touch.

Ingredients for 4 servings		Microwave cookware
275 g frozen asparagus spears *4 sole or plaice fillets (115 g each)* *15 g butter or margarine* *120 ml half cream or milk* *2 tablespoons dry white wine*	*1 tablespoon plain flour* *1/4 teaspoon salt* *1/4 teaspoon cayenne pepper* *50 g Cheddar cheese, grated* *Lemon Twists (page 132, optional) to garnish*	20 cm square baking dish

1 Unwrap frozen asparagus packet. On oven floor, place asparagus in packet. Heat on Medium-Low (30% power) for 2 minutes, or until spears separate easily.

2 On cutting board, place fish fillets, boned side down. On narrow end of each fish fillet, place equal amount of asparagus spears.

3 Starting at narrow end, roll up each fish fillet round asparagus spears. In baking dish, place fish bundles, seam side down.

4 On each fish bundle, dot butter or margarine. Cook, covered, on High (100% power) for 4–6 minutes, just until flesh flakes easily, rotating dish halfway through cooking. Transfer fish bundles to platter; keep warm.

5 Into cooking liquid in baking dish, whisk cream, wine, flour, salt and pepper. Cook on High for 3–4 minutes, until sauce thickens slightly, stirring twice. Into sauce, stir cheese. Cook on High for 1 minute; stir until smooth.

6 *To serve:* over fish bundles on serving platter, spoon cheese sauce. Garnish with Lemon Twists and serve immediately.

Whole Fish

STUFFED TROUT

Colour Index page 51. 345 cals per serving. Good source of vitamin A, thiamine, iron. Begin 35 minutes ahead.

Ingredients	For 4	For 2	For 1
Butter or margarine	*60 g*	*30 g*	*15 g*
Onion, chopped	*1 medium*	*1 small*	*1/2 small*
Carrot, chopped	*1 small*	*1/2 small*	*2 tablespoons*
Celery sticks, chopped	*2 small*	*1 small*	*1/2 small*
Garlic cloves, crushed	*2 cloves*	*1 clove*	*1/2 clove*
Walnuts, chopped	*30 g*	*2 tablespoons*	*1 tablespoon*
Fresh thyme leaves	*1 1/2 teaspoons*	*3/4 teaspoon*	*1/2 teaspoon*
Salt	*to taste*	*to taste*	*to taste*
Dry sherry or white wine	*3 tablespoons*	*1 1/2 tablespoons*	*2 1/2 teaspoons*
Dried breadcrumbs	*25 g*	*2 tablespoons*	*1 tablespoon*
Trout (225–275 g each), cleaned, with head removed	*4 trout*	*2 trout*	*1 trout*
Lemon slices and walnut halves	*garnish*	*garnish*	*garnish*
Microwave cookware	Large bowl 32.5 × 22.5 cm baking dish	Medium bowl 32.5 × 22.5 cm baking dish	Small bowl 30 × 20 cm baking dish
Time on High (100% power)			
Butter or margarine	45 seconds– 1 minute	45 seconds	30 seconds
With vegetables	5 minutes	3 minutes	2 minutes
With seasonings	2 minutes	1 1/2 (1:30) minutes	1 minute
Stuffed trout	4–5 minutes each batch	4–5 minutes	2 1/2 (2:30)– 3 minutes
Standing time	5 minutes	3 minutes	2 minutes

1 In bowl (see Chart), place butter or margarine. Heat, covered with kitchen paper, on High for time in Chart.

2 Into melted butter, stir onion, carrot, celery, garlic and nuts. Cook on High for time in Chart, stirring twice.

3 Add thyme, salt and one-third of sherry or wine. Cook on High for time in Chart, stirring once. Add breadcrumbs.

4 Sprinkle trout cavities with salt. Place equal amount stuffing in each.

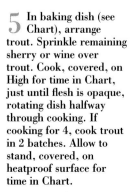

5 In baking dish (see Chart), arrange trout. Sprinkle remaining sherry or wine over trout. Cook, covered, on High for time in Chart, just until flesh is opaque, rotating dish halfway through cooking. If cooking for 4, cook trout in 2 batches. Allow to stand, covered, on heatproof surface for time in Chart.

6 *To serve:* transfer trout to warmed dinner plates. Garnish.

CAJUN TROUT

Colour Index page 51. 2 servings. 457 cals per serving. Good source of vitamin A, vitamin C, iron. Begin 35 minutes ahead.

45 g butter or margarine
1 large onion, chopped
1 green pepper, chopped
1 garlic clove, crushed
1 × 225 g can crushed tomatoes
1/2 teaspoon dried thyme
1/2 teaspoon dried oregano
1/4 teaspoon cayenne pepper
30 g cornmeal

1/4 teaspoon caster sugar
2 × 225–275 g rainbow trout, cleaned, with heads removed
Salt to taste
1 tablespoon vegetable oil
Lime Twists (page 132) to garnish
Hot Cooked Rice (page 293, optional)

1. In 2 litre microwave-safe casserole, place 30 g butter or margarine. Heat, covered with kitchen paper on High (100% power) for 45 seconds, or until melted.

2. Into melted butter or margarine, stir onion, green pepper and garlic. Cook on High for 5 minutes, or until softened, stirring twice.

3. Into onion mixture, stir tomatoes and half each of thyme, oregano and cayenne pepper. Cook on High for 5 minutes, or until flavours blend; set aside.

4. On greaseproof paper, mix cornmeal with sugar and remaining thyme, oregano and cayenne. Sprinkle trout lightly with salt. Dip each trout in cornmeal mixture, using hand to pat cornmeal on to trout to coat well.

5. Meanwhile, preheat browning dish according to manufacturer's instructions. On browning dish, place remaining butter or margarine and oil; add trout. Cook on High for 4–5 minutes, just until flesh flakes easily, turning fish over once.

6. *To serve:* transfer trout to warmed dinner plates; spoon sauce around. Garnish and, if you like, accompany with rice.

SERVING A WHOLE FISH
With sharp knife, carefully slit skin along back; if you like, remove skin and discard. Divide top side of fish into serving portions, cutting down to bone.

With palette knife, ease fish from bone. Lift each portion of fish and place on warmed dinner plate.

Slide palette knife under bone and lift to separate it from lower section. Continue portioning in same way.

COUNTRY-STYLE SEA BASS AND POTATOES

Colour Index page 52. 6 servings. 335 cals per serving. Good source of vitamin A, fibre. Begin 45 minutes ahead.

6 rashers streaky rindless bacon, chopped	*Salt and pepper to taste*
2 large onions, thickly sliced	*1 × 1.4 kg sea bass, cleaned, with head removed*
700 g small new potatoes, scrubbed and cut into quarters	*Rosemary sprigs to garnish*

1. In 32.5 × 22.5 cm microwave-safe baking dish, place bacon. Cook, covered with kitchen paper, on High (100% power) for 5–7 minutes, until browned, stirring halfway through cooking. Discard all but 3 tablespoons bacon fat.
2. To bacon, add onions and potatoes. Cook, covered, on High for 8–10 minutes, until potatoes are almost tender, stirring twice. Season.
3. With cooking liquid from vegetables, brush fish and fish cavity. With smooth strip of foil shield tail of fish.
4. Place fish on top of potatoes. Cook, covered, on High for 6–8 minutes, just until outer edges of flesh are opaque, removing foil and rotating dish halfway through cooking. Allow to stand, covered, on heatproof surface for 5 minutes.
5. *To serve:* on warmed serving platter, place fish and spoon potato mixture around. Garnish.

CHINESE RED SNAPPER

Colour Index page 49. 4 servings. 246 cals per serving. Good source of vitamin A, vitamin C, iron, fibre. Begin 25 minutes ahead.

1 × 1.1 kg red snapper, cleaned, with head removed	*4 large carrots, cut into matchstick-thin strips*
30 g butter or margarine, melted	*2 celery sticks, sliced*
6 spring onions, cut into 5 cm pieces	*1 garlic clove, sliced*
2 large red peppers, cut into matchstick-thin strips	*1 tablespoon vegetable oil*
	2 tablespoons dry sherry
	2 tablespoons soy sauce
	1/2 teaspoon ground ginger

1. With smooth strip of foil, shield tail of fish. In 32.5 × 22.5 cm microwave-safe baking dish, place fish. Brush with melted butter or margarine. Arrange next 4 ingredients round fish.
2. In medium microwave-safe bowl, place garlic and oil. Cook on High (100% power) for 1½ (1:30) – 2 minutes, until garlic is golden; discard garlic. Into oil, stir sherry, soy sauce and ginger. Pour over fish and vegetables.
3. Cook, covered, on High for 12–14 minutes, just until outer edges of fish are opaque, removing foil, rotating dish and stirring vegetables halfway through cooking. Allow to stand, covered, on heatproof surface for 5 minutes before serving.

The microwave is ideal for cooking larger whole fish such as salmon, trout, sea bass and red snapper: it seals in their delicate flavours. Use smooth strips of foil to shield tail of any whole fish that would otherwise overcook, but be sure to keep foil at least 2.5 cm away from oven walls.

SEA BASS WITH RIBBON VEGETABLES

Colour Index page 48. 138 cals per serving. Good source of vitamin A. Begin 25 minutes ahead.

Ingredients for 6 servings		Microwave cookware
1 × 1.4 kg sea bass, cleaned, with head removed	*1 garlic clove, crushed*	32.5 × 22.5 cm baking dish
30 g butter or margarine	*1/4 teaspoon pepper*	Small bowl
2 tablespoons dry sherry	*1/4 teaspoon salt*	Large bowl
1 tablespoon lime or lemon juice	*1 large carrot*	
	2 courgettes, preferably 1 yellow and 1 green	
	Salad leaves, and orange and lemon slices to garnish	

1 With smooth strip of foil, shield tail of fish. In baking dish, place fish; set aside. In small bowl, place butter or margarine and next 5 ingredients. Cook on High (100% power) for 1 minute, or until melted.

2 With some of melted mixture, brush fish and fish cavity; reserve remainder. Cook fish, covered, on High for 6–8 minutes, just until outer edges of flesh are opaque, removing foil and rotating dish halfway through cooking.

3 Meanwhile, with vegetable peeler, shred carrot and courgettes into long ribbons about 2.5 cm wide, pressing lightly with peeler so ribbons will be very thin.

4 When fish is cooked, carefully transfer to warmed serving platter; allow to stand, covered, for 5 minutes.

5 Meanwhile, in large bowl, gently toss vegetable ribbons and reserved melted mixture. Cook, covered, on High for 30 seconds.

6 *To serve:* arrange vegetables around fish. Garnish with salad leaves and orange and lemon slices. Serve immediately.

Whole and Canned Fish

PARTY POACHED SALMON

Colour Index page 54. 329 cals per serving. Good source of thiamine, niacin, vitamin B$_{12}$. Begin early in day or 1 day ahead.

Ingredients for 10 servings		Microwave cookware
1 large salmon or brown trout, (about 2 kg), cleaned and scaled, with head and tail left on *Salt and pepper to taste* *2 tablespoons lemon juice* *4 dill or parsley sprigs* *4 tablespoons dry white wine*	*1 thin cucumber* *Curly lettuce leaves and Lemon Twists (page 132) to garnish* *Green Mayonnaise Dressing (page 159)*	*38 cm oval baking dish or large oval or oblong plate*

1 Vandyke tail of fish by cutting it into a 'V' shape; shield tail with smooth strip of foil. In baking dish or on plate, place fish. (If too long, remove head and place alongside fish.) Sprinkle cavity of fish with salt, pepper and lemon juice. Place dill or parsley sprigs in cavity.

2 Over fish, sprinkle white wine. Cook, covered tightly with microwave cling film, on High (100% power) for 12–15 minutes, until flesh is opaque, turning dish or plate and removing foil halfway through cooking. Allow to stand, covered, for 15 minutes.

3 Meanwhile, with sharp knife, thinly slice cucumber. Alternatively, slice in food processor with slicing disc attached.

4 When fish is cool enough to handle, with sharp knife, carefully slit skin along back. Remove skin on top side and discard; drain off any liquid. On to serving platter, gently flip fish, skinned side down. Remove and discard remaining skin. If head has been removed, reassemble fish. Cover and leave to cool.

5 Beginning at tail end of fish, place 1 cucumber slice where tail joins body. Working towards head, cover fish with closely overlapping slices of cucumber, to resemble fish scales. Cover join between head and body.

6 *To serve:* garnish serving platter with curly lettuce leaves and Lemon Twists. Serve fish at room temperature, with Green Mayonnaise Dressing handed separately.

TUNA AND SPINACH LOAF

Colour Index page 51. 6 servings. 242 cals per serving. Good source of vitamin A, calcium, iron, fibre. Begin 40 minutes ahead.

2 tablespoons vegetable oil *1 onion, finely chopped* *1 lemon* *275 g frozen chopped spinach* *2 × 200 g cans tuna, drained*	*4 slices white bread* *120 ml soured cream* *2 eggs* *¼ teaspoon salt* *¼ teaspoon Tabasco sauce* *Parsley to garnish*

1. Lightly grease 22.5 × 12.5 cm microwave-safe loaf dish.

2. In medium microwave-safe bowl, combine oil and onion. Cook, covered, on High (100% power) for 2–3 minutes, until onion softens; set aside.

3. Thinly slice half of lemon; cover and reserve. Squeeze juice from remaining lemon half.

4. Remove frozen spinach from packet and place on microwave-safe plate. Heat on Medium-Low (30% power) for 5–6 minutes, until thawed, turning spinach over once. Squeeze spinach to remove as much liquid as possible.

5. In large bowl, finely flake tuna. With hands, finely tear bread. Add bread to tuna with onion mixture, lemon juice, spinach, soured cream, eggs, salt and Tabasco; mix well. Spoon into prepared loaf dish.

6. Cook, covered with greaseproof paper, on Medium-High (70% power) for 11–13 minutes, until knife inserted 2.5 cm from centre comes out clean, rotating dish halfway through cooking. (If ends of loaf begin to overcook, shield with 7.5 cm wide smooth strips of foil.) Allow loaf to stand, covered, on heatproof surface for 5 minutes.

7. Unmould loaf on to warmed serving platter. Garnish with reserved lemon slices and parsley sprigs, to serve.

Unmoulding the Loaf

With knife, loosen loaf from side of dish. Place serving platter upside down on dish and invert. Carefully remove dish to unmould loaf.

TUNA FISH CAKES FLORENTINE

Colour Index page 51. 6 servings. 190 cals per serving. Good source of vitamin A, iron. Begin 35 minutes ahead.

30 g butter or margarine	1 tablespoon chopped
275 g frozen chopped	capers
spinach	1 tablespoon grated
2 × 200 g cans tuna,	onion
drained and flaked	1 tablespoon lemon juice
30 g fresh breadcrumbs	Lemon wedges and
2 eggs	parsley to garnish

1. In large microwave-safe bowl, place butter or margarine. Heat, covered with kitchen paper, on High (100% power) for 45 seconds, or until melted; set aside.
2. Remove frozen spinach from packet and place on microwave-safe plate. Heat on Medium-Low (30% power) for 5–6 minutes, until thawed, turning spinach over once. Squeeze spinach to remove as much liquid as possible.
3. To melted butter or margarine, add spinach, tuna, breadcrumbs, eggs, capers, grated onion and lemon juice; mix well.
4. Shape tuna mixture into six 7.5 cm cakes. Place cakes on 30 cm round microwave-safe plate. Cook, covered with greaseproof paper, on Medium (50% power) for 12 minutes, or until firm, rearranging cakes halfway through cooking. Allow to stand, covered, on heatproof surface for 5 minutes before serving. Garnish.

LEMON AND LIME GARNISHES

Lemon is the traditional garnish for fish, and lime adds an extra touch of colour. The acidity of these fruits balances the oil content of mackerel, salmon and tuna, and brings out the flavour of more delicate white fish.

Lemon or lime loops: cut *1 lemon or lime* in half lengthways, then cut each half into 5 mm thick slices. Cut peel from fruit, leaving 1 cm attached. Curl peel under to form loop.

Lemon or lime bundles: place *lemon or lime half*, cut side down, in centre of small piece of muslin. Gather edges of cloth together; place *1 parsley sprig* at gathered edge and tie tightly with string.

Meal in Minutes *for 8 people*
Spanish Supper
Olives and tortilla chips
Paella, page 171
Crème Caramel, page 325 (double quantity) with strawberries
Sangria (below)

PREPARATION TIMETABLE

Early in day	Prepare Crème Caramel up to end of step 5, in 2 batches.
1½ hours ahead	Make Paella.
Just before serving	Fill serving bowls with olives and tortilla chips. Unmould Crème Caramel and decorate. Make Sangria.

SANGRIA

Sangria makes a delightful accompaniment to a Spanish style meal. Use a dry, fruity Spanish wine and a jug large enough to hold the cut up fruit. Be sure to serve the Sangria in large glasses so that each guest receives some wine-soaked fruit.

Into large jug, pour *250 ml each lemon juice* and *orange juice*. Add *200 g caster sugar*; stir to dissolve. Stir in *1.5 litres red wine, 120 ml brandy, 400 ml chilled soda water, 225 g sliced fruit (apple, banana, lemon, orange, peach, strawberry)* and *2 trays ice cubes.*

Prawns

PIQUANT PRAWNS

Colour Index page 50. 222 cals per serving. Good source of niacin, calcium, iron. Begin 25 minutes ahead.

Ingredients	For 4	For 2	For 1
Large raw prawns in their shells	900 g	450 g	225 g
Dried basil	1½ teaspoons	¾ teaspoon	½ teaspoon
Celery salt	1½ teaspoons	¾ teaspoon	½ teaspoon
Dried rosemary	1½ teaspoons	¾ teaspoon	½ teaspoon
Dried thyme	1½ teaspoons	¾ teaspoon	½ teaspoon
Dry mustard	1 teaspoon	½ teaspoon	¼ teaspoon
Fennel seed	1 teaspoon	½ teaspoon	¼ teaspoon
Cayenne pepper	to taste	to taste	to taste
Lager	120 ml	60 ml	2 tablespoons
Worcestershire sauce	1 teaspoon	½ teaspoon	¼ teaspoon
Lemon slices (optional)	4 slices	2 slices	1 slice
Hot Cooked Rice (page 293)	400 g	200 g	100 g
Chopped fresh herbs	to taste garnish	to taste garnish	to taste garnish
Parsley sprigs			
Microwave cookware	2 litre soufflé dish	2 litre soufflé dish	1 litre soufflé dish
Time on High (100% power)	8–10 minutes	4–6 minutes	2–3½ (3:30) minutes
Standing time	3–4 minutes	3 minutes	2 minutes

1 In colander, place prawns. Rinse under cold running water to clean; drain well.

2 In soufflé dish (see Chart), combine basil, celery, salt, rosemary, thyme, mustard, fennel seed and cayenne pepper until well mixed.

3 To herb mixture, add prawns; toss to coat prawns. Add lager and Worcestershire sauce; mix well.

4 Cook prawns, covered, on High for time in Chart, just until they turn pink, stirring twice. Allow to stand, covered, on heatproof surface for time in Chart.

5 Meanwhile, if you like, for each serving, prepare finger bowl by filling soup or dessert bowl with warm water and floating lemon slice on top.

6 To serve: arrange prawns in warmed soup plates. Fork hot rice and chopped fresh herbs together; spoon next to prawns. Garnish with parsley. If using finger bowls, place by each setting.

PRAWNS IN SAFFRON CREAM

Colour Index page 53. 6 servings. 205 cals per serving. Good source of vitamin A, vitamin C, iron. Begin 35 minutes ahead.

Good pinch of saffron threads
Water
4 medium carrots, cut into matchstick-thin strips
700 g large raw prawns, shelled and deveined (below)
60 ml lemon juice
60 ml dry vermouth or dry white wine
2 tablespoons finely chopped spring onion or onion
¼ teaspoon salt
250 ml half cream
2 teaspoons cornflour
350 g mange-touts

1. In 1 litre microwave-safe measuring jug, soak saffron threads in 1 tablespoon boiling water.
2. In 30 × 20 cm microwave-safe baking dish, place carrots and 60 ml water. Cook, covered, on High (100% power) for 4–6 minutes, until tender. Transfer to plate; cover and keep warm. Reserve cooking liquid in baking dish.
3. In 32.5 × 22.5 cm microwave-safe baking dish, place prawns, half each of lemon juice, vermouth or wine, onion and salt. Cook, covered, on High for 5–6 minutes, just until prawns turn pink, stirring halfway through cooking. Over small bowl, drain prawns; discard liquid; keep prawns warm.
4. To saffron mixture, add cream, cornflour and remaining lemon juice, vermouth or wine, onion and salt; stir until well blended. Cook, covered, on High for 4–6 minutes, until cream boils and thickens slightly, stirring once; keep warm.
5. To reserved carrot liquid in baking dish, add mange-touts. Cook, covered, on High for 4–5 minutes, until tender-crisp, stirring halfway through cooking. Add carrots to one side of dish, keeping vegetables separate. Cook, covered, on High for 1 minute.
6. Gently toss prawns in saffron cream. Spoon equal amounts on to warmed dinner plates. Arrange vegetables around prawn mixture.

SHELLING AND DEVEINING PRAWNS

Prawns may be shelled and deveined before or after cooking in the microwave, depending on the recipe.

Snip prawn along back, exposing vein. Peel back shell; pull prawn free.

Scrape away black or green vein; rinse prawn under cold running water.

CREOLE PRAWNS

Colour Index page 50. 4 servings. 463 cals per serving. Good source of vitamin A, niacin, vitamin C, calcium, iron. Begin 20 minutes ahead.

60 g butter or margarine	1 teaspoon dried thyme
3 small onions, cut into 1 cm wedges	2 teaspoons Worcestershire sauce
1 small green pepper, cut into 1 cm pieces	1 teaspoon prepared horseradish
3 garlic cloves, crushed	1 × 400 g can passatta (sieved tomatoes)
700 g large raw prawns, shelled and deveined (see Shelling and Deveining Prawns, opposite page)	Salt, pepper and Tabasco sauce to taste
¼ teaspoon ground cloves	400 g Hot Cooked Rice (page 293)

1. In 2.5 litre microwave-safe casserole, place butter or margarine. Heat, covered with kitchen paper, on High (100% power) for 45 seconds–1 minute, until melted.

2. Into melted butter or margarine, stir onions, green pepper, garlic, prawns, cloves and thyme. Cook, covered on High for 6 minutes, or just until prawns turn pink, stirring twice.

3. Into prawn mixture, stir Worcestershire sauce, horseradish and passatta. Cook on High for 4 minutes, or until flavours blend, stirring halfway through cooking. Add salt, pepper and Tabasco. Serve hot, ladled over hot rice.

BUYING PRAWNS

There are many varieties and sizes of raw and cooked prawns, in the shell and shelled, with and without their heads. Raw prawns cook superbly in the microwave, retaining their natural juiciness and flavour far more than when cooked conventionally. Medium and large prawns are widely available. King, jumbo and tiger prawns are very large, and best reserved for special occasions.

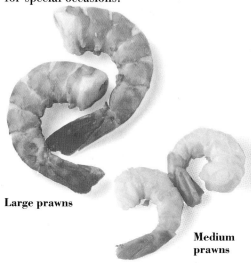

Large prawns

Medium prawns

Filled prawn dishes such as Stuffed Prawns Supreme (below) make an impressive addition to any dinner or buffet table. To ensure a neat and attractive finished result, it is essential to use large prawns and to grate or finely chop the stuffing ingredients.

STUFFED PRAWNS SUPREME

Colour Index page 53. 349 cals per serving. Good source of iron. Begin 45 minutes ahead.

Ingredients for 4 servings		Microwave cookware
450 g king or large raw prawns, shelled and deveined (see Shelling and Deveining Prawns, opposite page)	Cayenne pepper	32.5 × 22.5 cm baking dish
	1 egg, beaten	30 cm plate
	30 g butter or margarine, melted	
	2 tablespoons dry sherry	
150 g courgettes, grated	1 tablespoon lemon juice	
50 g red pepper, very finely chopped	2 tablespoons finely chopped pecan nuts	
25 g dried breadcrumbs	1 × 175 g goat cheese, cut into 8 slices	
	Lettuce leaves	

1 With sharp knife, cut each prawn along back, three-quarters of way through. Spread open and pound lightly to flatten.

2 Place courgettes in sieve over mixing bowl; press with back of spoon to remove excess liquid; discard liquid. In bowl, combine courgettes, red pepper, breadcrumbs, cayenne and egg.

3 Spoon equal amount of courgette mixture along centre of each prawn; fold prawn over filling. Arrange stuffed prawns in single layer in baking dish.

4 In ramekin or small bowl, combine melted butter or margarine, sherry and lemon juice; pour over stuffed prawns. Cook, covered with greaseproof paper, on Medium-High (70% power) for 6–8 minutes, until prawns turn pink, rotating dish halfway through cooking. Set aside, covered.

5 In shallow dish, place chopped pecans; press cheese slices into pecans to coat. Place on plate. Heat on Medium (50% power) for 1–2 minutes, until cheese softens slightly.

6 To serve: arrange lettuce leaves round edge of serving platter. Place stuffed prawns and pecan-coated cheese slices on platter; pour any remaining butter mixture over prawns. Serve immediately.

Prawns

'STIR-FRIED' PRAWNS AND BROCCOLI

Colour Index page 53. 222 cals per serving. Good source of vitamin A, vitamin C, iron. Begin 40 minutes ahead.

Ingredients	For 4	For 2	For 1
Large raw prawns, shelled and deveined (see Shelling and Deveining Prawns page 164)	24 (450 g)	12 (225 g)	6 (115 g)
Cornflour	2 teaspoons	1 teaspoon	1/2 teaspoon
Dry sherry	2 tablespoons	1 tablespoon	1 1/2 teaspoons
Grated root ginger	1/2 teaspoon	1/4 teaspoon	to taste
Broccoli, florets and stalks, sliced	450 g	225 g	115 g
Water	60 ml	2 tablespoons	1 tablespoon
Red pepper, sliced	1 large	1 medium	1 small
1 × 425 g can straw mushrooms, drained	1 can	1/2 can	1/4 can
Butter or margarine	15 g	1 1/2 teaspoons	1 teaspoon
Vegetable oil	1 tablespoon	1 1/2 teaspoons	1 teaspoon
Garlic cloves, crushed	2 cloves	1 clove	1/2 clove
Soy sauce (optional)	to taste	to taste	to taste
Microwave cookware	2 litre casserole	1 litre casserole	Small bowl
	Browning dish	Browning dish	Browning dish
Time on High (100% power)			
Broccoli	4–5 minutes	3–3 1/2 (3:30) minutes	2 1/2 (2:30) minutes
Butter mixture	1 minute	45 seconds	30 seconds
Prawns	2–3 minutes	1 1/2 (1:30)– 2 minutes	1 minute
Vegetables	2–3 minutes	1 1/2 (1:30)– 1 3/4 (1:45) minutes	1 minute

1 In mixing bowl, place prawns, cornflour, sherry and ginger; stir until blended. Cover and refrigerate for 15 minutes, stirring twice.

2 In casserole or bowl (see Chart), place broccoli and water. Cook, covered, on High for time in Chart; drain and rinse. Stir in red pepper and mushrooms.

4 On browning dish, place vegetables. Cook on High for time in Chart, stirring once.

5 Add prawns to vegetables; toss gently to mix. If you like, serve with soy sauce.

3 Preheat browning dish according to manufacturer's instructions. On browning dish, place butter or margarine, oil and garlic. Cook on High for time in Chart, stirring halfway through cooking. Add prawns to browning dish in single layer. Cook on High for time in Chart or just until prawns turn pink, stirring halfway through cooking. Remove prawns; cover and keep warm.

PRAWN AND RED PEPPER RISOTTO

Colour Index page 53. 6 servings. 437 cals per serving. Low in fat, sodium. Good source of calcium, fibre. Begin 40 minutes ahead.

3 tablespoons olive oil
125 g button mushrooms, cut into quarters or eighths
1 onion, finely chopped
1 celery stick, finely chopped
1 garlic clove, crushed
400 g arborio rice
750 ml Fish Stock (page 125) or stock from a cube
200 ml dry white wine

450 g medium raw prawns, shelled and deveined (see Shelling and Deveining Prawns, page 164)
125 g mange-touts, cut in half crossways
2 red peppers, cut into 2 cm pieces
1/2 teaspoon pepper
4 spring onions, finely chopped
2 tablespoons shredded fresh basil
Basil leaves to garnish

1. In deep 3 litre microwave-safe casserole, place oil, mushrooms, onion, celery and garlic. Cook, covered, on High (100% power) for 3–4 minutes, until vegetables soften, stirring halfway through cooking.
2. To vegetables, add rice; stir to combine. Add stock and white wine; stir again. Cook, loosely covered, on High for 15 minutes.
3. To vegetables and rice, add prawns, mange-touts, red peppers and pepper; stir gently. Cook, loosely covered, on High for 10 minutes.
4. To vegetables and rice, add spring onions and shredded basil; stir gently to combine. Allow to stand, covered, on heatproof surface for 7–10 minutes, until most of liquid is absorbed. Risotto should be creamy, not dry; rice should be *al dente* (tender yet firm to the bite). Serve hot, garnished with fresh basil leaves.

CRAB AND FENNEL RISOTTO: make as for Prawn and Red Pepper Risotto (above), substituting *2 thinly sliced fennel bulbs* for red pepper in step 3 and *450 g white crabmeat* for prawns. Add crabmeat with spring onions in step 4, just to heat through. If you like, stir in *1 tablespoon anise-flavoured liqueur* with spring onions and substitute *dill* for basil. 473 cals per serving. Good source of vitamin A, vitamin C, calcium, iron, fibre.

SZECHUAN LOBSTER

Colour Index page 53. 4 servings. 292 cals per serving. Good source of vitamin A, vitamin C, calcium, iron. Begin 50 minutes ahead.

4 cooked lobsters	2 teaspoons soy sauce
1 tablespoon groundnut or vegetable oil	1 teaspoon sesame oil
	225 g green beans
2 teaspoons rice wine vinegar or cider vinegar	3 spring onions, cut into 5 cm pieces
3 garlic cloves, crushed	1 green pepper, cut into matchstick-thin strips
70 g dry roasted cashews	
1 teaspoon chilli powder	

1. Remove meat from lobsters (See Lobster Thermidor, right, steps 1–3).

2. In 30 × 20 cm microwave-safe baking dish, combine oil, vinegar, garlic, cashews, chilli powder, soy sauce and sesame oil. Cook on High (100% power) for 2 minutes, or until flavours blend.

3. To cashew mixture, add green beans, spring onions and green pepper. Stir to coat with cashew mixture. Cook, covered, on High for 6–8 minutes, until beans are tender.

4. Add lobster meat to vegetables. Cook, covered, on High for 2–3 minutes, until lobster is hot. Spoon on to warmed dinner plates and serve immediately.

COOKING MUSSELS

Cooking mussels in the microwave is quick, simple and clean. All mussels should be thoroughly scrubbed with a stiff brush under cold running water to remove any sand and surface dirt; barnacles and beards should be scraped off with a small, sharp knife. Discard any mussels that are open or partially open. Place mussels in soufflé dish or casserole and cook, covered tightly with microwave cling film, on High (100% power) for time in recipe. If some mussels do not open, remove opened mussels and reserve; cover dish again and cook on High for 1–2 minutes longer. Remove opened mussels and place with others. Discard any that are not open; reserve juice according to recipe instructions.

LOBSTER THERMIDOR

Colour Index page 53. 322 cals per serving. Good source of calcium. Begin 45 minutes ahead.

Ingredients	For 4	For 2	For 1
Cooked lobsters (575 g each)	4 lobsters	2 lobsters	1 lobster
Butter or margarine	60 g	30 g	15 g
Mushrooms, cut into quarters	115 g	50 g	25 g
1 × 300 g can condensed cream of mushroom soup	1 can	1/2 can	1/4 can
Milk	60 ml	2 tablespoons	1 tablespoon
Medium sherry	2 tablespoons	1 tablespoon	1 1/2 teaspoons
Parsley	garnish	garnish	garnish
Microwave cookware	Large bowl	Medium bowl	Medium bowl
Time on High (100% power)			
Butter and mushrooms	4 minutes	3 minutes	2 minutes
With soup and milk	4 minutes	2 minutes	1 1/2 (1:30) minutes
With lobster	4 minutes	2 1/2 (2:30) minutes	1 1/2 (1:30) minutes

1 Prepare lobsters: break off claws and legs. With nut cracker, crack large claws. Remove claw meat from shell; place in mixing bowl.

2 With kitchen shears, cut thin underside shell from tail of each lobster; gently pull meat from shell. Place green meat (tomalley) and any roe (coral) in bowl with claw meat. Devein tail meat; cut into chunks. Add chunks to bowl.

3 Lift out bony portion from head shell; add green meat or roe to bowl. Discard sac and spongy grey gills from top of head. Break bony portion apart. Pick out any meat; add to bowl. Rinse whole lobster shells; set aside.

4 In bowl (see Chart), place butter or margarine and mushrooms. Cook on High for time in Chart. Stir in soup and milk. Cook on High for time in Chart, stirring halfway through cooking.

5 Into mushroom mixture, stir lobster meat and sherry. Cook on High for time in Chart, or until lobster is hot, stirring halfway through cooking.

6 To serve: place reserved lobster shells on warmed dinner plates; spoon equal amount of lobster mixture into each shell. Garnish with parsley.

Mussels and Scallops

When cooking mussels, it is essential to scrub the shells with a wire brush or stiff plastic brush, and to scrape any calcium and salt deposits from their surfaces. It is also necessary to remove barnacles and beards (string-like threads that attach mussels to their beds) by scraping them away with a sharp knife and rinsing under cold running water. Before cooking, discard any mussels with open shells. After cooking, discard any that remain closed.

MOULES MARINIÈRE

Colour Index page 52. 216 cals per serving. Good source of iron. Begin 35 minutes ahead.

Ingredients	For 4	For 2	For 1
Mussels	48	24	12
Olive or vegetable oil	60 ml	2 tablespoons	1 tablespoon
Onion, finely chopped	1	1/2	1/4
Garlic cloves, sliced	4 cloves	2 cloves	1 clove
Tomatoes, diced	4 tomatoes	2 tomatoes	1 tomato
Dry white wine	250 ml	120 ml	60 ml
Dried basil	1/2 teaspoon	1/4 teaspoon	good pinch
French bread (optional)	to serve	to serve	to serve
Microwave cookware	3 litre soufflé dish or bowl	2 litre soufflé dish or bowl	1.5 litre soufflé dish or bowl
Time on High (100% power)	5–7 minutes each batch	5–7 minutes	4–5 minutes

1 With stiff brush, scrub mussels under cold running water.

2 With small, sharp knife, scrape any barnacles from shells and scrape away beards. Rinse mussels.

3 In soufflé dish (see Chart), place mussels.

4 To mussels, add oil, onion, garlic, tomatoes, wine and basil.

5 Cook mussels, covered tightly with microwave cling film, on High for time in Chart, just until open.

6 To serve: arrange mussels in warmed soup plates with cooking liquid. If you like, serve with French bread.

MUSSELS IN CREAM AND GARLIC

Colour Index page 50. 4 servings. 410 cals per serving. Low in sodium. Good source of vitamin A, calcium, iron, zinc. Begin 25 minutes ahead.

2 kg mussels
4 tablespoons dry white wine
15 g butter or margarine
1 small onion, finely chopped
2 garlic cloves, crushed
250 ml whipping cream
4 tablespoons chopped parsley
1/2 teaspoon pepper

1. With stiff brush, scrub mussels under cold running water. With small, sharp knife, scrape any barnacles from shells and scrape away beards. Rinse mussels.
2. In 3 litre microwave-safe soufflé dish or bowl, place mussels; add wine. Cook, covered tightly with microwave cling film, on High (100% power) for 6–8 minutes, just until mussels open. Remove mussels; set aside.
3. Into jug, strain cooking liquid through muslin; rinse out soufflé dish or bowl.
4. Into cleaned soufflé dish or bowl, place butter or margarine, onion and garlic. Cook on High for 3 minutes, or until vegetables soften, stirring halfway through cooking.
5. To soufflé dish or bowl, add strained cooking liquid and cream. Cook on High for 2 minutes, or until sauce thickens and reduces slightly, stirring once; stir in parsley and pepper.
6. Discard top shells of mussels. Arrange mussels on large microwave-safe serving platter; pour over sauce. Cook on High for 1–2 minutes, until hot and bubbling. Serve immediately.

SCALLOPS IN CHIVE CREAM

Colour Index page 49. 4 servings. 220 cals per serving. Begin 25 minutes ahead.

450 g shelled scallops
30 g butter or margarine
1 onion, finely chopped
60 ml double or whipping cream
60 ml Chicken Stock (page 125) or stock from a cube
60 ml dry white wine
4 tablespoons finely chopped fresh chives
1 tablespoon cornflour dissolved in 2 tablespoons cold water
Salt and pepper to taste
Fresh chives to garnish

1. Rinse scallops under cold running water to remove any sand; pat dry.
2. In 30 × 20 cm microwave-safe baking dish, place butter or margarine and onion. Cook, covered with kitchen paper, on High (100% power) for 3–4 minutes, until onion is translucent and softened, stirring halfway through cooking.
3. To onion mixture, add scallops, cream, stock and wine. Cook, covered, on High for 4–6 minutes, just until scallops are opaque.
4. Into scallop mixture, stir chives and dissolved cornflour. Cook on High for 2–3 minutes, until thickened. Season.
5. To serve: spoon scallop mixture into 4 small dishes or large scallop shells. Garnish with chives.

Scallops and Oysters

CURRIED SCALLOPS

Colour Index page 50. 4 servings. 185 cals per serving. Good source of vitamin A. Begin 25 minutes ahead.

450 g shelled queen scallops	*2 large carrots, cut into matchstick-thin strips*
30 g butter or margarine	*2 tablespoons dry white wine*
1–1½ teaspoons curry powder	*Salt to taste*
1 onion, thinly sliced	*Coriander or parsley sprigs to garnish*
2 medium celery sticks, cut into matchstick-thin strips	

1. Rinse scallops under cold running water to remove any sand; pat dry.
2. In 30 × 20 cm microwave-safe baking dish, place butter or margarine. Heat, covered with kitchen paper, on High (100% power) for 45 seconds, or until melted. Add curry powder according to taste; stir until well blended. To mixture, add onion, celery and carrots; stir to coat with curry butter. Cook on High for 2–3 minutes, until carrots are tender-crisp.
3. To curry butter mixture, add scallops. Drizzle with white wine. Cook, covered, on High for 3–4 minutes, just until scallops are opaque, stirring twice. Season with salt.
4. *To serve:* arrange curried scallops on warmed dinner plates. Garnish with coriander or parsley.

SCALLOPS WITH BACON AND BASIL

Colour Index page 50. 2 servings. 600 cals per serving. Good source of vitamin A, calcium, iron. Begin 25 minutes ahead.

2 rashers rindless, streaky bacon, diced	*1 garlic clove, crushed*
200 g shelled scallops, cut in half crossways	*2 tablespoons dry white wine*
2 mushrooms, thinly sliced	*200 ml whipping cream*
1 small onion, thinly sliced	*¼ teaspoon white pepper*
	1 tablespoon shredded fresh basil

1. In deep 21.5 cm microwave-safe pie dish, place bacon. Cook, covered with kitchen paper, on High (100% power) for 2 minutes, or until just lightly browned. With slotted spoon, transfer bacon to kitchen paper to drain; set aside.
2. Into bacon fat in dish, stir scallops. Cook, covered, on High for 2–2½ minutes, just until scallops are opaque. Remove and keep warm.
3. To dish, add mushrooms, onion, garlic and wine; stir to combine. Cook, covered, on High for 3 minutes, or until vegetables soften, stirring halfway through cooking.
4. To vegetable mixture, add cream and pepper; stir. Cook on High for 3–5 minutes, until sauce thickens and reduces slightly, stirring twice. Stir in reserved bacon and scallops. Cook, covered, on High for 1 minute. Stir in basil and serve.

Oysters are sold fresh in the shell, shelled (shucked), frozen and canned. European and Portuguese oysters are small in size, and highly prized for their exquisite flavour when eaten raw. Oriental oysters are larger, and best used sliced in soups and stews.

CREAMED OYSTERS IN PUFF PASTRY

Colour Index page 50. 350 cals per serving. Good source of calcium, iron. Begin 25 minutes ahead.

Ingredients for 4 servings		Microwave cookware
4 rashers rindless bacon, chopped	*600 ml shelled oysters, with their liquid*	*30 × 20 cm baking dish*
1 small onion, chopped	*120 ml half cream*	
1 celery stick, chopped	*Salt and pepper to taste*	
1 garlic clove, crushed	*4 large or 8 medium vol-au-vents*	
½ teaspoon dried thyme	*Lemon Twists (page 132) and parsley sprigs to garnish*	
1 tablespoon plain flour		

1 In 30 × 20 cm baking dish, place bacon. Cook, covered with kitchen paper, on High (100% power) for 4–5 minutes, until browned, stirring twice. With slotted spoon, transfer bacon to kitchen paper to drain; set aside.

2 To bacon fat in dish, add onion, celery, garlic and thyme. Cook on High for 3–4 minutes, until onion is softened. Stir in flour until blended.

3 Over small mixing bowl, drain oysters: reserve 4 tablespoons liquid. Set oysters aside. Into onion mixture, stir reserved oyster liquid and half cream. Cook on High for 3–4 minutes, until mixture thickens, stirring twice.

4 To creamed mixture, add oysters; season. Cook on High for 1–2 minutes, just until edges of oysters begin to curl and sauce is hot. Allow to stand, covered, on heatproof surface for 5 minutes.

5 Meanwhile, warm vol-au-vents through in conventional oven at 180°C (350°F, gas mark 4) for about 5 minutes.

6 With sharp knife, cut out centres of vol-au-vents. Place vol-au-vents on warmed dinner plates; spoon in oyster mixture. Sprinkle over reserved bacon; garnish.

Crab

CRAB CAKES

Colour Index page 50. 119 cals each. Good source of vitamin A, calcium, iron. Begin 25 minutes ahead.

These Crab Cakes can be made with fresh, frozen or canned crabmeat, or with other shellfish or fish. Popular alternatives, for example, are tuna and salmon cakes made with canned fish. Shaped into tiny patties, Crab Cakes make attractive cocktail nibbles or accompaniments for soup – they go particularly well with Sweetcorn Chowder (page 133).

Ingredients for 12 crab cakes		Microwave cookware
450 g white crabmeat, thawed and drained if frozen 90 g fresh breadcrumbs 1/4 red or green pepper, finely diced 60 ml medium sherry 2 tablespoons finely chopped onion 1 egg, beaten 1/4 teaspoon Tabasco sauce, or to taste	45 g dried wholemeal breadcrumbs 2 teaspoons paprika 60 g butter or margarine, melted Lemon slices and coriander or parsley leaves Spicy Cocktail Sauce (page 159, optional)	25 cm round baking dish

1 Remove any shell and cartilage from crab. To crab, add fresh breadcrumbs and next 5 ingredients; toss.

2 On greaseproof paper, combine dried breadcrumbs and paprika.

3 Shape crab mixture into 12 cakes. For Mini Crab Cakes, shape into 24 small cakes.

4 Into melted butter or margarine, dip Crab Cakes until coated. Coat in breadcrumbs and paprika mixture.

5 In baking dish, place 6 large or 12 miniature cakes. Cook each batch, covered with greaseproof paper, on High for 3–5 minutes, until cakes are set, turning halfway through cooking.

6 Serve Crab Cakes hot, garnished with lemon and fresh coriander or parsley, and accompanied with Spicy Cocktail Sauce, if you like.

DEVILLED CRAB

Colour Index page 50. 4 servings. 308 cals per serving. Good source of calcium. Begin 20 minutes ahead.

450 g fresh white crabmeat 60 g butter or margarine 60 ml double or whipping cream 1 egg, beaten 2 tablespoons chopped parsley	1 tablespoon Dijon mustard 1 tablespoon lemon juice 1 teaspoon Worcestershire sauce 2 tablespoons dried breadcrumbs Lemon to garnish

1. Pick over crab to remove any pieces of shell or cartilage.
2. In 1 litre microwave-safe measuring jug, place butter or margarine. Heat, covered with kitchen paper, on High (100% power) for 45 seconds–1 minute, until melted.
3. To melted butter or margarine, add cream, egg, parsley, mustard, lemon juice, Worcestershire sauce and breadcrumbs; stir to blend.
4. Into cream mixture, gently stir crab until just mixed.
5. Into each of 4 microwave-safe ceramic scallop shells or ramekins, spoon one-quarter of crab mixture. Cook on High for 4–5 minutes, until hot. Garnish with lemon and serve immediately.

CHILLI CRAB

Colour Index page 50. 2 servings. 229 cals per serving. Low in fat. Good source of vitamin A, iron, zinc. Begin 25 minutes ahead.

1 large crab 150 ml tomato ketchup 2 tablespoons soy sauce 2 tablespoons water 1–2 tablespoons sweet or mild chilli sauce, to taste 1 tablespoon sugar	1 tablespoon rice wine vinegar 1 teaspoon chopped fresh root ginger 2 spring onions, sliced Spring Onion Tassels (page 132) to garnish

1. Prepare crab: on cutting board, place crab, shell side down. Twist off large claws and legs from body; set aside. With thumbs, prise up tail flap on underside; twist off and discard. Remove and discard dead man's fingers and soft substance from centre of body.
2. With cleaver or large heavy knife, crack claws and legs, discarding any shell and cartilage. Chop body of crab into 4–6 pieces.
3. In 500 ml microwave-safe measuring jug, combine ketchup and next 6 ingredients. Cook, covered, on High (100% power) for 4–5 minutes, until sauce boils and flavours blend, stirring twice. Stir in spring onions.
4. In deep 2 litre microwave-safe bowl, place crab pieces, claws and legs; pour over hot sauce. Cook, covered, on High for 3–4 minutes, until sauce boils and crab is hot, stirring halfway through cooking. Serve hot, garnished with Spring Onion Tassels.

Mixed Shellfish

PAELLA

Colour Index page 54. 297 cals per serving. Good source of niacin, iron.
Begin 1¼ hours ahead.

The paella of Spain has become a classic party dish all over the
world. The ingredients vary from one Spanish region to another,
but usually include large amounts of shellfish with chicken, sausages
and rice, giving the paella its contrast of textures, colours and
flavours. This microwave Paella uses a combination of different
shellfish, but it is not essential to use them all; if clams are difficult
to obtain, they can be omitted and the mussels increased.

1 Scrub mussels and clams under cold running water; with sharp knife, remove beards from mussels (page 168).

2 In soufflé dish, arrange clams in a ring round edge of dish. Place mussels in centre.

Ingredients for 8 servings		Microwave cookware
12 mussels *12 clams* *60 ml dry white wine* *225 g spicy-hot fresh pork sausages, cut into 2.5 cm lengths* *450 g chicken breasts, skinned, boned and cut into 5 cm strips* *2 garlic cloves, crushed* *½ teaspoon dried thyme* *¼ teaspoon salt* *1 green pepper, chopped*	*1 onion, chopped* *450 g raw king prawns, shelled and deveined (see Shelling and Deveining Prawns, page 164)* *175 g long-grain rice* *½ teaspoon crushed saffron threads* *250 ml Chicken Stock (page 125) or stock from a cube* *1 × 225 g can crushed tomatoes*	*3 litre soufflé dish*

3 To dish, add wine. Cook, covered, on High (100% power) for 3–5 minutes, just until shellfish open (see Cooking Mussels, page 167).

4 Discard top shells of shellfish; rinse shellfish in own liquid from shells to remove any sand. Place shellfish on plate; reserve.

5 Into jug, pour shellfish cooking liquid; leave to stand until sand settles. Spoon off clear cooking liquid and reserve; discard remainder.

6 In soufflé dish used for shellfish, place sausages. Cook, covered with kitchen paper, on High for 5 minutes, or until lightly browned. Remove to drain on kitchen paper. Reserve dripping.

7 In mixing bowl, place chicken. Add garlic, thyme and salt.

8 To sausage dripping in soufflé dish, add seasoned chicken. Cook, covered with kitchen paper, on High for 4–5 minutes, until chicken is tender, stirring halfway through cooking. Remove chicken; reserve.

9 To same soufflé dish, add green pepper, onion and prawns. Cook, covered, on High for 2–3 minutes, just until prawns turn pink, stirring halfway through cooking. Remove prawns and set aside.

10 To vegetables, add rice and saffron. Stir to coat. Cook on High for 2 minutes, stirring halfway through cooking.

11 Into rice, stir reserved shellfish cooking liquid, stock and tomatoes. Cook on High for 15 minutes, or until rice is tender; stir once.

12 Into rice mixture, carefully stir reserved sausage, chicken and shellfish.

13 Cook paella, covered, on High for 2–3 minutes, until hot. Be careful not to overcook.

14 *To serve:* place paella in warmed serving dish, arranging mussels and clams on top. Garnish and serve immediately.

Mixed Shellfish

BOUILLABAISSE

Colour Index page 54. 205 cals per serving. Begin 1¼ hours ahead.

Ingredients for 8 servings		Microwave cookware
12 mussels	½ teaspoon crushed	Large bowl
3 tablespoons olive or	saffron threads	
vegetable oil	1 uncooked lobster	
1 onion, finely chopped	(575 g)	
3 garlic cloves,	450 g sea bass or John	
crushed	Dory fillet, cut into	
3 large tomatoes,	5 cm pieces	
chopped	450 g cod steak, cut into	
1 bay leaf	5 cm pieces	
250 ml dry white wine	1 tablespoon anise-	
60 ml tomato purée	flavoured liqueur	
¼ teaspoon salt	Tabasco sauce to taste	
½ teaspoon dried	Chopped parsley to	
thyme	garnish	
500 ml Chicken Stock		
(page 125) or stock		
from a cube		

1 With stiff brush, scrub mussels to remove any sand: rinse under cold running water. Scrape away any barnacles and beards. In bowl, place mussels. Cook, covered, on High (100% power) for 2–3 minutes, just until open. Rinse each mussel in own liquid from shell to remove any sand. Place mussels on plate; reserve. Into jug, pour cooking liquid. Leave to stand until sand settles. Spoon off clear cooking liquid and reserve; discard remainder.

2 In bowl used for cooking mussels, combine oil, onion, garlic, tomatoes and bay leaf. Cook on High for 3–4 minutes, until onion softens, stirring twice. Add wine, next 5 ingredients and reserved cooking liquid. Cook on High for 12 minutes, until flavours blend, stirring every 3 minutes.

3 On cutting board, place lobster. Insert point of knife through back shell, where tail and body meet, to sever vein.

4 With knife, cut lobster in half lengthways through shell. Devein tail. Leave green meat (tomalley) and any roe (coral).

5 Remove sand sac from head; break off claws. Cut each claw across joints into 3 pieces. Crack claws. Cut lobster into chunks.

6 To tomato mixture, add lobster. Cook on High for 4 minutes, stirring once. Add fish. Cook on High for 2 minutes, or until opaque. Add liqueur, Tabasco and mussels; stir. Allow to stand, covered, for 5 minutes. Discard bay leaf. Ladle Bouillabaisse into soup bowls; garnish.

DELUXE OCEAN PIE

Colour Index page 54. 4 servings. 650 cals per serving. Good source of vitamin A, vitamin C, calcium, potassium, iron, fibre. Begin 1¼ hours ahead.

1 onion, finely chopped	125 g crab sticks, cut
60 g butter or margarine	into 2.5 cm pieces, or
2 tablespoons plain flour	1 × 170 g can
300 ml milk	crabmeat, drained and
4 button mushrooms, cut	picked over
into quarters	125 g frozen peas,
¼ teaspoon dried thyme	thawed and drained
½ teaspoon white	1 tablespoon chopped
pepper	parsley
1 × 250 g can mussels in	750 g old potatoes,
brine, drained, with	peeled
liquid reserved	2 tablespoons water
125 g shelled scallops,	280 ml single cream
cut in half crossways	¼ teaspoon salt
125 g medium raw	
prawns, shelled and	
deveined (see Shelling	
and Deveining	
Prawns, page 164)	

1. In 3 litre microwave-safe bowl, place onion and half of butter or margarine. Cook, covered, on High (100% power) for 3 minutes, or until onion softens, stirring once.

2. Into onion, stir flour until smooth and blended. Cook on High for 3 minutes, stirring halfway through cooking. Into flour mixture, gradually stir milk; cook on High for 3–4 minutes, until sauce thickens and is smooth, stirring twice.

3. To sauce, add mushrooms, thyme, ¼ teaspoon pepper and reserved mussel liquid; stir well to combine. Cook, covered, on High for 3–4 minutes, until mushrooms are tender, stirring halfway through cooking.

4. To mushroom sauce, add scallops and prawns. Cook, covered, on High for 3–4 minutes, just until scallops are opaque and prawns turn pink, stirring twice. Gently stir in crab stick pieces, mussels, peas and parsley. Transfer to oval 33 cm microwave-safe gratin dish or deep 26 cm round microwave-safe baking dish; set aside.

5. Cut potatoes in half lengthways; cut halves into 2 cm thick slices. In cleaned bowl used for sauce, place potato slices; add water. Cook, covered, on High for 10 minutes, or until tender; drain off liquid.

6. To potatoes, add remaining butter or margarine, cream, salt and remaining pepper. With mixer on low speed, beat potatoes until smooth. Into large piping bag fitted with star nozzle, spoon potato mixture. Over shellfish mixture in dish, pipe potato mixture in shell pattern, taking care to pipe right to edges. (Alternatively, spread potato over and mark with fork.)

7. Cook pie on High for 6–7 minutes, until piping hot, rotating dish a half turn every 2 minutes. Serve hot.

ITALIAN SHELLFISH STEW

Colour Index page 52. 8 servings. 166 cals per serving. Low in fat. Good source of vitamin A, vitamin C, iron. Begin 45 minutes ahead.

12 clams	*1 teaspoon dried*
2 tablespoons olive oil	*oregano*
1 large onion, chopped	*225 g large raw prawns,*
1 medium green pepper,	*shelled and deveined*
chopped	*(see Shelling and*
2 celery sticks,	*Deveining Prawns,*
chopped	*page 164)*
250 ml dry red wine	*225 g shelled scallops*
1 × 400 g can passatta	*8 crab sticks, cut in half*
(sieved tomatoes)	*lengthways*

1. With stiff brush, scrub clams under cold running water to remove any sand. In large microwave-safe bowl, place clams. Cook, covered, on High (100% power) for 4–6 minutes, until open.
2. Discard top clam shells; rinse each clam in own liquid from shell to remove any sand. Place clams on plate; reserve. Into jug, pour cooking liquid; leave to stand until sand settles. Spoon off clear cooking liquid and reserve; discard rest.
3. In bowl used for clams, combine oil and next 3 ingredients. Cook on High for 3–4 minutes, until softened. Add wine, passatta, oregano and reserved clam liquid. Cook on High for 10 minutes, stirring twice.
4. Into mixture, stir prawns and scallops. Cook, covered, on High for 3–5 minutes, until prawns turn pink and scallops are opaque, stirring once. Add crab sticks and reserved clams. Cook, covered, on High for 2 minutes, or until hot.

LOBSTER AND PRAWN STEW WITH CHICKEN

Colour Index page 52. 4 servings. 240 cals per serving. Good source of vitamin A, niacin. Begin 40 minutes ahead.

2 cooked lobsters (about	*150 g frozen sweetcorn*
575 g each)	*kernels, thawed*
30 g butter or margarine	*1 tablespoon cornflour*
1 onion, chopped	*dissolved in 120 ml*
2 tomatoes, chopped	*Chicken Stock (page*
1 teaspoon dried basil	*125) or stock from a*
225 g chicken breasts,	*cube*
skinned, boned and cut	*225 g shelled cooked*
into 5 cm pieces	*prawns*

1. Remove meat from lobsters (page 167). Cut meat into 5 cm pieces.
2. In 32.5 × 22.5 cm microwave-safe baking dish, place butter or margarine, onion, tomatoes and basil. Cook on High (100% power) for 3–4 minutes. Add chicken and sweetcorn. Cook on High for 4–6 minutes, until chicken is opaque, stirring twice.
3. Into chicken mixture, stir stock mixture and lobster. Cook on High for 2 minutes. Add prawns. Cook on High for 1–2 minutes, until sauce thickens and lobster is hot, stirring twice. Season.

TUNA AND TOMATO SAUCE

Colour Index page 49. 4 servings, 426 cals per serving (with pasta). Good source of thiamine, niacin, iron. Begin 15 minutes ahead.

225 g any pasta	**1.** Cook pasta conventionally.
1 tablespoon olive or	**2.** Meanwhile, in large microwave-safe bowl,
vegetable oil	place oil and next 4 ingredients. Cook,
1 onion, chopped	covered with kitchen paper, on High (100%
2 garlic cloves,	power) for 3–4 minutes, until onion is trans-
crushed	lucent, stirring halfway through cooking.
10 stoned black	**3.** To mixture, add tuna with oil from can,
olives, chopped	and red pepper flakes, breaking tuna into
1 tablespoon capers	bite-size pieces. Cook, loosely covered, on
1 × 200 g can tuna in	High for 2–3 minutes, until hot. Stir in tom-
oil	atoes and parsley. Cook, loosely covered, on
¼ teaspoon dried hot	High for 4–5 minutes, until bubbling, stirring
red pepper flakes	twice.
1 × 400 g can crushed	**4.** *To serve:* drain pasta and place on
tomatoes	warmed dinner plates; spoon over sauce.
4 tablespoons	
chopped parsley	

RED CLAM SAUCE

Colour Index page 49. 4 servings, 338 cals per serving (with pasta). Low in fat. Good source of vitamin A, vitamin C, iron. Begin 15 minutes ahead.

225 g any pasta	**1.** Cook pasta conventionally.
2 rashers rindless	**2.** Meanwhile, in large microwave-safe bowl,
streaky bacon,	place diced bacon. Cook, covered with
diced	kitchen paper, on High (100% power) for 2–3
1 small onion, diced	minutes, until browned.
1 × 400 g can crushed	**3.** To bacon, add onion. Cook, covered, on
tomatoes	High for 3 minutes, stirring twice.
½ teaspoon dried	**4.** Into mixture, stir crushed tomatoes and
mixed herbs	herbs. Cook, loosely covered, on High for 3–4
½ teaspoon dried	minutes, until hot. Stir in clams. Cook,
oregano	loosely covered, on High for 2 minutes.
1 × 275 g can whole	**5.** *To serve:* drain pasta and place on
baby clams, drained	warmed dinner plates; spoon over sauce.

SPICY PRAWN SAUCE

Colour Index page 49. 4 servings. 317 cals per serving (with pasta). Low in fat. Good source of vitamin A, calcium, iron, zinc, fibre. Begin 20 minutes ahead.

225 g any pasta	**1.** Cook pasta conventionally.
1 tablespoon olive oil	**2.** Meanwhile, in large microwave-safe bowl,
1 onion, finely	place oil, onion and garlic. Cook, covered
chopped	with kitchen paper, on High (100% power)
1 garlic clove, crushed	for 2–3 minutes, until vegetables soften, stir-
1 × 794 g can	ring once.
tomatoes	**3.** To bowl, add tomatoes with their liquid,
1 tablespoon tomato	tomato purée, chillies, thyme and oregano.
purée	Cook on High, loosely covered, for 5 minutes,
½ teaspoon crushed	stirring halfway through cooking to break up
dried red chillies	tomatoes. Uncover and cook on High for 5
½ teaspoon dried	minutes longer, or until sauce thickens
thyme	slightly, stirring twice.
½ teaspoon dried	**4.** To tomato sauce, add prawns. Cook,
oregano	covered, on High for 2 minutes, or until
225 g shelled cooked	heated through. Stir in half of parsley.
prawns	**5.** *To serve:* drain pasta and place on
4 tablespoons	warmed dinner plates; spoon over sauce.
chopped parsley	Sprinkle with remaining parsley.

Meal in Minutes *for 8 people*

Do-It-Yourself Shellfish Pasta Party

Melon and Parma ham
Grissini
Pasta with three Shellfish Sauces, page 173
Tossed mixed salad
Ice cream or sorbet of your choice
Espresso, page 130, with Florentines, page 365

PREPARATION TIMETABLE

1 day ahead	Early in day	1 hour ahead	30 minutes ahead	Just before serving
Make Florentines; store in airtight container.	*Prepare salad ingredients; store in polythene bags in refrigerator. Prepare shellfish sauces; cover and refrigerate. Slice melon; cover and refrigerate.*	*Arrange melon slices on large serving platter with Parma ham; if you like, wrap melon with Parma ham. Garnish platter with olives and basil leaves; cover.*	*Cook 3 kinds of pasta conventionally; keep warm. Meanwhile, reheat shellfish sauces in microwave. Place salad ingredients in bowl and toss with dressing of your choice.*	*Transfer pasta and shellfish sauces to warmed serving bowls; if you like, garnish with fresh basil or parsley. Prepare Espresso.*

Poultry

DEFROSTING, COOKING AND BROWNING POULTRY
JOINTED CHICKEN · CHICKEN BREASTS
CHICKEN PIECES · COOKED CHICKEN
POUSSINS · DUCKLING · TURKEY

Poultry

Poultry, a naturally tender food, is ideal for the fast, moist cooking of the microwave oven. Chicken, duckling, poussins and turkey all turn out successfully, although smaller portions rather than whole birds are easiest to cook. A whole chicken requires shielding and turning halfway through cooking; a whole turkey must be cooked conventionally if it is over 5 kg, but turkey breasts and pieces are delicious cooked in the microwave. Duckling is better microwaved, as excess fat is more easily removed. Poussins are excellent cooked whole or split in half. Microwaved chicken should be very juicy; if meat is dry or tough, it has been overcooked.

Because poultry skin is high in calories and cholesterol and rarely browns in the microwave oven, it should be removed when fat is not necessary for recipe. To look as appetising as possible, poultry should be glazed, simmered in a sauce, or coated. Plain microwaved chicken, however, is ideal for use in main course salads and other cold dishes.

If you are using a temperature probe when cooking chickens, make sure the weight of the bird is at least 1.5 kg. If the chicken is too small, the probe may touch a bone and cause an inaccurate reading. When cooking a whole bird, cover its wing and leg tips and the breastbone with smooth, small pieces of foil to prevent overcooking. Chicken pieces have to be arranged carefully for even cooking: place meatier pieces towards edges of dish and bonier parts towards centre, then rearrange pieces halfway through cooking. Prevent uneven cooking of boneless chicken breasts by tucking thin ends under. Because the microwave sometimes renders more fat from foods than conventional methods, use a rack to cook duckling pieces and cover loosely with greaseproof or waxed paper.

Poultry is done when flesh is opaque and fork-tender; juices should run clear when flesh is pierced in thickest part with a fork. Standing time is given in those individual poultry recipes where it is necessary to complete cooking before serving.

DINNER PARTY PRESENTATIONS

Transform a plain, boneless microwaved chicken breast (page 178) into impressive dinner party fare by slicing it evenly, then fanning out the slices on a pool of sauce. This quick presentation works with both hot and chilled cooked chicken.

A hot chicken breast (left) sliced and fanned on pool of Tomato Sauce (page 380), then garnished with fresh herb sprigs.

A sliced cold chicken breast (right), arranged on Creamy Avocado Sauce (page 218) with Orange Julienne (page 330). Garnished with avocado and parsley.

Defrosting Poultry

It is quick and easy to defrost poultry in the microwave – an absolute boon if you have forgotten to take something out of the freezer in time to defrost it conventionally. If possible, remove or loosen wrappings before defrosting, taking care not to tear poultry skin. If wrapping is left on, it will retain heat and poultry may begin to cook. Before cooking, rinse poultry under cold running water, then pat dry. To avoid any risk of food poisoning, check that poultry is completely defrosted and no ice crystals remain.

Defrosting a Whole Bird This can be done in less than 30 minutes; an average, family-sized chicken weighing about 1.5 kg, for example, will take only about 20 minutes. At end of defrosting time, remove bird from microwave and allow to stand in deep bowl of cold water for up to 30 minutes, depending on size of bird. This is to allow ice crystals in cavity to dissolve. Rinse bird under cold running water and pat dry before beginning to cook.

Defrosting Pieces Legs, breasts, wings, thighs and drumsticks can all be defrosted in 6–7 minutes per 450 g. Do not defrost for longer than this or poultry will lose its natural flavour and juiciness; if any areas seem to be starting to cook, shield them with smooth pieces of foil. At end of defrosting time, there should still be some ice crystals around bony areas; allow pieces to stand for 5 minutes, then rinse under cold running water and pat dry.

On microwave-safe rack set in microwave-safe baking dish, place bird. Defrost on Medium-Low (30% power) for 5–9 minutes per 450 g. Elevating bird on rack will raise it above juices that collect in bottom of dish and so prevent bird from beginning to cook. Pour off these juices twice during defrosting.

If poultry pieces have been frozen in a tray, remove this and any paper liner provided to absorb juices as soon as tray and paper can be separated from poultry. If left in place, defrosting time will be prolonged.

Halfway through defrosting time, turn bird breast side down. Cover bird with greaseproof or waxed paper to hold heat round bird as it defrosts.

If not in solid block, arrange boned breasts with thicker portions towards edge of dish. Break apart partially frozen pieces after half of defrosting time.

Towards end of defrosting, uncover bird and turn breast side up. Shield any warm spots with smooth pieces of foil. Legs, wing tips and highest portion of breast normally defrost soonest.

Rearrange pieces so that icier ones are towards edge of dish; defrost for remaining time. At end of defrosting, pieces will be cold to the touch and there will be some ice crystals.

Cooking Chicken

EXTRA-QUICK CHICKEN BREASTS

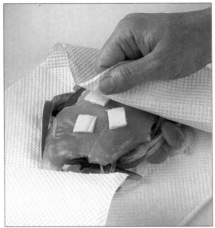

Barbecued
In microwave-safe casserole, place
1 × 225 g chicken breast, skinned and
boned. Cook, covered, on High (100%
power) for 2 minutes, rotating once. Brush
with *2 tablespoons barbecue sauce*. Cook,
covered, for 2–3 minutes, until juices run
clear. Stand for 2 minutes.

Poached
Pound *1 × 175 g chicken breast fillet* to 1 cm thickness. Place *115 g mixed thinly
sliced peppers, carrots, celery* and *onion* on 2 connected sheets of kitchen paper; top
with chicken. If you like, dot with *butter or margarine*; season. Fold sides of paper
parcel over chicken; tuck ends under. Place parcel on microwave-safe plate; sprinkle
with a little water. Cook 1 parcel on High (100% power) for 3½ (3:30)–4 minutes; 2
parcels for 5½ (5:30)–6 minutes. Allow to stand on heatproof surface for 3 minutes
before serving.

COOKING CHICKEN

Amount	Time	Power level
1 × 175 g chicken breast (*skinned and boned*)	3½ (3:30)– 4 minutes	High (100% power)
2 × 175 g chicken breasts (*skinned and boned*)	5½ (5:30)– 6 minutes	High
1 × 225 g chicken leg	5–5½ (5:30) minutes	High
2 × 225 g chicken legs	8–8½ (8:30) minutes	High
2 × 575 g poussins	14–16 minutes	High
Whole chicken	7–9 minutes per 450 g	Medium (50% power)

COOKING SMALL TURKEYS

Use a probe or microwave thermometer while bird is cooking,
or check temperature with a meat thermometer once it is out
of microwave. Turkey breast meat should register 76°C
(170°F); thigh and dark meat 79–82°C (175–180°F). Choose a
light, bread-type stuffing and mix and pack it lightly. Heavy
stuffings take too long to cook, so meat will overcook before
stuffing is ready; cooking stuffing in separate casserole is
recommended.

COOKING WHOLE BIRDS

Choose plump birds weighing at least 1.5 kg, but no more than 5 kg. Cover wing and leg tips and breastbone with smooth, small pieces of foil to prevent these areas from overcooking.

Larger birds may brown due to longer cooking times, otherwise brush bird with bottled barbecue sauce or a browning agent (see Browning Chicken, pages 180–181). Chicken is done when juices run clear if thickest part of thigh is pierced with fork.

As a rule of thumb, cook whole chicken on Medium (50% power) for 7–9 minutes per 450 g. Place bird breast side down, covered with greaseproof or waxed paper for half of cooking time; turn breast side up for remaining time.

If using thermometer, remove chicken when it reads 82–85°C (180–185°F); on standing, temperature will rise to 85–87°C (185–190°F). Always tent bird with foil to help hold in heat.

COOKING POULTRY PIECES

Poultry skin is high in calories and cholesterol. Replacing it with melted butter or margarine and a crumb coating is healthier, helps keep poultry moist and improves its appearance. If you like, use a rack underneath pieces to keep them free of pan juices.

COOKING DUCKLINGS

The microwave is ideal for turning out delicious duck. Before microwaving, pierce skin of duckling in many places to allow fat to drain and to prevent skin from splitting during cooking.

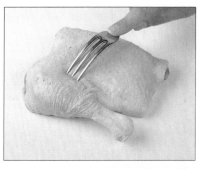

Loosely cover crumb-coated poultry with greaseproof or waxed paper, otherwise crumbs will become soggy. For best results, cook poultry pieces of about same size – pieces of different densities cook unevenly.

Places pieces on microwave-safe rack in microwave-safe baking dish to allow excess fat to drain off; turn frequently during cooking.

Arrange meatier portions towards edges of dish and bonier parts towards centre, rearranging halfway through cooking. Overcooking of boneless chicken breasts can be prevented by tucking thin ends under so that breasts cook evenly.

Leg portions take longer to cook than breast portions. Baste during cooking or serve with a sauce when finished.

Browning Chicken

Small poultry pieces do not look the same cooked in the microwave as they do when cooked conventionally. One reason is that the bird's fat does not have time to get hot enough to caramelise in the short microwave cooking time, which is the way conventionally cooked poultry becomes crisp and brown on the surface.

Another reason poultry pieces do not brown is because all the fat is just below the skin's surface, unlike with some meat, which is marbled with fat throughout. Larger birds, however, do brown because of their prolonged cooking time.

Great-tasting microwaved poultry sometimes needs a little help to make it look at its best. Commercial products such as browning agents, bottled sauces and dry coatings can be used to add colour, or the poultry pieces can be finished off under a conventional grill. Alternatively, a microwave browning dish can be used to cook poultry pieces from start to finish.

With honey and parsley glaze

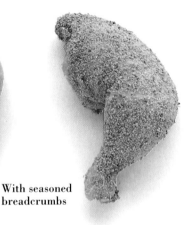
With seasoned breadcrumbs

With butter and paprika

With soy sauce

BROWNING CONVENTIONALLY AND WITH BROWNING DISH

Microwaved chicken pieces can be finished under a conventional grill for a few minutes until skin browns and crisps.

Using a microwave browning dish to cook small poultry pieces is another way to brown and crisp the surface. The dish is preheated to a high temperature and oil or fat heated on it. Uncooked pieces are then placed on the dish, and the combination of high temperature and hot oil or fat gives the food a crisp, brown finish.

Finishing microwaved chicken pieces under the conventional grill

These chicken pieces have been cooked in the microwave. Although completely cooked, they still look pale because there was insufficient time for the surfaces to brown.

After microwaving, place chicken pieces on grill pan and brown under preheated grill until skin is crisp and coloured. Turn pieces over halfway through grilling.

Using a browning dish

Preheat browning dish according to manufacturer's instructions; this heats up a concealed metal plate. When hot, add butter, margarine or oil according to recipe. *Do not touch dish.*

When butter or margarine is melted or oil is hot, add chicken piece with tongs; press lightly with spatula or fish slice. Cook according to recipe instructions, until underneath is browned.

With tongs, carefully turn chicken piece over. Continue cooking according to recipe until other side is browned and juices run clear. If cooking in batches, it may be necessary to reheat dish.

SAUCES

Adding extra colour to poultry pieces is easy to do by coating the skin with a sauce. Thin liquid preparations such as soy, teryaki and browning sauces are best diluted with a little water, oil, or melted butter or margarine, then lightly rubbed into the skin with the fingers. Thicker, stickier sauces, such as barbecue sauce and honey-based mixtures, jellies and glazes are best applied with a brush.

Barbecue sauce   Browning sauce   Redcurrant jelly   Honey

Rubbing in sauce

Dilute soy or browning sauce with a little water, oil or melted butter or margarine; this makes coating easier and also softens the flavour.

Before cooking, place chicken on plate or board; dip fingers into diluted sauce and gently rub into skin, covering surface completely.

Brushing with honey and lemon

Into honey, stir chopped herbs. Squeeze in lemon juice. Heat on High (100% power) for 30 seconds, to make glaze easier to apply.

Begin cooking chicken according to recipe. Towards end of cooking, brush with glaze; if applied too early, honey in glaze may burn.

DRY PREPARATIONS

Adding dry preparations before cooking enhances chicken pieces with extra colour and texture. The pieces can be brushed with melted butter or margarine, or oil, then sprinkled with powders or with dry microwave browning mixtures. Prepared coating mixes or breadcrumbs are applied after first dipping chicken pieces into beaten egg or milk. If you like, drizzle with melted butter or margarine.

Seasoned breadcrumbs   Prepared coating mix   Paprika   Microwave browning

Coating with crumbs

With tongs, dip chicken in lightly beaten egg or milk, coating evenly; shake off any excess.

In another dish, place seasoned bread-crumbs or prepared coating mix. Pat evenly on to chicken.

Sprinkling on powders

With pastry brush, lightly brush chicken with melted butter or margarine, or oil, to help powder stick to skin.

With chicken on plate, lightly sprinkle with powder. Paprika gives a colourful finish.

Jointed Chicken

COQ AU VIN

Colour Index page 56. 404 cals per serving. Good source of vitamin A, riboflavin, niacin, iron, fibre. Begin 55 minutes ahead.

Ingredients	For 4	For 2	For 1
Smoked bacon, diced	115 g	50 g	25 g
Carrots, diced	2 carrots	1 carrot	½ carrot
Mushrooms, cut into quarters	225 g	115 g	50 g
Chicken, jointed and skinned	1 × 1.1 kg	450 g	225 g
Frozen baby onions, thawed	125 g	60 g	30 g
Chopped tomatoes, canned	120 ml	60 ml	2 tablespoons
Dry red wine	250 ml	120 ml	60 ml
Dried thyme	¾ teaspoon	½ teaspoon	¼ teaspoon
Pepper	to taste	to taste	to taste
Cold butter, diced	45 g	30 g	15 g
Microwave cookware	32.5 × 22.5 cm baking dish	30 × 20 cm baking dish	20 cm square baking dish
Time on High (100% power)			
Smoked bacon	4 minutes	3 minutes	2 minutes
With vegetables	3 minutes	2 minutes	2 minutes
With chicken	15–20 minutes	10–12 minutes	8 minutes

1 In baking dish (see Chart), place bacon. Cook, covered with kitchen paper, on High for time in Chart, or until crisp, stirring twice.

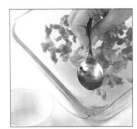

2 With spoon, discard excess fat from baking dish.

3 To bacon, add carrots and mushrooms. Cook on High for time in Chart, or until tender, stirring halfway through cooking.

4 To baking dish, add chicken, arranging in single layer over bacon and vegetables.

5 To chicken, add baby onions, tomatoes, wine and thyme. Cook, covered, on High for time in Chart, or until chicken juices run clear, rearranging pieces halfway through cooking.

6 Transfer chicken to warmed dish. Allow to stand, covered, while finishing sauce. Add pepper to sauce, then gradually whisk in cold butter until well blended. Spoon over chicken.

CHICKEN PAPRIKASH

Colour Index page 56. 4 servings. 468 cals per serving. Good source of vitamin A, niacin, vitamin C, iron, fibre. Begin 35 minutes ahead.

60 g butter or margarine
2 onions, sliced
1 medium red pepper, thinly sliced
2 tablespoons plain flour
1 × 400 g can tomatoes
1 tablespoon paprika
2 tablespoons tomato purée
1 chicken stock cube
60 ml water
1 × 1.1 kg chicken, jointed
Chives to garnish

1. In shallow 2.5 litre microwave-safe casserole, place butter or margarine, onions and red pepper. Cook, covered, on High (100% power) for 6–7 minutes, until tender-crisp, stirring twice.
2. Into onion and pepper mixture, stir flour. Add tomatoes with liquid and next 4 ingredients. Add chicken, arranging thicker, meatier pieces towards edges. Over chicken, spoon tomato sauce. Cook, covered, on High for 18–20 minutes, until juices run clear, rearranging pieces halfway through cooking. Skim fat. Allow to stand for 5 minutes; garnish.

LEMON CHICKEN

Colour Index page 56. 4 servings. 355 cals per serving. Good source of niacin, iron. Begin 45 minutes ahead.

4 tablespoons lemon juice
3 tablespoons olive or vegetable oil
1 garlic clove, crushed
25 g canned pimientos, thinly sliced
1 teaspoon dried basil
¼ teaspoon pepper
1 × 1.4 kg chicken, jointed and skinned
120 ml Chicken Stock (page 125) or stock from a cube
1 tablespoon cornflour dissolved in 2 tablespoons cold water
Salt to taste
45 g Melba Toast Crumbs (page 196) or golden dried breadcrumbs
1 teaspoon finely chopped lemon zest
Lemon Twists (page 132) and parsley sprigs to garnish

1. In 2.5 litre microwave-safe casserole, place lemon juice, 2 tablespoons oil, garlic, pimientos, basil and pepper. Add chicken pieces; stir to coat. Arrange chicken so that thicker, meatier pieces are towards edges of casserole. Add stock.
2. Cook chicken, covered, on High (100% power) for 15–18 minutes, until juices run clear, rearranging pieces occasionally. Stir in dissolved cornflour. Cook on High for 3 minutes, or until slightly thickened. Season with salt.
3. In mixing bowl, combine remaining oil, crumbs and lemon zest; sprinkle over chicken. Cook on High for 2 minutes. Allow to stand for 5 minutes; garnish.

CHICKEN CACCIATORE

Colour Index page 56. 4 servings. 560 cals per serving. Good source of thiamine, niacin, vitamin C, calcium, iron, fibre. Begin 45 minutes ahead.

2 tablespoons olive or vegetable oil	60 g stoned green olives, sliced
2 onions, chopped	1/2 × 450 g jar sauce for
1 medium green pepper, chopped	pasta (without meat)
2 garlic cloves, crushed	120 ml Chicken Stock (page 125)
1 tablespoon bottled pesto sauce or 2 teaspoons dried basil	1 × 1.1 kg chicken, jointed and skinned
1/2 teaspoon dried oregano	225 g spaghetti
	Salt and pepper to taste
	Basil leaves to garnish

1. In 2.5 litre microwave-safe casserole, combine oil, onions, green pepper, garlic, pesto sauce or basil and oregano. Cook on High (100% power) for 3–5 minutes, until onions and green pepper are slightly softened, stirring twice. Into onion mixture, stir olives, pasta sauce and stock.

2. To casserole, add chicken, arranging thicker, meatier pieces towards edges. Cook, covered, on High for 18–20 minutes, until chicken juices run clear, rearranging pieces halfway through cooking.

3. Meanwhile, cook spaghetti conventionally according to instructions on packet. Drain.

4. *To serve:* skim fat from chicken. Season with salt and pepper; allow to stand for 5 minutes. Arrange spaghetti and chicken on warmed dinner plates. Spoon sauce over chicken and garnish.

SPICY CRUMBED CHICKEN

Colour Index page 55. 4 servings. 277 cals per serving. Good source of niacin, iron. Begin 25 minutes ahead.

2 tablespoons Dijon mustard	1/2 teaspoon poultry seasoning
1 tablespoon clear honey	1/2 teaspoon paprika
1 tablespoon tomato purée	1/2 teaspoon celery salt
45 g golden dried breadcrumbs	Cayenne pepper to taste
	1 × 1.1 kg chicken, jointed and skinned

1. In mixing bowl, combine Dijon mustard, honey and tomato purée. On greaseproof paper, combine breadcrumbs and next 4 ingredients.

2. Coat chicken pieces, one at a time, in mustard and honey mixture, then roll in seasoned breadcrumbs.

3. In 32.5 × 22.5 cm microwave-safe baking dish, arrange chicken so that thicker, meatier pieces are towards edges. Cook, covered loosely with greaseproof paper, on High (100% power) for 11–13 minutes, until chicken juices run clear, rearranging pieces once. Allow to stand on heatproof surface for 5 minutes before serving.

These recipes using jointed whole chicken are also suitable for pieces of your choice – breasts, drumsticks or thighs – as long as their weight equals that of the chicken called for in the recipe.

CHICKEN MARENGO

Colour Index page 56. 524 cals per serving. Good source of riboflavin, niacin, iron, fibre. Begin 45 minutes ahead.

Ingredients for 4 servings		Microwave cookware
3 tablespoons olive or vegetable oil	1 × 230 g can chopped tomatoes	32.5 × 22.5 cm baking dish
2 onions, chopped	4 tablespoons chopped parsley	
225 g mushrooms, sliced	150 g shelled cooked prawns, thawed if frozen	
1/2 teaspoon dried rosemary	Parsley sprigs to garnish	
70 g plain flour	Hot Cooked Rice (page 293, optional)	
1/4 teaspoon salt		
Pepper to taste		
1 × 1.25 kg chicken, jointed		
250 ml dry white wine		

1 In frying pan over medium-high heat, heat 1 tablespoon oil. Add onions, mushrooms and rosemary. Cook until onions are golden, stirring occasionally. With slotted spoon, transfer onion mixture to baking dish.

2 On greaseproof paper, combine flour, salt and pepper. Coat chicken pieces in seasoned flour. In same frying pan, heat remaining oil. Add chicken and cook for 5 minutes, or until browned on all sides.

3 On top of onion mixture, arrange chicken so that thicker, meatier pieces are towards edges of dish. Discard oil from pan; pour in wine. Over medium heat, stir to loosen any sediment. Add tomatoes and parsley. Cook until mixture boils, stirring occasionally.

4 Over chicken pieces, pour tomato mixture. Cook, covered, on High (100% power) for 10–12 minutes, until chicken juices run clear, rearranging pieces halfway through cooking.

5 To chicken mixture, add prawns; spoon over cooking liquid. Cook on High for 1–2 minutes, just until prawns are hot.

6 *To serve:* arrange chicken and prawns on warmed serving dish or platter. Spoon over sauce and garnish with parsley. If you like, serve with rice.

Meal in Minutes *for 6 people*

French Bistro Dinner

French Onion Soup, page 131
Coq au Vin, page 182, for 6
Tossed mixed salad
French bread
French apple tart (bought) with whipped cream
Coffee or Espresso, page 130

PREPARATION TIMETABLE

Early in day or 2 hours ahead	*Prepare soup up to end of step 2; cover and refrigerate. Prepare salad ingredients; store in polythene bags in refrigerator. Prepare salad dressing of your choice.*
1 hour ahead	*Make Coq au Vin; keep warm. If you like, transfer to warmed casserole dish with cover.*
15 minutes ahead	*Ladle soup into microwave-safe bowls. Heat on High (100% power) until bubbling; complete recipe. Place salad ingredients in bowl and toss with dressing.*
Just before serving	*If you like, heat French bread on High for 1 minute. Whip cream to serve with French apple tart. Prepare coffee or Espresso to serve with or after apple tart.*

HONEY-SOY CHICKEN

Colour Index page 55. 4 servings. 530 cals per serving. Good source of vitamin A, niacin, vitamin C, iron. Begin 25 minutes ahead.

1 × 1.4 kg chicken, jointed	*2 tablespoons water*
4 tablespoons clear honey	*1 × 425 g can straw mushrooms or 1 can whole mushrooms, drained*
¼ teaspoon ground ginger	
1 garlic clove, crushed	*1 tablespoon sesame or vegetable oil*
2 tablespoons soy sauce	*1 tablespoon sesame seeds*
225 g mange-touts	
1 carrot, thinly sliced	*Coriander to garnish*

1. In 30 × 20 cm microwave-safe baking dish, arrange chicken so that thicker, meatier pieces are towards edges. In mixing bowl, combine honey, ginger, garlic and half of soy sauce; brush half over chicken. Cook, covered loosely with greaseproof paper, on High (100% power) for 13–15 minutes, until chicken juices run clear, re-arranging pieces once. Brush pieces with remaining mixture. Allow to stand, covered, while preparing vegetables.
2. In large microwave-safe bowl, place mange-touts, carrot and water. Cook, covered, on High for 4 minutes; drain. Stir in mushrooms, oil, sesame seeds and remaining soy sauce. Cook on High for 1–1½ (1:30) minutes, until hot. Arrange chicken and vegetable mixture on warmed serving platter; garnish with coriander. Serve immediately while piping hot.

QUICK CHICKEN STEW

Colour Index page 56. 4 servings. 597 cals per serving. Good source of vitamin A, niacin, vitamin C, iron, fibre. Begin 45 minutes ahead.

450 g potatoes	*½ teaspoon dried thyme*
3 carrots	*¼ teaspoon salt*
1 onion, chopped	*¼ teaspoon pepper*
325 ml chicken stock, made from a cube	*3 tablespoons plain flour*
	250 g frozen green beans
1 × 1.1 kg chicken, jointed	*Chopped thyme or dill sprigs to garnish*

1. Cut potatoes into 2.5 cm chunks; cut carrots lengthways into quarters, then crossways into 5 cm pieces. In 4 litre microwave-safe casserole, combine potatoes, carrots, onion and stock, reserving 80 ml. Place chicken on top so that thicker, meatier pieces are towards edges, sprinkle with thyme, salt and pepper. Cook, covered, on High (100% power) for 18 minutes, stirring occasionally.
2. Into reserved stock, stir flour until well blended; add to chicken mixture with frozen green beans; stir well. Cook, covered, on High for 8–10 minutes, until chicken and vegetables are tender, stirring once. Allow to stand on heatproof surface for 5 minutes. Spoon stew on to warmed serving plates and garnish.

Chicken Breasts

CHICKEN FRICASSÉE

Colour Index page 57. 4 servings. 455 cals per serving. Good source of vitamin A, riboflavin, niacin, calcium, iron, fibre. Begin 55 minutes ahead.

60 g butter or margarine
1 onion, chopped
½ teaspoon poultry seasoning
35 g plain flour
750 ml milk
450 g chicken breasts, skinned and boned

150 g each: frozen peas, baby carrots and diagonally cut green beans, thawed
2 egg yolks
Pepper to taste

1. In 2 litre microwave-safe casserole, place butter or margarine. Heat, covered with kitchen paper, on High (100% power) for 45 seconds–1 minute, until melted. Add onion and poultry seasoning. Cook on High for 2–3 minutes, until onion softens.
2. Into onion, stir flour. Cook on High for 1 minute. Gradually stir in milk until smooth. Cook on High for 10–12 minutes, stirring often.
3. Cut chicken into 4 cm chunks; add to sauce with vegetables. Cook on High for 10–12 minutes, until juices run clear, stirring twice.
4. In mixing bowl, lightly beat egg yolks. Stir in 120 ml cooking liquid until smooth. Return to chicken; stir. Cook on Medium (50% power) for 3 minutes, or until thickened, stirring twice; add pepper. Allow to stand, covered, for 5 minutes.

HERB AND CHEESE CHICKEN BREASTS

Colour Index page 58. 8 servings. 548 cals per serving. Good source of vitamin A, niacin, vitamin C, iron, fibre. Begin 35 minutes ahead.

225 g cream cheese, softened
2 tablespoons milk
2 spring onions, finely chopped
2 tablespoons finely chopped parsley
½ teaspoon dried thyme
Salt and pepper to taste
1 garlic clove, crushed
8 chicken breasts, boned

30 g dried breadcrumbs
1 teaspoon paprika
30 g butter or margarine, melted
1 head endive
575 g asparagus, cooked
350 g cherry tomatoes
120 ml vinaigrette dressing

1. In mixing bowl, combine first 8 ingredients.
2. Push fingers between skin and meat of each chicken breast to form pocket. Spread equal amount of cream cheese mixture in each pocket.
3. On greaseproof paper, combine breadcrumbs and paprika. Into melted butter, dip chicken breasts; roll in seasoned breadcrumbs to coat.
4. In 32.5 × 22.5 cm microwave-safe baking dish, place chicken. Cook, covered loosely with greaseproof paper, on High (100% power) for 15 minutes, or until fork-tender, rotating dish halfway through cooking.
5. Arrange chicken, endive, asparagus and tomatoes on platter. Serve dressing separately.

POACHED CHICKEN WITH VEGETABLES

Colour Index page 57. 324 cals per serving. Good source of niacin, iron, fibre. Begin 40 minutes ahead.

Ingredients	For 4	For 2	For 1
Butter or margarine	30 g	15 g	2 teaspoons
Vinaigrette dressing	60 ml	2 tablespoons	1 tablespoon
Leeks, sliced	4 small	2 small	1 small
Mushrooms, cut in half	115 g	50 g	25 g
Canned or bottled artichoke hearts, drained	250 g	125 g	60 g
Chicken Stock (page 125) or stock from a cube	250 ml	120 ml	60 ml
Chicken breasts, skinned and boned	4 breasts	2 breasts	1 breast
Cornflour	1 tablespoon	1½ teaspoons	¾ teaspoon
Cold water	2 tablespoons	1 tablespoon	1 teaspoon
Salt and pepper	to taste	to taste	to taste
Microwave cookware	32.5 × 22.5 cm baking dish	30 × 20 cm baking dish	20 cm square baking dish
Time on High (100% power) Vegetable mixture	4–5 minutes	3 minutes	2 minutes
With chicken	8–10 minutes	5–6 minutes	3–4 minutes
With cornflour	3 minutes	2–3 minutes	1–2 minutes

1 In baking dish (see Chart), place butter or margarine, vinaigrette, leeks, mushrooms and artichokes. Cook on High for time in Chart, or until vegetables are softened, stirring twice; stir in stock.

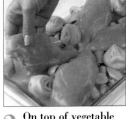

2 On top of vegetable mixture, arrange chicken so that thicker, meatier pieces are towards edges of dish.

3 Cook chicken, covered, on High for time in Chart, turning chicken over halfway through cooking.

4 To test if chicken is cooked, pierce with fork. Chicken is done when juices run clear.

5 With tongs or slotted spoon, carefully transfer chicken breasts to warmed serving platter. Allow to stand, covered, while finishing sauce. Dissolve cornflour in water. Pour into baking dish; stir until well blended. Cook mixture on High for time in Chart, or until thickened. Season with salt and pepper.

6 To serve: spoon vegetables and sauce over chicken breasts.

185

Chicken Breasts

Stuffed chicken breasts are extremely versatile, and any number of different fillings are suitable. They can be prepared well in advance and kept refrigerated until ready for cooking. The breasts should be pounded until thin, then folded over the filling with the thinner ends tucked under. Use wooden cocktail sticks to hold in the filling if necessary.

BROCCOLI-STUFFED CHICKEN BREASTS

Colour Index page 57. 341 cals per serving. Good source of vitamin A, niacin, vitamin C, calcium, iron, fibre. Begin 45 minutes ahead.

Ingredients for 6 servings		Microwave cookware
275 g frozen broccoli, thawed	60 g fresh breadcrumbs	32.5 × 22.5 cm baking dish
2 spring onions, finely chopped	1 tablespoon finely chopped parsley	Medium bowl
115 g mild Cheddar cheese, grated	1/2 teaspoon paprika	
6 large chicken breasts, skinned, boned and pounded to 5 mm thickness	3 tablespoons melted butter or margarine	
	1 tablespoon plain flour	
	Salt and pepper to taste	
3 × 25 g slices cooked ham, cut in half	250 ml milk	
	Parsley sprigs to garnish	

1 Chop thawed broccoli and drain well; place in mixing bowl. To broccoli, add onions and half of cheese.

2 On each pounded chicken breast, place 1 piece ham. Top with equal amounts of broccoli mixture.

3 Carefully fold chicken in half over broccoli filling; neatly tuck ends under.

4 In pie plate or on greaseproof paper, combine breadcrumbs, parsley and paprika. Brush chicken with melted butter or margarine, using about 1 tablespoon. Coat chicken with breadcrumb mixture.

5 In baking dish, place chicken. Cook, covered loosely with greaseproof paper, on High (100% power) for 10–12 minutes, until fork-tender, rotating dish once. Arrange chicken on warmed dinner plates or platter. Allow to stand, covered, while preparing sauce.

6 In medium bowl, place remaining melted butter or margarine. Add flour, salt and pepper; mix well. Gradually stir in milk. Cook on High for 3 1/2 (3:30) minutes, or until boiling, stirring twice. Add remaining cheese; stir until melted. Spoon round chicken; garnish.

CHICKEN KIEV

Colour Index page 56. 4 servings. 359 cals per serving. Good source of niacin. Begin 55 minutes ahead.

4 large chicken breasts, skinned and boned	30 g butter or margarine
Salt and pepper to taste	1 egg yolk
	45 g dried breadcrumbs
60 g chilled butter, cut into four 5 × 1 cm sticks	2 garlic cloves, crushed
	2 tablespoons chopped parsley
	1/2 teaspoon paprika

1. On cutting board, with dull edge of large knife or smooth edge of meat mallet, pound each chicken breast to 5 mm thickness. Season with salt and pepper. Place 1 stick butter lengthways in centre of each chicken breast. Fold ends over butter; roll up Swiss roll fashion so that butter is enclosed. Secure with cocktail sticks if necessary. Freeze the chicken breasts for 30 minutes, then remove cocktail sticks.

2. In small microwave-safe bowl, place 30 g butter or margarine. Heat, covered with kitchen paper, on High (100% power) for 45 seconds, or until melted. Stir in egg yolk. On greaseproof paper, combine breadcrumbs, garlic, parsley and paprika. Dip well chilled chicken pieces into butter or margarine and egg mixture; coat with breadcrumb mixture.

3. In 30 × 20 cm microwave-safe baking dish, place chicken pieces, at least 2.5 cm apart. Cook, covered loosely with greaseproof paper, on High for 8–9 minutes, until fork-tender, rotating dish halfway through cooking. Allow to stand for 4 minutes before serving.

TO MAKE CHICKEN KIEV FOR TWO, USE: *2 chicken breasts, 30 g chilled butter, 15 g butter or margarine, 1 egg yolk, 25 g dried breadcrumbs, 1 crushed garlic clove, 1 tablespoon chopped parsley and 1/4 teaspoon paprika.* Prepare as above, melting butter or margarine on High for 30–45 seconds and cooking chicken, covered loosely with greaseproof paper, in 20 cm square baking dish on High for 6–7 minutes. Allow chicken to stand for 3 minutes.

Preparing the Butter and Chicken Breasts

Chill butter thoroughly before use. With sharp knife, cut butter into 4 sticks, each measuring 5 × 1 cm.

With dull edge of large knife or smooth edge of meat mallet, pound chicken breasts to 5 mm thickness.

CHICKEN WITH CRANBERRIES AND WALNUTS

Colour Index page 58. 6 servings. 335 cals per serving. Good source of niacin, fibre. Begin 35 minutes ahead.

125 g cranberries	*2 tablespoons grated*
120 ml orange juice	*orange zest*
3 tablespoons sugar	*6 chicken breasts,*
3 tablespoons port	*skinned and boned*
¼ teaspoon salt	*5 tablespoons clear*
90 g walnuts, finely	*honey*
chopped	*1 tablespoon Orange*
25 g dried breadcrumbs	*Julienne (page 330)*

1. In 1 litre microwave-safe measuring jug, place 100 g cranberries, orange juice, sugar and port. Cook on High (100% power) for 4–6 minutes, until cranberries begin to pop, stirring twice. In food processor with knife blade attached or in blender, process mixture until smooth. Over medium microwave-safe bowl, press mixture through sieve; reserve.
2. On greaseproof paper, mix salt, walnuts, breadcrumbs and orange zest. Brush chicken with honey; coat with walnut mixture. Arrange in 32.5 × 22.5 cm microwave-safe baking dish. Cook, covered loosely with greaseproof paper, on High for 10 minutes, or until fork-tender, rotating dish once.
3. To reserved cranberry mixture, add Orange Julienne and remaining cranberries. Cook on High for 2–3 minutes; serve with chicken.

CREAMY CHICKEN BREASTS

Colour Index page 55. 4 servings. 442 cals per serving. Good source of vitamin A, niacin. Begin 25 minutes ahead.

30 g butter or margarine	*2 tablespoons plain flour*
3 spring onions, sliced	*1 teaspoon mild curry*
225 g asparagus,	*powder*
trimmed and cut into	*250 ml double or*
2.5 cm pieces	*whipping cream*
4 chicken breasts,	
skinned and boned	

1. In 30 × 20 cm microwave-safe baking dish, place butter or margarine. Heat, covered with kitchen paper, on High (100% power) for 45 seconds, or until melted. Stir in spring onions and asparagus. Place chicken breasts on top, with thicker, meatier parts towards edges of dish. Cook on High for 5–7 minutes, just until chicken turns opaque. Transfer chicken to plate; cover and keep warm.
2. In mixing bowl, combine flour and curry powder. Add to vegetables; stir until blended. Cook on High for 1 minute. Gradually stir in cream until smooth. Cook on High for 4–5 minutes, until sauce thickens.
3. Return chicken to dish; spoon over sauce. Cook on High for 1–2 minutes, until juices run clear. Serve hot.

A crumbed coating helps keep skinned chicken moist and tender during cooking as well as making it more attractive. Because chicken breasts vary in density, they should be flattened uniformly so that they cook more evenly in the microwave. To help prevent chicken from sticking to knife or meat mallet when pounding, place it between 2 sheets of greaseproof paper.

CHICKEN BREASTS PARMESAN

Colour Index page 57. 381 cals per serving. Good source of vitamin A, niacin, calcium, iron, fibre. Begin 35 minutes ahead.

Ingredients for 4 servings		Microwave cookware
4 medium chicken breasts, skinned and boned	*½ teaspoon paprika*	Medium bowl
	1 large onion, chopped	32.5 × 22.5 cm
	1 garlic clove, crushed	baking dish
45 g butter or margarine	*1 × 400 g can chopped tomatoes*	
1 egg	*70 g stoned black olives, sliced*	
30 g dried breadcrumbs	*5–6 tablespoons shredded fresh basil leaves*	
50 g Parmesan cheese, grated	*Pepper to taste*	
½ teaspoon dried oregano	*Basil leaves to garnish*	

1 Cut each chicken breast in half crossways. With dull edge of large knife or smooth edge of meat mallet, pound each chicken piece to 5 mm thickness.

2 In medium bowl, place 30 g butter or margarine. Heat, covered with kitchen paper, on High (100% power) for 45 seconds, or until melted. Cool slightly; beat in egg.

3 On greaseproof paper, combine breadcrumbs, Parmesan, oregano and paprika. Dip chicken pieces in butter mixture, then coat in breadcrumbs.

4 In baking dish, place chicken. Cook, covered loosely with greaseproof paper, on High for 6–8 minutes, or until fork-tender, rearranging chicken halfway through cooking. Allow to stand, covered, while preparing sauce.

5 In bowl used to melt butter or margarine, place remaining butter or margarine, onion and garlic. Cook on High for 4 minutes, stirring halfway through cooking. Add tomatoes, olives, basil and pepper.

6 Cook sauce on High for 2–3 minutes, until hot, stirring to combine. Serve chicken with sauce. Garnish with basil leaves.

Meal in Minutes *for 6 people*

Bank Holiday Picnic

Potato crisps and pretzels
Sweetcorn Chowder, page 133, with brown rolls
Devilled Chicken, right (double quantity)
Garden Vegetable and Pasta Salad, page 280
Pecan Pie, page 349
Apples and pears

Chicken Pieces

DEVILLED CHICKEN

Colour Index page 55. 4 servings. 293 cals per serving. Good source of riboflavin, niacin, iron. Begin 25 minutes ahead.

2 tablespoons mayonnaise	1/2 teaspoon cayenne pepper
2 tablespoons made mustard	1/2 teaspoon garlic salt
45 g golden dried breadcrumbs	1.1 kg chicken drumsticks and/or thighs, skinned
1 tablespoon finely chopped parsley	Lemon wedges and parsley to garnish

1. In mixing bowl, combine mayonnaise and mustard. On greaseproof paper, combine breadcrumbs, parsley, cayenne pepper and garlic salt.
2. Brush chicken pieces with mayonnaise mixture, then coat with crumb mixture.
3. In 32.5 × 22.5 cm microwave-safe baking dish, place chicken so that thicker, meatier pieces are towards edges of dish. Cook, covered with greaseproof paper, on High (100% power) for 11–13 minutes, until chicken juices run clear, rearranging once. Allow to stand on heatproof surface for 3 minutes.
4. *To serve:* arrange chicken pieces on warmed serving platter; garnish with lemon wedges and parsley sprigs.

'BARBECUED' CHICKEN

Colour Index page 55. 4 servings. 386 cals per serving. Good source of niacin, vitamin C, iron. Begin 25 minutes ahead.

2 onions, thinly sliced	2 teaspoons Worcestershire sauce
1 green pepper, cut into matchstick-thin strips	1 teaspoon chilli powder
1 garlic clove, crushed	8 medium chicken thighs (about 900 g)
150 ml tomato ketchup	Parsley to garnish
2 tablespoons brown sugar	

1. Prepare barbecue sauce: in medium microwave-safe bowl, place onions, green pepper, garlic, ketchup, brown sugar, Worcestershire sauce and chilli powder. Cook, covered, on High (100% power) for 8–10 minutes, until vegetables are tender, stirring twice; cover and set aside.
2. In 30 × 20 cm microwave-safe baking dish, arrange chicken thighs in single layer so that thicker, meatier pieces are towards edges of dish. Cook chicken, covered, on High for 10 minutes, rearranging halfway through cooking; discard drippings.
3. Over chicken, spoon barbecue sauce. Cook on High for 6–8 minutes, until chicken juices run clear, rearranging once.
4. *To serve:* arrange chicken thighs on warmed dinner plates. Garnish with parsley.

PREPARATION TIMETABLE

1 day ahead	*Make Devilled Chicken in batches; cool. Pack in portable container lined with kitchen paper; refrigerate. Make Sweetcorn Chowder; cover and refrigerate. Make Pecan Pie; cool. Pack in airtight container. Cook vegetables for salad; cover and refrigerate. Pack plates, napkins, cutlery and cups. Wrap fruit; pack potato crisps and pretzels.*
Early in day	*For salad, cook pasta conventionally; toss with vegetables and dressing and pack in portable container. Pack brown rolls in airtight container.*
Just before leaving	*Reheat Sweetcorn Chowder in microwave on Medium-High (70% power) for 5 minutes or until piping hot. Pour into wide-necked flask and seal tightly.*

Cooked Chicken

CURRIED CHICKEN THIGHS

Colour Index page 59. 4 servings. 233 cals per serving. Good source of niacin, calcium. Begin 1 day ahead.

250 ml plain yogurt	4 chicken thighs,
2 teaspoons curry	skinned
powder	45 g dried breadcrumbs
2 garlic cloves, crushed	2 tablespoons corn oil
1 tablespoon finely	Lime wedges and mint
chopped fresh	sprigs to garnish
coriander, basil or	
parsley	

1. In large microwave-safe bowl, combine yogurt, curry powder, garlic and coriander, basil or parsley. To mixture, add chicken thighs; stir to coat. Cover and refrigerate for 12–24 hours.
2. Thirty minutes before serving, remove chicken from marinade; set marinade aside in bowl. Coat chicken with breadcrumbs.
3. Preheat browning dish according to manufacturer's instructions; brush with oil. On dish, arrange chicken spoke-fashion. Cook on High (100% power) for 5 minutes. With tongs, turn chicken over. Cook on High for 5–7 minutes, until juices run clear. Allow to stand on heatproof surface while preparing sauce.
4. Cook marinade in bowl on Medium (50% power) for 3–4 minutes, until hot, stirring halfway through cooking. Spoon marinade on to warmed dinner plates; arrange chicken on top. Garnish with lime and mint and serve.

CHICKEN LIVERS WITH TOMATO SAUCE

Colour Index page 55. 4 servings. 219 cals per serving. Good source of vitamin A, riboflavin, niacin, vitamin C, iron. Begin 25 minutes ahead.

30 g butter or margarine	1 onion, finely chopped
450 g chicken livers, cut	2 tablespoons fruity
in half	brown sauce
½ × 225 g can chopped	½ teaspoon dried
tomatoes	oregano
60 ml Beef Stock (page	½ teaspoon dried thyme
125) or stock from a	Parsley to garnish
cube	

1. In 30 × 20 cm microwave-safe baking dish, place butter or margarine. Heat, covered with kitchen paper, on High (100% power) for 45 seconds, or until melted. Pierce chicken livers. Add to dish; stir. Cook, covered with kitchen paper, on High for 2–4 minutes, until livers lose raw appearance, stirring once. Remove livers.
2. To drippings in baking dish, add tomatoes, stock, onion, fruity sauce, oregano and thyme. Cook on High for 10 minutes, or until flavours blend and sauce thickens, stirring twice. Return chicken livers to baking dish. Cook on High for 1–2 minutes, until hot.
3. Spoon livers and sauce on to warmed dinner plates; garnish and serve immediately.

Cooked chicken can be combined with other ingredients and ready to serve in a matter of minutes. For Chicken à la King (below), you can use leftovers from any cooked whole chicken or pieces. Or, if you like, you can use the simple cooking method on page 178 for fresh chicken that adds only a few additional minutes cooking time.

CHICKEN À LA KING

Colour Index page 55. 568 cals per serving. Good source of niacin, calcium, iron. Begin 25 minutes ahead.

Ingredients for 4 servings		Microwave cookware
60 g butter or margarine	250 ml Chicken Stock (page 125)	1 litre measuring jug
1 onion, finely chopped	300 g cooked chicken meat, cubed	
1 small green pepper, finely chopped	1 canned pimiento, diced	
8 small mushrooms, cut into quarters	2 egg yolks	
35 g plain flour	Salt and pepper to taste	
250 ml milk	8 medium or 4 large vol-au-vents, warmed	
1 tablespoon dry sherry	Dill sprigs to garnish	

1 In measuring jug, place butter or margarine. Heat, covered with kitchen paper, on High (100% power) for 45 seconds–1 minute, until melted.

2 To melted butter or margarine, add onion, green pepper and mushrooms; stir to coat. Cook on High for 3–4 minutes, until onion softens slightly.

3 Into vegetable mixture, stir flour until blended. Cook on High for 1 minute, stirring once.

4 Into vegetable mixture, gradually stir milk, sherry and stock, until evenly blended. Cook sauce to High for 4–6 minutes, until thickened, stirring twice. To sauce, add cubed chicken and diced pimiento; mix together gently. Cook on High for 3 minutes, or until chicken is hot. In mixing bowl, with whisk, beat egg yolks. Stir 4 tablespoons sauce from chicken into beaten egg yolks.

5 Into remaining chicken mixture, pour egg yolk mixture, beating rapidly to prevent lumping. Season with salt and pepper.

6 To serve: spoon chicken and sauce into warmed vol-au-vents; garnish with dill sprigs and serve immediately.

189

Cooked Chicken

CHICKEN CRÊPES FLORENTINE

Colour Index page 58. 410 cals per serving. Good source of vitamin A, riboflavin, niacin, calcium, iron, fibre. Begin 55 minutes ahead.

Ingredients	For 4	For 2	For 1
Basic White Sauce (page 381)	500 ml	250 ml	120 ml
Parmesan cheese, grated	40 g	3 tablespoons	4 teaspoons
Frozen chopped spinach, thawed	275 g	150 g	75 g
Garlic clove, crushed	1 clove	½ clove	¼ clove
Butter or margarine	15 g	1½ teaspoons	1 teaspoon
Salt and pepper	to taste	to taste	to taste
Cooked chicken, cubed	300 g	150 g	75 g
Crêpes (see Making and Freezing Crêpes, below right)	8 crêpes	4 crêpes	2 crêpes
Microwave cookware	32.5 × 22.5 cm baking dish	30 × 20 cm baking dish	20 cm square baking dish
Time on High (100% power)			
Spinach mixture	3–5 minutes	3 minutes	2 minutes
Filled crêpes with sauce	5–7 minutes	5–6 minutes	3–4 minutes

1 Prepare Basic White Sauce; into sauce, stir Parmesan cheese. On to surface of sauce, lightly press dampened greaseproof paper, to prevent skin from forming; set aside and keep warm.

2 In baking dish (see Chart), place spinach, garlic and butter or margarine. Cook, covered with kitchen paper, on High for time in Chart, or until flavours blend, stirring twice. Season with salt and pepper.

3 Transfer spinach mixture to mixing bowl. To spinach mixture, add chicken; stir to combine. Clean baking dish with kitchen paper.

4 Place 1 crêpe at a time on work surface. Spoon equal amount of spinach and chicken mixture on to each crêpe.

5 Roll up each crêpe to enclose filling. In cleaned baking dish, place crêpes, seam side down, at least 5 mm apart.

6 Over filled crêpes, pour sauce. Cook on High for time in Chart, until bubbling. If you like and if dish is flameproof, brown under preheated grill.

CHICKEN RATATOUILLE

Colour Index page 58. 4 servings. 346 cals per serving. Good source of vitamin A, niacin, vitamin C, calcium, iron, fibre. Begin 40 minutes ahead.

2 tablespoons olive or vegetable oil
2 garlic cloves, crushed
1 large onion, chopped
1 medium green pepper, chopped
4 courgettes, preferably 2 yellow and 2 green, cut into 4 cm chunks
1 teaspoon dried basil
1 teaspoon dried oregano
300 g cooked chicken, cubed
1 × 230 g can chopped tomatoes
Salt and pepper to taste
115 g mozzarella cheese, grated
Parsley sprigs to garnish

1. In 32.5 × 22.5 cm microwave-safe baking dish, place oil, garlic, onion, green pepper, courgettes, basil and oregano; stir to combine. Cook, covered, on High (100% power) for 5 minutes. Uncover; stir. Cook on High for 5–10 minutes longer, until vegetables are tender, stirring twice during cooking.
2. To vegetable mixture, add chicken and tomatoes; stir to combine. Season with salt and pepper. Sprinkle with cheese. Cook on High for 5–7 minutes, until mozzarella cheese is melted and cubed chicken is hot, rotating baking dish halfway through cooking time.
3. If you like and if dish is flameproof, brown Chicken Ratatouille under preheated grill until cheese is bubbling and golden. Serve hot on warmed dinner plates, or cover and refrigerate to serve chilled later. Just before serving, garnish with parsley sprigs.

MAKING AND FREEZING CRÊPES

In bowl, whisk **95 g plain flour**, **¼ teaspoon salt** and **3 eggs** until smooth. Slowly whisk in **350 ml milk** and **1½ tablespoons melted butter** or **margarine**. Cover and refrigerate batter for 2 hours.

Brush bottom and sides of 18–20 cm frying pan with **melted butter** or **margarine**. Heat pan; pour in scant 60 ml batter. Tip pan to coat bottom. Over low heat, cook for 3 minutes, or until crêpe is set and underside browned. With fish slice, turn crêpe over; cook other side for 1 minute, or until golden. Slip crêpe on to greaseproof paper. Repeat with remaining batter to make 12 crêpes altogether, stacking with greaseproof paper between crêpes.

To freeze crêpes: wrap stack in foil; store in freezer for up to 2 months. To use, preheat conventional oven to 170°C (325°F, gas mark 3). Place wrapped, frozen crêpes on baking sheet; heat for 30 minutes, until hot.

Poussins

WHOLE STUFFED POUSSINS

Colour Index page 57. 2 servings. 1017 cals per serving. Good source of vitamin A, thiamine, riboflavin, niacin, calcium, iron, fibre. Begin 45 minutes ahead.

115 g small mushrooms, sliced
30 g butter or margarine
1 small courgette, shredded
50 g Gruyère cheese, grated
1 spring onion, chopped
Salt and pepper to taste
45 g long grain rice, cooked

2 × 575 g poussins
4 tablespoons parsley, thyme and lemon stuffing mix
1½ teaspoons paprika
Parsley sprigs and matchstick-thin strips of carrot and celery to garnish

1. In 1.5 litre microwave-safe casserole, place mushrooms and half of butter or margarine. Cook on High (100% power) for 2–2½ (2:30) minutes, stirring halfway through cooking. Into mushrooms, stir courgette, cheese, spring onion, salt, pepper and cooked rice; leave stuffing mixture to cool completely.
2. Rinse poussins under cold running water; pat dry with kitchen paper. Fill each bird's cavity with half of stuffing. Tie legs and tail of each bird with string. In small microwave-safe bowl, place remaining butter or margarine. Heat on High for 30–45 seconds, until melted. Brush melted butter or margarine on to birds.
3. On greaseproof paper, combine stuffing mix and paprika; use to coat poussins. On microwave-safe rack set in 30 × 20 cm microwave-safe baking dish, place birds. Cook, covered loosely with greaseproof paper, on High for 14–16 minutes, until juices run clear when birds are pierced with fork, rotating dish once. Allow to stand, covered, for 5 minutes.
4. To serve: remove string from poussins. Arrange birds on warmed plates. Garnish with parsley sprigs, carrot strips and celery.

Tying and Brushing the Poussins

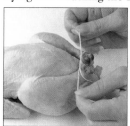

Using white cotton string, tie legs and tail of each bird. This prevents stuffing from falling out and gives bird a plump, attractive shape.

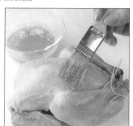

In small microwave-safe bowl, heat butter or margarine until melted. With pastry brush, apply butter or margarine all over surface of poussins. This helps coating to adhere to skin of birds.

POUSSIN HALVES WITH HERB STUFFING

Colour Index page 57. 708 cals per serving. Good source of niacin, iron. Begin 55 minutes ahead.

Ingredients	For 4	For 2	For 1
Poussins (575 g each)	4 poussins	2 poussins	1 poussin
Butter or margarine, softened	60 g	30 g	15 g
Garlic cloves, finely chopped	2 cloves	1 clove	1 small clove
Dried basil	1 teaspoon	½ teaspoon	¼ teaspoon
Dried thyme	1 teaspoon	½ teaspoon	¼ teaspoon
Dried oregano	1 teaspoon	½ teaspoon	¼ teaspoon
Worcestershire sauce	1 tablespoon	1½ teaspoons	1 teaspoon
Salt and pepper	to taste	to taste	to taste
Sautéed cherry tomatoes and basil leaves	garnish	garnish	garnish
Microwave cookware	32.5 × 22.5 cm baking dish with rack	32.5 × 22.5 cm baking dish with rack	20 cm square baking dish with rack
Time on High (100% power)	12–14 minutes each batch	12–14 minutes	7–10 minutes
Standing time	3–4 minutes	3–4 minutes	2–3 minutes

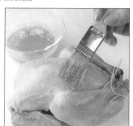

1 Rinse poussins under cold running water; pat dry with kitchen paper. Using kitchen scissors or sharp knife, cut each bird in half lengthways.

2 In small bowl, combine butter or margarine, garlic, basil, thyme and oregano; mix well.

3 One at a time, place half a bird on work surface, with breastbone facing towards you. Work fingers under skin at top of breast to make pocket, taking care not to tear skin.

6 Brush birds with Worcestershire sauce. Cook, covered loosely with greaseproof paper, on High for time in Chart, until juices run clear when birds are pierced with fork, rotating dish once. Season with salt and pepper. Allow to stand for time in Chart. Arrange poussin halves on warmed serving platter; garnish with tomatoes and basil leaves.

4 Into each pocket, spoon equal amount of garlic and herb mixture.

5 On rack in baking dish (see Chart), arrange poussins, breasts towards centre. If cooking for 4, cook birds in 2 batches.

Duckling

DUCKLING with ORANGE SAUCE

Colour Index page 59. 810 cals per serving. Good source of thiamine, riboflavin, niacin, iron. Begin 1½ hours ahead.

Ingredients for 4 servings		Microwave cookware
1 × 2.3 kg fresh or frozen (thawed) duckling, cut into quarters 1 orange 3 tablespoons cider vinegar 2 tablespoons sugar 350 ml Chicken Stock (page 125) or stock from a cube	2 teaspoons cornflour dissolved in 1 tablespoon cold water 2 tablespoons lemon juice 2 tablespoons brandy Salt and pepper to taste Parsley and orange slices to garnish	32.5 × 22.5 cm baking dish with rack

1 Trim excess skin and fat from duckling pieces. Rinse pieces under cold running water. Pat dry with kitchen paper. With fork, pierce skin of each piece about 10 times; this allows fat to drain off and prevents skin from splitting during cooking.

2 On rack in baking dish, arrange leg quarters, skin side down, in opposite corners, with bones towards centre. Cook, covered, on Medium (50% power) for 20 minutes, turning pieces over once. Prick skin with fork; turn pieces over again, placing skin side down. Add breast quarters, skin side down.

3 Cook, covered loosely with greaseproof paper, on Medium-High (70% power) for 20 minutes, turning pieces over and pricking skin once. Uncover and cook on High (100% power) for 5 minutes, or until juices run clear. Cover and allow to stand while preparing sauce.

4 Prepare sauce: with vegetable peeler, remove zest from orange, leaving bitter white pith behind. Stack zest and cut into fine strips. Into small bowl, squeeze juice from orange.

5 In measuring jug, combine vinegar and sugar. Cook, covered, on High for 3–5 minutes, just until mixture turns light golden, watching carefully since mixture burns easily and continues to cook and darken when removed from oven. Into mixture, stir orange zest and juice and stock. Cook, covered, on High for 5 minutes. Into orange mixture, stir dissolved cornflour. Cook on High for 2–4 minutes, until sauce thickens. Add lemon juice and brandy. Season.

6 *To serve:* arrange duckling pieces on warmed dinner plates; pour over sauce. Garnish with parsley and orange slices and serve immediately.

APRICOT GLAZED DUCKLING

Colour Index page 59. 4 servings. 847 cals per serving. Good source of thiamine, riboflavin, niacin, iron. Begin 1¼ hours ahead.

2 tablespoons made mustard 6 tablespoons apricot jam 2 tablespoons soy sauce 1 garlic clove, crushed ½ teaspoon ground ginger	1 × 2.3 kg fresh or frozen (thawed) duckling, cut into quarters Parsley sprigs to garnish

1. In 1 litre microwave-safe measuring jug, combine mustard, apricot jam, soy sauce, garlic and ground ginger. Cook on High (100% power) for 2 minutes, stirring twice; set aside while preparing duckling pieces.

2. Trim excess skin and fat from duckling pieces. Rinse pieces under cold running water. Pat dry with kitchen paper. With fork, pierce skin of each piece about 10 times; this allows fat to drain off and prevents duckling skin from splitting during cooking time.

3. Cook duckling as for Duckling with Orange Sauce (left) up to end of step 3, brushing pieces with apricot glaze twice in step 3, after skin has been pricked and when duckling is uncovered. Allow duckling to stand for 5 minutes.

4. If you like and if dish is flameproof-safe, place duckling under preheated grill for a few minutes to crisp up. Garnish dish with parsley sprigs before serving.

POULTRY GLAZES

Brushing whole birds or pieces with a glaze gives poultry an attractive appearance, as does brushing with melted butter or margarine mixed with chopped herbs or spice powders. Allow about 120 ml glaze for 1.8–2.7 kg birds, 250 ml for larger birds, and brush on poultry towards end of cooking; if applied too early, glaze may burn. For information on Browning Chicken, see pages 180–181.

Honey Barbecue Glaze: in 500 ml microwave-safe measuring jug, mix *120 ml clear honey, 1 tablespoon soy sauce* and *½ teaspoon ground ginger.* Heat on Medium-High (70% power) for 1 minute, stirring halfway through cooking. Makes about 120 ml.

Jelly Glaze: in 500 ml microwave-safe measuring jug, place *120 ml redcurrant jelly.* Heat on Medium-High (70% power) for 1 minute, stirring halfway through cooking. Makes 120 ml.

DUCKLING WITH OLIVES AND ALMONDS

Colour Index page 59. 4 servings. 818 cals per serving. Good source of thiamine, riboflavin, niacin, iron, fibre. Begin 1¼ hours ahead.

1 × 2.3 kg fresh or frozen (thawed) duckling, cut into quarters *3 onions, cut into 1 cm wedges* *150 g almond-stuffed green olives, or 115 g green stoned olives, and 35 g blanched almonds*	*350 ml Beef Stock (page 125) or stock from a cube* *3 tablespoons dry sherry* *2 teaspoons cornflour dissolved in 1 tablespoon cold water* *Salt and pepper to taste* *Lemon slices and coriander to garnish*

1. Cook duckling as for Duckling with Orange Sauce (opposite page) up to end of step 3. Transfer to warmed serving dish and allow to stand, covered, while preparing sauce.
2. Remove rack from baking dish and pour off all but 3 tablespoons dripping. Add onion wedges; stir. Cook on High (100% power) for 3–5 minutes, just until onions soften, stirring twice. Add almond-stuffed olives or olives and almonds; stir to coat. Cook on High for 1 minute.
3. Into mixture, stir stock. Cook on High for 3–4 minutes, until boiling, stirring twice. Stir in sherry and dissolved cornflour. Cook on High for 2–4 minutes, until sauce thickens, stirring occasionally. Season with salt and pepper. Pour sauce over duckling and garnish.

DUCKLING WITH CHERRY SAUCE

Colour Index page 59. 4 servings. 778 cals per serving. Low in sodium. Good source of thiamine, riboflavin, niacin, iron. Begin 1¼ hours ahead.

1 × 2.3 kg fresh or frozen (thawed) duckling, cut into quarters *1 tablespoon plain flour* *60 ml Chicken Stock (page 125) or stock from a cube*	*60 ml dry red wine* *1 × 225 g can cherries in syrup* *½ garlic clove, crushed* *1 tablespoon lemon juice* *Pepper to taste* *Watercress sprigs to garnish*

1. Cook duckling as for Duckling with Orange Sauce (opposite page) up to end of step 3. Transfer to warmed serving dish and allow to stand, covered, while preparing sauce.
2. Into 1 litre microwave-safe measuring jug pour 2 tablespoons duck dripping; add flour and stir until blended. Cook on High (100% power) for 30 seconds.
3. Into flour mixture, stir stock, wine, cherries with their syrup and garlic. Cook on High for 3–5 minutes, until sauce thickens, stirring twice.
4. Into cherry sauce, stir lemon juice; season with freshly ground black pepper. Spoon sauce over duckling and garnish.

When preparing duckling dishes that call for breasts only, it is important to remove skin and fat first. Because of the shortness of microwave cooking time, the fat does not have enough time to melt out and drain off, therefore the skin will not crisp. A browning dish will give the meat a more attractive appearance.

DUCK BREASTS WITH APPLE AND GREEN PEPPERCORNS

Colour Index page 58. 226 cals per serving. Good source of thiamine, niacin, iron. Begin 40 minutes ahead.

Ingredients for 4 servings		Microwave cookware
4 boneless duck breasts *1 dessert apple* *1 tablespoon sugar* *1 tablespoon vegetable oil* *1 teaspoon green peppercorns in brine, drained*	*120 ml Chicken Stock (page 125) or stock from a cube* *½ teaspoon cornflour dissolved in 1 teaspoon cold water* *Salt and pepper to taste* *Parsley to garnish*	Browning dish

1 Remove skin and fat from duck breasts; discard. Preheat browning dish according to manufacturer's instructions.

2 Meanwhile, core apple and cut into about 20 slices. In mixing bowl, combine apple slices and sugar. Brush browning dish with oil. Arrange duck breasts on browning dish.

3 Cook duck breasts on High (100% power) for 2–3 minutes, until rare, turning halfway through cooking. Transfer to warmed plate. Allow to stand, covered, while preparing sauce.

4 Reheat browning dish. Arrange apple slices in single layer on browning dish. Cook on High for 2 minutes. With tongs, transfer apple slices to warmed plate; set aside. Reheat browning dish; add peppercorns and stock. Cook on High for 3 minutes, or until bubbling.

5 To peppercorns and stock, add cornflour; stir. Cook on High for 2 minutes, or until sauce thickens. Season with salt and pepper.

6 *To serve:* cut each duck breast into slices and arrange on warmed dinner plate with apple slices; spoon over sauce. Garnish with parsley sprigs and serve immediately.

Meal in Minutes *for 8 people*

Harvest Supper

Curried Crab Dip, page 111 (double quantity), with
crudités and olives
Turkey Breast with Chestnut Stuffing, page 195
Cranberry Sauce, page 379
Mashed swede and mixed autumn vegetables
Sticky Walnut Tart, page 349, with whipped cream (optional)

MEXICAN PANCAKES

Colour Index page 57. 4 servings. 580 cals per serving. Good source of vitamin A, riboflavin, niacin, vitamin C, calcium, iron, fibre. Begin 45 minutes ahead.

450 g turkey breast fillets	*1 × 198 g can sweetcorn, drained*
1 teaspoon ground cumin	*8 crêpes (see Making and Freezing Crêpes, page 190)*
¼ teaspoon ground cloves	
1 tablespoon lime juice	*1 × 400 g can chopped tomatoes or passatta*
2 tablespoons groundnut or vegetable oil	*1 tablespoon double cream*
1 onion, chopped	*115 g mild Cheddar cheese, grated*
1 medium green pepper, chopped	*Lime wedges and coriander sprigs to garnish*
2 tomatoes, chopped	
2 tablespoons chopped fresh coriander	

1. Cut turkey breast into 4 cm chunks. In mixing bowl, combine turkey, cumin, cloves and lime juice. Allow to stand for 5 minutes.
2. Meanwhile, in large microwave-safe bowl, combine oil, onion, green pepper and tomatoes. Cook on High (100% power) for 3 minutes, or until softened, stirring twice.
3. To onion mixture, add turkey mixture and coriander. Cook on High for 6–8 minutes, just until turkey turns white, stirring twice. Into turkey mixture, stir sweetcorn.
4. Place 1 crêpe at a time on work surface. Spoon equal amount of turkey mixture on to each crêpe. Roll up each crêpe to enclose filling. In 32.5 × 22.5 cm microwave-safe baking dish, place crêpes, seam side down, at least 5 mm apart.
5. In medium microwave-safe bowl, combine tomatoes and cream. Cook on High for 4 minutes, or until hot and slightly reduced, stirring twice.
6. Over filled crêpes, pour sauce. Cook on High for 8–10 minutes, rotating dish halfway through cooking. Sprinkle cheese on top; garnish.

ITALIAN-STYLE PANCAKES: make as for Mexican Pancakes (above), using **1 crushed garlic clove, ½ teaspoon dried oregano, 1 tablespoon lemon juice** and **1 tablespoon bottled pesto sauce** in step 1 instead of the cumin, cloves and lime juice, and substituting **chopped fresh basil or parsley** for the coriander in step 3. Omit the sweetcorn in step 3 and use **1 × 300 g can red kidney beans, drained and rinsed**, together with **50 g diced mozzarella cheese**. In step 6, sprinkle over **2 tablespoons each grated Parmesan and pine nuts** instead of Cheddar cheese; garnish with **basil leaves** rather than lime and coriander.

PREPARATION TIMETABLE

1 day ahead	*Prepare dip, cover and refrigerate. Cut crudités; store in polythene bags in refrigerator. Make Cranberry Sauce, spoon into serving dish; cover and refrigerate.*
1¾ hours ahead	*Cook turkey and stuffing. Make tart. Cook swede and autumn vegetables conventionally; mash swede. Spoon swede and vegetables into microwave-safe serving dishes.*
10 minutes ahead	*While turkey is standing, arrange crudités and olives on platter; spoon dip into bowl. Reheat swede and autumn vegetable selection on High (100% power).*
Just before serving	*If you like, whip cream to serve with tart; spoon into piping bag and pipe decorative design on top of tart.*

Turkey breast, available as a roasting joint in some large supermarkets, is ideal for microwaving and, because cooking time is long enough, the skin will brown if cooked with butter or margarine and browning sauce. If you like, try a different stuffing (see Stuffings for Poultry, right), microwaving it separately in a casserole until thermometer registers 73°C (165°F).

TURKEY BREAST WITH CHESTNUT STUFFING

Colour Index page 59. 390 cals per serving. Good source of niacin, iron, fibre. Begin 1³/₄ hours ahead.

Ingredients for 8 servings		Microwave cookware
1 × 1.1–1.4 kg fresh turkey breast joint 115 g butter or margarine ¹/₂ teaspoon browning sauce 1 onion, chopped 2 celery sticks, chopped 180 g fresh bread cubes 70 g sultanas	2 tablespoons chopped parsley 1 × 450 g can whole chestnuts, drained 1¹/₂ teaspoons poultry seasoning Pepper to taste Parsley sprigs to garnish	32.5 × 22.5 cm baking dish

1 Rinse turkey joint; pat dry. In baking dish, place 60 g butter or margarine. Heat, covered with kitchen paper, on High (100% power) for 45 seconds–1 minute, until melted. Add browning sauce; stir.

2 Into browning sauce mixture in baking dish, place turkey breast joint, skin side down. With pastry brush, evenly coat skin of turkey with browning sauce mixture. Cook turkey breast joint, covered, on Medium (50% power) for 12–15 minutes per 450 g (about 1¹/₄–1¹/₂ hours).

3 Meanwhile, in frying pan over medium heat, melt remaining butter or margarine. Add onion and celery. Cook until softened, stirring occasionally.

4 Remove frying pan from heat; stir in bread cubes, sultanas, parsley, chestnuts, poultry seasoning and pepper. Toss to mix well; set aside.

5 About 20–30 minutes before end of calculated cooking time for turkey, carefully transfer turkey to plate. Add chestnut stuffing to turkey drippings in baking dish. Stir well to combine with drippings.

6 Place turkey joint, skin side up, on top of chestnut stuffing. Continue cooking, covered, on Medium for 20–30 minutes, until thermometer inserted in centre of joint reaches 70°C (160°F), rotating dish twice.

7 On heatproof surface, allow turkey and stuffing to stand in dish, tented with foil, for 10 minutes. Turkey will continue to cook and will reach 76°C (170°F) on meat thermometer.

8 *To serve:* place turkey joint on large warmed platter. Spoon stuffing round turkey. Garnish with parsley sprigs.

STUFFINGS FOR POULTRY

Shorten preparation time for stuffings by microwaving some of the ingredients, then cook stuffed large birds conventionally, or microwave stuffing separately on High (100% power) in a 30 × 20 cm baking dish until thermometer inserted in centre reaches 73°C (165°F). Spinach and Ricotta Stuffing takes 10 minutes; Bacon and Rice Stuffing takes 3 minutes.

Spinach and Ricotta Stuffing: in deep, large microwave-safe bowl, place **115 g diced butter or margarine**. Heat, covered with kitchen paper, on High (100% power) for 1¹/₂ (1:30)–2 minutes, until melted. Stir in **115 g thinly sliced mushrooms, 2 diced celery sticks** and **1 small chopped onion**. Cook, covered, on High for 3–4 minutes, until vegetables soften, stirring twice. Stir in **275 g frozen chopped spinach, thawed, drained and squeezed dry, 225 g ricotta cheese, 180 g fresh breadcrumbs, 1 egg, 1 tablespoon chopped parsley, ¹/₂ teaspoon poultry seasoning** and **pepper to taste**; mix well.

Bacon and Rice Stuffing: cook **175 g long grain rice** conventionally according to instructions on packet. Meanwhile, in 32.5 × 22.5 cm microwave-safe baking dish, place **12 diced rindless streaky bacon rashers**. Cook, covered with kitchen paper, on High (100% power) for 4–5 minutes, until browned, stirring twice. Transfer to kitchen paper to drain. Discard all but 3 tablespoons bacon fat; add **1 diced onion**. Cook, covered, on High for 2 minutes, or until softened. Stir in cooked rice and bacon.

Turkey

TURKEY ROLLS WITH CHEESE FILLING

Colour Index page 58. 470 cals per serving. Good source of vitamin A, niacin, calcium, iron. Begin 35 minutes ahead.

Ingredients	For 4	For 2	For 1
Sun-dried tomatoes (drained if packed in oil), chopped	4 tomatoes	2 tomatoes	1 tomato
Full-fat soft cheese with garlic and herbs	115 g	50 g	25 g
Mozzarella cheese, grated	25 g	2 tablespoons	1 tablespoon
Fresh basil leaves, shredded	4 leaves	2 leaves	1 leaf
Turkey breast fillets (75–115 g each)	4 fillets	2 fillets	1 fillet
Butter or margarine	30 g	15 g	2 teaspoons
Dried breadcrumbs	45 g	25 g	2 tablespoons
Salt	1/4 teaspoon	pinch	pinch
Microwave cookware	Small bowl 30 × 20 cm baking dish	Small bowl 30 × 20 cm baking dish	Small bowl 20 cm square baking dish
Time on High (100% power) Butter	45 seconds	30–45 seconds	15–30 seconds
Turkey	6–9 minutes	4–6 minutes	2½ (2:30)– 3½ (3:30) minutes
Standing time	4 minutes	3 minutes	2 minutes

1 In mixing bowl, combine chopped tomatoes, cheeses and basil; stir until blended.

2 If fillets come in more than one piece, slightly overlap. Spoon equal amount of filling on end of each.

3 Roll up fillets Swiss roll fashion. Secure with wooden cocktail sticks.

4 In bowl (see Chart), place butter or margarine. Heat, covered with kitchen paper, on High for time in Chart, or until melted.

5 In shallow dish or on greaseproof paper, mix breadcrumbs and salt. Dip turkey rolls in melted butter or margarine; coat in breadcrumbs.

6 In baking dish, arrange rolls, 2.5 cm apart. Cook, covered loosely with greaseproof paper, on High for time in Chart, until tender. Stand for time in Chart.

TURKEY AND NOODLE BAKE

Colour Index page 58. 4 servings. 700 cals per serving. Good source of vitamin A, thiamine, riboflavin, niacin, calcium, iron, fibre. Begin 55 minutes ahead.

225 g tagliatelle
45 g butter or margarine
3 tablespoons plain flour
500 ml milk
250 ml Chicken Stock (page 125) or stock from a cube
1 teaspoon poultry seasoning
4 slices Melba toast
3 medium celery sticks, diced
3 spring onions, sliced
275 g frozen peas, thawed
450 g turkey breast fillets, cut into 4 cm chunks
120 ml soured cream

1. Cook noodles conventionally according to instructions on packet. Drain and keep warm.
2. In 32.5 × 22.5 cm microwave-safe baking dish, place butter or margarine. Heat, covered with kitchen paper, on High (100% power) for 45 seconds–1 minute, until melted. Stir in flour until blended. Gradually stir in milk and stock; add poultry seasoning. Cook on High for 8–10 minutes, until sauce thickens, stirring twice.
3. Meanwhile, make Melba Toast Crumbs: place toasts in strong polythene bag. With rolling pin, roll until finely crushed.
4. Into sauce, stir celery, spring onions, peas, turkey chunks and noodles. Cook, covered, on High for 8 minutes, stirring twice. Add soured cream; stir well. Cook, covered, on Medium (50% power) for 5–8 minutes, rotating dish halfway through cooking.
5. Sprinkle with Melba Toast Crumbs. Cook on High for 2 minutes. Serve hot.

Making the Melba Toast Crumbs

Place Melba toasts in strong polythene bag. With rolling pin, go over bag until Melba toasts are finely crushed. Alternatively, process toasts in food processor with knife blade attached, or in blender, until finely crushed.

Meat

DEFROSTING AND COOKING MEAT · BEEF
QUICK OUTDOOR COOKING · FAST FOOD · PORK
MICROWAVING BACON · HAM · VEAL · LAMB · SAUSAGES
SAUSAGE SNACKS

Meat

Meat cooked in the microwave is generally tastier and juicier than if conventionally cooked and, of course, it is ready much sooner. Overcooking, especially on large rolled roasts, can be prevented by shielding ends with foil for part of the cooking time, which also ensures that the roast cooks evenly. Thinner ends of meat should always be shielded, as should bony portions. Small cuts cook successfully on High (100% power), but larger cuts, especially roasting joints, are more tender when cooked at a lower power level.

Meat that is well marbled with fat and contains even layers of fat on the outside will cook more evenly and will be more tender. Drippings, which attract microwave energy away from the meat, should be removed at intervals to prevent spatters and speed cooking.

Roasts with a good, even fat covering will brown due to their longer cooking times. Steaks, which are cooked for a shorter time, are best cooked on a browning dish to sear them attractively while retaining their tenderness. Hamburgers are best when prepared with a coating mixture, which will make them as flavoursome as grilled or barbecued burgers. Standing time is important for larger cuts as it allows them to complete cooking, and the internal temperature of the meat to rise to its final desired temperature. Temperature guidelines given in recipes should be followed when testing to see if meat is done (this is especially true of pork); appearance is not enough, as meat can look underdone although it is fully cooked.

Choose evenly shaped cuts: roasts should have a regular diameter; meat for stews and casseroles should be cut to uniform size; steaks, chops and cutlets should be of the same density throughout. For even cooking, turn roasts and stir or rotate casseroles. Arrange irregular pieces of meat with thicker ends towards edges of dish. Use a rack, if directed, to prevent meat from cooking unevenly in its own juices.

NEW WAYS WITH HAMBURGERS

A simple hamburger quickly cooked in the microwave can be dressed up with a variety of popular accompaniments to create unusual and tasty variations.

Plain burger in bagel, topped with raw onion rings (left). Served with coleslaw, potato salad, gherkin fan and stuffed olives.

Cheeseburger (page 209) on round of wholemeal toast, topped with goat's cheese slices (right). Served with radish and salad leaves.

Defrosting Meat

Defrosting frozen foods is one of the great uses of a microwave oven. It must be done carefully, however, if quality is to be retained. It is important to defrost meat evenly, to prevent some parts starting to cook before others have completely defrosted. Use a Medium-Low (30% power) or Defrost power level, or manually turn your oven on and off, allowing heat to even out during 'rest' periods.

DEFROSTING A LARGE ROASTING JOINT

Remove all wrapping quickly from frozen meat. This speeds defrosting because wrapping insulates bottom of roast.

Place meat on microwave-safe rack in microwave-safe baking dish, so meat does not sit in juices which could cause surface to start cooking.

Check for warm areas as meat defrosts, and shield these with smooth pieces of foil during defrosting; remove foil before starting to cook.

Using containers to fit
If transferring meat from packet to dish, choose one which fits food as closely as possible; this prevents defrosted edges from spreading out and starting to cook.

Separating pieces
As soon as possible, separate frozen burgers, steaks or other pieces which have been stacked; place in single layer on microwave-safe rack.

Breaking up minced beef
Break up minced beef with a fork as it defrosts; scrape off defrosted parts and set aside.

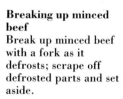

Covering with greaseproof or waxed paper
Covering meat loosely with greaseproof or waxed paper while defrosting helps retain heat for speedier defrosting.

Separating cubes/strips
As soon as sufficiently defrosted, separate cubes and strips of meat and arrange separately in dish, removing pieces as they defrost.

Testing with skewer
Thick meat cuts are defrosted when skewer can go through thickest part to centre.

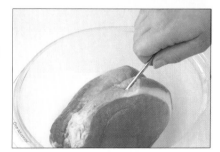

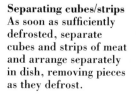

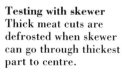

Cooking Meat

Careful choice and preparation of meat is essential for successful microwaving, and an understanding of how microwave ovens work helps explain most of the techniques. Microwave energy cooks food quickly but not evenly. Therefore, whenever possible, choose evenly-sized pieces of meat, or trim meat to make it more uniform in size; at the same time, trim fat so it is evenly distributed over the meat.

Arrange unevenly shaped pieces with thicker parts towards edges of dish where they will cook faster. Thin ends of meat, bone and cut edges tend to overcook, so shield them with smooth strips of foil.

PREPARING MEAT FOR MICROWAVE COOKING

Removing excess fat from minced meat
Before proceeding with recipe, place meat in microwave-safe colander set over microwave-safe bowl; cook on High (100% power); discard drippings from bowl. For 450 g beef, cook 4 minutes, stirring twice.

Even fat covering
While a certain amount of fat is desirable to tenderise and add flavour to meat, it should be evenly distributed as well as of uniform thickness; this helps meat cook evenly.

Trimming meat to size
Uniformity of size is important for even cooking in the microwave oven. If meat cubes are required, cut them to a uniform size.

Slashing sausages
To prevent frankfurters, sausages and other foods with skins or casings from bursting during cooking due to steam building up, slash or pierce them before cooking in the microwave.

Even diameter
Boned and rolled roasting joints that are not uniform in diameter should be unrolled, then trimmed and pounded to even them out before rolling them up again.

Tenderising roasts
Roasting joints, which cook more quickly in the microwave than in the conventional oven, benefit from meat tenderiser. Sprinkle meat with water, rub on tenderiser, then pierce with fork so that tenderiser penetrates surface of meat.

SHIELDING

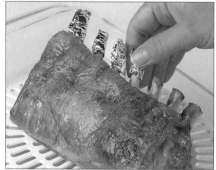

Ends of meat
To prevent cut ends of roasting joints from overcooking, shield with smooth 5 cm wide strips of foil. Remove or retain these during cooking as necessary. Shield 'hot spots' in same way.

Exposed bones
To prevent overcooking, shield bony areas or ends of bones such as those on lamb best end of neck with smooth strips of foil.

Long, thin sides of steaks
If steaks are irregular in size, shield longer sides with smooth, narrow strips of foil, to prevent them from overcooking. Remove foil halfway through cooking.

BROWNING

Browning conventionally
Meat that will not brown during microwaving – for example, a pot roast cooked in a roasting bag – can be first browned conventionally in a frying pan.

Coatings and browning agents
Coat meat with beaten egg and a dry topping such as breadcrumbs or herbs, or brush meat before and during cooking with a browning agent or glaze.

Browning dish
Browning dishes are used to sear and brown meat such as cutlets, chops, steaks and burgers while they are in the microwave.

COOKING TECHNIQUES FOR MEAT

Racks and trivets
Placing meat on rack prevents it from sitting and steaming in cooking juices and fats. Racks and trivets should also be used to elevate denser meat so microwaves reach bottom of food and it cooks more uniformly.

Standing time
It is important to let meat stand to complete cooking after removal from microwave; internal temperatures will rise 5°C–8°C during standing.

Roasting bags
Less tender meat cuts are best cooked in liquid, and roasting bags are ideal for this. Use plastic, nylon or cotton ties and vent to allow steam to escape; do not use metal ties.

Tenting
Keep meat warm during standing time by tenting with foil, shiny side in, or greaseproof or waxed paper.

Using a mould
A ring mould allows microwaves to penetrate from all sides, ensuring even cooking. This is especially important in dishes such as meat loaves that cannot be stirred.

Freezer-to-table casseroles
Fit smooth foil on to frozen surface. Place on microwave-safe rack; cook on High (100% power), rotating a quarter turn every 5 minutes until defrosted. Discard foil and continue cooking until piping hot and bubbling.

Beef Roasts

When choosing beef for cooking in the microwave oven, make sure there is an even marbling of fat throughout, for even cooking and moist, tender results.

ROAST FILLET OF BEEF WITH HERBS

Colour Index page 63. 170 cals per serving. Low in sodium, fat. Good source of vitamin B₁₂, niacin, iron, zinc. Begin 45 minutes ahead.

Ingredients for 10 servings		Microwave cookware
1 × 1.1 kg beef fillet roasting joint Water 1¼ teaspoons meat tenderiser 4 tablespoons dried breadcrumbs 1 tablespoon dried thyme 1 tablespoon dried oregano	1 tablespoon dried basil 1 tablespoon steak pepper ½ teaspoon garlic powder 2 tablespoons Dijon mustard Radishes and basil leaves to garnish	30 × 20 cm baking dish with rack 3 wooden cocktail sticks

1 Moisten meat with water; rub evenly with meat tenderiser. With fork, pierce meat deeply all over.

2 On rack in baking dish, place meat. Shield ends with smooth 5 cm wide strips of foil. Cook, covered loosely with greaseproof paper, on Medium (50% power) for 25 minutes, turning once and removing foil halfway through cooking.

3 Meanwhile, in small mixing bowl, combine breadcrumbs, thyme, oregano, basil, steak pepper and garlic powder.

4 Remove greaseproof paper from meat; turn meat over. Spread mustard evenly over meat and sprinkle with herb mixture; press with your fingers so that herbs adhere to mustard.

5 Along top of meat, insert 3 cocktail sticks, evenly spaced, about 2.5 cm deep. Cover meat with greaseproof paper, tenting paper over sticks. Cook on Medium for 7–10 minutes, or until meat thermometer inserted in centre of roast reaches 50°C (120°F) for medium-rare.

6 On heatproof surface, allow joint to stand, covered, for 5–8 minutes. Temperature will reach 57°C (135°F). Thinly slice beef across grain. Arrange on warmed serving platter and garnish with radishes and basil leaves. Skim fat from meat juices; serve separately in gravy boat.

ROAST RIB OF BEEF

Colour Index page 66. 6 servings. 274 cals per serving. Low in sodium. Good source of niacin, iron. Begin 1¼ hours ahead.

1 2-rib beef wing rib roasting joint, about 1.6 kg, with chine bone removed 1 teaspoon pepper 1 teaspoon dried thyme 1 teaspoon onion powder	½ teaspoon paprika 1 tablespoon vegetable oil Salt and pepper to taste Fresh thyme leaves to garnish

1. Trim any large areas of fat from meat.
2. In small mixing bowl, combine pepper, thyme, onion powder and paprika. Rub seasonings evenly over meat.
3. In frying pan over high heat, heat oil until very hot. Add meat and brown on all sides. On microwave-safe rack in 32.5 × 22.5 cm microwave-safe baking dish, place meat.
4. Shield ends of bone with smooth strips of foil. Cook on Medium (50% power) for 30–40 minutes, until meat thermometer inserted in centre of roast reaches 50°C (120°F) for medium-rare, removing foil halfway through cooking.
5. Transfer roast to warmed serving platter; tent with foil and allow to stand for 15–20 minutes. Temperature will reach 54–57°C (130–135°F). Season with salt and pepper.
6. Sprinkle roast with thyme leaves and serve with meat juices.

CARVING RIB OF BEEF

After cooking, rib of beef needs to stand 15–20 minutes – to complete cooking and allow juices to settle; this makes for easier carving. Transfer meat to warmed serving platter and tent with foil. Allow to stand while preparing gravy or last-minute vegetables. With practice, and good carving utensils, any roast can be carved on a garnished serving platter.

For easy carving of rib of beef at the table, it is essential to remove the chine bone before cooking – your butcher will do this for you. After standing time, cut meat into 5 mm thick slices with sharp carving knife; use long-tined fork to prevent roast from slipping on platter while carving. Transfer slices to warmed dinner plates; continue carving until all guests are served.

Beef Stir-Frys

STIR-FRIED BEEF IN OYSTER SAUCE

Colour Index page 64. 4 servings. 227 cals per serving. Good source of vitamin B$_{12}$, niacin, iron, zinc. Begin 35 minutes ahead.

450 g rump or fillet steak	5 tablespoons Beef Stock (page 125) or stock from a cube
1 tablespoon soy sauce	
1 tablespoon rice wine or dry sherry	2 tablespoons bottled oyster sauce
1 tablespoon vegetable oil	1–2 teaspoons cornflour dissolved in 1 tablespoon cold water
1 red pepper, cut into 2 cm pieces	
2.5 cm piece root ginger, peeled and cut into matchstick-thin strips	2 spring onions, thinly sliced

1. With sharp knife, cut steak across grain into thin strips. Place in mixing bowl. Add soy sauce and rice wine or sherry; stir well to mix. Cover the meat and leave to marinate in a cool place for 10–15 minutes.
2. Preheat browning dish according to manufacturer's instructions. Coat surface of browning dish with oil.
3. With slotted spoon, drain meat strips from marinade; place meat on browning dish. Press lightly with fish slice or spatula and stir quickly to brown meat. Cook on High (100% power) for 1–2 minutes, until beef is fork-tender. Transfer to plate; set meat aside and keep warm while preparing oyster sauce.
4. To drippings on browning dish, add red pepper, ginger, stock, oyster sauce, marinade from beef and cornflour. Cook on High for 1–2 minutes, or until mixture boils, stirring twice. Add spring onion slices and beef strips; cook on High for 1 minute, or until beef is hot. Serve immediately.

TIMETABLE FOR COOKING BEEF

Beef may look underdone when removed from microwave, so allow it to stand, tented with foil, to achieve its final temperature. As a general rule, remove it from microwave when the temperature is 5°C–8°C lower than temperature you require.

Beef	Remove at	Will rise to
Medium-rare	46°C–51°C	51°C–60°C
Medium	54°C–60°C	60°C–68°C
Well done	65°C–71°C	71°C–77°C

BEEF AND MANGE-TOUTS IN BLACK BEAN SAUCE

Colour Index page 64. 314 cals per serving. Good source of vitamin B$_{12}$, niacin, iron, zinc. Begin 35 minutes ahead.

Ingredients for 4 servings		Microwave cookware
450 g rump or fillet steak	1 fresh green chilli	Large bowl
2 tablespoons soy sauce	2 cm piece root ginger	
2 tablespoons rice wine or dry sherry	1 tablespoon vegetable oil	
1 teaspoon sugar	4 tablespoons bottled black bean sauce	
2 teaspoons cornflour dissolved in 2 teaspoons cold water	Spring Onion Tassels (page 132) to garnish	
125 g mange-touts		
2 spring onions		

1 With sharp knife, cut steak across grain into thin strips. Place in mixing bowl. Add soy sauce, rice wine or sherry and sugar; stir well to mix. Into beef mixture, stir cornflour; cover and leave to marinate for 10–15 minutes.

2 Meanwhile, cut mange-touts in half crossways if large. Trim spring onions; slice thinly on diagonal.

3 Wearing rubber gloves for protection, cut fresh chilli in half lengthways. Hold chilli under cold running water and rub to remove seeds. Slice chilli thinly; peel and finely chop root ginger.

4 In large bowl, place oil. Heat on High (100% power) for 1 minute. Add mange-touts, spring onions, chilli, ginger and black bean sauce; stir well to mix. Cook on High for 1–2 minutes until vegetables soften, stirring halfway through cooking.

5 To vegetable mixture, add beef and marinade. Cook on High for 2–3 minutes, until beef is fork-tender, stirring twice.

6 Spoon beef and vegetables on to warmed serving platter or dinner plates. Garnish with Spring Onion Tassels and serve immediately.

Beef Steaks

Try using a browning dish to cook steak in the microwave. It will give the meat a seared look without sacrificing tenderness. Make sure you press the steak lightly with a fish slice or spatula for even browning, as in the recipe for Steak au Poivre (below). Don't forget to reheat browning dish if cooking steaks in batches.

STEAK AU POIVRE

Colour Index page 60. 313 cals per serving. Good source of niacin, iron. Begin 25 minutes ahead.

Ingredients	For 4	For 2	For 1
Whole black peppercorns	2 tablespoons	1 tablespoon	2 teaspoons
Beef fillet steaks, cut at least 2.5 cm thick (175 g each)	4 steaks	2 steaks	1 steak
Dry red wine	3 tablespoons	2 tablespoons	1 tablespoon
Worcestershire sauce	2 teaspoons	1 teaspoon	½ teaspoon
Brandy	2 tablespoons	1 tablespoon	1 teaspoon
Whipping cream	120 ml	60 ml	2 tablespoons
Microwave cookware	Browning dish	Browning dish	Browning dish
Time on High (100% power) Steak	4½ (4:30)– 6 minutes	3–4½ (4:30) minutes	2–3 minutes
Wine mixture	4 minutes	3–3½ (3:30) minutes	2–2½ (2:30) minutes

1 Place peppercorns in polythene bag. With mallet or rolling pin, crush peppercorns. On greaseproof paper, evenly spread crushed peppercorns.

2 Into crushed peppercorns, press both sides of each steak until evenly coated. Preheat browning dish according to manufacturer's instructions.

3 On preheated browning dish, arrange steaks, pressing lightly with fish slice to brown evenly.

4 Cook steaks on High for time in Chart, turning over halfway through cooking. Transfer to platter; loosely cover and keep warm while preparing sauce.

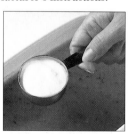

5 To browning dish, add wine, Worcestershire sauce, brandy and cream. Cook on High for time in Chart, or until sauce thickens, stirring twice.

6 *To serve:* place steaks on warmed dinner plates. Spoon sauce over steaks; serve immediately.

STEAK FORESTIÈRE

Colour Index page 60. 4 servings, 329 cals per serving. Good source of niacin, iron. Begin 25 minutes ahead.

2 rashers rindless streaky bacon, diced
4 beef fillet steaks, cut 2.5 cm thick
1 small onion, diced
4 mushrooms, cut into quarters
2 tomatoes, diced
60 ml Madeira
120 ml Beef Stock (page 125) or stock from a cube
½ teaspoon cornflour dissolved in 1 teaspoon cold water
Salt and pepper to taste

1. Preheat browning dish according to manufacturer's instructions. Add bacon. Cook on High (100% power) for 2–3 minutes, until bacon is browned, stirring halfway through cooking. With slotted spoon, transfer bacon to kitchen paper.
2. Reheat dish with bacon fat. Place steaks on dish, pressing lightly with fish slice. Cook on High for 3–4½ (4:30) minutes, turning over once. Transfer to platter; loosely cover and keep warm while preparing sauce.
3. Discard all but 1 teaspoon bacon fat. Add vegetables and stir to coat. Cook on High for 3–4 minutes, until softened, stirring twice. Add Madeira, stock and cornflour. Cook on High for 3–3½ (3:30) minutes, until sauce thickens, stirring halfway through cooking. Season and add reserved bacon. Place steaks on warmed dinner plates; spoon over sauce. Serve immediately.

STEAK WITH MUSHROOMS AND ARTICHOKES

Colour Index page 60. 4 servings, 374 cals per serving. Good source of riboflavin, niacin, iron, fibre. Begin 25 minutes ahead.

350 g mushrooms
1 × 397 g can artichoke hearts, drained and cut into halves
2 spring onions, chopped
30 g butter or margarine
1 tablespoon dry red wine
4 beef fillet steaks, cut 2.5 cm thick
½ teaspoon browning sauce
1 teaspoon dried mixed herbs
Salt and pepper to taste
Parsley to garnish

1. In 1 litre microwave-safe casserole, place mushrooms, artichokes and next 3 ingredients. Cook, covered, on High for 3 minutes, or until mushrooms are tender, stirring twice; set aside and keep warm.
2. On microwave-safe rack in microwave-safe baking dish, arrange steaks. In bowl, mix browning sauce with 1 teaspoon water. Brush on to both sides of meat; sprinkle with herbs and salt and pepper. Cook on Medium-High (70% power) for 6–8 minutes for medium-rare, rotating dish halfway through cooking.
3. Place steaks on warmed dinner plates. Spoon mushrooms and artichokes round steaks, garnish.

Beef Cubes and Strips

STEAK AND MUSHROOM PIE

Colour Index page 66. 8 servings. 317 cals per serving. Good source of iron. Begin 1¾ hours ahead.

30 g butter or margarine
4 small onions, sliced
225 g mushrooms, cut into quarters
700 g chuck steak, cut into 2.5 cm cubes
120 ml dry red wine
120 ml Beef Stock (page 125) or stock from a cube
2 tablespoons brown sauce

1 tablespoon tomato purée
2 tablespoons cornflour dissolved in 60 ml cold water
Salt and pepper to taste
225 g packet frozen shortcrust or puff pastry, thawed
1 egg yolk
Water

1. In shallow 21.5 cm microwave-safe pie dish, place butter or margarine. Heat, covered with kitchen paper, on High (100% power) for 45 seconds, or until melted. Add sliced onions and quartered mushrooms. Cook on High for 5–6 minutes, until onions are just softened but not browned, stirring twice.
2. To vegetables, add beef, wine, stock, brown sauce and tomato purée; stir until blended. Cook, covered, on Medium (50% power) for 40–60 minutes, until meat is fork-tender, stirring occasionally. Stir in dissolved cornflour. Cook on High for 2–3 minutes, until sauce thickens, stirring halfway through cooking; season. Allow mixture to cool completely.
3. Preheat conventional oven to 200°C (400°F, gas mark 6).
4. On lightly floured surface, with floured rolling pin, roll pastry into round about 5 cm larger than pie dish. Gently roll pastry on to rolling pin; place loosely over cooled meat mixture. With kitchen scissors, trim edge of pastry, leaving 2.5 cm overhang. Fold overhang under; bring up over dish rim; make Pastry Edge (page 340) of your choice.
5. Cut several slits in pastry top. In small cup, beat egg yolk with 1 teaspoon water. Brush pastry with egg yolk mixture. If you like, reroll pastry scraps and, with decorative cutter, cut out shapes; place on top of pie. Brush pastry shapes with a little egg yolk mixture. Bake pie conventionally for 20 minutes, or until pastry is light golden brown.

Decorating the Top of Pie

With tip of small sharp knife, slash pastry top to allow steam to escape.

Cut out leaves or other shapes and decorate top of glazed pie.

STEAK AND KIDNEY PUDDING

Colour Index page 66. 656 cals per serving. Good source of vitamin A, vitamin B₁₂, riboflavin, niacin, calcium, iron, zinc. Begin 1¼ hours ahead.

Ingredients for 4 servings		Microwave cookware
1 tablespoon vegetable oil 1 onion, chopped 225 g mushrooms, cut into halves 4 tablespoons plain flour 450 g rump steak, cut into thin strips 4 lamb kidneys, skinned, cored and cut into 1 cm pieces 250 ml red wine or Beef Stock (page 125) or stock from a cube ½ teaspoon dried thyme	¼ teaspoon pepper 1 bay leaf 2 tablespoons chopped parsley 100 g self-raising flour 50 g wholemeal flour 1 teaspoon baking powder ¼ teaspoon ground allspice Salt to taste 75 g shredded beef suet 1 egg, beaten 4–6 tablespoons water 1 tablespoon milk	Large bowl 1 litre pudding basin

1 In large bowl, place oil, onion and mushrooms. Cook on High (100% power) for 4–5 minutes, until onion and mushrooms are softened.

2 On large plate, place plain flour. Toss steak and kidneys in flour; stir into onion and mushroom mixture. Cook on High for 3–4 minutes. Stir in wine or stock, thyme, pepper and bay leaf. Cook, loosely covered, on High for 10 minutes, stirring occasionally. Discard bay leaf. Stir in parsley; cool.

3 Meanwhile, in large mixing bowl, combine self-raising and wholemeal flours, baking powder, allspice and salt; stir in shredded suet. Make well in centre; stir in egg and enough cold water to mix to soft dough. Knead dough lightly until smooth; form into ball.

4 Cut off one-quarter of pastry. On lightly floured surface, roll out into round to fit top of pudding basin; reserve. Roll out remaining pastry and use to line basin.

5 Into lined pudding basin, spoon steak and kidney mixture. Fold over excess pastry and dampen edges. Place pastry round on top; crimp edges together to seal. If you like, reroll pastry trimings and cut out shapes; place on top of pudding. Brush with milk to glaze.

6 Cover pudding basin loosely with microwave cling film, allowing for pastry to rise. Cook on High for 8–10 minutes, until pastry is done. Allow to stand, covered, for 5 minutes. Serve hot, from basin wrapped in table napkin.

Beef Cubes and Strips

BEEF BOURGUIGNON

Colour Index page 66. 449 cals per serving. Good source of vitamin A, riboflavin, niacin, iron. Begin 1¹/₂ hours ahead.

Ingredients for 4 servings		Microwave cookware
4 rashers rindless streaky bacon, diced 225 g mushrooms, cut into quarters 2 carrots, diced 2 celery sticks, diced 450 g chuck steak, cut into 4 cm cubes 250 ml dry red wine 250 ml Beef Stock (page 125) or stock from a cube	1 tablespoon tomato purée 1 teaspoon sugar 1 bay leaf ¹/₂ teaspoon dried thyme 225 g frozen baby onions, thawed 30 g butter or margarine, softened 2 tablespoons plain flour Salt and pepper to taste Parsley sprigs to garnish	32.5 × 22.5 cm baking dish

1 In baking dish, place diced bacon. Cook, covered with kitchen paper, on High (100% power) for 4–5 minutes, until bacon is browned, stirring twice. With slotted spoon, transfer bacon to kitchen paper to drain; keep warm.

2 To bacon fat in baking dish, add mushrooms, carrots and celery; stir to combine. Cook on High for 4–6 minutes, until vegetables are softened, stirring twice.

3 To vegetables, add beef; stir to coat with bacon fat. Add red wine, stock, tomato purée, sugar, bay leaf and thyme. Cook, covered, on Medium (50% power) for 45–55 minutes, until meat is fork-tender, stirring occasionally.

4 To beef and vegetable mixture, add onions. Cook, covered, on Medium for 5 minutes; skim fat from surface and discard bay leaf. In small mixing bowl, combine butter or margarine and flour to form smooth paste (beurre manié).

5 Into beef and vegetable mixture, stir small pieces of beurre manié, a few at a time, until blended. Cook on High for 3–4 minutes, until thickened and piping hot, stirring twice. Allow to stand, loosely covered, for 5 minutes. Season with salt and pepper.

6 *To serve:* transfer beef and vegetables to warmed serving dish; sprinkle over reserved diced bacon. Garnish with parsley sprigs.

BEEF STROGANOFF

Colour Index page 60. 4 servings. 344 cals per serving. Good source of vitamin A, vitamin B₁₂, riboflavin, iron, zinc, fibre. Begin 25 minutes ahead.

1 tablespoon vegetable oil 450 g fillet steak, cut into thin strips 1 tablespoon butter or margarine 1 onion, chopped 225 g button mushrooms, sliced	1¹/₂ tablespoons plain flour 1 teaspoon Worcestershire sauce 250 ml soured cream Salt and pepper to taste 2 tablespoons chopped parsley

1. Preheat browning dish according to manufacturer's instructions. Coat surface of browning dish with half of oil. Place half of steak strips on browning dish; quickly press with fish slice and stir to brown meat.

2. Cook steak on High (100% power) for 30–50 seconds, until sealed, turning once; transfer to bowl. Repeat with remaining oil and steak. Loosely cover bowl; set aside.

3. In 20 cm square microwave-safe baking dish, place butter or margarine. Heat on High for 1 minute, or until melted. Stir in onion and mushrooms. Cook on High for 3–4 minutes until softened, stirring once. Stir in flour. Cook on High for 2 minutes, stirring once.

4. To vegetable mixture, add Worcestershire sauce, soured cream, salt and pepper, and any juices from meat. Cook on High for 2–3 minutes, stirring often; do not boil. Add meat and cook on High for 2 minutes, or until fork-tender. Stir in parsley; serve.

BEEF GOULASH

Colour Index page 67. 6 servings. 296 cals per serving. Good source of vitamin A, vitamin C, iron. Begin 1¹/₂ hours ahead.

2 tablespoons olive or vegetable oil 2 large onions, sliced 2 green peppers, cut into thin strips 4 garlic cloves, crushed 2 tablespoons paprika 700 g braising steak, cut into 5 × 1 cm strips	1 × 400 g can or jar passatta (sieved Italian tomatoes) 120 ml Beef Stock (page 125) or stock from a cube Salt and pepper to taste Buttered noodles (optional)

1. In 32.5 × 22.5 cm microwave-safe baking dish, place oil, onions, green peppers, garlic and paprika. Cook, covered with kitchen paper, on High (100% power) for 5–6 minutes; stir twice.

2. To vegetables, add beef strips, passatta and stock; stir. Cook, covered, on Medium (50% power) for 45–60 minutes, until meat is fork-tender, stirring occasionally. Allow to stand, loosely covered, for 5 minutes.

3. Season goulash with salt and pepper. If you like, serve over buttered noodles.

OLD-FASHIONED BEEF STEW

Colour Index page 67. 6 servings. 376 cals per serving. Good source of vitamin A, niacin, vitamin C, iron fibre. Begin 1¾ hours ahead.

30 g butter or margarine	3 small turnips, cut into
2 large onions, cut into	5 cm chunks
wedges	700 g chuck steak, cut
4 carrots, cut into	into 4 cm cubes
7.5 cm pieces, then	350 ml Beef Stock (page
lengthways into	125) or stock from a
quarters	cube
3 celery sticks, cut into	½ teaspoon dried thyme
7.5 cm pieces, then	1 bay leaf
lengthways into	2 tablespoons tomato
quarters	purée
6 small potatoes, cut in	Salt and pepper to taste
half	

1. In 32.5 × 22.5 cm microwave-safe baking dish, place butter or margarine. Heat, covered with kitchen paper, on High (100% power) for 45 seconds, until melted.
2. To melted butter or margarine, add onions, carrots, celery, potatoes and turnips. Cook on High for 5–6 minutes, until softened; stir twice.
3. To vegetables, add beef, stock, thyme, bay leaf and tomato purée. Cook, covered, on Medium (50% power) for 45–60 minutes, or until meat is fork-tender, stirring occasionally. Allow to stand, loosely covered, for 10–15 minutes. Discard bay leaf and season before serving.

BEEF CARBONNADE

Colour Index page 67. 8 servings. 268 cals per serving. Good source of iron. Begin 1½ hours ahead.

3 rashers rindless	1 tablespoon browning
streaky bacon, diced	sauce
3 large onions, thinly	1 bay leaf
sliced	1 tablespoon cornflour
900 g chuck steak, cut	dissolved in 2
into 4 cm cubes	tablespoons cold water
350 ml stout	1 tablespoon red wine
250 ml Beef Stock (page	vinegar
125) or stock from a	Salt and pepper to taste
cube	

1. In 32.5 × 22.5 cm microwave-safe baking dish, place bacon. Cook, covered with kitchen paper, on High (100% power) for 4–5 minutes, until bacon is browned, stirring twice. With slotted spoon, transfer bacon to kitchen paper to drain.
2. Into bacon fat in dish, stir onions. Cook on High for 7–10 minutes, until onions are soft and tender, stirring occasionally.
3. Into onions, stir beef and next 4 ingredients. Cook, covered, on Medium (50% power) for 45–60 minutes, until meat is fork-tender, stirring occasionally. Skim fat. Stir in dissolved cornflour. Cook on High for 3–4 minutes, until sauce thickens slightly, stirring twice. Allow to stand, loosely covered, for 10–15 minutes.
4. Before serving, discard bay leaf. Into stew, stir vinegar, salt and pepper.

Meal in Minutes *for 8 people*

Superfast Barbecue

Mexican Dip, page 112 (double quantity) with crudités and potato crisps
'Barbecued' Chicken, page 188
Barbecue Steak with Spicy Vegetables, page 208
Corn-on-the-Cob with Flavoured Butter, page 273
Hot French bread
Vanilla Ice Cream, page 332, and chocolate ice cream (bought)
Strawberries and melon slices

PREPARATION TIMETABLE	
1 day ahead	*Make Vanilla Ice Cream; store in freezer. Make Mexican Dip; cover and refrigerate.*
2 hours ahead	*Prepare vegetables for crudités; store in polythene bags in refrigerator. Prepare strawberries and melon, arrange on attractive serving platter and cover; if you like, store in refrigerator.*
1 hour ahead	*Prepare 'Barbecued' Chicken up to end of step 2, to be finished later on barbecue. Assemble Mexican Dip, crudités and crisps. Preheat barbecue and cook Barbecue Steak with Spicy Vegetables.*
15 minutes before serving	*Brush chicken with barbecue sauce and complete cooking on barbecue. Cook Corn-on-the-Cob and melt Flavoured Butters as in recipes. Heat French bread in microwave on High (100% power).*

Quick Outdoor Cooking

Use the microwave to make outdoor cooking quick and easy:
while meat is cooking on the barbecue, the vegetable
accompaniment can be cooked in the microwave. Barbecue
Steak with Spicy Vegetables works perfectly using
this method.

BARBECUE STEAK WITH SPICY VEGETABLES

6 servings. 276 cals per serving. Good source of vitamin B$_{12}$, niacin, iron,
zinc. Begin 45 minutes ahead.

*1 very thick slice rump
  steak (about 700 g),
  trimmed of fat*
Vegetable oil
1 celery stick, chopped
*1 small green pepper,
  sliced*
*1 small onion, thinly
  sliced*
3 tablespoons water
*120 ml bottled chilli
  sauce*
*1 tablespoon plain
  flour*
*2 tablespoons dark soft
  brown sugar*
*$^{1}/_{4}$ teaspoon garlic
  powder*
$^{1}/_{4}$ teaspoon salt
*Large pinch of
  cayenne pepper*

1. Preheat barbecue. With sharp knife,
score both sides of steak; brush with oil.
Place steak on oiled grid of barbecue. Cook
for 7–10 minutes each side, until done to
your liking, brushing occasionally with more
oil.
2. Meanwhile, in 30 × 20 cm microwave-safe
baking dish, place celery, pepper and onion.
Cook, covered, on High (100% power) for
4–6 minutes, until softened, stirring twice.
3. Into vegetable mixture, stir water and
next 6 ingredients. Cook, covered, on
Medium (50% power) for 13 minutes, rotating dish halfway through cooking.
4. Transfer steak to cutting board; with
knife held in slanting position almost parallel
to cutting surface, cut thin slices across width
of steak. Arrange slices on warmed serving
platter and surround with vegetable mixture.

QUICK BARBECUE SAUCES

Each one of these easy sauces makes enough for 1 large barbecued
steak to serve 6 people, or 6 hamburgers. They taste good on
grilled meats and fish as well.

Sweet and Sour Sauce: in 500 ml
microwave-safe measuring jug, place **120 ml
bottled chilli sauce, 2 tablespoons each
cider vinegar** and **brown sugar, 1 teaspoon
salt** and **$^{1}/_{4}$ teaspoon ground cumin
(optional)**. Cook on High (100% power) for
3–3$^{1}/_{2}$ (3:30) minutes, until bubbling, stirring
twice. Makes 180 ml.

Soy and Apricot Sauce: in 500 ml
microwave-safe measuring jug, place **8
tablespoons apricot jam, 2 thinly sliced
spring onions, 2 tablespoons soy sauce, 1
teaspoon each cider vinegar** and **dry
mustard** and **$^{1}/_{4}$ teaspoon ground ginger.**
Cook on High (100% power) for 1$^{1}/_{2}$ (1:30)–2
minutes, until bubbling, stirring twice.
Makes 150 ml.

Herb Butter Sauce: in 500 ml microwave-
safe measuring jug, place **60 g butter, 1
tablespoon each vegetable oil** and **lemon
juice, $^{1}/_{2}$ teaspoon dried herbs (eg basil,
thyme, rosemary, dill), $^{1}/_{4}$ teaspoon salt** and
pinch of pepper. Cook on High (100% power)
for 1 minute, stirring twice. Makes 80 ml.

Beef Brisket

SALT BEEF AND CABBAGE

Colour Index page 65. 6 servings. 520 cals per
serving. Good source of vitamin A, niacin, vitamin
C, iron, fibre. Begin 2 hours ahead.

*1 × 1.6 kg joint salted
  beef brisket*
2 onions, sliced
2 celery sticks, sliced
1 carrot, sliced
8 whole allspice
10 whole cloves
6 black peppercorns
2 bay leaves
350 ml ginger ale
600 ml water
*1 small cabbage, cut
  into 8–10 wedges*
Salt and pepper to taste

1. In large roasting bag, place meat, onions,
celery, carrot, allspice, cloves, peppercorns, bay
leaves, ginger ale and 250 ml water. Close bag
loosely with plastic or nylon tie (do not use metal
tie), leaving vent. Place bag in 32.5 × 22.5 cm
microwave-safe baking dish.
2. Cook meat on High (100% power) for 5 minutes. Reduce power level to Medium-Low (30%
power) and cook for 1–1$^{1}/_{2}$ hours longer, until
meat is fork-tender, turning bag over every 20
minutes.
3. Carefully open roasting bag and transfer meat
to cutting board. Tent with foil and allow to stand
for 15–20 minutes. Reserve bag with vegetables
and cooking liquid.
4. Meanwhile, pour remaining water into same
baking dish. Add cabbage wedges. Cook, covered,
on High for 11–14 minutes, until tender-crisp,
stirring halfway through cooking. To cabbage,
add vegetables from bag and 60 ml cooking liquid.
Cook, covered, on High for 2 minutes, or until
cabbage is tender. Discard bay leaves; season.
5. *To serve:* thinly slice meat across grain.
Arrange meat on warmed serving platter with
vegetables.

'BARBECUED' BRISKET

Colour Index page 65. 6 servings. 279 cals per
serving. Good source of niacin, iron.
Begin 1$^{3}/_{4}$ hours ahead.

*1 × 1.4 kg beef brisket
  roasting joint*
2 onions, sliced
*120 ml bottled barbecue
  sauce*
120 ml apple juice
*1 tablespoon soft brown
  sugar*
*1 teaspoon
  Worcestershire sauce*
*1 tablespoon grated
  horseradish*
*$^{1}/_{4}$ teaspoon ground
  cloves*

1. In large roasting bag, place meat and all other
ingredients. Close bag with plastic or nylon tie (do
not use metal tie). Place bag in 32.5 × 22.5 cm
microwave-safe baking dish.
2. Cook brisket on High (100% power) for 5 minutes. Reduce power level to Medium-Low (30%
power) and cook for 1–1$^{1}/_{4}$ hours longer, until
meat is fork-tender, turning bag over every 20
minutes. Allow to stand in bag for 15 minutes.
3. *To serve:* thinly slice meat across grain. Serve
with cooking sauce spooned over meat.

Minced Beef

CHEESEBURGERS

Colour Index page 60. 4 servings. 406 cals per serving. Good source of riboflavin, niacin, calcium, iron. Begin 25 minutes ahead.

1 onion, sliced	2 teaspoons cornflour
115 g mushrooms, sliced	1 teaspoon meat
30 g butter or margarine	tenderiser
1¼ teaspoons paprika	½ teaspoon black
450 g minced beef	pepper
75 g Cheddar, Fontina,	1 teaspoon browning
or Gruyère cheese,	sauce
grated, or 50 g blue	4 slices white bread,
cheese, crumbled	toasted (optional)
2 tablespoons iced water	

1. In 25 cm round microwave-safe baking dish, place onion, mushrooms, 15 g butter or margarine and ¼ teaspoon paprika. Cook, covered, on High (100% power) for 5–6 minutes, until vegetables are tender, stirring twice. Spoon mixture into small mixing bowl; set aside.
2. In medium mixing bowl, combine beef, cheese and iced water. Shape into 4 patties. On greaseproof paper, mix cornflour, tenderiser, pepper and remaining paprika. In 250 ml microwave-safe glass jug, place remaining butter or margarine. Heat on High for 30 seconds, or until melted; stir in browning sauce. Brush on patties; coat with cornflour mixture.
3. In baking dish used for cooking vegetables, place burgers. Cook, covered loosely with greaseproof paper, on Medium-High (70% power) for 5 minutes, rotating dish halfway through cooking. Spoon onion and mushroom mixture over burgers. Cook on Medium-High for 1 minute longer, or until hot. If you like, serve on toast.

HEATING HAMBURGER BUNS

Heating hamburger buns in the microwave is fast and easy, and the same technique can be used for heating pitta bread. Use kitchen paper when heating bread, rolls and other baked goods as it absorbs moisture and prevents sogginess.

Wrap 2 hamburger buns in kitchen paper. Place on paper plate or directly on oven floor. Cook on High (100% power) for 12–17 seconds, until buns are warm. For 1 bun, heat on High for 10–15 seconds.

Minced meat of all kinds works well for burgers cooked in the microwave, although meat with a 10% fat content is best if you are watching calories. When making Surprise Burgers (below), take care not to overhandle the meat or the end result will be rubbery and tough.

SURPRISE BURGERS

Colour Index page 60. 380 cals per serving. Good source of niacin, iron. Begin 20 minutes ahead.

Ingredients	For 4	For 2	For 1
Minced beef	450 g	225 g	115 g
Water	1 tablespoon	1½ teaspoons	¾ teaspoon
Salt	to taste	to taste	to taste
Pepper	to taste	to taste	to taste
Canned pimientos, diced	4 tablespoons	2 tablespoons	1 tablespoon
Stoned black olives, thinly sliced	4 large	2 large	1 large
Bottled chilli sauce	60 ml	2 tablespoons	1 tablespoon
Hamburger buns	4 buns	2 buns	1 bun
Microwave cookware	30 × 20 cm baking dish with rack	22.5 cm square baking dish with rack	Shallow 21.5 cm pie dish
Time on High (100% power) Burgers After rotating	3 minutes 1½ (1:30)–3 minutes	2 minutes 1½ (1:30)–2 minutes	1 minute 1½ (1:30) minutes

1 In mixing bowl, combine beef, water, salt and pepper; divide mixture into 2 portions per serving.

2 On greaseproof paper, shape each portion into 8.5 cm patty. In bowl, mix pimientos, olives and chilli sauce.

3 Top half of patties with equal amounts of pimiento mixture, to within 5 mm of edges.

4 On top of each patty with filling, place plain patty. With fingers, gently press edges together to seal.

5 On rack in baking dish or pie dish (see Chart), place burgers. Cook on High for time in Chart.

6 With fish slice, turn burgers over; rotate dish. Cook on High for time in Chart, or until burgers are done to your liking. Serve in hamburger buns.

Minced Beef

PARTY BURGERS

Colour Index page 67. 106 cals per serving. Low in cholesterol. Begin early in day.

For easy entertaining, dishes such as these Party Burgers can be prepared up to a certain point and frozen, then removed from the freezer and microwaved just before serving.

Ingredients for 12 servings		Microwave cookware
225 g sirloin steak, minced 25 g Cheddar cheese, grated, or blue cheese, finely crumbled ¹/₂ teaspoon meat tenderiser ¹/₂ teaspoon browning sauce ¹/₂ teaspoon Worcestershire sauce 3 tablespoons chopped parsley	2 teaspoons crushed black peppercorns ¹/₂ teaspoon dried basil 6 slices white bread 45 g butter or margarine, melted Garnishes: lettuce, cherry tomato slices, small white onion slices, canned sliced mushrooms or chopped pimiento, cheese or bacon	Platter 30 × 20 cm baking dish with rack

1 Combine minced sirloin, cheese, meat tenderiser, browning sauce and Worcestershire sauce; shape into 15 × 4 cm log. Wrap in greaseproof paper; freeze for 1 hour, or until firm.

2 In small mixing bowl, combine parsley, pepper and basil. Using 5 cm round biscuit cutter, cut 2 rounds from each slice of bread; toast. Dip edges of toast in melted butter or margarine, then in parsley mixture. Place in freezer container; cover and freeze.

3 When meat is firm, cut crossways into twelve 1 cm thick slices. On baking sheet lined with greaseproof paper, freeze patties until firm. Place in freezer container; cover and return to freezer.

4 About 15 minutes before serving, on platter, arrange toast rounds in single layer. Heat on High (100% power) for 20 seconds, or until thawed; set aside.

5 On rack in baking dish, place burgers. Cook on Medium (50% power) for 5–5¹/₂ (5:30) minutes for medium-rare, rotating dish halfway through cooking.

6 On toast rounds, place burgers. Garnish with lettuce, cherry tomato slices, small white onion slices, canned sliced mushrooms or chopped pimiento, cheese or bacon. Heat cheese-topped burgers just until cheese melts.

BEST-EVER BURGERS

Colour Index page 60. 2 servings. 344 cals per serving. Good source of vitamin A, niacin, calcium, iron. Begin 25 minutes ahead.

1 large carrot 1 small courgette 45 g butter or margarine 225 g minced beef 1 teaspoon cornflour ¹/₂ teaspoon meat tenderiser	¹/₂ teaspoon paprika ¹/₄ teaspoon pepper ¹/₂ teaspoon browning sauce 2 small onions, sliced 2 tablespoons dry red wine

1. With vegetable peeler, shred carrot and courgette. Place in 1 litre microwave-safe casserole. Add 15 g butter or margarine; cover and set aside.
2. Shape minced beef into two 2 cm thick oval patties. On greaseproof paper, mix cornflour, meat tenderiser, paprika and pepper. In 250 ml microwave-safe glass jug, place 15 g butter or margarine. Heat on High (100% power) for 30 seconds, or until melted; stir in browning sauce. Brush on patties; coat with cornflour mixture.
3. In 20 cm square microwave-safe baking dish, place burgers, onions and remaining butter or margarine. Cook, covered loosely with greaseproof paper, on Medium-High (70% power) for 4–5 minutes for medium-rare, rotating dish once. Transfer burgers to platter; keep warm. Into same baking dish, stir wine. Cook, covered, on High for 4 minutes; keep warm.
4. Cook vegetable mixture, covered, on High for 2–3 minutes, until tender-crisp, stirring once. Spoon onion mixture over burgers; accompany with vegetables.

KEEMA CURRY

Colour Index page 61. 4 servings. 348 cals per serving. Low in salt. Good source of vitamin A, riboflavin, thiamine, niacin, calcium, iron, fibre. Begin 25 minutes ahead.

1 tablespoon vegetable oil 1 large onion, sliced 2 garlic cloves, chopped 1 green pepper, chopped 2 cm piece root ginger, finely chopped 1 teaspoon garam masala 1 teaspoon turmeric	1 tablespoon ground coriander ¹/₂ teaspoon chilli powder 450 g minced beef 4 tomatoes, peeled, seeded and chopped 225 g frozen peas, thawed

1. In large microwave-safe bowl, place oil and next 4 ingredients. Cook on High (100% power) for 3–4 minutes, until softened, stirring once. Stir in spices. Cook on High for 2 minutes.
2. To vegetable mixture, add minced beef. Cook on High for 5 minutes or until beef is no longer pink, stirring twice.
3. Into meat mixture, stir tomatoes. Cook on High for 10 minutes. Stir in peas. Cook on High for 5 minutes, or until peas are hot.

CHILLI CON CARNE

Colour Index page 61. 6 servings. 250 cals per serving. Good source of vitamin A, vitamin C, iron, fibre. Begin 25 minutes ahead.

450 g minced beef	2 teaspoons tomato
1 onion, chopped	purée
3 garlic cloves, crushed	120 ml water
1 green pepper, diced	1 × 400 g can red kidney
2 tablespoons chilli	beans
powder	Soured cream, grated
1 teaspoon dried	Cheddar cheese and
oregano	chopped fresh
1 bay leaf	coriander to garnish
2 teaspoons ground	Tortilla chips (optional)
cumin (optional)	
1 × 400 g can chopped	
tomatoes	

1. In microwave-safe colander set over microwave-safe bowl, place minced beef. Cook on High (100% power) for 4 minutes, or until beef is no longer pink, stirring twice. Discard all but 3 tablespoons meat drippings from bowl.

2. In 2 litre microwave-safe casserole, combine drippings, minced beef, onion, garlic, green pepper, chilli powder, oregano and bay leaf. If you like, add cumin. Cook on High for 3 minutes, stirring twice.

3. To mixture, add chopped tomatoes, tomato purée and water; stir well to combine. Cook, covered with kitchen paper, on High for 5 minutes, stirring twice; discard bay leaf.

4. Drain and rinse beans; stir into meat mixture. Cook, covered with kitchen paper, on High for 3 minutes, or until hot, stirring once.

5. Serve chilli in individual bowls garnished with soured cream, Cheddar cheese and chopped coriander. If you like, serve with tortilla chips.

QUICK AND EASY CHILLI

Colour Index page 61. 8 servings. 385 cals per serving. Good source of niacin, iron, fibre. Begin 25 minutes ahead.

700 g minced beef	2 × 400 g cans tomatoes
2 onions, coarsely	65 g tomato purée
chopped	1 × 400 g can red kidney
2 garlic cloves, crushed	beans, drained
1 tablespoon mild chilli	275 g frozen sweetcorn
powder	kernels, thawed
1 medium courgette, cut	
into 2.5 cm chunks	

1. In 3 litre microwave-safe casserole, place beef, onions, garlic and chilli powder. Cook, covered, on High (100% power) for 5–7 minutes, until beef is no longer pink, stirring twice.

2. To meat mixture, add courgette, tomatoes with their liquid and tomato purée. Cook, covered, on High for 11–13 minutes, until courgette is tender, stirring twice. To mixture, add beans and sweetcorn. Cook, covered, on High for 3–5 minutes, until hot.

INDIVIDUAL MEAT LOAVES

Colour Index page 61. 470 cals per serving. Good source of riboflavin, niacin, calcium, iron. Begin 25 minutes ahead.

Ingredients	For 4	For 2	For 1
1 medium cucumber (about 225 g), peeled	1 cucumber	1/2 cucumber	1/4 cucumber
Minced beef	450 g	225 g	115 g
Fresh breadcrumbs	45 g	20 g	3 tablespoons
Grated onion	1 tablespoon	1 1/2 teaspoons	3/4 teaspoon
Salt	to taste	to taste	to taste
Pepper	to taste	to taste	to taste
Eggs/Water	1 egg	3 tablespoons water	1 1/2 tablespoons water
Processed cheese slices	8 slices	4 slices	2 slices
Salad and parsley sprigs	garnish	garnish	garnish
Microwave cookware	30 × 20 cm baking dish	20 cm square baking dish	20 cm square baking dish
Time on Medium-High (70% power)			
Meat loaves	9 minutes	4 minutes	2 minutes
With cheese topping	2 minutes	1 minute	30 seconds
Standing time	3 minutes	2 minutes	2 minutes

1 Cut cucumber in half lengthways; with spoon, remove seeds. Cut several slices for garnish; reserve. Coarsely shred remaining cucumber.

2 In mixing bowl, combine shredded cucumber and all remaining ingredients except cheese. Divide mixture into required number of servings.

3 Reserve half of cheese slices; fold each remaining slice into 4 × 2 × 1 cm chunk.

4 Shape each portion of meat around 1 chunk of cheese to make 10 × 5 cm loaf. In baking dish (see Chart), arrange loaves. Cook, covered loosely with greaseproof paper, on Medium-High for time in Chart.

5 Remove greaseproof paper; rotate dish. Top each loaf with 1 slice remaining cheese. Cook on Medium-High for time in Chart. Allow to stand, covered, for time in Chart.

6 *To serve:* arrange meat loaves on warmed serving platter. Garnish with salad, parsley and reserved cucumber slices.

Minced Beef

Minced beef is extremely versatile as it can be combined with so many different flavourings and seasonings to make a host of tasty dishes in the microwave. It cooks very quickly and absorbs the flavours of other ingredients really well, even during the short microwave cooking time.

CONTINENTAL MEAT LOAF

Colour Index page 63. 380 cals per serving. Good source of niacin, calcium, iron. Begin 45 minutes ahead.

Ingredients for 6 servings		Microwave cookware
1 × 225 g can or jar sauerkraut, drained 1 tablespoon brown sugar 1 medium celery stick, finely chopped 2 tablespoons water 700 g minced beef 90 g fresh breadcrumbs	120 ml milk 1/4 teaspoon pepper 1 egg 2 slices Gruyère cheese Thousand Island dressing (bottled) Radish Flowers (page 116) and parsley to garnish	Medium bowl 30 × 20 cm baking dish

1 In mixing bowl, combine sauerkraut and sugar; set aside. In medium bowl, place celery and water. Cook, covered, on High (100% power) for 3 minutes, or until celery is tender.

2 To celery, add minced beef, breadcrumbs, milk, pepper and egg; stir to combine. In baking dish, pat half of mixture into flat 22.5 × 15 cm oval.

3 On to meat, evenly spoon sauerkraut mixture, to within 1 cm of edges. Top with cheese slices, folding to fit if necessary. On greaseproof paper, shape remaining meat mixture into 23.5 × 16 cm oval.

4 Over cheese-topped meat in baking dish, invert plain meat oval; remove paper. With fingers, gently press edges together to seal.

5 Cook meat loaf, covered loosely with greaseproof paper, on Medium-High (70% power) for 20 minutes, or until meat thermometer inserted in centre reaches 74°C (165°F), rotating dish after 10 minutes. Allow to stand on heatproof surface for 5 minutes.

6 *To serve:* drizzle about 4 tablespoons Thousand Island dressing over meat loaf. Cut meat loaf crossways into thick slices. Garnish with Radish Flowers and parsley. If you like, serve extra dressing separately.

MEAT LOAF MILANESE

Colour Index page 63. 6 servings. 350 cals per serving. Good source of niacin, vitamin C, iron, fibre. Begin 45 minutes ahead.

450 g small red potatoes, cut in half 250 g frozen French beans 60 ml water 1 small onion, chopped 1 celery stick, chopped 1 tablespoon lemon juice 700 g minced beef	45 g dried breadcrumbs 1 teaspoon browning sauce 1 egg, lightly beaten Dry red wine 1 teaspoon dried basil 1 × 400 g can tomatoes, chopped 1 teaspoon sugar

1. In 2 litre microwave-safe casserole, place potatoes, frozen French beans and water. Cook, covered, on High (100% power) for 12 minutes, or until potatoes are tender, stirring twice. Drain; allow to stand, covered.

2. In 2.5 litre microwave-safe bowl, place onion, celery and lemon juice. Cook, covered, on High for 3 minutes. Add beef, breadcrumbs, browning sauce, egg, 120 ml wine and 1/2 teaspoon basil; mix well. In 30 × 20 cm microwave-safe baking dish, shape meat mixture into 20 × 10 cm loaf.

3. Cook meat, covered loosely with greaseproof paper, on Medium-High (70% power) for 15 minutes, rotating dish a half turn halfway through cooking. Allow to stand, covered, while preparing sauce.

4. In medium microwave-safe bowl, place tomatoes with their liquid, sugar, 2 tablespoons wine and remaining basil. Cook, covered, on High for 5 minutes, or until bubbling, stirring twice.

5. Serve meat loaf with vegetables; hand tomato and basil sauce separately.

MEAT LOAF VARIATIONS
Adapt the Individual Meat Loaves recipe (page 211) by trying one of these variations:

Cheesy Meat Loaf: in mixing bowl, combine *450 g minced beef, 1 egg, 45 g fresh breadcrumbs, 1 tablespoon grated onion, 1/4 teaspoon pepper* and *1/4 teaspoon dried oregano*. In 30 × 20 cm microwave-safe baking dish, shape meat into loaf. Cook, covered loosely with greaseproof paper, on Medium-High (70% power) for 10–12 minutes, rotating dish once. Remove paper and rotate dish. Top with *4 slices processed cheese* and *1 peeled and sliced tomato*. Cook on Medium-High for 2 minutes. Allow to stand for 3 minutes.

Pineapple Meat Loaf: prepare as for Cheesy Meat Loaf (above), omitting oregano, cheese and tomato. Top with slices from *1 × 225 g can sliced pineapple*. Cook on Medium-High for 2 minutes. Allow to stand for 3 minutes.

PASTA POT

Colour Index page 66. 6 servings. 418 cals per serving. Good source of vitamin A, thiamine, niacin, vitamin C, iron, fibre. Begin 1¼ hours ahead.

450 g minced beef	*75 g tomato purée*
1 tablespoon olive oil	*120 ml water*
2 onions, chopped	*225 g large pasta shells*
1 large carrot, chopped	*1 garlic clove, crushed*
2 celery sticks, chopped	*Grated Parmesan*
1 teaspoon dried basil	*cheese (optional)*
1 teaspoon dried	
oregano	
2 × 400 g cans chopped	
tomatoes	

1. In microwave-safe colander set over microwave-safe bowl, place minced beef. Cook on High (100% power) for 5–6 minutes, until beef is no longer pink, stirring twice. Discard drippings from bowl.
2. In 30 × 20 cm microwave-safe baking dish, combine oil, onions, carrot, celery, basil and oregano. Cook on High for 5–6 minutes, until vegetables are softened, stirring twice.
3. Into vegetable mixture, stir cooked beef, chopped tomatoes, tomato purée and water. Cook on High for 10 minutes, or until slightly thickened, stirring twice.
4. Cook pasta conventionally according to instructions on packet.
5. Into beef mixture, stir garlic. Cook on High for 5 minutes, stirring once.
6. Drain pasta; fold into beef mixture. If you like, sprinkle with Parmesan cheese. Cook, covered loosely with greaseproof paper, on High for 7–10 minutes, until hot. Allow to stand, loosely covered, for 10 minutes before serving.

PREPARING MINCED BEEF

Precooking is an ideal way to prepare minced beef for use in casseroles and stews because it reduces the calorie count by getting rid of excess fat, making it healthier for you and your family.

Place raw minced beef in plastic or other microwave-safe colander set over microwave-safe bowl.

Cook beef on High (100% power) until no longer pink, stirring twice to break up pieces. Discard drippings from bowl.

You and your microwave oven can produce traditional slow-cooking dishes, like Stuffed Cabbage (below), in a fraction of the time and without losing that authentic taste. The combination of minced beef, rice, raisins and seasonings makes a flavoursome stuffing that can be varied by adding different herbs.

STUFFED CABBAGE

Colour Index page 65. 573 cals per serving. Good source of vitamin A, thiamine, niacin, vitamin C, calcium, iron, fibre. Begin 1¼ hours ahead.

Ingredients for 4 servings		Microwave cookware
1 × 900 g cabbage	*2 × 400 g cans chopped*	32.5 × 22.5 cm baking dish
1 large onion, finely	*tomatoes*	
chopped	*2 beef stock cubes*	
1 large carrot, finely	*Large pinch of ground*	
chopped	*cloves*	
90 g long-grain rice	*1 tablespoon brown*	
70 g raisins	*sugar*	
450 g minced beef	*½ teaspoon cider*	
2 tablespoons fruity	*vinegar*	
brown sauce	*75 g tomato purée*	
¼ teaspoon ground	*Parsley to garnish*	
allspice		
Pepper to taste		

1 Discard tough outer leaves from cabbage. Remove 8 large leaves for cabbage rolls. (Reserve remaining cabbage to use another day.)

2 In baking dish, place cabbage leaves. Cook, covered, on High (100% power) for 3–4 minutes, until leaves wilt. Remove to kitchen paper to cool while preparing stuffing.

3 In mixing bowl, combine onion, carrot, rice, raisins, minced beef, brown sauce, allspice and pepper. With small, sharp knife, remove ribs from cabbage leaves.

4 On centre of each cabbage leaf, place equal amount of beef stuffing mixture.

5 Fold 2 sides of cabbage leaf towards centre over meat, overlapping edges. From 1 narrow edge, roll Swiss roll fashion. In baking dish used for wilting cabbage leaves, arrange cabbage rolls, seam side down.

6 In 1 litre measuring jug, combine tomatoes, stock cubes, cloves, brown sugar, vinegar and tomato purée. Pour over cabbage rolls. Cook, covered, on Medium (50% power) for 30–40 minutes, until fork-tender, spooning sauce over and rotating dish halfway through cooking. Arrange cabbage rolls on warmed serving platter, spoon sauce round rolls and garnish.

The microwave produces delicious fast food in next to no time, ideal for American-style snacks after school, and perfect for teaching teenagers how to cook. And for your own peace of mind, it's safer than conventional cooking.

TEX-MEX TREATS

Use leftovers from homemade chilli recipes (page 211) or canned chilli to cook these 2 taste-tempting treats.

Chilli Taco: on small microwave-safe plate, place *1 taco shell*. Heat on High (100% power) for 45 seconds. Spoon *2 tablespoons chilli con carne* into taco shell. Heat on High for 30 seconds. Sprinkle over *3 tablespoons grated Cheddar cheese*. Serve with *lettuce* and *tomato*. 1 serving.

Tamale Pie: in microwave-safe soup plate, place *8 tablespoons chilli con carne*. Top with *3 tablespoons canned sweetcorn, 2 tablespoons grated Cheddar cheese* and *2 tablespoons crumbled tortilla chips*. Cook on High (100% power) for 1¹/₂ (1:30)–2 minutes, or until hot. 1 serving.

SUPERQUICK BURGERS

2 servings.
Begin 10 minutes ahead.

225 g minced beef
2 hamburger buns
2 leaves lettuce
2 slices tomato
Potato crisps

1 Shape beef into 2 patties, about 2.5 cm thick. Line 21.5 cm microwave-safe shallow pie dish with kitchen paper; place patties on top.

2 Cook, covered with kitchen paper, on High (100% power) for 2–3 minutes, turning patties over halfway through cooking. Allow to stand for 2 minutes. Place in buns with lettuce and tomato. Serve with potato crisps.

EASY SLOPPY JOES

4 servings.
Begin 15 minutes ahead.

450 g minced beef
1 tablespoon dried onion flakes
¹/₂ teaspoon garlic salt
¹/₄ teaspoon pepper
120 ml bottled barbecue sauce
2 tablespoons dried parsley flakes
4 hamburger buns
Lettuce and cherry tomatoes

1 In microwave-safe colander set over large microwave-safe bowl, combine beef and onion. Cook on High (100% power) for 4–5 minutes, until beef is no longer pink, stirring twice.

2 Discard drippings. Place meat in bowl with garlic salt and next 3 ingredients. Cook on Medium (50% power) for 4–5 minutes. Spoon on to buns and serve with lettuce and tomatoes.

EASY PIZZAS

4 servings.
Begin 10 minutes ahead.

4 muffins, split and toasted
1 × 300 g can sauce for pasta
8 slices mozzarella cheese
Assorted pizza toppings: pepperoni sausage, olives, grated Parmesan or other cheese, sliced mushrooms, red or green pepper strips

1 Over each muffin half, spread 1 tablespoon sauce. Top each with 1 slice mozzarella cheese and topping of your choice.

2 On paper plate, place 4 pizza halves. Cook on High (100% power) for 1–2 minutes, until cheese melts. Repeat with remaining 4 halves.

1 In microwave-safe colander set over large microwave-safe bowl, place minced beef. Cook on High (100% power) for 4–5 minutes, until beef is no longer pink, stirring twice. Discard drippings from bowl. Place meat in bowl.

2 Into beef, stir mushroom slices and onion soup mix. In mixing bowl, combine flour and next 3 ingredients; stir into beef mixture. Cook on High for 4–6 minutes, stirring twice. Serve with noodles, cream and parsley.

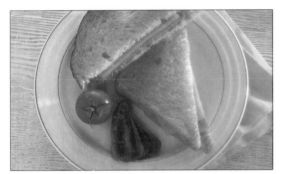

1 On 2 slices toast, spread equal amount of mustard. Place 1 slice ham on each. Cover each with 1 slice cheese and remaining toast slice.

2 On paper plates, place sandwiches. Cook on High (100% power) for 20–30 seconds, just until cheese melts. Cut in half and serve with gherkins and cherry tomatoes.

1 Place beef in microwave-safe colander set over a large microwave-safe bowl. Cook on High (100% power) for 4–5 minutes, until beef is no longer pink, stirring twice.

2 Discard dripping. Place meat in bowl. Stir in chilli sauce and next 3 ingredients. Cook on High for 4–6 minutes, until hot, stirring twice. Serve with accompaniments.

QUICK BEEF STROGANOFF

4 servings.
Begin 25 minutes ahead.

450 g minced beef
$^1/_2 \times 200$ g can button mushrooms, drained and sliced
$^1/_2$ packet French onion soup mix
2 tablespoons plain flour
$^1/_4$ teaspoon garlic powder
2 tablespoons tomato ketchup
250 ml soured cream
Cooked noodles, soured cream and parsley

HAM AND CHEESEMELTS

2 servings.
Begin 20 minutes ahead.

4 slices white bread, toasted
2 teaspoons made mustard
2 slices cooked ham
2 slices Gruyère cheese
2 gherkins
2 cherry tomatoes

SOUTH-OF-THE-BORDER BEEF DINNER

4 servings.
Begin 20 minutes ahead.

450 g minced beef
1–2 tablespoons bottled chilli sauce
1 tablespoon dried onion flakes
$^1/_2$ teaspoon garlic salt
1×225 g can refried beans
Assorted accompaniments: soured cream, radishes, fresh coriander, tortilla chips, taco sauce

KIDS COOKING
The microwave is one of the safest cooking appliances, but if the children are using it, get them to read these guidelines before they start.

1 Always read the recipe through completely to make certain you understand it and have all the necessary ingredients and cookware.

2 Use only the amounts given in the recipe and cook for the recommended times on the given power.

3 Always use oven gloves. While the oven may feel cool, the dishes will be hot from the heat of the food.

4 Be sure cookware is microwave-safe. Ask an adult to mark microwave-safe items with an 'M', using an indelible marker.

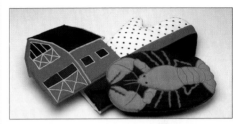

5 When using cling film or covers, carefully lift off cooked food so that steam escapes away from your face and fingers.

DO NOT
* Turn on microwave with nothing in it.
* Put any metal or foil in microwave.
* Cook an egg in its shell.
* Make microwave popcorn in anything other than manufacturer's container or bag.

Pork Roasts

Choose roasting joints which are uniform in diameter. Allow about 22 minutes per 450 g for a boneless joint and 20 minutes per 450 g for a joint on the bone. Turn the meat over and rotate the dish halfway through cooking; meat is done when thermometer inserted in several places reaches 77°C (170°F).

LOIN OF PORK WITH APRICOT STUFFING

Colour Index page 67. 163 cals per serving. Good source of vitamin A, riboflavin, thiamine, niacin, iron. Begin 1½ hours ahead.

Ingredients for 12 servings		Microwave cookware
15 g butter or margarine 1 onion, chopped 1 large celery stick, chopped 1 medium cooking apple, cored and chopped 115 g dried apricots, chopped	½ teaspoon poultry seasoning 75 g fresh bread cubes 1 tablespoon vegetable oil 1 × 900 g boneless pork loin Pepper to taste Parsley sprigs to garnish	30 × 20 cm baking dish

1 In baking dish, place butter or margarine and next 4 ingredients. Cook on High (100% power) for 3 minutes, or until onion is softened, stirring twice. Into mixture, stir poultry seasoning and bread cubes; mix well. Push towards sides of dish.

2 In frying pan over high heat, heat oil. Add meat and quickly brown meat on all sides. Season with pepper.

3 In centre of baking dish with stuffing, place meat. Cook, covered, on Medium (50% power) for 15 minutes.

4 Turn meat over and rotate dish. Cook, covered, on Medium for 20–30 minutes longer, until meat thermometer inserted in several places reaches 74°C (165°F).

5 On heatproof surface, allow meat to stand in dish, tented with foil, for 10–15 minutes. Temperature will reach 77°C (170°F).

6 To serve: thinly slice pork; arrange on warmed serving platter with apricot stuffing. Garnish with parsley sprigs.

LOIN OF PORK WITH GARLIC

Colour Index page 64. 10 servings. 196 cals per serving. Good source of thiamine, niacin. Begin 55 minutes ahead.

20 garlic cloves
350 ml Chicken Stock (page 125) or stock from a cube
1 × 1.1 kg boneless pork loin

Salt and pepper to taste
Lemon juice to taste
Watercress to garnish

1. In 30 × 20 cm microwave-safe baking dish, place garlic cloves and stock. Cook, covered, on High (100% power) for 10 minutes.
2. Season meat. In frying pan over high heat, quickly brown meat on all sides.
3. In centre of baking dish with garlic and stock, place meat. Cook, covered, on Medium (50% power) for 30–35 minutes, until a meat thermometer inserted in several places reaches 74°C (165°F), turning meat over and rotating dish after 15 minutes. Transfer roast to warmed serving platter; allow to stand, tented with foil, on heatproof surface for 10–15 minutes. Temperature will reach 77°C (170°F).
4. Meanwhile, in food processor with knife blade attached or in blender, process garlic and stock until smooth. Add salt, pepper and lemon juice.
5. To serve: thinly slice pork and garnish with watercress. Serve immediately, with garlic sauce handed separately.

HASH BROWN PORK AND POTATOES

Colour Index page 62. 4 servings. 366 cals per serving. Good source of thiamine. Begin 20 minutes ahead.

280 g boneless roast pork, cubed
300 g boiled potatoes, cubed
1 large onion, chopped
½ teaspoon dried thyme
Salt and pepper to taste

2 eggs
2 tablespoons double or whipping cream
30 g butter or margarine
Paprika to taste

1. Preheat browning dish according to manufacturer's instructions. Meanwhile, in large bowl, combine pork, potatoes and onion. Add thyme, salt and pepper; stir.
2. In small bowl, with fork, combine eggs and cream. Add to pork mixture; stir.
3. Place butter or margarine on browning dish. Add pork mixture, pressing lightly with fish slice or spatula. Cook on High for 7–10 minutes, until mixture is set, rotating dish halfway through cooking.
4. If you like, with fish slice, slide hash on to serving platter; brown under preheated grill. Sprinkle with paprika.

Pork Loin and Fillet (Tenderloin)

PORK WITH VEGETABLES

Colour Index page 62. 4 servings. 440 cals per serving. Good source of vitamin A, thiamine, niacin, vitamin C, iron, fibre. Begin 25 minutes ahead.

450 g boneless pork loin, cut into 5 mm thick slices
15 g butter or margarine
1 spring onion, finely chopped
1 chicken stock cube
120 ml water
350 g baby carrots
450 g asparagus, cut into 5 cm pieces
2 heads chicory, cut in half lengthways
80 ml single cream
1 tablespoon plain flour
2 tablespoons made mustard
1 tablespoon brandy (optional)

1. On cutting board, with dull edge of large knife or smooth edge of meat mallet, pound pork slices to 3 mm thickness. In 30 × 20 cm microwave-safe baking dish, place pork, butter or margarine, spring onion, stock cube and 60 ml water. Cook, covered, on High (100% power) for 8–10 minutes, until pork is tender and juices run clear, re-arranging slices once. Cover and set aside on heat-proof surface.
2. Into shallow 2-litre microwave-safe casserole, pour remaining water; add carrots. Cook, covered, on High for 4 minutes. Stir in asparagus. Cook, covered, on High for 4–5 minutes, until tender. To vegetables, add chicory; set aside.
3. Remove pork to microwave-safe platter. Into mixture in baking dish, whisk cream and flour until blended. Cook on High for 2–3 minutes, until sauce thickens, stirring once. Stir in mustard and, if you like, brandy.
4. To serve: spoon vegetables round pork; pour sauce over pork and vegetables. Cook on High for 1–2 minutes, until hot.

COOKING PORK CHOPS
Choose loin chops (with or without bone) cut 2–2.5 cm thick.

4 × 175 g chops	2 × 175 g chops	1 × 175 g chop
Microwave cookware		
30 × 20 cm baking dish with rack	25 × 15 cm baking dish with rack	21.5 cm pie dish with rack
Time on Medium-Low (30% power)		
20–30 minutes	11–14 minutes	7–9 minutes

On rack in baking dish or pie dish, place chops. Cook, covered, for time in Chart, until juices run clear, turning chops over and rotating dish halfway through cooking.

Stir-frying is the traditional oriental method of quickly cooking slivers of meat and vegetables in very little oil. Even less oil is necessary when you use a browning dish in the microwave oven, as in Stir-Fry with Pork (below), so microwave 'stir-frying' is delicious *and* nutritious!

STIR-FRY WITH PORK

Colour Index page 61. 350 cals per serving. Good source of vitamin A, riboflavin, thiamine, niacin, vitamin C, iron, fibre. Begin 25 minutes ahead.

Ingredients for 4 servings		Microwave cookware
450 g pork fillet (tenderloin)	225 g courgettes, preferably yellow	Browning dish
2 tablespoons dry sherry	225 g mushrooms	250 ml measuring jug
2 tablespoons soy sauce	2 tablespoons vegetable oil	2 litre casserole
1 teaspoon cornflour	30 g butter or margarine	
1/4 teaspoon ground ginger	1 tablespoon lemon juice	
3 spring onions, cut into thin strips	115 g mange-touts	
3 large carrots	2 tablespoons water	
	Spinach leaves to garnish	

1 With knife held in slanted position, cut pork crossways into thin slices. In mixing bowl, combine sherry, soy sauce, cornflour and ginger. Add pork slices and spring onions; stir to coat. Preheat browning dish according to manufacturer's instructions.

2 Meanwhile, with knife, cut carrots and courgettes into matchstick-thin strips. Trim and slice mushrooms. Set vegetables aside.

3 Coat surface of browning dish with oil. Add pork and onion mixture; stir quickly to brown. Cook on High (100% power) for 1½ (1:30)–2 minutes. Remove from browning dish; set aside.

4 In glass jug, place butter or margarine and lemon juice. Cook, covered with kitchen paper, on High for 45 seconds, or until butter or margarine is melted.

5 In casserole, place carrots, mange-touts and water. Cook, covered, on High for 5–5½ (5:30) minutes, stirring once; drain. To casserole, add courgettes, mushrooms and lemon butter. Cook, covered, on High for 3–4 minutes, until vegetables are tender-crisp, stirring once. Place pork and onion mixture on top of vegetables. Cook, covered, on High for 1 minute, or until pork is hot.

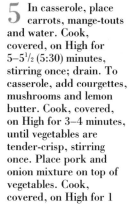

6 To serve: arrange pork and vegetable mixture on warmed dinner plates. Garnish with spinach leaves.

Meal in Minutes *for 6 people*
Calypso Party

Crab-Filled Mushrooms, page 118 (double quantity)
Pork Jambalaya, page 219
Marinated Okra, page 265
Tossed green salad
Crème Brûlée, page 325, for 6
Fresh fruit platter

PREPARATION TIMETABLE

Early in day	*Prepare mushrooms up to end of step 2. Prepare salad leaves; store in polythene bags in refrigerator. Prepare fruit, sprinkle cut fruit with lemon juice; cover and refrigerate. Prepare okra up to end of step 3. Prepare Crème Brûlée up to end of step 3.*
1¹⁄₂ hours ahead	*Complete Crème Brûlée. Cook Pork Jambalaya.*
10 minutes before serving	*While meat is standing, complete Crab-Filled Mushrooms. Drain okra; place in serving dish and garnish. Place salad leaves in bowl and toss with dressing of your choice.*

Pork Loin

SPICY PORK TURNOVERS

Colour Index page 68. 4 servings. 630 cals per serving. Good source of riboflavin, thiamine, niacin, calcium, iron. Begin 2 hours ahead.

450 g boneless pork loin, trimmed of fat and minced	*140 g plain flour*
1 onion, finely chopped	*60 g cornmeal*
2¹⁄₂ teaspoons chilli powder	*50 g Cheddar cheese, grated*
40 g raisins	*60 g white vegetable fat*
30 g slivered almonds	*5–6 tablespoons water*
2 tablespoons tomato purée	*Coriander leaves to garnish*
5 pimiento-stuffed olives, chopped	*Creamy Avocado Sauce (below, optional)*

1. In 30 × 20 cm microwave-safe baking dish, place pork and onion. Cook, covered with kitchen paper, on High (100% power) for 5–7 minutes, until pork is no longer pink, stirring occasionally.

2. Into pork mixture, stir chilli powder, raisins, almonds, tomato purée and chopped olives. Cook, covered with kitchen paper, on High for 8–10 minutes, until raisins are plump and sauce thickens slightly, stirring occasionally. Set aside to cool while preparing pastry.

3. In mixing bowl, combine flour and cornmeal; add cheese and vegetable fat. With fingers or 2 knives used scissor fashion, cut and rub in cheese and vegetable fat until mixture resembles crumbs. Into mixture, sprinkle water, 1 tablespoon at a time. Mix lightly with fork, until pastry just holds together. Shape into ball; flatten slightly. Wrap in greaseproof paper and refrigerate for about 1 hour, or until well chilled.

4. On lightly floured surface, with floured rolling pin, roll out half of pastry into round about 3 mm thick. Using 12.5 cm round plate as guide, cut out 4 rounds from pastry. Repeat with remaining pastry, rerolling trimmings, to make 8 rounds in all.

5. On to half of 1 pastry round, spoon one-eighth of pork filling. Brush pastry edge lightly with water; fold pastry over filling. With fork, firmly press edges together to seal. Place turnovers on ungreased large baking sheet. Repeat with remaining pastry rounds and pork filling.

6. Preheat conventional oven to 200°C (400°F, gas mark 6). Bake turnovers conventionally for 15 minutes, or until golden brown. Transfer to warmed serving platter and garnish with coriander. If you like, serve with Creamy Avocado Sauce.

CREAMY AVOCADO SAUCE: in food processor with knife blade attached or in blender, process *1 ripe avocado* until smooth with *375 ml plain yogurt, 2 sliced spring onions, 1 tablespoon lime juice* and *1 teaspoon ground cumin*. Season with *Tabasco sauce to taste.*

PORK JAMBALAYA

Colour Index page 67. 6 servings. 292 cals per serving. Good source of vitamin A, thiamine, vitamin C, iron. Begin 1¹/₂ hours ahead.

45 g butter or margarine	Large pinch of cayenne
3 tablespoons plain flour	pepper
2 large onions, chopped	1 tablespoon tomato
2 garlic cloves, crushed	purée
3 medium celery sticks,	1 medium green pepper,
chopped	diced
450 g boneless pork loin,	1 medium red pepper,
cut into 4 cm cubes	diced
500 ml Chicken Stock	4 spring onions, sliced
(page 125) or stock	60 g long-grain rice
from a cube	Salt and pepper to taste
¹/₂ teaspoon poultry	
seasoning	
¹/₂ teaspoon filé powder	

1. In deep 2.5 litre microwave-safe casserole, place butter or margarine. Heat, covered with kitchen paper, on High (100% power) for 45 seconds–1 minute, until melted.
2. Into melted butter or margarine, stir flour until blended. Cook on High for 5–7 minutes, until golden brown, stirring frequently.
3. To flour mixture, add onions, garlic, celery and pork cubes; stir until vegetables and meat are coated with flour mixture. Stir in stock, poultry seasoning, filé powder, cayenne pepper and tomato purée. Cook, covered, on Medium (50% power) for 30 minutes, or until pork is cooked, stirring occasionally.
4. Into mixture, stir peppers, onions and rice. Cook, covered, on Medium for 15–20 minutes, until rice is tender but still firm; season with salt and pepper. Allow to stand, covered, on heat-proof surface for 10 minutes. Transfer to warmed serving dish and serve immediately.

FILÉ Filé powder is derived from ground sassafras leaves. It is used as a thickener and flavouring in traditional Creole and Cajun dishes, such as gumbo. It can be added straight to cooking juices or dissolved in water first. If not available, you can substitute dried rubbed sage for an alternative flavouring.

SWEDISH MEATBALLS

Colour Index page 64. 401 cals per serving. Low in salt. Good source of vitamin A, vitamin B₁₂, niacin, iron. Begin 45 minutes ahead.

Ingredients for 6 servings		Microwave cookware
45 g butter or margarine, softened	¹/₂ teaspoon pepper	Small bowl
1 onion, chopped	¹/₂ teaspoon grated nutmeg	24 cm round flan dish
225 g boneless pork loin, trimmed of fat and minced	¹/₄ teaspoon salt	Large bowl
125 g minced beef	4 tablespoons chopped fresh dill	
125 g minced veal	2 tablespoons plain flour	
45 g dried breadcrumbs	250 ml Beef Stock (page 125) or stock from a cube	
1 egg, beaten	125 ml soured cream	
60 ml double cream	Gravy browning (optional)	
60 ml club soda or light ale		

1 In small bowl, place 15 g butter or margarine and chopped onion. Cook on High (100% power) for 3–4 minutes, until onion is softened, stirring halfway through cooking.

2 In mixing bowl, with fork, combine minced pork, beef and veal. Add softened onion, breadcrumbs, egg, cream, club soda or light ale, pepper, nutmeg and salt, and 2 tablespoons chopped dill. Stir well to mix; mixture will be soft.

3 With wet hands, form mixture into 2 cm balls. Brush flan dish with 15 g butter or margarine. Arrange half of meatballs in 2 circles on dish.

4 Cook meatballs on High for 6–8 minutes, turning over and rearranging after 3 minutes; transfer to large bowl and keep warm. Repeat with remaining butter or margarine and meatballs.

5 To drippings in flan dish, add flour; stir to combine. Cook on High for 1 minute. Stir in stock and soured cream. Cook on High for 3–4 minutes, until sauce thickens and bubbles, stirring often. If you like, add 1 teaspoon gravy browning.

6 Over meatballs, pour sauce. Cook on High, covered, for 2–3 minutes, until heated through. Serve hot, garnished with remaining chopped dill.

Bacon is best cooked in the microwave; it does not curl or shrink as it does when cooked conventionally, and cleaning up is easier. Bacon rashers vary in thickness, as well as in sugar and fat content; to ensure that bacon cooks evenly, choose rashers of equal thickness and with similar fat-to-lean ratio. To separate bacon rashers easily, heat pack on High (100% power) for 15–30 seconds.

Do not let bacon rashers overlap or they will not cook properly. When done, bacon will be evenly browned. It should then be left to stand for about 5 minutes before serving, until it is crisp.

Cooking bacon

On microwave-safe plate or paper plate, place 2 sheets kitchen paper, one on top of another. Place 2 bacon rashers on paper; cover with another sheet paper. Cook on High (100% power) for 1½ (1:30)–2 minutes. Alternatively, cook on special microwave bacon rack. Allow to stand for 5 minutes.

Cooking bacon in batches

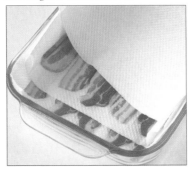

In 30 × 20 cm microwave-safe baking dish, place 2 layers kitchen paper. Arrange 5 bacon rashers on paper; cover with 2 sheets paper. Add 5 more bacon rashers, then 1 more sheet paper. Cook on High (100% power) for 7½ (7:30)–9 minutes, rotating dish once. Allow to stand for 5 minutes.

PAPER
Plain white absorbent kitchen paper and paper napkins can be safely used in the microwave; patterned and coloured paper and napkins should not be used as dyes can transfer to foods or oven floor during heating process.

Smoked Pork Loin and Spareribs

SMOKED PORK AND BEAN BAKE

Colour Index page 61. 6 servings. 282 cals per serving. Good source of thiamine, calcium, iron, fibre. Begin 25 minutes ahead.

1 small onion, thinly sliced	4 tablespoons tomato purée
110 g brown sugar	1 × 400 g can white kidney (cannellini) beans, drained and rinsed
2 tablespoons dark molasses or treacle	
1 tablespoon dry mustard	1 × 450 g smoked boneless pork loin roast, cut into 6 slices
1 tablespoon Worcestershire sauce	
60 ml cider vinegar	Parsley to garnish

1. In 2 litre microwave-safe casserole, place onion, brown sugar, molasses or treacle, mustard, Worcestershire sauce, vinegar and tomato purée; stir to combine. Cook, covered, on High (100% power) for 5–7 minutes, until onion softens slightly and sauce is blended, stirring twice.
2. Into mixture, stir beans. Add pork slices, pushing them down into bean mixture. Cook, covered, on Medium (50% power) for 15 minutes, or until flavours are blended and pork slices are hot, stirring occasionally. Serve in casserole, garnished with parsley sprigs.

SAVOURY SPARERIB CHOPS

Colour Index page 64. 4 servings. 473 cals per serving. Good source of vitamin A, thiamine, vitamin C, iron.
Begin 55 minutes ahead.

1 large onion, chopped	2 tablespoons brown sugar
1 large green pepper, cut into thin strips	1 chicken stock cube
2 tablespoons vegetable oil	½ teaspoon caraway seeds, crushed
2 tablespoons paprika	1 kg small sparerib chops, well trimmed
450 g sauerkraut	
1 × 225 g can tomato sauce	Soured cream (optional)

1. In 3 litre microwave-safe casserole, place onion, green pepper and oil. Cook, covered, on High (100% power) for 6 minutes, or until vegetables soften, stirring twice. Add paprika; stir. Cook on High for 1 minute.
2. Into mixture, stir undrained sauerkraut, tomato sauce, brown sugar, stock cube and caraway seeds. Place chops in casserole; coat with sauce. Cook, covered, on High for 35–40 minutes, until meat is fork-tender, turning chops over and rotating casserole after 15 minutes.
3. *To serve:* with fish slice, transfer chops to warmed serving platter. Spoon sauce over. If you like, serve with soured cream.

Ham and Gammon Steaks

GLAZED HAM

Colour Index page 67. 8 servings. 324 cals per serving. Good source of riboflavin, thiamine, niacin, iron, zinc. Begin 1½ hours ahead.

40 g soft brown sugar	1 × 2 kg boneless fully
4 tablespoons apple	cooked honey roast
sauce	ham
2 tablespoons made	Whole cloves (optional)
mustard	2 tablespoons water

1. *Prepare glaze:* in 500 ml measuring jug, combine brown sugar, apple sauce and mustard. Cook on High (100% power) for 3–4 minutes, until syrupy, stirring twice.
2. With sharp knife, remove excess fat from ham, leaving 5 mm layer of fat. Score fat in decorative diamond pattern. If you like, insert 1 whole clove in each diamond shape.
3. Into 3 litre microwave-safe casserole, place ham, fat side uppermost. Spoon water into base of casserole. Cook, covered, on Medium-Low (30% power) for 1 hour, turning ham over every 20 minutes.
4. Uncover ham; brush with prepared glaze. Cook, uncovered, on Medium-Low for 20 minutes longer, until meat thermometer inserted in several places reaches 54°C (130°F), brushing with glaze every 5 minutes.
5. On heatproof surface, allow ham to stand, tented with foil, for 10–15 minutes before serving. Temperature will reach 60°C (140°F).

HAM AND BEAN CASSEROLE

Colour Index page 62. 6 servings. 296 cals per serving. Good source of vitamin A, thiamine, niacin, calcium, iron, fibre. Begin 25 minutes ahead.

1 onion, chopped	1 chicken stock cube
1 garlic clove, crushed	½ teaspoon dried
1 tablespoon vegetable	rosemary
oil	¼ teaspoon pepper
2 × 400 g cans white	60 ml water
kidney (cannellini)	450 g boneless fully
beans	cooked smoked ham
2 celery sticks, thinly	½ head escarole
sliced	
2 carrots, coarsely	
shredded	

1. In 3 litre microwave-safe casserole, place onion, garlic and oil. Cook, covered, on High (100% power) for 5 minutes, or until onion softens, stirring twice.
2. Drain and rinse 1 can beans. To casserole, add drained beans, remaining can beans with their liquid, celery, carrots, stock cube, rosemary, pepper and water; stir. Cook, covered, on High for 12–15 minutes, until hot, stirring twice.
3. Meanwhile, with knife, cut ham into 2 cm cubes. Tear escarole into bite-sized pieces.
4. Into bean mixture, stir ham and escarole. Cook, covered, on High for 2–3 minutes, until escarole wilts, stirring halfway through cooking. Serve immediately.

GAMMON STEAKS WITH ORANGE AND HONEY GLAZE

Colour Index page 64. 404 cals per serving. Good source of thiamine, iron, zinc. Begin 35 minutes ahead.

Mustard and spices give a piquant flavour to Gammon Steaks with Orange and Honey Glaze, and the decorative orange garnish adds a touch of sweetness which helps offset the salty taste of the gammon. If you like, you can used canned pineapple slices in natural juice instead of the oranges used here.

Ingredients for 2 servings		Microwave cookware
2 large oranges	¼ teaspoon ground	500 ml measuring jug
1 tablespoon coarse-	ginger	24 cm round flan dish
grained mustard	2 × 175 g gammon	
2 tablespoons clear	steaks	
honey	Parsley to garnish	
¼ teaspoon ground		
cinnamon		
¼ teaspoon ground		
ginger		

1 With vegetable peeler, remove strips of peel from 1 orange, taking care to remove as little of the bitter white pith as possible. Cut peel into julienne strips.

2 Squeeze juice from orange. Into measuring jug, pour orange juice; add mustard, honey, cinnamon, ginger and julienne strips of orange peel. Cook, loosely covered, on High (100% power) for 3–4 minutes, until sauce is bubbling and syrupy.

3 Meanwhile, with sharp knife, remove peel and pith from remaining orange; cut between membranes to remove segments. Set orange segments aside.

4 Remove rind and trim fat from gammon steaks; with kitchen shears, snip around edges of each gammon steak at 1 cm intervals (this helps prevent steaks from curling during cooking).

5 In flan dish, place gammon steaks. Cook, covered with greaseproof paper, on High for 2 minutes. With orange glaze, brush gammon steaks. Cook, covered with greaseproof paper, on High for 2 minutes. Allow to stand for 1–2 minutes.

6 Serve gammon steaks hot, with glaze poured over, garnished with reserved orange segments and parsley sprigs.

Veal Roasts

HOLIDAY VEAL ROAST

Colour Index page 68. 433 cals per serving. Good source of vitamin A, niacin, calcium, iron. Begin 2 hours ahead.

Ingredients for 12 servings		Microwave cookware
1 × 1.8 kg boneless veal breast, trimmed of excess fat	30 g butter or margarine, melted	32.5 × 22.5 cm baking dish
275 g frozen chopped spinach, thawed	½ teaspoon browning sauce	500 ml measuring jug
115 g Fontina or Cheddar cheese, grated	1 onion, diced	
25 g Parmesan cheese, grated	Water	
1 egg	Sweet Pepper Medley (right, optional)	
¼ teaspoon salt	1 tablespoon plain flour	
200 g canned pimientos, drained		

SWEET PEPPER MEDLEY

On cutting board, with sharp knife, cut *10 large peppers (red, green and yellow)* into 2.5 cm strips. With same sharp knife, thinly slice *1 large onion*. In 4 litre microwave-safe casserole, place pepper strips, sliced onion, *3 tablespoons vegetable oil, 1 teaspoon dried oregano* and ¼ *teaspoon salt*. Cook pepper mixture, covered, on High (100% power) for 10–12 minutes until vegetables are tender-crisp, stirring occasionally. Serve hot as accompaniment to roasts. 12 servings. 71 cals per serving.

1 On cutting board, spread veal breast flat. With rolling pin or meat mallet, pound meat to 45 × 25 cm rectangle, about 2.5 cm thick.

2 Drain spinach well. In mixing bowl, combine spinach, cheeses, egg and salt; spread evenly over surface of meat.

3 If pimientos are thick, cut each horizontally in half, then into 4 cm pieces. Arrange pimientos randomly over spinach mixture.

4 Starting from 1 narrow end, roll up meat tightly; tie with string at 2.5 cm intervals. In small mixing bowl, combine melted butter or margarine and browning sauce.

5 Over meat, brush melted mixture. In baking dish, mix onion and 60 ml water. Into onion mixture, place meat, seam side up. Cook meat, covered, on Medium (50% power) for 30 minutes.

6 With fork, turn seam side down; rotate casserole. Cook meat, covered, on Medium for 25–30 minutes longer, until meat thermometer inserted in centre reaches 71°C (160°F).

7 On heatproof surface, allow meat to stand, tented with foil, for 15 minutes. Temperature will reach 77°C (170°F).

8 If you like, during meat standing time, make Sweet Pepper Medley. When meat has reached desired temperature, strain meat juices from baking dish into measuring jug. With spoon, skim fat from surface. In small bowl, combine flour and 2 tablespoons water until smooth.

9 Into meat juices in measuring jug, stir flour mixture. Cook on High (100% power) for 4–6 minutes, until gravy thickens slightly, stirring halfway through cooking.

10 With sharp knife, cut veal into slices, removing and discarding string as you carve. Arrange slices on warmed serving platter, with Sweet Pepper Medley if you like. Serve gravy separately.

STUFFED SHOULDER OF VEAL

Colour Index page 68. 10 servings. 443 cals per serving. Good source of riboflavin, thiamine, niacin, calcium, iron. Begin 2 hours ahead.

225 g fresh (not dried) spinach-filled ravioli in 2.5–4 cm squares	250 ml dry white wine
50 g thinly sliced Parma ham, diced	250 ml Beef Stock (page 125) or stock from a cube
50 g provolone cheese, diced	1½ tablespoons cornflour dissolved in 3 tablespoons cold water
3 spring onions, sliced	Salt and pepper to taste
½ teaspoon dried basil	Parsley sprigs to garnish
2 tablespoons olive or vegetable oil	
1 × 1.8 kg boned veal shoulder roasting joint	

1. In mixing bowl, combine ravioli, Parma ham, provolone, spring onions, basil and 1 tablespoon olive or vegetable oil; set aside.

2. On cutting board, place veal shoulder, fat side down. To make veal evenly thick, with sharp knife held parallel to cutting surface, cut off horizontal slices from thick parts of veal. Press cut off slices where needed along edges of meat to make 45 × 25 cm rectangle. Then, if necessary, pound meat with dull edge of large knife or smooth edge of meat mallet to make about 2.5 cm thick throughout.

3. Along centre of meat, spoon ravioli mixture. Pull meat up and over stuffing. With heavy string, tie meat at 5 cm intervals.

4. In frying pan over medium-high heat, heat remaining oil. Add stuffed meat and quickly brown on all sides. On microwave-safe rack in 32.5 × 22.5 cm microwave-safe baking dish, place meat, seam side up.

5. Into frying pan, pour wine and stock; stir to loosen any sediment. Over high heat, bring liquid to the boil; pour over meat in baking dish.

6. Cook meat, covered, on Medium (50% power) for 20 minutes. Turn meat seam side down. Cook, covered, on Medium for 20–30 minutes longer, until a meat thermometer inserted in centre of roast reaches 71°C (160°F). Remove roast to warmed serving platter and tent with foil. Allow to stand for 10–15 minutes; temperature will reach 77°C (170°F).

7. Meanwhile, into 500 ml microwave-safe measuring jug, strain meat juices from baking dish. With spoon, skim off excess fat. Add dissolved cornflour and cook on High (100% power) for 5-6 minutes, until gravy thickens, stirring twice. Season with salt and pepper. With sharp knife, cut roast into slices, removing and discarding string as you carve. Arrange slices on warmed serving platter; pour over gravy. Garnish with parsley and serve immediately.

To hold in heat and reduce spatter when cooking a roast, meat can be tented loosely with greaseproof or waxed paper. To prevent paper sticking to fat or skin, brush 'food side' of paper with a little vegetable oil. Remove paper and tent with foil during standing time, according to instructions in recipe.

ROAST LOIN OF VEAL WITH PURÉE OF SWEDE

Colour Index page 68. 235 cals per serving. Low in fat. Good source of iron, fibre. Begin 1½ hours ahead.

Ingredients for 8 servings		Microwave cookware
450 g swede	1 × 1.4 kg boned and rolled loin of veal	32.5 × 22.5 cm baking dish
1 small onion, chopped	60 ml Chicken Stock (page 125) or stock from a cube	
2 garlic cloves, crushed	Salt and pepper to taste	
2 tomatoes, chopped	Watercress sprigs to garnish	
½ teaspoon ground cumin		
30 g butter or margarine		

1. With sharp knife, peel swede; cut into 2.5 cm chunks. In baking dish, combine swede, onion, garlic, tomatoes, cumin and butter or margarine.

2. Cover vegetables in baking dish with kitchen paper. Heat on High (100% power) for 45 seconds–1 minute, until butter or margarine is melted, stirring once. With spoon, push vegetables to sides of dish.

3. In centre of dish, place meat; add stock. Cook, covered, on Medium (50% power) for 20 minutes.

4. With fork, turn meat over. Cook, covered, on Medium for 20–30 minutes longer, until meat thermometer inserted in centre of roast reaches 71°C (160°F). Transfer roast to warmed serving platter. Allow to stand, tented with foil, for 10–15 minutes. Temperature will reach 74–77°C (165–170°F).

5. During meat standing time, prepare sauce: in food processor with knife blade attached or in blender, process vegetables and cooking juices until smooth; season. With sharp knife, cut veal into thin slices, removing and discarding string as you carve.

6. Pour small amount of sauce on to each of 8 warmed dinner plates; arrange slices of veal on sauce. Garnish with watercress sprigs and serve immediately.

Veal Escalopes and Knuckle

VEAL MARSALA

Colour Index page 62. 376 cals per serving. Good source of niacin, iron. Begin 25 minutes ahead.

Ingredients	For 4	For 2	For 1
Veal escalopes, 1 cm thick (about 115 g each)	4 escalopes	2 escalopes	1 escalope
Butter or margarine	60 g	30 g	15 g
Paprika	1/2 teaspoon	1/4 teaspoon	pinch
Dry Marsala	120 ml	60 ml	30 ml
Dried breadcrumbs, made from Italian or French bread	70 g	45 g	25 g
Chopped parsley or other fresh herbs	garnish	garnish	garnish
Microwave cookware	Shallow 21.5 cm pie dish	Shallow 21.5 cm pie dish	Shallow 21.5 cm pie dish
	32.5 × 22.5 cm baking dish	30 × 20 cm baking dish	20 cm square baking dish
Time on High (100% power) Marsala mixture	3–4 minutes	2–3 minutes	1 1/2 (1:30)– 2 minutes
Veal escalopes	5–8 minutes	3–5 minutes	2–3 minutes
Reheating Marsala mixture	1–2 minutes	1 minute	30 seconds

1 On cutting board, with dull edge of large knife or smooth edge of meat mallet, pound veal escalopes until about 3 mm thick.

2 In pie dish (see Chart), place butter or margarine, paprika and Marsala. Cook, covered with kitchen paper, on High for time in Chart, or until melted, stirring twice.

3 On greaseproof paper, spread breadcrumbs. Dip escalopes in Marsala mixture, then in breadcrumbs, coating on both sides. Reserve remaining mixture.

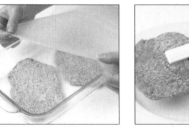

4 In baking dish (see Chart), place escalopes, 5 mm apart. Cook, covered loosely with greaseproof paper, on High for time in Chart, until juices run clear.

5 Place escalopes on warmed platter; keep warm. Reheat reserved Marsala mixture on High for time in Chart.

6 Drizzle Marsala mixture over escalopes on platter. Sprinkle with chopped parsley or other herbs to garnish. Serve immediately.

VEAL WITH SPINACH

Colour Index page 62. 4 servings. 430 cals per serving. Good source of vitamin A, riboflavin, niacin, calcium, iron. Begin 25 minutes ahead.

90 g butter or margarine
2 tablespoons lemon juice
1/2 chicken stock cube
1 garlic clove, crushed
60 ml water
1/2 teaspoon paprika
75 g dried breadcrumbs
1/4 teaspoon salt
450 g veal escalopes, each 5 mm thick
275 g spinach leaves
350 g cherry tomatoes

1. In 3 litre microwave-safe casserole, place first 5 ingredients. Cook, covered, on High (100% power) for 3 1/2 (3:30)–4 minutes, stirring halfway through cooking.
2. On greaseproof paper, mix paprika, breadcrumbs and salt. On cutting board, with smooth edge of meat mallet, pound escalopes until about 3 mm thick. Dip escalopes in butter mixture, then in breadcrumbs. Toss spinach and tomatoes in remaining butter mixture.
3. In 32.5 × 22.5 cm microwave-safe baking dish, place escalopes. Cook, covered, on High for 8 minutes, rearranging escalopes once. Transfer to warmed serving platter; keep warm. In same dish, place spinach and tomato mixture. Cook, covered, on High for 3–4 minutes, until spinach wilts. Serve immediately, with veal.

OSSO BUCO

Colour Index page 68. 4 servings. 495 cals per serving. Good source of riboflavin, thiamine, niacin, iron. Begin 2 hours ahead.

3 tablespoons olive oil
2 onions, chopped
2 celery sticks, chopped
2 garlic cloves, crushed
4 slices veal knuckle (shin), cut 5 mm thick
250 ml dry white wine
1 × 225 g can chopped tomatoes
120 ml Beef Stock (page 125) or stock from a cube
7 g dried mushrooms
1 teaspoon dried basil
1 teaspoon dried oregano
1/2 teaspoon dried rosemary
1/2 bay leaf
200 g arborio rice
Salt and pepper to taste

1. In 32.5 × 22.5 cm microwave-safe baking dish, combine 2 tablespoons oil, onions, celery and garlic. Cook on High (100% power) for 4–5 minutes, until vegetables soften, stirring twice.
2. In frying pan over high heat, heat 1 tablespoon oil. Add veal pieces and brown on both sides. Arrange veal pieces on top of vegetables in baking dish, at least 2.5 cm apart.
3. Into frying pan, pour wine; stir to loosen sediment. Over high heat, bring to the boil; pour over veal. Add tomatoes and next 6 ingredients.
4. Into meat, stir rice. Cook on High for 12–15 minutes, until rice is tender, stirring occasionally. Discard bay leaf and season.

Meal in Minutes *for 6 people*

Easter Lunch

Tartlets with Asparagus and Brie Filling, page 117
Glazed Ham, page 221
Hot Pepper Jelly, page 376, Sweetcorn Relish, page 377
Special Mixed Vegetables, page 274
Light Lemon and Almond Tart, page 348

PREPARATION TIMETABLE

Up to 1 week ahead	*Make Hot Pepper Jelly and Sweetcorn Relish.*
1 day ahead	*Make Light Lemon and Almond Tart but do not decorate; store in airtight container.*
Early in day	*Make Tartlets with Asparagus and Brie Filling; loosely cover. Prepare and cook Special Mixed Vegetables; cover.*
1½ hours ahead	*Cook Glazed Ham; allow to stand. Decorate lemon and almond tart.*
Just before serving	*Reheat vegetables on High (100% power). If you like, reheat Tartlets with Asparagus and Brie Filling on High.*

DECORATING A HAM
Scoring the fat on top of a ham gives it an attractive finish for a festive occasion or celebration.

With sharp knife, score fat on top of ham in decorative diamond pattern. Insert 1 whole clove in each diamond shape; cook and glaze according to recipe instructions.

Veal Stews and Meat Glazes

VEAL RAGOÛT

Colour Index page 68. 657 cals per serving. Good source of vitamin A, riboflavin, niacin, calcium, iron, fibre. Begin 1½ hours ahead.

Ingredients for 4 servings		Microwave cookware
450 g stewing veal, cut into 4 cm chunks	225 g frozen baby onions	2 litre soufflé dish or casserole
500 ml water	8 large button mushrooms	
30 g butter or margarine	1 tablespoon plain flour	
1 large carrot, diced	250 ml double cream	
1 large celery stick, diced	2 egg yolks	
1 garlic clove, crushed	¼ teaspoon salt	
1 teaspoon dried thyme	Pepper to taste	
1 bay leaf		
250 ml Chicken Stock (page 125) or stock from a cube		

1 In soufflé dish or casserole, place veal; add water. Cook, covered, on High (100% power) for 8–10 minutes, until water boils. With fish slice or slotted spoon, transfer veal to kitchen paper to drain. Into mixing bowl, pour cooking liquid through muslin-lined sieve; set aside.

2 In dish or casserole used for veal, place butter or margarine. Heat, covered with kitchen paper, on High for 45 seconds, or until melted. Add carrot and next 4 ingredients. Cook on High for 5–7 minutes, until softened, stirring twice. To vegetables, add veal and stock; stir. Cook, covered, on Medium (50% power) for 20 minutes, stirring often.

3 To dish or casserole, add onions and mushrooms; stir. Cook, covered, on Medium for 15–25 minutes longer, until meat is fork-tender.

4 In another mixing bowl, place flour. Gradually add 120 ml reserved cooking liquid, stirring until smooth. Add flour mixture to ragoût. Cook on High for 3–5 minutes, until sauce thickens slightly, stirring twice.

5 Meanwhile, in bowl used for flour, combine cream and egg yolks. Stir small amount of hot cooking liquid from ragoût into cream mixture. Slowly pour cream mixture back into ragoût, stirring to prevent lumping.

6 Discard bay leaf. Cook ragoût on Medium-Low (30% power) for 2–3 minutes, until mixture thickens slightly, stirring twice. Season with salt and pepper.

VEAL STEW PROVENÇALE

Colour Index page 68. 4 servings. 377 cals per serving. Good source of vitamin A, niacin, vitamin C, iron. Begin 1½ hours ahead.

450 g stewing veal, cut into 4 cm chunks
70 g plain flour
¼ teaspoon salt
¼ teaspoon pepper
2 tablespoons olive or vegetable oil
3 small onions, chopped
1 green pepper, chopped
1 red pepper, chopped
250 ml dry white wine
1 beef stock cube
1 tablespoon tomato purée
1 teaspoon dried thyme
1 teaspoon dried rosemary
1 teaspoon dried oregano
2 teaspoons browning sauce (optional)
2 garlic cloves, crushed
10 stoned black olives

1. Trim fat from veal. On greaseproof paper, combine flour, salt and pepper. Lightly coat veal chunks in seasoned flour.

2. In frying pan over high heat, heat oil. Add veal chunks and quickly brown on all sides. With slotted spoon, remove veal to 2 litre microwave-safe casserole.

3. In same frying pan, over medium-high heat, cook onions and green and red peppers until softened, stirring frequently. Add to veal.

4. In 1 litre measuring jug, combine wine, stock cube, tomato purée, thyme, rosemary, oregano and, if you like, browning sauce. Pour over veal. Cook, covered, on Medium (50% power) for 30 minutes, stirring occasionally.

5. Add crushed garlic and olives; stir. Cook, covered, on Medium for 15–20 minutes longer, until veal is fork tender.

MEAT GLAZES

These glazes are ideal for dressing up plain cooked pork, lamb, ham and veal.

Orange and Mincemeat Glaze: in blender at low speed, blend **8 tablespoons drained mincemeat** and **4 tablespoons orange marmalade** until smooth. Makes about 175 ml.

Curry and Orange Glaze: in small bowl, combine **150 ml golden syrup, 1 tablespoon curry powder** and **1 tablespoon grated orange zest** until blended. Makes 150 ml.

Tomato and Onion Glaze: in 1 litre measuring jug, cook **15 g butter or margarine** and **2 tablespoons finely chopped onion** on High (100% power) for 1 minute, or until onion softens. Stir in **1 × 225 g can chopped tomatoes, 2 tablespoons dark brown sugar** and **1 teaspoon Worcestershire sauce**; mix well to combine. Cook, covered, on High for 3–5 minutes, until glaze thickens slightly. Makes about 250 ml.

Lamb Roasts

ZESTY LEG OF LAMB

Colour Index page 64. 8 servings. 221 cals per serving. Good source of niacin, iron. Begin 55 minutes ahead.

1 × 1.6–1.8 kg leg of lamb, shank end	2 garlic cloves, crushed
4 tablespoons mango chutney	1 tablespoon red wine vinegar
2 tablespoons Dijon mustard	1 tablespoon Worcestershire sauce

1. With sharp knife, trim any large pieces of fat from lamb. Place lamb on microwave-safe rack in 32.5 × 22.5 cm microwave-safe baking dish.
2. In 500 ml microwave-safe measuring jug, combine chutney and next 4 ingredients. Cook on High (100% power) for 3–4 minutes, until bubbling, stirring halfway through cooking. With brush, coat lamb with half of mixture.
3. Shield thin end of leg with smooth strips of foil. Cook on High for 5 minutes. Reduce power level to Medium (50% power) and cook for 15–20 minutes longer, until meat thermometer inserted in centre reaches 57°C (135°F), for medium-rare, removing foil, turning roast over and brushing with remaining mixture halfway through cooking.
4. Remove lamb to platter. Allow to stand, tented with foil, for 10–15 minutes; temperature will reach 65–68°C (150–155°F).

LAMB PILAF

Colour Index page 69. 8 servings. 286 cals per serving. Low in sodium. Good source of calcium, iron. Begin 1¼ hours ahead.

30 g butter or margarine	300 g roast lamb, cut into 4 cm cubes
1 large onion, finely chopped	150 g frozen peas, thawed
1 green pepper, chopped	Salt and pepper to taste
265 g long-grain rice	250 ml plain yogurt
1 tablespoon curry powder	2 spring onions, thinly sliced
750 ml Chicken Stock (page 125) or stock from a cube	⅓ small cucumber, diced
	Mint to garnish

1. In 32.5 × 22.5 cm microwave-safe baking dish, place butter or margarine. Heat, covered with kitchen paper, on High (100% power) for 45 seconds, or until melted.
2. Into melted butter or margarine, stir onion and next 3 ingredients. Cook on High for 3–4 minutes, until vegetables soften, stirring once.
3. To vegetable mixture, add stock and lamb. Cook on Medium (50% power) for 25–35 minutes, until rice is tender, stirring occasionally.
4. Into lamb mixture, stir peas. Season with salt and pepper. Cook, covered, on Medium for 5 minutes, or until tender. Allow to stand, covered, on heatproof surface for 20 minutes. Meanwhile, combine yogurt, spring onions and cucumber; season.
5. *To serve:* top each portion of pilaf with yogurt sauce; garnish with mint.

For roast lamb that is medium-rare, remove meat from microwave when its temperature registers 57°C (135°F). Left to stand, tented with foil, its temperature will rise to 65°C–68°C (150°F–155°F). For a well-done roast, remove lamb from microwave when temperature is 65°C–71°C (150°F–160°F). Left to stand, its temperature will rise to 79°C (175°F).

APRICOT-GLAZED RACK OF LAMB

Colour Index page 65. 829 cals per serving. Good source of vitamin A, niacin, iron, fibre. Begin 45 minutes ahead.

Ingredients for 4 servings		Microwave cookware
½ teaspoon browning sauce 1 teaspoon water 1 × 1.1 kg best end of neck of lamb (ask butcher to chine joint for easier carving) 8 tablespoons apricot jam	1 tablespoon lemon juice 1 tablespoon made mustard ¼ teaspoon salt 2 × 400 g cans small whole carrots, drained Watercress sprigs to garnish	30 × 20 cm baking dish with rack Large bowl

1 In mixing bowl, combine browning sauce with water. Brush on lamb. Shield bone ends of ribs with smooth strips of foil.

2 On rack in baking dish, place lamb, fat side up. Cook, covered loosely with greaseproof paper, on Medium-High (70% power) for 8 minutes.

3 Meanwhile, in mixing bowl, combine apricot jam, lemon juice, mustard and salt. Spoon 4 tablespoons apricot mixture into large bowl; set aside.

4 Discard foil from bone ends. Cook on Medium-High for 7–8 minutes longer for medium-rare, until meat thermometer inserted in centre reaches 57°C (135°F). After cooking, brush with apricot mixture.

5 On heatproof surface, allow lamb to stand, tented with foil, for 5–10 minutes. Temperature will reach 65°C–68°C (150°F–155°F). Meanwhile, into reserved apricot mixture in large bowl, stir carrots. Cook, covered, on High (100% power) for 3–5 minutes, until hot, stirring twice.

6 *To serve:* place lamb on warmed serving platter; spoon carrots round. Garnish with watercress sprigs. If you like, decorate with cutlet frills.

227

Lamb Cutlets and Chops

MARINATED LAMB CUTLETS WITH HERBED PEAS

Colour Index page 69. 217 cals per serving. Good source of niacin, zinc, fibre. Begin early in day or 1 day ahead.

Ingredients	For 4	For 2	For 1
Mint and apple jelly	2 tablespoons	1 tablespoon	2 teaspoons
Dijon mustard	2 tablespoons	1 tablespoon	2 teaspoons
Garlic cloves, finely chopped	2 cloves	1 clove	1/2 clove
Mint leaves, chopped	3 tablespoons	2 tablespoons	2 1/2 teaspoons
Lamb cutlets, each 2.5 cm thick	8 cutlets	4 cutlets	2 cutlets
Frozen peas	275 g	150 g	65 g
Water	2 tablespoons	1 tablespoon	1 1/2 teaspoons
Butter or margarine	15 g	1 1/2 teaspoons	3/4 teaspoon
Mint sprigs	garnish	garnish	garnish
Microwave cookware	Browning dish 1.5 litre soufflé dish	Browning dish 1.5 litre soufflé dish	Browning dish 21.5 cm pie dish
Time on High (100% power) Cutlets	3–4 1/2 (4:30) minutes each batch	3–4 1/2 (4:30) minutes	2–2 1/2 (2:30) minutes
Peas	4–5 minutes	2 1/2 (2:30)–3 1/2 (3:30) minutes	1 1/2 (1:30)–2 minutes

1 In dish large enough to hold lamb cutlets in single layer, combine mint and apple jelly, mustard, garlic and half of mint.

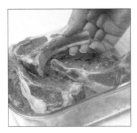

2 To mixture, add lamb cutlets, turning to coat. Cover dish and refrigerate for 2 hours or overnight, turning cutlets occasionally.

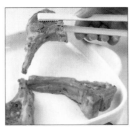

3 Preheat browning dish according to manufacturer's instructions. On browning dish, arrange cutlets with bones towards centre.

4 Cook cutlets on High for time in Chart, turning halfway through cooking. If cooking for 4, cook in batches, reheating browning dish between batches. Remove cutlets; cover and keep warm.

5 In soufflé dish or pie dish (see Chart), place peas and water. Cook, covered, on High for time in Chart, until peas are tender; drain. Toss with butter or margarine and remaining mint.

6 To serve: place 2 cutlets on each warmed dinner plate. Spoon herbed peas around; garnish with mint sprigs.

BACON-WRAPPED LAMB CHOPS

Colour Index page 62. 4 servings. 496 cals per serving (with sauce). Good source of niacin, iron, fibre. Begin 25 minutes ahead.

Redcurrant and Orange Sauce (below)
4 rashers streaky bacon
15 g butter or margarine
8 stoned prunes
8 dried apricot halves

2 slices white bread, cubed
1/4 teaspoon dried thyme
1/4 teaspoon dried basil
4 lamb loin chops, each 4 cm thick

1. Prepare Redcurrant and Orange Sauce. In 22.5 cm microwave-safe shallow pie dish, place bacon. Cook, covered with kitchen paper, on High (100% power) for 1 1/2 (1:30)–2 minutes, just until bacon begins to curl. Transfer bacon to kitchen paper to drain.
2. To bacon fat in pie dish, add butter or margarine. Heat, covered with kitchen paper, on High for 30–45 seconds, until melted. Add prunes, apricots, bread cubes, thyme and basil; stir to coat. Set aside.
3. To remove bones from lamb chops, with sharp knife and starting at 1 side of backbone, cut through meat along bone, keeping knife blade against bone. Cut down both sides of bone to separate bone from meat, making sure that meat remains in 1 piece. Trim off any excess fat from chops.
4. Fill each chop where bone has been removed with equal amount of filling. Push meat tightly round filling. To keep filling in place, wrap 1 bacon rasher tightly round side of each chop; secure with wooden cocktail stick.
5. On microwave-safe rack in 30 × 20 cm microwave-safe baking dish, place lamb chops. Cook on High for 3–5 minutes, until chops are cooked through to your liking, rotating dish halfway through cooking.
6. To serve: reheat Redcurrant and Orange Sauce on High for 1 minute. Place lamb chops on warmed serving platter. Serve sauce separately.

REDCURRANT AND ORANGE SAUCE

Makes about 120 ml. 27 cals per tablespoon. Begin 10 minutes ahead.

2 teaspoons grated orange zest
120 ml orange juice

4 tablespoons redcurrant jelly
1 teaspoon honey

1. In 500 ml microwave-safe measuring jug, combine orange zest, orange juice, redcurrant jelly and honey; stir until smooth.
2. Cook sauce on High (100% power) for 4–5 minutes, until boiling and slightly thickened, stirring occasionally. Serve warm.

Lamb Noisettes and Kebabs

LAMB NOISETTES WITH ORANGE

Colour Index page 62. 8 servings. 504 cals per serving. Good source of niacin, iron, zinc. Begin 25 minutes ahead.

75 g butter or margarine	½ teaspoon grated orange zest
1 teaspoon browning sauce	¼ teaspoon cider vinegar
8 lamb noisettes (boneless loin chops), each 2.5 cm thick	8 × 7.5 cm bread rounds, toasted
120 ml mayonnaise	4 tablespoons chopped parsley
½ teaspoon dried rosemary	8 orange slices
½ teaspoon dried thyme	Rosemary to garnish

1. In small microwave-safe bowl, place 45 g butter or margarine. Heat, covered with kitchen paper, on High (100% power) for 45 seconds–1 minute, until melted. Add browning sauce; brush on noisettes.

2. Arrange noisettes in 32.5 × 22.5 cm microwave-safe baking dish. Cook, covered loosely with greaseproof paper, on Medium-High (70% power) for 9–12 minutes for medium-rare, turning noisettes over occasionally. In mixing bowl, combine mayonnaise and next 4 ingredients.

3. In small microwave-safe bowl, place remaining butter or margarine. Heat, covered with kitchen paper, on High for 45 seconds, or until melted. Dip edges of toast in melted butter and roll in parsley to coat. Arrange toast on warmed serving platter; top each with orange slice and lamb noisette. Spoon over mayonnaise mixture; garnish.

LEMON AND LIME THAI KEBABS

Colour Index page 69. 4 servings. 368 cals per serving. Good source of vitamin A, niacin, vitamin C, iron. Begin early in day or 1 day ahead.

3 tablespoons lemon juice	1 garlic clove, crushed
2 tablespoons lime juice	450 g stewing lamb, cut into 4 cm chunks
2 tablespoons chopped fresh mint	1 papaya, peeled, seeded and cut into 5 cm chunks
½ teaspoon ground coriander	1 green pepper, cut into 4 cm chunks
½ teaspoon ground cumin	400 g Hot Cooked Rice (page 293)
1 tablespoon Worcestershire sauce	
2 tablespoons olive oil	

1. In large bowl, combine first 9 ingredients. Cover and refrigerate for 2 hours or overnight.

2. On eight 20–25 cm wooden skewers, thread lamb alternately with papaya and green pepper. Arrange on 25–30 cm microwave-safe platter. Cook on High (100% power) for 5–7 minutes, until lamb is fork-tender, turning over once. Spoon rice on to serving platter. Place kebabs on top.

Meal in Minutes *for 4 people*

Mother's Day Lunch

Celebration Prawns, page 119, for 4
Apricot-Glazed Rack of Lamb, page 227
Wild Rice and Mushroom Pilaf, page 292
Mint Jelly, page 376
Dinner rolls
Orange Chiffon Pie, page 346

PREPARATION TIMETABLE

Up to 1 week ahead	*Make Mint Jelly. Prepare Celebration Prawns up to end of step 4.*
1 day ahead	*Make Orange Chiffon Pie but do not decorate; store in airtight container.*
Early in day	*Cook Wild Rice and Mushroom Pilaf; cover and set aside.*
45 minutes ahead	*Cook rack of lamb; allow to stand. Decorate chiffon pie.*
About 15 minutes before serving	*Reheat pilaf on High (100% power). If you like, heat dinner rolls on High. Complete Celebration Prawns.*

Lamb Stews

Lamb, like any meat that has been cut into uniform cubes, cooks quickly and evenly in the microwave. For the almond garnish in Lamb Curry (below) place 40 g flaked almonds in shallow microwave-safe pie dish. Heat on High (100% power) for 1–1½ minutes, until lightly browned, stirring twice.

LAMB CURRY

Colour Index page 69. 402 cals per serving. Good source of vitamin A, thiamine, niacin, vitamin C, calcium, iron, fibre. Begin 1½ hours ahead.

Ingredients for 4 servings		Microwave cookware
1 lemon wedge	75 g dried apricots, diced	32.5 × 22.5 cm baking dish
2 cooking apples	250 ml Chicken Stock (page 125) or stock from a cube	
30 g butter or margarine		
2 tablespoons curry powder	1 tablespoon tomato purée	
1 large onion, cut into 5 cm chunks	275 g frozen peas, thawed	
1 green pepper, cut into 5 cm chunks	120 ml plain yogurt	
450 g stewing lamb, cut into 4 cm chunks	Toasted almonds and coriander to garnish	

1 In mixing bowl, place lemon wedge; fill bowl with cold water. Peel, core and cut apples into 4 cm chunks; place in lemon water to prevent discoloration.

2 In baking dish, place butter or margarine. Heat, covered with kitchen paper, on High (100% power) for 45 seconds, or until melted.

3 Into melted butter or margarine, stir curry powder, onion, green pepper and apple. Cook on High for 3–4 minutes, until vegetables are warm, stirring halfway through cooking.

4 Into vegetable mixture, stir lamb chunks, apricots, stock and tomato purée. Cook, covered, on Medium (50% power) for 45–60 minutes, until lamb is fork-tender, stirring occasionally.

5 Into lamb mixture, stir peas. Cook on High for 3–4 minutes, until hot, stirring halfway through cooking.

6 Into curry, gradually stir yogurt, until blended. Serve hot, garnished with toasted almonds and coriander leaves.

MOROCCAN LAMB WITH COUSCOUS

Colour Index page 69. 6 servings. 337 cals per serving. Good source of vitamin A, niacin, iron, fibre. Begin 2 hours ahead.

2 tablespoons olive or vegetable oil	½ teaspoon dried thyme
2 carrots, cut into 7.5 cm chunks, then lengthways into quarters	Large pinch of cayenne pepper
	150 g okra
2 large onions, sliced	1 × 400 g can chick peas, drained and rinsed
450 g stewing lamb, cut into 4 cm chunks	
350 ml tomato juice	350 ml Chicken Stock (page 125) or stock from a cube
2 tablespoons red wine vinegar	
1 cinnamon stick	¼ teaspoon turmeric
1 bay leaf	175 g quick-cooking couscous
1 teaspoon ground cumin	
1 teaspoon ground coriander	

1. Into 32.5 × 22.5 cm microwave-safe baking dish, pour oil. Heat, covered with kitchen paper, on High (100% power) for 45 seconds–1 minute, until oil is hot.

2. Into oil, stir carrots, onions and lamb. Cook on High for 5–6 minutes, until onions soften, stirring twice.

3. Meanwhile, in 1 litre microwave-safe measuring jug, combine tomato juice, vinegar, cinnamon stick, bay leaf, cumin, coriander, thyme and cayenne pepper; stir into lamb mixture. Cook, covered, on Medium (50% power) for 30–40 minutes, until carrots are tender, stirring occasionally.

4. Into lamb mixture, stir okra and chick peas. Cook, covered, on Medium for 15–20 minutes, until lamb is fork-tender, stirring occasionally; discard bay leaf. Allow lamb to stand, covered, on heatproof surface while preparing couscous.

5. In same measuring jug, combine stock and turmeric. Cook, covered, on High for 4–6 minutes, until boiling. Add couscous. Allow to stand, covered, on heatproof surface for 5 minutes. With fork, fluff up couscous.

6. *To serve:* spoon couscous on to warmed serving platter; top with lamb and vegetable mixture.

COUSCOUS Couscous is precooked semolina derived from durum wheat, forming fine, yellow, rice-like pellets. The traditional way to cook couscous involves steaming it over a highly spiced stew. A quick-and-easy modern alternative using the microwave, is to place couscous in boiling stock or water with spices such as turmeric added to taste, then to leave it to absorb the liquid. Fluff up with a fork before serving.

Lamb Stew and Minced Lamb

LAMB STEW WITH FETA

Colour Index page 69. 6 servings. 432 cals per serving. Good source of thiamine, niacin, calcium, iron. Begin 2 hours ahead.

2 tablespoons olive oil	450 g ripe tomatoes,
2 large onions, chopped	coarsely chopped
2 garlic cloves, crushed	120 ml dry white wine
450 g stewing lamb, cut	2 courgettes, cut into
into 4 cm cubes	4 cm chunks
1 teaspoon dried	225 g elbow macaroni,
rosemary	cooked
1 teaspoon dried	225 g feta cheese,
oregano	crumbled
2 tablespoons stoned	2 tablespoons chopped
black olives	fresh dill

1. In 32.5 × 22.5 cm microwave-safe baking dish, place oil and next 6 ingredients. Cook on High (100% power) for 5–6 minutes, until lamb is no longer pink, stirring halfway through cooking.
2. Into mixture, stir tomatoes and wine. Cook, covered, on Medium (50% power) for 45 minutes, stirring occasionally. Stir in courgettes. Cook, covered, on Medium for 15–20 minutes longer, until meat is fork-tender, stirring occasionally.
3. Combine macaroni, feta and dill. Spoon on to microwave-safe serving platter; spoon over stew. Cook, covered, on High for 4–5 minutes, until hot.

SHEPHERD'S PIE

Colour Index page 64. 6 servings. 421 cals per serving. Good source of vitamin B_{12}, riboflavin, thiamine, niacin, iron, zinc, fibre. Begin 45 minutes ahead.

1 tablespoon vegetable	2 teaspoons
oil	Worcestershire sauce
1 large onion, chopped	1/2 teaspoon dried thyme
6 mushrooms, chopped	1/2 teaspoon pepper
675 g minced lamb	4 tablespoons chopped
2 tablespoons plain flour	parsley
1 × 225 g can tomatoes	1 × 126 g packet instant
2 tablespoons tomato	mashed potato
purée	

1. In large microwave-safe bowl, place oil, onion and mushrooms. Cook on High (100% power) for 4–5 minutes, until vegetables are softened, stirring halfway through cooking.
2. To vegetable mixture, add lamb; stir to combine. Cook on High for 7–8 minutes, until meat is no longer pink, stirring twice. Skim off any excess fat. Stir in flour. Cook on High for 1 minute; stir.
3. To meat mixture, add tomatoes and next 4 ingredients; stir to mix and break up tomatoes. Cook on High for 10–12 minutes, until mixture thickens, stirring often. Stir in parsley. Transfer to 33 cm oval microwave-safe baking dish.
4. Make up potato according to packet instructions. Spread over meat mixture; rough up surface with fork. Cook on High for 10–12 minutes, until bubbling, turning dish every 4 minutes.

MOUSSAKA

Colour Index page 69. 375 cals per serving. Good source of vitamin A, B_{12}, niacin, iron, zinc, fibre. Begin 1 1/4 hours ahead.

Ingredients for 6 servings		Microwave cookware
450 g aubergines	1/2 teaspoon dried thyme	30 × 20 cm baking
2 tablespoons water	175 g feta cheese,	dish
1 tablespoon olive oil	crumbled	Large bowl
1 large onion, chopped	4 tablespoons chopped	500 ml measuring jug
2 garlic cloves,	fresh coriander or	
crushed	parsley	
450 g minced lamb	1/4 teaspoon pepper	
1 × 225 g can	25 g butter or margarine	
tomatoes, drained	30 g plain flour	
2 tablespoons tomato	250 ml milk	
purée	1/4 teaspoon paprika	
2 teaspoons dried	Coriander to garnish	
oregano		

1 Cut aubergines into 5 mm thick slices. In baking dish, place half of slices, overlapping them if necessary; sprinkle with 1 tablespoon water. Cook, covered, on High (100% power) for 4–5 minutes until tender, turning dish once. Transfer to kitchen paper to drain. Repeat with remaining aubergines and water.

2 In large bowl, place olive oil, onion and garlic. Cook on High for 2–3 minutes, until onion softens. Stir in lamb, breaking up any lumps with fork. Cook on High for 5–6 minutes, until meat is no longer pink, stirring twice.

3 To bowl, add tomatoes; stir to break up large pieces. Stir in tomato purée, oregano and thyme. Cook on High for 8–10 minutes, until tomato liquid is absorbed. Add half of feta cheese, chopped coriander or parsley and pepper.

4 Line base and sides of cleaned baking dish with aubergine slices. Spoon in meat mixture, layering in any remaining aubergine slices; set aside.

5 In measuring jug, place butter or margarine. Heat on High for 45 seconds–1 minute, until melted. Stir in flour until smooth and blended. Cook on High for 1 minute. Gradually stir in milk. Cook on High for 4–5 minutes, until sauce thickens, stirring often. Stir in remaining feta cheese.

6 Over meat mixture in dish, pour sauce, allowing edges of aubergines to show. Cook on High for 10–12 minutes, until hot and bubbling, turning dish a half turn every 4 minutes. Allow to stand on heatproof surface for 5 minutes. Sprinkle top with paprika and garnish before serving.

Sausages

KNACKWURST AND POTATO SUPPER

Colour Index page 65. 677 cals per serving. Good source of thiamine, niacin, vitamin C, iron, fibre. Begin 40 minutes ahead.

Knackwurst and Potato Supper adapts easily to many variations. For example, instead of knackwurst use frankfurters, salami, ham or liverwurst, or even hard-boiled eggs for a different flavour. You can also use any kind of potato, since cooking times are all the same.

Ingredients for 4 servings		Microwave cookware
900 g potatoes, well scrubbed, cut into 4 cm chunks 2 rashers streaky bacon, diced 1 onion, chopped 2 tablespoons brown sugar 1 tablespoon plain flour 3 tablespoons cider vinegar	1 tablespoon made mustard ½ teaspoon salt ¼ teaspoon pepper 450 g knackwurst sausages Endive leaves Coarsely chopped sweet pickled cucumber or sliced beetroot to garnish	2 litre casserole 3 litre casserole

1 In 2 litre casserole, place potatoes and 120 ml water. Cook, covered, on High (100% power) for 10 minutes, stirring once; drain. Cover and set aside.

2 In 3 litre casserole, place diced bacon. Cook, covered with kitchen paper, on High for 2–3 minutes, until bacon is browned. Transfer to kitchen paper to drain.

3 To bacon fat in casserole, add chopped onion. Cook on High for 3–4 minutes, until onion softens, stirring halfway through cooking.

4 Into onion mixture, stir brown sugar, flour, vinegar, mustard, salt, pepper and 150 ml water, until mixture is well blended. Cook on High for 3 minutes, or until flavours blend, stirring halfway through cooking.

5 With small, sharp knife, cut several diagonal slashes in each knackwurst. To onion mixture, add knackwurst and potatoes. Cook, covered, on High for 6–8 minutes, until potatoes are tender, stirring twice.

6 To serve: line serving platter with endive leaves; spoon knackwurst and potato mixture on to leaves. Sprinkle with bacon and garnish.

FRANKFURTER AND RED CABBAGE CASSEROLE

Colour Index page 63. 4 servings. 452 cals per serving. Good source of thiamine, niacin, vitamin C, calcium, iron, zinc, folic acid, fibre. Begin 35 minutes ahead.

30 g butter or margarine
2 cooking apples
2 onions, thinly sliced
1 red cabbage (about 700 g), thinly shredded
80 ml apple juice
1 tablespoon sugar
3 tablespoons red wine vinegar
450 g frankfurters, cut into 5 cm pieces

1. In 32.5 × 22.5 cm microwave-safe baking dish, place butter or margarine. Heat, covered with kitchen paper, on High (100% power) for 45 seconds.
2. Core and dice 1 apple. Into butter or margarine, stir onions and diced apple. Cook on High for 5 minutes, or until softened, stirring twice.
3. Into apple mixture, stir cabbage and next 3 ingredients. Cook, covered, on High for 7–10 minutes, until cabbage is tender, stirring once.
4. Cut remaining apple into wedges; add to mixture with frankfurters. Cook, covered, on High for 5–7 minutes, until frankfurters are hot, stirring twice.

CUMBERLAND SAUSAGES WITH GLAZED ONIONS

Colour Index page 63. 4 servings. 522 cals per serving. Good source of vitamin B_{12}, iron. Begin 35 minutes ahead.

30 g butter or margarine
45 g onions, sliced
120 ml Beef Stock (page 125) or stock from a cube
1 tablespoon soy sauce
1 tablespoon soft brown sugar
¼ teaspoon dried thyme
2 tablespoons chopped parsley
450 g Cumberland sausages (about 8), at room temperature
1 tablespoon vegetable oil

1. In large microwave-safe bowl, combine butter or margarine and next 5 ingredients. Cook, covered, on High (100% power) for 5 minutes, stirring once.
2. Uncover bowl. Cook on High for 15–20 minutes longer, until onions are tender and liquid has evaporated, stirring occasionally. Stir in chopped parsley; cover and set aside.
3. Preheat browning dish according to manufacturer's instructions. Pierce each sausage in several places. Coat browning dish with oil. Add sausages and press to brown on underside; turn sausages over. Cook on High for 4–6 minutes, turning over and rearranging twice.
4. Push sausages under onion mixture. Cook on High for 2 minutes, or until onions are heated through, stirring once. Serve hot.

Tex-Mex Buffet

Margaritas
Guacamole (below) with fresh vegetables and fruit, olives and tortilla chips
Chilli con Carne, page 211
Spicy Pork Turnovers, page 218 (double quantity)
Mexican Pancakes, page 194
Lime or lemon sorbet (bought)
Mexican Wedding Biscuits, page 365 (double quantity)

PREPARATION TIMETABLE

1 day ahead	*Make Mexican Wedding Biscuits; store in airtight container. Cook Chilli con Carne; cover and refrigerate. Make ice for Margaritas.*
Early in day	*Prepare Spicy Pork Turnovers up to end of step 5; do not bake. Prepare Mexican Pancakes up to end of step 4 and prepare sauce as in step 5. Cover pancakes and sauce and refrigerate. Prepare fresh vegetables; store in polythene bags in refrigerator.*
2 hours ahead	*Prepare glasses for Margaritas by dipping rims in lime juice and salt. Make Guacamole; cover and refrigerate.*
15 minutes before serving	*Complete Spicy Pork Turnovers. Reheat Chilli con Carne on High (100% power), until bubbling. Pour sauce over pancakes and finish in microwave as in recipe. Assemble Guacamole, vegetables, fruit, olives and tortilla chips. Make Margaritas as guests arrive.*

GUACAMOLE

Set the Mexican mood when your guests arrive by serving spicy hot Guacamole as a first course.

Peel and dice **2 tomatoes**. Chop **1 onion**. Crush **2 garlic cloves**. In bowl, mash flesh of **4 avocados** with **4 tablespoons lemon juice**. Add tomatoes, onion, garlic, **Tabasco sauce** and **salt to taste**; stir. Spoon into serving bowl; garnish with **sliced fresh green chillies** and **coriander sprigs** if you like.

Sausages

SAUSAGE AND PEPPERS

Colour Index page 65. 6 servings. 445 cals per serving. Good source of thiamine, vitamin C, iron, fibre. Begin 45 minutes ahead.

700 g spicy-hot fresh pork sausages	*1 × 400 g can chopped tomatoes*
¹/₂ teaspoon browning sauce	*2 tablespoons tomato purée*
1 teaspoon water	*¹/₂ teaspoon salt*
3 large green, yellow and/or red peppers, each cut into 2 cm strips	*¹/₄ teaspoon pepper*
	¹/₄ teaspoon fennel seeds, crushed
2 onions, each cut into 6 wedges	

1. With sharp knife, slash sausages. Place on microwave-safe rack in 32.5 × 22.5 cm microwave-safe browning dish. Mix browning sauce with water; brush on sausages. Cook, covered, on High (100% power) for 9–10 minutes, until meat is no longer pink, turning sausages over and rotating dish halfway through cooking. Remove sausages and rack; keep sausages warm.
2. To dripping in baking dish, add peppers and onions. Cook, covered, on High for 12–13 minutes, until softened, stirring twice.
3. Cut sausages into 2.5 cm pieces. Into pepper and onion mixture, stir sausages, tomatoes and remaining ingredients. Cook, covered, on High for 5–6 minutes until flavours blend, stirring halfway through cooking. Serve immediately.

FRANKFURTER AND VEGETABLE MEDLEY

Colour Index page 63. 6 servings. 342 cals per serving. Good source of thiamine, vitamin C, iron, fibre. Begin 35 minutes ahead.

2 onions, each cut into 8 wedges	*1 teaspoon dried oregano*
1 yellow or green pepper, cut into pieces	*450 g frankfurters, cut into 2.5 cm pieces*
2 garlic cloves, crushed	*1 × 400 g can tomatoes*
2 tablespoons olive or vegetable oil	*1 × 400 g can chick peas, drained*
1 aubergine (about 450 g), cut into 5 × 2 cm pieces	*¹/₄ teaspoon salt*
	¹/₄ teaspoon pepper
1 courgette, cut into 2.5 cm pieces	

1. In 3 litre microwave-safe casserole, place onions, pepper, garlic and oil. Cook, covered, on High (100% power) for 2–3 minutes, until vegetables are slightly softened, stirring once.
2. Into mixture, stir aubergine, courgette and oregano. Cook, covered, on High for 10–12 minutes, until tender-crisp, stirring twice.
3. To vegetable mixture, add frankfurters, tomatoes with their liquid, chick peas, salt and pepper. Cook, covered, on High for 2–3 minutes, until vegetables are tender, stirring once.

Frankfurters heat up in seconds in the microwave, and if you cook them in their buns there's no need for washing up. Just remember to slash or pierce the skins with a knife or fork before putting them in the oven.

Hot Dogs in Buns
Place **slashed frankfurter** in **long soft roll** and wrap in kitchen paper; place on paper plate. Heat on High (100% power) for 30–40 seconds, until hot. For 2 frankfurters in buns, heat on High for 1–1¹/₄ (1:15) minutes.

Hot Dog Melt
Make slit lengthways in **frankfurter** and fill with **1 slice processed cheese**. Place on paper plate. Heat on High (100% power) for 30–40 seconds, until hot. Serve with **potato crisps**.

Mini Frankfurters and Beans
In microwave-safe soup bowl, place contents of **1 × 400 g can baked beans**. Place in centre of microwave-safe dinner plate. Cook, covered loosely with greaseproof paper, on High (100% power) for 2–3 minutes, until bubbling. Meanwhile, push wooden cocktail sticks into **8 cocktail frankfurters**. Arrange in circle round bean-filled bowl. Heat on High for 45 seconds–1 minute, until hot. Serve with **mustard**. 2 servings.

Chilli Dogs
In medium microwave-safe bowl, place contents of **1 × 425 g can chilli beans** or **400 g Chilli con Carne** (page 211). Cook, covered, on High (100% power) for 4–5 minutes, until bubbling, stirring twice; set aside. Wrap **4 hot dogs** in **long soft rolls** in kitchen paper; place in circle on oven floor. Heat on High for 2–3 minutes, until hot. Unwrap; place on platter. Top hot dogs with **chilli, soured cream, bottled taco sauce** and **coriander**. 4 servings.

Vegetables and Salads

CHARTS FOR MICROWAVING VEGETABLES · INDIVIDUAL VEGETABLES
MIXED VEGETABLE DISHES · CHICKEN SALADS · MEAT SALADS
WARM SALADS · VEGETABLE SALADS · PRAWN SALADS

Vegetables and Salads

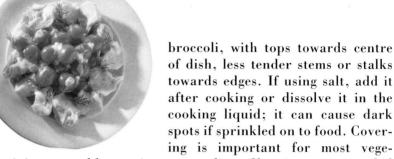

Cooking vegetables is one of the things the microwave does best; fresh vegetables cook quickly with a minimum amount of water, so they retain nutrients and have the taste, colour and texture of fresh-from-the-garden produce. A microwave enables you to cook small portions with a minimum of trouble and is ideal for peeling vegetables such as garlic, onions and tomatoes (see Cook's Tips, page 30), and for precooking vegetables for the barbecue in order to prevent them from charring (see page 265).

Charts for cooking vegetables in the microwave (pages 237–251) give cooking instructions for a wide variety of fresh vegetables and several popular frozen ones. For best results, remember the following tips: pierce skins of whole vegetables; make sure vegetables are uniform in size – small pieces and quantities cook more quickly, as do freshly picked young vegetables; slice dense vegetables such as potatoes and swedes; arrange vegetables with tender tops, like asparagus and broccoli, with tops towards centre of dish, less tender stems or stalks towards edges. If using salt, add it after cooking or dissolve it in the cooking liquid; it can cause dark spots if sprinkled on to food. Covering is important for most vegetables; microwave cling film is recommended because it holds in heat and steam. To prevent it from splitting, vent it by turning back a small corner or by puncturing the film.

Frozen vegetables are tastier when cooked in the microwave, and they keep more of their nutrients. Some are used straight from the freezer in recipes, but cooking charts are included for portions of some of the most popular frozen vegetables. Many fresh vegetables require blanching before freezing; instructions are given on page 260. After patting dry, pack in freezer containers, leaving headspace, or pack in polythene bags, pressing out all air. Seal, label and freeze. Smaller vegetables such as shelled peas can be open frozen; freeze until firm, then pack.

TOMATO GARNISHES WITH FLAIR

The deep red colour and year-round availability of tomatoes makes them an ideal choice for garnishing vegetable dishes and salads with style.

Tomato Rose: cut thin slice from tomato bottom without cutting completely through (left), then peel continuous strips of skin, keeping it attached.

Roll up strips, skin side out, towards slice cut from bottom of tomato (above). Gently flare rolled strip to resemble rose.

Tomato Hoops: hollow out small tomato (above right), leaving 5 mm ring; discard seeds.

Fill hoops with cooked dwarf beans (right) or matchstick-thin strips of carrot.

Cooking Vegetables in the Microwave

These vegetable cooking charts will be an invaluable help as a reference for the basic preparation and cooking of a wide variety of vegetables. You will be able to use your favourite vegetables in other microwave recipes or on their own with a little lemon juice, butter or margarine, salt and pepper, or a sauce.

Because vegetables vary in size, texture and density, it is important to follow instructions carefully. Remember to rotate the dish a half turn or stir the vegetables during cooking, rearranging larger pieces if necessary. Cover tightly to keep in heat; this helps vegetables cook more quickly and evenly.

Key			
Microwave cookware	Water	Time	Standing time

ARTICHOKE, GLOBE

Rinse artichokes under cold running water. Cut off stalks and 2.5 cm of tops. With kitchen shears, trim thorny tips of leaves. Brush cut edges with lemon juice to prevent discoloration. Pull off any loose leaves from round bottoms.

About 67 cals per serving			
	For 4	**For 2**	**For 1**
	4 artichokes (about 350 g each)	2 artichokes (about 350 g each)	1 artichoke (about 350 g)
cookware	Wrap each individually in cling film; *arrange on oven floor in circle*	Wrap each individually in cling film; *arrange on oven floor*	Wrap in cling film; *place on oven floor*
water	Whatever clings after rinsing	Whatever clings after rinsing	Whatever clings after rinsing
time	16 minutes; *rotate each artichoke halfway through cooking*	10 minutes; *rotate each artichoke halfway through cooking*	7 minutes; *rotate halfway through cooking*
standing	5 minutes	5 minutes	5 minutes

Cook artichokes, wrapped, on High (100% power) for time in Chart. Allow to stand, still wrapped, for time in Chart. Artichokes are done when an outer leaf as well as one close to centre core can be pulled out without resistance.

ARTICHOKE, JERUSALEM (PIECES)

Scrub under cold running water. Separate larger knobs and tubers for easier peeling; peel. Cut knobs and tubers into 1 cm pieces.

85 cals per serving			
	For 4	**For 2**	**For 1**
	700 g	350 g	175 g
cookware	2 litre casserole	21.5 cm pie dish	Small bowl
water	5½ tablespoons	4 tablespoons	2 tablespoons
time	7–8 minutes; *stir halfway through cooking*	4–5 minutes; *stir halfway through cooking*	2½ (2:30)–3 minutes; *stir halfway through cooking*
standing	5 minutes	5 minutes	3 minutes

Cook Jerusalem artichokes and water, covered, on High (100% power) for time in Chart. Allow to stand, covered, for time in Chart. Jerusalem artichoke pieces are done when centres are tender-crisp if pierced with tip of sharp knife. Drain.

ASPARAGUS (SPEARS)

Select asparagus with 1 cm thick stalks. Hold base of stalk firmly and bend stalk; end will break off at spot where it becomes too tough to eat. Discard ends; trim scales if stalks are gritty.

About 15 cals per serving			
	For 4	**For 2**	**For 1**
	15–16 spears (about 450 g)	7–8 spears (about 225 g)	3–4 spears (about 115 g)
cookware	30 × 20 cm baking dish; *arrange tips overlapping in centre*	20 cm square baking dish; *arrange tips facing in same direction*	20 cm plate; *arrange tips facing in same direction*
water	2 tablespoons	1 tablespoon	2 teaspoons
time	4½ (4:30)–6 minutes; *rotate dish halfway through cooking*	2½ (2:30)–3 minutes; *rotate dish halfway through cooking*	1½ (1:30)–2 minutes
standing	3–5 minutes	3–5 minutes	3–5 minutes

Cook asparagus and water, covered, on High (100% power) for time in Chart. Allow to stand, covered, for time in Chart. Asparagus spears are done when tender-crisp. Drain.

ASPARAGUS (PIECES)

Prepare as for asparagus spears (p. 237).
Cut spears crossways into 2.5–4 cm pieces.

About 15 cals per serving		
For 4	**For 2**	**For 1**
15–16 spears (about 450 g)	7–8 spears (about 225 g)	3–4 spears (about 115 g)
1 litre casserole; *add only stalks, not tips, at start of cooking*	1 litre casserole; *add only stalks, not tips, at start of cooking*	Small bowl; *place tips under stalk pieces*
2 tablespoons	1 tablespoon	1 teaspoon
4–5 minutes; *stir stalks after 2½ (2:30) minutes, then stir in tips*	2–2½ (2:30) minutes; *stir stalks after 1 minute, then stir in tips*	1–1½ (1:30) minutes
3–5 minutes	3–5 minutes	3–5 minutes

Cook only asparagus stalks and water, covered, on High (100% power) for time in Chart; when stalk pieces are bright green and crisp, stir in tips. Allow to stand, covered, for time in Chart. Asparagus pieces are done when tender-crisp. Drain.

AUBERGINE (PIECES)

Prepare just before cooking because flesh turns brown if exposed to air. Rinse under cold running water and pat dry. Trim off stalk end. Cut aubergine into 1 cm pieces.

21 cals per serving		
For 4	**For 2**	**For 1**
1 large aubergine (about 700 g)	1 medium aubergine (350 g)	½ medium aubergine (about 175 g)
3 litre casserole	1.5 litre casserole	1 litre casserole
4 tablespoons	2 tablespoons	1 tablespoon
8–9 minutes; *stir halfway through cooking*	6–7 minutes; *stir halfway through cooking*	3–4 minutes; *stir halfway through cooking*
5 minutes	5 minutes	5 minutes

Cook aubergine and water, covered, on High (100% power) for time in Chart. Allow to stand, covered, for time in Chart. Aubergine pieces are done when tender. Drain.

BEAN, BROAD (FROZEN)

130 cals per serving		
For 4	**For 2**	**For 1**
575 g	275 g	150 g
2 litre casserole	1 litre casserole	Small bowl
120 ml	4 tablespoons	1 tablespoon
10–12 minutes; *stir every 3 minutes*	7–8 minutes; *stir twice during cooking*	2–3 minutes; *stir halfway through cooking*
5 minutes	5 minutes	5 minutes

Cook frozen broad beans and water, covered, on High (100% power) for time in Chart. Allow to stand, covered, for time in Chart. Broad beans are done when tender. Drain.

BEAN, FRENCH

Rinse under cold running water.
Top and tail.

25 cals per serving		
For 4	**For 2**	**For 1**
450 g	225 g	115 g
20 cm square baking dish	Shallow 21.5 cm pie dish	Small bowl
250 ml	120 ml	80 ml
12–14 minutes; *stir every 4 minutes*	6–7 minutes; *stir halfway through cooking*	3½ (3:30)–4½ (4:30) minutes; *stir halfway through cooking*
5 minutes	5 minutes	5 minutes

Cook beans and water, covered, on High (100% power) for time in Chart. Allow to stand, covered, for time in Chart. French beans are done when tender-crisp. Drain.

BEAN, RUNNER

Rinse under cold running water.
Top and tail, then cut into 2.5 cm
lengths.

22 cals per serving		
For 4	**For 2**	**For 1**
450 g	225 g	115 g
2 litre casserole	1 litre casserole	1 litre casserole
4 tablespoons	2 tablespoons	1 tablespoon
10–14 minutes; *stir 3 times during cooking*	4–6 minutes; *stir halfway through cooking*	3–4 minutes; *stir halfway through cooking*
2 minutes	2 minutes	1 minute

Cook beans and water, covered, on High (100% power) for time
in Chart. Allow to stand, covered, for time in Chart. Runner
beans are done when tender-crisp. Drain.

BEETROOT

Cut off tops; leave part of stalks
and roots on beetroot. Scrub;
take care not to damage skins as
this will cause beetroot to 'bleed'
during cooking. Cut off stalks
and roots and peel after standing.
Skin will peel off easily if it is
peeled from bottom to top. If you
like, when handling beetroot,
wear rubber gloves to prevent
staining hands.

27 cals per serving		
For 4	**For 2**	**For 1**
8 beetroot (about 115 g each)	4 beetroot (about 115 g each)	2 beetroot (about 115 g each)
30 × 20 cm baking dish; *arrange along long edges with root ends overlapping in centre*	1 litre casserole; *arrange round edge with root ends overlapping in centre*	1 litre casserole; *arrange with root ends overlapping in centre*
None	None	None
20 minutes; *turn beetroot over and rotate dish halfway through cooking*	12 minutes; *turn beetroot over and rotate dish halfway through cooking*	7½ (7:30) minutes; *turn beetroot over and rotate dish halfway through cooking*
5 minutes	5 minutes	5 minutes

Cook beetroot, covered, on High (100% power) for time in Chart.
Allow to stand, covered, for time in Chart. Beetroot are done
when tender in centre if pierced with sharp knife.

BROCCOLI (SPEARS)

Remove large leaves and trim
woody stalk ends. Cut through
stalks lengthways 2–3 times.
Rinse under cold running
water.

About 20 cals per serving		
For 4	**For 2**	**For 1**
450 g	225 g	115 g
30 × 20 cm baking dish; *arrange with florets overlapping in centre*	Shallow 21.5 cm pie dish; *arrange spears facing in same direction*	20 cm plate; *arrange spears facing in same direction*
4 tablespoons	4 tablespoons	Whatever clings after rinsing
5–6 minutes; *rotate dish halfway through cooking*	3½ (3:30)–4 minutes; *rotate dish halfway through cooking*	1½ (1:30)–1¾ (1:45) minutes
5 minutes	3–4 minutes	3–4 minutes

Cook broccoli and water, covered, on High (100% power) for
time in Chart. Allow to stand, covered, for time in Chart.
Broccoli spears are done when tender-crisp. Drain.

BROCCOLI (PIECES)

Remove large leaves and trim
woody stalk ends. Cut stalks
and florets into bite-sized
pieces. Rinse under cold
running water.

About 30 cals per serving		
For 4	**For 2**	**For 1**
450 g	225 g	115 g
2 litre casserole	1 litre casserole	Small bowl
4 tablespoons	2 tablespoons	1 tablespoon
6–7 minutes; *stir halfway through cooking*	3½ (3:30)–4 minutes; *stir halfway through cooking*	1½ (1:30)–2 minutes; *stir halfway through cooking*
5 minutes	5 minutes	5 minutes

Cook broccoli and water, covered, on High (100% power) for
time in Chart. Allow to stand, covered, for time in Chart.
Broccoli pieces are done when tender-crisp. Drain.

BRUSSELS SPROUTS

Look for firm, fresh, bright green sprouts with tight-fitting outer leaves free from black spots. Puffy or soft sprouts are usually poor in quality. Remove any yellow leaves and trim stalks. Rinse under cold running water.

About 43 cals per serving		
For 4	**For 2**	**For 1**
575 g	275 g	150 g
2 litre casserole	21.5 cm pie dish	Small bowl
4 tablespoons	4 tablespoons	2 tablespoons
8–9 minutes; *stir halfway through cooking*	6–7 minutes; *stir halfway through cooking*	3–3½ (3:30) minutes; *stir halfway through cooking*
5 minutes	5 minutes	5 minutes

Cook Brussels sprouts and water, covered, on High (100% power) for time in Chart. Allow to stand, covered, for time in Chart. Brussels sprouts are done when centres are tender-crisp if pierced with tip of sharp knife. Drain.

CABBAGE, GREEN AND WHITE (WEDGES)

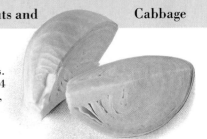

Discard any tough outer leaves. Cut cabbage in half, then into 4 wedges; cut cores from wedges, leaving just enough to retain shapes. Rinse.

About 25 cals per serving		
For 4	**For 2**	**For 1**
1 cabbage (about 450 g)	½ cabbage (about 225 g; 2 wedges)	1 wedge cabbage (about 115 g)
Square baking dish; *arrange spoke fashion*	Square baking dish; *arrange 2.5 cm apart*	Shallow 21.5 cm pie dish
4 tablespoons	4 tablespoons	3 tablespoons
12 minutes; *rotate dish halfway through cooking*	6–7 minutes; *rotate dish halfway through cooking*	3½ (3:30)–4 minutes
5 minutes	3 minutes	3 minutes

Cook cabbage and water, covered, on High (100% power) for time in Chart. Allow to stand, covered, for time in Chart. Cabbage wedges are done when tender-crisp. Drain.

CABBAGE, CHINESE LEAF (SHREDS)

Trim stalk end. Rinse leaves under cold running water. Cut crossways into 4 cm shreds.

About 9 cals per serving		
For 4	**For 2**	**For 1**
600 g	300 g	150 g
3 litre casserole	2 litre casserole	1 litre casserole
4 tablespoons	2 tablespoons	Whatever clings after rinsing
4–5 minutes; *stir halfway through cooking*	3–4 minutes; *stir halfway through cooking*	2–3 minutes; *stir halfway through cooking*
3–4 minutes	3 minutes	2–3 minutes

Cook Chinese leaf and water, covered, on High (100% power) for time in Chart. Allow to stand, covered, for time in Chart. Drain. Chinese leaf shreds are done when tender-crisp; the volume will be reduced by about half. Drain.

CABBAGE, GREEN AND WHITE (SHREDDED)

Discard any tough outer leaves. Cut cabbage in half, then cut into wedges; cut cores from wedges. Shred cabbage by hand with knife or in food processor.

About 25 cals per serving		
For 4	**For 2**	**For 1**
700 g	350 g	175 g
2 litre casserole	1 litre casserole	Small bowl
4 tablespoons	2 tablespoons	1 tablespoon
6–7 minutes; *stir every 3 minutes*	4–5 minutes; *stir halfway through cooking*	2–3 minutes; *stir halfway through cooking*
5 minutes	5 minutes	3 minutes

Cook cabbage and water, covered, on High (100% power) for time in Chart. Allow to stand, covered, for time in Chart. Cabbage shreds are done when tender-crisp. Drain.

CABBAGE, RED (SHREDDED)

Prepare as for shredded green or white cabbage (left).

Red cabbage is usually served shredded. Vinegar is added to cooking liquid to prevent cabbage from turning an unappetising blue.

About 15 cals per serving		
For 4	**For 2**	**For 1**
350 g	175 g	90 g
1 litre casserole	Small bowl	Small bowl
4 tablespoons water *plus 4 tablespoons white vinegar; toss well*	3 tablespoons water *plus 3 tablespoons white vinegar; toss well*	2 tablespoons water *plus 2 tablespoons white vinegar; toss well*
14–16 minutes; *stir halfway through cooking*	10–12 minutes; *stir halfway through cooking*	5–6 minutes; *stir halfway through cooking*
5 minutes	5 minutes	5 minutes

Cook cabbage, water and vinegar, covered on High (100% power) for time in Chart. Allow to stand, covered, for time in Chart. Red cabbage shreds are done when tender-crisp. Drain.

CARROT (SLICES)

Scrape or peel; rinse under cold running water. Top and tail. Cut crossways into 5 mm thick slices.

About 24 cals per serving		
For 4	**For 2**	**For 1**
450 g	225 g	115 g
1 litre casserole; *arrange larger slices around edge*	Shallow 21.5 pie dish; *arrange larger slices around edge*	Small bowl
120 ml	4 tablespoons	2 tablespoons
7–9 minutes; *stir twice during cooking*	5–6½ (6:30) minutes; *stir halfway through cooking*	2½(2:30)–3½ (3:30) minutes; *stir halfway through cooking*
5 minutes	5 minutes	5 minutes

Cook carrots and water, covered, on High (100% power) for time in Chart. Allow to stand, covered, for time in Chart. Carrot slices are done when larger and smaller pieces are equally tender-crisp. Drain.

CARROT (WHOLE)

Scrape or peel; rinse under cold running water. Top and tail.

About 24 cals per serving		
For 4	**For 2**	**For 1**
450 g	225 g	115 g
20 cm square dish; *alternate narrow ends*	21.5 cm pie dish; *alternate narrow ends*	20 cm plate; *alternate narrow ends*
4 tablespoons	4 tablespoons	2 tablespoons
7–9 minutes; *rearrange carrots halfway through cooking*	5–6½ (6:30) minutes; *rearrange carrots halfway through cooking*	2½ (2:30) minutes; *rotate plate halfway through cooking*
5 minutes	5 minutes	5 minutes

Cook carrots and water, covered, on High (100% power) for time in Chart. Allow to stand, covered, for time in Chart. Carrots are done when thickest sections are tender-crisp if pierced with tip of sharp knife. Drain.

CARROT, BABY (WHOLE)

Scrape or peel; rinse under cold running water. Top and tail.

27 cals per serving		
For 4	**For 2**	**For 1**
700 g	350 g	175 g
20 cm square baking dish	Shallow 21.5 cm pie dish	Small bowl
175 ml	120 ml	4 tablespoons
10–12 minutes; *stir halfway through cooking*	7–9 minutes; *stir halfway through cooking*	3½ (3:30)–4 minutes; *stir halfway through cooking*
5 minutes	5 minutes	5 minutes

Cook carrots and water, covered, on High (100% power) for time in Chart. Allow to stand, covered, for time in Chart. Baby carrots are done when tender-crisp. Drain.

CAULIFLOWER
(WHOLE)

Keeping cauliflower whole, remove leaves and cut out core. Rinse under cold running water.

About 25 cals per serving		
For 4	**For 2**	**For 1**
1 cauliflower (about 900 g)	1 cauliflower (about 450 g)	½ cauliflower (about 225 g)
21.5 cm pie dish	21.5 cm pie dish	21.5 cm pie dish
4 tablespoons	3 tablespoons	2 tablespoons
8–9 minutes; *rotate dish halfway through cooking*	5–6 minutes; *rotate dish halfway through cooking*	3–5 minutes; *rotate dish halfway through cooking*
5 minutes	5 minutes	5 minutes

Cook cauliflower and water, covered, on High (100% power) for time in Chart. Allow to stand, covered, for time in Chart. Cauliflower is done when stalk end is fork-tender. Drain.

CELERIAC (PIECES)

Cut off roots. Peel and cut out any pitted areas. Rinse celeriac under cold running water. Cut into 1 cm thick pieces.

About 40 cals per serving		
For 4	**For 2**	**For 1**
1 large celeriac (about 700 g)	½ large celeriac (about 350 g)	1 medium celeriac (about 175 g)
2 litre casserole	1 litre casserole	Small bowl
120 ml	4 tablespoons	2 tablespoons
9–10 minutes; *stir every 3 minutes*	4–5 minutes; *stir halfway through cooking*	2½ (2:30)–3 minutes
5 minutes	5 minutes	3 minutes

Cook celeriac and water, covered, on High (100% power) for time in Chart. Allow to stand, covered, for time in Chart. Celeriac pieces are done when tender-crisp. Drain.

CAULIFLOWER (FLORETS)

Remove outer green leaves and core. Separate into florets; large florets can be cut in half for more even cooking. Rinse under cold running water.

About 25 cals per serving		
For 4	**For 2**	**For 1**
900 g	450 g	225 g
2 litre casserole; *arrange larger florets round edge*	1 litre casserole; *arrange larger florets round edge*	Small bowl
4 tablespoons	4 tablespoons	2 tablespoons
8–9 minutes; *stir every 3 minutes*	5–6 minutes; *stir halfway through cooking*	3–4 minutes; *stir halfway through cooking*
5 minutes	5 minutes	3–4 minutes

Cook cauliflower and water, covered, on High (100% power) for time in Chart. Allow to stand, covered, for time in Chart. Cauliflower florets are done when tender-crisp. Drain.

CELERY (SLICES)

Remove leaves; trim root end. Scrub sticks under cold running water. With vegetable peeler, peel off any coarse strings. Cut sticks crossways into 5 mm thick slices.

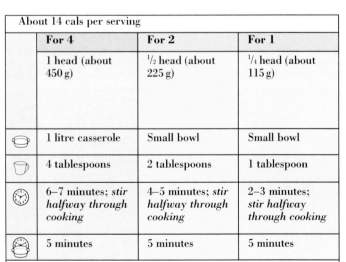

About 14 cals per serving		
For 4	**For 2**	**For 1**
1 head (about 450 g)	½ head (about 225 g)	¼ head (about 115 g)
1 litre casserole	Small bowl	Small bowl
4 tablespoons	2 tablespoons	1 tablespoon
6–7 minutes; *stir halfway through cooking*	4–5 minutes; *stir halfway through cooking*	2–3 minutes; *stir halfway through cooking*
5 minutes	5 minutes	5 minutes

Cook celery and water, covered, on High (100% power) for time in Chart. Allow to stand, covered, for time in Chart. Celery slices are done when tender-crisp. Drain.

CELERY HEART (HALVES)

Rinse under cold running water. Trim tops and bottoms; cut in half lengthways. Remove any coarse outer sticks and leafy centre of each heart.

About 15 cals per serving		
For 4	**For 2**	**For 1**
450 g	225 g	115 g
20 cm square baking dish	20 cm square baking dish	Shallow 21.5 cm pie dish
175 ml	120 ml	120 ml
8–9 minutes; *turn halves over and rearrange halfway through cooking*	6–7 minutes; *turn halves over and rearrange halfway through cooking*	4–5 minutes; *turn halves over and rearrange halfway through cooking*
5 minutes	5 minutes	5 minutes

Cook celery hearts and water, covered, on High (100% power) for time in Chart. Allow to stand, covered, for time in Chart. Celery hearts are done when tender-crisp. Drain.

CELERY HEART
(PIECES)

Prepare as for celery hearts (above), then cut into 2.5–7.5 cm pieces.

About 15 cals per serving		
For 4	**For 2**	**For 1**
450 g	225 g	115 g
1 litre casserole; *arrange larger pieces round edge*	Shallow 21.5 cm pie dish; *arrange larger pieces round edge*	Small bowl
4 tablespoons	2 tablespoons	1 tablespoon
7–8 minutes; *stir halfway through cooking*	4–5 minutes; *stir halfway through cooking*	2–3 minutes; *stir halfway through cooking*
5 minutes	5 minutes	5 minutes

Cook celery hearts and water, covered, on High (100% power) for time in Chart. Allow to stand, covered, for time in Chart. Celery heart pieces are done when tender-crisp. Drain.

CHICORY

Rinse under cold running water. Remove any bruised leaves. Trim root ends without disconnecting leaves. With point of sharp knife, cut out bitter cone-shaped core in base of each head.

About 16 cals per serving		
For 4	**For 2**	**For 1**
8 heads (about 115 g each)	4 heads (about 115 g each)	2 heads (about 115 g each)
30 × 20 cm baking dish; *arrange along narrow ends with tips pointing towards centre*	20 cm square baking dish; *alternate tips*	Shallow 21.5 cm pie dish; *alternate tips*
250 ml	150 ml	150 ml
16–18 minutes; *turn each head over and rotate dish halfway through cooking*	12–14 minutes; *turn each head over and rotate dish halfway through cooking*	8–10 minutes; *turn each head over and rotate dish halfway through cooking*
5 minutes	5 minutes	5 minutes

Cook chicory and water, covered, on High (100% power) for time in Chart. Allow to stand, covered, for time in Chart. Chicory is done when tender. Drain.

CHRISTOPHINE
(ALSO CALLED CHAYOTE)

These are pear-shaped members of the squash family, 7.5–15 cm long. Select firm, very young ones. Rinse under cold running water; pat dry. With fork, pierce skin of each in several places.

About 48 cals per serving		
For 4	**For 2**	**For 1**
2 christophines (about 350 g each)	1 christophine (about 350 g)	1 christophine (about 350 g)
Wrap individually in cling film; *arrange in circle on oven floor*	Wrap in cling film; *place in centre of oven floor*	Wrap in cling film; *place in centre of oven floor*
None	None	None
10–12 minutes; *turn and rearrange halfway*	7–8 minutes; *turn and rearrange halfway*	7–8 minutes; *turn and rearrange halfway*
5 minutes	5 minutes	5 minutes

Cook christophines, wrapped, on High (100% power) for time in Chart. Allow to stand, still wrapped, for time in Chart. Christophines are done when thickest area of flesh can be pierced easily down to stone with tip of sharp knife. Cut in half lengthways; discard stone. Use pulp only. For 1, refrigerate half.

COURGETTE (SLICES)

Select courgettes which are uniform in size with same diameter top to bottom for even cooking.

Rinse under cold running water. Top and tail; do not peel. Cut crossways into 5 mm thick slices.

About 16 cals per serving			
	For 4	**For 2**	**For 1**
	450 g	225 g	115 g
🍲	1 litre casserole; *arrange larger slices round edge*	1 litre casserole; *arrange larger slices round edge*	Small bowl
🥤	2 tablespoons	1 tablespoon	1 teaspoon
🕐	6–7 minutes; *stir halfway through cooking*	4–5 minutes; *stir halfway through cooking*	2–2½ (2:30) minutes; *stir halfway through cooking*
⏲	5 minutes	5 minutes	3 minutes

Cook courgettes and water, covered, on High (100% power) for time in Chart. Allow to stand, covered, for time in Chart. Courgette slices are done when tender-crisp. Drain.

FENNEL (SLICES)

Rinse under cold running water. Cut off root ends and leaves from bulbs. Cut bulbs in half lengthways, then slice crossways into 5 mm thick slices.

15 cals per serving			
	For 4	**For 2**	**For 1**
	2 bulbs (about 225 g each)	1 bulb (about 225 g)	1 bulb (about 225 g, use half; refrigerate remainder)
🍲	20 cm square baking dish	Shallow 21.5 cm pie dish	Small bowl
🥤	250 ml	120 ml	4 tablespoons
🕐	10–12 minutes; *stir every 3–4 minutes*	7–8 minutes; *stir halfway through cooking*	4–4½ (4:30) minutes; *stir halfway through cooking*
⏲	5 minutes	5 minutes	5 minutes

Cook fennel and water, covered, on High (100% power) for time in Chart. Allow to stand, covered, for time in Chart. Fennel slices are done when tender-crisp. Drain.

GREENS, SPRING AND KALE

Use only tender, green leaves. Discard any damaged, dry or yellow leaves and coarse stalks. Wash under cold running water; drain.

Spring greens – about 30 cals per serving; kale – about 50 cals per serving			
	For 4	**For 2**	**For 1**
	900 g	450 g	225 g
🍲	4 litre casserole	3 litre casserole	1 litre casserole
🥤	250 ml	175 ml	120 ml
🕐	18–20 minutes; *stir every 6 minutes*	10–12 minutes; *stir every 3 minutes*	6–8 minutes; *stir every 2 minutes*
⏲	5 minutes	5 minutes	5 minutes

Cook greens and water, covered, on High (100% power) for time in Chart. Allow to stand, covered, for time in Chart. Greens are done when leaves and stalks are tender. Drain.

GREENS, SWISS CHARD

Prepare as for spring greens (above).

About 30 cals per serving			
	For 4	**For 2**	**For 1**
	900 g	450 g	225 g
🍲	4 litre casserole	3 litre casserole	1 litre casserole
🥤	Whatever clings after washing	Whatever clings after washing	Whatever clings after washing
🕐	12–14 minutes; *stir every 3 minutes*	8–9 minutes; *stir halfway through and at end of cooking*	5–6 minutes; *stir halfway through and at end of cooking*
⏲	5 minutes	5 minutes	5 minutes

Cook chard, covered, on High (100% power) for time in Chart. Allow to stand, covered, for time in Chart. Chard is done when leaves and stalks are tender. Drain.

KOHLRABI (SLICES)

Cut off tops and discard. Peel thinly and cut into 5 mm thick slices. Rinse under cold running water.

About 20 cals per serving		
For 4	**For 2**	**For 1**
450 g	225 g	115 g
1 litre casserole; *arrange larger slices round edge*	Shallow 21.5 cm pie dish; *arrange larger slices round edge*	Small bowl
4 tablespoons	2 tablespoons	1 tablespoon
13–14 minutes; *stir halfway through cooking*	9–10 minutes; *stir halfway through cooking*	5–6 minutes; *stir halfway through cooking*
5 minutes	5 minutes	5 minutes

Cook kohlrabi and water, covered, on High (100% power) for time in Chart. Allow to stand, covered, for time in Chart. Kohlrabi slices are done when tender. Drain.

MANGE-TOUT

Rinse under cold running water. Top and tail; remove strings along both sides of pods if necessary.

24 cals per serving		
For 4	**For 2**	**For 1**
225 g	115 g	50 g
20 cm square baking dish	Shallow 21.5 cm pie dish	Small bowl
2 tablespoons	1 tablespoon	1½ teaspoons
4–5 minutes; *stir halfway through cooking; test after 4 minutes*	2–3 minutes; *stir halfway through cooking; test after 2½ (2:30) minutes*	1–1½ (1:30) minutes; *stir halfway through cooking; test after 1 minute*
30 seconds–1 minute	30 seconds–1 minute	30 seconds–1 minute

Cook mange-touts and water on High (100% power) for time in Chart. Allow to stand for time in Chart. Mange-touts are done when tender-crisp. Drain.

LEEK (HALVES)

Trim off roots and leaf ends, leaving 2.5–5 cm above white parts. Cut each leek in half lengthways. Carefully wash under cold running water to remove all sand.

Divide leeks into number of servings. Tie loosely into bundles with string.

About 60 cals per serving		
For 4	**For 2**	**For 1**
8 leeks (about 900 g)	4 leeks (about 450 g)	2 leeks (about 225 g)
30 × 20 cm baking dish; *arrange bundles along edges with centre empty*	20 cm square baking dish	Small bowl
350 ml	250 ml	120 ml
18–20 minutes; *turn leeks over halfway through cooking*	15–18 minutes; *turn leeks over halfway through cooking*	10–12 minutes; *turn leeks over halfway through cooking*
5 minutes	5 minutes	5 minutes

Cook leeks and water, covered, on High (100% power) for time in Chart. Allow to stand, covered, for time in Chart. Leek halves are done when tender. Drain and untie.

MARROW (PIECES)

Select marrows that are firm and not too large. Peel and cut in half; scoop out seeds. Cut flesh into 2.5 cm slices or into chunks.

18 cals per serving		
For 4	**For 2**	**For 1**
450 g	225 g	115 g
2 litre casserole	1 litre casserole	1 litre casserole
2 tablespoons	1 tablespoon	1½ teaspoons
8–10 minutes; *stir halfway through cooking*	5–6 minutes; *stir halfway through cooking*	3–4 minutes; *stir halfway through cooking*
3 minutes	2 minutes	1 minute

Cook marrow pieces, covered, on High (100% power) for time in Chart. Allow to stand, covered, for time in Chart. Marrow pieces are done when tender. Drain.

MUSHROOM (WHOLE)

Do not peel or soak: soaking makes mushrooms soggy. Instead, rinse under cold running water and pat dry. Cut off thin slice from base of each stalk.

34 cals per serving (without butter or margarine)		
For 4	**For 2**	**For 1**
450 g	225 g	115 g
2 litre casserole	1 litre casserole	Small bowl
1 tablespoon water; *or melted butter or margarine*	1½ teaspoons water; *or melted butter or margarine*	¾ teaspoon water; *or 1½ teaspoons melted butter or margarine*
5–7 minutes; *stir twice during cooking*	4–6 minutes; *stir twice during cooking*	1½ (1:30)–2 minutes; *stir halfway through cooking*
3–4 minutes	3–4 minutes	1–2 minutes

Cook mushrooms and water or melted butter or margarine, covered, on High (100% power) for time in Chart. Allow to stand, covered, for time in Chart. Mushrooms are done when tender. Drain if cooked with water.

MUSHROOM (SLICES)

Prepare as for whole mushroom (above). With sharp knife, cut vertically into slices.

34 cals per serving (without butter or margarine)		
For 4	**For 2**	**For 1**
450 g	225 g	115 g
2 litre casserole	1 litre casserole	Small bowl
1 tablespoon water; *or 30 g melted butter or margarine; stir well to coat*	1½ teaspoons water; *or 15 g melted butter or margarine; stir well to coat*	¾ teaspoon water; *or 1½ teaspoons melted butter or margarine; stir well to coat*
5–7 minutes; *stir halfway through cooking*	4–6 minutes; *stir halfway through cooking*	1½ (1:30)–2 minutes; *stir halfway through cooking*
3–4 minutes	3–4 minutes	1–2 minutes

Cook mushrooms and water or melted butter or margarine, covered, on High (100% power) for time in Chart. Allow to stand, covered, for time in Chart. Mushroom slices are done when tender. Drain if cooked with water.

OKRA (WHOLE)

Select pods 6–10 cm long. Wash okra under cold running water.   Cut off stalks without cutting into pods.

20 cals per serving		
For 4	**For 2**	**For 1**
450 g	225 g	115 g
30 × 20 cm baking dish; *arrange larger pods along outer edges*	Shallow 21.5 cm pie dish; *arrange larger pods along outer edges*	Small bowl; *place smaller pods on bottom*
250 ml *plus 1 teaspoon white vinegar*	150 ml *plus ½ teaspoon white vinegar*	80 ml *plus ¼ teaspoon white vinegar*
7–8 minutes; *stir halfway through cooking; check if done after 3 further minutes*	5–6 minutes; *stir halfway through cooking; check if done after 2 further minutes*	2½–3 minutes; *stir halfway through cooking; check if done after 1 further minute*
5 minutes	5 minutes	5 minutes

Cook okra, water and vinegar, covered, on High (100% power) for time in Chart. Allow to stand, covered, for time in Chart. Okra are done when pods are tender-crisp.

ONION (WHOLE)

Select onions of uniform size, about 7.5 cm in diameter. Cut off tops. Trim root ends   just enough to allow onions to stand upright; peel.

About 40 cals per serving		
For 4	**For 2**	**For 1**
4 onions (about 700 g)	2 onions (about 350 g)	1 onion (about 175 g)
20 cm square baking dish; *arrange in circle*	21.5 cm pie dish; *arrange in centre of dish*	Small bowl
None	None	None
9–10 minutes; *rotate dish halfway through cooking*	6–7 minutes; *rotate dish halfway through cooking*	3½ (3:30)–4 minutes; *rotate bowl halfway through cooking*
5 minutes	5 minutes	5 minutes

Cook onions, covered, on High (100% power) for time in Chart. Allow to stand, covered, for time in Chart. Whole onions are done when tender-crisp if pierced with tip of sharp knife.

ONION, SMALL PICKLING

For even cooking, select onions of uniform size.

Peel onions; leave a little of their root ends to help onions hold shape during cooking.

40 cals per serving		
For 4	**For 2**	**For 1**
700 g	350 g	175 g
2 litre casserole	1 litre casserole	Small bowl
1 tablespoon	1 tablespoon	1 teaspoon
7–8 minutes; *stir halfway through cooking*	4–6 minutes; *stir halfway through cooking*	2½ (2:30)–3 minutes; *stir once*
5 minutes	5 minutes	5 minutes

Cook onions and water, covered, on High (100% power) for time in Chart. Allow to stand, covered, for time in Chart. Onions are done when centres are tender and outer skins are slightly resistant if pierced with tip of sharp knife. Drain.

PARSNIP (WHOLE)

Scrub under cold running water. Top and tail.

About 75 cals per serving		
For 4	**For 2**	**For 1**
450 g	225 g	115 g
20 cm square baking dish; *arrange with narrow ends alternating*	20 cm square baking dish; *arrange with narrow ends alternating*	20 cm square baking dish; *arrange with narrow ends alternating*
120 ml	120 ml	120 ml
7–9 minutes; *turn parsnips over and rearrange halfway through cooking; do not rearrange if parsnips in centre are smaller than those at edges*	5–7 minutes; *turn parsnips over and rearrange halfway through cooking; do not rearrange if parsnips in centre are smaller than those at edges*	3–4 minutes; *turn parsnips over and rearrange halfway through cooking*
5 minutes	5 minutes	5 minutes

Cook parsnips and water, covered, on High (100% power) for time in Chart. Allow to stand, covered, for time in Chart. Parsnips are done when tender if pierced with tip of sharp knife. Drain.

PARSNIP (PIECES)

Prepare as for whole parsnip (below left). If mature parsnips are used, remove woody cores. Cut into 4 cm long pieces.

About 75 cals per serving		
For 4	**For 2**	**For 1**
450 g	225 g	115 g
1 litre casserole; *arrange larger pieces round edge*	Shallow 21.5 cm pie dish; *arrange larger pieces round edge*	Small bowl
120 ml	4 tablespoons	2 tablespoons
7–9 minutes; *stir every 3 minutes*	5–7 minutes; *stir halfway through cooking*	3–4 minutes; *stir halfway through cooking*
5 minutes	5 minutes	5 minutes

Cook parsnips and water, covered, on High (100% power) for time in Chart. Allow to stand, covered, for time in Chart. Parsnip pieces are done when tender. Drain.

PEAS

Shell peas by pressing pods between thumb and forefinger until open.

About 150 cals per serving		
For 4	**For 2**	**For 1**
900 g	450 g	225 g
1 litre casserole	Small bowl	Small bowl
4 tablespoons	2 tablespoons	1 tablespoon
6–7 minutes; *stir halfway through cooking*	4–5 minutes; *stir halfway through cooking*	2–2½ (2:30) minutes; *stir halfway through cooking*
3–5 minutes	3–5 minutes	3–5 minutes

Cook peas and water, covered, on High (100% power) for time in Chart. Allow to stand, covered, for time in Chart. Shelled peas are done when tender. Drain.

PEPPER (STRIPS)

Rinse under cold running water. Cut slice from stalk end; remove core, seeds and white membranes. Cut peppers in half lengthways; cut each half lengthways into 1 cm wide strips.

About 25 cals per serving		
For 4	**For 2**	**For 1**
4 peppers (115–150 g each)	2 peppers (115–150 g each)	1 pepper (115–150 g each)
2 litre casserole	1 litre casserole	Small bowl
3 tablespoons	2 tablespoons	1 tablespoon
5½ (5:30)–7 minutes; *stir after 3 minutes*	4–5 minutes; *stir after 3 minutes*	2–3 minutes; *stir halfway through cooking*
5 minutes	5 minutes	5 minutes

Cook peppers and water, covered, on High (100% power) for time in Chart; after stirring, check texture of peppers and stop cooking when slightly less done than desired. Allow to stand, covered, for time in Chart. Pepper strips are done when tender-crisp. Drain.

POTATO, BAKING

(WHOLE)

Buy oval-shaped potatoes of uniform size. Scrub under cold running water. Pierce several times.

About 100 cals per serving		
For 4	**For 2**	**For 1**
4 baking potatoes (about 225 g each)	2 baking potatoes (about 225 g each)	1 potato (about 225 g)
Arrange in circle on kitchen paper on oven floor	Arrange on kitchen paper on oven floor	Place in centre of kitchen paper on oven floor
None	None	None
14–16 minutes; *turn potatoes over and rearrange halfway through cooking*	7–8 minutes; *turn potatoes over and rearrange halfway through cooking*	4–6 minutes; *turn potato over halfway through cooking*
5 minutes; *wrap in foil or clean tea towel before standing*	5 minutes; *wrap in foil or clean tea towel before standing*	5 minutes; *wrap in foil or clean tea towel before standing*

Cook potatoes on High (100% power) for time in Chart. Allow to stand, wrapped, for time in Chart. Baking potatoes are done when tender if squeezed.

POTATO, ALL-PURPOSE

(CHUNKS)

Peel potatoes and remove any blemishes; rinse under cold running water. Cut into 2.5 cm chunks.

About 75 cals per serving		
For 4	**For 2**	**For 1**
4 potatoes (about 175 g each)	2 potatoes (about 175 g each)	1 potato (about 175 g)
20 cm square baking dish	Shallow 21.5 cm pie dish	1 litre measuring jug
175 ml	120 ml	4 tablespoons
10–12 minutes; *stir halfway through cooking*	6–8 minutes; *stir halfway through cooking*	5–6 minutes; *stir halfway through cooking*
5 minutes	5 minutes	5 minutes

Cook potatoes and water, covered, on High (100% power) for time in Chart. Allow to stand, covered, for time in Chart. Potato chunks are done when tender if pierced with tip of sharp knife. Drain.

POTATO, NEW (WHOLE)

Scrub potatoes under cold running water. With fork, pierce each potato once. Or, with vegetable peeler, peel strip round centre of each.

78 cals per serving		
For 4	**For 2**	**For 1**
450 g	225 g	115 g
Shallow 21.5 cm pie dish; *arrange larger potatoes round edge*	Small bowl	Small bowl
4 tablespoons	2 tablespoons	1 tablespoon
6–7 minutes; *turn potatoes over halfway through cooking*	3½ (3:30)–4 minutes; *turn potatoes over halfway through cooking*	2–2½ (2:30) minutes; *turn potatoes over halfway through cooking*
5 minutes	5 minutes	3–5 minutes

Cook potatoes and water, covered, on High (100% power) for time in Chart. Allow to stand, covered, for time in Chart. Potatoes are done when tender if pierced with knife. Drain.

POTATO (SLICES)

Scrub under cold running water. Potatoes can be cooked with their skins on or peeled. Cut into 5 mm thick slices.

About 75 cals per serving		
For 4	**For 2**	**For 1**
4 potatoes (about 115 g each)	2 potatoes (about 115 g each)	1 potato (about 115 g)
20 cm square baking dish; *arrange larger slices round edges*	Shallow 21.5 cm pie dish; *arrange larger slices round edge*	Shallow 21.5 cm pie dish; *arrange larger slices round edge*
120 ml	120 ml	80 ml
7–9 minutes; *stir halfway through cooking*	4¹⁄₂ (4:30)–5 minutes; *stir halfway through cooking*	3–3¹⁄₂ (3:30) minutes; *stir halfway through cooking*
5 minutes	5 minutes	5 minutes

Cook potatoes and water, covered, on High (100% power) for time in Chart. Allow to stand, covered, for time in Chart. Potato slices are done when tender. Drain.

SPINACH

Discard any yellowish and wilted leaves. Remove stalks from spinach. Wash leaves under cold running water to remove any sand; roughly chop leaves.

About 40 cals per serving		
For 4	**For 2**	**For 1**
600 g	275 g	150 g
3 litre casserole	3 litre casserole	2 litre casserole
Whatever clings after washing	Whatever clings after washing	Whatever clings after washing
6–7 minutes; *stir halfway through cooking*	5¹⁄₂ (5:30)–6¹⁄₂ (6:30) minutes; *stir halfway through cooking*	3–3¹⁄₂ (3:30) minutes; *stir halfway through cooking*
4 minutes	3 minutes	3 minutes

Cook spinach, covered, on High (100% power) for time in Chart. Allow to stand, covered, for time in Chart. Spinach is done when leaves are wilted. Drain.

POTATO, SWEET (WHOLE)

Buy oval-shaped sweet potatoes of uniform size. Scrub under cold running water; pierce several times. If they have tapered ends, arrange ends pointing towards centre as they will cook more rapidly than rest of vegetable. If ends seem tender halfway through cooking, shield them with smooth, thin strips of foil.

About 161 cals per serving		
For 4	**For 2**	**For 1**
4 sweet potatoes or yams (about 225 g each)	2 sweet potatoes or yams (about 225 g each)	1 sweet potato or yam (about 225 g)
Arrange on kitchen paper on oven floor	Arrange on kitchen paper on oven floor	Place on kitchen paper on oven floor
None	None	None
10–11 minutes; *turn sweet potatoes or yams over and rearrange halfway through*	7–8 minutes; *turn sweet potatoes or yams over halfway through cooking*	4–5 minutes; *turn sweet potato or yam over halfway through cooking*
5 minutes; *wrap in foil or clean tea towel before standing*	5 minutes; *wrap in foil or clean tea towel before standing*	5 minutes; *wrap in foil or clean tea towel before standing*

Cook sweet potatoes or yams on High (100% power) for time in Chart. Allow to stand, wrapped, for time in Chart. Sweet potatoes or yams are done when tender if pierced with tip of sharp knife.

SQUASH, ACORN (HALVES)

This is a variety of winter squash. Wash under cold running water. To soften slightly for easier cutting, pierce each squash several times; heat on High (100% power) for 1–1¹⁄₂ (1:30) minutes per squash. Cut in half lengthways; discard seeds.

About 75 cals per serving		
For 4	**For 2**	**For 1**
2 squash (about 700 g each)	1 squash (about 700 g)	1 small squash (about 450 g)
Wrap each half individually in cling film; *arrange in circle on oven floor*	Wrap each half individually in cling film; *place on oven floor*	Wrap each half individually in cling film; *place on oven floor*
None	None	None
12–14 minutes; *rearrange halfway through cooking*	9 minutes; *rearrange halfway through cooking*	7 minutes; *rearrange halfway through cooking*
5 minutes	5 minutes	5 minutes

Cook squash, wrapped, on High (100% power) for time in Chart. Allow to stand, still wrapped, for time in Chart. Acorn squash halves are done when flesh is tender.

249

SQUASH, BUTTERNUT (HALVES AND QUARTERS)

Rinse under cold running water and pat dry. Cut in half lengthways; if squash is heavier than 900 g, cut into quarters. With spoon, scoop out seeds.

About 120 cals per serving			
	For 4	**For 2**	**For 1**
	1 large squash (about 1.4 kg)	1 medium squash (about 900 g)	1 small squash (about 575 g)
🍲	Wrap individually in cling film; *arrange on oven floor, alternating narrow ends*	Wrap individually in cling film; *arrange on oven floor, alternating narrow ends*	Wrap in cling film; *arrange on oven floor, alternating narrow ends*
🥤	None	None	None
🕐	20–24 minutes; *rearrange pieces halfway through cooking*	10–12 minutes; *rearrange halves halfway through cooking*	7–8 minutes; *rearrange halves halfway through cooking*
🍲	5 minutes	5 minutes	5 minutes

Cook squash, wrapped, on High (100% power) for time in Chart. Allow to stand, still wrapped, for time in Chart. Butternut squash is done when flesh is tender and can be scooped easily from shell; any pale yellow areas will continue to cook during standing. If any area remains pale yellow after standing, continue to cook, rewrapped, for 30 seconds at a time until rich yellow-orange.

SQUASH, SPAGHETTI (HALVES)

Rinse under cold running water. Cut squash in half lengthways. Scrape out seeds and membranes; discard.

About 66 cals per serving			
	For 4	**For 2**	**For 1**
	1 large squash (1.8–2 kg)	1 medium squash (about 900 g)	1 small squash (about 575 g)
🍲	Wrap each half individually in cling film; *arrange on oven floor*	Wrap each half individually in cling film; *arrange on oven floor*	Wrap each half individually in cling film; *arrange on oven floor*
🥤	None	None	None
🕐	22–24 minutes; *rearrange halves halfway through cooking*	12–14 minutes; *rearrange halves halfway through cooking*	9–10 minutes; *rearrange halves halfway through cooking*
🍲	5 minutes	5 minutes	5 minutes

Cook squash halves, wrapped, on High (100% power) for time in Chart. Allow to stand, still wrapped, for time in Chart. Spaghetti squash is done when fork can easily pull and separate squash strands. Texture is crisp compared with other squash.

SWEDE (CHUNKS)

Cut into quarters. Peel and cut into 2 cm chunks.

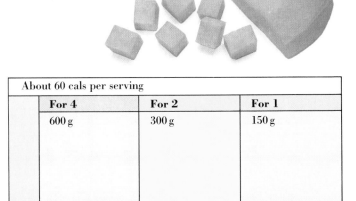

About 60 cals per serving			
	For 4	**For 2**	**For 1**
	600 g	300 g	150 g
🍲	1 litre casserole	1 litre casserole	1 litre casserole
🥤	120 ml	4 tablespoons	4 tablespoons
🕐	17–19 minutes; *stir twice during cooking*	12–14 minutes; *stir twice during cooking*	7–9 minutes; *stir halfway through cooking*
🍲	5 minutes	5 minutes	5 minutes

Cook swede and water, covered, on High (100% power) for time in Chart. Allow to stand, covered, for time in Chart. Swede chunks are done when tender. Drain.

SWEETCORN, BABY

Rinse baby sweetcorn under cold running water. Trim off any brown bits on tips or stalk ends.

16 cals per serving			
	For 4	**For 2**	**For 1**
	350 g	175 g	75 g
🍲	20 cm square baking dish	Shallow 21.5 cm pie dish	Small bowl
🥤	120 ml	4 tablespoons	2 tablespoons
🕐	5–6 minutes; *stir halfway through cooking*	3–4 minutes; *stir halfway through cooking*	2–3 minutes; *stir halfway through cooking*
🍲	3 minutes	2 minutes	1 minutes

Cook baby sweetcorn and water, covered, on High (100% power) for time in Chart. Allow to stand, covered, for time in Chart. Baby sweetcorn is done when tender-crisp if pierced with tip of sharp knife. Drain.

SWEETCORN (WHOLE),
see CORN-ON-THE-COB
(page 273)

SWEETCORN (FROZEN KERNELS)

About 80 cals per serving		
For 4	**For 2**	**For 1**
575 g	275 g	150 g
1 litre casserole	Small bowl	Small bowl
4 tablespoons	4 tablespoons	1 tablespoon
8–9 minutes; *stir halfway through cooking*	5–7 minutes; *stir halfway through cooking*	1½(1:30)–2½ (2:30) minutes; *stir halfway through cooking*
5 minutes	3–5 minutes	1–2 minutes

Cook frozen sweetcorn kernels and water, covered, on High (100% power) for time in Chart. Allow to stand, covered, for time in Chart. Frozen sweetcorn kernels are done when hot. Drain.

TURNIP (CHUNKS)

Peel. Rinse under cold running water. Cut into 2 cm thick chunks.

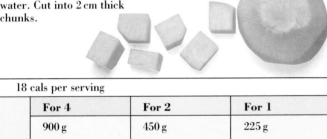

18 cals per serving		
For 4	**For 2**	**For 1**
900 g	450 g	225 g
2 litre casserole	1 litre casserole	Small bowl
120 ml	4 tablespoons	2 tablespoons
8–9½ (9:30) minutes; *stir halfway through cooking*	5–7 minutes; *stir halfway through cooking*	3½ (3:30)–4 minutes; *stir halfway through cooking*
5 minutes	5 minutes	5 minutes

Cook turnips and water, covered, on High (100% power) for time in Chart. Allow to stand, covered, for time in Chart. Turnip chunks are cooked when tender. Drain.

YAM, cook as for potato, sweet (page 249)

SPECIAL TECHNIQUES FOR VEGETABLES

Use the microwave to help cook vegetables in a special way: purées, ribbons and rings can make a simple vegetable look really special. Impress your guests by serving a colourful selection of puréed vegetables, or delicate vegetable ribbons or rings following the easy instructions below. Use your imagination to create different combinations of colours, flavours and shapes.

Vegetable purées are particularly good to serve at dinner parties because they can be made in advance and reheated in the microwave; they go well with roast meats and grilled chicken. The ribbons and rings can be served uncooked as a salad with a favourite dressing.

Vegetable purées Root vegetables such as potatoes, carrots and parsnips cook very quickly in the microwave; leafy green vegetables such as spinach and broccoli remain bright and green.

Cook vegetables, covered, on High (100% power) for 2 minutes longer than time in Charts, or until soft, then drain well. In food processor with knife blade attached, process vegetable to smooth purée. Add 30 g melted butter or margarine, season with salt and pepper, and process again. If you like, add 1–2 tablespoons double or whipping cream. Using ice-cream scoop or spoon, shape purée on to microwave-safe plates. Reheat on High for 45–60 seconds, until hot.

Ribbon vegetables With vegetable peeler, shred 1 large carrot, 1 medium courgette and 1 white radish (mooli) into long ribbons, about 2.5 cm wide, pressing lightly with peeler so ribbons will be very thin. In large microwave-safe bowl, toss vegetables with 15 g melted butter or margarine. Cook, covered, on High (100% power) for 30 seconds–1 minute, until tender-crisp.

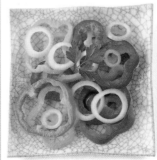

Vegetable rings With sharp knife, cut 3 peppers (green, yellow and red) and 1 small onion into rings; remove cores, seeds and membranes from peppers. In 32.5 × 22.5 cm microwave-safe baking dish, toss vegetables with 15 g melted butter or margarine, or 1 tablespoon olive oil, or 1 tablespoon water. Cook, covered, on High (100% power) for 1–2 minutes, until tender-crisp. Serve hot, or refrigerate to serve chilled later with a favourite salad dressing.

Asparagus and Aubergines

ASPARAGUS BUNDLES

Colour Index page 70. 68 cals per serving. Low in cholesterol, sodium. Good source of vitamin A. Begin 25 minutes ahead.

Ingredients	For 4	For 2	For 1
Medium asparagus spears	*450 g*	*225 g*	*115 g*
Spring onions	*2 onions*	*1 onion*	*1 onion*
Water	*2 tablespoons*	*1 tablespoon*	*1½ teaspoons*
Butter or margarine	*30 g*	*15 g*	*1½ teaspoons*
Diced canned pimiento	*2 tablespoons*	*1 tablespoon*	*1½ teaspoons*
Lemon juice	*1 tablespoon*	*1½ teaspoons*	*½ teaspoon*
Microwave cookware	30 × 20 cm baking dish Small bowl	30 × 20 cm baking dish Small bowl	30 × 20 cm baking dish Small bowl
Time on High (100% power) Asparagus	5–7 minutes	3–5 minutes	1½(1:30)–2½ (2:30) minutes
Butter mixture	45 seconds	30 seconds	15 seconds

1 Hold base of each asparagus stalk firmly and bend; end will break off at spot where it becomes too tough to eat. Discard tough ends; trim scales if stalks are gritty.

2 With sharp knife, cut spring onions where white ends and green starts. Cut green halves in half lengthways. Thinly slice white ends and reserve.

3 Divide asparagus into bundles, with tips pointing in same direction. Use green ends of spring onions to tie up asparagus bundles.

4 In baking dish (see Chart), arrange asparagus bundles with tips overlapping in centre and tougher, thicker ends pointing towards edges.

5 Sprinkle bundles with water. Cook, covered, on High for time in Chart, until tender-crisp, rotating dish once. Drain; loosely cover and set aside. In small bowl (see Chart), place reserved onions, butter or margarine and pimiento. Cook, covered with kitchen paper, on High for time in Chart. Stir in lemon juice.

6 Over asparagus bundles in baking dish, spoon spring onion and pimiento mixture. Serve immediately.

ASPARAGUS WITH CELERY AND WALNUTS

Colour Index page 70. 4 servings. 58 cals per serving. Low in cholesterol, sodium. Begin 25 minutes ahead.

2 teaspoons olive or vegetable oil
2 tablespoons chopped walnuts
3 celery sticks
350 g medium asparagus spears
1 garlic clove, crushed
Salt to taste

1. In 21.5 cm shallow microwave-safe pie dish combine oil and walnuts. Heat on High (100% power) for 1–3 minutes, until walnuts are lightly toasted, stirring once. With slotted spoon, remove nuts to kitchen paper to drain.
2. Meanwhile, with sharp knife, cut celery sticks diagonally into 5 cm pieces. Discard tough ends and trim scales from asparagus. Cut asparagus diagonally into 5 cm pieces.
3. Into oil remaining in pie dish, stir celery, asparagus and garlic. Cook on High for 6–8 minutes, until asparagus is tender-crisp, stirring twice. Add salt and walnuts and toss lightly. Arrange on warmed serving platter.

SZECHUAN AUBERGINE

Colour Index page 72. 4 servings. 73 cals per serving. Low in cholesterol. Good source of fibre. Begin 25 minutes ahead.

1 aubergine (about 450 g)
1 teaspoon sugar
1 teaspoon cornflour
1 tablespoon finely chopped peeled root ginger or 1¼ teaspoons ground ginger
175 ml Chicken Stock (page 125) or stock from a cube
1 tablespoon soy sauce
½ teaspoon Tabasco sauce
1 tablespoon groundnut or vegetable oil
1 spring onion, thinly sliced
Spring Onion Tassel (page 132) to garnish

1. Preheat browning dish according to manufacturer's instructions. Meanwhile, cut aubergine into 10 × 1 × 1 cm strips; set aside.
2. In mixing bowl, combine sugar, cornflour and ginger. Gradually stir in stock, soy and Tabasco sauces until blended.
3. Coat browning dish with half of the oil. On browning dish, arrange half of the aubergine strips. Cook on High (100% power) for 3–4 minutes, until aubergine softens, stirring once. With fish slice, transfer aubergine to kitchen paper to drain. Repeat with remaining oil and aubergine.
4. Return all aubergine to browning dish. Stir in ginger and soy mixture. Cook on High for 3–4 minutes, until slightly thickened, stirring halfway through cooking. Stir in spring onion.
5. *To serve:* transfer aubergine mixture to serving platter. Serve hot or cover and refrigerate to serve chilled later. Garnish before serving.

BABY AUBERGINE BROCHETTES WITH SATAY SAUCE

Colour Index page 74. 4 servings. 191 cals per serving. Low in cholesterol. Good source of vitamin C, fibre. Begin 35 minutes ahead.

4 tablespoons peanut butter	Water
1 teaspoon tomato purée	2 tablespoons olive oil
1 tablespoon soy sauce	½ teaspoon dried oregano
2 tablespoons lime or lemon juice	12 baby aubergines, total weight about 450 g
1 green chilli, deseeded and thinly sliced	Tomatoes and fresh coriander leaves to garnish
2 cm root ginger, peeled and finely chopped	
2 cloves garlic, chopped	

1. Prepare sauce: in 500 ml microwave-safe measuring jug, combine peanut butter, tomato purée, soy sauce, lime or lemon juice, chilli, ginger, half of garlic and 50 ml water. Cook, covered, on High (100% power) for 2–3 minutes, until boiling, stirring twice; set aside.
2. In small microwave-safe bowl, combine olive oil, remaining chopped garlic and oregano. Cook on High for 25 seconds. Allow to stand while preparing aubergines.
3. With sharp knife, cut slits in 1 side of 1 aubergine at 1 cm intervals. Turn aubergine over and cut slits in other side, in between first slits. Do not remove stalk end. Repeat with each of remaining aubergines.
4. Beginning at bottom end, push each aubergine on to short wooden skewer. Gently pull out each aubergine to create concertina effect.
5. Brush each aubergine with oil and garlic mixture; arrange half of aubergines spoke-fashion on 30 cm microwave-safe platter. Cook on High for 3–4 minutes, until tender, turning aubergines over and rearranging halfway through cooking. Keep warm while cooking remaining aubergines. Reheat sauce on High for 45 seconds. Pour sauce over aubergines, garnish with tomatoes and coriander and serve immediately.

Preparing the Aubergines for Cooking

Cut slits down 1 side of aubergine at 1 cm intervals, without cutting right through. Repeat on other side.

Push each aubergine on to wooden skewer. Gently pull out aubergine to create concertina effect.

AUBERGINES WITH TABBOULEH STUFFING

Colour Index page 77. 303 cals per serving. Low in cholesterol. Good source of vitamin C, calcium, iron, fibre. Begin 1¼ hours ahead.

This nutritious vegetarian main course has a Middle Eastern flavour, with its stuffing of bulgur, garlic, raisins and mint – known as tabbouleh. Bulgur, also known as cracked wheat, is a nutritious grain used in Middle Eastern cooking; it is available in health food shops and some large supermarkets.

Ingredients for 4 main course servings		Microwave cookware
2 aubergines (about 350 g each)	2 tablespoons capers, drained	30 × 20 cm baking dish
Salt	70 g bulgur, soaked	30 × 20 cm platter
2 onions, chopped	1 tablespoon finely chopped fresh mint or	
3 celery sticks, chopped	½ teaspoon dried mint	
3 tablespoons olive or vegetable oil	½ teaspoon dried thyme	
3 garlic cloves, crushed	80 ml tomato juice	
1 small green pepper, chopped	1 tablespoon lemon juice	
75 g raisins	Pepper to taste	
120 ml Vegetable Stock (page 125) or water	Lemon wedges and mint leaves to garnish	

1. With sharp knife, cut each aubergine in half lengthways. Cut out centre of each half, leaving a 1 cm shell. Finely chop aubergine centres; set aside.

2. Sprinkle hollowed-out halves with salt. On double thickness of kitchen paper, place aubergine halves, cut side down. Allow to stand for 20 minutes.

3. In baking dish, place onions, celery and 2 tablespoons oil. Cook on High (100% power) for 3–4 minutes, until vegetables soften slightly, stirring halfway through cooking.

4. To baking dish, add garlic, green pepper, raisins, stock or water and chopped aubergine centres. Cook on High for 10–12 minutes, until aubergine is tender, stirring occasionally. Stir in capers, bulgur, mint, thyme, tomato juice and lemon juice. Season. Rinse salt off aubergine halves; pat dry.

5. With remaining oil, lightly brush aubergine halves. Arrange on platter. Cook on High for 5 minutes, or until fork-tender (do not cook longer or shells will collapse when filled).

6. Into each aubergine half, spoon equal amount of bulgur mixture. Cook on High for 4–6 minutes, just until filling is hot. Garnish with lemon wedges and mint and serve immediately.

Beans

BROAD BEANS WITH BUTTERED BREADCRUMBS

Colour Index page 70. 153 cals per serving. Good source of fibre.
Begin 20 minutes ahead.

Ingredients	For 4	For 2	For 1
Butter or margarine	*30 g*	*15 g*	*1½ teaspoons*
Fresh white or brown breadcrumbs	*30 g*	*15 g*	*2 tablespoons*
Frozen broad beans, defrosted	*275 g*	*150 g*	*75 g*
Water	*2 tablespoons*	*1 tablespoon*	*1½ teaspoons*
Grated Parmesan or Cheddar cheese	*2 tablespoons*	*1 tablespoon*	*1½ teaspoons*
Microwave cookware	Pie dish	Pie dish	Pie dish
	Medium bowl	Small bowl	Soup bowl
Time on High (100% power)			
Butter or margarine	45 seconds	30–45 seconds	15 seconds
Breadcrumbs	2–2½ (2:30) minutes	1½ (1:30)–1¾ (1:45) minutes	1–1¼ (1:15) minutes
Broad beans	6–8 minutes	4–5 minutes	2–3 minutes

1 In 21.5 cm pie dish, place butter or margarine. Heat, covered with kitchen paper, on High for time in Chart, until melted.

2 Into melted butter or margarine, stir breadcrumbs. Cook on High for time in Chart, until crumbs are dried and golden, stirring twice. Set aside.

3 In bowl (see Chart), place broad beans and water. Cook, covered, on High for time in Chart, until tender, stirring once; drain. Stir in cheese. Transfer to warmed serving dish; sprinkle with buttered breadcrumbs and serve immediately.

FRENCH BEANS WITH PEANUT SAUCE

Colour Index page 71. 243 cals per serving. Low in cholesterol. Good source of vitamin A, niacin, vitamin C, iron, fibre. Begin 25 minutes ahead.

Ingredients	For 4	For 2	For 1
Garlic cloves	*2 cloves*	*1 clove*	*½ clove*
Red pepper	*1 pepper*	*½ pepper*	*¼ pepper*
Crunchy peanut butter	*8 tablespoons*	*4 tablespoons*	*2 tablespoons*
Vegetable Stock (page 125) or stock from a cube	*120 ml*	*60 ml*	*2 tablespoons*
Soy sauce	*1 tablespoon soy sauce*	*1½ teaspoons soy sauce*	*¾ teaspoon soy sauce*
Cider vinegar	*1 tablespoon vinegar*	*1½ teaspoons vinegar*	*¾ teaspoon vinegar*
Sesame oil	*¼ teaspoon*	*to taste*	*to taste*
Finely chopped peeled root ginger or ground ginger	*1 tablespoon or 1½ teaspoons*	*1½ teaspoons or ¾ teaspoon*	*¾ teaspoon or ¼ teaspoon*
Tabasco sauce	*to taste*	*to taste*	*to taste*
French beans	*450 g*	*225 g*	*115 g*
Water	*4 tablespoons*	*2 tablespoons*	*1 tablespoon*
Coriander sprigs and red pepper strips	*garnish*	*garnish*	*garnish*
Microwave cookware	500 ml glass jug	250 ml glass jug	250 ml glass jug
	30 × 20 cm baking dish	20 cm square baking dish	20 cm square baking dish
Time on High (100% power)			
Sauce	1–1½ (1:30) minutes	45 seconds–1 minute	30–45 seconds
French beans	7–10 minutes	4–5 minutes	3–4 minutes

1 Chop garlic; dice red pepper. In jug (see Chart), combine garlic, pepper, peanut butter, stock, soy, vinegar, sesame oil, ginger and Tabasco. Cook on High for time in Chart, stirring once.

2 In baking dish (see Chart), place beans; add water. Cook, covered, on High for time in Chart, until tender-crisp, stirring once. Drain.

3 Over drained beans in baking dish, pour peanut sauce; toss to coat beans.

4 Transfer beans and sauce to serving platter. Serve hot or cover and refrigerate to serve chilled later. Garnish before serving.

Beetroot

Cooking fresh beetroot in the microwave is very quick and easy. Simply cut off the leafy tops, leaving on part of the stalks and roots, then scrub beetroot under cold running water; take care not to damage the skins or this may cause 'bleeding'. Cook in the microwave and allow to cool, covered, as in step 1 of Fresh Beetroot with Endive (below), then cut off the stalks and roots and peel from bottom to top. Very large beetroot cook better if individually wrapped in microwave cling film and arranged in a circle on the oven floor.

1 In baking dish, place beetroot and water. Cook, covered, on High (100% power) for 17–20 minutes, until tender, rotating twice. Cool.

2 In large mixing bowl, whisk oil, vinegar, sugar, mustard, oregano and salt; set aside. Drain and rinse beetroot.

FRESH BEETROOT WITH ENDIVE

Colour Index page 74. 143 cals per serving. Low in cholesterol. Good source of fibre. Begin 50 minutes ahead.

Ingredients for 6 servings		Microwave cookware
8 fresh beetroot (about 900 g without tops)	1 tablespoon sugar	32.5 × 22.5 cm baking dish
120 ml water	1 tablespoon made mustard	
60 ml olive or vegetable oil	1/2 teaspoon dried oregano	
3 tablespoons red wine vinegar	1/4 teaspoon salt	
	1/2 small head endive	

3 With rubber glove for protection, peel beetroot and cut into 5 mm thick slices; cut slices into 5 mm wide strips. Toss strips in bowl of dressing.

4 Tear endive into bite-sized pieces. Transfer beetroot and dressing to warmed serving dish; add endive and serve immediately.

SWEET AND SOUR BEETROOT

Colour Index page 70. 62 cals per serving. Low in cholesterol, fat. Good source of fibre. Begin 15 minutes ahead.

Ingredients	For 4	For 2	For 1
Can sliced beetroot	1 × 400 g	1 × 225 g	1/2 × 225 g
Liquid from can	120 ml	60 ml	2 tablespoons
Cider vinegar	3 tablespoons	4 teaspoons	2 teaspoons
Caster sugar	2 tablespoons	1 tablespoon	1 1/2 teaspoons
Salt	1/4 teaspoon	to taste	to taste
Cornflour	1 1/2 teaspoons	1 teaspoon	1/2 teaspoon
Orange Julienne (page 330)	garnish	garnish	garnish
Microwave cookware	2 litre casserole or bowl	1 litre casserole or bowl	Soup bowl
Time on High (100% power)			
Sauce	2–3 minutes	1 1/2 (1:30)–2 minutes	1–1 1/4 (1:15) minutes
Beetroot	3–4 minutes	2–2 1/2 (2:30) minutes	45 seconds–1 minute

1 In casserole or bowl (see Chart), combine beetroot liquid, vinegar, sugar, salt and cornflour until blended.

2 Cook mixture on High for time in Chart, or until sauce thickens, stirring twice.

3 To sauce, add sliced beetroot; stir to coat. Cook on High for time in Chart, or until hot, stirring once.

4 To serve: spoon beetroot and sauce into warmed serving dish. Garnish with Orange Julienne.

Broccoli

BROCCOLI MORNAY

Colour Index page 74. 211 cals per serving. Good source of vitamin A, vitamin C, calcium, fibre. Begin 40 minutes ahead.

Ingredients for 4 servings		Microwave cookware
450 g broccoli	50 g Cheddar cheese	1 litre
45 g butter or	Salt and pepper to taste	measuring jug
margarine	2 tablespoons water	20 cm square
2 tablespoons plain	15 g fresh breadcrumbs	baking dish
flour	1 small onion, finely	Small bowl
250 ml milk	chopped	
Pinch of dry mustard		

1 Remove large leaves from broccoli and trim woody stalk ends. Cut through stalks lengthways 2–3 times. Rinse well and set aside.

2 In measuring jug, place 30 g butter or margarine. Heat, covered with kitchen paper, on High (100% power) for 45 seconds, or until melted. Stir in flour until smooth and blended. Gradually whisk in milk and dry mustard. Cook on High for 3–4 minutes, until sauce thickens and is smooth, whisking twice.

3 Grate Cheddar cheese. To sauce, gradually add cheese, whisking until melted and smooth. Season with salt and pepper. Cover and keep warm.

4 In baking dish, arrange broccoli with florets pointing towards centre of dish and stalks towards edges. Sprinkle over water. Cook, covered, on High for 6–8 minutes, until tender-crisp, rotating dish halfway through cooking. Drain broccoli; rearrange in attractive pattern in same baking dish or warmed serving dish.

5 Over broccoli, pour cheese sauce; cover and keep warm. In small bowl, place remaining butter or margarine. Heat, covered with kitchen paper, on High for 30–45 seconds, until melted. Into melted butter or margarine, stir breadcrumbs and onion. Cook on High for 2–3 minutes, until crumbs are dried and golden, stirring twice.

6 To serve: sprinkle golden breadcrumb topping evenly over broccoli and cheese sauce in dish. Serve immediately.

NEAPOLITAN BROCCOLI

Colour Index page 70. 4 servings. 113 cals per serving. Low in cholesterol. Good source of vitamin A, vitamin C, fibre. Begin 25 minutes ahead.

2 tablespoons olive or vegetable oil	2 tablespoons capers
	5 stoned black olives
1 red or green pepper, thinly sliced	700 g broccoli
	1½ teaspoons red wine vinegar
1 garlic clove, finely chopped	Flaked almonds to garnish
2 spring onions, sliced	

1. In 2 litre microwave-safe casserole, place oil, red or green pepper, garlic, spring onions, capers and olives. Cook on High (100% power) for 5–6 minutes, until pepper softens, stirring twice.
2. Meanwhile, with sharp knife, remove large leaves from broccoli and trim woody stalk ends.
3. To vegetable mixture, add broccoli; stir to coat. Cook, covered, on High for 7–10 minutes, until broccoli is tender, stirring twice. Add vinegar; toss. Serve hot or cover and refrigerate to serve chilled later. Garnish before serving.

SAUCES FOR VEGETABLES

Use to add zest to plain cooked fresh or frozen vegetables.

Lemon Butter Sauce: in 500 ml microwave-safe measuring jug, place **60 g butter or margarine.** Heat, covered with kitchen paper, on High (100% power) for 45 seconds–1 minute, until melted. Stir in **1 tablespoon lemon juice, 1 tablespoon chopped parsley, ½ teaspoon salt** and **pinch of cayenne pepper.** Makes about 80 ml. 90 cals per tablespoon.

Fines Herbes Sauce: prepare Lemon Butter Sauce (above), substituting **3 tablespoons dry white wine** for lemon juice; add **2 tablespoons chopped chives** and **1 teaspoon chopped fresh dill.** Makes about 80 ml. 95 cals per tablespoon.

Mustard and Chive Sauce: in large microwave-safe bowl, place **60 g butter or margarine.** Heat, covered with kitchen paper, on High (100% power) for 45 seconds–1 minute, until melted. Stir in **35 g plain flour** until blended. Cook on High for 1 minute, stirring once. Gradually stir in **500 ml milk.** Cook on High for 3–5 minutes, until sauce thickens, stirring twice. Stir in **1 tablespoon Dijon mustard** and **1 tablespoon chopped chives.** Makes about 500 ml. 26 cals per tablespoon.

Broccoli and Brussels Sprouts

BROCCOLI WITH SESAME SAUCE

Colour Index page 73. 4 servings. 99 cals per serving. Low in cholesterol. Good source of vitamin A, vitamin C, calcium, iron, fibre.
Begin 25 minutes ahead.

1 tablespoon sesame seeds	2 tablespoons soy sauce
1 tablespoon sesame oil	2 spring onions, finely sliced
1 tablespoon vegetable oil	450 g broccoli
1 clove garlic, chopped	4 tablespoons water

1. Make sesame sauce: on flat plate, spread sesame seeds. Cook on High (100% power) for 2–3 minutes, until golden, stirring often. In mixing bowl, combine sesame seeds, oils, garlic, soy sauce and spring onions; set aside.
2. With sharp knife, remove large leaves from broccoli and trim woody stalk ends. Separate stalks from heads. Peel stalks and cut into 2 cm pieces. Break heads into small florets.
3. In 22 cm round microwave-safe baking dish, arrange broccoli with florets in centre, stalks round edge. Sprinkle over water. Cook on High (100% power) for 5 minutes, or until tender-crisp, rearranging or stirring twice.
4. Into large bowl of iced water, plunge broccoli. Drain in colander, then drain on kitchen paper. Arrange in serving dish and pour over sesame sauce. Serve cold.

PARTY BRUSSELS SPROUTS

Colour Index page 71. 6 servings. 108 cals per serving. Good source of vitamin C, fibre. Begin 25 minutes ahead.

2 rashers rindless streaky bacon, diced	575 g frozen Brussels sprouts
450 g baby onions, peeled and trimmed	1 teaspoon dried thyme
60 ml water	

1. In 3 litre microwave-safe casserole, place bacon. Cook on High (100% power) for 2–3 minutes, until browned. With slotted spoon, transfer bacon to kitchen paper to drain.
2. Into bacon fat in casserole, stir onions and water. Cook, covered, on High for 4 minutes, stirring halfway through cooking.
3. To onions, add Brussels sprouts and thyme. Cook, covered, on High for 10–12 minutes, until sprouts are tender-crisp, stirring halfway through cooking.
4. Sprinkle bacon over vegetables. Toss to mix and serve immediately.

BRUSSELS SPROUTS WITH CHESTNUTS

Colour Index page 75. 79 cals per serving. Good source of vitamin C, fibre. Begin 35 minutes ahead.

Ingredients	For 4	For 2	For 1
Trimmed Brussels sprouts	275 g	150 g	75 g
Vegetable Stock (page 125) or water	120 ml	60 ml	3 tablespoons
Butter or margarine	1 tablespoon	1½ teaspoons	1 teaspoon
Peeled cooked chestnuts (below)	8	6	4
Salt and pepper	to taste	to taste	to taste
Lemon juice (optional)	½ teaspoon	¼ teaspoon	to taste
Microwave cookware	30 × 20 cm baking dish	20 cm square baking dish	Soup bowl
Time on High (100% power) Brussels sprouts	7–9 minutes	5–6 minutes	3½(3:30)–4½ (4:30) minutes
With chestnuts	5–6 minutes	3–3½(3:30) minutes	1½(1:30)–2½ (2:30) minutes

1 In baking dish or bowl (see Chart), place Brussels sprouts; add stock or water. Cook, covered tightly with cling film, on High for time in Chart, or until tender-crisp, stirring twice.

2 To Brussels sprouts, add butter or margarine and peeled cooked chestnuts. Cook on High for time in Chart, or until flavours blend. Season with salt and pepper.

3 If you like, just before serving, sprinkle lemon juice over Brussels sprouts.

PEELING AND COOKING CHESTNUTS

Make horizontal cut through shells of 120 g chestnuts, cutting across rounded side. Do not cut through meat.

In 1 litre measuring jug, place chestnuts and 250 ml water. Heat, covered, on High (100% power) for 2½ (2:30)–4 minutes, until boiling; boil for 1 minute longer.

Allow to stand for 7 minutes. Peel off shells and skins; reboil any that do not open. In shallow dish, in single layer, cook nuts on High for 1½ (1:30) minutes, or until tender.

Meal in Minutes *for 8 people*

Chinese New Year Party

Dim sum (bought)
Szechuan Lobster, page 167
'Stir-Fried' Prawns and Broccoli, page 166, for 4
Stir-Fry with Pork, page 217
Szechuan Aubergine, page 252
Hot Cooked Rice, page 293
Fortune cookies and China tea

PREPARATION TIMETABLE

Early in day	*Prepare all vegetables and store in polythene bags in refrigerator. Slice pork for Stir-Fry with Pork; cover and refrigerate. Prepare Szechuan Lobster up to end of step 1; cover and refrigerate. Prepare Szechuan Aubergine up to end of step 4; place on serving platter, cover and refrigerate.*
1 hour ahead	*Prepare 'Stir-Fried' Prawns and Broccoli up to end of step 2. Complete Szechuan Lobster, arrange in warmed serving dish, cover and keep warm. Cook rice; keep warm. Place cookies in bowls.*
30 minutes ahead	*Complete 'Stir-Fried' Prawns and Broccoli and Stir-Fry with Pork; arrange in warmed serving dishes, cover and keep warm. Prepare bought dim sum according to packet instructions and place in bamboo steamers or bowls. Make China tea.*

Cabbage

SWEET-AND-SOUR SHREDDED RED CABBAGE

Colour Index page 74. 8 servings. 37 cals per serving. Low in cholesterol, fat. Good source of vitamin C, fibre. Begin 35 minutes ahead.

1 small red cabbage (about 700 g), shredded	*1 bay leaf*
2 tablespoons brown sugar	*Salt and pepper to taste*
60 ml red wine vinegar	*Apple slices and parsley sprig to garnish*

1. In 3 litre microwave-safe casserole, combine cabbage, sugar, vinegar and bay leaf. Cook, covered, on High (100% power) for 15 minutes, stirring twice.
2. Uncover; stir. Cook on High for 5–10 minutes longer, until cabbage is done to your liking. Discard bay leaf. Season with salt and pepper.
3. Spoon cabbage on to warmed serving platter; garnish with apple slices and parsley sprig. Serve immediately.

CREAMY CABBAGE

Colour Index page 74. 8 servings. 124 cals per serving. Good source of vitamin C, fibre. Begin 45 minutes ahead.

45 g butter or margarine	*120 ml double or whipping cream*
30 g fresh breadcrumbs	*Salt and pepper to taste*
2 onions, thinly sliced	
1 green cabbage (about 700 g), shredded	

1. In 3 litre microwave-safe casserole, place 30 g butter or margarine. Heat, covered with kitchen paper, on High (100% power) for 45 seconds, or until melted. Into melted butter or margarine, stir breadcrumbs. Cook on High for 3–4 minutes, until crumbs are dried and golden, stirring twice. Transfer to small bowl. Set aside.
2. In same casserole, place remaining butter or margarine and onions. Cook, covered with kitchen paper, on High for 5–6 minutes, until onions soften, stirring twice.
3. To onion mixture, add cabbage; stir to coat. Cook, covered, on High for 10–12 minutes, until cabbage is tender, stirring occasionally. Into mixture, stir cream. Season with salt and pepper.
4. Sprinkle cabbage with breadcrumbs. Cook on High for 3–4 minutes, until cabbage is hot and cream bubbles. If you like and if casserole is flameproof, brown lightly under preheated grill.

Carrots

GLAZED CARROTS

Colour Index page 71. 4 servings. 88 cals per serving. Good source of vitamin A, fibre. Begin 25 minutes ahead.

450 g carrots, cut into 5 mm thick slices
60 ml Chicken Stock (page 125) or stock from a cube
2 teaspoons sugar
15 g butter or margarine
Salt and pepper to taste
Parsley sprig to garnish

1. In 21.5 cm microwave-safe shallow pie dish, combine carrots, stock and sugar. Cook, covered, on High (100% power) for 5–7 minutes, until carrots are tender-crisp, stirring twice.
2. Uncover; cook on High for 3–5 minutes longer, until carrots are tender and liquid has almost evaporated, stirring twice.
3. To carrot mixture, add butter or margarine; stir until carrots are glazed. Season with salt and pepper. Transfer carrots to warmed serving dish; garnish and serve immediately.

GINGER-ORANGE CARROTS

Colour Index page 71. 4 servings. 58 cals per serving. Low in cholesterol, fat. Good source of vitamin A, fibre. Begin 25 minutes ahead.

450 g carrots, peeled and cut into matchstick-thin strips
1 tablespoon orange juice
2 teaspoons finely grated orange zest
2 teaspoons soy sauce
4 tablespoons finely grated peeled root ginger or 1 teaspoon ground ginger
2 spring onions, thinly sliced

1. In 21.5 cm microwave-safe shallow pie dish, place carrots and orange juice. Cook, covered, on High (100% power) for 7–9 minutes, until carrots are tender-crisp, stirring occasionally.
2. To carrot mixture, add orange zest, soy sauce, ginger and spring onions. Stir to combine well. Cook on High for 1–2 minutes, until carrot mixture is hot.
3. Spoon mixture on to serving platter. Serve hot or cover and refrigerate to serve chilled later.

Making 'Baby' Carrots

With sharp knife, cut medium carrots into 7.5 cm pieces. With vegetable peeler, shape each piece until about 1 cm in diameter, tapering to a point at one end. Use trimmings in salads or stocks.

Carrots may be prepared in a variety of ways. Baby carrots are best microwaved whole if they are a similar size, but larger carrots can be cut into matchstick-thin strips or slices. For a quick lunchtime snack or vegetable accompaniment, try grating carrots and combining them with another vegetable, as in Carrot and Potato Pancakes (below).

CARROT AND POTATO PANCAKES

Colour Index page 74. 112 cals per serving. Good source of vitamin A, fibre. Begin 35 minutes ahead.

Ingredients for 4 servings		Microwave cookware
2 carrots 1 baking potato, peeled (about 225 g) 2 tablespoons plain flour 1/4 teaspoon salt 1/4 teaspoon baking powder	1 egg 1 small onion, finely chopped Pepper to taste 15 g butter or margarine Dill sprigs to garnish Apple sauce and soured cream (optional)	Shallow 21.5 cm pie dish Browning dish

1 Into a little cold water in mixing bowl, coarsely grate carrots and potato (water prevents potato discolouring). In colander, drain carrots and potato.

2 In pie dish, place grated carrots and potato. Cook, covered, on High (100% power) for 5 minutes, or until tender-crisp. In colander, drain carrots and potato; set aside.

3 Meanwhile, in large bowl, combine flour, salt and baking powder until blended. Add egg and onion; stir until blended.

4 Into egg mixture, stir carrot and potato mixture and pepper. Preheat browning dish according to manufacturer's instructions. Add butter or margarine; stir to coat dish.

5 Drop mounds of carrot and potato mixture on to browning dish; flatten slightly. Cook on High for 2½ (2:30) minutes, until set, turning pancakes over halfway through cooking. (If necessary, cook in batches, reheating browning dish between batches.)

6 To serve: arrange hot pancakes on warmed serving platter. Garnish with dill sprigs. If you like, serve pancakes with apple sauce and soured cream.

<table>
<tr><td colspan="2">

Blanching Vegetables

</td></tr>
</table>

Blanching vegetables for the freezer helps preserve their flavours. Prepare according to the charts on pages 237–251, then blanch in the microwave for the minimum time below: the vegetable should be bright in colour and evenly heated through. Chill in iced water for as long as blanching time. Drain, pat dry and freeze.

Method	High (100% power)

ASPARAGUS (PIECES)
Amount to buy: 15–16 spears (about 450 g)
Blanching quantity: about 450 g

Blanch, covered, in 2 litre casserole with 4 tablespoons water, stirring once.	2½ (2:30)–3½ (3:30) minutes

BEANS, GREEN (WHOLE)
Amount to buy: 450 g
Blanching quantity: about 225 g

Blanch, covered, in 1.5 litre casserole with 120 ml water, stirring halfway through cooking.	2½ (2:30)–3½ (3:30) minutes

BROCCOLI (SPEARS) AND CAULIFLOWER (FLORETS)
Broccoli – Amount to buy: 700 g
   Blanching quantity: about 225 g
Cauliflower: 450 g
   Blanching quantity: 300 g

Blanch, covered, in 2 litre casserole with 4 tablespoons water, rearranging halfway through cooking	Broccoli: 4–6 minutes Cauliflower: 4–5 minutes

CARROTS (SLICES)
Amount to buy: 450 g
Blanching quantity: about 225 g

Blanch, covered, in 1.5 litre casserole with 4 tablespoons water, stirring halfway through cooking.	4½ (4:30)–5½ (5:30) minutes

PEAS (SHELLED)
Amount to buy: 1 kg
Blanching quantity: about 225 g

Blanch, covered, in 1 litre casserole with 4 tablespoons water, stirring halfway through cooking.	3–4½ (4:30) minutes

Cauliflower

CAULIFLOWER WITH LEMON AND DILL SAUCE

Colour Index page 72. 8 servings. 89 cals per serving. Good source of vitamin C, fibre. Begin 25 minutes ahead.

1 large cauliflower (about 1.4 kg)	2 tablespoons lemon juice
60 ml water	1 tablespoon chopped fresh dill
45 g butter or margarine	
1 garlic clove, crushed	Salt and pepper to taste
1 tablespoon plain flour	Lemon slices and dill
175 ml half cream	sprigs to garnish

1. Keeping cauliflower whole, remove large leaves and cut out core. In 3 litre microwave-safe casserole, place cauliflower cored side up; add water. Cook, covered, on High (100% power) for 9–10 minutes, until cauliflower is tender-crisp, rotating casserole once. Allow to stand, covered, on heatproof surface while preparing sauce.
2. In 1 litre microwave-safe measuring jug, place butter or margarine and garlic. Heat, covered with kitchen paper, on High for 45 seconds–1 minute, until butter or margarine is melted. Stir in flour until blended. Cook on High for 1 minute, stirring once. Into flour mixture, gradually stir cream. Cook on High for 2–3 minutes, until sauce thickens slightly, stirring twice. Into sauce, stir lemon juice, dill and salt and pepper.
3. Drain cauliflower; place on warmed serving platter. Spoon sauce over; garnish.

CAULIFLOWER WITH MINTY HOT SPINACH SAUCE

Colour Index page 72. 6 servings. 42 cals per serving. Low in cholesterol, fat. Good source of vitamin A, vitamin C, calcium, iron, fibre. Begin 25 minutes ahead.

275 g frozen spinach, defrosted	1 medium cauliflower, trimmed, rinsed and cut into florets
4 tablespoons fresh mint leaves	60 ml water
½ teaspoon crushed red pepper flakes	120 ml plain yogurt
1 garlic clove	Salt to taste

1. Squeeze and drain spinach. In food processor with knife blade attached or in blender, process spinach, mint leaves, red pepper flakes and garlic in batches until smooth.
2. In 2 litre microwave-safe casserole, place cauliflower and water. Cook, covered, on High (100% power) for 5 minutes, stirring once. Drain.
3. To cauliflower, add spinach mixture; stir well to combine. Cook, covered, on High for 5–7 minutes, until cauliflower is tender, stirring occasionally during cooking.
4. Into vegetable mixture, stir yogurt and salt. Serve hot or cover and refrigerate to serve chilled later.

Celeriac and Chicory

CELERIAC PURÉE

Colour Index page 75. 6 servings. 142 cals per serving. Good source of fibre.
Begin 35 minutes ahead.

450 g celeriac, peeled and diced	45 g butter or margarine
225 g red potatoes, peeled and diced	60 ml double or whipping cream
250 ml Vegetable Stock (page 125) or water	Salt and pepper to taste

1. In 2 litre microwave-safe casserole, place celeriac and potatoes; add stock or water. Cook, covered, on High (100% power) for 10–15 minutes, until tender, stirring twice.
2. In food processor with knife blade attached or in blender, process celeriac and potatoes. Add butter or margarine, cream and salt and pepper; process until smooth.
3. Return purée to casserole. Cook on High for 3–4 minutes, until hot, stirring twice.

CHICORY WITH CHEESE SAUCE

Colour Index page 74. 4 servings. 215 cals per serving. Good source of calcium.
Begin 45 minutes ahead.

4 heads chicory	2 tablespoons plain flour
120 ml Vegetable Stock (page 125) or water	175 ml half cream
1 tablespoon lemon juice	115 g Gruyère or Cheddar cheese, grated
1/2 teaspoon sugar	1 egg yolk
30 g butter or margarine	Salt and pepper to taste

1. Trim root ends from chicory. Cut each head in half lengthways. In 32.5 × 22.5 cm microwave-safe baking dish, arrange chicory, cut side down, with stalk ends towards edges. Add stock or water, lemon juice and sugar. Cook, covered, on High (100% power) for 7–10 minutes, until chicory is tender-crisp, rearranging chicory and rotating dish once. Drain liquid from dish and reserve. Turn chicory cut side up; cover and set aside.
2. In large microwave-safe bowl, place butter or margarine. Heat, covered with kitchen paper, on High for 45 seconds, or until melted. Stir in flour until smooth. Cook on High for 1 minute, stirring once. Gradually stir in cream and reserved cooking liquid. Cook on High for 3–4 minutes, until sauce thickens, stirring twice. Add cheese; stir until melted.
3. In mixing bowl, lightly beat egg yolk; stir in 4 tablespoons cheese sauce, taking care that yolk does not curdle. Slowly pour egg mixture back into remaining sauce, beating rapidly to prevent lumping. Season.
4. Over chicory, pour sauce. Cook on Medium (50% power) for 3–5 minutes, until hot.

Chicory is normally used as a salad vegetable, but it is equally delicious braised. Remember to arrange the heads with the delicate, leafy tips pointing towards the centre of the dish and the denser stalk ends towards the edges; this ensures even cooking.

BRAISED CHICORY

Colour Index page 74. 78 cals per serving.
Begin 35 minutes ahead.

Ingredients	For 4	For 2	For 1
Chicory	4 heads	2 heads	1 head
Vegetable Stock (page 125)	250 ml	120 ml	60 ml
Spring onions, sliced	2 onions	1 onion	1/2 onion
Dried thyme	1/2 teaspoon	1/4 teaspoon	to taste
Dried basil	1/2 teaspoon	1/4 teaspoon	to taste
Butter or margarine	30 g	15 g	1 1/2 teaspoons
Caster sugar	1 teaspoon	1/2 teaspoon	1/4 teaspoon
Lemon juice	1 teaspoon	1/2 teaspoon	1/4 teaspoon
Salt and pepper	to taste	to taste	to taste
Microwave cookware	32.5 × 22.5 cm baking dish	20 cm square baking dish	20 cm square baking dish
Time on High (100% power) Chicory Stock mixture	12–15 minutes 5 minutes	8–10 minutes 3–3 1/2 (3:30) minutes	4–6 minutes 1 1/2 (1:30)–2 minutes

1 Trim root ends from heads of chicory; cut each chicory in half lengthways. In baking dish (see Chart), arrange chicory, cut side down, with stalk ends towards edges and leafy tips towards centre.

2 Over chicory, pour stock; add spring onions, thyme and basil. Cook, covered, on High for time in Chart, or until chicory is tender, rearranging chicory and rotating dish halfway through cooking.

3 With fish slice, remove chicory to warmed serving platter, arranging cut side up. Cover and keep warm.

4 To same baking dish, add butter or margarine, sugar, lemon juice, salt and pepper.

5 Cook mixture on High for time in Chart, or until bubbling, stirring once.

6 To serve: spoon hot cooking liquid over chicory. Serve immediately.

Courgettes

Courgettes of any size make ideal containers for savoury vegetable stuffings. If you have extra large courgettes, they can be served as a main course dish; with nutty brown rice and a crisp side salad, they make a well-balanced and filling vegetarian meal. The Stuffed Courgettes (below) are delicious as an accompaniment to lamb or fish; they are also very good served cold as a first course. To save time, they can be prepared ahead up to the end of step 4, then cooked at the last minute.

STUFFED COURGETTES

Colour Index page 77. 87 cals per serving. Low in cholesterol, sodium. Begin 35 minutes ahead.

Ingredients for 2 servings		Microwave cookware
2 medium courgettes, cut in half	2 tablespoons dried breadcrumbs	30 × 20 cm baking dish
1½ teaspoons olive or vegetable oil	1 tablespoon grated Parmesan cheese	
½ red pepper, diced	Salt to taste	
½ tomato, diced	Lemon Twists (page 132) and basil leaves to garnish	
1 small garlic clove, crushed		
Pinch dried thyme		

1 With teaspoon, scoop out flesh from each courgette half, leaving 5 mm thick shell. Reserve courgette flesh.

2 In baking dish, arrange courgette shells, cut side down. Cook, covered, on High (100% power), for 2–3 minutes, until tender but not soft. With fish slice, transfer shells to platter. Set aside.

3 Dice reserved courgette flesh. In same baking dish, place diced courgette, olive or vegetable oil, diced red pepper, diced tomato, garlic and thyme; stir well. Cook on High for 2–3 minutes, until tender, stirring halfway through cooking.

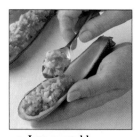

4 Into vegetable mixture, stir breadcrumbs and Parmesan. Season with salt. With spoon, mound an equal amount of vegetable mixture in each courgette shell.

5 In cleaned baking dish, arrange stuffed courgettes with stalk ends towards edges. Cook on High for 2–3 minutes, until hot. On heatproof surface, stand, loosely covered, for 2 minutes.

6 Arrange stuffed courgettes on warmed serving platter. Garnish with Lemon Twists and basil leaves and serve.

COURGETTE LINGUINE WITH SUN-DRIED TOMATOES AND PINE NUTS

Colour Index page 77. 4 servings. 195 cals per serving. Low in cholesterol. Good source of iron. Begin 35 minutes ahead.

4 medium courgettes
2 tablespoons olive or vegetable oil
1 garlic clove, crushed
25 g pine nuts
45 g sun-dried tomatoes in oil, drained and chopped

2 teaspoons chopped fresh basil or 1 teaspoon dried
Salt and pepper to taste
Basil leaves to garnish

1. With sharp knife, top and tail courgettes. Cut each courgette lengthways into 6 slices. Cut each courgette slice lengthways into 5 mm wide strips. Set strips aside.

2. In 32.5 × 22.5 cm microwave-safe baking dish, place olive or vegetable oil, crushed garlic and pine nuts. Cook on High (100% power) for 2–3 minutes, until pine nuts are lightly toasted, stirring twice.

3. Into garlic and pine nut mixture, stir courgette strips, sun-dried tomatoes and chopped fresh or dried basil. Cook, covered, on High for 5–7 minutes, until courgette strips are tender-crisp, stirring halfway through cooking. Add salt and pepper to taste.

4. Transfer courgette strips to warmed serving platter. Garnish with basil leaves and serve immediately while piping hot.

Making the Courgette Linguine

With sharp knife, cut each courgette lengthways into 6 slices. Cut each slice lengthways again into 5 mm wide strips. When cooked, courgette strips will resemble linguine (very thin pasta), hence the name of the recipe.

A NO-MESS TRICK FOR STEAMING VEGETABLES: To ensure even cooking, use vegetables of similar size or density (such as broccoli and cauliflower florets) or cut vegetables into pieces of uniform size (such as sticks of carrot and courgette). Lightly moisten 1 sheet kitchen paper; place vegetables on top. Bring all corners of paper to centre and twist to close. Place on oven floor. Cook 225 g vegetables on High (100% power) for 4–5 minutes, until tender-crisp.

VEGETABLE PRESENTATION

Simply cooked vegetables make an elegant presentation for a special occasion.

Matchstick Carrots and Parsnips: cooked matchstick-thin strips of carrot and parsnip in a lattice pattern accentuate the colour and pattern of a pretty plate.

Asparagus Parcels: asparagus spears tied with a strip of cooked leek echo the shape of a long plate. Lemon Twists (page 132) give the finishing touch.

Spinach Filled Tomatoes: hollowed-out tomatoes filled with Creamed Spinach (page 271) look stunning nestled in a fluted-edged white plate.

New Potatoes in Radicchio Cups: crisp leaves of colourful radicchio make an ideal shell for small new potatoes garnished with a sprig of fresh dill.

LEEKS WITH HAM IN CHEESE SAUCE

Colour Index page 75. 367 cals per serving. Good source of calcium, iron, fibre. Begin 50 minutes ahead.

Ingredients	For 4	For 2	For 1
Large leeks (225 g each)	*4 leeks*	*2 leeks*	*1 leek*
Chicken Stock (page 125) or stock from a cube	*120 ml*	*60 ml*	*3 tablespoons*
Butter or margarine	*30 g*	*15 g*	*2 teaspoons*
Plain flour	*2 tablespoons*	*1 tablespoon*	*2 teaspoons*
Half cream	*250 ml*	*120 ml*	*60 ml*
Gruyère or Cheddar cheese, grated	*115 g*	*50 g*	*25 g*
Salt and pepper	*to taste*	*to taste*	*to taste*
Cooked ham slices (about 15 g each)	*8 slices*	*4 slices*	*2 slices*
Parsley	*garnish*	*garnish*	*garnish*
Microwave cookware	30 × 20 cm baking dish	20 cm square baking dish	20 cm square baking dish
Time on High (100% power)			
Leeks	5–7 minutes	3–4 minutes	2–2½ (2:30) minutes
Sauce	3–3½ (3:30) minutes	2–2½ (2:30) minutes	1–1½ (1:30) minutes
Leeks with sauce	5–6 minutes	3–3½ (3:30) minutes	1½ (1:30)–2 minutes

1 Cut roots from leeks; trim leek tops. Cut leeks in half lengthways. Carefully rinse leeks under cold running water to remove any sand.

2 In baking dish (see Chart), arrange leek halves, cut side down, in single layer.

3 Over leeks, pour stock; add butter or margarine. Cook, covered, on High for time in Chart, until tender, rearranging once. Remove leeks; stir flour into cooking liquid.

4 To flour mixture, gradually add cream. Cook on High for time in Chart, until sauce thickens, stirring twice. Add cheese; stir until melted. Season.

5 Wrap each leek half in 1 slice of ham. Place wrapped leeks in cheese sauce. Cook, covered, on High for time in Chart, or until leeks are hot and sauce is bubbling.

6 *To serve:* sprinkle leeks with chopped parsley; transfer to warmed dinner plates. Spoon sauce over leeks and serve immediately.

Meal in Minutes *for 4 people*

Middle Eastern-style Family Supper

Fresh Tomato Soup, page 127, chilled
Aubergines with Tabbouleh Stuffing, page 253
Hot pitta bread
Tossed green salad
Goat cheese with dried fruit and nuts

PREPARATION TIMETABLE

Early in day	*Prepare Fresh Tomato Soup; cover and refrigerate. Prepare salad ingredients; store in polythene bags in refrigerator. Prepare salad dressing of your choice and refrigerate.*
1 hour ahead	*Cook Aubergines with Tabbouleh Stuffing; cover and set aside. Arrange an assortment of cheese, dried fruit and nuts on serving plate; cover and set aside.*
Just before serving	*Ladle soup into individual bowls and garnish. Reheat stuffed aubergines on High (100% power) until hot; garnish. Under preheated grill, lightly toast pitta breads; arrange on warmed platter. Place salad ingredients in bowl and toss with dressing.*

MUSHROOMS À LA GRECQUE

Colour Index page 72. 6 servings. 199 cals per serving. Low in cholesterol, sodium. Begin 25 minutes ahead.

120 ml olive or vegetable oil	*120 ml dry white wine*
120 ml Vegetable Stock (page 125) or stock from a cube	*60 ml tarragon vinegar or white wine vinegar*
3 garlic cloves, thinly sliced	*2 bay leaves*
2 small onions, cut into 5 mm wedges	*1 teaspoon dried thyme*
2 small tomatoes, cut into chunks	*12 black peppercorns*
	12 whole coriander seeds (optional)
	450 g button mushrooms, trimmed

1. In 2 litre microwave-safe casserole place all ingredients except mushrooms. Cook on High (100% power) for 5–7 minutes, until bubbling, stirring halfway through cooking.
2. Into tomato mixture, stir mushrooms. Cook, covered, on High for 10 minutes, or until tender, stirring occasionally. Discard bay leaves.
3. Serve hot or cover and refrigerate to serve chilled later.

ORIENTAL MUSHROOMS

Colour Index page 75. 4 main course servings. 123 cals per serving. Low in cholesterol. Good source of thiamine, iron. Begin 45 minutes ahead.

1 small boneless pork chop (about 115 g)	*1 teaspoon rice wine or cider vinegar*
1 teaspoon cornflour	*2 garlic cloves, crushed*
120 ml Vegetable Stock (page 125) or stock from a cube	*225 g mushrooms, sliced*
	115 g mange-touts, cut in half
2 teaspoons finely chopped peeled root ginger or 1 teaspoon ground ginger	*1 small tomato, cut into matchstick-thin strips*
1 tablespoon soy sauce	

1. Thinly slice pork. Cut slices into slivers. In small bowl, combine cornflour, stock, ginger, soy sauce, vinegar and garlic. Add pork; stir to coat. Cover and marinate for 10 minutes.
2. Preheat browning dish according to manufacturer's instructions. With slotted spoon, arrange pork in single layer on browning dish; reserve marinade. Cook on High (100% power) for 3–4 minutes, until pork is cooked, stirring halfway through cooking. Remove pork to warmed serving platter; cover and keep warm.
3. Reheat browning dish. On dish, place mushrooms. Cook on High for 3–4 minutes, until softened, stirring halfway through cooking.
4. To mushrooms, add mange-touts, tomato, reserved marinade and cooked pork. Cook on High for 3–4 minutes, until sauce bubbles and thickens, stirring twice. Arrange on warmed serving platter with pork. Serve immediately.

Okra

OKRA, HAM AND TOMATOES

Colour Index page 72. 4 main course servings. 63 cals per serving. Low in cholesterol. Good source of vitamin C, fibre. Begin 25 minutes ahead.

1 onion, diced	*¼ teaspoon Tabasco*
45 g cooked ham, diced	*sauce*
1 × 400 g can chopped	*1 tablespoon lemon juice*
tomatoes	*Hot Cooked Rice (page*
275 g okra	*293, optional)*

1. In 32.5 × 22.5 cm microwave-safe baking dish, combine diced onion and ham. Cook on High (100% power) for 3 minutes, or until onion softens, stirring mixture halfway through cooking.
2. Into ham mixture, stir tomatoes, okra and Tabasco sauce. Cook on High for 6–9 minutes, until okra is hot and tomatoes are bubbling, stirring twice.
3. Into vegetable and ham mixture, stir lemon juice until evenly blended. If you like, serve with Hot Cooked Rice.

MARINATED OKRA

Colour Index page 77. 4 servings. 145 cals per serving. Low in cholesterol, sodium. Begin 1 day ahead.

120 ml olive or vegetable	*275 g okra*
oil	*Parsley to garnish*
80 ml tarragon vinegar	
or white wine vinegar	
½ teaspoon dry mustard	
½ teaspoon sugar	
½ teaspoon dried thyme	
¼ teaspoon dried hot	
red pepper flakes	

1. In 1.5 litre microwave-safe casserole, combine oil, vinegar, mustard, sugar, thyme and red pepper flakes. Cook on High (100% power) for 3 minutes, or until flavours blend, stirring halfway through cooking.
2. To oil and vinegar mixture, add okra; stir to coat. Cook on High for 3–5 minutes, until okra is hot, stirring twice.
3. Cover casserole and refrigerate for 4 hours or overnight, stirring occasionally.
4. *To serve:* drain marinade from okra. Arrange okra on serving platter and garnish with parsley. Serve chilled.

Barbecuing Vegetables

Use the microwave to precook vegetables for the barbecue and cut down barbecuing time. Your vegetables will have that delicious outdoor flavour, yet stay tender-crisp without charring. Cook vegetables in 4 tablespoons water, covered, on High (100% power) for time in Chart, or until almost tender; drain. Skewer and cook on barbecue over high heat, brushing with oil and turning until browned.

Vegetable	Amount	In Microwave	On Barbecue
Asparagus	*450 g*	4–6 minutes	2 minutes
Aubergine	*1 medium, about 375 g, cut into 8 wedges*	4–6 minutes	3–5 minutes
Carrots	*450 g*	6–8 minutes	5 minutes
Cauliflower	*1 head, about 575 g*	6–8 minutes	5 minutes
Chicory	*4 heads, about 115 g each*	4–5 minutes	2 minutes
Courgettes	*2 medium, cut in half lengthways*	3–5 minutes	5 minutes
Fennel	*2 bulbs, about 450 g each, cut in half lengthways*	9–11 minutes	5 minutes
Leeks	*4 medium, cut in half lengthways*	4–5 minutes	5 minutes
Mushrooms	*450 g medium-size*	4–6 minutes	5 minutes
Onions	*2 large, cut into 4 cm thick chunks*	6–8 minutes	5 minutes
Peppers	*4 medium, stalks and seeds removed*	8–10 minutes	5 minutes

When preparing vegetables for kebabs, prevent the outsides of onion, courgette and red pepper chunks from charring on the barbecue by precooking them in the microwave. Place vegetables in baking dish with 4 tablespoons water. Cook, covered, on High (100% power) for 3–4 minutes, until tender-crisp, stirring twice.

Preparing the Vegetables for Kebabs

In microwave-safe baking dish, place chunks of onion, courgette and red pepper. Add 4 tablespoons water. Cook, covered, on High (100% power) for 3–4 minutes, until tender-crisp, stirring twice; drain.

When vegetables are cool enough to handle, thread them carefully on to kebab skewers. Finish cooking on grid of barbecue, brushing lightly with oil and turning frequently until evenly browned.

Onions

STUFFED ONIONS

Colour Index page 75. 113 cals per serving. Good source of fibre. Begin 45 minutes ahead.

Ingredients	For 4	For 2	For 1
Large onions	4 onions	2 onions	1 onion
Vegetable Stock (page 125) or stock from a cube	120 ml	60 ml	3 tablespoons
Butter or margarine	30 g	15 g	1½ teaspoons
Celery sticks	1 stick	½ stick	¼ stick
Small red or yellow pepper	1 pepper	½ pepper	¼ pepper
Dried mixed herbs	1 teaspoon	½ teaspoon	¼ teaspoon
Fresh wholemeal breadcrumbs	60 g	30 g	15 g
Microwave cookware	2 litre soufflé dish	1 litre soufflé dish	Small bowl
Time on High (100% power)			
Hollowed-out onions	5–7 minutes	4–6 minutes	2½ (2:30)–3 minutes
Butter or margarine	45 seconds	30–45 seconds	30 seconds
Vegetable mixture	3–5 minutes	2–3 minutes	1½ (1:30)–2 minutes
Stuffed onions	4–6 minutes	2–3 minutes	1½ (1:30)–2 minutes
Standing time	5 minutes	3 minutes	2 minutes

1 Cut small slice from base of each onion so they stand upright. Hollow out centres, leaving 2 cm thick shells. Reserve centres. In dish or bowl (see Chart), place onions.

2 Over onions, pour stock. Cook, covered, on High for time in Chart, rotating dish once. Remove onions. To stock, add butter or margarine. Cook on High for time in Chart.

3 Finely chop red pepper, celery and reserved onion centres. Add to stock with mixed herbs. Cook on High for time in Chart.

6 Place onions in same dish or bowl. Cook on High for time in Chart, until hot, rotating dish or bowl halfway through cooking. Allow to stand, loosely covered, on heatproof surface, for time in Chart.

4 Add breadcrumbs to stuffing; mix well.

5 Fill hollowed-out onions with equal amounts of stuffing.

CREAMED ONIONS

Colour Index page 72. 8 servings. 82 cals per serving. Low in cholesterol, sodium. Begin 25 minutes ahead.

30 g butter or margarine
1 small onion, finely chopped
2 tablespoons plain flour
350 ml milk
¼ teaspoon salt
¼ teaspoon pepper
Grated nutmeg to taste
450 g frozen baby onions, thawed
Paprika (optional)

1. In 1 litre microwave-safe measuring jug, place butter or margarine. Heat, covered with kitchen paper, on High (100% power) for 45 seconds, or until melted.
2. To melted butter or margarine, add chopped onion. Cook on High for 2–3 minutes, until onion softens, stirring once. Stir in flour until blended. Cook on High for 1 minute, stirring once.
3. Into onion mixture, gradually stir milk. Cook on High for 3–4 minutes, until sauce thickens and is smooth, stirring twice. Season with salt, pepper and nutmeg.
4. In 21.5 cm round microwave-safe baking dish, combine baby onions and onion sauce. Cook on High for 3–5 minutes, until sauce bubbles, stirring halfway through cooking. Just before serving, if you like, sprinkle with paprika.

SWEET AND SOUR ONIONS

Colour Index page 75. 8 servings. 69 cals per serving. Begin 40 minutes ahead.

450 g onions, sliced
3 tablespoons butter or margarine
1 tablespoon sugar
120 ml Beef Stock (page 125) or stock from a cube
4 tablespoons red wine
1 tablespoon red wine vinegar
Salt and pepper to taste

1. In 21.5 cm microwave-safe shallow pie dish, combine onions, butter or margarine, sugar, stock and wine. Cook, covered, on High (100% power) for 5 minutes, stirring halfway through cooking.
2. Uncover; stir. Cook on High for 15–20 minutes longer, until onions brown and cooking liquid evaporates, stirring occasionally.
3. Into onions, stir red wine vinegar. Cook on High for 5 minutes, or until vinegar evaporates, stirring halfway through cooking.
4. Season with salt and pepper. Transfer to warmed serving dish. Serve hot.

Peas

PETITS POIS À LA FRANÇAISE

Colour Index page 70. 6 servings. 161 cals per serving. Good source of thiamine, iron, fibre. Begin 20 minutes ahead.

1 small head Cos or other crisp lettuce	*450 g frozen peas, defrosted*
6 rashers rindless streaky bacon, diced	*Pepper to taste chopped parsley*
1 onion, chopped	

1. On cutting board, cut lettuce in half lengthways. With cut side down, slice lettuce crossways into 1 cm shreds; set aside.
2. In 3 litre microwave-safe casserole or 30 × 20 cm baking dish, place diced bacon. Cook on High (100% power) for 3–4 minutes, until browned, stirring halfway through cooking. Add onion; stir to mix with bacon. Cook on High for 2 minutes, or until onion is softened, stirring halfway through cooking.
3. To onion and bacon, add peas. Cook for 2 minutes, or until peas are hot; stir in shredded lettuce. Cook, covered, on High for 3–4 minutes, until lettuce is wilted, stirring twice. Add pepper and stir in parsley. Serve immediately.

PEAS WITH BACON AND ONIONS

Colour Index page 72. 4 servings. 105 cals per serving. Good source of fibre. Begin 15 minutes ahead.

2 rashers rindless streaky bacon, diced	*225 g frozen baby onions, defrosted*
275 g frozen peas, defrosted	*Salt and pepper to taste*

1. In 21.5 cm microwave-safe shallow pie dish, place bacon. Cook, covered with kitchen paper, on High (100% power) for 2–3 minutes, until bacon is browned, stirring occasionally. With slotted spoon, remove bacon to kitchen paper to drain. Discard all but 1 tablespoon bacon fat.
2. Into bacon fat, stir peas and onions. Cook, covered, on High for 3–5 minutes, until peas and onions are hot, stirring halfway through cooking.
3. *To serve:* season pea and onion mixture with salt and pepper. Spoon mixture into warmed serving dish; sprinkle with reserved bacon.

LEMON PEAS

Colour Index page 73. 81 cals per serving. Good source of fibre. Begin 15 minutes ahead.

Ingredients	For 4	For 2	For 1
Butter or margarine	1 tablespoon	1½ teaspoons	¾ teaspoon
Frozen peas, defrosted	275 g	150 g	75 g
Finely grated lemon zest	2 teaspoons	1 teaspoon	½ teaspoon
Water	1 tablespoon	2 teaspoons	1 teaspoon
Salt	¼ teaspoon	to taste	to taste
Pepper	to taste	to taste	to taste
Lemon slices and fresh mint sprigs	garnish	garnish	garnish
Microwave cookware	2 litre casserole	1 litre casserole	500 ml measuring jug
Time on High (100% power) Butter or margarine	30–45 seconds	30 seconds	15–30 seconds
Peas	4–5 minutes	2–3 minutes	1½ (1:30)– 2½ (2:30) minutes

1 In casserole or measuring jug (see Chart), place butter or margarine. Heat, covered with kitchen paper, on High for time in Chart, until melted.

2 Into melted butter or margarine, stir peas, grated lemon zest, water, salt and pepper. Cook peas, covered, on High for time in Chart, or until tender, stirring occasionally.

3 *To serve:* transfer peas to warmed serving dish; garnish with lemon slices and fresh mint sprigs. Serve immediately.

MANGE-TOUTS AND SUGAR SNAP PEAS

Both these edible pea pods are delicious cooked in the microwave. Mange-touts, also known as snow peas, have thin, delicate skins and contain peas that are not fully formed. Sugar snap peas, a newer variety, are shorter and rounder than mange-touts and have thicker pods containing fully formed peas. Both can be eaten raw or cooked as a vegetable using any recipe for peas. Check page 245 for preparation tips and cooking times. Both are quick-cooking, although sugar snap peas require slightly longer than mange-touts.

Potatoes

NEW POTATOES WITH BUTTER AND CHIVES

Colour Index page 73. 215 cals per serving. Good source of vitamin C, fibre.
Begin 25 minutes ahead.

Ingredients	For 4	For 2	For 1
New potatoes, unpeeled and well scrubbed	700 g	350 g	150 g
Butter or margarine	45 g	25 g	2 teaspoons
Chopped fresh chives	4 tablespoons (15 g)	2 tablespoons	1 tablespoon
Salt and pepper	to taste	to taste	to taste
Microwave cookware	30 × 20 cm baking dish	20 cm square baking dish	20 cm square baking dish
Time on High (100% power)	8–10 minutes	5–7 minutes	3–4 minutes

1 With canelle knife (page 320) or vegetable peeler, remove strip of peel from centre of each potato; discard.

2 In baking dish (see Chart), place potatoes and butter or margarine. Cook, covered, on High for time in Chart, or until tender, stirring halfway through cooking.

3 Into potatoes, stir chopped chives. Season with salt and pepper. Serve immediately, spooning chive butter over potatoes.

QUICK POTATO SNACKS
Use your microwave to cook quick and easy after-school snacks. Children will love these tasty treats and they can be ready in next to no time.

Cheesy Potato Slices: in 32.5 × 22.5 cm baking dish, arrange *12 unpeeled potato slices, each 5 cm in diameter and 5 mm thick.* Sprinkle lightly with *dried oregano.* Cook, covered, on High (100% power) for 3½ (3:30)–4 minutes. Top each slice with about *2 teaspoons grated Cheddar cheese.* Cook on High for 30 seconds, or just until cheese melts.
2 servings. 153 cals per serving.

Pizza Potatoes: wash *1 medium baking potato (about 175 g)* under cold running water; do not peel. With fork, pierce potato in several places. On oven floor, place kitchen paper; place potato on top. Cook on High (100% power) for 5 minutes, or until potato feels soft when pierced with tip of sharp knife. Cut potato in half lengthways. Place halves on paper plate. Top each half with *1 tablespoon tomato ketchup, 1 tablespoon grated mozzarella cheese* and *2 slices pepperoni sausage.* Cook on High for 1–1½ (1:30) minutes, until cheese melts. 2 servings. 235 cals per serving.

POTATOES AU GRATIN

Colour Index page 75. 235 cals per serving. Good source of vitamin C, iron, fibre.
Begin 35 minutes ahead.

One of the best ways to cook potatoes is in the microwave, since this retains their full flavour, texture and nutritional value. When microwaving potatoes, cut slices the same thickness to ensure even cooking.

Ingredients for 8 servings		Microwave cookware
60 g butter or margarine	¼ teaspoon pepper	25 cm round baking dish
1 small onion, finely chopped	¼ teaspoon paprika	
25 g dried breadcrumbs	1.4 kg potatoes, peeled or unpeeled	
¼ teaspoon salt	60 ml water	
	50 g Fontina or Cheddar cheese, grated	

1 In baking dish, place butter or margarine and onion. Cook, covered, on High (100% power) for 2–3 minutes, stirring once.

2 In mixing bowl, combine breadcrumbs, salt, pepper, paprika and onion. Cut potatoes into 3 mm thick slices.

3 In dish used for onion, arrange potatoes. Add water. Cook, covered, on High for 13–15 minutes, until tender, rotating once.

4 Drain off water from potatoes, pressing with fish slice.

Over potatoes, sprinkle cheese, then onion and breadcrumb mixture. Cook on High for 1½ (1:30) minutes, or until cheese melts.

MASHED POTATOES

Colour Index page 73. 4 servings. 233 cals per serving. Good source of vitamin C, fibre. Begin 25 minutes ahead.

700 g potatoes, peeled and diced	¼ teaspoon pepper
250 ml water	60–120 ml half cream
60 g butter or margarine	Chopped chives to garnish
¼ teaspoon salt	Almost Instant Gravy (below, optional)

1. In 2 litre microwave-safe glass bowl, place potatoes and water. Cook, covered, on High (100% power) for 10–15 minutes, until potatoes are very tender, stirring occasionally. Drain.
2. To potatoes, add butter or margarine, salt and pepper. With mixer at low speed, beat until ingredients are combined and potato mixture is fluffy. To potato mixture, gradually add cream, beating until smooth. Cook, covered, on High for 3–5 minutes, until hot, stirring halfway through cooking.
3. Transfer to serving dish; garnish. If you like, serve Almost Instant Gravy separately.

ALMOST INSTANT GRAVY: in 1 litre microwave-safe measuring jug, place **1 tablespoon butter or margarine, or chicken or meat dripping.** Heat, covered with kitchen paper, on High (100% power) for 30–45 seconds, until melted and hot. Add **1 tablespoon plain flour**; stir until smooth. Gradually blend in **250 ml Chicken or Beef Stock (page 125) or stock from a cube.** Cook on High for 3–5 minutes, until gravy boils and thickens, stirring twice. Season with **salt and pepper to taste.** If you like, add ¼ **teaspoon gravy browning** for colour. Makes 250 ml. 11 cals per tablespoon.

HOME STYLE POTATOES WITH BACON AND ONIONS

Colour Index page 73. 4 servings. 188 cals per serving. Good source of vitamin C, fibre. Begin 25 minutes ahead.

3 rashers rindless streaky bacon, diced	700 g potatoes, peeled and diced
1 large onion, sliced	Salt and pepper to taste

1. In 30 × 20 cm microwave-safe baking dish, place bacon. Cook, covered with kitchen paper, on High (100% power) for 3–4 minutes, until bacon is browned, stirring halfway through cooking. With slotted spoon, transfer bacon to kitchen paper to drain. Discard all but 2 tablespoons bacon fat.
2. Into bacon fat, stir onion and potatoes. Cook on High for 12–15 minutes, until potatoes are tender, stirring occasionally. Stir in reserved bacon and season before serving.

STUFFED POTATOES ORIENTALE

Colour Index page 75. 453 cals per serving. Good source of niacin, vitamin C, iron. Begin 45 minutes ahead.

Ingredients	For 4	For 2	For 1
Baking potatoes (about 225 g each), well scrubbed	4 potatoes	2 potatoes	1 potato
Chicken breasts, skinned, boned and cut into 5 mm thick strips	450 g	225 g	115 g
Vegetable oil	1 tablespoon	1½ teaspoons	¾ teaspoon
Cornflour	2 teaspoons	1 teaspoon	½ teaspoon
Garlic clove, finely chopped	1 clove	½ clove	¼ clove
Ground ginger	½ teaspoon	¼ teaspoon	to taste
Frozen mixed vegetables for stir-frying	275 g	150 g	75 g
Soy sauce	2 tablespoons	1 tablespoon	to taste
Chinese sweet chilli sauce	to taste	to taste	to taste
Salt and pepper	to taste	to taste	to taste
Butter or margarine	60 g	30 g	15 g
Microwave cookware	1 litre baking dish	1 litre baking dish	Shallow 21.5 cm pie dish
Time on High (100% power)			
Potatoes	14–16 minutes	7–8 minutes	4–6 minutes
Chicken	4–5 minutes	2–3 minutes	1–2 minutes
With vegetables	4–6 minutes	2–4 minutes	1–2 minutes

1 Pierce potatoes several times. Place on kitchen paper on oven floor (in circle if cooking 4). Cook on High for time in Chart, turning over once.

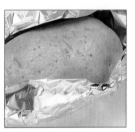

2 Wrap each potato in foil; set aside while preparing filling.

3 In baking dish or pie dish (see Chart), combine chicken, oil, cornflour, garlic and ground ginger.

4 Cook chicken mixture, covered, on High for time in Chart, or until chicken is no longer pink, stirring halfway through cooking.

5 Into chicken mixture, stir frozen vegetables, soy sauce and chilli sauce. Season.

6 Cook on High for time in Chart, or until vegetables are tender, stirring once. Stir until sauce is smooth. Remove potatoes from foil. Cut lengthways slit on top of each potato. Place equal amount of butter or margarine in each slit. With fork, fluff potatoes, then top each with chicken and vegetable mixture. Place on warmed serving platter and serve immediately.

Potatoes

Potatoes can be baked in the microwave in a matter of minutes – see the chart on page 248 for exact cooking instructions and timings. Sweet potatoes make an appetising change from plain baked potatoes and Twice-Baked Sweet Potatoes (below) are especially delicious.

TWICE-BAKED SWEET POTATOES

Colour Index page 77. 147 cals per serving. Good source of vitamin A, fibre. Begin 40 minutes ahead.

Ingredients	For 4	For 2	For 1
Yellow- or orange-fleshed sweet potatoes, well scrubbed	2 large	1 large	1 small
Plain low-fat yogurt	60 ml	2 tablespoons to taste	1 tablespoon to taste
Mild chilli powder	1/4 teaspoon		
Butter or margarine	30 g	15 g	1 1/2 teaspoons
Salt	to taste	to taste	to taste
Microwave cookware	Baking tray Dinner plate	Baking tray Dinner plate	Baking tray Dinner plate
Time on High (100% power) Sweet potatoes With stuffing	8–10 minutes 4–5 minutes	5–7 minutes 2 1/2 (2:30)– 3 minutes	3–5 minutes 1–2 minutes

1 With fork, pierce skin of each sweet potato several times. On baking tray (see Chart), place kitchen paper; place sweet potatoes on top, with narrow ends pointing towards centre.

2 Cook sweet potatoes on High for time in Chart, or until tender, turning over and rearranging halfway through cooking. Wrap in foil; allow to stand for 5 minutes. Remove foil.

3 On cutting board, with sharp knife, cut each sweet potato in half lengthways.

4 With spoon, scoop flesh from sweet potatoes into bowl, leaving 5 mm thick shells; reserve shells. On dinner plate (see Chart), arrange sweet potato shells.

5 In bowl with mixer at low speed, beat sweet potato flesh, yogurt, chilli powder and butter or margarine until well mixed and fluffy. Season with salt.

6 Spoon mashed sweet potato mixture into reserved shells. Reheat on High for time in Chart, or until hot. Serve immediately.

CURRIED POTATOES WITH PEAS

Colour Index page 73. 6 servings. 149 cals per serving. Low in cholesterol, fat, sodium. Good source of iron, fibre. Begin 25 minutes ahead.

2 tablespoons groundnut or vegetable oil	1 teaspoon lemon juice
1 onion, chopped	1 teaspoon garam masala
1 clove garlic, chopped	1 teaspoon turmeric
2 cm root ginger, peeled and chopped	1/2 teaspoon chilli powder
450 g potatoes, peeled and cut into 2 cm pieces	225 g frozen peas, defrosted
1 × 225 g can tomatoes, drained	1 tablespoon chopped fresh coriander
2 teaspoons ground coriander	Chilli Flower (page 116) to garnish

1. In 3 litre microwave-safe bowl, place oil, onion, garlic and ginger. Cook on High (100% power) for 3–4 minutes, stirring once.
2. To bowl, add potatoes and next 6 ingredients. Cook, covered, on High for 5 minutes, or until liquid boils, stirring once. Uncover and cook for 7–8 minutes, until potatoes are tender and liquid has almost evaporated, stirring twice.
3. Stir in peas and coriander. Cook on High for 5 minutes, or until sauce has thickened. Garnish.

SWEET POTATO BAKE

Colour Index page 77. 10 servings. 279 cals per serving. Low in sodium. Good source of vitamin A, fibre. Begin 1 1/2 hours ahead.

1.4 kg orange-fleshed sweet potatoes	1/2 teaspoon vanilla essence
90 g butter or margarine	30 g fresh wholemeal breadcrumbs
250 ml single cream	60 g shelled walnuts, finely chopped
Ground mixed spice	
50 g brown sugar	

1. Pierce skin of each sweet potato several times. On oven floor, place kitchen paper. Arrange sweet potatoes spoke-fashion on top. Cook on High (100% power) for 20–25 minutes until soft, turning over and rearranging once. Wrap in foil; allow to stand for 5 minutes. Remove foil. Cut each sweet potato in half lengthways. Scoop out flesh into mixing bowl; reserve. Discard shells.
2. In 21.5 cm microwave-safe shallow pie dish, place butter or margarine. Heat, covered with kitchen paper, on High for 1–1 1/2 (1:30) minutes.
3. To sweet potatoes, add 4 tablespoons melted butter or margarine, cream and next 3 ingredients; beat until smooth. Spoon into deep 21.5 cm microwave-safe pie dish.
4. Into melted butter or margarine remaining in pie dish, stir breadcrumbs and walnuts. Cook on High for 5–6 minutes, until breadcrumbs are crisp and nuts are toasted, stirring every minute. Sprinkle on top of sweet potato mixture. Cook on High for 7–10 minutes, until hot. Allow to stand, loosely covered, for 5 minutes.

Spinach

CREAMED SPINACH

Colour Index page 75. 4 servings. 140 cals per serving. Good source of vitamin A, riboflavin, vitamin C, calcium, iron, fibre. Begin 40 minutes ahead.

575 g fresh spinach	*¹/₄ teaspoon salt*
30 g butter or margarine	*¹/₄ teaspoon pepper*
2 tablespoons plain flour	*Grated nutmeg to taste*
350 ml milk	*Lemon slices to garnish*

1. With sharp knife, remove stalks from spinach. Rinse spinach under cold running water; drain lightly. In 3 litre microwave-safe casserole, place spinach with water remaining on leaves. Cook, covered, on High (100% power) for 5–7 minutes, until leaves are wilted, stirring twice. Drain; set aside.

2. In 2 litre microwave-safe measuring jug, place butter or margarine. Heat, covered with kitchen paper, on High for 45 seconds, or until melted. Into melted butter or margarine, stir flour until smooth and blended. Cook on High for 1 minute, stirring once.

3. Into flour mixture, gradually stir milk. Cook on High for 4–6 minutes, until sauce thickens and is smooth, stirring occasionally. Season with salt, pepper and nutmeg.

4. Into sauce, stir spinach. Cook on High for 3–5 minutes, until spinach is hot. Spoon into warmed serving dish and garnish with lemon slices.

ALTERNATIVE SERVING IDEAS

For a special occasion, Creamed Spinach can be served in a vegetable shell such as an artichoke bottom or hollowed-out tomato (as on page 263), or in an individual serving dish (below) with Buttered Crumb Topping and dill sprig garnish.

Buttered Crumb Topping: in 500 ml microwave-safe measuring jug, heat *30 g butter or margarine* on High (100% power) for 45 seconds, or until melted. Stir in *30 g fresh breadcrumbs* and ¹/₄ *teaspoon dried thyme or basil*. Cook, covered, on High for 2–2¹/₂ (2:30) minutes, until crumbs are dried and golden.

SPINACH GNOCCHI WITH BUTTER AND PARMESAN

Colour Index page 77. 233 cals per serving. Good source of vitamin A, calcium, fibre. Begin 2 hours ahead.

Spinach gnocchi – ricotta and spinach Italian-style 'dumplings' spiced with Parmesan for extra flavour – make a light lunch or supper when served with salad and crusty Italian bread, but are equally delicious as an accompaniment to roast veal.

Ingredients for 8 servings		Microwave cookware
2 tablespoons melted butter or margarine	*2 eggs*	30 × 20 cm baking dish
275 g frozen chopped spinach, defrosted and well drained	*140 g plain flour*	500 ml measuring jug
	50 g Parmesan cheese, grated	
115 g ricotta cheese	*¹/₄ teaspoon salt*	
1 small onion, finely chopped	*¹/₄ teaspoon pepper*	
	Grated nutmeg to taste	
	90 g butter or margarine	

1 In baking dish, place 2 tablespoons melted butter or margarine, spinach, ricotta cheese and chopped onion; stir well to mix. Cook on High (100% power) for 5 minutes.

2 To spinach mixture, add eggs, half of flour and half of Parmesan; season with salt, pepper and nutmeg. Stir until blended. Refrigerate, loosely covered, until cool enough to handle. Fill 5 litre saucepan halfway with water. On stove, bring to the boil.

3 Meanwhile, roll 1 tablespoon spinach and ricotta mixture in remaining flour on greaseproof paper and form into oval shape with floured hands. Repeat with remaining mixture.

4 To boiling water, carefully add half of spinach and ricotta ovals (gnocchi). Cook for about 7 minutes, or until gnocchi are slightly puffed and set.

5 With slotted spoon, transfer gnocchi to kitchen paper to drain. Repeat with remaining gnocchi. Meanwhile, in measuring jug, place 90 g butter or margarine. Heat, covered with kitchen paper, on High for 1–1¹/₂ (1:30) minutes, until melted.

6 *To serve:* arrange gnocchi on warmed serving platter. Pour melted butter or margarine over gnocchi; sprinkle with remaining Parmesan and serve immediately.

Squash

The many different types of squash available, including butternut, acorn and spaghetti squash, lend themselves beautifully to microwaving. You can microwave them whole (don't forget to pierce the skin) or cut them in half and serve them with Flavoured Butter (page 273). Below, the cooked squash is pulled up with forks to resemble strands of spaghetti.

SPAGHETTI SQUASH WITH MEAT SAUCE

Colour Index page 76. 564 cals per serving. Good source of thiamine, niacin, vitamin C, iron. Begin 55 minutes ahead.

Ingredients for 4 servings		Microwave cookware
1 spaghetti squash (about 1 kg)	1 × 400 g can chopped tomatoes	32.5 × 22.5 cm baking dish
450 g pork sausagemeat	2 tablespoons tomato purée	
1 small onion, diced	1 teaspoon dried basil	
1 green pepper, diced	salt to taste	

1 With fork, pierce squash in several places. On oven floor, place 2 sheets kitchen paper, one on top of the other; place squash on paper.

2 Cook squash on High (100% power) for 12–15 minutes, until flesh is tender when pierced with sharp knife, turning over halfway through cooking. Wrap in foil; allow to stand while preparing sauce.

3 In baking dish, place sausagemeat and onion. Cook, covered with kitchen paper, on High for 5–7 minutes, until meat is no longer pink, stirring often to break up lumps.

4 To sausagemeat mixture, add green pepper, tomatoes, tomato purée and basil; stir to mix. Cook on High for 15–18 minutes, until vegetables are tender and sauce thickens slightly, stirring occasionally. Season with salt.

5 Split squash in half lengthways; discard seeds. With 2 forks, lift up flesh of squash to form spaghetti-like strands; transfer to warmed large serving platter.

6 To serve: spoon sausagemeat sauce over spaghetti squash.

ACORN SQUASH WITH ORANGE AND HONEY GLAZE

Colour Index page 76. 4 servings. 236 cals per serving. Low in sodium.
Begin 40 minutes ahead.

2 acorn squash (about 700 g each)	60 g butter or margarine Orange slices and
1 teaspoon grated orange zest	parsley sprigs to garnish
4 tablespoons honey	

1. With fork, pierce squash in several places. For easier cutting, heat squash on High (100% power) for 2–2¹/₂ (2:30) minutes until slightly softened. With sharp knife, cut squash in half lengthways; remove seeds and discard.
2. In 30 × 20 cm microwave-safe baking dish, place squash halves, cut side down, with thicker ends towards edges. Cook, covered, on High for 8–10 minutes, until tender, rotating dish halfway through cooking.
3. Turn squash cut side up. In each cavity, place one-quarter of orange zest, honey and butter or margarine. Cook on High for 5–7 minutes, until bubbling, rotating dish halfway through cooking.
4. On heatproof surface, allow to stand, covered, for 5 minutes. Garnish before serving.

MAPLE BUTTERNUT SQUASH

Colour Index page 76. 4 servings. 176 cals per serving. Low in cholesterol, sodium. Good source of vitamin A. Begin 55 minutes ahead.

1 small butternut squash (about 575 g)	1 small onion, diced
30 g butter or margarine	4 tablespoons maple syrup
1 cooking apple, peeled, cored and diced	Apple slices and parsley sprigs to garnish

1. With fork, pierce squash in several places. On oven floor, place 2 sheets kitchen paper, one on top of the other; place squash on top. Cook on High (100% power) for 10–15 minutes, until flesh is tender when pierced with sharp knife, turning squash over halfway through cooking. Set aside until cool enough to handle.
2. In 1 litre microwave-safe casserole, place butter or margarine. Heat, covered with kitchen paper, on High for 45 seconds, or until melted. Into melted butter or margarine, stir apple and onion. Cook on High for 3–5 minutes, until apple and onion are tender, stirring twice.
3. With sharp knife, cut squash in half lengthways; discard seeds. With large spoon, scoop out flesh. In food processor with knife blade attached or in blender, process squash, in several batches if necessary. To squash, add apple and onion mixture and maple syrup.
4. In same casserole, pour blended mixture. Cook on High for 10–12 minutes, until mixture thickens slightly, stirring often. Garnish.

Sweetcorn

CREAMED SWEETCORN WITH PEPPERS

Colour Index page 70. 4 servings. 152 cals per serving. Good source of fibre. Begin 25 minutes ahead.

30 g butter or margarine	1/4 teaspoon dried
2 small onions, thinly sliced	oregano
	60 ml half cream
1 small green pepper, cut into strips	1 small tomato, cut into thin wedges
4 corn-on-the-cob, husked, or 1 × 330 g can sweetcorn kernels, drained	1 teaspoon salt
	Pepper to taste

1. In 30 × 20 cm microwave-safe baking dish, place butter or margarine. Heat, covered with kitchen paper, on High (100% power) for 45 seconds–1 minute, until melted.
2. To melted butter or margarine, add onions and green pepper; stir to coat. Cook on High for 4–5 minutes, until onions are softened, stirring once.
3. Meanwhile, if using fresh corn-on-the-cob, with sharp knife, cut kernels from cobs.
4. Into onion mixture, stir oregano, sweetcorn and cream. Cook, covered, on High for 5–7 minutes, until sweetcorn is tender, stirring twice. For canned sweetcorn, cook, covered, on High for 3–5 minutes. Add tomato. Cook on High for 1–2 minutes, until tomato is hot but still firm. Season.

SWEETCORN PUDDING

Colour Index page 72. 4 servings. 244 cals per serving. Begin 25 minutes ahead.

2 tablespoons plain flour	15 g butter or margarine
1 tablespoon caster sugar	1 × 330 g can sweetcorn kernels, drained
2 eggs	2 tablespoons dried breadcrumbs
250 ml half cream	Paprika to taste
1 teaspoon salt	
1/4 teaspoon pepper	

1. In 2 litre microwave-safe glass bowl, blend flour and sugar. Add eggs; beat until smooth. Into egg mixture, gradually blend cream. Cook on Medium (50% power) for 4–5 minutes, until mixture thickens, stirring twice. Season with salt and pepper.
2. In 21.5 cm microwave-safe shallow pie dish, place butter and sweetcorn. Cook on High (100% power) for 2–3 minutes, until butter melts, stirring twice. Add breadcrumbs; stir until well mixed.
3. To sweetcorn, add egg mixture; stir. Cook, covered, on Medium for 5–7 minutes, until a knife inserted in centre comes out clean. Allow to stand, loosely covered, on heatproof surface for 5 minutes. Sprinkle top of pudding with paprika just before serving.

Corn-on-the-Cob

Corn-on-the-cob cooks perfectly in the microwave. Simply remove the husks and silks, then rinse and wrap each ear tightly in microwave cling film. Cook 1 ear on High (100% power) for 3–4 minutes; 2 ears for 5–6 minutes; 3 ears for 7–8 minutes; 4 ears for 9–11 minutes. Halfway through cooking, turn the ears over and rearrange, moving the front ears to the back and vice versa for even, thorough cooking.

Serve corn-on-the-cob with Flavoured Butter (below) or, using a sharp knife, cut cooked kernels from each ear and serve as a vegetable accompaniment or add to salads or hot main dishes.

Preparing Corn-on-the-Cob

Just before cooking, remove outer husks and silks from cobs.

Rinse under cold running water; remove any remaining silks with vegetable brush.

After cooking, hold each ear at an angle. With sharp knife, cut down ear to remove kernels.

FLAVOURED BUTTER

Colour Index page 71. Each butter makes enough for 4 ears of corn. 78 cals per tablespoon. Begin 15 minutes ahead.

Golden Spiced Butter: in 500 ml microwave-safe measuring jug, place *45 g butter or margarine, 1 tablespoon lemon juice, 1/2 teaspoon curry powder* and *1/2 teaspoon Dijon mustard*. Stir ingredients until well mixed. Heat, covered, on High (100% power) for 45 seconds–1 minute, until butter or margarine is melted, stirring once.

Three Pepper Butter: in 500 ml microwave-safe measuring jug, place *45 g butter or margarine, 3 tablespoons finely chopped green pepper, 1/4 teaspoon crushed black peppercorns* and *1/4 teaspoon cayenne pepper*. Stir ingredients until well mixed. Heat, covered, on High (100% power) for 45 seconds–1 minute, until butter or margarine is melted, stirring once.

Fresh Herb Butter: in 500 ml microwave-safe measuring jug, place *45 g butter or margarine* and *2 teaspoons lemon juice*. Stir ingredients until well mixed. Heat, covered, on High (100% power) for 45 seconds–1 minute, until butter or margarine is melted, stirring once. Into melted butter mixture, stir *1 teaspoon chopped fresh herbs*.

Mixed Vegetable Dishes

Microwaving brings out the best in different vegetables cooked together in the same dish. In the selection in Special Mixed Vegetables (below), all the vegetables have different densities and water content, so they each microwave at different speeds. To prevent the vegetables from cooking unevenly, they are added to the microwave in stages.

SPECIAL MIXED VEGETABLES

Colour Index page 76. 107 cals per serving. Low in cholesterol. Good source of vitamin A, vitamin C, fibre. Begin 45 minutes ahead.

Ingredients for 8 servings		Microwave cookware
4 spring onions	2 tablespoons soy sauce	Medium bowl
450 g carrots	60 ml water	4 litre casserole
3 tablespoons vegetable oil	450 g broccoli	
¼ teaspoon dried hot red pepper flakes	1 medium red pepper	
	225 g button mushrooms	

1 On cutting board, with sharp knife, cut spring onions diagonally into 2.5 cm pieces and carrots into 5 mm thick slices.

2 In medium bowl, place spring onions, oil and red pepper flakes. Cook on High (100% power) for 3 minutes, until tender-crisp, stirring once. Stir in soy sauce. Cover; set aside.

3 In casserole, place carrots and water. Cook, covered, on High for 8–10 minutes, until carrots are tender-crisp, stirring halfway through cooking.

4 Meanwhile, with sharp knife, cut broccoli into 5 × 2.5 cm pieces. Cut red pepper into matchstick-thin strips. Set aside.

5 To carrots, add broccoli. Cook, covered, on High for 5 minutes, stirring once. Add mushrooms. Cook, covered, on High for 5 minutes longer, or until vegetables are tender, stirring halfway through cooking. Drain liquid from vegetables.

6 To vegetables, add red pepper strips and spring onion mixture. Toss to coat well. Arrange vegetables on warmed serving platter and serve immediately.

MASHED HARVEST VEGETABLES

Colour Index page 76. 8 servings. 135 cals per serving. Good source of vitamin C, fibre. Begin 45 minutes ahead.

700 g butternut squash or pumpkin	1 tablespoon orange-flavour liqueur
700 g swede	1 teaspoon finely grated orange zest
120 ml water	
60 g butter or margarine	Pinch of ground cinnamon
2 tablespoons dark brown sugar	Orange Julienne (page 330) and parsley sprig to garnish
¼ teaspoon salt	

1. With fork, pierce skin of butternut squash several times. For easier cutting, heat squash on High (100% power) for 2–2½ (2:30) minutes until slightly softened. Peel squash or pumpkin and swede. Cut each into 2 cm pieces.
2. In 4 litre microwave-safe casserole, place squash or pumpkin, swede and water. Cook, covered, on High for 18 minutes, or until vegetables are very tender, stirring occasionally.
3. To vegetable mixture, add butter or margarine, sugar, salt, liqueur, orange zest and cinnamon. With potato masher, mash thoroughly.
4. Spoon mixture into microwave-safe serving dish. Reheat on High for 2 minutes, or until hot; garnish.

GARDEN VEGETABLE MEDLEY

Colour Index page 76. 6 servings. 182 cals per serving. Low in cholesterol, sodium. Good source of vitamin A, vitamin C, iron, fibre. Begin 45 minutes ahead.

450 g potatoes, peeled	1 small garlic clove, crushed
2 small aubergines (about 225 g each)	60 ml vegetable oil
2 onions	2 tablespoons cider vinegar
4 red or yellow peppers	
2 courgettes (about 225 g each)	¼ teaspoon dried oregano
60 ml water	1 medium tomato

1. Cut potatoes into 4 cm chunks. Cut each aubergine lengthways into quarters. Cut each onion into 6 wedges. Cut peppers into 2.5 cm strips. Cut courgettes into 2.5 cm slices.
2. In 32.5 × 22.5 cm microwave-safe baking dish, place potatoes and water. Cook, covered, on High (100% power) for 5 minutes, stirring once. Drain.
3. To potato chunks, add aubergines and remaining ingredients except tomato; stir. Cook, covered, on High for 15 minutes, stirring twice.
4. Cut tomato into 8 wedges; add to vegetable mixture. Cook, covered, on High for 4–5 minutes, until vegetables are tender, stirring halfway through cooking. Serve hot or cover and refrigerate to serve chilled later.

RATATOUILLE

Colour Index page 76. 8 servings. 115 cals per serving. Low in cholesterol. Good source of vitamin C, fibre. Begin 45 minutes ahead.

60 ml olive oil	*2 teaspoons dried*
1 large onion, diced	*oregano*
2 garlic cloves, crushed	*1 teaspoon sugar*
1 red or green pepper,	*¼ teaspoon salt*
cut into 2.5 cm pieces	*2 large tomatoes, each*
1 aubergine (about	*cut into 8 wedges*
700 g), cut into 2.5 cm	*2 tablespoons tomato*
chunks	*purée*
3 courgettes, cut into	*Basil leaves to garnish*
2.5 cm chunks	

1. In 32.5 × 22.5 cm microwave-safe baking dish, place oil, onion and garlic. Cook on High (100% power) for 3–4 minutes, until onion softens, stirring halfway through cooking.

2. Stir in red or green pepper, aubergine and courgettes. Cook, covered, on High for 10–12 minutes, until aubergine and courgettes are slightly softened, stirring twice during cooking.

3. Into aubergine mixture, stir oregano, sugar, salt, tomatoes and tomato purée. Cook on High for 15–18 minutes, until vegetables are tender and juices thicken slightly, stirring occasionally.

4. Spoon ratatouille on to serving platter; serve hot or cover and refrigerate to serve chilled later; garnish before serving.

RATATOUILLE-FILLED PEPPERS: prepare *Ratatouille* (above) up to end of step 3. Cut *4 medium peppers (red, green and/or yellow)* in half lengthways; remove seeds and stalks. Brush peppers on all sides with *1 tablespoon vegetable oil.* Arrange, cut side down, in single layer in 30 × 20 cm microwave-safe baking dish. Cook, covered, on High (100% power) for 3–4 minutes, just until softened; cool slightly. Spoon equal amounts of Ratatouille into pepper halves and arrange on serving platter. If you like, reheat filled peppers on microwave-safe platter on Medium-High (70% power) for 3–4 minutes.

Oiling and Arranging the Peppers

With pastry brush, lightly and evenly brush oil over pepper halves.

Place oiled peppers, cut side down, in single layer in baking dish. Cook, covered, as above.

When cooking a variety of fresh seasonal vegetables in the microwave, be sure to arrange them so that the thicker parts are pointing towards the edges of the dish, where they will receive most microwave energy. If necessary, overlap the pieces slightly, as in the recipe for Spring Vegetables with Lemon and Chive Butter (below).

SPRING VEGETABLES WITH LEMON AND CHIVE BUTTER

Colour Index page 73. 141 cals per serving. Low in cholesterol. Good source of vitamin A, vitamin C, fibre. Begin 25 minutes ahead.

Ingredients for 6 servings		Microwave cookware
700 g asparagus	*2 tablespoons finely*	30 × 20 cm
3 small courgettes	*chopped chives*	baking dish
(preferably yellow) or	*1 tablespoon made*	Small bowl
summer squash	*mustard*	
2 bunches radishes	*2 tablespoons lemon*	
6 medium carrots	*juice*	
120 ml water	*1 tablespoon Lemon*	
60 g butter or	*Julienne (page 330)*	
margarine	*¼ teaspoon salt*	

1 With sharp knife, trim tough ends from asparagus. Rinse under cold running water to remove any sand. With knife, cut courgettes or squash into quarters lengthways; trim radishes; cut carrots in half lengthways.

2 In baking dish, arrange carrots so that tips are overlapping in centre; add water. Cook, covered, on High (100% power) for 4 minutes.

3 On top of carrots in baking dish, arrange asparagus so that tips are overlapping in centre.

4 Arrange courgettes or squash and radishes in layers on top of carrots and asparagus. Cook, covered, on High for 8–10 minutes, until vegetables are tender-crisp, rotating dish halfway through cooking.

5 In small bowl, combine butter or margarine, chives, mustard, lemon juice, Lemon Julienne and salt. Cook on High for 2½ (2:30)–3 minutes, until butter is melted.

6 *To serve:* arrange vegetables on warmed serving platter. Top with lemon and chive butter.

Main Course Chicken Salads

OLD-FASHIONED CHICKEN SALAD

Colour Index page 78. 399 cals per serving. Good source of niacin.
Begin 55 minutes ahead.

Ingredients	For 4	For 2	For 1
Chicken breasts, skinned and boned	4 breasts	2 breasts	1 breast
Chicken Stock (page 125) or stock from a cube	2 tablespoons	1 tablespoon	2 teaspoons
Celery stick, diced	1 stick	½ stick	¼ stick
Small onion, finely chopped	1 onion	½ onion	¼ onion
Canned pimiento, diced	2 tablespoons	1 tablespoon	1 teaspoon
Mayonnaise	150 ml	80 ml	3 tablespoons
Lemon juice	1 tablespoon	1½ teaspoons	½ teaspoon
Poultry seasoning	½ teaspoon	¼ teaspoon	to taste
Salt	to taste	to taste	to taste
Microwave cookware	Pie dish	Pie dish	Pie dish
Time on High (100% power)	5–7 minutes	3½ (3:30)–5 minutes	2½ (2:30)–3½ (3:30) minutes

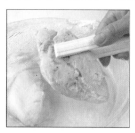

1 In 21.5 cm pie dish (see Chart), place chicken and stock. Cook, covered, on High for time in Chart, until juices run clear, turning pieces over and rotating dish once. Allow to stand, loosely covered, on heatproof surface.

2 Meanwhile, prepare dressing: in mixing bowl, combine celery, onion, pimiento, mayonnaise, lemon juice and poultry seasoning; mix well.

3 Drain chicken; cut into chunks. Stir into dressing; mix well. Season with salt. For best flavour, cover and refrigerate for 30 minutes before serving.

SALAD DRESSINGS

Vinaigrette Dressing: in small mixing bowl, whisk 1 diced small red onion, 60 ml olive oil, 60 ml red wine vinegar, ¼ teaspoon dried oregano and ¼ teaspoon salt until blended.

Zesty Mayonnaise Dressing: in small mixing bowl, whisk 120 ml mayonnaise, 3 tablespoons milk, 2 tablespoons lemon juice, 1 tablespoon made mustard, ½ teaspoon salt, ¼ teaspoon pepper and ¼ teaspoon dried basil until blended.

CHICKEN CLUB SALAD

Colour Index page 78. 2 main course servings. 338 cals per serving. Good source of niacin, iron. Begin 40 minutes ahead.

2 chicken breasts (about 175 g each), skinned and boned
Pinch of dried thyme
4 rashers rindless streaky bacon

2 slices bread
Lettuce leaves
1 tomato, sliced
Vinaigrette Dressing (below left)

1. In 21.5 cm microwave-safe shallow pie dish, place chicken breasts. Sprinkle with thyme. Cook, covered with greaseproof paper, on High (100% power) for 5–6 minutes, until chicken juices run clear, turning pieces over and rotating dish halfway through cooking. Discard cooking juices. Cover and refrigerate.
2. Meanwhile, on double thickness of kitchen paper, place bacon rashers. Cook, covered with kitchen paper, on High for 3½ (3:30) minutes, until browned; set aside.
3. With sharp knife, cut chicken crossways into 5 mm thick slices. Toast bread; cut into quarters. On dinner plates, arrange lettuce leaves, tomato, chicken and toast triangles. Chop bacon; sprinkle over salad. Serve with Vinaigrette Dressing.

CHICKEN AND POTATO SALAD WITH ZESTY DRESSING

Colour Index page 79. 6 main course servings. 414 cals per serving. Good source of niacin, vitamin C, iron, fibre. Begin 1¼ hours ahead.

1 × 1.6 kg chicken, jointed and skinned
700 g small new potatoes, cut into 1 cm thick slices
60 ml water
1 yellow pepper, sliced
1 small red onion, sliced
10 stoned black olives, cut in half

60 ml milk
80 ml mayonnaise
60 ml soured cream
2 tablespoons prepared horseradish
2 tablespoons lemon juice
¼ teaspoon salt

1. In 32.5 × 22.5 cm microwave-safe baking dish, place chicken legs, thighs and wings at edges of dish, breasts in centre. Cook, covered, on High (100% power) for 22–24 minutes, until chicken juices run clear, turning over and rearranging pieces halfway through cooking. Set aside to cool.
2. In 2 litre microwave-safe casserole, place potatoes and water. Cook, covered, on High for 8–9 minutes, stirring once. Drain; set aside to cool.
3. Cut reserved chicken into bite-sized pieces; discard bones. Place chicken pieces, potatoes, pepper, onion and olives in large bowl; toss.
4. In small bowl, combine milk and remaining ingredients. Pour dressing over salad in bowl, or serve separately.

Main Course Meat Salads

ANTIPASTO SALAD

Colour Index page 78. 6 main course servings. 431 cals per serving. Good source of vitamin A, vitamin C, calcium. Begin 25 minutes ahead.

*1 small cauliflower, cut
  into florets
2 tablespoons water
3 small courgettes, cut
  into 1 cm slices
Vinaigrette Dressing
  (page 276)
297 g can artichoke
  hearts, drained
Salad leaves*

*3 medium carrots, cut
  into matchstick-thin
  strips
225 g smoked Gouda,
  mozzarella or other
  cheese, sliced
225 g salami, cut into
  chunks
2 tomatoes, cut into
  wedges*

1. In 25 cm round microwave-safe baking dish, place cauliflower and water. Cook, covered, on High (100% power) for 5 minutes, stirring once. To dish, add courgettes. Cook, covered, for 3–5 minutes, until vegetables are tender-crisp. With slotted spoon, transfer vegetables to mixing bowl. Pour over half of Vinaigrette Dressing; toss.
2. In same microwave-safe dish, place artichoke hearts. Heat, covered, on High for 1–2 minutes, until hot.
3. On platter, arrange salad leaves, cooked vegetables, carrots, cheese, salami and tomatoes. Serve remaining dressing separately.

DELICATESSEN SALAD

Colour Index page 78. 6 main course servings. 365 cals per serving. Good source of niacin, calcium, iron, fibre. Begin 50 minutes ahead.

*900 g small new
  potatoes, peeled and
  diced
175 ml Chicken Stock
  (page 125) or stock
  from a cube
1/4 teaspoon caraway
  seeds
1/4 teaspoon pepper
4 rashers rindless
  streaky bacon, diced*

*2 celery sticks, sliced
1 onion, chopped
1 tablespoon plain flour
20 ml cider vinegar
3 tablespoons brown
  sugar
Salad leaves
225 g sliced cooked
  meats
115 g Cheddar cheese,
  cut into strips*

1. In 3 litre microwave-safe casserole, combine potatoes, stock, caraway seeds and pepper. Cook, covered, on High (100% power) for 11–13 minutes, until potatoes are tender, stirring halfway through cooking. Drain cooking liquid, reserving 60 ml. Cover potatoes; set aside.
2. In medium microwave-safe bowl, place bacon. Cook, covered with kitchen paper, on High for 4–5 minutes, until browned. Transfer to kitchen paper to drain. Into bacon fat in bowl, stir celery and onion. Cook on High for 3 minutes.
3. To celery and onion mixture, add flour, reserved cooking liquid, vinegar and sugar; stir. Cook on High for 3–5 minutes, until mixture thickens, stirring once. Pour over potatoes; add bacon. Stand for 10 minutes. Arrange leaves on platter with potatoes, meats and cheese.

Both hot and cold pasta can be combined with a selection of crisply cooked vegetables and thin slivers of meat to make a hearty salad. In Thai-Style Beef and Noodle Salad (below), crushed red pepper, spring onions, fresh mint and cashews create an authentic Thai flavour. This dish can be served hot, or prepared well in advance to serve chilled later.

THAI-STYLE BEEF AND NOODLE SALAD

Colour Index page 79. 905 cals per serving. Good source of vitamin A, riboflavin, thiamine, vitamin C, iron. Begin 1½ hours ahead or early in day.

Ingredients for 4 main course servings		Microwave cookware

450 g beef fillet
120 ml groundnut or
  vegetable oil
2 tablespoons lime or
  lemon juice
2 tablespoons soy
  sauce
2 tablespoons cider
  vinegar
2 tablespoons caster
  sugar
	1/4 teaspoon dried hot
	  red pepper flakes
	250 g medium egg
	  noodles
	2 tablespoons shredded
	  fresh mint leaves
	1 small red pepper, diced
	4 spring onions, thinly
	  sliced
	35 g dry-roasted
	  unsalted cashews
		Large bowl
		Browning dish

1 On cutting board, with sharp knife, cut beef crossways into 3 mm thick slices. Cut each slice into thin strips.

2 In mixing bowl, combine oil, lime or lemon juice, soy sauce, vinegar, sugar and pepper flakes. Add beef; stir to coat. Cover and marinate for 30 minutes.

3 Over large bowl, set sieve. Drain beef; reserve marinade. Preheat browning dish according to manufacturer's instructions.

4 Spread half of beef on browning dish. Cook on High (100% power) for 1–2 minutes, just until beef is done to your liking, stirring halfway through cooking. Remove beef; set aside and keep warm. Reheat browning dish and cook remaining beef slices.

5 Meanwhile, cook noodles conventionally according to instructions on packet. Drain; add to reserved marinade in bowl and toss well to mix. Heat noodles on High for 2–3 minutes until hot.

6 Toss noodles with shredded mint, diced red pepper, spring onions and cashews. Place on serving platter. Arrange beef over noodles. Serve hot or cover and refrigerate to serve chilled later.

Warm Salads

Various salad leaves such as endive, watercress, rocket and radicchio are delicious served wilted with a warm dressing. Escarole, with its pungent flavour, is a particularly good choice.

SPINACH SALAD WITH HOT BACON DRESSING

Colour Index page 78. 153 cals per serving. Low in cholesterol. Good source of vitamin A. Begin 20 minutes ahead.

Ingredients	For 4	For 2	For 1
Fresh young spinach leaves	*275 g*	*150 g*	*75 g*
Rindless streaky bacon, diced	*4 rashers*	*2 rashers*	*1 rasher*
Cider vinegar	*1 tablespoon*	*1¹/₂ teaspoons*	*³/₄ teaspoon*
Dijon mustard	*1 tablespoon*	*1¹/₂ teaspoons*	*³/₄ teaspoon*
Caster sugar	*1 teaspoon*	*¹/₂ teaspoon*	*¹/₄ teaspoon*
Red onion, sliced	*1 medium*	*1 small*	*¹/₂ small*
Microwave cookware	Large bowl Pie dish	Medium bowl Pie dish	Small bowl Pie dish
Time on High (100% power)			
Bacon	4–5 minutes	2–3 minutes	1–1¹/₂ (1:30) minutes
Dressing	1–2 minutes	30 seconds– 1 minute	15–30 seconds
Salad	2–3 minutes	1–1¹/₂ (1:30) minutes	45 seconds– 1 minute

1 Into bowl (see Chart), tear spinach into bite-sized pieces. In 21.5 cm pie dish, place bacon. Cook, covered with kitchen paper, on High for time in Chart, or until browned, stirring twice.

2 With fish slice, transfer bacon to kitchen paper to drain.

3 Into bacon fat in pie dish, stir vinegar, mustard and sugar. Cook, covered with kitchen paper, on High for time in Chart, or until hot.

4 To spinach, add onion and hot dressing; toss to coat well. Sprinkle reserved bacon over spinach. Cook salad on High for time in Chart, just until spinach wilts.

LEAVES FOR SALADS

While lettuce remains the favourite salad ingredient, there is a wide variety of more unusual leaves available to add interest to your salads, such as lamb's lettuce, rocket, Swiss chard, chicory, endive, escarole, lollo rosso and radicchio. Try varying different colours and shapes in your salad bowl, tossing them together with your favourite dressing.

Radicchio: ruby-red leaves with bitter flavour; used frequently in Italian salads.

Lamb's Lettuce: a spring and summer salad green, wild or cultivated. Spoon-shaped leaves are tangy; good with other leaves.

Curly Endive: somewhat bitter tasting; outer leaves are darker and stronger in flavour than inner ones.

Lollo Rosso: curly leaves, often tinged with red; oak leaf lettuce looks similar.

Escarole: wide flat leaves, curled at edges; slightly bitter taste.

WARM SALAD OF ROCKET, SWEETCORN, BLACK BEANS AND AVOCADO

Colour Index page 78. 8 servings. 140 cals per serving. Low in cholesterol. Good source of fibre. Begin 20 minutes ahead.

3 rashers rindless streaky bacon, diced	*180 g rocket leaves, shredded*
1 large onion, sliced	*2 tablespoons red wine vinegar*
2 garlic cloves, crushed	*Salt and pepper to taste*
275 g frozen sweetcorn kernels, defrosted	*Avocado slices to garnish*
1 × 400 g can black or red kidney beans, drained and rinsed	

1. In 32.5 × 22.5 cm microwave-safe baking dish, place bacon. Cook, covered with kitchen paper, on High (100% power) for 3–4 minutes, until bacon is browned, stirring twice. With tongs, transfer bacon to kitchen paper to drain.
2. Into bacon fat in dish, stir onion, garlic, sweetcorn and beans. Cook, covered, on High for 4–5 minutes, until onion softens, stirring once.
3. Into vegetable mixture, stir rocket and vinegar. Cook on High for 2–4 minutes, until rocket is wilted, stirring once. Season salad.
4. *To serve:* spoon salad on to warmed dinner plates; garnish each portion with avocado slices and sprinkle with diced bacon.

PEPPER SALAD

Colour Index page 78. 6 servings. 166 cals per serving. Low in cholesterol. Good source of vitamin A, vitamin C, calcium. Begin 25 minutes ahead.

1 large Spanish onion (about 450 g)	*1/2 teaspoon fennel seeds, crushed*
2 red peppers	*1/4 teaspoon salt*
2 green peppers	*80 g stoned black olives, cut in half*
2 yellow peppers	*115 g feta cheese, crumbled*
2 tablespoons olive or vegetable oil	
2 tablespoons white wine vinegar	
1 teaspoon sugar	

1. With sharp knife, cut onion into 8 wedges. Separate each wedge to loosen onion layers. Cut red, green and yellow peppers into 1 cm strips.
2. In 32.5 × 22.5 cm microwave-safe baking dish, place oil and onion. Cook on High (100% power) for 3–4 minutes, until onion softens slightly, stirring once.
3. To onion mixture, add green, red and yellow peppers. Cook, covered, on High for 7–10 minutes, until all pepper strips are tender, stirring occasionally.
4. In large bowl, combine vinegar, sugar, fennel seeds and salt. Add pepper and onion mixture, olives and feta cheese. Toss gently to mix well. Serve warm or cover and refrigerate to serve chilled later.

Warm salads make a welcome alternative to plainly cooked green vegetables. They are also delicious served as a first course. An appetiser salad should be light and tangy – to whet the appetite for heartier dishes to come.

WARM SALAD OF ARTICHOKE HEARTS AND CHERRY TOMATOES

Colour Index page 79. 186 cals per serving. Begin 55 minutes ahead.

Ingredients for 6 servings		Microwave cookware
115 g butter or margarine	*1 tablespoon tarragon vinegar*	32.5 cm × 22.5 cm baking dish
2 × 297 g cans artichoke hearts, drained	*1 tablespoon dry white wine*	500 ml measuring jug
350 g cherry tomatoes	*1/4 teaspoon dried tarragon*	Medium bowl
1/2 teaspoon finely chopped onion	*1 egg yolk*	
	Salt and pepper to taste	
	Dill sprigs to garnish	

1 In baking dish, place 15 g butter or margarine. Heat, covered with kitchen paper, on High (100% power) for 30 seconds, or until melted. To dish, add artichokes. Heat on High for 2–3 minutes, or until hot, stirring twice.

2 Add tomatoes. Cook on High for 2–3 minutes, until hot, stirring once. Keep hot. In measuring jug, place onion, vinegar, wine and tarragon. Cook on High for 2–3 minutes, until liquid evaporates.

3 Into medium bowl, spoon onion mixture.

4 Into onion mixture in bowl, stir egg yolk. In measuring jug used for onion, place remaining butter or margarine. Heat, covered, with kitchen paper, on High for 1–1 1/2 (1:30) minutes, until melted.

5 Beating constantly with whisk, pour hot butter or margarine in thin stream into onion mixture until mixture thickens. Season with salt and pepper. Cook on Medium (50% power) for 30 seconds–1 minute, stirring every 15 seconds, until hot and slightly thickened.

6 *To serve:* arrange artichoke hearts in circle on warmed serving platter. Arrange cherry tomatoes in centre; pour over warm sauce. Garnish with dill sprigs and serve immediately.

Vegetable Salads

Pasta shapes combine beautifully with a variety of garden vegetables; prepare them in advance and, if you like, reheat them in the microwave. Use the smaller shells, bow ties and spirals to turn any salad from a light and tasty accompaniment to a satisfying main course everyone will enjoy.

GARDEN VEGETABLE AND PASTA SALAD

Colour Index page 79. 438 cals per serving. Good source of vitamin A, thiamine, riboflavin, vitamin C, calcium, iron, fibre. Begin 55 minutes ahead.

Ingredients for 6 main course servings		Microwave cookware
80 ml cider vinegar 60 ml olive or vegetable oil 1 teaspoon dried oregano 1/4 teaspoon dried hot red pepper flakes 1/4 teaspoon salt 6 spring onions, chopped 115 g French beans 3 carrots, sliced 60 ml water 225 g farfalle (bow tie) pasta	450 g broccoli, cut into bite-sized pieces 2 courgettes, cut into 1 cm thick slices 115 g Cheddar cheese, cubed 115 g Gruyère cheese, cubed 175 g cherry tomatoes	30 × 20 cm baking dish

1 In large mixing bowl, combine vinegar, oil, oregano, red pepper flakes, salt and spring onions. In baking dish, place beans, carrots and water. Cook on High (100% power) for 6–8 minutes, until tender-crisp, stirring once.

2 With slotted spoon, transfer French beans and carrots to dressing in bowl; toss to coat. Cover and set aside. Cook pasta shapes conventionally according to instructions on packet.

3 Meanwhile, in baking dish used for beans and carrots, place broccoli. Cook, covered, on High for 6–7 minutes, until tender-crisp, stirring once. Transfer to bowl with vegetables and dressing; toss to mix.

4 In baking dish used for broccoli, place courgette slices. Cook, covered, on High for 3–4 minutes, until courgette slices are tender-crisp, stirring halfway through cooking. With slotted spoon, transfer courgette slices to bowl with French beans, carrots, broccoli and dressing; toss to mix together thoroughly.

5 When pasta is al dente (tender yet firm to the bite), drain thoroughly in colander.

6 To vegetables in bowl, add pasta, cheese cubes and cherry tomatoes. Toss gently and transfer to serving dish. Serve warm or cover and refrigerate to serve chilled later.

LENTILS VINAIGRETTE

Colour Index page 79. 8 servings. 183 cals per serving. Low in cholesterol. Good source of iron, fibre. Begin 2½ hours ahead or early in day.

6 tablespoons olive or vegetable oil
1 onion, chopped
1 teaspoon dried thyme
1 bay leaf
190 g lentils
750 ml water
2 tablespoons red wine vinegar

2 tablespoons chopped fresh basil, mint or parsley
3 spring onions, sliced
1 green pepper, diced
1 large tomato, diced
Salt and pepper to taste

1. In 30 × 20 cm microwave-safe baking dish, place 2 tablespoons oil, onion, thyme and bay leaf. Cook on High (100% power) for 3–5 minutes, until onion softens, stirring twice.
2. Into onion mixture, stir lentils and water. Cook, covered, on High for 15–20 minutes, until lentils are tender but not mushy, stirring occasionally. Drain; discard bay leaf.
3. In mixing bowl, combine remaining oil, vinegar, chopped basil, mint or parsley, spring onions, green pepper and tomato; add to lentil mixture in baking dish. Toss well. Season with salt and pepper.
4. Cover salad and refrigerate for at least 2 hours to blend flavours before serving.

HIGH-FIBRE SALAD

Colour Index page 79. 8 servings. 247 cals per serving. Low in cholesterol. Good source of fibre. Begin 2¼ hours ahead or early in day.

2 tablespoons sugar
120 ml olive or vegetable oil
120 ml cider vinegar
1/4 teaspoon salt
1 × 450 g can chopped French beans
1 × 425 g can chick peas

2 × 400 g cans red kidney beans
1 onion, chopped
4 tablespoons chopped sweet pickled cucumber
1/2 small green pepper, chopped

1. In 1 litre microwave-safe measuring jug, combine sugar, oil, vinegar and salt. Heat on High (100% power) for 3–5 minutes, until mixture boils and sugar dissolves.
2. Meanwhile, drain and rinse French beans, chick peas and kidney beans. In mixing bowl, place peas and beans, onion, pickle and green pepper. Pour dressing over salad; mix well.
3. Cover salad and refrigerate for at least 2 hours to blend flavours before serving.

WILD RICE SALAD

Colour Index page 79. 8 servings. 187 cals per serving. Low in cholesterol. Begin 1¹/₂ hours ahead.

750 ml water	4 spring onions, sliced
80 g wild rice	1 cooking apple, peeled,
90 g long-grain rice	cored and diced
60 ml olive or vegetable	2 celery sticks, sliced
oil	25 g pine nuts
1 tablespoon cider	35 g raisins
vinegar	Salt to taste
1 tablespoon lemon juice	
¹/₄ teaspoon ground	
coriander (optional)	

1. Into 2 litre microwave-safe glass bowl, pour water. Heat on High (100% power) for 5–7 minutes, until boiling.

2. Into water, stir wild rice. Cook, covered tightly with microwave cling film, on High for 20 minutes. Uncover; stir in long-grain rice. Cover again and cook on High for 15–20 minutes longer, until rice is tender. Drain in sieve and rinse under cold running water until cooled.

3. Meanwhile, in mixing bowl, combine oil, vinegar, lemon juice and, if you like, coriander. Into dressing, stir spring onions, apple, celery, pine nuts and raisins. Stir in rice and salt.

4. Cover salad and allow to stand for 30 minutes to blend flavours before serving. Serve at room temperature or cover and refrigerate to serve chilled later.

CLASSIC POTATO SALAD

Colour Index page 78. 6 servings. 170 cals per serving. Good source of fibre. Begin 25 minutes ahead.

700 g potatoes, cut into	¹/₄ teaspoon salt
2 cm chunks	¹/₄ teaspoon pepper
60 ml water	1 celery stick, thinly
80 ml mayonnaise	sliced
1 tablespoon milk	1 hard-boiled egg
1 teaspoon vinegar	(below), finely chopped

1. In 2 litre microwave-safe casserole, place potatoes and water. Cook, covered, on High (100% power) for 7–9 minutes, until tender, stirring twice. Drain; allow potatoes to cool slightly.

2. In mixing bowl, combine mayonnaise, milk, vinegar, salt and pepper. Add potatoes, celery and egg; toss to coat well. Serve immediately or cover and refrigerate to serve chilled later.

HARD-BOILED EGGS: break *1 egg* into 175 ml ramekin; prick yolk in several places. Cook, covered, on Medium (50% power) for 1¹/₂ (1:30)–2¹/₂ (2:30) minutes. Allow to stand on heatproof surface for 2 minutes, until yolk and white are firmly set. Cook 2 eggs for 2¹/₂ (2:30)–3¹/₂ (3:30) minutes; 3 eggs for 3–4 minutes.

TOMATO ASPIC

Colour Index page 79. 38 cals per serving. Low in cholesterol, fat. Begin early in day.

Ingredients	For 4	For 2	For 1
Tomato juice	500 ml	250 ml	120 ml
Water	175 ml	90 ml	3 tablespoons
Celery stick, sliced	1 stick	¹/₂ stick	¹/₄ stick
Lemon slices	2 slices	1 slice	¹/₂ slice
Tabasco sauce	to taste	to taste	to taste
Powdered gelatine	1 tablespoon	1¹/₂ teaspoons	³/₄ teaspoon
Cider vinegar	1¹/₂ teaspoons	³/₄ teaspoon	¹/₃ teaspoon
Caster sugar	¹/₂ teaspoon	¹/₄ teaspoon	to taste
Salt	¹/₄ teaspoon	to taste	to taste
Plain low-fat yogurt and chives	garnish	garnish	garnish
Microwave cookware	2 litre jug or glass bowl	1 litre measuring jug	500 ml measuring jug
Time on High (100% power)			
Tomato mixture	5–7 minutes	3–5 minutes	2–2¹/₂ (2:30) minutes
With gelatine	3–4 minutes	2–3 minutes	1–1¹/₂ (1:30) minutes

1 Into jug or bowl (see Chart), pour tomato juice and water. Add celery, lemon and Tabasco sauce. Cook, covered, on High for time in Chart, stirring once.

2 Over mixing bowl, set sieve. Pour mixture through sieve. Discard vegetables and return tomato mixture to jug or bowl.

3 Sprinkle gelatine evenly over tomato mixture; allow to stand for 1 minute to soften slightly.

4 Cook mixture, covered, on High for time in Chart, until gelatine completely dissolves, stirring twice. Stir in vinegar, sugar and salt. Taste and adjust seasoning.

5 Into 120 ml ramekins or individual moulds, ladle tomato mixture. Cover and refrigerate until firmly set.

6 *To serve:* dip ramekins or moulds in warm water. With knife, loosen aspic from sides. Place small plate upside down over each and invert. Shake gently and remove ramekin or mould. Garnish.

Meal in Minutes *for 6 people*

Summer Salad Supper

Delicatessen Salad, page 277
Prawn Salad with Mange-Touts, right
Warm Salad of Rocket, Sweetcorn, Black Beans and
Avocado, page 279
Tossed green salad and hot bread rolls
Fresh fruit platter
Banana Coconut Pie, page 344

PREPARATION TIMETABLE

Early in day	*Make Prawn Salad with Mange-Touts. Prepare green salad ingredients; store in polythene bags in refrigerator. Prepare salad dressing of your choice. Arrange fresh fruit assortment on platter; loosely cover. Prepare Banana Coconut Pie up to end of step 5.*
1¼ hours ahead	*Make Delicatessen Salad and arrange on serving platter. Make Warm Salad of Rocket, Sweetcorn, Black Beans and Avocado; spoon into warmed serving dish.*
Just before serving	*Complete Banana Coconut Pie. Toss salad ingredients with dressing. Wrap rolls in kitchen paper and heat on High (100% power).*

Prawn Salads

PRAWN SALAD WITH MANGE-TOUTS

Colour Index page 79. 4 servings. 268 cals per serving. Good source of vitamin A, vitamin C, iron. Begin 2 hours ahead.

450 g large raw prawns, shelled and deveined	*60 ml olive or vegetable oil*
150 g mange-touts, cut in half crossways	*2 tablespoons dry white wine*
1 small red pepper, thinly sliced	*2 tablespoons lemon juice*
275 g frozen baby sweetcorn, defrosted	*1 tablespoon chopped fresh dill*
4 spring onions, sliced	*Salt and pepper to taste*

1. In 32.5 × 22.5 cm microwave-safe baking dish, place prawns, mange-touts, red pepper, sweetcorn, onions, oil and white wine. Cook, covered, on High (100% power) for 5–7 minutes, until prawns just turn pink, stirring halfway through cooking.
2. Stir in lemon juice and dill; season with salt and pepper. Transfer to serving dish, cover and refrigerate for 1–2 hours.

PRAWN SALAD SUPREME

Colour Index page 79. 6 servings. 377 cals per serving. Good source of vitamin C, iron, fibre. Begin 45 minutes ahead.

450 g large raw prawns, shelled and deveined	*1 × 400 g can chick peas, drained*
1 tablespoon lemon juice	*1 small red pepper, thinly sliced*
1 tablespoon sherry	*70 g stoned black olives, cut in half*
450 g small new potatoes, unpeeled and cut into quarters	*Zesty Mayonnaise Dressing (page 276)*
2 tablespoons water	
225 g French beans	

1. In 25 cm round microwave-safe baking dish, arrange prawns in circle with tails pointing towards centre. Sprinkle with lemon juice and sherry. Cook, covered, on High (100% power) for 3–4 minutes, just until prawns turn pink, turning prawns over and rotating dish halfway through cooking. Drain, cover and refrigerate.
2. Meanwhile, in 1 litre microwave-safe casserole, place potatoes and water. Cook, covered, on High for 7–9 minutes, until tender, stirring once. With slotted spoon, transfer potatoes to colander. Cool potatoes under cold running water; transfer to large mixing bowl.
3. To water remaining in casserole, add French beans. Cook, covered, on High for 4–5 minutes, until tender-crisp, stirring once. Transfer beans to colander; cool under cold running water. To potatoes in bowl, add French beans, chick peas, red pepper, olives and reserved prawns. Pour dressing over and toss gently. Serve immediately or cover and refrigerate to serve chilled later.

Pasta, Grains and Nuts

PASTA SHAPES · MAIN COURSE PASTA
LAYERED PASTA DISHES AND SAUCES
MAIN COURSE RICE · PILAFS
BARLEY, BULGUR AND CORNMEAL · NUTS

Pasta, Grains and Nuts

Microwaving pasta is usually no faster than conventional cooking: the microwave is best used to cook the delicious sauces to acccompany pasta – they are so quick and easy to prepare and cook in the microwave that many can be ready in the same time it takes to boil the pasta. Although specific types of pasta are given in the recipes in this chapter, as in Penne with Cheese, Red Pepper and Olive Sauce (page 286), other pasta such as spaghetti, fettuccine, bow ties and tagliatelle can be substituted.

Layered and filled pasta dishes do cook more quickly in the microwave, however, and recipes usually call for a single piece of cookware which saves on washing up. The microwave is perfect, too, for reheating pasta dishes because tenderness and flavour are retained. Place a single serving on a microwave-safe dinner plate. Cook, covered, on Medium-High (70% power) for 2 minutes, or until plate is warm underneath and food is hot.

Microwave cooking is the preferred cooking method for rice because there is no need to heat the cooking liquid before adding the rice to it. For other grains such as bulgur and couscous, where the cooking liquid should be boiled first, the liquid can be heated in the microwave before it is combined with the grain.

Nourishing breakfasts can be made instantly in the microwave with quick-cooking grains. Try Breakfast Porridge: for each serving, pour 150 ml water into 1 litre microwave-safe measuring jug or a cereal bowl; heat on High (100% power) for 1½ (1:30)–2 minutes, until boiling. Stir in 25 g quick-cooking porridge oats and a pinch of salt. Cook on High for 1–2 minutes, until mixture thickens; stir well. If you like, stir in 2 tablespoons strawberry or apricot jam. Stir well and serve immediately.

Nuts can be blanched, peeled and toasted in the microwave. On page 294 you will find easy-to-follow instructions for these techniques, plus quick-cooking ideas for a delicious variety of nuts flavoured with spices, herbs and seasonings.

ATTRACTIVELY MOULDED RICE

Moulded rice always looks attractive and is so easy to prepare. Use large moulds or rings for parties, small moulds for individual servings. Lightly oil moulds and fill with Hot Cooked Rice (page 293), gently pressing down. Turn out on to an attractive plate or platter. Serve hot or chilled.

Saffron-flavoured rice ring (left) *filled with chopped cooked ham and cherry tomatoes; garnished with mixed salad leaves.*

White and wild rice moulded together in ramekin (right). *Here with poached salmon garnished with mayonnaise and dill, lemon slices and mixed salad leaves.*

Pasta Shapes

Pasta is available in a wide variety of shapes, sizes and colours. Italian delicatessens often have a large selection of the more unusual and hard-to-find types. Teamed with a quick microwave sauce, pasta makes a fast and nutritious meal for any occasion.

Fusilli: *spirals or coils of various lengths*

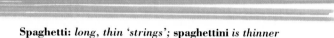

Spaghetti: *long, thin 'strings';* **spaghettini** *is thinner*

Wholewheat spaghetti: *made from wholewheat flour*

Cappelletti: *small hat-shaped pasta*

Small Pasta Shapes: *letters, shells, bows, stars and animals; for soups and children's dishes*

Linguine: *thin, flat ribbon noodles*

Tagliatelle/Fettuccine: *flat ribbon noodles, about 5 mm wide*

Lasagne: *extra wide noodles, sometimes with ruffled edges*

Egg noodles: *flat noodles wider than tagliatelle/fettuccine, available in white or green*

Shells: *shell shapes in various sizes; extra-large shells can be stuffed*

Cannelloni: *large smooth tubes for stuffing; sometimes available ridged*

Rotelle or Corkscrews: *short spiral, coil or spring shapes*

Wheels: *cartwheel or wagon-wheel shapes*

Penne: *short tubular 'quills' with angled ends*

Farfalle: *bow tie or butterfly shapes*

Rigatoni: *short-cut, straight, ridged tubes*

Main Course Pasta

SPAGHETTI BOLOGNESE

Colour Index page 80. 560 cals per serving. Good source of vitamin A, riboflavin, thiamine, niacin, vitamin C, iron. Begin 25 minutes ahead.

Ingredients	For 4	For 2	For 1
Carrot, chopped	1 carrot	1/2 carrot	1/4 carrot
Water	2 tablespoons	1 tablespoon	2 teaspoons
Minced beef	350 g	175 g	75 g
Mushrooms, cut into quarters	115 g	50 g	25 g
Small onion, chopped	1 onion	1/2 onion	1/4 onion
Small courgette, chopped	1 courgette	1/2 courgette	1/4 courgette
Garlic clove, crushed	1 clove	to taste	to taste
Canned tomatoes	1 × 400 g can	1 × 225 g can	1/2 × 225 g can
Tomato purée	4 tablespoons	2 tablespoons	1 tablespoon
Dried basil	1/2 teaspoon	1/4 teaspoon	to taste
Dry red wine (optional)	2 tablespoons	1 tablespoon	1 1/2 teaspoons
Salt and pepper	to taste	to taste	to taste
Spaghetti or other pasta	225 g	115 g	50 g
Parsley	garnish	garnish	garnish
Microwave cookware	3 litre soufflé dish	2 litre soufflé dish	1 litre soufflé dish
Time on High (100% power)			
Carrot	3–5 minutes	2–3 minutes	1–2 minutes
With minced beef	4–6 minutes	3–4 minutes	2–3 minutes
With tomatoes	8–10 minutes	6–7 minutes	4–5 minutes

1 In soufflé dish (see Chart), place carrot and water. Cook, covered, on High for time in Chart, or until carrot is tender. Drain.

2 To carrot, add minced beef, mushrooms, onion, courgette and garlic; stir. Cook, covered, on High for time in Chart, or until meat just loses its pink colour, stirring twice.

3 To vegetable and meat mixture, add tomatoes with their liquid, tomato purée and basil. If you like, add wine. Season with salt and pepper. Stir well.

4 Cook sauce on High for time in Chart, until sauce bubbles, stirring often.

5 Meanwhile, cook pasta conventionally according to instructions on packet; drain.

6 To serve: place pasta on warmed dinner plates; ladle sauce over. Garnish.

PENNE WITH CHEESE, RED PEPPER AND OLIVE SAUCE

Colour Index page 80. 4 servings. 589 cals per serving. Good source of vitamin A, thiamine, vitamin C, calcium, iron. Begin 20 minutes ahead.

2 onions, thinly sliced
2 large red peppers, very thinly sliced
60 ml olive or vegetable oil
225 g penne or other pasta
115 g mozzarella cheese, cut into 5 mm cubes
115 g Fontina or Cheddar cheese, grated
75 g stoned black olives, cut in half
4 tablespoons shredded basil leaves or finely chopped parsley
Salt and pepper to taste

1. In 30 × 20 cm microwave-safe baking dish, combine onions, red peppers and oil. Cook, covered, on High (100% power) for 10–12 minutes, until vegetables are tender, stirring twice.
2. Meanwhile, cook pasta conventionally according to instructions on packet; drain.
3. Toss pasta and vegetable mixture together with cheeses, olives, basil or parsley, salt and pepper. Serve immediately.

TAGLIATELLE WITH BACON, MUSHROOMS AND PEAS

Colour Index page 80. 4 servings. 581 cals per serving. Good source of vitamin A, riboflavin, thiamine, niacin, calcium, iron, fibre. Begin 25 minutes ahead.

4 rashers rindless streaky bacon, diced
115 g mushrooms, cut into halves
2 spring onions, sliced
2 tablespoons plain flour
250 ml single cream
250 ml milk
1/4 teaspoon salt
1/4 teaspoon pepper
225 g tagliatelle or other pasta
275 g frozen peas, defrosted
50 g Parmesan cheese, grated

1. In 3 litre microwave-safe casserole, place bacon. Cook, covered with kitchen paper, on High (100% power) for 4–5 minutes, until browned, stirring halfway through cooking. With slotted spoon, transfer to kitchen paper to drain.
2. To bacon fat, add mushrooms and spring onions. Cook on High for 2 minutes. Stir in flour until smooth and blended. Gradually stir in cream and milk. Season with salt and pepper. Cook, covered, on High for 8–10 minutes, until sauce thickens, stirring often. Meanwhile, cook pasta conventionally according to instructions on packet.
3. Into sauce, stir peas. Cook, covered, on High for 1–2 minutes, until hot.
4. Drain pasta. Toss pasta and sauce together. Transfer to warmed serving dish; sprinkle with Parmesan and diced bacon. Serve immediately.

FETTUCCINE PRIMAVERA

Colour Index page 81. 4 servings. 726 cals per serving. Good source of vitamin A, riboflavin, thiamine, niacin, vitamin C, calcium, iron, fibre. Begin 40 minutes ahead.

3 small leeks, trimmed	*225 g fettuccine or other*
30 g butter or margarine	*pasta*
450 g broccoli	*2 tablespoons plain flour*
8 mushrooms, sliced	*500 ml half cream*
2 courgettes, cut into	*2 tomatoes, diced*
5 mm thick slices	*175 g Fontina or mild*
2 medium peppers	*Cheddar cheese,*
(green and red), cut	*grated*
into 1 cm chunks	*Salt and pepper to taste*
2 carrots, cut into 5 mm	
thick slices	

1. Cut leeks in half lengthways; carefully wash under cold running water. Cut into 2.5 cm pieces.
2. In 3 litre microwave-safe casserole, place butter or margarine and leeks. Cook, covered, on High (100% power) for 3–4 minutes, until softened, stirring twice.
3. With sharp knife, trim woody stalk ends from broccoli. Separate florets from stalks; peel stalks and slice. Stir broccoli and next 4 ingredients into leeks. Cook, covered, on High for 8–10 minutes, until vegetables are tender-crisp, stirring twice. Meanwhile, cook pasta according to instructions on packet.
4. In medium microwave-safe bowl, place flour. Gradually stir in cream until smooth. Cook on High for 5–7 minutes, until sauce bubbles and thickens, stirring occasionally.
5. Drain pasta. To vegetables, add pasta, tomatoes, cheese and sauce; toss. Cook on High for 3–5 minutes, until hot, stirring twice. Season.

CHEESE TORTELLONI WITH BROCCOLI AND PINE NUTS

Colour Index page 80. 8 servings. 307 cals per serving. Low in cholesterol. Good source of vitamin A, riboflavin, thiamine, niacin, vitamin C, calcium, iron, fibre. Begin 25 minutes ahead.

700 g broccoli	*450 g fresh or frozen*
80 ml olive oil	*cheese-filled tortelloni*
25 g pine nuts	*25 g Parmesan cheese,*
2 garlic cloves, crushed	*grated*
1/4 teaspoon dried hot	*Salt to taste*
red pepper flakes	
(optional)	

1. Trim woody stalk ends from broccoli. Separate florets from stalks; peel stalks and slice.
2. In 30 × 20 cm microwave-safe baking dish, combine broccoli and next 4 ingredients. Cook, covered, on High (100% power) for 6–9 minutes, until broccoli is tender-crisp, stirring twice.
3. Meanwhile, cook pasta conventionally according to instructions on packet; drain. In warmed large bowl, lightly toss pasta, broccoli, Parmesan and salt.

You can make colourful and delicious combinations of your favourite fresh vegetables and pasta shapes in the microwave. In the recipe for Chicken and Vegetable Pasta (below), pasta spirals or shells can be used instead of farfalle.

CHICKEN AND VEGETABLE PASTA

Colour Index page 81. 499 cals per serving. Good source of vitamin A, riboflavin, thiamine, niacin, vitamin C, calcium, iron, fibre. Begin 35 minutes ahead.

Ingredients for 4 servings		Microwave cookware
450 g chicken breasts, skinned and boned	*175 ml water*	*3 litre casserole*
450 g broccoli	*225 g mushrooms, cut into halves*	
80 ml soy sauce	*4 spring onions, cut into*	
2 tablespoons cornflour, dissolved in 2 tablespoons sherry	*2.5 cm pieces*	
	175 g radishes, sliced	
	225 g farfalle (bow ties) or other pasta	
2 tablespoons sesame or vegetable oil		
1 garlic clove, crushed		
1/2 teaspoon ground ginger		

1 With sharp knife, cut chicken crossways into thin strips; set aside. Trim woody stalk ends from broccoli. Separate florets from stalks; peel stalks and slice. Set aside.

2 In casserole, combine soy sauce, dissolved cornflour, oil, garlic, ginger and water. Cook on High (100% power) for 5 minutes, or until sauce thickens, stirring halfway through cooking.

3 To sauce, add broccoli, mushrooms and spring onions; stir to coat. Cook, covered, on High for 5–7 minutes, until vegetables are tender-crisp, stirring halfway through cooking.

4 Into vegetable mixture, stir chicken and radishes. Cook, covered, on High for 3–4 minutes, until chicken is fork-tender, stirring halfway through cooking.

5 Meanwhile, cook pasta conventionally according to instructions on packet; drain and transfer to warmed large bowl.

6 *To serve:* add chicken and vegetables to pasta and toss to mix. Serve immediately.

Layered Dishes and Sauces

Save on preparation, cooking and washing up by using the microwave for cooking the sauce and the top of the stove for cooking the pasta. The microwave Lasagne (below) is a sumptuous Italian-style dish: rich, meat-based sauce layered with ricotta and mozzarella cheeses and pasta.

LASAGNE

Colour Index page 83. 281 cals per serving. Good source of vitamin A, riboflavin, thiamine, niacin, calcium, iron. Begin 1³/₄ hours ahead.

Ingredients for 10 servings		Microwave cookware
450 g minced beef 2 × 450 g jars sauce for pasta (without meat) ¹/₂ × 175 g can tomato purée 450 g ricotta cheese 2 eggs 300 g lasagne (about 14 sheets)	450 g mozzarella cheese, thinly sliced 50 g Parmesan cheese, grated	2 litre soufflé dish 32.5 × 22.5 cm baking dish

1 In soufflé dish, place minced beef. Cook on High (100% power) for 5–7 minutes, until meat just loses its pink colour, stirring occasionally.

2 Into minced beef, stir pasta sauce and tomato purée until blended. Cook, covered, on High for 5–7 minutes, until boiling, stirring occasionally. Uncover and cook on High for 5–7 minutes longer.

3 Meanwhile, in mixing bowl, beat ricotta and eggs until smooth. Cook pasta conventionally according to instructions on packet; drain.

4 Cover bottom of baking dish with one-third of meat sauce. Arrange one-third of pasta over sauce, overlapping if necessary. Top with one-third of ricotta mixture and one-third of mozzarella. Repeat layers twice, finishing with mozzarella.

5 Cook lasagne, covered, on Medium (50% power) for 25–35 minutes, until cheese melts and meat sauce bubbles, rotating dish halfway through cooking. Allow lasagne to stand, covered loosely with foil, on heatproof surface for 15–20 minutes.

6 Uncover lasagne. With spoon, sprinkle top of lasagne evenly with Parmesan. Serve hot on warmed dinner plates.

CANNELLONI WITH SPINACH AND MUSHROOMS

Colour Index page 83. 4 servings. 630 cals per serving. Good source of vitamin A, riboflavin, thiamine, niacin, vitamin C, calcium, iron, fibre. Begin 1¹/₄ hours ahead.

2 tablespoons vegetable oil 2 garlic cloves, finely chopped 150 g mushrooms, sliced 575 g frozen chopped spinach, defrosted 225 g cream cheese Salt, grated nutmeg and cayenne pepper to taste	8 sheets lasagne, cooked 500 ml Creamy Tomato Sauce (below) or Basic White Sauce (page 381) Parsley sprigs to garnish

1. In 32.5 × 22.5 cm microwave-safe baking dish, place oil, garlic and mushrooms. Cook, covered, on High (100% power) for 2–3 minutes, until mushrooms are tender, stirring twice.
2. Squeeze spinach to remove excess moisture. Stir into mushroom mixture. Cook on High for 5–7 minutes, stirring twice. Stir in cream cheese until well blended. Season with salt, nutmeg and cayenne pepper. Transfer spinach mixture to mixing bowl.
3. With sharp knife, cut each lasagne sheet crossways in half. Spread 2 tablespoons spinach mixture on each half sheet. Roll up sheets Swiss roll fashion.
4. In same baking dish, arrange rolls, seam side down, in single layer. Pour tomato or white sauce over rolls. Cook, covered, on High for 5 minutes. Reduce power level to Medium (50% power) and cook for 10–15 minutes longer, until sauce bubbles, rotating dish halfway through cooking. Allow to stand, loosely covered, on heatproof surface for 10 minutes. Garnish with parsley and serve immediately.

CREAMY TOMATO SAUCE

Colour Index page 80. Makes 500 ml. 246 cals per 250 ml. Begin 20 minutes ahead.

³/₄ × 400 g can chopped tomatoes 120 ml double or whipping cream ¹/₂ teaspoon dried oregano	1 tablespoon shredded basil leaves or 1¹/₂ teaspoons dried 2 garlic cloves, crushed Salt and pepper to taste

1. In 2 litre microwave-safe jug or bowl, combine tomatoes, cream, oregano, basil and garlic.
2. Cook sauce on High (100% power) for 10–15 minutes, until sauce thickens slightly and flavours blend, stirring occasionally. Season with salt and pepper. Serve hot over pasta of your choice.

CHEESE-FILLED JUMBO SHELLS

Colour Index page 81. 4 servings. 316 cals per serving. Good source of vitamin A, calcium. Begin 55 minutes ahead.

450 g jumbo pasta shells (about 20 shells)	1 egg
450 g ricotta cheese	15 g parsley, chopped
115 g mozzarella cheese, grated	Salt and pepper to taste
25 g Parmesan cheese, grated	1 × 450 g jar sauce for pasta (without meat)
	Chopped parsley and grated Parmesan cheese to garnish

1. Cook pasta conventionally according to instructions on packet. Drain immediately under warm running water to stop cooking (cold water causes shells to break); drain again.
2. In large bowl, combine ricotta, mozzarella, Parmesan, egg and chopped parsley. Season with salt and pepper.
3. With spoon, fill each shell with equal amount of cheese mixture. Into 32.5 × 22.5 cm microwave-safe baking dish, pour half of pasta sauce. Arrange shells, filled side up, in single layer in dish. Pour remaining sauce over shells. Cook, covered, on High (100% power) for 5 minutes. Reduce power level to Medium (50% power) and cook for 10–15 minutes longer, until sauce bubbles, rotating dish halfway through cooking. Allow to stand, loosely covered, on heatproof surface for 10 minutes before serving.
4. *To serve:* on warmed serving platter, arrange filled shells; spoon over sauce. Garnish with chopped parsley and grated Parmesan cheese. Serve immediately.

MADE-IN-MINUTES BOLOGNESE SAUCE

Colour Index page 80. Makes 1.5 litres. 410 cals per 250 ml. Begin 25 minutes ahead.

450 g minced beef	4 tablespoons tomato purée
115 g mushrooms, sliced	
1 onion, chopped	1/2 teaspoon dried basil
1 garlic clove, crushed	1/2 teaspoon dried thyme
2 × 400 g cans tomatoes	1/4 teaspoon salt
1 teaspoon sugar	

1. In large microwave-safe bowl, place minced beef, mushrooms, onion and garlic. Cook on High (100% power) for 5 minutes, or until meat just loses its pink colour, stirring occasionally.
2. Into meat mixture, stir tomatoes with liquid, sugar, tomato purée, basil, thyme and salt. Cook, covered, on High for 8 minutes, stirring occasionally. Reduce power level to Medium (50% power) and cook for 10 minutes longer, stirring occasionally. Serve hot over pasta of your choice.

Vary the fillings for large pasta shells or tubes. Instead of the usual cheese or tomato fillings, try minced beef or veal, as in the recipe for Cannelloni Milanese (below). These can make a substantial evening meal served with a crunchy mixed salad.

CANNELLONI MILANESE

Colour Index page 83. 839 cals per serving. Good source of riboflavin, thiamine, niacin, calcium, iron. Begin 1 1/2 hours ahead.

Ingredients for 4 servings		Microwave cookware
1 tablespoon olive oil	1 tablespoon tomato purée	32.5 × 22.5 cm baking dish
1 onion, chopped	70 g currants	
2 celery sticks, chopped	30 g pine nuts	
225 g minced beef	225 g cannelloni tubes	
225 g minced veal	500 ml Basic White Sauce (page 381) or Creamy Tomato Sauce (page 288)	
1 teaspoon dried oregano		
1 teaspoon dried basil	50 g Parmesan cheese, grated	
1 bay leaf	Basil leaves to garnish	
1 × 225 g can chopped tomatoes		

1 In baking dish, combine oil, onion and celery. Cook, covered, on High (100% power) for 3–4 minutes, until vegetables are soft, stirring halfway through cooking.

2 Into vegetables, stir minced beef and veal. Cook on High for 8–10 minutes, until meat just loses its pink colour, stirring occasionally. Stir in oregano, basil, bay, tomatoes, tomato purée, currants and pine nuts. Cook on High for 10–15 minutes, stirring occasionally.

3 Meanwhile, cook pasta conventionally according to instructions on packet. Drain under warm running water to stop cooking; drain again; cover and keep warm. From meat mixture, discard cooking juices; transfer meat mixture to mixing bowl.

4 With spoon, fill each cannelloni tube with equal amount of meat mixture. In baking dish used for cooking meat mixture, arrange tubes in single layer.

5 Over tubes, pour white or tomato sauce. Cook, covered, on High for 5 minutes. Reduce power level to Medium (50% power) and cook for 10–15 minutes longer, until sauce bubbles, rotating dish once.

6 Over cannelloni, sprinkle Parmesan. Allow to stand on heatproof surface, loosely covered, for 10–15 minutes. Garnish with basil just before serving.

Main Course Rice

ARROZ CON POLLO

Colour Index page 82. 644 cals per serving. Good source of thiamine, niacin, vitamin C, iron. Begin 55 minutes ahead.

Ingredients	For 4	For 2	For 1
Olive or vegetable oil	4 tablespoons	2 tablespoons	1 tablespoon
Onion, chopped	1 large	1 small	½ small
Celery sticks, chopped	2 sticks	1 stick	½ stick
Green pepper, chopped	1 large	1 small	½ small
Smoked ham, chopped	115 g	50 g	25 g
Turmeric	½ teaspoon	¼ teaspoon	¼ teaspoon
Long-grain rice	175 g	90 g	45 g
Chicken Stock (page 125) or stock from a cube	500 ml	250 ml	120 ml
Bay leaf	1 leaf	½ leaf	to taste
Chicken pieces	700 g	350 g	150 g
Plain flour	70 g	70 g	45 g
Salt	to taste	to taste	to taste
Canned pimiento and parsley	garnish	garnish	garnish
Microwave cookware	32.5 × 22.5 cm baking dish	22.5 cm square baking dish	20 cm square baking dish
Time on High (100% power) Chicken and rice	5 minutes	4 minutes	2½ (2:30) minutes
Time on Medium (50% power) Chicken and rice	25–30 minutes	10–15 minutes	7–10 minutes
Standing time	5 minutes	5 minutes	3 minutes

1 In frying pan, combine half of oil and next 5 ingredients. Stir-fry for 2 minutes.

2 In baking dish, place vegetable and ham mixture, rice, stock and bay leaf; stir.

3 Coat chicken in flour. In remaining oil in frying pan, cook chicken 5 minutes, until browned.

4 With tongs, place chicken pieces on top of vegetable and rice mixture in baking dish.

5 Cook, covered tightly with cling film, on High for time in Chart, or until stock boils. Reduce power to Medium and cook for time in Chart; turn chicken once.

6 On heatproof surface, allow to stand, covered, for time in Chart, or until liquid is absorbed and rice is tender. Add salt. Garnish just before serving.

SAUSAGE, RICE AND BEANS

Colour Index page 83. 4 servings. 562 cals per serving. Good source of thiamine, niacin, calcium, iron, fibre. Begin 35 minutes ahead.

225 g fresh pork sausages with herbs
1 onion, sliced
2 garlic cloves, crushed
1 × 425 g can red kidney beans, drained and rinsed
1 × 400 g can chopped tomatoes
½ beef stock cube
1 teaspoon dried oregano
800 g Hot Cooked Rice (page 293)
25 g Parmesan cheese, grated
Basil leaves to garnish

1. With sharp knife, cut sausages into 4 cm pieces; place in 30 × 20 cm microwave-safe baking dish. Cook, covered with kitchen paper, on High (100% power) for 5 minutes, until meat is no longer pink, stirring occasionally. Add onion and garlic. Cook on High for 2–3 minutes, until onion is hot, stirring halfway through cooking.
2. To sausage mixture, add beans, tomatoes, stock cube and oregano; stir. Cook, covered, on Medium (50% power) for 10–15 minutes, until mixture bubbles, stirring occasionally. Stir in rice. Cook on High for 3–5 minutes, until hot. Just before serving, stir in Parmesan; garnish.

CHINESE-STYLE RICE WITH PORK

Colour Index page 82. 4 servings. 393 cals per serving. Good source of thiamine, iron. Begin 35 minutes ahead.

225 g boneless pork loin, cut into 2.5 cm cubes
1 onion, chopped
1 celery stick, sliced
1 medium red pepper, chopped
1 tablespoon groundnut or vegetable oil
175 g long-grain rice
500 ml Beef Stock (page 125) or stock from a cube
2 tablespoons soy sauce
2 garlic cloves, crushed
1 tablespoon finely chopped peeled root ginger
Dash of Tabasco sauce
4 tablespoons chopped fresh coriander or parsley

1. In 30 × 20 cm microwave-safe baking dish, combine pork, onion, celery, red pepper and oil. Cook on High (100% power) for 3–5 minutes, until meat is no longer pink, stirring twice.
2. Into meat mixture, stir rice and stock. Cook, covered tightly with microwave cling film, on High for 5 minutes. Reduce power level to Medium (50% power) and cook for 20–25 minutes longer, until liquid is absorbed and rice is tender.
3. Meanwhile, in mixing bowl, combine soy sauce, garlic, root ginger, Tabasco sauce and chopped coriander or parsley. Pour over hot rice, mix well and serve immediately.

MILANESE-STYLE RISOTTO

Colour Index page 81. 4 servings. 333 cals per serving. Good source of calcium, iron. Begin 40 minutes ahead.

30 g butter or margarine	Pinch of powdered
1 onion, finely chopped	saffron
2 garlic cloves, crushed	150 g frozen peas,
230 g arborio rice	defrosted
500 ml Chicken Stock	50 g Parmesan cheese,
(page 125) or stock	grated
from a cube	Salt and pepper to taste
2 tablespoons lemon	Basil leaves to garnish
juice	

1. In 30 × 20 cm microwave-safe baking dish, place butter or margarine, onion and garlic. Cook on High (100% power) for 2–3 minutes, until onion softens, stirring twice. Add rice; stir to coat. Cook on High for 3 minutes, stirring twice.
2. Into rice mixture, stir stock, lemon juice and saffron. Cook, loosely covered, on High for 15–20 minutes.
3. Into risotto, stir peas. Cook, loosely covered, on High for 2–3 minutes. Stir in Parmesan; season with salt and pepper. Allow to stand, covered, on heatproof surface for 5 minutes, until most of liquid is absorbed. Risotto should be creamy, not dry; rice should be *al dente* (tender yet firm to the bite). Serve hot, garnished with basil.

RED BEANS AND RICE

Colour Index page 82. 4 servings. 534 cals per serving. Low in cholesterol. Good source of thiamine, calcium, iron, fibre. Begin 40 minutes ahead.

3 rashers rindless	2 tablespoons tomato
streaky bacon, diced	purée
1 onion, diced	2 × 425 g cans red
1 celery stick, diced	kidney beans, drained
1 bay leaf	and rinsed
1 teaspoon ground	Tabasco sauce to taste
cumin	800 g Hot Cooked Rice
1 teaspoon dried	(page 293)
oregano	Parsley sprigs to
1/4 teaspoon cayenne	garnish
pepper	

1. In 30 × 20 cm microwave-safe baking dish, place bacon. Cook, covered with kitchen paper, on High (100% power) for 3–4 minutes, until bacon is browned, stirring twice. With slotted spoon, transfer bacon to kitchen paper to drain.
2. Into bacon fat, stir onion and next 5 ingredients. Cook on High for 3–4 minutes, until vegetables soften, stirring twice.
3. Into vegetables, stir tomato purée and kidney beans. Cook on Medium (50% power) for 10–15 minutes, until mixture thickens slightly, stirring occasionally. Add Tabasco sauce.
4. *To serve:* on warmed dinner plates, ladle bean mixture over rice; sprinkle with diced bacon. Garnish with parsley.

SAVOURY RICE

Colour Index page 81. 398 cals per serving. Good source of vitamin A, calcium, iron. Begin 45 minutes ahead.

Ingredients	For 4	For 2	For 1
Butter or margarine	30 g	15 g	2 teaspoons
Onion, chopped	1 medium	1 small	1/2 small
Green pepper, chopped	1 medium	1 small	1/2 small
Long-grain rice	175 g	90 g	45 g
Chicken Stock (page 125) or stock from a cube	500 ml	250 ml	120 ml
Cheddar or Fontina cheese, grated	115 g	50 g	25 g
Soured cream	120 ml	60 ml	2 tablespoons
Salt and pepper	to taste	to taste	to taste
Parsley or coriander sprigs	garnish	garnish	garnish
Microwave cookware	30 × 20 cm baking dish	20 cm square baking dish	20 cm square baking dish
Time on High (100% power)			
Butter or margarine	45 seconds	30–45 seconds	30 seconds
With vegetables and rice	3–4 minutes	2–3 minutes	1–2 minutes
With stock	5 minutes	4 minutes	2 minutes
Time on Medium (50% power)			
Vegetables, rice and stock	15–20 minutes	10–12 minutes	7–10 minutes
With cheese	2–3 minutes	2 minutes	1 1/2 (1:30) minutes

1 In baking dish (see Chart), place butter or margarine. Heat, covered, on High for time in Chart, or until melted.

2 To melted butter or margarine, add onion, green pepper and rice; stir to coat.

3 Cook, covered tightly with microwave cling film, on High for time in Chart, or until vegetables soften, stirring once.

4 Into vegetables and rice, pour stock; stir. Cook, covered tightly with cling film, on High for time in Chart, or until rice mixture boils.

5 Reduce power level to Medium and cook for time in Chart, or until liquid is absorbed and rice is tender.

6 Into rice mixture, stir cheese and soured cream. Season. Cook, covered, on Medium for time in Chart. Garnish.

Meal in Minutes *for 8 people*

Simple Spaghetti Supper

Salami and pepper platter
Spaghetti Bolognese, page 286, for 8
Tossed green salad
Garlic Bread, page 308 (double quantity)
Gorgonzola cheese and crackers
Neapolitan ice cream and fan wafers (bought)

PREPARATION TIMETABLE	
Early in day	*Prepare Spaghetti Bolognese up to end of step 4, in 2 batches. Cover sauce and refrigerate. Prepare salad ingredients: store in polythene bags in refrigerator. Prepare salad dressing of your choice.*
45 minutes ahead	*Prepare Garlic Bread but do not cook; wrap in kitchen paper and set aside. Arrange selection of sliced salami and fresh peppers on serving platter. Place Gorgonzola on serving platter with crackers and cover until required.*
Just before serving	*Cook spaghetti conventionally. Meanwhile, reheat Bolognese sauce on High (100% power) until bubbling. Drain spaghetti: place on warmed dinner plates and ladle over sauce; garnish. Heat Garlic Bread in microwave. Place salad ingredients in bowl and toss with dressing.*

Pilafs

INDIAN PILAF

Colour Index page 82. 4 servings. 383 cals per serving. Good source of iron.
Begin 45 minutes ahead.

30 g butter or margarine	*500 ml Chicken Stock*
1 onion, diced	*(page 125) or stock*
2 garlic cloves, crushed	*from a cube*
1 teaspoon ground	*4 tablespoons chopped*
cumin	*fresh coriander or*
1 teaspoon ground	*parsley*
coriander	*45 g flaked almonds*
175 g long-grain rice	*Coriander sprigs to*
35 g seedless raisins	*garnish*

1. In 30×20 cm microwave-safe baking dish, place butter or margarine. Heat, covered with kitchen paper, on High (100% power) for 45 seconds, or until melted.
2. To butter or margarine, add onion, garlic and ground spices; stir. Cook, covered, on High for 3–4 minutes, until onion softens, stirring twice. Stir in rice. Cook, covered, on High for 2 minutes.
3. Into rice, stir raisins and stock. Cook, covered tightly with microwave cling film, on High for 5 minutes. Reduce power level to Medium (50% power) and cook for 20 minutes longer, or until liquid is absorbed and rice is tender. Add chopped coriander or parsley; stir. Allow to stand, loosely covered, on heatproof surface 5 minutes.
4. Meanwhile, in shallow microwave-safe pie dish, place almonds. Heat on High for $2–2^{1}/_{2}$ (2:30) minutes, until browned, stirring twice.
5. *To serve:* transfer pilaf to warmed serving platter. Top with almonds and garnish.

WILD RICE AND MUSHROOM PILAF

Colour Index page 83. 4 servings. 236 cals per serving. Good source of iron.
Begin $1^{1}/_{4}$ hours ahead.

750 ml water	*115 g mushrooms, sliced*
1 chicken stock cube	*$^{1}/_{4}$ teaspoon poultry*
160 g wild rice	*seasoning*
45 g butter or margarine	*Salt to taste*
1 onion, chopped	

1. Into 2 litre microwave-safe casserole, pour water. Heat on High (100% power) for 6–8 minutes, until boiling. Stir in stock cube and wild rice. Cook, covered tightly with cling film, on High for 30–40 minutes, until wild rice is tender. Allow to stand, loosely covered, on heatproof surface while preparing mushrooms.
2. In 30×20 cm microwave-safe baking dish, place butter. Heat, covered with kitchen paper, on High for 45 seconds, or until melted. Stir in onion, mushrooms and seasonings. Cook, covered, on High for 5–7 minutes, until vegetables soften, stirring twice. Stir into rice. Cook, covered, on High for 3–5 minutes, stirring twice.

Barley, Bulgur and Cornmeal

BARLEY WITH WILD MUSHROOMS

Colour Index page 83. 4 servings. 260 cals per serving. Low in cholesterol, sodium. Begin 40 minutes ahead.

2 tablespoons vegetable oil	7 g dried wild mushrooms, broken into 1 cm pieces
200 g pearl barley	
750 ml Beef Stock (page 125) or stock from a cube	Salt to taste
	Parsley sprigs to garnish

1. In 2 litre microwave-safe casserole, place oil and barley. Cook, covered, on High (100% power) for 5 minutes, stirring twice.
2. To barley, add stock and wild mushrooms; stir to mix well. Cook, covered, on High for 20–30 minutes, until liquid is absorbed and barley is tender, stirring occasionally. Season and garnish.

BULGUR PILAF WITH PEPPERS

Colour Index page 82. 8 servings. 139 cals per serving. Low in cholesterol, sodium. Good source of vitamin C, iron. Begin 45 minutes ahead.

750 ml Chicken Stock (page 125) or stock from a cube	3 medium peppers (green, yellow, red), cut into 1 cm chunks
160 g bulgur (cracked wheat)	Salt to taste
2 tablespoons olive or vegetable oil	2 tablespoons shredded basil leaves
2 garlic cloves, crushed	
8 mushrooms, sliced	

1. Into 1 litre microwave-safe measuring jug, pour stock. Heat on High (100% power) for 5–7 minutes, until boiling. In mixing bowl, place bulgur; pour boiling stock over bulgur. Allow to stand, covered, on heatproof surface 30 minutes.
2. Meanwhile, in 30 × 20 cm microwave-safe baking dish, combine oil, garlic, mushrooms and green, yellow and red peppers. Cook on High for 8–10 minutes, until vegetables are tender, stirring occasionally.
3. Drain bulgur well, squeezing out excess moisture. Stir into pepper and mushroom mixture; add salt. Cook, covered, on High for 4–5 minutes, until hot. Stir in basil. Serve hot or cover and refrigerate to serve chilled later.

MAKING HOT COOKED RICE

To make 400 g Hot Cooked Rice in microwave: in large microwave-safe bowl, combine **140 g long-grain rice, 280 ml water** and **¼ teaspoon salt**. Cook, covered, on High (100% power) for 5 minutes. Reduce power level to Medium (50% power) and cook for 15–20 minutes longer, until liquid is absorbed and rice is tender.

Treat your family to a change with cornmeal, finely ground corn that can be white or yellow and is also called polenta and maize meal. Yellow cornmeal is used in the recipe for Polenta with Meat Sauce (below). After cooking, present it in a variety of ways by cutting it with crescent-shaped, star-shaped or heart-shaped cutters, before topping it with Made-in-Minutes Bolognese Sauce.

POLENTA WITH MEAT SAUCE

Colour Index page 83. 612 cals per serving. Good source of vitamin A, niacin, calcium, iron. Begin 50 minutes ahead.

Ingredients for 4 servings		Microwave cookware
1 litre Chicken Stock (page 125) or stock from a cube	Pinch of cayenne pepper	2 litre jug or bowl
190 g polenta (cornmeal)	Salt and pepper to taste	30 cm serving platter
60 g butter or margarine	500 ml Made-in-Minutes Bolognese Sauce (page 289)	
115 g mozzarella cheese, grated	25 g Parmesan cheese, grated	
	Basil leaves to garnish	

1 In jug or bowl, put stock and polenta. Cook on High (100% power) for 12–15 minutes, until very thick, stirring occasionally.

2 To polenta, add butter or margarine, mozzarella, cayenne, salt and pepper; stir. Line 32.5 × 22.5 cm tin with oiled greaseproof.

3 Spread polenta mixture in even layer in tin. Allow to cool while preparing sauce.

4 With biscuit cutter or knife, cut shapes from cooled polenta. Arrange on serving platter.

5 Over polenta, spoon sauce. Cook on High for 7–10 minutes, until both polenta and sauce are hot.

6 *To serve:* sprinkle polenta and sauce with Parmesan; garnish with basil leaves.

Spiced nuts are always a popular appetiser to serve with drinks or at parties. In the microwave oven, they are so quick and easy to make that you can always have some on hand for unexpected guests. Using Bombay Mixed Nuts (below) as a guide, you can vary the flavours depending on what nuts and spices you have.

BOMBAY MIXED NUTS

Colour Index page 38. Makes 350 g. 70 cals per tablespoon. Low in cholesterol. Begin 25 minutes ahead.

350 g unsalted mixed nuts	*1½ teaspoons ground cumin*
1 tablespoon vegetable oil	*½ teaspoon ground coriander*
1 tablespoon chilli powder	*1 teaspoon sea salt*

1. In 22.5 cm square microwave-safe baking dish, place nuts and oil; stir to coat with oil. Cook on High (100% power) for 2 minutes.

2. Combine remaining ingredients; add to nuts and toss well to combine. Cook on High for 3 minutes, stirring twice. With slotted spoon, transfer nuts to kitchen paper to drain and cool. Store nuts in airtight container; use within 2 weeks.

Hot Pepper Pecans: prepare as for Bombay Mixed Nuts (left), using *350 g pecan halves* instead of mixed nuts. In step 2, use *4 teaspoons soy sauce* and *¼ teaspoon Tabasco sauce.* Makes 350 g. 75 cals per tablespoon.

Curried Almonds: prepare as for Bombay Mixed Nuts (left), using *450 g blanched whole almonds* instead of mixed nuts. In step 2, use *2 tablespoons curry powder* and *½ teaspoon salt.* Makes 450 g. 66 cals per tablespoon.

Herby Pistachios: prepare as for Bombay Mixed Nuts (left), using *350 g pistachios* instead of mixed nuts. In step 2, use *¼ teaspoon dried thyme* and *¼ teaspoon paprika.* Makes 350 g. 65 cals per tablespoon.

Cashews with Chilli: prepare as for Bombay Mixed Nuts (left), using *350 g unsalted cashews* instead of mixed nuts. In step 2, use *1 tablespoon chilli powder* and *½ teaspoon salt.* Makes 350 g. 66 cals per tablespoon.

Toasting Coconut

In shallow 21.5 cm microwave-safe pie dish, spread *200 g desiccated coconut.* Heat on High (100% power) for 5–6 minutes, until toasted, stirring twice.

Peeling Chestnuts

With sharp knife, slit shells of *120 g chestnuts.* Place in 1 litre microwave-safe measuring jug with *250 ml water.* Heat, covered, on High (100% power) for 2½ (2:30)–4 minutes, until boiling; boil 1 minute longer. Allow to stand for 5–10 minutes. Peel shells and inner skins. Reboil any not open.

Blanching Almonds

Into 1 litre microwave-safe bowl, pour *250 ml water.* Heat on High (100% power) for 3–4 minutes, until boiling. Add *140 g whole shelled almonds.* Heat on High for 1 minute; drain. When cool, rub off skins with fingers or between kitchen paper; dry on paper.

Toasting Nuts

In shallow microwave-safe pie dish, place *75 g shelled nuts.* Heat on High (100% power) for 2½ (2:30)–4 minutes, until lightly browned, stirring occasionally.

Breads and Sandwiches

TEA BREADS · FRUIT-FLAVOURED BUTTERS · SCONES
HOT CHICKEN, TURKEY, PORK AND BEEF SANDWICHES
CREATIVE SANDWICHES · QUICK CANAPÉS
SIMPLE CHEESE SPREADS · HOT CHEESE SANDWICHES · PIZZAS

Breads and Sandwiches

Traditional, hard-crusted breads and rolls cannot be cooked successfully in the microwave, because of its moist heat, but tea breads and scones are suitable for microwave cooking, as this chapter illustrates so well. They are delicious eaten plain, or served with a spread – try sweet Fruit-Flavoured Butters (page 299) or savoury cheese flavoured spreads (page 307). During cooking in the microwave oven, tea breads should be elevated on a microwave-safe trivet or rack, or on a ramekin turned upside down, and loaf dishes should be rotated frequently. Tea breads are done when they spring back if lightly touched with a finger, and when a cocktail stick inserted in the centre comes out clean. They may look paler than when conventionally baked, and may be moist to the touch: any moist spots will dry during standing time in the dish. Sandwiches are popular for almost every meal, from afternoon snacks to hearty one-dish suppers, and in this chapter there is a wide assortment of different shapes, sizes and fillings to choose from,

guaranteed to suit all tastes. A wide range of breads has been used as sandwich bases, including sliced white, wholemeal, French loaves, croissants, pitta breads and bagels, and on page 298 you will find a selection of unusual and interesting breads to experiment with, all of which are widely available in supermarkets.

Most breads reheat successfully in the microwave, if they are wrapped in kitchen paper to absorb moisture. You can also reheat breads and rolls in a straw basket, provided it has no metal parts. A roll or hamburger bun can be reheated in 10–15 seconds on High (100% power), so too can a Danish pastry, but take care when handling the sugar coating as it will be very hot to the touch. Baked goods should be just warmed through or they will become tough.

Use your microwave, too, for defrosting and warming frozen breads and pancakes, taking individual slices or single items from the freezer and defrosting them as needed.

SANDWICHES WITH A DIFFERENCE
Use the microwave to soften Simple Cheese Spreads (page 307) and any other firm fillings, to create sandwiches with a difference for a lunch or light supper. Make pretty open-faced sandwiches with a variety of thinly sliced meats, fish, shellfish or vegetables.

Wholemeal toast triangles (below) topped with Smoked Salmon and Chive Spread and latticed smoked salmon; fresh herbs are used as a garnish.

Wholemeal bread rounds (below) spread with cream cheese and topped with hard-boiled egg slices and prawns; garnished with chervil.

Tortilla chips (above) topped with refried beans, soured cream and taco sauce; garnished with coriander and Lime Twists (page 132).

Rye bread sandwiches (above) filled with cooked ham and Cheddar Cheese Spread; garnished with salad leaves.

Tea Breads

CRANBERRY AND NUT BREAD

Colour Index page 86. 12 servings. 182 cals per serving. Begin 40 minutes ahead.

70 g plain flour	95 g fresh or frozen
85 g digestive biscuits,	cranberries, coarsely
finely crushed	chopped
1/2 teaspoon bicarbonate	1 tablespoon grated
of soda	orange zest
1/2 teaspoon baking	1 egg
powder	120 ml milk
110 g dark brown sugar	80 ml vegetable oil
60 g chopped walnuts	60 ml orange juice

1. Line bottom of 21.5 × 12.5 cm microwave-safe loaf dish with kitchen paper; set aside.
2. In large mixing bowl, combine flour and next 6 ingredients. Stir in zest.
3. In 1 litre measuring jug, whisk egg, milk, oil and orange juice until blended. Into flour mixture, pour egg mixture all at once. Stir just until flour is moistened.
4. Into prepared loaf dish, spoon mixture. Elevate on trivet or rack, or on ramekins turned upside down. Cook, covered loosely with greaseproof paper, on Medium (50% power) for 7–10 minutes, until bread springs back when lightly touched, rotating dish a quarter turn every 2 minutes. Allow bread to stand in dish on heatproof surface for 10 minutes.
5. On to rack, invert bread; carefully remove kitchen paper; turn bread right way up. Cool.

DATE AND WALNUT BREAD

Colour Index page 86. 12 servings. 183 cals per serving. Good source of thiamine, calcium. Begin 45 minutes ahead.

75 g butter or margarine	1 teaspoon ground
75 g soft brown sugar	mixed spice
100 ml milk	1/2 teaspoon salt
1 egg, beaten	100 g chopped dates
100 g plain flour	50 g chopped walnuts
100 g self-raising flour	2 tablespoons amber
1 teaspoon baking	sugar crystals
powder	(optional)

1. Lightly grease 21.5 × 12.5 cm microwave-safe loaf dish. In large mixing bowl, cream butter or margarine and sugar until light and fluffy. Gradually beat in milk and egg.
2. In medium mixing bowl, combine flours, baking powder, spice and salt; fold into creamed mixture. Stir in dates and walnuts.
3. Into prepared loaf dish, spoon batter; smooth top. If you like, sprinkle with sugar crystals. Elevate dish on microwave-safe trivet or rack, or on ramekins turned upside down. Cook, covered loosely with greaseproof paper, on Medium (50% power) for 15–20 minutes, until bread springs back when lightly touched, rotating dish a quarter turn every 2 minutes. Allow bread to stand in dish for 10 minutes. On to rack, invert bread; turn bread right way up. Slice when cool.

Tea breads are traditionally made without yeast, relying on bicarbonate of soda and baking powder to rise. The cranberries in Cranberry and Nut Bread (left) make this an attractive snack when served with pats of butter or margarine, while Courgette Tea Bread (below) makes an unusual teatime or morning coffee treat served with Orange Butter (page 299).

COURGETTE TEA BREAD

Colour Index page 86. 158 cals per serving. Begin 35 minutes ahead.

Ingredients for 12 servings		Microwave cookware
30 g cornflakes	2 tablespoons poppy	21.5 × 12.5 cm
140 g plain flour	seeds	loaf dish
150 g caster sugar	2 eggs	Trivet, rack or
1 1/2 teaspoons baking	80 ml vegetable oil	ramekins
powder	125 g courgette, shredded	
1/2 teaspoon salt	1 teaspoon grated lemon	
60 g chopped walnuts	zest	

1 Line bottom of loaf dish with kitchen paper; set aside. Crumble cornflakes.

2 In large mixing bowl, combine flour, cornflake crumbs, sugar, baking powder, salt, chopped walnuts and poppy seeds.

3 In 1 litre measuring jug, with whisk, beat eggs. Stir in oil, courgette and lemon zest.

4 Into flour mixture, pour courgette mixture all at once. Stir just until flour is moistened.

5 Into prepared loaf dish, spoon batter. Elevate dish on trivet or rack, or on ramekins turned upside down. Cook, covered loosely with greaseproof paper, on Medium (50% power) for 7–10 minutes, until bread springs back when lightly touched, rotating dish a quarter turn every 2 minutes. Allow bread to stand in dish on heatproof surface for 10 minutes.

6 On to rack, invert bread; carefully remove kitchen paper; turn bread right way up. Slice when cool. If you like, wrap in polythene and store in refrigerator for up to 1 week.

There is such a variety of different breads available at the supermarket, that it is difficult to know which to choose. Here is a selection of some of the most attractive, to add interest to your sandwiches and snacks. They can all be heated in the microwave, wrapped in kitchen paper, for a few seconds on High (100% power).

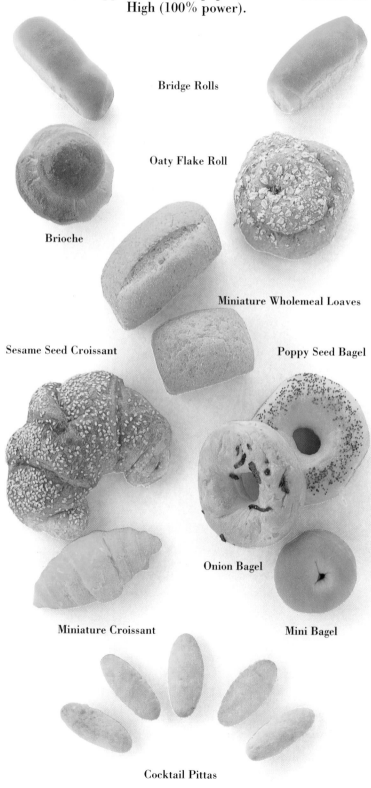

Bridge Rolls

Oaty Flake Roll

Brioche

Miniature Wholemeal Loaves

Sesame Seed Croissant

Poppy Seed Bagel

Onion Bagel

Miniature Croissant

Mini Bagel

Cocktail Pittas

Tea Breads

GINGERBREAD

Colour Index page 86. 12 servings. 188 cals per serving. Good source of calcium, iron. Begin 55 minutes ahead.

100 g plain flour	1 teaspoon ground
50 g self-raising flour	mixed spice
100 g soft brown sugar	115 g butter or
1 teaspoon bicarbonate	margarine
of soda	2 eggs
1 teaspoon ground	75 ml soured cream
ginger	4 tablespoons black
1/2 teaspoon salt	treacle

1. Lightly grease 21.5 × 12.5 cm microwave-safe loaf dish. In bowl, combine first 7 ingredients.
2. In 1 litre microwave-safe measuring jug, place butter or margarine. Heat, covered with kitchen paper, on High (100% power) for 2–3 minutes, just until melted. Cool slightly; beat in eggs, soured cream and treacle.
3. In centre of flour, make well. Pour in egg mixture; stir until blended. Pour into prepared loaf dish and smooth top. Elevate dish on microwave-safe trivet or rack, or on ramekins turned upside down; shield corners with smooth pieces of foil.
4. Cook gingerbread on Medium-High (70% power) for 12–15 minutes, until top springs back when lightly touched, rotating dish a quarter turn every 2 minutes and removing foil halfway through. Allow to stand in dish for 7 minutes. Invert on to rack; turn right way up. Cool.

CARROT AND PINEAPPLE TEA BREAD

Colour Index page 84. 12 servings. 155 cals per serving. Good source of vitamin A, vitamin C. Begin 25 minutes ahead.

100 g butter or	1 teaspoon ground
margarine	ginger
100 g soft brown sugar	2 teaspoons black
2 eggs, beaten	treacle
100 g plain flour	1 × 237 g can crushed
2 teaspoons baking	pineapple, drained
powder	1 carrot, finely grated

1. Lightly grease 21.5 × 12.5 cm microwave-safe loaf dish. In large mixing bowl, cream butter or margarine and sugar until light and fluffy. Gradually beat in eggs.
2. In medium mixing bowl, combine flour, baking powder and ginger; fold into creamed mixture. Stir in remaining ingredients.
3. Into prepared loaf dish, spoon batter; smooth top. Elevate dish on microwave-safe trivet or rack, or on ramekins turned upside down. Cook, covered loosely with greaseproof paper, on Medium (50% power) for 6 minutes. Increase power level to High (100% power) and cook for 6–7 minutes longer, until bread springs back when lightly touched, rotating dish 3–4 times.
4. Allow to stand in dish for 10 minutes. Invert on to rack; turn bread right way up. Cool.

FRUIT-FLAVOURED BUTTERS

These quick-and-easy Fruit-Flavoured Butters, turn simple tea breads into something really special. They can be made in a matter of seconds and taste equally good on breakfast toast too!

To soften butter for Fruit-Flavoured Butters: in small microwave-safe bowl, place *115 g butter.* Heat, covered with kitchen paper, on Medium-Low (30% power) for 30–40 seconds, until the butter has just softened.

Orange Butter: into softened butter (above), stir *grated zest of 1 orange* and *2 tablespoons orange juice.*
8 servings. 108 cals per serving.

Strawberry or Raspberry Butter: into softened butter (above), stir *2 tablespoons strawberry or raspberry jam.*
8 servings. 116 cals per serving.

Cinnamon and Apple Butter: into softened butter (above), stir *2 tablespoons apple sauce or apple and pear spread* and *1/2 teaspoon ground cinnamon.*
8 servings. 109 cals per serving.

Scones rise well and cook quickly in the microwave, so if unexpected guests arrive, it won't take you many minutes to bake a batch of fresh warm scones for a teatime treat. The Savoury Scones (below) look attractive with their different toppings, but you can leave them plain if you don't have the ingredients to hand. To make sweet scones, substitute caster sugar for the grated Parmesan cheese in the mixture and omit the cayenne pepper. If you like, you can add 2 tablespoons sultanas or raisins to the mixture, at the same time as the beaten egg and milk.

SAVOURY SCONES

Colour Index page 84. 158 cals per serving. Good source of thiamine, calcium. Begin 25 minutes ahead.

Ingredients for 14 scones		Microwave cookware
200 g plain wholewheat flour *150 g plain white flour* *4 teaspoons baking powder* *45 g grated Parmesan cheese* *1/2 teaspoon cayenne pepper*	*75 g cold butter or margarine* *175 ml milk* *2 eggs* *poppy seeds* *sesame seeds* *caraway seeds*	30 cm round plate 500 ml measuring jug

1 Line plate with non-stick baking parchment. In large mixing bowl, combine flours, baking powder, Parmesan cheese and cayenne pepper.

2 With 2 round-bladed knives or pastry blender, cut butter or margarine into flour until mixture resembles fine breadcrumbs. Into measuring jug, pour milk. Add 1 egg and beat well to mix.

3 In centre of flour mixture, make well; pour in beaten egg and milk. Mix lightly to form soft dough. Knead on lightly floured surface until smooth; form into ball.

4 On lightly floured surface, roll out dough to 2 cm thickness. Using 5 cm round biscuit cutter, cut out 14 scones, re-rolling dough once. Turn scones upside down so pressed down edges face upwards.

5 Beat remaining egg; brush on top of scones to glaze. Sprinkle 5 scones with poppy seeds, 5 with sesame seeds and 4 with caraway seeds. On lined plate, arrange 7 scones in circle.

6 Cook scones on High (100% power) for 2–3 minutes, until almost dry on top, rotating plate twice. Allow to stand on heatproof surface for 2 minutes; transfer to rack. Repeat with remaining 7 scones. Serve warm or cool.

Hot Chicken and Turkey Sandwiches

Remember that several thin slices of meat or poultry microwave more efficiently than 1 thick slice, so slice meat thinly across the grain, or use pounded cutlets or minced meat, as in the recipes for hearty sandwiches here. Microwave the sandwiches only for the time given – they are best served warm, not hot. Overcooking can also dry out the fillings.

CHICKEN CLUB SANDWICHES

Colour Index page 87. 424 cals per serving. Good source of niacin, iron, fibre. Begin 55 minutes ahead.

Ingredients for 4 servings		Microwave cookware
8 rashers rindless streaky bacon 1 egg, beaten 70 g stuffing mix for chicken 4 chicken breasts, skinned and boned	8 slices wholemeal bread, toasted 4 large lettuce leaves 2 tomatoes, sliced Mayonnaise (optional)	32.5 × 22.5 cm baking dish

1 In baking dish, place bacon rashers. Cook, covered with kitchen paper, on High (100% power) for 8–9 minutes. Transfer to kitchen paper to drain. Discard all but 2 teaspoons bacon fat; let dish cool slightly.

2 Into bacon fat in dish, pour beaten egg. With fork, stir until well mixed; set aside.

3 In food processor with knife blade attached or in blender, process stuffing mix until fine crumbs form. Place stuffing crumbs on greaseproof; set aside.

4 With dull edge of large knife or smooth edge of meat mallet, pound each chicken breast to 5 mm thickness. Cut each crossways in half. Dip chicken breast pieces into egg mixture, then coat in stuffing crumbs.

5 In cleaned baking dish, place coated chicken. Cook, covered loosely with greaseproof, on High for 6–8 minutes, until juices run clear, rearranging pieces halfway through cooking. Allow to stand on heatproof surface for 5 minutes.

6 On 4 slices wholemeal toast, arrange lettuce leaves and tomato slices. Top each slice with 2 pieces chicken and 2 rashers bacon. If you like, top with mayonnaise. Cover with remaining toast slices. Cut each sandwich diagonally into quarters; if you like, secure with cocktail sticks.

HOT TURKEY OPEN SANDWICHES WITH GRAVY

Colour Index page 85. 2 servings. 320 cals per serving. Good source of niacin, iron, fibre. Begin 15 minutes ahead.

15 g butter or margarine
1 tablespoon plain flour
250 ml Chicken Stock (page 125) or stock from a cube
4 drops gravy browning
Salt and pepper to taste
2 slices wholemeal bread, toasted
225 g cooked turkey meat, thinly sliced

1. In 1 litre microwave-safe measuring jug, place butter or margarine. Heat on High (100% power) for 30–45 seconds, until melted.
2. To melted butter or margarine, add flour. Stir until blended. Gradually stir in stock until smooth. Cook on High for 4–6 minutes, until gravy boils and thickens, stirring occasionally. Stir in gravy browning. Season gravy with salt and pepper.
3. On 2 microwave-safe dinner plates, arrange toast. Top with equal amounts of turkey; pour over gravy. Cook on High for 2-3 minutes, until turkey is warm.

SMOKED TURKEY AND GRUYERE ON CROISSANTS

Colour Index page 84. 4 servings. 408 cals per serving. Good source of niacin, calcium. Begin 10 minutes ahead.

4 croissants
225 g smoked turkey or chicken, thinly sliced
1 large tomato, thinly sliced
225 g Gruyère cheese, thinly sliced
4 teaspoons Dijon mustard

1. If you like, preheat conventional oven to 200°C (400°F, gas mark 6). Heat croissants for 5 minutes while preparing filling.
2. On large microwave-safe platter, arrange smoked turkey in 4 portions, leaving at least 2.5 cm between each portion. Top each with sliced tomato and cheese, cutting cheese to fit. Cook on High (100% power) for 2–4 minutes, until cheese just melts and turkey is warm.
3. With serrated knife, slice each croissant horizontally in half. Spread bottom halves of croissants with mustard.
4. With spatula, arrange each portion of turkey on bottom half of each croissant. Replace top halves of croissants. Serve immediately.

Hot Pork and Beef Sandwiches

PORK BARBECUE SANDWICHES

Colour Index page 84. 4 servings. 641 cals per serving. Good source of riboflavin, thiamine, niacin, iron. Begin 25 minutes ahead.

450 g boneless pork loin, cut into 4 slices (each 5 mm thick)	4 hamburger buns or large soft bread rolls, split
2 egg yolks	250 ml bottled barbecue sauce
70 g dried breadcrumbs	
Salt and pepper to taste	120 g coleslaw

1. With dull edge of large knife or smooth edge of meat mallet, pound pork slices to 3 mm thickness. On plate, with fork, beat egg yolks. Spread breadcrumbs on greaseproof paper.
2. Into egg mixture, dip each pork slice, then coat with crumbs.
3. In 32.5 × 22.5 cm microwave-safe baking dish, place pork slices. Cook, covered loosely with greaseproof, on High (100% power) for 8–9 minutes, until tender, rearranging halfway through cooking. Season with salt and pepper.
4. Meanwhile, lightly toast buns or rolls under preheated grill. On bottom half of each, place 1 pork slice. Spoon over barbecue sauce, then coleslaw. Replace top halves of buns or rolls.

ROAST BEEF AND BRIE SIZZLER

Colour Index page 84. 4 servings. 588 cals per serving. Good source of riboflavin, thiamine, niacin, calcium, iron. Begin 25 minutes ahead.

1 loaf French bread, about 30 cm long	225 g roast beef, thinly sliced
30 g butter or margarine	225 g Brie cheese, thinly sliced
1/4 teaspoon dried tarragon	
1 teaspoon Dijon mustard	

1. With serrated knife, diagonally cut French bread into 8 thin slices; set aside.
2. In small microwave-safe bowl, place butter or margarine. Heat, covered with kitchen paper, on Medium (50% power) for 15–30 seconds, until softened. Stir in tarragon and mustard. Spread 1 side of each bread slice with butter mixture.
3. Preheat browning dish according to manufacturer's instructions. On greaseproof paper, place half of bread slices, buttered sides down. Arrange roast beef and Brie on bread. Cover with remaining bread, buttered sides up. Place sandwiches on browning dish; press with spatula. Cook on High (100% power) for 3–4 1/2 (4:30) minutes, until sandwiches are golden, turning over and pressing lightly with spatula after 2–2 1/2 (2:30) minutes. Serve immediately.

STEAK SANDWICHES

Colour Index page 86. 692 cals per serving. Good source of riboflavin, thiamine, niacin, calcium, iron. Begin 35 minutes ahead.

Ingredients	For 4	For 2	For 1
Sirloin steak, 2 cm thick	450 g	225 g	115 g
Green pepper, sliced	1 pepper	1/2 pepper	1/4 pepper
Red onion, sliced	1 small	1/2 onion	1/4 onion
French bread, about 60 cm long, or individual loaves (petits pains)	1 large loaf or 4 petits pains	1/2 large loaf or 2 petits pains	1/4 large loaf or 1 petit pain
Dijon Mustard	2 tablespoons	1 tablespoon	1 1/2 teaspoons
Gruyère or Cheddar cheese, grated	115 g	50 g	25 g
Microwave cookware	Browning dish 30 cm platter	Browning dish 22.5 cm plate	Browning dish 17.5 cm plate
Time on High (100% power)			
Steak	5–7 minutes	3–4 minutes	2–3 minutes
Pepper-onion mixture	5–6 minutes	3–4 minutes	2–3 minutes
Sandwiches	2–2 1/2 (2:30) minutes	1–2 minutes	45 seconds–1 1/2 (1:30) minutes

1 Preheat browning dish according to manufacturer's instructions. Place steak on browning dish, pressing firmly with fish slice.

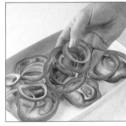

2 Cook steak on High for time in Chart, until almost done to your liking, turning over once. Remove from dish; keep warm. Reheat dish.

3 In meat drippings in browning dish, place green peppers and red onion rings.

4 Cook mixture on High for time in Chart, until tender, stirring twice. Meanwhile, if using French bread, cut crossways into 15 cm sections. Split each section or petit pain horizontally in half; toast lightly.

5 On platter or plate (see Chart), arrange bottom halves of bread; thinly spread with mustard. Thinly slice steak across grain.

6 Arrange steak slices on bottom halves of bread; top with pepper and onion mixture. Sprinkle over cheese. Cook on High for time in Chart, or until cheese just melts. Cover with top halves of bread and serve immediately.

Meal in Minutes *for 4 people*

Breakfast in a Hurry

Fresh fruit juice of your choice
Chilled grapefruit and orange segments
Scrambled Eggs and Bacon, page 139
Toast with jam, marmalade or honey
Café au Lait (below)

PREPARATION TIMETABLE

15 minutes ahead	Make Scrambled Eggs and Bacon.
10 minutes ahead	Spoon jam, marmalade or honey into small bowl. Mix fruit in individual bowls.
Just before serving	Make coffee and heat milk for Café au Lait. Toast bread conventionally. Pour fruit juice into glasses. Complete Café au Lait.

CAFÉ AU LAIT

This French-style breakfast coffee can be made in minutes in your microwave, and you can use any blend of coffee you like.

In 1 litre microwave-safe measuring jug, heat **500 ml milk**, covered, on High (100% power) for 2–3 minutes, until almost boiling. Remove from oven; stir in **500 ml hot black coffee**. Pour into 4 large cups. Top with **whipped cream**; sprinkle each with ¼ **teaspoon cocoa powder**.

Hearty Hot Beef Sandwiches

EASY BEEF TORTILLAS

Colour Index page 85. 4 servings. 323 cals per serving. Good source of niacin, iron. Begin 10 minutes ahead.

450 g minced beef	*4 canned corn tortillas*
1 onion, chopped	*4 lettuce leaves*
1 garlic clove, crushed	*Grated cheese, soured*
1 × 225 g can tomato	*cream and taco sauce*
sauce	*(optional)*
1 teaspoon chilli powder	

1. In microwave-safe plastic colander set over large microwave-safe bowl, place minced beef, onion and garlic. Cook on High (100% power) for 5–6 minutes, until meat is no longer pink, stirring twice. Discard fat from bowl.
2. In same bowl, combine meat mixture and next 2 ingredients. Cook, covered, on High for 3 minutes, or until hot, stirring once.
3. Place 1 tortilla between lightly moistened kitchen paper; repeat with remainder. Place each on oven floor and heat on High for 30 seconds.
4. *To serve:* place tortillas on warmed dinner plates. On each tortilla, arrange 1 lettuce leaf and one-quarter of meat mixture. If you like, serve with grated cheese, soured cream and taco sauce.

MEXICAN-STYLE ACCOMPANIMENTS

Easy Beef Tortillas taste good on their own, or serve them with the following accompaniments: chopped coriander, chopped jalapeño peppers, corn relish and grated Cheddar cheese.

Chopped Coriander

Chopped Jalapeño Peppers

Corn Relish

Grated Cheese

CHILLI IN A BUN

Colour Index page 85. 4 servings. 529 cals per serving. Good source of niacin, vitamin C, iron. Begin 20 minutes ahead.

1 onion, chopped	2 tablespoons water
1 green pepper, chopped	Salt and pepper to taste
1 celery stick, chopped	4 hamburger buns, split
450 g minced beef	and toasted
120 ml tomato ketchup	
2 tablespoons bottled	
chilli sauce	

1. In 30 × 20 cm microwave-safe baking dish, place chopped onion, green pepper, celery and minced beef. Cook on High (100% power) for 5–6 minutes, until meat is no longer pink, stirring often. Drain off fat.
2. To meat mixture, add ketchup, chilli sauce and water; stir. Cook on High for 5–7 minutes, until flavours blend, stirring occasionally. Season with salt and pepper.
3. Arrange bottom halves of toasted buns on warmed dinner plates and spoon one-quarter of minced beef mixture over each. Replace tops of buns and serve immediately.

MEATBALL 'SUBMARINES'

Colour Index page 87. 4 servings. 602 cals per serving. Good source of vitamin A, riboflavin, thiamine, niacin, iron. Begin 35 minutes ahead.

1 small onion, diced	Salt and pepper to taste
1 garlic clove, crushed	1 × 450 g jar sauce for
50 g mushrooms, finely	pasta (without meat)
chopped	4 individual French
450 g minced beef	loaves (petits pains),
30 g fresh breadcrumbs	split and toasted
(1 slice)	
1/2 teaspoon dried basil	

1. In mixing bowl, combine onion, garlic, mushrooms, minced beef, breadcrumbs and basil. Season with salt and pepper.
2. Shape minced beef mixture into 12 meatballs. In 30 × 20 cm microwave-safe baking dish, arrange meatballs 2.5 cm apart. Cook, covered with kitchen paper, on High (100% power) for 4–5 minutes, until meatballs are no longer pink, rearranging halfway through cooking.
3. Over meatballs, pour pasta sauce; stir gently to coat. Cook, covered, on High for 5–7 minutes, until sauce bubbles and flavours blend, stirring occasionally.
4. Arrange bottom halves of French loaves on warmed dinner plates. Place 3 meatballs on each half and top with any remaining pasta sauce. Replace top halves of loaves and serve immediately with knives and forks.

Try toasting bread for a delicious nutty flavour as in the recipe for Reuben Sandwiches (below). Day-old bread, buns, croissants and rolls are perfect for making sandwiches. Because they are slightly dry, they absorb enough moisture from the microwaved fillings to refresh them but not make them soggy.

REUBEN SANDWICHES

Colour Index page 85. 526 cals per serving. Good source of calcium, iron, fibre. Begin 20 minutes ahead.

Ingredients	For 4	For 2	For 1
Salt beef, thinly sliced	225 g	115 g	50 g
Sauerkraut, drained	175 g	80 g	60 g
Emmenthal cheese slices	4 slices	2 slices	1 slice
Rye bread slices	8 slices	4 slices	2 slices
Thousand Island dressing	120 ml	60 ml	2 tablespoons
Dill pickled cucumbers	4 cucumbers	2 cucumbers	1 cucumber
Microwave cookware	32.5 × 22.5 cm baking dish	30 × 20 cm baking dish	20 cm square baking dish
Time on High (100% power)	5–6 minutes	3–4 minutes	2–3 minutes

1 In baking dish (see Chart), arrange thinly sliced salt beef in 50 g portions, leaving at least 2.5 cm between each portion and shaping them to fit size of rye bread slices.

2 Over salt beef, spoon sauerkraut; cover with Emmenthal cheese slices.

3 Cook fillings on High for time in Chart, or until cheese melts and salt beef is warm, rotating dish halfway through cooking. Meanwhile, lightly toast rye bread conventionally.

4 With dressing, evenly spread 1 side of each slice of toasted rye bread. Arrange half of slices on warmed serving platter.

5 With spatula, place salt beef and cheese fillings on top of toasts on platter. Top with remaining toast slices, dressing side down.

6 Cut each sandwich in half; secure with cocktail sticks. Serve hot, with dill pickled cucumbers.

Hallowe'en Supper

Meatball 'Submarines', page 303 (double quantity)
Bought pizza, or pizza of your choice, page 310 (double quantity)
Chocolate Ice Cream Pie, page 331
Butterscotch Squares, page 362
Toffee apples
Butter Caramels, page 370
Popcorn, peanuts, potato crisps and potato sticks
Fresh fruit juice

PREPARATION TIMETABLE

1 day ahead	**Early in day**	**2 hours ahead**	**15 minutes ahead**	**Just before serving**
Make Butterscotch Squares and Butter Caramels; store in airtight containers. Prepare Chocolate Ice Cream Pie and freeze; do not decorate.	Prepare Meatball 'Submarines' up to end of step 2; cover and refrigerate. Chill fruit juice.	If making pizza, prepare and cook in microwave.	Put out popcorn, peanuts, potato crisps and potato sticks. Arrange toffee apples on plate. Put out Butterscotch Squares and Butter Caramels.	Complete Meatball 'Submarines'. Reheat bought or homemade pizza in microwave. Decorate Chocolate Ice Cream Pie.

Creative Sandwiches

PITTA POCKETS WITH SOUVLAKI

Colour Index page 84. 4 servings. 486 cals per serving. Good source of riboflavin, thiamine, niacin, calcium, iron. Begin 25 minutes ahead.

1 tablespoon olive or vegetable oil
450 g boneless lamb steak or beef fillet
1 small red onion, sliced
½ small cucumber, peeled, cut in half lengthways, seeded and sliced
8 large stoned black olives, sliced
2 tablespoons chopped fresh dill or ¾ teaspoon dried

2 tomatoes, each cut into 8 wedges
75 g feta cheese, diced
Salt and pepper to taste
4 pitta breads
Plain yogurt, lemon wedges and mint sprigs to garnish

1. Preheat browning dish according to manufacturer's instructions. Lightly brush dish with 1 teaspoon oil. Place meat on browning dish, pressing firmly with fish slice. Cook on High (100% power) for 4–7 minutes, until done to your liking, turning meat over and pressing with fish slice after 3–4 minutes. Allow meat to stand, covered, on heatproof surface for 5 minutes.
2. Meanwhile, in mixing bowl, place remaining oil, onion, cucumber, olives, dill, tomatoes and feta cheese; stir to mix. Season mixture with salt and pepper.
3. With sharp knife, thinly slice meat across grain. To vegetable mixture in bowl, add meat and cooking juices; toss lightly.
4. Lightly toast pitta breads under preheated grill until hot and softened. Cut each one in half crossways and separate to form 2 pockets.
5. *To serve:* into each pitta pocket, spoon equal amount of meat and vegetable mixture. Garnish with yogurt, lemon wedges and mint sprigs.

Making the Pitta Pockets

Lightly toast pitta breads under preheated grill until hot and softened. With serrated knife, cut each pitta in half crossways and separate to form 2 pockets. Into each pitta pocket, spoon equal amount of meat and vegetable filling.

WARM VEGETABLE SALAD WITH CHEESE IN PITTA

Colour Index page 84. 570 cals per serving. Good source of vitamins A and C, riboflavin, thiamine, niacin, calcium, iron, fibre. Begin 20 minutes ahead.

Ingredients	For 4	For 2	For 1
Carrot, thinly sliced	1 carrot	½ carrot	¼ carrot
Water	3 tablespoons	2 tablespoons	1 tablespoon
Red onion, sliced	1 large	1 small	½ small
Red or green pepper, sliced	1 pepper	½ pepper	¼ pepper
Celery stick, sliced	1 stick	½ stick	¼ stick
Broccoli, cut into florets, and stalks, peeled and sliced	450 g	225 g	115 g
Mushrooms, sliced	115 g	50 g	25 g
Vinaigrette dressing	4 tablespoons	2 tablespoons	1 tablespoon
Tomatoes, diced	2 medium	1 medium	1 small
Cheddar cheese, diced	225 g	115 g	50 g
Pitta bread	4 breads	2 breads	1 bread
Microwave cookware	2 litre soufflé dish	1 litre soufflé dish	Shallow 21.5 cm pie dish
Time on High (100% power) Carrot	2–3 minutes	1½ (1:30)– 2 minutes	1–1½ (1:30) minutes
With other vegetables	5–7 minutes	4–5 minutes	2–3 minutes

1 In soufflé dish or pie dish (see Chart), place carrot and water. Cook, covered, on High for time in Chart, until carrot is lightly cooked; drain.

2 Into carrot, stir red onion, red or green pepper, celery, broccoli and mushrooms.

3 To vegetable mixture, add vinaigrette dressing; stir to coat. Cook, covered, on High for time in Chart, or until vegetables are tender, stirring twice.

4 While vegetables are hot, add tomatoes and cheese; stir gently until cheese begins to melt. Lightly toast pitta breads under preheated grill until hot and softened.

5 With serrated knife, cut each pitta bread in half crossways and separate to form 2 pockets.

6 *To serve:* into each pitta pocket, spoon equal amount of vegetable and cheese mixture. Spoon over any remaining vinaigrette. Serve immediately.

Quick Canapés

Canapés for spur-of-the-moment cocktail parties can be made in minutes in the microwave, yet your guests will think you've spent hours preparing them in the kitchen! The recipes on this page all have an Italian flavour, and would be ideal served with an Italian aperitif such as martini, or an Italian dry white wine like Frascati or Soave. All the ingredients for the canapés are widely available in supermarkets, and most keep well in the storecupboard – just perfect for impromptu entertaining.

NUTTY GOAT CHEESE TOASTS

Colour Index page 86. Makes 15. 131 cals each. Good source of vitamin A, riboflavin, thiamine, niacin, calcium, iron.
Begin 35 minutes ahead.

Ingredients for 15		Microwave cookware
4 tablespoons finely chopped walnuts 1 × 175 g goat cheese log 50 g sun-dried tomatoes, drained if packed in oil	½ French stick Olive oil	Serving platter

1 In shallow dish, place finely chopped walnuts. Carefully roll goat cheese log in walnuts until evenly coated. Wrap goat cheese log in cling film; chill in refrigerator for 20 minutes, or until firm.

2 Meanwhile, with sharp knife, cut sun-dried tomatoes into 30 matchstick-thin strips; set strips aside.

3 With serrated knife, cut French stick into fifteen 1 cm thick slices, discarding rounded end. Preheat grill to hot.

4 Meanwhile, in grill pan, arrange French stick slices in rows. Place under preheated grill for 2 minutes, or until slices are golden brown on both sides, turning them over once.

5 With sharp knife, cut chilled goat cheese log into 15 slices. Place 1 cheese slice on top of each piece of toast. Arrange 2 strips of sun-dried tomato in lattice pattern on top of each cheese slice.

6 On serving platter, arrange toasts. Heat on Medium (50% power) for 1–2 minutes, until cheese softens slightly. Drizzle each toast with a little olive oil and serve hot.

PIZZA TARTLETS

Colour Index page 86. Makes 16. 145 cals each filled tartlet. Low in cholesterol.
Begin 35 minutes ahead.

1 × 50 g can anchovy fillets in olive oil, well drained
75 g stoned black olives
16 × 5 cm bought tartlet shells

250 ml bottled sauce for pasta (without meat)
115 g mozzarella cheese, grated
Basil leaves to garnish

1. Rinse anchovy fillets thoroughly under cold running water. Pat dry with kitchen paper. Cut each anchovy fillet in half crossways, then cut each half lengthways to make 4 thin strips. Cut black olives into thin rings. Set both anchovy strips and olives aside for garnish.
2. Preheat conventional oven to 180°C (350°F, gas mark 4). Arrange tartlet shells on baking sheet and place in preheated oven for about 5 minutes, or until heated through.
3. Into small microwave-safe bowl, pour sauce for pasta. Heat sauce on High (100% power) for 3–5 minutes, until piping hot, stirring twice.
4. On microwave-safe serving platter, arrange warmed tartlet shells. Into each tartlet shell, spoon equal amount of sauce for pasta; sprinkle evenly with grated mozzarella cheese. Arrange anchovy strips on top of each filled tartlet in lattice pattern; arrange 2 black olive rings in centre of lattice.
5. Heat tartlets on Medium (50% power) for 1–2 minutes, just until mozzarella cheese begins to melt, rotating platter and rearranging tartlets once. Garnish tartlets with basil leaves just before serving. Serve warm.

SAVOURY BREADSTICKS

Colour Index page 85. Makes 12 breadsticks. 37 cals each breadstick. Low in cholesterol, fat.
Begin 15 minutes ahead.

6 rashers rindless streaky bacon
12 grissini (Italian breadsticks)

1. Line 32.5 × 22.5 cm microwave-safe baking dish with kitchen paper; set aside.
2. With sharp knife, cut each bacon rasher in half lengthways.
3. Around each grissini, wrap 1 bacon piece, spiral fashion.
4. In lined baking dish, arrange grissini. Cook, covered with kitchen paper, on High (100% power) for 4½ (4:30)–6 minutes, until bacon is browned, rotating dish and rearranging grissini halfway through cooking.

Simple Cheese Spreads

These delicious homemade spreads made with a variety of cheeses can be served on your favourite bread, rolls, crackers and scones. After making, serve them immediately, or cover and store in the refrigerator. To soften refrigerated spreads, place small quantity in microwave-safe container. Heat on High (100% power) for 5 seconds at a time, until just spreadable.

BASIC YOGURT CHEESE

Makes about 250 ml. 9 cals per tablespoon. Good source of riboflavin, calcium. Begin 1 day ahead.

250 ml plain yogurt
Salt and ground
  white pepper to
  taste

1. Set sieve over bowl. Line sieve with double thickness of muslin or coffee filter. In sieve, place yogurt. Allow yogurt to drain overnight in refrigerator.
2. Discard liquid. Spoon yogurt cheese into bowl. Season with salt and white pepper.

APRICOT CHEESE SPREAD: make Basic Yogurt Cheese (above); stir in **2 tablespoons apricot jam** and **½ teaspoon ground ginger**. Makes 250 ml. 14 cals per tablespoon.

SMOKED SALMON AND CHIVE SPREAD

Makes about 225 g. 22 cals per tablespoon. Begin 5 minutes ahead.

75 g cream cheese
75 g curd cheese
1 tablespoon milk
3 tablespoons
  chopped chives
50 g smoked salmon,
  chopped
1 teaspoon lemon
  juice
Ground white pepper
  to taste

1. In 500 ml microwave-safe measuring jug, heat cheeses on Medium (50% power) for 1–2 minutes, until softened.
2. To cheese mixture, add milk, chopped chives, salmon and lemon juice; stir until blended. Season with pepper.

CREAM CHEESE AND CHIVE SPREAD: make spread (above), omitting smoked salmon and lemon juice. Makes 175 g. 23 cals per tablespoon.

STILTON SPREAD

Makes about 200 g. 30 cals per tablespoon. Begin 5 minutes ahead.

115 g Stilton or other
  blue cheese,
  crumbled
75 g cream cheese
2 tablespoons finely
  chopped spring
  onion
1 tablespoon milk

1. In 1 litre microwave-safe measuring jug, place cheeses and spring onion. Heat on Medium (50% power) for 1–2 minutes, until cheeses are softened.
2. To cheese mixture, add milk; stir until smooth.

STILTON WALNUT SPREAD: make Stilton spread (above); stir in **25 g finely chopped walnuts**. Makes 225 g. 32 cals per tablespoon.

CHEDDAR CHEESE SPREAD

Makes 350 g. 49 cals per tablespoon. Good source of calcium. Begin 5 minutes ahead.

115 g butter or
  margarine
225 g Cheddar
  cheese, grated
3–4 tablespoons milk
2 spring onions,
  finely chopped
¼ teaspoon Tabasco
  sauce

1. In 1 litre microwave-safe measuring jug, place butter or margarine. Heat on Medium (50% power) for 30 seconds–1 minute, until softened.
2. Into butter or margarine, beat cheese. Add milk; stir until well blended. Stir in spring onions and Tabasco sauce.

CURRIED CHEDDAR CHEESE SPREAD: make Cheddar Cheese Spread (above); stir in **1 tablespoon curry paste** and **2 tablespoons chopped fresh coriander**. Makes 375 g. 55 cals per tablespoon.

Hot Cheese Sandwiches

CROQUE MONSIEUR

Colour Index page 87. 340 cals per serving. Good source of thiamine, calcium, iron. Begin 35 minutes ahead.

Ingredients	For 4	For 2	For 1
Eggs	2 eggs	1 egg	1 egg
Milk	120 ml	60 ml	60 ml
White bread slices	8 slices	4 slices	2 slices
Cooked ham slices	4 slices	2 slices	1 slice
Emmenthal or Gruyère cheese slices	4 slices	2 slices	1 slice
Butter or margarine	30 g	15 g	2 teaspoons
Microwave cookware	Browning dish	Browning dish	Browning dish
Time on High (100% power) Sandwiches	3–4 minutes each batch	3–4 minutes	1½ (1:30)– 2½ (2:30) minutes
Standing time	2 minutes	1 minute	1 minute

1 In shallow dish, with fork, beat eggs and milk until blended. Arrange half of bread slices on cutting board.

2 Top each slice bread with 1 slice ham and 1 slice cheese, trimming to fit if necessary. Top with remaining bread; set aside.

3 Preheat browning dish according to manufacturer's instructions. On browning dish, place butter or margarine.

4 Into egg mixture, dip each sandwich, to coat both sides of bread.

5 On browning dish, place sandwiches, pressing lightly with fish slice. Cook on High for time in Chart, until sandwiches are golden, turning sandwiches over halfway through cooking. (If cooking for 4, cook sandwiches in 2 batches, reheating browning dish between batches.)

6 On kitchen paper, allow sandwiches to stand for time in Chart. With serrated knife, cut diagonally in half; serve immediately.

MOZZARELLA GARLIC BREAD

Colour Index page 85. 6 pieces. 235 cals each. Good source of calcium. Begin 10 minutes ahead.

45 g butter or margarine, softened
1 garlic clove, crushed
¾ teaspoon dried oregano
1 loaf Italian or French bread, about 45 cm long
50 g mozzarella cheese, grated

1. In mixing bowl, combine softened butter or margarine, garlic and oregano. With serrated knife, cut bread crossways into three 15 cm sections. Split each section horizontally in half to make 6 halves of bread.
2. Spread cut side of each piece of bread with garlic butter. Sprinkle mozzarella evenly over buttered sides. Arrange bread in a circle on kitchen paper on oven floor. Cook on High (100% power) for 45 seconds, or just until cheese begins to melt.

GARLIC BREAD: prepare as above, omitting mozzarella cheese. Cook on High (100% power) for 30 seconds, or just until garlic butter melts.

MUFFINS WITH MELTED CHEESE AND TUNA

Colour Index page 85. 4 servings. 432 cals per serving. Good source of calcium, iron. Begin 15 minutes ahead.

75 g cream cheese
1 onion, chopped
1 celery stick, chopped
40 g sweet pickled gherkins, chopped
35 g pimiento-stuffed green olives, chopped
2 tablespoons mayonnaise
Tabasco sauce (optional)
1 × 200 g can tuna in brine, drained
4 muffins, split
4 slices processed cheese

1. In small microwave-safe bowl, place cream cheese. Heat on Medium-Low (30% power) for 1½ (1:30)–2 minutes, until softened.
2. To cream cheese, add chopped onion, celery, gherkins, olives and mayonnaise; stir until blended. If you like, add Tabasco sauce to taste. Fold in tuna, stirring to break up.
3. Lightly toast bottom halves of muffins under preheated grill. On microwave-safe platter, arrange toasted bottom halves of muffins. Spoon equal amount of tuna mixture on to each half and top with 1 slice processed cheese. Cook on High for 2–3 minutes, until cheese melts and tuna mixture is warm.
4. Meanwhile, toast top halves of muffins. When cheese is melted, replace top halves of toasted muffins. Serve immediately.

DESIGNER BAGELS

Colour Index page 85. Makes 12 bagel halves. 65 cals each. Begin 25 minutes ahead.

6 × 6 cm bagels	*Garnish:*
50 g ricotta cheese,	*Sliced stoned black*
crumbled	*olives, chopped sun-*
40 g Smoked Salmon	*dried tomatoes,*
and Chive Spread	*shredded basil leaves,*
(page 307)	*red pepper strips,*
60 g Orange Butter	*Orange Julienne (page*
(page 299)	*330)*

1. With serrated knife, split bagels. On cutting board, place bagel halves cut side up. Spread 4 bagel halves with ricotta, 4 bagel halves with Smoked Salmon and Chive Spread and 4 bagel halves with Orange Butter
2. On microwave-safe serving platter lined with kitchen paper, place 6 bagel halves. Heat on Medium-Low (30% power) for 1½ (1:30) minutes, or just until topping is softened. Repeat with remaining 6 bagel halves.
3. On ricotta topped bagels, arrange olives, sun-dried tomatoes and basil. Garnish salmon and chive topped bagels with red pepper strips; garnish Orange Butter topped bagels with Orange Julienne. Serve warm.

MOZZARELLA FRENCH BREAD

Colour Index page 86. 8 servings. 296 cals per serving. Good source of calcium. Begin 40 minutes ahead.

225 g mozzarella cheese,	*2 tablespoons olive or*
diced	*vegetable oil*
45 g pimiento-stuffed	*Salt to taste*
green olives, chopped	*1 loaf French bread,*
4 spring onions, sliced	*about 60 cm long*
2 slices Parma ham,	
diced	

1. In mixing bowl, combine mozzarella, olives, spring onions, Parma ham, oil and salt; set aside.
2. With serrated knife, cut French bread crossways into four 15 cm sections. With spoon or fingers, scoop out bread, leaving a 1 cm thick crust.
3. Fill each hollowed-out piece of bread with some of cheese mixture.
4. Wrap each piece loosely in kitchen paper. On oven floor, place bread. Heat on Medium (50% power) for 45 seconds–1½ (1:30) minutes, just until cheese begins to soften. Do not overcook or bread will become too chewy. Cut each piece into 12 slices. Serve immediately.

Cheese is one of the most versatile foods, and your microwave will help transform simple cheese sandwiches into tasty snacks or original main course dishes. For a change, try using Brie instead of Camembert in the toasted sandwiches below, but be careful in all the cheese sandwich recipes to microwave only for the time given; if you overcook cheese even slightly in the microwave, it will become rubbery and stringy.

TOASTED SANDWICHES WITH CAMEMBERT AND PEARS

Colour Index page 87. 280 cals each. Begin 35 minutes ahead.

Ingredients for 4 servings		Microwave cookware
8 thin slices white bread	*1 ripe pear*	Small bowl
30 g butter or margarine	*8 mint leaves*	Browning dish
1 × 125 g Camembert cheese, chilled	*Pear slices and mint leaves to garnish*	

1 With serrated knife, remove crusts from bread. In small bowl, place butter or margarine. Heat, covered with kitchen paper, on Medium (50% power) for 15–30 seconds, until softened but not melted.

2 Spread 1 side of each slice of bread with softened butter or margarine. Cut chilled Camembert into thin slices; arrange on unbuttered sides of 4 bread slices, cutting cheese to fit.

3 Cut pear into quarters lengthways; remove core, but do not peel. Cut each quarter into 4 slices lengthways.

4 Arrange pear slices on top of Camembert. Place 2 mint leaves in centre of each sandwich. Top with remaining slices of bread, buttered sides up. Preheat browning dish according to manufacturer's instructions.

5 On browning dish, place 2 sandwiches, pressing lightly with fish slice. Cook on High (100% power) for 3–5 minutes, until sandwiches are golden, turning over and pressing after 2–3 minutes. Set aside; keep warm. Reheat browning dish and repeat with remaining sandwiches.

6 *To serve:* cut each sandwich diagonally into quarters. Garnish with pear slices and mint leaves. Serve warm.

Pizza

CALZONE

Colour Index page 87. 504 cals per serving (without extra fillings). Good source of iron. Begin 35 minutes ahead.

Ingredients for 2 servings		Microwave cookware
1 × 145 g packet pizza base mix *115 ml warm water* *1 × 450 g jar sauce for pasta (without meat)* *25 g mozzarella cheese, grated* *1 teaspoon olive oil* *Basil leaves to garnish*	*Fillings:* *Diced green or red pepper, shredded Parma ham, thinly sliced pepperoni, thinly sliced mushrooms, well-drained canned anchovy fillets*	*Browning dish* *1 litre measuring jug*

1 In mixing bowl, combine pizza base mix and water to form dough. Knead well on lightly floured surface for 5 minutes; divide in half. Roll out each half, then shape into 15 cm circle with fingers.

2 On to half of each dough circle, spoon 60 ml pasta sauce; reserve remaining sauce. Sprinkle with mozzarella. Top with fillings of your choice (above). With pastry brush, moisten edge of each circle with water.

3 Fold each circle of dough in half to enclose filling; press edges together to seal, crimping to decorate. Preheat browning dish according to manufacturer's instructions. Lightly brush with oil.

4 With fish slice, carefully place calzone on browning dish. Cook on High (100% power) for 2–3 minutes, until lightly browned on underside.

5 Turn calzone over with fish slice; cook on High for 3–4 minutes longer. Transfer to warmed dinner plates; allow to stand, covered, for 3–5 minutes. Meanwhile, pour reserved sauce into measuring jug. Heat, covered, on High for 2–3 minutes, until hot, stirring twice.

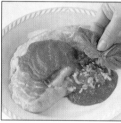

6 Over calzone on dinner plates, spoon hot pasta sauce; garnish with basil leaves. Serve immediately.

FOUR SEASONS PIZZA

Colour Index page 87. 4 servings. 367 cals per serving. Good source of vitamin A, thiamine, vitamin C, calcium, iron, fibre. Begin 35 minutes ahead.

1 × 145 g packet pizza base mix
115 ml warm water
1 teaspoon vegetable oil
2 tablespoons bottled pesto sauce or 1 tablespoon dried basil
1 × 175 g jar artichoke hearts, drained and sliced

200 g canned pimientos, drained and sliced
50 g Parma ham, thinly sliced
2 tomatoes, sliced
25 g Parmesan cheese, grated

1. In mixing bowl, combine pizza base mix and water to form dough. Knead well on lightly floured surface for 5 minutes, then roll out to 25 cm circle. Make 1 cm rim round edge; crimp rim with fingers.

2. Preheat 22.5 cm round browning dish according to manufacturer's instructions. Lightly brush with oil. Carefully transfer dough to browning dish. With fork, prick dough to prevent puffing. Spread with pesto sauce or sprinkle with dried basil.

3. With knife, lightly mark dough into quarters. Arrange artichoke hearts, pimientos, Parma ham and tomatoes separately on each quarter. Sprinkle Parmesan evenly over pizza. Cook on High (100% power) for 10 minutes, or until crust is firm and vegetables are tender, piercing crust with fork occasionally. Serve hot.

MEDITERRANEAN PIZZA

Colour Index page 87. 4 servings. 520 cals per serving. Good source of calcium, iron. Begin 35 minutes ahead.

1 × 145 g packet pizza base mix
115 ml warm water
2 tablespoons olive or vegetable oil
1 large red onion, thinly sliced

½ teaspoon dried rosemary
¼ teaspoon dried basil
¼ teaspoon dried thyme
Salt and pepper to taste
225 g soft goat or feta cheese, crumbled

1. In mixing bowl, combine pizza base mix and water to form dough. Knead well on lightly floured surface for 5 minutes, then roll out to 25 cm circle. Make a 1 cm rim round edge; press with fork to make decorative edge.

2. Preheat 22.5 cm round browning dish according to manufacturer's instructions. Lightly brush with 1 teaspoon oil. Carefully transfer dough to browning dish. With fork, prick dough.

3. In small bowl, combine onion slices, remaining oil and herbs. Season with salt and pepper.

4. Over dough, spread onion mixture; top with cheese. Cook pizza on High (100% power) for 10 minutes, or until crust is firm, piercing crust with fork occasionally. Serve hot.

Fruit and Desserts

**CHARTS FOR MICROWAVING FRUIT · FRUIT DESSERTS
CREAMY DESSERTS · CHOCOLATE DESSERTS
ICE CREAM AND SORBETS · PUDDINGS · CHEESECAKES**

Fruit and Desserts

Fruit cooked in the microwave keeps its shape better and looks more attractive than conventionally cooked fruit. Using the charts on pages 313–315, a wide range of fresh and dried fruits, some with added sugar for extra sweetness, can be quickly prepared. Plainly cooked apples, peaches, pears and plums can be served hot or cold as accompaniments to roast meats and poultry, or served chilled with their cooking juices as delicious and nutritious desserts. More elaborate fruit dishes are given amongst the recipes in this chapter, such as poached peaches and pears in sweet sauces, apples caramelised with sugar and spices, cherries in a red wine sauce, creamy soufflés, and sorbets.

Many dessert recipes contain delicate ingredients that benefit particularly from microwave cooking. Egg-based creams and mousses that can curdle will be smooth and creamy with only occasional stirring when cooked on Medium (50% power). Better-than-ever cheesecakes can be made in half the normal baking time. These delicate mixtures should be elevated on a trivet, rack or ramekin, then cooked on Medium, and rotated occasionally for even cooking throughout. Remove a cheesecake from the oven while still soft in the centre, then allow to stand for about 30 minutes, during which time it will set without cracking.

The delicious puddings in this chapter are a particular treat when made in the microwave. They cook quickly, and the milk-based mixtures do not stick or scorch. These, too, are usually elevated and cooked on Medium power.

Chocolate melts perfectly in the microwave without any special equipment such as a double boiler. Do not cover it, however, as the moisture that builds up inside a cover or lid can drop on to the chocolate as it melts and make it stiff. Remove chocolate from the oven when it begins to look soft and changes from dull to shiny, bearing in mind that pieces and squares will retain their shapes until the chocolate is removed from the microwave and stirred.

INSTANT DESSERTS
Create an easy, last-minute dessert by combining ice cream or sorbet with canned fruit or fresh bakery goods, then topping with a sweet sauce. Use bottled sweet sauces or make a quick microwave sweet sauce (pages 382–383).

Peach Melba (left): canned peach half filled with vanilla ice cream, set on Melba Sauce and decorated with mint leaves.

Apple Tart à la Mode (right): bought apple tartlet and scoop of vanilla ice cream with Butterscotch Sauce spooned over. Decorated with mint leaves.

Cooking Fruit in the Microwave

Fruit cooked in the microwave keeps its fresh flavour and retains its shape because it doesn't need constant stirring.

Microwave cling film is the best choice for covering a dish of fruit to be microwaved. 'Vent' the film a little, turning back a small corner or puncturing it to allow steam to escape.

Key				
Microwave cookware	Sugar	Water	Time	Standing time

APPLE (WHOLE)

Wash under cold running water and pat dry, then core and peel one-third of the way down from tops.

About 132 cals per serving		
For 4	**For 2**	**For 1**
4 cooking apples (about 225 g each)	2 cooking apples (about 225 g each)	1 cooking apple (about 225 g)
20 cm square baking dish	20 cm square baking dish	Small
None	None	None
7–9 minutes; *rotate apples and dish halfway through cooking*	4–5 minutes; *rotate apples and dish halfway through cooking*	2–3 minutes
5 minutes	5 minutes	5 minutes

Cook apples, standing upright and covered, on High (100% power) for time in Chart. Allow to stand, covered, for time in Chart. Whole apples are done when tender yet retaining their shapes.

APPLE (SLICES)

Wash under cold running water, then core and, if you like, peel. Cut each apple in half lengthways; cut each half lengthways into eighths.

About 108 cals per serving		
For 4	**For 2**	**For 1**
4 cooking apples (about 175 g each)	2 cooking apples (about 175 g each)	1 cooking apple (about 175 g)
2 litre casserole	1 litre casserole	Small bowl
2 teaspoons	1 teaspoon	$1/2$ teaspoon
4 tablespoons water *plus* $1/2$ *teaspoon lemon juice*	2 tablespoons water *plus* $1/4$ *teaspoon lemon juice*	1 tablespoon water *plus* $1/4$ *teaspoon lemon juice*
9–11 minutes; *stir 3 times during cooking*	5–6 minutes; *stir halfway through cooking*	2–3 minutes; *stir halfway through cooking*
5 minutes	5 minutes	5 minutes

Stir sugar, water and lemon juice together. Add apple and stir to coat. Cook, covered, on High (100% power) for time in Chart. Allow to stand, covered, for time in Chart. Apple slices are done when tender yet retaining their shapes.

CHERRY

Wash under cold running water and drain. Remove stalks and stones. Cherries boil vigorously and foam towards end of cooking. Do not allow to boil over.

80 cals per serving		
For 4	**For 2**	**For 1**
450 g (weight before removing stones)	225 g (weight before removing stones)	115 g (weight before removing stones)
2 litre casserole	1 litre casserole	Small bowl
1 tablespoon	2 teaspoons	1 teaspoon
4–5 minutes; *stir halfway through cooking*	3–4 minutes; *stir halfway through cooking*	$1^{1}/2$ (1:30)–2 minutes; *stir halfway through cooking*
2–3 minutes	2–3 minutes	2–3 minutes

Cook cherries and water, covered, on High (100% power) for time in Chart. Allow to stand, covered, for time in Chart. Cherries are done when tender.

PEACH (WHOLE)

Rinse under cold running water. To peel, dip whole peaches in rapidly boiling water for 15–20 seconds, then dip them into bowl of cold water; pull off skins.

About 40 cals per serving			
	For 4	**For 2**	**For 1**
	4 peaches (about 115 g each)	2 peaches (about 115 g each)	1 peach (about 115 g)
🍲	20 cm square baking dish	Shallow 23.5 cm pie dish	Small bowl
🥤	None	None	None
⏰	3–6 minutes; *rotate dish halfway through cooking*	2–3$\frac{1}{2}$ (3:30) minutes; *rotate dish halfway through cooking*	45 seconds–2 minutes
⏲	2 minutes	2 minutes	2 minutes

Cook peaches, standing upright and covered, on High (100% power) for time in Chart. Allow to stand, covered, for time in Chart. Peaches are done when tender yet retaining their shapes.

PEAR (SLICES)

Prepare as whole pears (below left). If you like, peel. Cut lengthways into eighths.

About 112 cals per serving			
	For 4	**For 2**	**For 1**
	4 pears (about 175 g each)	2 pears (about 175 g each)	1 pear (about 175 g)
🍲	2 litre casserole	1 litre casserole	Small bowl
🥄	2 teaspoons	1 teaspoon	$\frac{1}{2}$ teaspoon
🥤	4 tablespoons water *plus $\frac{1}{2}$ teaspoon lemon juice*	2 tablespoons water *plus $\frac{1}{4}$ teaspoon lemon juice*	1 tablespoon water *plus 1–2 drops lemon juice*
⏰	10–12 minutes; *stir 3 times during cooking*	7–9 minutes; *stir halfway through cooking*	3–5 minutes; *stir halfway through cooking*
⏲	5 minutes	3–5 minutes	2–3 minutes

Stir sugar, water and lemon juice together. Add pears and stir to coat. Cook, covered, on High (100% power) for time in Chart. Allow to stand, covered, for time in Chart. Pear slices are done when tender yet retaining their shapes.

PEAR (WHOLE)

Rinse under cold running water. With apple corer, remove cores from base of pears but do not remove stalks. Peel pears. To prevent turning brown, brush exposed flesh with lemon juice.

About 139 cals per serving			
	For 4	**For 2**	**For 1**
	4 large pears (about 225 g each)	2 large pears (about 225 g each)	1 large pear (about 225 g)
🍲	20 cm square baking dish	Shallow 23.5 cm pie dish	Small bowl
🥤	None	None	None
⏰	5–7 minutes; *rotate pears, then rotate dish halfway through cooking*	4–6 minutes; *rotate pears, then rotate dish halfway through cooking*	2–3 minutes
⏲	5 minutes	5 minutes	5 minutes

Cook pears, standing upright and covered, on High (100% power) for time in Chart. Allow to stand, covered, for time in Chart. Pears are done when tender yet retaining their shapes.

PINEAPPLE (PIECES)

Cut off about 2.5 cm from top and base of fruit. Cut pineapple in half lengthways, then into quarters. Cut away fibrous woody cores. Cut off peel, cutting close to fruit. Cut out any remaining eyes. Cut pineapple quarters in half lengthways, then cut crossways into 1–2 cm thick pieces.

About 50 cals per serving			
	For 4	**For 2**	**For 1**
	1 pineapple (1.6–1.8 kg)	1 pineapple (1.6–1.8 kg; use half and refrigerate remainder)	1 pineapple (1.6–1.8 kg; use one-quarter and refrigerate remainder)
🍲	2 litre casserole	1 litre casserole	Small bowl
🥤	None	None	None
⏰	8–9 minutes; *stir halfway through cooking*	4–5 minutes; *stir halfway through cooking*	2$\frac{1}{2}$ (2:30)–3 minutes; *stir halfway through cooking*
⏲	5 minutes	5 minutes	5 minutes

Cook pineapple, covered, on High (100% power) for time in Chart. Allow to stand, covered, for time in Chart. Pineapple pieces are done when tender.

PLUM (HALVES)

Wash plums under cold running water. Pat dry. Cut each plum in half and remove stone.

About 80 cals per serving		
For 4	**For 2**	**For 1**
8 plums (about 50 g each)	4 plums (about 50 g each)	2 plums (about 50 g each)
30 × 20 cm baking dish; *arrange round edges*	Shallow 23.5 cm pie dish; *arrange round edge*	Shallow 23.5 cm pie dish
None	None	None
3–4 minutes; *rotate dish halfway through cooking*	2–3 minutes; *rotate dish halfway through cooking*	1–2 minutes; *rotate dish halfway through cooking*
3–4 minutes	3–4 minutes	2–3 minutes

Cook plums, covered, on High (100% power) for time in Chart. Allow to stand, covered, for time in Chart. Plum halves are done when tender.

DRIED FRUIT (APRICOTS, PEACHES AND PRUNES)

About 188 cals per serving for each fruit		
For 4	**For 2**	**For 1**
225 g (weight after removing any stones)	115 g (weight after removing any stones)	50 g (weight after removing any stones)
1.5 litre casserole	1 litre casserole	500 ml measuring jug
4 tablespoons	2 tablespoons	1 tablespoon
500 ml	250 ml	125 ml
10–12 minutes; *stir in sugar halfway through cooking*	6–7 minutes; *stir in sugar halfway through cooking*	4–5 minutes; *stir in sugar at start of cooking*
30 minutes	30 minutes	30 minutes

Cook dried fruit and water, covered, on High (100% power) for time in Chart, stirring in sugar when indicated. Allow to stand, covered, for time in Chart. Dried apricots, peaches and prunes are done when tender.

RHUBARB (PIECES)

Wash rhubarb and trim any discoloured ends; cut off any leaves and discard. Cut rhubarb crossways into 2.5 cm pieces.

Rhubarb boils vigorously towards end of cooking; do not allow to boil over.

About 140 cals per serving		
For 4	**For 2**	**For 1**
700 g	350 g	175 g
4 litre casserole	2 litre casserole	1 litre casserole
150 ml	80 ml	2½ tablespoons
4 tablespoons	2 tablespoons	1 tablespoon
7–8 minutes; *stir halfway through cooking and stir in sugar before final minute*	4–6 minutes; *stir halfway through cooking and stir in sugar before final minute*	2½ (2:30)–3 minutes; *stir halfway through cooking and stir in sugar before final minute*
10 minutes	10 minutes	10 minutes

Cook rhubarb and water, covered, on High (100% power) for time in Chart, stirring in sugar when indicated. Allow to stand, covered, for time in Chart. Rhubarb pieces are done when tender.

DRIED FRUIT (FIGS)

210 cals per serving		
For 4	**For 2**	**For 1**
350 g	175 g	75 g
1.5 litre casserole	1 litre casserole	500 ml measuring jug
500 ml water *plus 2 teaspoons lemon juice*	250 ml water *plus 1 teaspoon lemon juice*	125 ml water *plus ½ teaspoon lemon juice*
12–15 minutes; *stir halfway through cooking*	7–8 minutes; *stir halfway through cooking*	3–5 minutes; *stir halfway through cooking*
30 minutes	30 minutes	30 minutes

Cook dried figs, water and lemon juice, covered, on High (100% power) for time in Chart. Allow to stand, covered, for time in Chart. Dried figs are done when plump and soft.

Fruit for Garnishing

Many new and exciting fruits from exotic places are now widely available. They make ideal garnishes for simple microwave dishes by providing additional colour and flavour as well as interesting shapes.

Date: use whole or chopped as topping for cakes, biscuits, desserts, tea breads and salads.

Lychee: peel off skin, remove stone and use halves or quarters on fruit salads and stir-fry dishes.

Kumquat: cut into slices to top fruit salads, stir-fry dishes and desserts.

Pomegranate: juicy seeds make an unusual topping for cheesecakes, ice creams and sorbets.

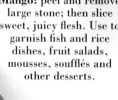

Mango: peel and remove large stone; then slice sweet, juicy flesh. Use to garnish fish and rice dishes, fruit salads, mousses, soufflés and other desserts.

Prickly Pear: peel thorny skin as you would peel an apple. Use on salads.

Papaya: halve and remove seeds; peel and slice. Serve on rice dishes, breakfast cereals and pies.

Fig: cut in half lengthways; serve with cooked meats or cheese.

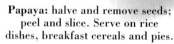

Kiwi Fruit: peel and slice. Use on fish, poultry and desserts.

Passion Fruit: cut in half crossways, then spoon out seeds and juice to use as topping for sorbets and other desserts.

Star Fruit: use this citrus-flavoured fruit to garnish fish, vegetables and desserts.

Apple Desserts

SPICED APPLE SLICES

Colour Index page 88. 4 servings. 157 cals per serving. Low in fat, sodium. Good source of fibre. Begin 25 minutes ahead.

350 ml apple juice	3 whole cloves
55 g brown sugar	3 allspice berries
2 teaspoons grated	4 small apples
lemon zest	2 tablespoons lemon
2 × 7.5 cm long	juice
cinnamon sticks	

1. In 30 × 20 cm microwave-safe baking dish, combine apple juice, brown sugar, lemon zest, cinnamon sticks, cloves and allspice. Cook on High (100% power) for 7–9 minutes, until sugar dissolves and liquid boils, stirring occasionally.
2. Meanwhile, peel and core apples. Slice crossways into 5 mm thick rings. If you like, cut edges with fluted biscuit cutter for a more decorative effect. Sprinkle apple rings with lemon juice.
3. To spiced liquid in baking dish, add half of apple rings. Cook on High for 3–5 minutes, until tender, turning over halfway through cooking. With slotted spoon, transfer rings to warmed serving dish; keep warm. Repeat with remaining apple rings. Strain liquid over apple rings in dish.
4. Serve spiced apple rings warm or cover and refrigerate to serve chilled later.

APPLE VARIETIES

Some apples lose their shape when baked, while others may be too tart for eating. Use this chart to guide your choice, but always choose firm, unblemished fruit.

Variety	E	B	C
Bramley's		•	•
Cox's Orange Pippin	•	•	•
Crispin	•		
Discovery	•		
Golden Delicious	•		•
Granny Smith's	•		
Jonathans	•	•	•
Macintosh Reds	•		
Red Delicious	•		
Russets	•		•
Worcester Pearmain	•		

Key
E Eating
B Baking
C Cooking

DELUXE BAKED APPLES

Colour Index page 89. 360 cals per serving. Low in sodium. Begin 40 minutes ahead.

Ingredients	For 4	For 2	For 1
Large dessert apples	4 apples	2 apples	1 apple
Butter or margarine, softened	30 g	15 g	2 teaspoons
Seedless raisins or currants	4 tablespoons	2 tablespoons	1 tablespoon
Finely chopped walnuts	2 tablespoons	1 tablespoon	2 teaspoons
Ground cinnamon	1/2 teaspoon	1/4 teaspoon	pinch
Apple juice	60 ml	2 tablespoons	1 tablespoon
Golden syrup	175 ml	120 ml	60 ml
Microwave cookware	20 cm square baking dish	22.5 × 12.5 cm loaf dish	Small bowl
Time on High (100% power)			
Filled apples	7–9 minutes	4–6 minutes	2–2 1/2 (2:30) minutes
Syrup	3–5 minutes	2–3 minutes	1–1 1/2 (1:30) minutes

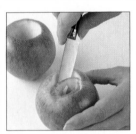

1 Starting from stalk ends, core apples, taking care not to go through to the base and making opening about 4 cm in diameter. Peel apples one-third of the way down.

2 In baking dish, loaf dish or bowl (see Chart), arrange apples, peeled ends up. In mixing bowl, combine butter or margarine, raisins or currants, walnuts and cinnamon.

3 Into hollow centre of each apple, spoon equal amount of spiced mixture. In jug, combine apple juice and golden syrup.

4 Over and around filled apples, pour apple juice and syrup mixture. Cook, covered, on High for time in Chart, until apples are tender, basting with syrup and rearranging apples twice during cooking.

5 With fish slice or slotted spoon, transfer apples to warmed serving platter. Set aside and keep warm. Cook syrup remaining in dish on High for time in Chart, until slightly thickened.

6 Over apples, spoon syrup. Serve hot or cover and refrigerate to serve chilled later.

Apple Desserts

APPLE CARAMEL DESSERT

Colour Index page 89. 314 cals per serving. Low in sodium. Good source of fibre. Begin 55 minutes ahead.

Ingredients for 6 servings		Microwave cookware
105 g plain flour	50 g caster sugar	Shallow flameproof
45 g dark brown sugar	3 tablespoons cold water	21.5 cm pie dish
1/2 teaspoon ground cinnamon	8 small apples, peeled, cored and thickly sliced	
30 g white vegetable fat, chilled	Ice cream or double or whipping cream	
75 g butter or margarine, chilled		
2–3 tablespoons iced water		

1 In food processor with knife blade attached, process flour, dark brown sugar and cinnamon until blended. Add vegetable fat and 45 g chilled butter or margarine; process until mixture resembles coarse crumbs. (Or use fingertips.)

2 Into mixture, sprinkle 2 tablespoons iced water; process just until mixture begins to hold together. If necessary, add another tablespoon iced water. Do not overprocess or mixture will be tough. Shape into ball; flatten slightly. Wrap in greaseproof paper and refrigerate for 30 minutes.

3 Prepare caramel: in pie dish, place remaining butter or margarine. Heat, covered with kitchen paper, on High (100% power) for 45 seconds, or until melted. Stir in sugar and cold water. Cook on High for 6–9 minutes, without stirring, just until mixture turns golden, watching carefully since caramel burns easily and continues to cook and darken when removed from oven.

4 Stir caramel once to distribute colour evenly; carefully arrange apple slices in concentric circles in caramel (there will be enough for 2–3 layers); cool slightly. On lightly floured surface, with floured rolling pin, roll dough into 21.5 cm round, 5 mm thick.

5 On top of apples, place dough. Cook on High for 7–10 minutes, until surface looks dry. Lightly brown under preheated grill. Allow to stand on heatproof surface for 5 minutes. With knife, loosen dessert from side of pie dish.

6 Invert serving plate on to pie dish; turn pie dish upside down on to plate. Carefully remove pie dish to unmould dessert. With rubber spatula, loosen any slices sticking to pie dish; place on top of dessert. If you like, accompany with ice cream or cream.

APPLE SPICED PUDDING

Colour Index page 89. 6 servings. 213 cals per serving. Good source of fibre. Begin 35 minutes ahead.

30 g butter or margarine	1 teaspoon vanilla essence
175 ml unsweetened apple sauce	1/2 teaspoon ground cinnamon
60 g fresh wholemeal breadcrumbs	1/4 teaspoon ground ginger
35 g plain flour	Pinch of allspice
55 g dark brown sugar	Crystallised ginger to decorate
3 eggs	
1/2 teaspoon baking powder	
60 ml double or whipping cream	

1. Lightly grease 1 litre microwave-safe bowl. Line bottom of bowl with greaseproof paper; lightly grease paper. Set aside.
2. In food processor with knife blade attached or in blender, process butter or margarine and remaining ingredients, except crystallised ginger, until smooth and well blended.
3. Into lined bowl, pour mixture. Cook, covered, on Medium (50% power) for 12 minutes, or until knife inserted in centre comes out clean. Allow to stand, covered, on heatproof surface for 10 minutes before serving.
4. *To serve:* invert bowl on to platter. Carefully remove bowl to unmould pudding. Serve warm or cover and refrigerate to serve chilled later. Before serving, decorate with crystallised ginger.

APPLE AND WALNUT CRUMBLE

Colour Index page 89. 8 servings. 246 cals per serving. Low in sodium. Good source of fibre. Begin 35 minutes ahead.

60 g shelled walnuts, chopped	1/2 teaspoon ground ginger
70 g plain flour	60 g chilled butter or margarine, cubed
75 g dark brown sugar	5 large cooking apples
1 teaspoon ground cinnamon	1 tablespoon lemon juice
1/2 teaspoon grated nutmeg	

1. In food processor with knife blade attached, process walnuts and next 5 ingredients until blended. Add butter or margarine; process until mixture resembles coarse crumbs. (Or use fingertips.) Set aside.
2. Peel, core and slice apples. In round 1.5 litre microwave-safe casserole, place apple slices. Sprinkle with lemon juice.
3. Over apple slices, sprinkle walnut and crumb mixture. Cook on High (100% power) for 14–16 minutes, until apple slices are tender. If you like, and if casserole is flameproof, brown under preheated grill. Serve warm or cover and refrigerate to serve chilled later.

Banana and Cherry Desserts

GLAZED BANANAS WITH ORANGE

Colour Index page 88. 4 servings. 258 cals per serving. Low in sodium. Good source of vitamin C, fibre. Begin 15 minutes ahead.

4 medium bananas	*¼ teaspoon ground*
2 medium oranges	*cinnamon*
45 g butter or margarine	*35 g pecan nut halves*
3 tablespoons light	*Orange Julienne (page*
brown sugar	*330) to decorate*

1. Peel bananas and cut into 5 cm pieces. Peel oranges; with sharp knife, separate into segments, removing membranes and any pith. Set aside.
2. In 1 litre microwave-safe measuring jug, place butter or margarine. Heat, covered with kitchen paper, on High (100% power) for 45 seconds–1 minute, until melted. Add brown sugar and cinnamon. Cook on High for 2–4 minutes, until sugar dissolves and mixture boils, stirring twice.
3. To butter and sugar mixture, add bananas, orange segments and pecans; stir. Cook on High for 2–3 minutes, until fruit is hot, stirring twice.
4. Spoon glazed fruit and nuts into warmed serving dish. Decorate and serve warm.

TO FLAMBÉ: place Glazed Bananas with Orange (above) in heatproof serving dish. In 250 ml microwave-safe glass jug, heat ***60 ml dark rum*** on High (100% power) for 30–45 seconds, until hot. Pour over fruit; ignite with long match. Let flames subside before serving.

CHERRIES IN RED WINE

Colour Index page 88. 6 servings. 110 cals per serving. Low in cholesterol, fat, sodium. Begin 15 minutes ahead.

500 ml dry red wine	*2 teaspoons cornflour*
115 g redcurrant jelly	*dissolved in 2*
1 × 7.5 cm long	*tablespoons cold water*
cinnamon stick	*Ice cream (optional)*
450 g fresh sweet	
cherries, stoned, or	
1 × 425 g can dark	
sweet cherries, drained	

1. Into 2 litre microwave-safe glass bowl, pour red wine; add redcurrant jelly and cinnamon stick. Cook on High (100% power) for 3–4 minutes, until mixture boils. Remove cinnamon stick.
2. Into wine mixture, stir cherries. Cook on High for 3–4 minutes, stirring halfway through cooking. Stir in dissolved cornflour. Cook on High for 2–3 minutes, until mixture thickens, stirring twice.
3. *To serve:* spoon into dessert dishes and serve warm or cover and refrigerate to serve chilled later. If you like, serve with ice cream.

ZABAGLIONE WITH CHERRIES

Colour Index page 90. 218 cals per serving. Low in sodium. Begin 45 minutes ahead.

Zabaglione is a rich and versatile dessert. It can be served on its own or with a variety of fruit: strawberries, raspberries and peaches work well. Alternatively, it can be used to create a fruit gratin in a flameproof gratin dish: arrange fruit in a single layer, spoon zabaglione over, then brown lightly under preheated grill and dust with icing sugar immediately before serving.

Ingredients for 4 servings		Microwave cookware
450 g cherries, stoned, or 1 × 425 g can pitted sweet cherries, drained	*50 g caster sugar 3–4 tablespoons kirsch or dry or sweet Marsala Orange Julienne (page 330), to decorate*	1 litre measuring jug
5 egg yolks		

1 Into wine goblets or dessert dishes, spoon cherries; set aside.

2 In measuring jug, with mixer at high speed, beat egg yolks and sugar until thick and lemon coloured. Cook on Medium (50% power) for 1½ (1:30)–2 minutes, until mixture is thick and fluffy, beating halfway through cooking.

3 To egg mixture, add kirsch or Marsala. Beat well.

4 Cook egg mixture on Medium for 30 seconds–1½ (1:30) minutes, until thickened and hot, beating every 30 seconds. Do not boil or mixture will curdle. With mixer at high speed, beat zabaglione for 10–15 minutes, until it is fluffy and mounds slightly when dropped from a spoon.

5 Over cherries in goblets or dessert dishes, spoon zabaglione.

6 Decorate each serving with sprinkling of Orange Julienne. Serve immediately.

Peach and Pear Desserts

All these attractive fruit dishes make delicious desserts, and the fruits used are naturally sweet, so only a minimal amount of sugar is needed. If you like, you can substitute strawberries for the raspberries in the sauce used in Elegant Poached Peaches (below); or try using different fruit suitable for poaching, such as ripe nectarines instead of peaches.

ELEGANT POACHED PEACHES

Colour Index page 92. 276 cals per serving. Good source of vitamin A, vitamin C, fibre. Begin 4 hours ahead or early in day.

Ingredients for 4 servings		Microwave cookware
750 ml water Sugar 1 tablespoon grenadine syrup 4 large ripe peaches 300 g fresh or frozen raspberries 1/2 teaspoon almond essence	6 amaretti biscuits or crisp macaroons Raspberries and mint leaves to decorate	2 litre glass jug or bowl

1 In glass jug or bowl, combine water, 100 g sugar and grenadine syrup. Cook, covered, on High (100% power) for 5–6 minutes, until boiling, stirring once. Uncover and cook on High for 5 minutes longer, stirring twice. Cut peaches in half and twist apart; remove stones.

2 In hot syrup, place peaches. Cook on High for 4–6 minutes, until tender. Cool slightly; remove skins. Refrigerate peaches in syrup until cold. In food processor with knife blade attached or in blender, purée raspberries. Sieve purée to remove seeds.

3 Into raspberry purée, stir almond essence and 2 tablespoons syrup from peaches; sweeten to taste. Cover and refrigerate.

4 With slotted spoon, remove peach halves from syrup and arrange cut side down in dish to drain. Reserve peach syrup.

5 Into mixing bowl, coarsely crumble biscuits. To crumbs, add 1–2 tablespoons reserved peach syrup; stir to moisten. Use to fill peach halves.

6 To serve: on to each of 4 dessert dishes, pour one-quarter of raspberry purée. Place 2 peach halves on top, filled sides up. Serve chilled, decorated with raspberries and mint.

RASPBERRY POACHED PEARS WITH CHOCOLATE AND RASPBERRY SAUCE

Colour Index page 91. 6 servings. 316 cals per serving. Good source of fibre.
Begin 4 hours ahead or early in day.

300 g fresh or frozen raspberries
65 g caster sugar
1 tablespoon lemon juice
6 large pears
1 tablespoon cornflour dissolved in 2 tablespoons water
25 g plain chocolate, chopped
120 ml double or whipping cream
1 tablespoon icing sugar
Mint leaves to decorate

1. In food processor with knife blade attached or in blender, purée raspberries. Over 3 litre microwave-safe casserole, set fine sieve. Press raspberry purée through sieve to remove seeds. Into purée, stir sugar and lemon juice; set aside.
2. Peel pears. Starting from base, core pears, being careful not to go through the tops. Do not remove stalks.
3. In raspberry purée in casserole, arrange pears spoke-fashion, with wide ends towards edge and stalk ends towards centre, overlapping stalk ends if necessary. Spoon raspberry purée over pears. Cook on High (100% power) for 15–20 minutes, until pears are nearly tender, turning halfway through cooking.
4. Into casserole, stir dissolved cornflour until blended. Cook, covered, on High for 2–5 minutes, until purée thickens slightly and pears are tender. Cover and refrigerate for about 3 hours, until flavours blend, spooning raspberry purée over pears occasionally.
5. Just before serving, in 500 ml microwave-safe measuring jug, place 250 ml raspberry purée from casserole. Cook on High for 2–3 minutes, until sauce is very hot. Remove from oven. Add chopped chocolate; stir until chocolate melts.
6. In small bowl, with mixer at medium speed, whip cream and icing sugar until soft peaks form.
7. To serve: on to 6 dessert dishes, pour chocolate and raspberry sauce, reserving some for glaze; place pears on top. Spoon some of reserved sauce over each pear to glaze. Decorate with mint and serve with whipped cream.

CANELLE KNIFE
For a decorative effect, use this to cut thin strips from peeled or unpeeled fruit such as apples, pears, lemons and oranges.

Pear and Pineapple Desserts

POACHED PEARS WITH CHOCOLATE SAUCE

Colour Index page 89. 4 servings. 168 cals per serving. Low in sodium. Begin 40 minutes ahead.

2 medium pears	4 teaspoons cocoa
80 ml water	powder
60 g caster sugar	60 ml double or
1/2 teaspoon vanilla	whipping cream
essence	Mint leaves to decorate

1. Peel pears; cut in half lengthways. With small spoon, remove cores. On cutting board, place pear halves, cut side down. With sharp knife, starting 1 cm from stalk end, slice each pear half lengthways several times, leaving pear connected at stalk end. Press down on each pear half to fan slices slightly. Set aside.
2. In 21.5 cm microwave-safe shallow pie dish, combine water and sugar. Add vanilla essence. Cook on High (100% power) for 5–7 minutes, until sugar dissolves and syrup boils, stirring occasionally. With fish slice, transfer pear fans to pie dish; arrange spoke-fashion, with wide ends towards edge and stalk ends towards centre. Spoon syrup over each pear fan. Cook, covered, on High for 3–5 minutes, until tender; reserve syrup.
3. Into 500 ml microwave-safe measuring jug, spoon cocoa. With fork or whisk, slowly beat in cream until blended but not whipped. Stir in 80 ml reserved syrup. Cook on High for 3–5 minutes, until sauce thickens slightly, stirring frequently. (If sauce is too thick, stir in more syrup.)
4. *To serve:* on to each of 4 dessert dishes, pour one-quarter of sauce. Arrange pear fans on top. Decorate with mint and serve warm.

SPICED PINEAPPLE

Colour Index page 88. 4 servings. 75 cals per serving. Low in fat, sodium. Good source of fibre. Begin 25 minutes ahead.

1 small pineapple	Lime Julienne (page
2 tablespoons brown	330) and mint leaves to
sugar	decorate
Pinch ground ginger or	
cinnamon	

1. With sharp knife, remove leaves and stalk end from pineapple. Remove peel and eyes. Cut pineapple in half lengthways; remove core. Cut each half crossways into 1 cm thick slices.
2. In shallow, round microwave-safe baking dish, place pineapple slices. Cook, covered, on High (100% power) for 3–4 minutes.
3. Meanwhile, in mixing bowl, combine brown sugar and ginger or cinnamon. Over pineapple, evenly sprinkle sugar and spice mixture. Cook on High for 1–2 minutes, just until sugar melts.
4. *To serve:* transfer spiced pineapple slices to warmed serving dish. Decorate with Lime Julienne and mint leaves; serve immediately.

CARAMEL PEARS IN STRAWBERRY SAUCE

Colour Index page 89. 250 cals per serving. Low in sodium. Good source of vitamin C, fibre. Begin 45 minutes ahead.

Ingredients	For 4	For 2	For 1
Large pears	4 pears	2 pears	1 pear
Lemon juice	4 teaspoons	2 teaspoons	1 teaspoon
Water	5 tablespoons	4 tablespoons	3 tablespoons
Fresh or frozen strawberries	300 g	150 g	75 g
Sugar	150 g	90 g	90 g
Double or whipping cream	3 tablespoons	2 tablespoons	2 tablespoons
Microwave cookware	20 cm square baking dish	22.5 × 12.5 cm loaf dish	Small bowl
	1 litre glass jug	500 ml glass jug	250 ml glass jug
Time on High (100% power)			
Pears	10–12 minutes	5–6 minutes	2–3 minutes
Caramel	2–4 minutes	2–4 minutes	2–4 minutes
With cream	1 minute	1 minute	1 minute
Standing time	2 minutes	2 minutes	2 minutes

1 Peel pears. Starting from base, core pears; take care not to go through tops. Do not remove stalks. With Canelle Knife (opposite page) or prongs of fork, cut spiral stripes into pears. Brush pears with lemon juice.

2 In baking dish, loaf dish or small bowl (see Chart), place pears; add water, reserving 1 tablespoon. Cook, covered, on High for time in Chart, until pears are tender, rotating dish halfway through cooking. Set aside.

3 Meanwhile, in food processor with knife blade attached or in blender, purée strawberries and one-third of sugar. Over small bowl, set fine sieve. Press purée through sieve to remove seeds; set aside.

4 Prepare caramel: in glass jug (see Chart), place remaining sugar; add reserved water. Cook on High for time in Chart, without stirring, just until mixture turns light golden, watching carefully since caramel burns easily and continues to cook and darken when removed from oven.

5 To caramel, gradually add cream, stirring constantly. Cook on High for time in Chart; stir. Allow to stand for time in Chart; stir until blended.

6 On to serving dish or dessert dishes, pour strawberry purée; place pears on top. Spoon caramel over pears and serve immediately.

Candlelit Dinner

Chilled Champagne
Chilli Prawn Cocktail *(below)*
Steak au Poivre, *page 204, for 2*
Asparagus Bundles, *page 252, for 2*
Sauté potatoes
Crème Brûlée, *page 325*

PREPARATION TIMETABLE

Early in day	*Make Crème Brûlée; cover and refrigerate. Chill Champagne.*
2 hours ahead	*Prepare Chilli Prawn Cocktail up to end of step 1 and Asparagus Bundles up to end of step 4; cover and refrigerate.*
45 minutes ahead	*Make sauté potatoes conventionally; keep warm. Prepare Steak au Poivre up to end of step 4. Complete Asparagus Bundles; keep warm.*
Just before serving	*Complete Steak au Poivre. Complete Chilli Prawn Cocktail.*

CHILLI PRAWN COCKTAIL
Large or jumbo prawns are the best choice for this starter.

Line 2 serving bowls with *salad leaves*. Arrange *115 g shelled and deveined cooked large prawns* in each bowl.

Spoon over *bottled chilli sauce to taste*. Garnish with *Lemon Twists* (page 132) just before serving.

Plum and Strawberry Desserts

PLUM KUCHEN

Colour Index page 90. 6 servings. 389 cals per serving. Good source of vitamin A, thiamine, niacin, calcium, iron, fibre. Begin 50 minutes ahead.

25 g butter or margarine, softened	*10 plums*
Brown sugar	*45 g Melba Toast Crumbs (page 196)*
2 × 145 g packets pizza base mix	*115 g butter or margarine, chilled and cubed*
230 ml warm water	

1. Lightly grease a 22.5 cm square baking dish. Sprinkle with 1 tablespoon brown sugar.
2. In mixing bowl, combine pizza base mix and water to form dough. Knead well on lightly floured surface for 5 minutes. Press dough evenly into baking dish. Spread with remaining softened butter or margarine.
3. Cut plums in half; remove stones. Cut plums into quarters. Press, skin down, into pizza base.
4. In food processor with knife blade attached, process Melba Toast Crumbs, 110 g brown sugar and cubed butter or margarine until mixture resembles coarse crumbs. (Or use fingertips.) Sprinkle evenly over plums; press lightly. Cook on High (100% power) for 14–16 minutes, shielding corners with foil for first 5 minutes and piercing dough with a fork halfway through cooking.
5. If you like and if dish is flameproof, brown kuchen under preheated grill. Allow to stand on heatproof surface for 5 minutes before serving.

STRAWBERRIES 'NOUVELLES'

Colour Index page 91. 6 servings. 141 cals per serving. Low in sodium. Good source of vitamin C, fibre. Begin 2½ hours ahead or early in day.

250 ml half cream	*½ teaspoon vanilla essence*
2 tablespoons caster sugar	*15 g plain chocolate, chopped*
Pinch of salt	*18 strawberries, cut into halves*
2 egg yolks	
1 tablespoon orange-flavour liqueur	

1. In medium microwave-safe bowl, place cream, sugar and salt. Cook on High (100% power) for 3 minutes, or until boiling, stirring once.
2. In 500 ml measuring jug, beat egg yolks. Stir small amount hot mixture into egg yolks. Slowly pour egg mixture back into remaining hot mixture, beating rapidly to prevent lumping. Cook on Medium (50% power) for 3 minutes, or until slightly thickened, beating twice. Stir in liqueur and vanilla.
3. Reserve half of custard. To remainder, add chocolate; stir until melted. Refrigerate both sauces until well chilled.
4. *To serve:* on to dessert plates, spoon equal amounts of each sauce; place strawberries on top.

Mixed Fruit Desserts

DRIED FRUIT COMPOTE

Colour Index page 89. 8 servings. 171 cals per serving. Low in fat, sodium. Good source of vitamin A, fibre. Begin 40 minutes ahead.

350 ml water	4 whole cloves
60 ml cider vinegar	Orange Julienne from 1
1 × 7.5 cm long	orange (page 330)
cinnamon stick	65 g dried apricot halves
1 vanilla pod, split	90 g stoned prunes
lengthways or 1	75 g glacé cherries
teaspoon vanilla	(optional)
essence	70 g dried figs
6 allspice berries	

1. Into 2 litre microwave-safe casserole, pour water and vinegar; add cinnamon stick, vanilla pod or essence, allspice, cloves and Orange Julienne, reserving some for decoration. Cook, covered, on High (100% power) for 5–7 minutes, until mixture boils and sugar dissolves, stirring occasionally.
2. To spiced syrup, add dried fruit. Cook on High for 8–10 minutes, until fruit plumps, stirring occasionally. With slotted spoon, transfer fruit to serving dish.
3. Cook syrup in casserole on High for 10–15 minutes, until slightly thickened. Over serving dish containing fruit, set sieve. Pour hot syrup through sieve to remove spices. Serve compote warm or cover and refrigerate to serve chilled later. Decorate with reserved Orange Julienne before serving.

RED FRUIT COMPOTE

Colour Index page 88. 8 servings. 113 cals per serving. Low in fat, sodium. Good source of vitamin C, fibre. Begin 20 minutes ahead.

1 × 425 g can pitted	2 tablespoons orange-
sweet cherries	flavour liqueur
300 g strawberries	1 kiwi fruit, peeled and
250 g raspberries	thinly sliced, to
1 tablespoon cornflour	decorate
4 tablespoons	
redcurrant jelly	

1. Drain cherries, reserving 120 ml syrup; set aside. If strawberries are large, cut in half lengthways or into quarters.
2. In 30 × 20 cm microwave-safe baking dish, combine cherries, strawberries and raspberries. Cook, covered, on High (100% power) for 2½ (2:30)–3 minutes, until just warm. Spoon into warmed serving dish; cover and keep warm.
3. In 500 ml microwave-safe measuring jug, dissolve cornflour in reserved syrup. Stir in redcurrant jelly. Cook on High for 2½ (2:30)–4 minutes, until thickened. Stir in orange-flavour liqueur. Pour over compote and serve immediately, or cover and refrigerate to serve chilled later. Decorate with kiwi fruit just before serving.

For the busy working woman, the microwave is a great help in preparing ahead. The Light Cheese Ring with Fruit (below) is ideal for a buffet supper table since it can be made the day before and refrigerated, then simply unmoulded when ready to serve. Try a combination of any of your favourite fruit for the centre.

LIGHT CHEESE RING WITH FRUIT

Colour Index page 91. 286 cals per serving. Good source of fibre. Begin 4½ hours ahead or early in day.

Ingredients for 8 servings		Microwave cookware
450 g low-fat cottage cheese	1 tablespoon grated orange zest	2 litre glass jug or bowl
450 g low-fat soft cheese	Sliced strawberries, sliced kiwi fruit, sliced	Medium bowl
100 g caster sugar	nectarines and	1.5 litre ring mould
2 tablespoons plain flour	pineapple chunks	
3 eggs	Mint sprigs to decorate	

1 Over 2 litre jug or bowl, set sieve. With spoon, press cottage cheese through sieve until smooth.

2 In medium bowl, place soft cheese. Heat on Medium (50% power) for 2–3 minutes, until softened.

3 To cottage cheese in jug or bowl, add soft cheese, sugar, flour, eggs and grated orange zest. With fork, beat until smooth. Cook on High (100% power) for 5–8 minutes, until cheese mixture is very hot, beating 3 times during cooking.

4 With pastry brush, lightly oil ring mould. Pour cheese mixture into ring mould. Cook on Medium for 6–8 minutes, until almost set. Allow to stand on heatproof surface for 30 minutes. Cover and refrigerate for 2–3 hours, until well chilled and firm.

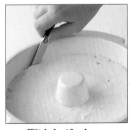

5 With knife, loosen cheese ring from side of ring mould. Invert mould on to serving platter. Carefully remove mould.

6 *To serve:* spoon prepared fruit into centre of cheese ring. Decorate with mint sprigs. Serve chilled.

Creamy Desserts

STRAWBERRY CHARLOTTE

Colour Index page 91. 313 cals per serving. Low in sodium.
Begin early in day or 1 day ahead.

Ingredients for 12 servings		Microwave cookware
About 20 sponge fingers	*4 eggs, separated*	*2 litre glass jug or bowl*
575 g frozen strawberries, defrosted	*100 g caster sugar* ½ *teaspoon almond essence*	
15 g powdered gelatine (2 tablespoons)	*500 ml double or whipping cream*	
500 ml milk	*Strawberries, to decorate*	

1 Line bottom of 2 litre soufflé dish with greaseproof. Trim 1 end of sponge fingers to fit dish. Line dish with sponge fingers, cut side up. In food processor or blender, purée strawberries. In glass jug or bowl, evenly sprinkle gelatine over milk; allow to stand for 1 minute. Heat on High (100% power) for 4–6 minutes, until small bubbles form round edge, stirring twice.

2 In mixing bowl, with mixer at high speed, beat egg yolks and half of sugar until thick and lemon coloured. Stir small amount of hot milk into egg yolk mixture. Slowly pour egg mixture back into remaining hot milk, beating rapidly to prevent lumping. Cook on Medium (50% power) for 5–6 minutes, until mixture thickens slightly and coats back of spoon, stirring twice. Do not boil or custard will curdle. Into large bowl, pour custard.

3 Into custard, stir strawberry purée and almond essence. Cover and refrigerate for about 45 minutes, or until strawberry mixture mounds slightly when dropped from a spoon, stirring occasionally.

4 In medium bowl, with mixer at high speed, whisk egg whites until soft peaks form. Gradually sprinkle in remaining sugar, 2 tablespoons at a time, whisking well after each addition, until sugar completely dissolves and whites stand in stiff, glossy peaks. Spoon on top of strawberry mixture. In same bowl, with same beaters, and with mixer at medium speed, whip cream until soft peaks form. Spoon over strawberry mixture, reserving one-quarter.

5 With rubber spatula or whisk, gently fold whipped cream and whisked egg whites into strawberry mixture. Carefully spoon into prepared soufflé dish. Cover and refrigerate for 4 hours, or until set.

6 *To serve:* with palette knife, loosen charlotte from side of dish. Invert dish on to chilled serving platter. Carefully remove dish to unmould charlotte; remove paper. Decorate with reserved cream and strawberries.

CRÈME PÂTISSIÈRE

Colour Index page 88. Makes 750 ml. 299 cals per 250 ml. Low in sodium. Begin 25 minutes ahead.

500 ml milk
50 g caster sugar
3 tablespoons plain flour
5 egg yolks
½ *teaspoon vanilla essence*

1. Into 2 litre microwave-safe glass bowl, pour milk. Heat on High (100% power) for 4–6 minutes, until small bubbles form round edge.

2. In mixing bowl, with fork or whisk, combine sugar and flour. Add egg yolks, one at a time, beating well after each addition.

3. Stir small amount of hot milk into egg mixture. Slowly pour egg mixture back into remaining hot milk, beating rapidly to prevent lumping. Cook on High for 2–3 minutes, until mixture thickens, beating every minute. Do not boil. Stir in vanilla essence.

4. On to surface of hot custard, press dampened greaseproof paper to prevent skin forming. Refrigerate until chilled.

5. Over bowl, set fine sieve. Press custard through sieve to remove any lumps. Use chilled Crème Pâtissière plain, or with flavourings (below), in tartlets and tarts and decorate with fresh fruit or other toppings. Crème Pâtissière can also be used as a filling in cakes, profiteroles and éclairs.

CRÈME PÂTISSIÈRE

Plain Crème Pâtissière (above) can be varied with different flavours and used to fill these prettily shaped tartlet shells.

Almond Filling
Prepare Crème Pâtissière (above), substituting ½ ***teaspoon almond essence*** for the vanilla essence.

Orange Filling
Prepare Crème Pâtissière (above), substituting ***1 tablespoon orange-flavour liqueur*** and ***1 teaspoon grated orange zest*** for the vanilla essence.

Mocha Filling
Prepare Crème Pâtissière (above). At end of step 3, stir in ***40 g plain chocolate chips*** and ½ ***teaspoon instant coffee powder*** until chocolate is melted.

CRÈME BRÛLÉE

Colour Index page 92. 4 servings. 419 cals per serving. Low in sodium. Good source of vitamin A. Begin early in day or 1 day ahead.

350 ml double or whipping cream	2 tablespoons dark soft brown sugar
3 egg yolks	4 large strawberries to decorate
3 tablespoons caster sugar	
1/2 teaspoon vanilla essence	

1. Into 1 litre microwave-safe measuring jug, pour cream. Heat on High (100% power) for 3–5 minutes, until small bubbles form round edge of cream.

2. In mixing bowl, with whisk, beat egg yolks and sugar. Stir small amount hot cream into egg mixture. Slowly pour egg mixture back into remaining hot cream, beating rapidly to prevent lumping. Cook on Medium (50% power) for 4–6 minutes, until mixture thickens, stirring frequently. Do not boil. Stir in vanilla essence.

3. Into four 120 ml flameproof ramekins, pour hot mixture. Cover and refrigerate for about 6 hours, or until well chilled.

4. About 1 hour before serving, preheat grill. Evenly sprinkle brown sugar over each ramekin so that cream is completely covered; arrange in flameproof baking dish. To prevent custard from curdling, place ice cubes between ramekins. Grill for 3–4 minutes, until sugar melts and forms shiny crust; refrigerate for about 30 minutes, or until crust hardens. Before serving, place ramekins on small plates and decorate with strawberries.

Sprinkling the Sugar and Adding the Ice Cubes

With spoon, sprinkle sugar evenly over surface of cream mixture to cover completely.

To prevent cream from curdling, place ice cubes between ramekins before grilling.

MAKING CARAMEL

Caramel is easy and quick to prepare in the microwave, but it is essential to watch the mixture carefully, without stirring, and to remove it from the oven as soon as it starts to turn golden, since it continues to cook and darken (even burn) afterwards.

To clean measuring jug after making caramel: fill with warm water and heat on High (100% power) until water boils.

CRÈME CARAMEL

Colour Index page 92. 226 cals per serving. Low in sodium. Good source of calcium. Begin 2 1/2 hours ahead or early in day.

Ingredients for 4 servings		Microwave cookware
100 g caster sugar	1 teaspoon vanilla essence	1 litre glass jug
3 tablespoons water		4 × 175 ml ramekins
300 ml milk		30 × 20 cm
4 eggs		baking dish

1 In glass jug, place half of sugar; add water. Cook on High (100% power) for 4–6 minutes, without stirring, just until mixture turns light golden, watching carefully since caramel burns easily and continues to cook and darken when removed from oven. As soon as caramel is light golden, take jug out of oven. Allow to cool for 30 seconds.

2 Into ramekins, pour caramel, swirling to coat bottoms of dishes; set aside to harden. Into same cleaned jug (see Making Caramel, below left), pour milk. Heat on High for 4–6 minutes, until small bubbles form round edge. In mixing bowl, with whisk, beat eggs and remaining sugar until blended. Stir small amount of hot milk into egg mixture. Slowly pour egg mixture into remaining hot milk, beating rapidly to prevent lumping. Stir in vanilla essence.

3 Over large jug, set fine sieve. Strain custard mixture through sieve to remove any lumps. In baking dish, place ramekins.

4 Into ramekins, pour custard mixture. Fill baking dish with water to within 2.5 cm of top of ramekins. Cook on Medium-High (70% power) for 10–14 minutes, until custards are set but centres are still soft, carefully rotating dish 3 times during cooking.

5 Remove ramekins from baking dish. Allow custards to stand, covered, on heatproof surface for 5 minutes, or until firmly set. Cover and refrigerate until ready to serve.

6 *To serve:* with small palette knife, loosen custards from sides of ramekins. Invert each custard on to chilled dessert plate. Carefully remove ramekin, allowing caramel syrup to drip on to custard. Serve chilled.

Creamy Desserts

ICED LEMON SOUFFLÉS

Colour Index page 92. 216 cals per serving. Low in sodium.
Begin early in day or 1 day ahead.

Ingredients for 8 servings		Microwave cookware
2 teaspoons plain flour 150 g caster sugar 175 ml milk 2 eggs, separated 4 medium lemons	250 ml double or whipping cream Lemon slices and mint leaves to decorate	1 litre measuring jug

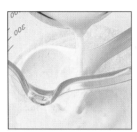

1 In measuring jug, with whisk, combine flour and 100 g sugar until blended. Gradually pour in milk, stirring until smooth. Cook on High (100% power) for 4–6 minutes, until mixture thickens and boils, stirring occasionally. In small mixing bowl, with whisk, beat egg yolks. Stir small amount hot milk into egg yolks.

2 Into remaining hot milk mixture, slowly pour egg yolk mixture, beating rapidly to prevent lumping. Cook on Medium (50% power) for 2–3 minutes, until custard thickens, stirring often. Do not boil. Pour into large mixing bowl. On to surface of hot custard, lightly press dampened greaseproof paper to prevent skin forming. Refrigerate for 1 hour, or until chilled.

3 Grate 1 tablespoon zest from lemons and squeeze 150 ml juice. Stir lemon zest and juice into chilled custard.

4 In medium mixing bowl, with mixer at high speed, whisk egg whites until soft peaks form. Gradually sprinkle in remaining sugar, 1 tablespoon at a time, whisking well after each addition, until sugar completely dissolves and whites stand in stiff, glossy peaks. Spoon on top of lemon custard. In same bowl and with same beaters, whip cream until soft peaks form.

5 To egg whites and lemon custard, add whipped cream; with rubber spatula or whisk, gently fold whipped cream and whisked egg whites into custard. Into 8 freezerproof glasses or dishes, spoon soufflé mixture; freeze for about 4 hours or overnight.

6 Before serving, allow soufflés to stand at room temperature for about 10 minutes to soften slightly; decorate with lemon slices and mint leaves.

RHUBARB RICE CREAM

Colour Index page 93. 8 servings. 181 cals per serving. Low in sodium. Good source of vitamin A, vitamin C, calcium, fibre.
Begin 3½ hours ahead or early in day.

250 ml milk
250 ml water
150 g caster sugar
2 tablespoons short-grain rice
700 g rhubarb, sliced
120 ml double or whipping cream
1 tablespoon icing sugar
¼ teaspoon vanilla essence

1. In 4 litre microwave-safe casserole, combine milk and next 3 ingredients. Allow to stand for 5 minutes. Stir in rhubarb. Cook, covered, on High (100% power) for 20–25 minutes, stirring every 5 minutes. Spoon mixture into dessert dishes; cover and refrigerate for 2½ hours, until well chilled.
2. In mixing bowl, with mixer at medium speed, whip cream with icing sugar and vanilla essence until soft peaks form. Pipe or spoon on top of each dessert.

RASPBERRY CREAM PARFAITS

Colour Index page 92. 6 servings. 327 cals per serving. Low in sodium.
Begin 3½ hours ahead or early in day.

300 g fresh or frozen raspberries
2 tablespoons water
1 tablespoon powdered gelatine
½ teaspoon lemon juice
100 g caster sugar
350 ml double or whipping cream
2 egg whites

1. In food processor with knife blade attached or in blender, purée raspberries. Over large mixing bowl, set fine sieve. Press raspberry purée through sieve to remove seeds. Into small microwave-safe bowl, pour water. Evenly sprinkle gelatine over; allow to stand for 1 minute to soften. Heat on High (100% power) for 1–2 minutes, until gelatine dissolves, stirring twice. Do not boil. Stir into raspberry sauce.
2. Into raspberry mixture, stir lemon juice and half of sugar. Cover and refrigerate for 15–20 minutes, until mixture mounds slightly when dropped from spoon, stirring often.
3. In medium mixing bowl, with mixer at medium speed, whip cream until soft peaks form. Fold half of cream into raspberry mixture; reserve remainder.
4. In bowl, with mixer at high speed, whisk egg whites until soft peaks form. Gradually sprinkle in remaining sugar, 1 tablespoon at a time, whisking well after each addition, until sugar dissolves and whites stand in stiff, glossy peaks. Fold into raspberry mixture.
5. Place 1 spoonful of raspberry mixture in each parfait glass. Top with 1 spoonful reserved whipped cream. Repeat layering once more. Cover and refrigerate until set. Serve chilled.

Creamy and Chocolate Desserts

TIRAMISÚ

Colour Index page 93. 16 servings. 296 cals per serving. Good source of vitamin A, calcium. Begin 4 hours ahead or early in day.

225 g sponge cake mix	350 ml double or whipping cream
1 egg	60 g icing sugar
75 ml water	40 ml coffee liqueur
1/2 teaspoon almond essence	40 ml strong coffee
450 g mascarpone or cream cheese	1 teaspoon vanilla essence
	Cocoa

1. Line bottom of 18 cm round microwave-safe baking dish with doubled greaseproof.
2. In mixing bowl, with mixer at low speed, beat cake mix, egg, water and almond essence until blended, constantly scraping bowl. Increase speed to medium; beat for 2 minutes, occasionally scraping bowl. Spoon mixture into prepared dish.
3. Elevate dish on microwave-safe trivet or rack, or on ramekins turned upside down. Cook on High (100% power) for 10–12 minutes, until cake springs back when lightly touched, rotating dish twice. Allow to stand in dish on heatproof surface for 5 minutes. With knife, loosen cake from sides of dish. Invert on to rack; remove paper. Cool.
4. In 1 litre microwave-safe measuring jug, place cheese. Heat on High for 1–2 minutes, until softened. With mixer at low speed, blend cheese, cream, icing sugar, liqueur, coffee and vanilla.
5. Cut cooled cake into small pieces. Place half in large serving bowl. Pour in a third of cheese mixture; repeat layers. Cover and refrigerate until chilled. Dust with cocoa before serving.

CHOCOLATE-DIPPED FRUIT

Colour Index page 90. Makes 14–30 pieces. About 31 cals per piece. Begin 35 minutes ahead.

75 g plain or white chocolate	14 large strawberries; or 24 grapes (about 225 g); or segments from 2 oranges
1 teaspoon white vegetable fat	

1. Line baking sheet with greaseproof paper. In 500 ml microwave-safe glass jug, place chocolate and vegetable fat. Heat on High (100% power) for 1 1/2 (1:30)–2 minutes, until melted, stirring once. Remove from oven; stir until smooth.
2. Dip fruit halfway into melted chocolate. Gently shake of excess chocolate; place dipped fruit on lined baking sheet.
3. Allow chocolate-dipped fruit to stand for about 10 minutes, until chocolate sets. Do not refrigerate. Serve same day.

CHOCOLATE AND CHESTNUT CREAM

Colour Index page 93. 430 cals per serving. Low in sodium. Good source of calcium, iron, fibre. Begin 4 1/2 hours ahead or early in day.

Ingredients for 12 servings		Microwave cookware
500 ml milk 1 × 437 g can unsweetened chestnut purée 150 g caster sugar 50 g plain chocolate, chopped 4 eggs, separated	15 g powdered gelatine (2 tablespoons) 600 ml double or whipping cream Chocolate Curls (page 360) to decorate	2 litre glass jug or bowl

1 Prepare collar for 1.5 litre soufflé dish: from roll of greaseproof paper or foil, tear off 60 cm strip; fold lengthways into 60 × 15 cm strip. Wrap strip around outside of dish so collar stands 7.5 cm above rim. Secure with tape and set aside.

2 In glass jug or bowl, combine milk, chestnut purée and 100 g sugar. Heat on High (100% power) for 6–8 minutes, until small bubbles form round edge. Remove from oven; stir until smooth and well blended. Add chopped chocolate and stir until melted.

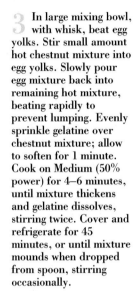

3 In large mixing bowl, with whisk, beat egg yolks. Stir small amount hot chestnut mixture into egg yolks. Slowly pour egg mixture back into remaining hot mixture, beating rapidly to prevent lumping. Evenly sprinkle gelatine over chestnut mixture; allow to soften for 1 minute. Cook on Medium (50% power) for 4–6 minutes, until mixture thickens and gelatine dissolves, stirring twice. Cover and refrigerate for 45 minutes, or until mixture mounds when dropped from spoon, stirring occasionally.

4 In medium mixing bowl, with mixer at high speed, whisk egg whites until soft peaks form. Gradually whisk in sugar until whites stand in stiff, glossy peaks and sugar is completely dissolved. Spoon on top of chocolate chestnut mixture. In same bowl and with same beaters, whip 500 ml cream until soft peaks form. With rubber spatula, fold cream and whisked egg whites into chocolate and chestnut mixture.

5 Into prepared soufflé dish, spoon chocolate and chestnut mixture; cover and refrigerate for about 2 1/2 hours or until set.

6 *To serve:* remove collar from soufflé dish. In small bowl, with mixer at medium speed, whip remaining cream until soft peaks form; spoon into piping bag fitted with rosette tube. Decorate top of dessert with piped whipped cream and Chocolate Curls. Serve chilled.

Chocolate Desserts

CHOCOLATE MOUSSE TORTE

**Colour Index page 92. 297 cals per serving. Low in sodium.
Begin 4½ hours ahead or early in day.**

Ingredients for 16 servings		Microwave cookware

350 ml milk
¼ teaspoon salt
Sugar
1 tablespoon powdered
  gelatine
4 eggs, separated
225 g plain chocolate
30 g butter or margarine
	125 g shelled nuts,
	  chopped
	500 ml double or
	  whipping cream
	Chocolate Rounds (page
	  360 optional)
		Large bowl
		Small bowl

1 In large bowl, combine milk, salt and 70 g sugar; evenly sprinkle gelatine over mixture. Allow to stand for 1 minute to soften gelatine slightly. Stir. Cook on High (100% power) for 3 minutes, until gelatine completely dissolves, stirring halfway through cooking. Do not boil.

2 In small bowl, whisk egg yolks; stir in small amount hot milk mixture. Slowly pour egg mixture into remaining hot milk, beating to prevent lumping. Cook on Medium (50% power) for 4 minutes, or until thickened slightly, stirring occasionally. Add 175 g chocolate; stir until melted. Cover and chill for 20 minutes. In small bowl, place remaining chocolate and butter or margarine. Heat, covered with kitchen paper, on High for 1½ (1:30) minutes, or until melted. Stir in nuts, reserving 1 tablespoon.

3 Over bottom of lightly oiled 22.5 × 7.5 cm springform tin, spread chocolate and nut mixture in even layer. Place tin in freezer for about 15 minutes, until chocolate and nut mixture sets into crust.

4 In medium mixing bowl, with mixer at high speed, whisk egg whites until soft peaks form. Gradually sprinkle in 50 g sugar, whisking well after each addition, until sugar dissolves and whites stand in stiff, glossy peaks. Spoon on top of cooled chocolate custard. In same bowl, with same beaters, and with mixer at medium speed, whip 300 ml cream until soft peaks form.

5 With rubber spatula or whisk, gently fold cream and egg whites into chocolate custard mixture. Spoon mousse over chocolate and nut crust in tin. Cover and refrigerate for about 3 hours, or until set.

6 With knife, loosen mousse from side of springform tin. Remove side of tin. In small bowl, with mixer at medium speed, whip remaining cream until soft peaks form; spoon into piping bag fitted with rosette tube. Decorate top of torte with piped whipped cream and sprinkle with reserved nuts. If you like, decorate with Chocolate Rounds. Serve chilled.

CHOCOLATE CREAM LOAF

Colour Index page 93. 16 servings. 299 cals per serving. Low in sodium. Begin early in day.

350 g frozen raspberries,
  defrosted
3 tablespoons caster
  sugar
6 egg yolks
350 ml double or
  whipping cream
	3 tablespoons finely
	  chopped pistachio nuts
	350 g plain chocolate
	115 g butter or
	  margarine

1. In food processor with knife blade attached or in blender, process raspberries and sugar until puréed. Press purée through fine sieve to remove seeds. Cover and refrigerate sauce.

2. In medium microwave-safe bowl, with whisk, beat egg yolks and 120 ml cream. Cook on Medium (50% power) for 3½ (3:30)–4 minutes, until egg yolk mixture coats back of spoon, stirring occasionally. Do not boil. Cover and refrigerate for 10 minutes, stirring once.

3. Line 22.5 × 12.5 cm loaf tin with foil. Evenly sprinkle bottom with nuts. Set aside.

4. In large microwave-safe bowl, place chocolate and butter or margarine. Heat, covered with kitchen paper, on High for 2–3 minutes, until melted. Remove from oven; stir until smooth. In small mixing bowl, with mixer at medium speed, whip remaining cream until soft peaks form. With whisk, beat egg yolk mixture into melted chocolate mixture. With rubber spatula, fold in cream.

5. Spoon mixture into prepared loaf tin. Refrigerate for about 3 hours, or until firm. With knife, loosen loaf from sides of tin. Invert loaf on to serving platter. Cut into slices and serve, chilled, with raspberry sauce.

RICH CHOCOLATE MOUSSE

Colour Index page 93. 4 servings. 171 cals per serving. Low in sodium. Begin early in day.

75 g plain chocolate,
  chopped
3 eggs, separated
	1 teaspoon vanilla
	  essence

1. In medium microwave-safe bowl, place chocolate. Heat on High (100% power) for 1–1½ (1:30) minutes, until melted. Remove from oven; stir until smooth.

2. In small bowl, with fork, beat egg yolks and vanilla essence. Slowly pour mixture into melted chocolate, beating until blended. Cook on Medium (50% power) for 30 seconds, stirring twice.

3. In bowl, with mixer at high speed, whisk egg whites until stiff peaks form. With rubber spatula or whisk, gently fold whisked egg whites into chocolate mixture until blended.

4. Into each of 4 glasses or dessert dishes, spoon one-quarter of chocolate mixture. Cover and refrigerate for at least 4 hours, or until firm.

TINY CHOCOLATE CONES

Colour Index page 93. Makes 25 cones. 54 cals each. Low in sodium. Begin early in day.

115 g plain chocolate, chopped	½ teaspoon vanilla essence
30 g butter or margarine	70 g shelled macadamia nuts, finely chopped
2 tablespoons double or whipping cream	

1. To form cones, cut twenty-five 8.5 cm foil squares. Fold each square diagonally in half to make triangle. Hold each triangle with long side towards you. Bring lower right point over to meet top point. Roll left side of foil around right side to form cone with tight point at bottom; secure with tape. Repeat with remaining foil squares.

2. In medium microwave-safe bowl, place chocolate and butter or margarine. Heat, covered with kitchen paper, on High (100% power) for 2–2½ (2:30) minutes, until melted. Remove from oven; stir until smooth. Stir in cream and vanilla essence. Set bowl over iced water. With whisk, beat mixture until fluffy. Fold in nuts, reserving 1 tablespoon.

3. Spoon chocolate mixture into piping bag fitted with medium rosette tube. Pipe into foil cones. Sprinkle with reserved nuts. Refrigerate for about 1 hour, until set.

WHITE CHOCOLATE MOUSSE

Colour Index page 90. 8 servings. 242 cals per serving. Low in sodium. Begin 55 minutes ahead.

175 g white chocolate	250 ml double or whipping cream
3 tablespoons milk	Raspberries and mint leaves to decorate
2 eggs	
½ teaspoon vanilla essence	

1. In medium microwave-safe bowl, place chopped white chocolate. Heat on High (100% power) for 2–3 minutes, until chocolate is melted, stirring twice. Remove from oven; stir until smooth.

2. In small bowl with fork or whisk, beat milk and eggs. Gradually beat egg mixture into melted chocolate until blended. Cook chocolate mixture on Medium (50% power) for 2½ (2:30)–3 minutes, until thickened slightly, stirring halfway through cooking. Do not boil. Stir in vanilla essence. Cover and refrigerate for about 30 minutes, until well chilled, stirring occasionally.

3. With mixer at medium speed, beat chilled chocolate mixture for 1 minute. In bowl, with same beaters, and with mixer at medium speed, whip cream until soft peaks form. With rubber spatula or whisk, gently fold cream into chocolate mixture. Spoon into serving dish or dessert dishes. Serve immediately or cover and refrigerate to serve chilled later. Decorate before serving.

CHOCOLATE ALMOND DESSERT

Colour Index page 93. 616 cals per serving. Good source of iron. Begin 3½ hours ahead or early in day.

Ingredients for 8 servings		Microwave cookware
50 g seedless raisins, chopped	½ teaspoon baking powder	2 litre soufflé dish
2 tablespoons almond-flavour liqueur	30 g dried breadcrumbs	500 ml measuring jug
225 g plain chocolate	6 amaretti biscuits or crisp macaroons, crushed	Trivet, rack or ramekin
60 g butter or margarine, softened	1 tablespoon caster sugar	
110 g light soft brown sugar	Chocolate Cream Icing (page 359)	
3 eggs, separated	Flaked almonds to decorate	

1 Line bottom of soufflé dish with double thickness of greaseproof paper. In small bowl, combine chopped raisins and almond-flavour liqueur. Set aside.

2 In measuring jug, place chocolate. Heat on High (100% power) for 2½ (2:30) minutes, until melted, stirring once. Remove from oven; stir until smooth. Set aside.

3 With mixer, beat butter or margarine and brown sugar until fluffy. Beat in egg yolks one at a time. Fold in melted chocolate, baking powder, breadcrumbs and crushed biscuits. Add raisins and liquid. Whisk egg whites until soft peaks form. Add sugar, whisking until whites stand in stiff, glossy peaks. Gently fold egg whites into chocolate mixture.

4 Into prepared soufflé dish, evenly spoon chocolate mixture. Elevate soufflé dish on trivet or rack, or on ramekin turned upside down. Cook on High (100% power) for 6–8 minutes, just until set, rotating dish every 2 minutes.

5 Allow dessert to stand, covered, on heatproof surface for 10 minutes. With palette knife, loosen dessert from dish. Invert on to serving platter; remove greaseproof paper. Leave to cool completely.

6 With palette knife, cover top and side of cake with Chocolate Cream Icing, making decorative swirls. Decorate with flaked almonds.

Chocolate

All milk-based chocolate desserts, or those with a high milk content, turn out well when cooked in the microwave – because they do not stick or scorch as they tend to do when cooked conventionally. Nutty Chocolate Delight (below) is especially popular with children. Easy to make in the microwave, it is irresistible when topped with whipped cream.

NUTTY CHOCOLATE DELIGHT

Colour Index page 93. 438 cals per serving. Good source of calcium. Begin 2½ hours ahead or early in day.

Ingredients for 6 servings		Microwave cookware
100 g caster sugar 35 g plain flour ¼ teaspoon salt ¼ teaspoon ground cinnamon 500 ml milk 60 g butter or margarine 75 g plain chocolate 1 egg, beaten	1 teaspoon vanilla essence 55 g shelled nuts, chopped 120 ml double or whipping cream Ground cinnamon to decorate	2 litre glass jug or bowl

1 In glass jug or bowl, combine sugar, flour, salt, cinnamon and milk; add butter or margarine and chocolate. Cook on High (100% power) for 5–7 minutes, until bubbling and slightly thickened, stirring often. In bowl, mix egg with a little of hot chocolate mixture.

2 Into remaining hot chocolate mixture, slowly pour egg mixture, beating rapidly to prevent lumping. Cook on Medium (50% power) for 2–3 minutes, until thickened, stirring often. Do not boil or pudding will curdle. Stir in vanilla essence and nuts.

3 Into each of 6 glasses or dessert dishes, pour equal amount of hot mixture.

4 On to surface, lightly press dampened greaseproof paper, to prevent skin from forming. Refrigerate for about 2 hours, or until well chilled and set.

5 In mixing bowl, with mixer at medium speed, whip cream until soft peaks form.

6 *To serve:* top each dessert with whipped cream; lightly sprinkle with cinnamon. Serve chilled.

CHOCOLATE PUDDING

Colour Index page 91. 8 servings. 274 cals per serving. Begin 45 minutes ahead.

60 g butter or margarine 140 g plain flour ½ teaspoon instant coffee powder (optional) 2 teaspoons baking powder 150 g caster sugar 6 tablespoons cocoa powder	120 ml half cream 1 teaspoon vanilla essence 75 g light brown sugar 25 g shelled walnuts, chopped 250 ml water Icing sugar

1. In 500 ml microwave-safe measuring jug, place butter or margarine. Heat, covered with kitchen paper, on High (100% power) for 45 seconds–1 minute, until melted. Set aside.

2. In medium mixing bowl, combine flour, coffee powder (if using), baking powder, 100 g sugar and 3 tablespoons cocoa. Into melted butter or margarine, stir cream and vanilla essence. Stir cream mixture into flour mixture until smooth. Pour into 21.5 cm microwave-safe deep pie dish.

3. In small mixing bowl, combine brown sugar, walnuts and remaining sugar and cocoa. Evenly sprinkle over mixture. Carefully pour water over top. Elevate pie dish on microwave-safe trivet or rack, or on ramekin turned upside down. Cook on Medium (50% power) for 12–15 minutes, until pudding rises and is almost set, rotating every 3 minutes. Allow to stand on heatproof surface for 15 minutes. Dust with icing sugar; serve warm.

ORANGE, LEMON AND LIME JULIENNE
Julienne garnish can intensify the flavours of a dish as in Glazed Bananas with Orange (page 319), or provide a zesty contrast, as in Sweet and Sour Beetroot (page 255).

With vegetable peeler, remove zest from orange, lemon or lime, leaving bitter white pith behind. Stack zest and cut into fine strips.

Or use zester to remove fine strips of zest as shown. Zester is best for thinner skin of limes.

CHOCOLATE AND COCONUT DESSERT CUPS

Colour Index page 90. Makes 6. 233 cals each. Low in sodium. Begin 40 minutes ahead.

75 g plain chocolate, chopped
2 teaspoons white vegetable fat
95 g desiccated coconut

500 ml ice cream
Chocolate-Dipped Fruit (page 327)

1. Place six 6 cm paper cake cases on tray; place 6 more cases inside to make double thickness.
2. In small microwave-safe bowl, place chocolate and vegetable fat. Heat on High (100% power) for 1½ (1:30)–2 minutes, until melted and smooth, stirring occasionally. Stir in coconut. Into each paper case, place 1 rounded tablespoon chocolate and coconut mixture. Press mixture on to bottom and up side of each paper case. Place in freezer for about 10 minutes, or until firm.
3. Lift out chilled chocolate cups; carefully remove paper cases and discard. Spoon equal amount of ice cream into each cup. Top with Chocolate-Dipped Fruit and serve immediately.

CHOCOLATE ICE CREAM PIE
Ice cream pies are always a popular choice for a party. Use the microwave to create this delicious version by softening peanut butter (page 29) and ice cream (page 31) for easy spreading.

In *Digestive Biscuit Crust* (page 339), evenly spread *500 ml softened vanilla ice cream.*

In small bowl, combine *120 ml golden syrup* and *85 ml peanut butter, softened*; spread evenly over ice cream.

Sprinkle pie with *50 g chopped peanuts or other nuts*. Top with *500 ml softened chocolate ice cream.*

Freeze ice cream pie for about 4 hours, or until firm. Decorate with *whipped cream and chopped nuts.*

CHOCOLATE PROFITEROLES

Colour Index page 94. 179 cals each. Begin 1½ hours ahead.

Ingredients for 12 profiteroles		Microwave cookware
250 ml water 100 g butter or margarine ½ teaspoon salt 150 g plain flour 4 eggs	Chocolate Glaze (below) Crème Pâtissière (page 324), chilled, or Vanilla Ice Cream (page 332)	2 litre glass jug or bowl

1. Lightly brush 1 large baking sheet with oil. Preheat conventional oven to 200°C (400°F, gas mark 6).

2. In glass jug or bowl, combine water, butter or margarine and salt. Heat on High (100% power) for 5–7 minutes, until boiling.

3. Into boiling water and butter or margarine mixture, pour flour all at once. With wooden spoon, beat mixture vigorously until it is smooth, forms a ball and leaves side of jug or bowl. (The warmth of the boiling mixture cooks the flour.)

4. To flour mixture, add eggs, one at a time, beating well after each addition until mixture is smooth and satiny. Allow mixture to stand until slightly cooled.

5. On to greased baking sheet, drop mixture in 12 mounds, 5 cm apart. Bake conventionally for 35 minutes, or until golden. Turn off oven; leave puffs in oven for 10 minutes to dry.

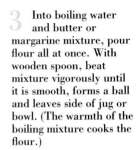

6. Remove puffs from oven and place on racks. Leave puffs to cool.

7. Make Chocolate Glaze: in 1 litre microwave-safe measuring jug, place *75 g plain chocolate drops, 15 g butter, 1½ teaspoons milk* and *1½ teaspoons golden syrup.*

8. Cook chocolate mixture on High for 2–3 minutes, until chocolate melts, stirring halfway through cooking. Remove from oven. Stir until smooth.

9. *To serve:* when puffs are cool, cut off tops. Fill shells with chilled Crème Pâtissière or ice cream. Replace tops and drizzle with warm Chocolate Glaze. Serve immediately.

Ice Cream and Sorbets

The custard and syrup bases for ice creams and sorbets are quick to make in the microwave, and the resulting desserts are delicious on their own – or served with fruit and toppings. Be sure to cool custards and syrups completely before freezing so that they freeze quickly and the consistency of the ice cream or sorbet is smooth.

VANILLA ICE CREAM

Colour Index page 94. 178 cals per serving. Low in sodium. Begin early in day.

Ingredients for 8 servings or 750 ml		Microwave cookware
100 g caster sugar 4 teaspoons plain flour ¹/₄ teaspoon salt 350 ml milk 1 egg 1 egg yolk	175 ml double or whipping cream 1 teaspoon vanilla essence	2 litre glass jug or bowl

1 In glass jug or bowl, combine sugar, flour and salt; stir in milk until smooth. Cook on High (100% power) for 4–6 minutes, until mixture boils and thickens slightly, stirring occasionally.

2 In mixing bowl with whisk, beat egg and egg yolk. Stir small amount hot milk mixture into beaten eggs.

3 Into remaining hot milk mixture, slowly pour egg mixture, beating rapidly to prevent lumping.

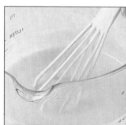

4 Cook custard on Medium (50% power) for 2–3 minutes, until thickened, beating frequently. Do not boil or custard will curdle. On to surface of hot custard, lightly press dampened greaseproof paper to prevent skin forming. Refrigerate for about 2 hours, or until well chilled, stirring occasionally.

5 Into 1.5–2 litre container of electric ice cream maker, pour chilled custard, cream and vanilla essence. Freeze mixture according to manufacturer's instructions. When freezing is finished, ice cream will be soft. With spoon, scoop ice cream into freezerproof serving dish. Pack down ice cream; smooth surface and, if you like, make decorative pattern on top. Cover with freezer film. Place dish in freezer for at least 2 hours, until ice cream is firm.

6 To serve: soften ice cream slightly by heating on Medium-Low (30% power) for 30 seconds–1 minute. Remove from serving dish with ice cream scoop.

MANGO SORBET

Colour Index page 94. 4 servings. 164 cals per serving. Low in fat, sodium. Good source of vitamin A, vitamin C. Begin early in day.

250 ml water
100 g caster sugar
1 ripe mango (about 450 g), peeled and cut into 1 cm chunks
1 tablespoon lime juice
2 tablespoons dark rum
Lime Julienne (page 330) to decorate

1. Into 1 litre microwave-safe measuring jug, pour water; add sugar. Cook on High (100% power) for 3–4 minutes, until sugar dissolves and mixture begins to boil, stirring halfway through cooking. Cook on High for 5 minutes longer, stirring occasionally. Cover and refrigerate for about 45 minutes, or until chilled.
2. In food processor with knife blade attached or in blender, purée mango, lime juice and rum.
3. Into cooled syrup, stir mango purée. Pour into 22.5 cm square baking dish. On to surface, press dampened greaseproof paper. Freeze for about 3 hours, or until sorbet is partially frozen, stirring occasionally.
4. Into chilled large mixing bowl, spoon sorbet. With mixer at medium speed, beat until smooth but still frozen. Transfer to freezerproof dish; smooth surface. Cover and freeze until firm.
5. To serve: allow sorbet to stand at room temperature for 5–10 minutes to soften. Decorate with Lime Julienne and serve immediately.

KIWI FRUIT SORBET

Colour Index page 94. 4 servings. 143 cals per serving. Low in cholesterol, fat, sodium. Good source of vitamin C. Begin early in day.

250 ml water
100 g caster sugar
4 ripe kiwi fruit, peeled, cut into quarters and cored
1 tablespoon lemon juice
Mint leaves to decorate

1. Into 1 litre microwave-safe measuring jug, pour water; add sugar. Cook on High (100% power) for 3–4 minutes, until sugar dissolves and mixture begins to boil, stirring halfway through cooking. Cook on High for 5 minutes longer, stirring occasionally. Cover and refrigerate for about 45 minutes, or until chilled.
2. In food processor with knife blade attached or in blender, purée kiwi fruit and lemon juice.
3. Into cooled syrup, stir kiwi fruit purée. Pour into 22.5 cm square baking dish. On to surface, press dampened greaseproof paper. Freeze for about 3 hours, stirring occasionally.
4. Into chilled large mixing bowl, spoon sorbet. With mixer at medium speed, beat until smooth but still frozen. Transfer to freezerproof dish; smooth surface. Cover and freeze until firm.
5. To serve: allow sorbet to stand at room temperature for 5–10 minutes to soften. Decorate with mint leaves and serve immediately.

Valentine's Dessert Party

Strawberry Charlotte, page 324
Tartlets filled with Crème Pâtissière, page 324, and fruit
Caramel Pears in Strawberry Sauce, page 321, for 4 (double quantity)
Black Forest Gâteau, page 357
Pink Champagne

PREPARATION TIMETABLE

Early in day	**4 hours ahead**	**3 hours ahead**	**30 minutes ahead**	**Just before serving**
Chill Champagne. Prepare Strawberry Charlotte up to end of step 5.	*Prepare Caramel Pears in Strawberry Sauce up to end of step 5, in 2 batches. Make Black Forest Gâteau; cover loosely and refrigerate.*	*Make Crème Pâtissière in flavours of your choice; cover and refrigerate. Prepare fruit for tartlets; cover and refrigerate. Complete Strawberry Charlotte as in step 6. Refrigerate until ready to serve.*	*If you like, reheat tartlet shells to crisp; set aside to cool. Fill tartlet shells with Crème Pâtissière and decorate with fruit; arrange on serving platter.*	*Complete Caramel Pears in Strawberry Sauce as in step 6.*

Puddings

Use your microwave to make traditional bread-based desserts. These puddings are a delicious and economical way to use up any day-old bread you may have left over, as in Old-Fashioned Bread and Butter Pudding (below), in which the crusts are removed for an attractive presentation. For a nutritious change, substitute wholemeal bread for the white bread.

OLD-FASHIONED BREAD AND BUTTER PUDDING

Colour Index page 90. 290 cals per serving. Good source of calcium. Begin 45 minutes ahead.

Ingredients for 10 servings		Microwave cookware
12 slices day-old white bread, crusts removed 60 g butter or margarine, softened 500 ml half cream 250 ml milk 4 eggs 150 g caster sugar	½ teaspoon ground cinnamon Pinch of grated nutmeg Pinch of ground cloves 1 teaspoon vanilla essence Icing sugar	Shallow 2 litre baking dish 1 litre measuring jug Trivet, rack or ramekins

1 Cut bread slices diagonally in half to form triangles. Arrange slices on baking sheet; toast lightly. Spread each triangle with softened butter or margarine.

2 In baking dish, working from outer edge towards centre, arrange toast triangles in overlapping circles.

3 Into measuring jug, pour cream and milk. Heat on High (100% power) for 4–6 minutes, until small bubbles form round edge.

4 In medium mixing bowl, with mixer at medium speed, beat eggs, sugar, spices and vanilla essence until blended. Stir small amount hot milk mixture into egg mixture. Slowly pour egg mixture back into remaining hot milk mixture, beating rapidly to prevent lumping.

5 Over toast in baking dish, carefully ladle custard. Elevate baking dish on trivet or rack, or on ramekins turned upside down.

6 Cook pudding on Medium (50% power) for 14–16 minutes, until knife inserted 2.5 cm from edge comes out clean, rotating dish twice. Allow to stand on heatproof surface until slightly cooled. Just before serving, dust with icing sugar. Serve warm.

SYRUP SPONGE PUDDING

Colour Index page 91. 4 servings. 278 cals per serving. Good source of calcium. Begin 35 minutes ahead.

50 g butter or margarine, softened
50 g caster sugar
1 egg, beaten
1 teaspoon grated lemon zest

½ teaspoon vanilla essence
100 g self-raising flour
45–60 ml milk
Golden syrup

1. In mixing bowl, cream butter or margarine and sugar until light and fluffy. Slowly beat in egg, lemon zest and vanilla. Lightly fold in flour alternately with milk until soft dough is formed.
2. Grease inside of 600 ml microwave-safe pudding basin; place 2 tablespoons golden syrup in bottom of basin. Spoon dough into basin.
3. Cook, covered tightly with microwave-safe cling film, on High (100% power) for 3–4 minutes, until pudding is well risen and cocktail stick inserted in centre comes out clean, turning basin every minute.
4. On heatproof surface, allow pudding to stand for 2 minutes. With sharp knife, loosen edges of pudding from basin; unmould on to serving dish. Allow to stand, loosely covered, for 2 minutes. Serve immediately.

CREAMY RICE PUDDING

Colour Index page 90. 6 servings. 283 cals per serving. Low in sodium. Good source of calcium. Begin 50 minutes ahead.

750 ml milk
175 g short-grain rice
1 teaspoon vanilla essence
2 egg yolks
3 tablespoons caster sugar

120 ml double or whipping cream
¼ teaspoon ground cinnamon
¼ teaspoon ground allspice
70 g raisins

1. In 2 litre microwave-safe casserole, combine milk, rice and vanilla. Cook on High (100% power) for 5 minutes, or until boiling. Reduce power level to Medium-High (70% power) and cook for 20–30 minutes longer, until tender, stirring often.
2. In small bowl, with whisk, beat egg yolks and next 4 ingredients until blended. Stir small amount rice mixture into egg mixture. Pour egg mixture back into remaining rice mixture, stirring rapidly to prevent lumping. Stir in raisins. Cook on Medium (50% power) for 3–4 minutes, until slightly thickened, stirring every minute.
3. On heatproof surface, allow pudding to stand, covered, for 5 minutes. Serve warm or cover and refrigerate to serve chilled later.

Puddings and Cheesecakes

CHOCOLATE AND CINNAMON BREAD PUDDING

Colour Index page 90. 10 servings. 280 cals per serving. Begin 45 minutes ahead.

12 slices cinnamon-flavoured raisin loaf	*250 ml milk*
	4 eggs
75 g plain chocolate, melted	*150 g caster sugar*
	1½ teaspoons vanilla essence
500 ml half cream	

1. Remove crusts from bread. With serrated knife, cut slices diagonally in half to form triangles. In shallow 2 litre microwave-safe baking dish, arrange half of triangles in single layer, overlapping if necessary. Drizzle half of melted chocolate over triangles. Arrange remaining triangles in single layer on top; set aside.
2. Into 1 litre microwave-safe glass measuring jug, pour half cream and milk. Heat, covered, on High (100% power) for 4–6 minutes, until small bubbles form round edge.
3. In mixing bowl, with whisk, beat eggs, sugar and vanilla. Stir small amount hot cream mixture into egg mixture. Slowly pour egg mixture back into remaining hot cream mixture, beating rapidly to prevent lumping. Ladle custard over bread. Drizzle with remaining melted chocolate.
4. Elevate baking dish on microwave-safe trivet or rack, or on ramekins turned upside down. Cook on Medium (50% power) for 14–16 minutes, until knife inserted 2.5 cm from edge comes out clean, rotating dish twice. Allow to stand on heatproof surface until slightly cooled. Serve warm or cover and refrigerate to serve chilled later.

RICH NOODLE PUDDING

Colour Index page 91. 8 servings. 319 cals per serving. Begin 45 minutes ahead.

225 g egg noodles (tagliatelle)	*2 tablespoons caster sugar*
90 g butter or margarine, melted	*35 g sultanas*
60 g fresh breadcrumbs	*35 g dried apricots, diced*
225 g cottage cheese	*1 teaspoon ground cinnamon*
175 ml soured cream	
1 egg, beaten	

1. Lightly grease 30 × 20 cm microwave-safe and flameproof baking dish. Cook noodles conventionally according to instructions on packet. Drain and keep warm.
2. In small bowl, mix half of melted butter or margarine with breadcrumbs; set aside.
3. In large bowl, combine cottage cheese, soured cream, beaten egg and sugar until blended. Stir in noodles, sultanas, apricots and cinnamon. Add remaining melted butter or margarine; stir. Pour into baking dish. Cook, covered, on Medium (50% power) for 10–12 minutes, until set.
4. Sprinkle pudding with crumb mixture. Brown under preheated grill. Allow to stand on heatproof surface for 5 minutes before serving.

CREAMY CHEESECAKE

Colour Index page 94. 420 cals per serving. Begin early in day or 1 day ahead.

Ingredients for 12 servings		Microwave cookware
90 g butter or margarine, melted	*2 tablespoons grated lemon zest*	*250 ml glass jug*
130 g digestive biscuits, finely crushed	*1 teaspoon vanilla essence*	*22.5 × 5 cm round baking dish*
150 g sugar	*Fresh berries, or soured cream and canned pie filling*	*Large bowl*
700 g cream cheese		*Trivet, rack or ramekin*
3 tablespoons plain flour		
3 eggs		
60 ml milk		

1 In glass jug, place butter or margarine. Heat, covered with kitchen paper, on High (100% power) for 1–1½ (1:30) minutes, until melted. In medium bowl, with fork, place biscuit crumbs and 50 g sugar. Pour in melted butter or margarine; stir with fork until well blended. Brush bottom and side of baking dish lightly with oil.

2 Line bottom of baking dish with non-stick baking parchment. With spoon, press one-third of crumb mixture on to side of dish to form side of crust. Set aside with remaining crumb mixture.

3 In large bowl, place cream cheese. Heat on Medium (50% power) for 2–3 minutes, until softened. With mixer, beat cream cheese until smooth; gradually beat in remaining sugar. Add flour, eggs, milk, lemon zest and vanilla; beat for 5 minutes. Cook on High for 5–8 minutes, until hot, beating 3 times. Spoon into prepared baking dish; smooth top.

4 With spoon, lightly press remaining crumb mixture evenly on to surface of cheese mixture to form crust. Elevate dish on trivet or rack, or on ramekin turned upside down.

5 Cook cheesecake on Medium for 6–10 minutes, until softly set, rotating dish twice. Do not overcook or cheesecake will not be creamy. Allow to stand in dish on heatproof surface for about 30 minutes, until set. Cover and refrigerate for at least 4 hours, until well chilled.

6 *To serve:* with palette knife, loosen cheesecake from side of dish. Invert dish on to serving platter to unmould cheesecake; remove parchment. If you like, top cheesecake with fresh berries, or with soured cream and canned pie filling.

Cheesecakes

For cheesecakes such as the lighter-than-traditional Individual Raspberry Cheesecakes (below), attractive microwave-safe cookware can double up as serving dishes. This easy way of cooking and serving in individual ramekins makes a nice presentation, eliminates having to unmould the desserts – and saves on the washing-up!

INDIVIDUAL RASPBERRY CHEESECAKES

Colour Index page 94. 437 cals per serving. Begin 3½ hours ahead or early in day.

Ingredients for 8 servings		Microwave cookware
60 g butter or margarine	150 g caster sugar	1 litre measuring jug
80 g digestive biscuits, finely crushed	2 eggs	Large bowl
275 g frozen raspberries, defrosted	1 teaspoon vanilla essence	8 × 120 ml ramekins
500 g cream cheese	Icing sugar to taste	

1 In jug, place butter or margarine. Heat, covered with kitchen paoer, on High (100% power) for 45 seconds–1 minute. Stir in crushed biscuits.

2 In food processor with knife blade attached or in blender, purée raspberries. Over bowl, set fine sieve. Press purée through sieve to remove seeds; set aside.

3 In large bowl, place cream cheese. Heat on Medium (50% power) for 2–3 minutes, until softened. With mixer, beat cheese, caster sugar, eggs, vanilla and 120 ml raspberry purée until smooth. Cook on High for 4–6 minutes, until very hot, beating 3 times during cooking. Remove from oven; beat until smooth. Lightly press crumb mixture on to bottoms of ramekins to form crust.

4 On top of crumb crusts in ramekins, spoon cream cheese mixture; smooth surface. On oven floor, arrange ramekins in circle, at least 2.5 cm apart. Cook on Medium for 3–4 minutes, until almost set, rearranging ramekins twice. On heatproof surface, allow cheesecakes to stand in ramekins for 15 minutes, or until set.

5 Sweeten remaining raspberry purée with icing sugar. Refrigerate cheesecakes and raspberry purée until well chilled.

6 To serve: spoon a little raspberry purée in decorative swirl pattern on top of each cheesecake. Place ramekins on dessert dishes and serve chilled. Serve remaining purée separately.

CHOCOLATE AND AMARETTI CHEESECAKE

Colour Index page 94. 12 servings. 542 cals per serving. Good source of vitamin A. Begin early in day or 1 day ahead.

120 g amaretti biscuits (about 40 biscuits) or crisp macaroons, crushed	700 g cream cheese
	200 g caster sugar
	3 eggs
90 g butter or margarine, melted	60 ml milk
	¼ teaspoon almond essence
75 g plain chocolate, chopped	250 ml double or whipping cream, whipped

1. In mixing bowl, with fork, combine biscuit crumbs and melted butter or margarine until well blended. Line 22.5 × 5 cm round microwave-safe baking dish with double thickness of greaseproof paper. With spoon, press one-third of crumb mixture on to side of dish to form side of crust. Set aside with remaining crumb mixture.
2. In large microwave-safe bowl, place chocolate and cream cheese. Heat on Medium (50% power) for 2–3 minutes, until cream cheese softens and chocolate melts, stirring halfway through cooking. With mixer at medium speed, beat until smooth. Add sugar, eggs, milk and almond essence; beat until blended, occasionally scraping bowl. Cook on High (100% power) for 5–8 minutes, until very hot, beating 3 times.
3. Into prepared dish, pour cheesecake mixture. With spoon, lightly press remaining crumbs evenly on to surface to form crust. Elevate dish on microwave-safe trivet or rack, or ramekin turned upside down. Cook on Medium (50% power) for 6–8 minutes, until softly set. Allow to stand in dish on heatproof surface for 30 minutes, until set. Cover and refrigerate for 4–5 hours, or overnight.
4. To serve: with palette knife, loosen cheesecake from side of dish. Invert dish on to platter. Carefully remove dish to unmould cheesecake; remove greaseproof paper. Decorate cheesecake with whipped cream. Serve remaining whipped cream separately.

CHEESECAKE TOPPINGS
Dress up a basic cheesecake with a mouth-watering topping. Spread with *soured cream* and top with fresh fruit, such as *hulled and sliced strawberries, whole blueberries*, or *kiwi fruit slices*. Or brush with *melted redcurrant jelly* for an elegant glazed finish. Or use canned fruit filling such as *cherry pie filling* with *1 tablespoon grated lemon zest* and ½ *teaspoon lemon juice* added. Or pipe *whipped cream* in decorative rosettes and decorate with *Chocolate Curls (page 360) or berries*.

Pies and Tarts

PASTRY SHELLS, BISCUIT AND PASTRY CRUSTS
DECORATIVE PASTRY EDGES · FRUIT PIES AND TARTS
CUSTARD AND CREAM PIES · CHIFFON PIES AND TARTS
NUT PIES, TARTS AND TARTLETS

Pies and Tarts

A combination of microwave and conventional cooking is ideal for producing quick-to-prepare, mouth-watering pies and tarts. Although shortcrust pastry cooked in the microwave turns out crisp and flaky, it looks better when cooked in a conventional oven: while your pastry shell is baking, you can use the microwave to prepare a delicious fruit, custard, cream, chiffon or nutty filling.

To create a shiny top on a double crust pie, brush it with lightly beaten egg white before baking; for a golden-brown glaze, use beaten whole egg; for an even richer colour, apply beaten egg yolk. To add a little sparkle to a pastry crust, sprinkle it lightly with caster sugar.

As an alternative to conventional pastry crusts and shells, crusts made with digestive or ginger biscuits and chocolate or vanilla wafer biscuits can be cooked in the microwave. When making a biscuit crust, press the crumbs firmly and evenly on to the bottom and up the side of the pie dish, then after microwaving, let the crust cool on a rack before filling. When filled with ice cream, ready prepared mousse or canned pie filling, biscuit crusts can make almost instant desserts.

The egg-enriched fillings of custard and cream pies and tarts work particularly well in the microwave. Cooked on Medium (50% power), these fillings are creamy and smooth. If you press dampened grease-proof directly on to the surface of the warm custard, it will prevent a skin from forming while the custard chills. Chiffon pies and tarts depend on both gelatine and whisked egg whites for their lightness and height; some also have whipped cream folded into their fillings. Cooking the filling on Medium results in a smooth mixture that blends well with whisked egg whites.

Your microwave can also help provide the finishing touches to your cooked pie or tart. Use it to toast almonds or coconut, to soften chocolate for making Chocolate Curls, or to make a delicious glaze from fruit jelly or jam to set off a fruit filling (see Glazes for Pies and Tarts, page 346).

PRETTY TARTS AND TARTLETS

Conventionally baked tart shells or bought tartlet shells make ideal bases for last-minute pastry treats. Using a variety of fillings such as jams, ice cream, instant puddings and mousses topped with berries or tropical fruit, you can make almost instant desserts fit for any occasion.

Bought tartlet shells filled with Mocha Crème Pâtissière (page 324) and topped with piped cream (left). Candied cake decorations add a decorative touch.

Bought tartlet shells filled with mango, nectarine and kumquat slices (right). Decorated with whipped cream and mint leaves.

Pastry Shell, Biscuit and Pastry Crusts

PASTRY SHELL

Colour Index page 95. Makes 22.5–25 cm shell.
1,622 cals. Begin 2¹/₂ hours ahead.

225 g plain flour
2 teaspoons caster
  sugar
¹/₄ teaspoon salt
50 g white vegetable fat

50 g butter or
  margarine, chilled
3–4 tablespoons iced
  water

1. In mixing bowl, combine flour, sugar and salt.
With 2 knives used scissors fashion or fingertips,
cut or rub in vegetable fat and butter or margarine until mixture resembles crumbs.
2. Into mixture, sprinkle water, 1 tablespoon at a
time, mixing lightly with fork until pastry just
holds together. Shape into ball; flatten slightly.
Wrap in greaseproof paper or foil and refrigerate
for about 1 hour, or until well chilled.
3. Preheat conventional oven to 220°C (425°F,
gas mark 7). On lightly floured surface, with
floured rolling pin, roll pastry into round about
2.5 cm larger than 22.5 or 25 cm flan tin with
removable bottom. Roll pastry on to rolling pin;
transfer to flan tin and unroll, pressing pastry on
to bottom and up side of tin.
4. Trim edge of pastry even with top of tin. With
fork, prick bottom and side in many places. Line
with foil; add beans, lentils or rice (see Baking the
Pastry Blind, page 341). Bake conventionally for
10 minutes. Remove beans, lentils or rice and foil;
prick pastry again. Bake for 15 minutes longer, or
until golden. Allow to cool on rack.

DIGESTIVE BISCUIT CRUST

Colour Index page 95. Makes 21.5 cm crust.
1255 cals. Begin 1¹/₄ hours ahead.

90 g butter or margarine
125 g digestive biscuits,
  finely crushed

¹/₂ teaspoon ground
  cinnamon

1. In shallow 21.5 cm microwave-safe pie dish,
place butter or margarine. Heat, covered with
kitchen paper, on High (100% power) for 1–1¹/₂
(1:30) minutes, until melted. Stir in biscuit
crumbs and cinnamon. Press on to bottom and up
side of pie dish.
2. Elevate pie dish on microwave-safe trivet or
rack, or on ramekin turned upside down. Cook
on High for 1–2 minutes, until warm. Cool on
rack.

GINGER BISCUIT CRUST: prepare as for
Digestive Biscuit Crust (above), using gingernut
biscuits. 1,236 cals.

VANILLA OR CHOCOLATE WAFER CRUST:
prepare as for Digestive Biscuit Crust (above),
using vanilla or chocolate wafer biscuits. 1,335
cals.

When making pastry, handle it as little as possible. If pastry
becomes too soft to handle, shape it into a ball, then flatten it
slightly with a floured rolling pin and wrap it in greaseproof
paper or foil; refrigerate for 30 minutes or until firm. When
rolling into a round, use a floured rolling pin and roll from centre
to edge. Add more flour if pastry begins to stick to work surface.

PASTRY CRUST

Colour Index page 95. 1,312 cals. Begin 2¹/₂ hours ahead.

When making this Pastry Crust in a conventional oven, check
the pie or tart recipe first to see if the filling is to be
microwaved in the crust. If so, bake the pastry in a pie dish
that can be used in both a conventional and a microwave
oven.

Ingredients for 21.5 cm crust

175 g plain flour
¹/₄ teaspoon salt
80 g white vegetable fat

2–3 tablespoons iced
  water

1 In mixing bowl,
combine flour and
salt. With 2 knives used
scissors fashion or
fingertips, cut or rub in
vegetable fat until
mixture resembles
crumbs.

2 Into mixture,
sprinkle water, 1
tablespoon at a time,
mixing lightly with fork
until pastry just holds
together. Shape pastry
into ball, flatten slightly
and wrap in greaseproof
or foil; refrigerate for
about 1 hour, or until
firm and well chilled.

3 On lightly floured
surface, with floured
rolling pin, roll pastry
into round about 5 cm
larger than shallow
21.5 cm pie dish (see
recipe introduction,
above).

4 Gently roll pastry on
to rolling pin;
transfer to pie dish and
unroll, pressing pastry on
to bottom and up side of
dish.

5 Trim edge of pastry,
leaving 2.5 cm
overhang. Fold overhang
under; bring up over pie
dish rim; make Pastry
Edge (page 340) of your
choice. Preheat
conventional oven to
220°C (425°F, gas mark 7).

6 With fork, prick
bottom and side of
pastry. Bake
conventionally for 15
minutes, or until golden.
(If pastry puffs up, gently
press into pie dish with
spoon.) Cool on rack.

Fluted Edge: pinch to form stand-up edge. Place 1 index finger on inside edge of pastry; with index finger and thumb of other hand, pinch pastry to make flute. Repeat round edge, leaving 5 mm space between each flute.

Sharp Fluted Edge: pinch to form stand-up edge. Vary Fluted Edge by using pointed edge of biscuit cutter or back of knife to make deeper indentations in pastry.

Leaf Edge: with sharp knife or leaf-shaped cutter, cut out leaves from rolled out pastry. Press each leaf on to lightly moistened pastry edge, overlapping leaves slightly to cover edge.

Pinched Edge: pinch to form stand-up edge. Pinch pastry edge at an angle between thumb and knuckle of index finger. Repeat round edge, rotating pie dish clockwise.

Fork-Scalloped Edge: pinch to form stand-up edge. Place thumb against outside pastry edge and press towards centre while pressing down next to it with fork. Repeat round edge, leaving alternate fork marks and ruffle effect.

Plaited Edge: prepare double quantity of pastry for Pastry Crust (page 339), using half to line pie dish. Roll out remaining pastry 5 mm thick and cut into 5 mm wide strips. Gently plait strips together and press on to lightly moistened pastry edge. Join ends of plait together to cover edge completely.

Pastry Crust

PASTRY FOR DOUBLE CRUST PIE

Makes 21.5 cm double crust. 2,296 cals. Begin 2½ hours ahead.

280 g plain flour
1 teaspoon salt
150 g white vegetable fat
4–5 tablespoons water

1. In mixing bowl, combine flour and salt. With 2 knives used scissors fashion or fingertips, cut or rub in vegetable fat until mixture resembles crumbs.

2. Into mixture, sprinkle water, 1 tablespoon at a time, mixing lightly with fork until pastry just holds together. Shape into 2 balls, 1 slightly larger; flatten slightly. Wrap both in greaseproof or foil and refrigerate for about 1 hour, or until well chilled.

3. On lightly floured surface, with floured rolling pin, roll larger ball into round 5 cm larger than shallow 21.5 cm pie dish. Roll pastry on to rolling pin; transfer to pie dish and unroll, pressing pastry on to bottom and up side of dish.

4. Fill pastry shell according to recipe instructions. For lid, roll smaller ball as for shell. Moisten edge of shell with water. Centre lid over filling. Trim pastry edges, leaving 2.5 cm overhang. Fold overhang under, then bring up over dish rim; make Sharp Fluted Edge (left). Cut slashes or design in centre. Brush with Milk or Egg Glaze (page 346). If you like, decorate top with shapes cut from trimmings; brush with glaze. Bake conventionally.

Decorating the Double Crust Pie

With small sharp knife, slash pastry lid to allow steam to escape. Brush with Milk or Egg Glaze (page 346).

With rolled-out pastry trimmings, cut out leaves or other shapes and arrange on top of glazed pie. Brush shapes with same glaze.

Fruit Pies and Tarts

APPLE, PEAR AND CRANBERRY TART

Colour Index page 98. 10 servings. 318 cals per serving. Good source of thiamine, vitamin C, calcium, fibre. Begin 2¹/₂ hours ahead.

Ingredients for Pastry for Double Crust Pie (page 340)	*2 tablespoons plain flour*
3 medium cooking apples, peeled, cored and thinly sliced	*¹/₂ teaspoon ground cinnamon*
2 pears, peeled, cored and thinly sliced	*¹/₄ teaspoon ground ginger*
95 g cranberries	*1 tablespoon grated orange zest*
100 g sugar	*1 egg yolk*
	1 tablespoon water

1. Preheat conventional oven to 220°C (425°F, gas mark 7). Prepare pastry according to recipe on page 340, up to end of step 2. In step 3, use 25 cm flan tin with removable bottom.
2. Trim edge of pastry even with top of tin. With fork, prick bottom and side in many places. Line with foil; add beans, lentils or rice. Bake conventionally for 10 minutes. Remove beans, lentils or rice and foil; prick pastry again. Bake for 5 minutes longer, or until golden. Leave oven at same setting.
3. In large microwave-safe bowl, combine fruit and next 5 ingredients. Cook, covered, on High (100% power) for 10–12 minutes, until apples are tender and juices thicken, stirring twice. Allow to cool slightly.
4. On lightly floured surface, with floured rolling pin, roll out remaining pastry 5 mm thick. With floured biscuit cutters, cut out decorative shapes. Spoon fruit mixture into prepared pastry shell. Place pastry shapes on top of filling.
5. In small mixing bowl, beat egg yolk and water until blended. Lightly brush pastry shapes with egg mixture. Bake conventionally for 10–15 minutes, until pastry is golden. Serve warm.

Baking the Pastry Blind

Line pastry with piece of foil cut slightly larger than flan tin. Press foil on to bottom and up side of pastry shell.

Fill foil lining with beans, lentils or rice to prevent shell from puffing during baking. After baking, remove beans, lentils or rice and foil; prick pastry again and return to oven, until golden.

DELUXE APPLE PIE

Colour Index page 96. 295 cals per serving. Good source of fibre. Begin 3¹/₂ hours ahead.

Unlike traditional apple pie, which has a top pastry crust, this microwave Deluxe Apple Pie has an unusual oat-based crumble topping that is both quick and nourishing.

Ingredients for 10 servings		Microwave cookware
6 medium cooking apples, peeled, cored and cut into 4 cm chunks *Plain flour* *70 g caster sugar* *2 teaspoons lemon juice* *¹/₂ teaspoon ground cinnamon* *¹/₂ teaspoon grated lemon zest* *¹/₄ teaspoon grated nutmeg*	*Pastry Crust (page 339)* *110 g brown sugar* *20 g quick-cooking rolled oats, uncooked* *60 g butter or margarine, chilled* *Cheddar cheese, ice cream or whipped cream (optional)*	Shallow 21.5 cm pie dish (for Pastry Crust) Large bowl Trivet, rack or ramekin

1 In large bowl, combine apple chunks, 2 tablespoons flour and next 5 ingredients. Cook covered, on High (100% power) for 5 minutes. Uncover; stir. Cook on High for 5–7 minutes longer, until apples are tender, stirring twice.

2 Into cool Pastry Crust, spoon hot apple mixture to make an even layer. Set aside.

3 In mixing bowl, combine brown sugar, oats, butter or margarine and 35 g flour. With 2 knives used scissors fashion or fingertips, cut or rub in butter or margarine until mixture resembles coarse crumbs.

4 Over apple filling, sprinkle crumb mixture. Elevate pie dish on trivet or rack, or on ramekin turned upside down.

5 Cook pie on High for 7–10 minutes, until topping is crisp, rotating pie dish halfway through cooking.

6 Serve pie warm or cover and refrigerate to serve chilled later. If you like, serve with Cheddar cheese, ice cream or whipped cream.

Fruit Pies and Tarts

SUMMER FRUIT TART

Colour Index page 96. 276 cals per serving. Good source of vitamins A and C, calcium, iron, fibre. Begin 2½ hours ahead.

For a seasonal treat, try this Summer Fruit Tart – biscuit crust filled with vanilla custard and topped with a mixture of juicy and colourful seasonal fresh fruit.

Ingredients for 10 servings		Microwave cookware
90 g butter or margarine	3 egg yolks	Shallow 21.5 cm pie dish
1 tablespoon brown sugar	1½ teaspoons vanilla essence	Trivet, rack or ramekin
100 g plain sweet biscuits, finely crushed	4 tablespoons redcurrant jelly	Medium bowl
100 g caster sugar	1 tablespoon water	Small bowl
2 tablespoons cornflour	575 g fresh seasonal fruit	
500 ml half cream or single cream	1 kiwi fruit, peeled and sliced	

1. In pie dish, place butter or margarine and brown sugar. Heat, covered with kitchen paper, on High (100% power) for 1–1½ (1:30) minutes, until butter or margarine melts and sugar dissolves, stirring halfway through cooking. Stir in biscuit crumbs.

2. On to bottom and up side of pie dish, press crumb mixture. Elevate on trivet or rack, or on ramekin turned upside down. Cook on High for 1 minute. Allow to cool on rack. In medium bowl, combine sugar and cornflour. Whisk in cream and egg yolks.

3. Cook mixture on High for 5–6 minutes, until custard thickens slightly and coats back of spoon, stirring often. Stir in vanilla essence. Pour into cool biscuit crust.

4. On to surface of hot custard in biscuit crust, lightly press dampened greaseproof paper (this helps prevent skin forming on top of custard). Refrigerate for 2 hours, or until custard is firm and set.

5. In small bowl, combine redcurrant jelly and water. Heat on High for 1½ (1:30) – 2 minutes, until jelly is melted and smooth, stirring often. Hull strawberries and cut in half. If you like, reserve 1 whole berry for decoration.

6. On top of custard, carefully arrange fresh seasonal fruit and sliced kiwi fruit. If you like, decorate with whole strawberry. With pastry brush, coat fruit with jelly glaze. Refrigerate for 15 minutes, or until glaze is set.

QUICK FRENCH APRICOT TART

Colour Index page 98. 10 servings. 243 cals per serving. Good source of vitamin A, thiamine, fibre. Begin 1¼ hours ahead.

120 ml double cream	Bought 21.5 cm tart
2 egg yolks	shell
3 tablespoons sugar	2 × 425 g cans apricot
1 tablespoon plain flour	halves, drained
½ teaspoon almond	25 g flaked almonds,
essence	toasted

1. Into 1 litre microwave-safe measuring jug, pour cream. Heat on High (100% power) for 2–3 minutes, until bubbles form round edge.

2. In mixing bowl, with whisk, beat egg yolks, sugar, flour and almond essence. Stir small amount hot cream into egg mixture. Slowly pour egg mixture back into remaining hot cream, beating rapidly to prevent lumping. Cook on Medium (50% power) for 3–5 minutes, until custard thickens slightly and coats back of spoon, stirring often.

3. On microwave-safe serving platter, place tart shell. Arrange apricots in tart shell. Pour custard over apricots. Cook on Medium for 7–10 minutes, until custard is softly set, rotating platter halfway through cooking. Sprinkle almonds over surface. Allow to stand on heatproof surface for 10 minutes; continue cooling on rack. Serve at room temperature, or cover and refrigerate to serve chilled later.

RASPBERRY CUSTARD TART

Colour Index page 98. 10 servings. 250 cals per serving. Good source of vitamin A, thiamine, riboflavin, calcium, iron, fibre. Begin 1¼ hours ahead.

4 tablespoons raspberry	Crème Pâtissière (page
jam	324)
Pastry Crust (page 339)	250 g raspberries

1. In small microwave-safe bowl, place raspberry jam. Heat on High (100% power) for 1–2 minutes, until spreadable, stirring once.

2. In bottom of cool Pastry Crust, evenly spread warm raspberry jam. Spread Crème Pâtissière evenly over jam. On to surface of Crème Pâtissière, gently press dampened greaseproof paper (this helps prevent skin forming). Refrigerate for about 40 minutes, or until cold.

3. Remove greaseproof paper. Arrange raspberries neatly on top of Crème Pâtissière. Serve immediately, or cover and refrigerate to serve chilled later.

Custard and Cream Pies

CHOCOLATE WALNUT PIE

Colour Index page 97. 10 servings. 362 cals per serving. Good source of thiamine, riboflavin, calcium, iron. Begin early in day.

Ingredients for Pastry Crust (page 339)	*1 teaspoon vanilla essence*
60 g butter or margarine	*3 eggs*
50 g plain chocolate, chopped	*125 g shelled walnuts, chopped*
100 g caster sugar	*Whipped cream and walnut halves to decorate*
120 ml milk	
35 g plain flour	
2 tablespoons golden syrup	

1. Prepare Pastry Crust, using shallow 21.5 cm microwave-safe and conventional ovenproof dish; cool on rack. In large microwave-safe glass bowl, place butter or margarine and chocolate. Heat, covered with kitchen paper, on High (100% power) for 45 seconds–1 minute, until melted, stirring twice.
2. Into mixture, whisk sugar, milk, flour, golden syrup, vanilla and eggs until blended. Stir in walnuts. Cook on Medium (50% power) for 5–6 minutes, until mixture coats back of spoon, stirring often.
3. Spoon chocolate mixture into Pastry Crust. Elevate pie dish on microwave-safe trivet or rack, or ramekin turned upside down. Cook on Medium for 10–12 minutes, until mixture is puffed and set, rotating dish halfway through cooking. Allow pie to cool completely on rack. Decorate with whipped cream and walnut halves.

PEACHES AND CREAM PIE

Colour Index page 96. 10 servings. 283 cals per serving. Good source of vitamin A, riboflavin, calcium, iron. Begin 2 hours ahead.

6 peaches, peeled, stoned and sliced	*Crème Pâtissière (page 324)*
100 g caster sugar	*1 tablespoon peach jam*
1 tablespoon plain flour	*Digestive Biscuit Crust (page 339)*
1/2 teaspoon vanilla essence	

1. In large microwave-safe bowl, place peach slices, sugar, flour and vanilla essence; toss to coat. Cook, covered, on High (100% power) for 8–10 minutes, until peaches are tender and juices thicken, stirring twice. Set aside.
2. Into Crème Pâtissière, beat peach jam. Pour mixture into cool biscuit crust. Arrange peach slices on top. Cover and refrigerate for 30 minutes, or until well chilled.

Custard makes a perfect base for fruit such as the peaches in Peaches and Cream Pie (below left). In Lemon Meringue Pie (below), the creamy texture of custard contrasts delightfully with fluffy meringue and crisp pastry.

LEMON MERINGUE PIE

Colour Index page 96. 291 cals per serving. Begin 3 1/2 hours ahead.

Ingredients for 10 servings		Microwave cookware
40 g cornflour	*1 teaspoon grated lemon zest*	1 litre measuring jug
250 g caster sugar	*Pastry Crust (page 339)*	
350 ml water	*1/4 teaspoon cream of tartar*	
4 eggs, separated		
120 ml lemon juice		
15 g butter or margarine		

1 In measuring jug, combine cornflour and 150 g sugar. Gradually add water, stirring until smooth. Cook on High (100% power) for 3–5 minutes, until mixture thickens, stirring often.

2 In small mixing bowl, with whisk, beat egg yolks. Stir small amount hot cornflour mixture into egg yolks. Slowly pour egg yolk mixture back into remaining hot cornflour mixture, beating rapidly to prevent lumping.

3 Cook custard on Medium (50% power) for 2–3 minutes, until custard thickens slightly and coats back of spoon, stirring often. Do not boil or custard will curdle.

4 To hot custard, add lemon juice, butter or margarine and lemon zest, stirring until butter or margarine melts. Pour into cool Pastry Crust. On to surface of hot custard, lightly press dampened greaseproof (this helps prevent skin forming). Refrigerate for about 30 minutes, or until set.

5 Preheat conventional oven to 200°C (400°F, gas mark 6). In large mixing bowl, with mixer at high speed, whisk egg whites and cream of tartar until soft peaks form. Gradually sprinkle in remaining sugar, whisking until sugar completely dissolves and whites stand in stiff, glossy peaks.

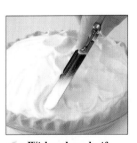

6 With palette knife, spread whisked egg whites over custard to edge of pastry. Swirl to make attractive design. Bake conventionally for 10 minutes, or until golden. Serve warm or refrigerate to cool slightly.

Cream Pies

BANANA COCONUT PIE

Colour Index page 95. 434 cals per serving. Begin early in day.

Use the microwave to make the lusciously creamy filling in this Banana Coconut Pie. When the pie is assembled, refrigerate until ready to serve, then sprinkle over toasted coconut at the last moment.

Ingredients for 10 servings		Microwave cookware

330 ml milk
4 eggs, separated
150 g caster sugar
¼ teaspoon salt
15 g powdered gelatine
  (2 tablespoons)
250 ml double cream
	1½ teaspoons vanilla
	  essence
	Pastry Shell (page 339),
	  made in 21.5 cm flan
	  tin
	1 large banana, sliced
	50 g desiccated coconut
		1 litre measuring jug
		Shallow 21.5 cm pie
		  dish

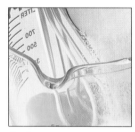

1 Into measuring jug, pour milk; add egg yolks, 100 g sugar and salt. Whisk until blended. Evenly sprinkle gelatine over mixture; allow to stand for 1 minute to soften slightly. Cook on High (100% power) for 4–6 minutes, until custard thickens slightly and coats back of spoon, stirring often. Do not boil or custard will curdle.

2 Into large mixing bowl, pour custard. Cover and refrigerate for 30–40 minutes, until custard mounds slightly when dropped from spoon, stirring often.

3 In another large mixing bowl, with mixer at high speed, whisk egg whites until soft peaks form. Gradually sprinkle in remaining sugar, whisking until sugar completely dissolves and whites stand in stiff, glossy peaks. Spoon on top of chilled custard. In same bowl, whip cream and vanilla essence until soft peaks form. Spoon over custard.

4 With rubber spatula or whisk, gently fold whipped cream and whisked egg whites into custard; set aside. Remove side of tin from cool Pastry Shell. Cover bottom of shell with banana slices.

5 Over banana slices, carefully spoon custard mixture in an even layer. Cover and refrigerate for about 3 hours, or until set. In pie dish, spread coconut. Heat on High for 3–4 minutes, until toasted, stirring often.

6 Just before serving, sprinkle toasted coconut over pie. Serve at room temperature.

CHOCOLATE CREAM PIE

Colour Index page 98. 10 servings. 393 cals per serving. Good source of vitamin A, riboflavin, calcium. Begin early in day.

500 ml milk
50 g caster sugar
45 g plain flour
3 egg yolks
45 g butter or margarine
50 g plain chocolate,
  chopped
1 teaspoon vanilla
  essence
	Vanilla or Chocolate
	  Wafer Crust (page
	  339)
	250 ml double or
	  whipping cream

1. Into 2 litre microwave-safe measuring jug or bowl, pour milk. Heat on High (100% power) for 3–5 minutes, until small bubbles form round edge.
2. In 1 litre measuring jug, combine sugar and flour. Gradually pour in hot milk, stirring until smooth. Pour milk mixture back into 2 litre jug or bowl. Cook on High for 6–8 minutes, until thick and smooth, stirring occasionally.
3. In 1 litre measuring jug, whisk egg yolks. Stir small amount hot milk mixture into egg yolks. Slowly pour egg mixture back into remaining hot milk mixture, beating rapidly to prevent lumping. Cook on Medium (50% power) for 2–3 minutes, until custard is very thick, stirring often. Do not boil or custard will curdle.
4. Into custard, stir butter or margarine and chocolate until melted and smooth. Stir in vanilla essence. Pour chocolate custard into cool wafer crust. On to surface of chocolate custard, lightly press dampened greaseproof (this helps prevent skin forming). Refrigerate pie for about 3 hours, or until set.
5. In small mixing bowl, with mixer at medium speed, whip cream until soft peaks form. With rubber spatula, swirl whipped cream over filling to edge of wafer crust. Spoon remaining cream into piping bag fitted with medium rosette tube; pipe cream round edge of pie.

Lining the Pie Dish with Biscuit Crumbs

In pie dish, combine finely crushed biscuits, sugar and melted butter or margarine. With back of metal spoon, firmly press mixture on to bottom and up side of pie dish.

Chiffon Pies and Tarts

MINTY CHOCOLATE TART

Colour Index page 95. 10 servings. 321 cals per serving. Begin 4½ hours ahead or early in day.

1 tablespoon powdered gelatine	250 ml double or whipping cream
100 g caster sugar	Chocolate Wafer Crust (page 339)
120 ml water	
3 eggs, separated	Chocolate Curls to decorate (page 360)
60 ml crème de menthe	
120 ml cold coffee	

1. In 1 litre microwave-safe measuring jug, combine gelatine and 50 g sugar. In 500 ml measuring jug, with fork, beat water and egg yolks. Gradually stir egg yolk mixture into gelatine mixture until blended. Cook on Medium (50% power) for 1–2 minutes, until mixture thickens slightly and coats back of spoon, stirring often. Do not boil. Pour into large mixing bowl and stir in crème de menthe and coffee. Cover and refrigerate for 20 minutes, until custard mounds slightly when dropped from spoon, stirring often.
2. In medium mixing bowl, with mixer at high speed, whisk egg whites until soft peaks form. Gradually sprinkle in remaining sugar, whisking until sugar completely dissolves and whites stand in stiff, glossy peaks. Spoon on top of custard.
3. In same bowl, with same beaters and mixer at medium speed, whip cream until soft peaks form. Spoon over custard. With rubber spatula or whisk, gently fold whisked egg whites and whipped cream into custard. Spoon into cool wafer crust. Cover and refrigerate for about 3 hours, or until set. Decorate with Chocolate Curls.

FLAVOURED WHIPPED CREAM
Whipped cream is an ideal finish for pies of all kinds, as well as cakes and desserts.

Basic Whipped Cream: in mixing bowl, whip **350 ml double or whipping cream** and **30 g icing sugar** until peaks form. Fold in ½ **teaspoon vanilla essence**. 56 cals per tablespoon.

Chocolate Whipped Cream: prepare Basic Whipped Cream. Fold in **225 g plain chocolate, melted and cooled**. 104 cals per tablespoon.

Coffee Whipped Cream: prepare Basic Whipped Cream, folding in **1 teaspoon instant coffee powder** with icing sugar. 57 cals per tablespoon.

Orange Whipped Cream: prepare Basic Whipped Cream, folding in **1 teaspoon grated orange zest** and **dash of orange flower water** with vanilla essence. 57 cals per tablespoon.

BLACK BOTTOM PIE

Colour Index page 96. 299 cals per serving. Begin 3½ hours ahead.

Ingredients for 10 servings		Microwave cookware
300 ml milk	50 g plain chocolate, chopped	1 litre measuring jug
3 eggs, separated	Ginger Biscuit Crust (page 339)	
100 g caster sugar	120 ml double cream, whipped	
2¼ teaspoons cornflour		
1 tablespoon powdered gelatine		
1 teaspoon vanilla essence		
1 tablespoon dark rum		

1 In measuring jug, heat milk on High (100% power) for 3–4 minutes, until small bubbles form round edge. In medium mixing bowl, with whisk, beat egg yolks, 50 g sugar and cornflour. Whisk small amount hot milk into egg yolk mixture. Slowly pour egg yolk mixture back into remaining hot milk, beating rapidly to prevent lumping.

2 Evenly sprinkle gelatine over custard mixture: allow to stand for 1 minute to soften slightly. Cook on Medium (50% power) for 2–3 minutes, until custard thickens slightly and coats back of spoon, stirring often. Stir in vanilla essence.

3 Into small mixing bowl, pour half of custard; stir in rum. Cover and refrigerate for about 30 minutes, or until custard mounds slightly when dropped from spoon, stirring often. Meanwhile, into remaining custard, stir chocolate until melted. Spread chocolate custard evenly in cool biscuit crust; cover and refrigerate.

4 In medium mixing bowl, with mixer at high speed, whisk egg whites until soft peaks form. Gradually sprinkle in remaining sugar, whisking until sugar completely dissolves and whites stand in stiff, glossy peaks. Spoon on top of chilled rum custard.

5 With rubber spatula or whisk, gently fold whisked egg whites into rum custard. Spoon on to chocolate custard in crust, taking care not to overfill. Cover and refrigerate for 10 minutes. Spoon any remaining rum custard on top. Cover and refrigerate for about 20 minutes, or until set. Spoon whipped cream into piping bag fitted with medium rosette tube.

6 Pipe cream round edge of pie. Alternatively, with palette knife, spread whipped cream over pie in attractive design. Serve at room temperature.

Chiffon Pies and Tarts

STRAWBERRY CHIFFON PIE

Colour Index page 97. 298 cals per serving. Good source of vitamin C. Begin 3 hours ahead.

Ingredients for 10 servings		Microwave cookware
600 g strawberries	*2 eggs, separated*	1 litre measuring jug
150 g caster sugar	*80 ml double or*	
1 tablespoon lemon	*whipping cream*	
juice	*Digestive Biscuit Crust*	
1 teaspoon cornflour	*(page 339)*	
1 tablespoon powdered	*Fruit Glaze for Pies and*	
gelatine	*Tarts (below right)*	
250 ml water		

1 Hull and slice strawberries, reserving 1 whole berry for decoration. Cover and refrigerate half of sliced berries. In mixing bowl, combine remaining sliced berries, 50 g sugar and lemon juice; toss lightly. With fork, crush berries lightly; set aside. In measuring jug, combine 50 g sugar, cornflour and gelatine.

2 Into sugar mixture, stir 250 ml water. Cook on High (100% power) for 3–4 minutes, until mixture thickens slightly and coats back of spoon, stirring often. In small mixing bowl, whisk egg yolks. Stir in small amount hot gelatine mixture. Slowly pour egg yolk mixture back into remaining hot gelatine mixture, beating rapidly. Cook on Medium (50% power) for 2–3 minutes, until custard thickens.

3 Into custard, stir crushed strawberry mixture. Cover and refrigerate for about 45 minutes, or until custard mounds slightly when dropped from spoon, stirring often.

4 In large mixing bowl, with mixer at high speed, whisk egg whites until soft peaks form. Gradually sprinkle in remaining sugar, whisking until sugar completely dissolves and whites stand in stiff, glossy peaks. Spoon over chilled custard. In same bowl, whip cream until soft peaks form. Spoon over custard. Gently fold cream and egg whites into custard.

5 Into cool biscuit crust, spoon strawberry chiffon mixture. Cover and refrigerate for about 30 minutes, or until set.

6 Cover top of pie with berries. Place whole berry in centre. Brush glaze over top of pie. Refrigerate for 15 minutes, or until glaze is set.

ORANGE CHIFFON PIE

Colour Index page 95. 10 servings. 381 cals per serving. Begin 3 hours ahead.

150 g caster sugar
1 tablespoon powdered gelatine
1 teaspoon grated orange zest
250 ml orange juice
2 tablespoons lemon juice
3 eggs, separated
350 ml double cream
Digestive Biscuit Crust (page 339)

1. In 1 litre microwave-safe measuring jug, combine 100 g sugar, gelatine, zest and orange and lemon juices. Cook on High (100% power) for 3–4 minutes, until small bubbles form round edge, stirring twice.

2. In small mixing bowl, whisk egg yolks. Stir in small amount hot gelatine mixture. Slowly pour egg yolk mixture back into remaining hot gelatine mixture, beating rapidly to prevent lumping. Cook on Medium (50% power) for 3–5 minutes, until custard thickens slightly, stirring often. Pour into large mixing bowl. Cover and refrigerate for about 45 minutes, or until custard mounds slightly when dropped from spoon, stirring often.

3. In another large mixing bowl, with mixer at high speed, whisk egg whites until soft peaks form. Gradually sprinkle in remaining sugar, whisking until sugar completely dissolves and whites stand in stiff, glossy peaks. Spoon over chilled custard. In same bowl, with same beaters and mixer at medium speed, whip 120 ml cream until soft peaks form. Spoon over custard.

4. Gently fold whipped cream and whisked egg whites into custard. Spoon into cool biscuit crust. Cover and refrigerate for about 30 minutes, or until set. Whip remaining cream until peaks form. Use to pipe round edge of pie.

GLAZES FOR PIES AND TARTS

Milk or Egg Glaze: before baking a double crust pie conventionally, brush top lightly with milk, half cream or undiluted evaporated milk, to enhance browning. For a shiny top, brush with whisked egg white; for a richer, golden brown colour, brush with beaten egg yolk.

Fruit glazes are the ideal way to set off the colours of fresh fruit tarts. Use sieved apricot jam to complement pale or yellow fruit, and redcurrant jelly or sieved strawberry jam for berries or plums.

Fruit Glaze: in 250 ml microwave-safe glass jug, combine *4 tablespoons jelly or jam* and *1 tablespoon water*. Heat on High (100% power) for 1½ (1:30)–2 minutes, until glaze coats back of spoon, stirring often. For jam, press glaze through fine sieve until smooth. Lightly brush over fruit.

HIGHLAND CREAM PIE

Colour Index page 98. 10 servings. 352 cals per serving. Good source of vitamin A, riboflavin. Begin 4 hours ahead.

300 ml milk	*Pastry Crust (page 339)*
100 g caster sugar	*¼ teaspoon grated*
1 tablespoon powdered	*nutmeg*
gelatine	*Chocolate Curls (page*
3 eggs, separated	*360) to decorate*
2 tablespoons whisky	
250 ml double or	
whipping cream	

1. Into 1 litre microwave-safe measuring jug, pour milk. Heat on High (100% power) for 3–4 minutes, until small bubbles form round edge.

2. In small mixing bowl, combine 50 g sugar and gelatine. With whisk, beat in egg yolks and whisky. Stir small amount hot milk into egg yolk mixture. Slowly pour egg yolk mixture back into remaining hot milk, beating rapidly to prevent lumping. Cook on Medium (50% power) for 2–3 minutes, until custard thickens slightly and coats back of spoon, stirring often. Pour into large mixing bowl. Cover and refrigerate for about 45 minutes, or until custard mounds slightly when dropped from spoon, stirring often.

3. After custard has chilled, in another large mixing bowl, with mixer at high speed, whisk egg whites until soft peaks form. Gradually sprinkle in remaining sugar, whisking until sugar completely dissolves and whites stand in stiff, glossy peaks. Spoon over chilled custard. In same bowl, whip cream until soft peaks form. Spoon cream over custard.

4. With rubber spatula or whisk, gently fold whipped cream and whisked egg whites into custard. Spoon into cool Pastry Crust; sprinkle top with grated nutmeg. Refrigerate pie for about 3 hours, or until set. Decorate with Chocolate Curls before serving.

Grating Chocolate

With grater, coarsely grate plain chocolate (or grate in food processor with grating disc attached). Sprinkle over any dessert or cake for a special effect, or use to cover uneven surfaces on sides of iced cakes. Store any leftover grated chocolate in airtight container in refrigerator.

Light and creamy chiffon fillings are ideal for use in a variety of crusts – pastry, biscuit crumb or coconut.

COCONUT CREAM PIE

Colour Index page 98. 346 cals per serving. Low in sodium. Good source of vitamin A, riboflavin, fibre. Begin 4 hours ahead.

Ingredients for 10 servings		Microwave cookware
165 g desiccated coconut	*¼ teaspoon almond essence*	*30 × 20 cm baking dish*
30 g icing sugar	*250 ml double or whipping cream*	*1 litre measuring jug*
45 g butter or margarine, softened	*Whipped cream and toasted coconut to decorate*	
300 ml milk		
100 g caster sugar		
1 tablespoon powdered gelatine		
3 eggs, separated		

1 In baking dish, place coconut. Heat on High (100% power) for 5–6 minutes, until toasted, stirring often. In mixing bowl, combine 115 g toasted coconut, icing sugar and butter or margarine.

2 With back of spoon, press mixture on to bottom and up side of shallow 21.5 cm pie dish; refrigerate.

3 Into measuring jug, pour milk. Heat on High (100% power) for 3–4 minutes until small bubbles form round edge.

4 In small mixing bowl, combine sugar and gelatine. With whisk, beat in egg yolks and almond essence. Stir small amount hot milk into egg yolk mixture. Slowly pour egg yolk mixture back into remaining hot milk, beating rapidly to prevent lumping. Cook on Medium (50% power) for 2–3 minutes, until custard thickens slightly and coats back of spoon, stirring often. Pour into large mixing bowl. Cover and refrigerate for about 45 minutes, or until custard mounds slightly when dropped from spoon, stirring often.

5 In another large mixing bowl, with mixer at high speed, whisk egg whites until soft peaks form. Gradually sprinkle in remaining sugar, whisking until sugar completely dissolves and whites stand in stiff, glossy peaks. Spoon over chilled custard. In same bowl, with same beaters and mixer at medium speed, whip cream until soft peaks form. Spoon over custard.

6 With rubber spatula or whisk, gently fold remaining toasted coconut, whipped cream and whisked egg whites into custard. Spoon into chilled coconut crust. Cover and refrigerate pie for about 3 hours, or until set. Just before serving, decorate pie with whipped cream and toasted coconut.

Nut Pies, Tarts and Tartlets

AMARETTO PIE

Colour Index page 97. 266 cals per serving. Begin early in day.

This light Amaretto Pie has the delicate flavour of almonds in both the amaretti biscuit crumb crust and the custard filling. Create a special look by piping cream in a Lattice Design, then decorate with toasted sliced almonds.

Ingredients for 10 servings		Microwave cookware

90 g butter or margarine
About 30 amaretti
  biscuits or crisp
  macaroons, crushed
50 g caster sugar
1 tablespoon powdered
  gelatine
3 eggs, separated
Water
	80 ml amaretto (almond-
	  flavoured liqueur)
	250 ml double or
	  whipping cream
	Whipped cream and
	  toasted flaked almonds
	  to decorate
		Shallow 21.5 cm pie
		  dish
		Trivet, rack or
		  ramekin
		1 litre measuring jug

1 In pie dish, place butter or margarine. Heat, covered with kitchen paper, on High (100% power) for 1–1½ (1:30) minutes, until melted. Stir in crumbs. With spoon, press mixture firmly on to bottom and up side of pie dish. Elevate dish on trivet or rack, or on ramekin turned upside down. Cook on High for 1 minute. Cool on rack.

2 In measuring jug, combine sugar and gelatine. In small bowl, with whisk, beat egg yolks and 120 ml water. Gradually stir egg yolk mixture into gelatine mixture until blended. Cook on Medium (50% power) for 1–2 minutes, until custard thickens slightly and coats back of spoon, stirring often. Do not boil or custard will curdle. Stir in amaretto.

3 Pour custard into large mixing bowl. Cover and refrigerate for about 45 minutes, or until custard mounds slightly when dropped from spoon, stirring often.

4 In another large mixing bowl, with mixer at high speed, whisk egg whites until soft peaks form. Spoon over custard. In same bowl, with same beaters and mixer at medium speed, whip cream. Spoon over custard.

5 With rubber spatula or whisk, gently fold whipped cream and whisked egg whites into custard. Spoon into cooled amaretti crust. Cover and refrigerate for about 3 hours, or until set.

6 Just before serving, pipe whipped cream in Lattice Design on top of pie (see Decorating with Whipped Cream, right), then decorate with toasted flaked almonds.

LIGHT LEMON AND ALMOND TART

Colour Index page 96. 10 servings. 584 cals per serving. Good source of vitamin A, thiamine, riboflavin, calcium, fibre. Begin 3½ hours ahead.

500 ml double or
  whipping cream
300 g caster sugar
1 teaspoon vanilla
  essence
¼ teaspoon almond
  essence
1 tablespoon grated
  lemon zest

1 tablespoon lemon juice
115 g slivered almonds
Pastry Shell (page 339)
25 g flaked almonds
Lemon Julienne (page
  330) to decorate

1. Into 2 litre microwave-safe measuring jug or bowl, pour 350 ml cream; add sugar. Cook on High (100% power) for 10 minutes, or until sugar completely dissolves, stirring occasionally. Stir in vanilla and almond essence, lemon zest, lemon juice and slivered almonds. Pour mixture into cool Pastry Shell. Bake in conventional oven at 180°C (350°F, gas mark 4) for 10–15 minutes, until golden; cool on rack.

2. In shallow 21.5 cm microwave-safe dish, place flaked almonds. Heat on High for 3½ (3:30)–4½ (4:30) minutes, until almonds are toasted, stirring occasionally. Set aside.

3. In mixing bowl, with mixer at medium speed, whip remaining cream until peaks form. Spoon whipped cream into piping bag fitted with medium rosette tube and pipe round edge of tart. Sprinkle over toasted flaked almonds and decorate with Lemon Julienne.

DECORATING WITH WHIPPED CREAM

When used as a topping, piped whipped cream complements a custard or chiffon filling, or it can be used as a contrast on rich or nutty tarts. Be careful not to overwhip cream for piping; it should just hold its shape. Spoon whipped cream into piping bag fitted with medium rosette tube.

Zig-Zag Edge: pipe a continuous border round edge of tart where filling meets edge. As you pipe, move tube to left and right.

Lattice Design: pipe 4 lines of cream, 5 cm apart, over tart. Pipe 4 more lines diagonally across first lines to create lattice effect.

STICKY WALNUT TART

Colour Index page 96. 10 servings. 373 cals per serving. Good source of thiamine, calcium. Begin 1½ hours ahead.

50 g butter or margarine	1 teaspoon vanilla essence
3 eggs	175 g shelled walnuts, chopped
175 g dark soft brown sugar	Pastry Crust (page 339)
5 tablespoons golden syrup	
1 teaspoon ground cinnamon	

1. In small microwave-safe bowl, place butter or margarine. Heat, covered loosely with kitchen paper, on High (100% power) for 30 seconds – 1 minute, until melted. Cool slightly.
2. In large mixing bowl, beat eggs. Add melted butter or margarine, sugar, golden syrup, cinnamon and vanilla; beat until smooth. Stir in chopped walnuts.
3. Into cool Pastry Crust, pour syrup mixture. Elevate pie dish on microwave-safe trivet or rack, or on ramekin turned upside down. Cook on Medium (50% power) for 16–19 minutes, until set, rotating dish a half turn 3 times during cooking. Allow to stand on heatproof surface for 10 minutes; continue cooling on rack. Serve at room temperature.

PECAN PIE

Colour Index page 97. 10 servings. 371 cals per serving. Good source of vitamin A, iron. Begin 3½ hours ahead.

60 g butter or margarine	3 eggs
250 ml golden syrup	Pastry Crust (page 339) made in shallow 25 cm pie dish
50 g dark brown sugar	
1 teaspoon vanilla essence	110 g pecan nut halves

1. In microwave-safe jug or bowl, place butter or margarine. Heat, covered with kitchen paper, on High (100% power) for 45 seconds–1 minute, until melted.
2. Into melted butter or margarine, beat golden syrup, sugar, vanilla and eggs until blended. Cook on Medium (50% power) for 6–8 minutes, until mixture coats back of spoon, stirring often. Pour into cool Pastry Crust. Arrange pecans on top, cutting them in half lengthways if you like.
3. Bake pie in conventional oven at 180°C (350°F, gas mark 4) for 10–15 minutes, until knife inserted 2.5 cm from edge comes out clean. Allow pie to cool on rack.

You can use nuts as a main ingredient, as in Pecan Pie (below left), or to add texture and flavour to other ingredients, as in the mincemeat filling in Mincemeat and Apple Tartlets (below).

MINCEMEAT AND APPLE TARTLETS

Colour Index page 97. 684 cals each. Low in cholesterol. Good source of thiamine, calcium, iron, fibre. Begin 2½ hours ahead.

Ingredients for 10 tartlets		Microwave cookware
Double quantity of chilled pastry for Pastry Shell (page 339)	1 large cooking apple, peeled, cored and diced	2 litre measuring jug or bowl
Milk	110 g soft brown sugar	
850 g prepared mincemeat	1 tablespoon lemon juice	
125 g walnuts, coarsely chopped	60 ml brandy or rum (optional)	

1 On lightly floured surface, with floured rolling pin, roll pastry 3 mm thick. With floured 10 cm round cutter, cut out 10 rounds. Reserve pastry trimmings.

2 On to bottom and up side of each of ten 7.5 cm fluted tartlet tins, gently press 1 pastry round. Prick with fork. Arrange tartlet tins in 2 baking tins. Bake in conventional oven at 220°C (425°F, gas mark 7) for 20–25 minutes. Cool for 10 minutes.

3 Loosen tartlet shells from tins with knife, then carefully remove tartlet shells and place on rack. Allow to cool completely. Leave oven heat at 220°C (425°F, gas mark 7).

4 Meanwhile, reroll pastry trimmings. With small decorative cutters, cut out shapes and place on baking sheet. Brush with milk. Bake conventionally for 15–20 minutes, until golden. Allow to cool on rack.

5 In jug or bowl, combine mincemeat, walnuts, apple, brown sugar and lemon juice. If you like, stir in brandy or rum. Cook, covered, on High (100% power) for 5 minutes, stirring twice. Uncover; stir. Cook on High for 5–7 minutes longer, until apple is tender and flavours are blended, stirring halfway through cooking.

6 To serve: spoon warm mincemeat mixture into tartlet shells, mounding it up slightly in centre. Place pastry shapes carefully on top of mincemeat. Serve warm.

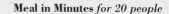

Meal in Minutes *for 20 people*

Summer Pie Party

Summer fruit cup
Minty Chocolate Tart, page 345
Strawberry Chiffon Pie, page 346
Lemon Meringue Pie, page 343
Summer Fruit Tart, page 342
Peaches and Cream Pie, page 343
Raspberry Custard Tart, page 342
Summer berry selection

PREPARATION TIMETABLE

1 day ahead
Make Minty Chocolate Tart, but do not decorate; cover and refrigerate. Prepare Strawberry Chiffon Pie up to end step 5; cover and refrigerate. Prepare pastry shells and biscuit crusts for remaining pies and tarts; cover and refrigerate.

Early in day
Make custard and cream fillings for Lemon Meringue Pie, Summer Fruit Tart and Peaches and Cream Pie; fill, cover and refrigerate. Prepare fruit cup; cover and refrigerate.

About 2 hours ahead
Make custard filling for Raspberry Custard Tart; fill, cover and refrigerate. Complete Strawberry Chiffon Pie, Lemon Meringue Pie, Summer Fruit Tart and Peaches and Cream Pie. Arrange summer berries in bowls; cover and refrigerate.

Just before serving
Decorate Minty Chocolate Tart. Top Raspberry Custard Tart with raspberries. Remove summer berries from refrigerator. Place ice cubes, citrus fruit slices and mint sprigs in glasses for fruit cup.

Cakes, Biscuits and Sweets

SIMPLE CAKES · LAYERED CAKES · SPECIAL CAKES
CHOCOLATE DECORATIONS · TRAY BAKES AND BROWNIES
SHORTBREAD · CREATIVE BISCUITS · CAKE DECORATIONS
CHOCOLATE BISCUITS · HARD AND SOFT SWEETS
CHOCOLATES AND CHEWY SWEETS

Cakes, Biscuits and Sweets

Microwaved cakes are light textured, moist and delicious. In keeping with the time-saving qualities of microwave cooking, this chapter includes a range of cakes based on packet mixes as well as on a simple sponge. You can produce family-pleasing cakes each time you bake in the microwave by following these simple tips: elevate cake dishes on microwave-safe trivets or racks, or on ramekins turned upside down, and rotate dishes halfway through cooking so that cakes will be cooked evenly throughout. Cakes should be removed from the microwave if they spring back when they are touched gently in the centre with a fingertip. Any moist spots on the top of a microwaved cake will dry during standing time in the dish, and the cake will begin to pull away from the sides of the dish by the end of standing time. The cake is done when a fine skewer inserted in the centre comes out clean. To cool a cake completely after standing time, invert it on to a wire cooling rack and remove the lining paper. To keep moist, wrap cakes when cool.

In addition to large family-sized cakes and special gâteaux, a wide range of small cakes, plus everyday and elegant biscuits, can be made in the microwave. When removed from the microwave, the biscuits are soft; allow them to stand as instructed, then remove them to a wire cooling rack to cool completely and become crisp and firm. Plain biscuits and cakes can be made to look more appealing or tailored to special occasions with the Cake Decorations that are featured on pages 366–367.

Sweets and candies cook easily in the microwave, and washing up afterwards is much easier than it is when making them by conventional methods. When boiling sugar mixtures for fudge or other sweets in the microwave, it is important to cook them to exactly the right stage. The Cold Water Test on page 369 provides an accurate and simple way of judging when the correct temperature for the sugar mixture has been reached, and yet it requires no special equipment.

PRETTY GIFTS

Use your microwave oven to make Christmas baking more fun.
Make any of the delicious biscuits and sweets from this chapter,
then pack them in pretty tins and boxes lined with colourful
paper. These gifts will be as much fun to give as receive.

Pistachio Bites (page 372), *Chocolate Mallow Fudge* (page 371) and *Mint Imperials* (page 369) *arranged in a heart-shaped tin* (left).

Mint Imperials (page 369) *and Tiny Chocolate Cones* (page 329) *are packed together to make an attractive gift* (right), *for someone with a sweet tooth.*

Simple Cakes

VICTORIA SANDWICH CAKE

Colour Index page 100. 12 servings. 357 cals per serving. Good source of vitamin A, calcium. Begin 3 hours ahead or early in day.

175 g butter or margarine, softened	*175 g self-raising flour*
175 g caster sugar	*½ teaspoon baking powder*
3 eggs, beaten	*3–4 tablespoons milk*
½ teaspoon vanilla essence	*200 ml double or whipping cream*
Yellow food colouring (optional)	*200 g strawberry jam*
	Icing sugar for dusting

1. Grease bottom and sides of 21 cm round microwave-safe cake dish; line bottom with kitchen paper or greaseproof paper.
2. In large mixing bowl, with mixer at low speed, beat butter or margarine and sugar until light and fluffy, occasionally scraping bowl.
3. Into butter mixture, gradually beat eggs, vanilla and, if you like, 1–2 drops yellow food colouring. Gently fold in flour and baking powder alternately with milk; mixture should have soft, dropping consistency.
4. Spoon half of mixture into prepared dish and smooth surface. Elevate dish on microwave-safe trivet or rack, or on ramekin turned upside down. Cook on High (100% power) for 2½–3½ minutes, until cake springs back when lightly touched with finger, rotating dish halfway through cooking.
5. On heatproof surface, allow cake to stand in dish for 5 minutes. Invert cake on to rack, remove lining paper; leave cake to cool completely.
6. Grease and line dish again. Spoon in remaining mixture and smooth surface. Cook and cool as for first cake layer.
7. Pour cream into small bowl. With mixer at medium speed, whip cream until soft peaks form.
8. On serving plate, place 1 cake layer; spread with strawberry jam. Spread or pipe cream on to jam and top with second cake layer. Dust top of cake with icing sugar. Refrigerate until ready to serve.

PINEAPPLE UPSIDE-DOWN CAKE

Colour Index page 100. 427 cals per serving. Good source of iron. Begin 1¼ hours ahead.

Pineapple Upside-Down Cake is a family favourite as well as one of the most popular choices for novice bakers. It is quick and easy to make in the microwave oven, and it rises just as well as when conventionally baked. Whipped cream or vanilla ice cream is the perfect accompaniment.

Ingredients for 8 servings		Microwave cookware
200 g light soft brown sugar	*175 g self-raising flour*	30 × 20 cm baking dish Trivet, rack or ramekins
115 g butter or margarine	*½ teaspoon baking powder*	
1 × 400 g can pineapple rings, drained	*½ teaspoon salt*	
	75 ml sunflower oil	
	3 eggs	
Maraschino cherries	*1 teaspoon vanilla essence*	
	Yellow food colouring	

1 In baking dish, place brown sugar and butter or margarine. Cook on High (100% power) for 3–5 minutes, until butter or margarine melts, stirring twice.

2 In sugar mixture, arrange pineapple. Place 1 cherry in each ring and extra cherries between. In large mixing bowl, combine flour, baking powder and salt. In medium mixing bowl, beat oil and eggs; stir in vanilla and 1–2 drops colouring. Add oil mixture to flour mixture; beat for 30 seconds.

3 Over fruit arrangement in baking dish, carefully pour batter; smooth surface. Elevate baking dish on trivet or rack, or on ramekins turned upside down.

4 Cook cake on High for 10–12 minutes, until centre springs back when lightly touched with finger, rotating dish halfway through cooking. Allow cake to stand in dish on heatproof surface for 10 minutes.

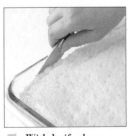

5 With knife, loosen cake from sides of dish. Invert dish on to serving plate. Carefully remove dish to turn out cake. With rubber spatula, loosen any pineapple rings sticking to baking dish and replace on cake.

6 *To serve:* cut cake into 8 portions. Serve warm or cover and refrigerate to serve chilled later.

Simple and Layered Cakes

Chocolate and peanut butter make an unusual combination, but once you try it you'll find it is irresistible. Here a scrumptious mixture of plain chocolate and peanut butter, melted with ease and no mess in the microwave, is used to ice Peanut Butter Fairy Cakes (below). For extra texture in this super-rich icing, you can use chunky instead of smooth peanut butter.

PEANUT BUTTER FAIRY CAKES

Colour Index page 100. 310 cals each. Begin 1¼ hours ahead or early in day.

Ingredients for 12 cakes		Microwave cookware
½ × 500 g packet American yellow cake mix 1 egg 130 g peanut butter	175 ml milk Peanut Butter and Chocolate Icing (below)	Bun dish

1. In large mixing bowl, with mixer at low-speed, beat together dry cake mix, egg, peanut butter and milk until thoroughly blended, constantly scraping bowl. Increase mixer speed to medium; beat 2 minutes longer, occasionally scraping bowl.

2. Line 6 bun dish cups with double thickness of paper liners. Spoon half of mixture into cups, filling them only half full.

3. Cook cakes on Medium (50% power) for 4–5½ (5:30) minutes, until they spring back when lightly touched with finger, rotating dish halfway through cooking.

4. Lift cakes from bun dish cups; remove outer papers. Place cakes on rack to cool. Meanwhile, reline bun dish cups and repeat with remaining mixture. Allow cakes to cool completely.

5. Prepare Peanut Butter and Chocolate Icing: in small microwave-safe bowl, place *170 g plain chocolate pieces*. Heat on High (100% power) for 1–2 minutes, until melted. Stir in *130 g peanut butter* until smooth and well blended.

6. With palette knife, spread top of cakes immediately with Peanut Butter and Chocolate Icing.

SUNNY ORANGE LAYER CAKE

Colour Index page 99. 10 servings. 390 cals per serving. Good source of vitamin A, calcium. Begin early in day.

100 g Lemon Curd Filling (below) *175 g self-raising flour* *1½ teaspoons baking powder* *100 g caster sugar* *90 ml sunflower oil* *3 eggs*	*75 ml frozen orange juice concentrate, defrosted* *Grated zest of 1 orange* *Orange Whipped Cream (page 345) for icing* *Mandarin orange segments for decoration*

1. Prepare Lemon Curd Filling. Grease bottom and sides of 21 cm round microwave-safe cake dish. Line bottom with kitchen paper or grease-proof paper.
2. In large mixing bowl, combine flour, baking powder and sugar. In medium mixing bowl, beat oil, eggs, orange juice concentrate and orange zest. Add oil mixture to flour mixture and, with mixer at low speed, beat for 30 seconds, or until blended, occasionally scraping bowl.
3. Spoon half of mixture into prepared dish and smooth surface. Elevate dish on microwave-safe trivet or rack, or on ramekin turned upside down. Cook on High (100% power) for 2½–3½ minutes, until cake springs back when lightly touched with finger, rotating dish halfway through cooking.
4. On heatproof surface, allow cake to stand in dish for 5 minutes. Invert cake on to rack, remove lining paper; leave cake to cool completely.
5. Grease and line dish again. Spoon in remaining mixture and smooth surface. Cook and cool as for first cake layer.
6. Prepare Orange Whipped Cream. On serving plate, place 1 cake layer; spread with Lemon Curd Filling. Top with second cake layer. Cover top and sides of cake with Orange Whipped Cream; refrigerate for 15 minutes. Decorate cake top with mandarin orange segments before serving.

LEMON CURD FILLING: in 1 litre microwave-safe measuring jug, combine *1 tablespoon grated lemon zest, 3 tablespoons lemon juice, 175 g butter or margarine* and *200 g caster sugar*. Cook on High (100% power) for 1–2 minutes, until butter or margarine melts, stirring once. In small mixing bowl, with whisk, beat *3 eggs*. Stir small amount of hot butter mixture into beaten eggs. Slowly pour egg mixture back into remaining hot butter mixture, beating rapidly to prevent lumping. Cook on Medium (50% power) for 2–3 minutes, until mixture is very thick, stirring occasionally. Do not boil or mixture will curdle. On to surface of hot filling, lightly press dampened greaseproof paper to prevent skin forming. Refrigerate for about 3 hours, or until well chilled. Makes enough to fill two sandwich cakes. 2,245 cals.

CARROT CAKE

Colour Index page 100. 10 servings. 467 cals per serving (without icing). Good source of vitamin A, calcium, iron. Begin 3 hours ahead or early in day.

175 g self-raising flour	*150 ml sunflower oil*
1 teaspoon bicarbonate of soda	*175 g grated carrots (about 3 medium carrots)*
1 teaspoon baking powder	*50 g sultanas*
1 teaspoon ground cinnamon	*50 g chopped walnuts*
1/2 teaspoon ground ginger	*Cream Cheese Icing (below)*
1/2 teaspoon ground allspice	*Walnut halves for decoration*
1/2 teaspoon grated nutmeg	
175 g caster sugar	
3 eggs	

1. Grease bottom and sides of 21 cm round microwave-safe cake dish; line bottom with kitchen paper or greaseproof paper.
2. In large mixing bowl, combine flour, bicarbonate of soda, baking powder, spices and sugar. In medium mixing bowl, beat eggs with oil. Add oil mixture to flour mixture and, with mixer at low speed, beat for 30 seconds, or until blended, occasionally scraping bowl. Stir in carrots, sultanas and walnuts.
3. Spoon half of mixture into prepared dish and smooth surface. Elevate dish on microwave-safe trivet or rack, or on ramekin turned upside down. Cook on High (100% power) for 4–6 minutes, until cake springs back when lightly touched with finger, rotating cake dish halfway through cooking.
4. On heatproof surface, allow cake to stand in dish for 5 minutes. Invert cake on to rack, remove lining paper; leave cake to cool completely.
5. Grease and line dish again. Spoon in remaining mixture and smooth surface. Cook and cool as for first cake layer.
6. Prepare Cream Cheese Icing. On serving plate, place 1 cake layer; spread with icing. Top with second cake layer. Cover top and sides of cake with remaining icing. Decorate with walnut halves.

CREAM CHEESE ICING: place ***100 g cream cheese*** in medium microwave-safe bowl. Heat on Medium (50% power) for 1–2 minutes, until softened. With mixer at low speed, beat in ***1 tablespoon milk*** until smooth. Gradually add ***225 g sifted icing sugar*** and ***1 teaspoon vanilla essence***; beat until smooth. Makes enough to fill and ice one sandwich cake. 2,374 cals.

TWO-TONED LAYER CAKE

Colour Index page 100. 474 cals per serving. Good source of calcium, iron. Begin 3 hours ahead or early in day.

Ingredients for 12 servings		Microwave cookware
1 × 500 g packet American yellow cake mix *60 ml corn oil* *3 eggs*	*3 tablespoons cocoa* *Chocolate Cream Icing (page 359)* *6 × 68 g prepared chocolate mousses*	*21 cm round cake dish* *Trivet, rack or ramekin*

1 Grease bottom and sides of cake dish; line bottom with kitchen paper or greaseproof paper. In large mixing bowl, with mixer at low speed, beat cake mix with oil, eggs and 250 ml water until blended, constantly scraping bowl. Increase speed to high; beat for 2 minutes. Spoon half of mixture into prepared dish; smooth surface.

2 Elevate cake dish on trivet or rack, or on ramekin turned upside down. Cook on High (100% power) for 2 1/2–3 1/2 minutes, until cake springs back when lightly touched with finger, rotating dish halfway through cooking. Allow cake to stand in dish on heatproof surface for 5 minutes.

3 On to wire cooling rack, invert cake; remove lining paper. Allow cake to cool completely.

4 Meanwhile, grease and line cake dish again. Add cocoa powder to remaining cake mixture; stir until well blended. Spoon mixture into prepared dish and smooth surface. Cook and cool as for first cake layer (steps 2 and 3).

5 Meanwhile, prepare Chocolate Cream Icing. With serrated knife, cut each cake layer horizontally in half. On serving platter, place 1 yellow cake layer, cut side up.

6 On yellow cake layer on platter, spread one-third of chocolate mousse. Top with 1 chocolate cake layer, cut side down; spread with one-third of chocolate mousse. Repeat layering, ending with chocolate cake layer. Spread top and side of cake with Chocolate Cream Icing. Cover loosely and refrigerate to serve chilled.

Layered Cakes

STRAWBERRY CREAM LAYER CAKE

Colour Index page 99. 597 cals per serving. Good source of vitamin A, riboflavin, thiamine, vitamin C, calcium, iron, fibre. Begin 3 hours ahead.

Ingredients for 8 servings		Microwave cookware
Ingredients for Victoria Sandwich Cake (page 353). *450 g fresh straw-berries, hulled and cut into quarters lengthways* *2 tablespoons sugar*	*350 ml double or whipping cream* *3 tablespoons icing sugar* *1 teaspoon vanilla essence* *About 10 whole strawberries for decoration*	*21 cm round cake dish Trivet, rack or ramekin*

1 Grease bottom and sides of cake dish; line bottom with kitchen paper or greaseproof paper. Prepare mixture for Victoria Sandwich Cake.

2 Spoon one-third of cake mixture into prepared dish; smooth surface. Elevate dish on trivet or rack, or on ramekin turned upside down. Cook on High (100% power) for 1½–2½ minutes, until cake springs back when lightly touched with finger, rotating dish halfway through cooking. Allow cake to stand in dish on heatproof surface for 5 minutes.

3 On to wire cooling rack, invert cake; remove lining paper. Allow cake to cool completely. Meanwhile, grease and line dish again. Spoon in half of remaining cake mixture; smooth surface. Cook and cool as for first cake. Repeat with remaining cake mixture to make 3 cakes altogether.

4 In mixing bowl, place quartered strawberries and sugar; stir gently until sugar dissolves. In another mixing bowl, whip cream, icing sugar and vanilla until soft peaks form. Place 1 cake on serving platter. Spread with one-third of whipped cream.

5 On top of cream, spoon half of strawberry mixture. Place second cake on top of strawberry mixture. Spread with one-third of whipped cream and top with remaining strawberry mixture. Cover with remaining cake and spread with remaining whipped cream.

6 *To serve:* arrange 1 whole strawberry in centre of cake. Hull remaining whole strawberries, cut in half lengthways and place round edge of cake. Refrigerate cake if not serving immediately.

WHITE CHOCOLATE AND STRAWBERRY GÂTEAU

Colour Index page 99. 12 servings. 616 cals per serving. Good source of vitamin A, thiamine, vitamin C, calcium. Begin early in day.

Double quantity of ingredients for White Chocolate Mousse (page 329)
Ingredients for Victoria Sandwich Cake (page 353)

650 g fresh strawberries
Strawberry Fans (below) for decoration

1. Prepare double quantity of White Chocolate Mousse; cover with cling film and refrigerate.
2. Grease bottom and sides of 21 cm round microwave-safe cake dish; line bottom with kitchen paper or greaseproof paper. Prepare mixture for Victoria Sandwich Cake.
3. Spoon half of cake mixture into prepared dish; smooth surface. Elevate dish on microwave-safe trivet or rack, or on ramekin turned upside down. Cook on High (100% power) for 2½–3½ minutes, until cake springs back when lightly touched with finger, rotating dish halfway through cooking.
4. On heatproof surface, allow cake to stand in dish for 5 minutes. Invert cake on to rack; remove lining paper. Allow cake to cool completely.
5. Meanwhile, grease and line cake dish again. Spoon in remaining cake mixture; smooth surface. Cook and cool as for first cake layer. Hull and slice strawberries.
6. On serving platter, place 1 cake layer. Spread with one-third of White Chocolate Mousse. Cover with sliced strawberries. Top with remaining cake layer. Cover top and side of cake with remaining White Chocolate Mousse.
7. Decoratively arrange Strawberry Fans on top of gâteau. Keep refrigerated until ready to serve.

Making the Strawberry Fans

Select firm whole strawberries with stalks. Starting just below stalk end, thinly slice each strawberry lengthways several times, leaving strawberry connected at stalk end.

With fingertips, gently press down on each strawberry to fan slices slightly.

BLACK FOREST GÂTEAU

Colour Index page 99. 441 cals per serving. Begin early in day.

Ingredients for 12 servings		Microwave cookware
1 × 500 g packet American devil's food cake mix 250 ml water 60 ml corn oil 3 eggs 1 × 400 g can stoned dark sweet cherries in light syrup	4 tablespoons kirsch 115 g plain chocolate 350 ml double or whipping cream 1 tablespoon caster sugar Maraschino cherries and Chocolate Curls (page 360) for decoration	21 cm round cake dish Trivet, rack or ramekin

1 Grease bottom and sides of cake dish; line bottom with kitchen paper or greaseproof paper. In large mixing bowl, with mixer at low speed, beat cake mix, water, oil and eggs until blended, constantly scraping bowl. Increase speed to medium; beat 2 minutes, occasionally scraping bowl.

2 Into dish, pour half of mixture; smooth surface. Elevate on trivet or rack, or on ramekin turned upside down. Cook on High (100% power) 6–8 minutes, until cake springs back when lightly touched with finger, rotating dish once. Allow to stand in dish on heatproof surface for 5 minutes.

3 On to wire cooling rack, invert cake; remove lining paper. Allow cake to cool completely. Meanwhile, grease and line dish again. Spoon in remaining cake mixture; smooth surface. Cook and cool as for first cake layer.

4 Meanwhile, drain cherries, reserving 2 tablespoons syrup. Cut each cherry in half; set aside. In medium mixing bowl, combine reserved syrup and 3 tablespoons kirsch; set aside.

5 With hand grater or in food processor with grating disc attached, coarsely grate chocolate; set aside. Place 1 cake layer on serving platter.

6 With fork, prick cake layer on platter. Evenly spoon half of cherry and kirsch syrup over. In mixing bowl, whip cream, sugar and remaining kirsch until soft peaks form. Evenly spread one-quarter of cream mixture over cake layer. Spoon cherries on to cream.

7 Over cherries, place remaining cake layer. With fork, prick top; evenly spoon over remaining cherry and kirsch syrup.

8 Cover top and side of cake with two-thirds of remaining whipped cream. Decorate cake with grated chocolate, remaining whipped cream, maraschino cherries and Chocolate Curls (see Decorating the Cake above). Keep refrigerated until ready to serve.

DECORATING THE CAKE

A simple microwave cake can be turned into something special with a decoration of cream, chocolate and maraschino cherries.

With spoon, gently press grated chocolate on to side of cream-covered cake until evenly coated.

Spoon remaining whipped cream into piping bag fitted with medium rosette tube.

Pipe decorative border around top edge of cake.

Decorate top of cake with maraschino cherries and Chocolate Curls.

Meal in Minutes *for 6 people*

Afternoon Tea Party

Strawberry Cream Layer Cake, page 356
Lemon Tuiles, page 364
Assorted sandwiches of your choice
Tea with milk or lemon

PREPARATION TIMETABLE	
Early in day	*Make Lemon Tuiles; store in airtight container. Make cake for Strawberry Cream Layer Cake; cool and wrap in cling film.*
2 hours ahead	*Prepare selection of sandwiches with white and wholemeal bread and fillings of your choice such as smoked salmon, thinly sliced cucumber, egg mayonnaise and thinly sliced ham. With serrated knife, cut off crusts, then cut diagonally into quarters to make triangles; wrap in cling film and refrigerate.*
30 minutes ahead	*Fill small jugs with milk and cut lemon slices for tea; cover and refrigerate. Complete Strawberry Cream Layer Cake.*
Just before serving	*Arrange Lemon Tuiles and sandwiches on attractive serving plates. Make tea.*

Layered Cakes

CHOCOLATE CREAM SANDWICH

Colour Index page 99. 12 servings. 353 cals per serving. Good source of vitamin A, riboflavin, calcium. Begin 2 hours ahead or early in day.

Ingredients for Victoria Sandwich Cake (page 353)
Half quantity of Crème Pâtissière (page 324)
Chocolate Glaze (below)
Glacé Icing (below)

1. Grease bottom and sides of 21 cm round microwave-safe cake dish; line bottom with kitchen paper or greaseproof paper.
2. Prepare mixture for Victoria Sandwich Cake.
3. Spoon half of cake mixture into prepared dish; smooth surface. Elevate dish on microwave-safe trivet or rack, or on ramekin turned upside down. Cook on High (100% power) for $2\frac{1}{2}$–$3\frac{1}{2}$ minutes, until cake springs back when lightly touched with finger, rotating dish halfway through cooking.
4. On heatproof surface, allow cake to stand in dish for 5 minutes. Invert cake on to rack; remove lining paper. Allow cake to cool completely.
5. Meanwhile, grease and line dish again. Spoon in remaining cake mixture; smooth surface. Cook and cool as for first cake layer.
6. On serving platter, place 1 cake layer. Spread with Crème Pâtissière. Top with second cake layer. Cover top of cake with Chocolate Glaze; feather with Glacé Icing. Refrigerate at least 15 minutes before serving.

CHOCOLATE GLAZE: in 1 litre microwave-safe measuring jug, place *75 g plain chocolate chips, 15 g butter, $1\frac{1}{2}$ teaspoons milk* and *$1\frac{1}{2}$ teaspoons golden syrup*. Cook on High for 2–3 minutes, until chocolate melts, stirring once. Remove from oven; stir until smooth.

GLACÉ ICING: in small bowl, combine *90 g icing sugar* and *1 tablespoon milk*.

Feathering with the Glacé Icing

Spoon Glacé Icing into piping bag fitted with small round tube and pipe parallel horizontal lines at regular intervals over top of cake.

Hold skewer or knife at right angle to piped lines. Starting at edge, draw lines at same regular intervals over top of cake, alternating direction of lines.

Special Cakes

Use your microwave to make the different stages of cake making quick and easy, as in this version of the classic French Christmas cake, Bûche de Noël (below).

BÛCHE DE NOËL

Colour Index page 99. 410 cals per serving. Good source of iron.
Begin 3½ hours ahead or early in day.

Ingredients for 14 servings		Microwave cookware
100 g butter, softened *100 g caster sugar* *2 eggs, separated* *100 g self-raising flour* *2 tablespoons ground* *almonds* *1 teaspoon baking* *powder*	*90 g cocoa* *125 ml milk* *4 tablespoons golden* *syrup* *4 × 68 g containers* *chocolate mousse* *Chocolate Cream Icing* *(right)*	*23 × 31 cm baking dish* *or tray* *Trivet, rack or* *ramekins*

1 Line bottom of dish or tray with non-stick baking parchment. In large mixing bowl, beat butter and 90 g sugar until light and fluffy. Beat in egg yolks. Mix next 4 ingredients; stir into butter mixture alternately with milk. Stir in golden syrup.

2 In medium mixing bowl, with mixer at high speed, beat egg whites until soft peaks form. Gradually sprinkle in remaining sugar, beating well after each addition, and beat until sugar completely dissolves and whites stand in stiff, glossy peaks.

3 With rubber spatula or whisk, gently fold beaten egg whites into cake mixture until evenly blended. Spoon mixture into prepared dish or tray.

4 With palette knife, evenly spread mixture in dish or tray, smoothing surface. Elevate on trivet or rack, or on ramekins turned upside down. Cook on High (100% power) for 6–9 minutes, until cake springs back when lightly touched with finger, rotating dish or tray halfway through cooking.

5 Evenly sift extra cocoa on to clean tea towel. When cake is done, immediately invert on to towel; remove paper. Starting from 1 long end, roll cake with towel, Swiss roll fashion. Cool completely, seam side down, on rack.

6 Carefully unroll cooled cake; spread evenly with chocolate mousse. Starting at same long end, roll up cake without towel. Place cake, seam side down, on serving platter.

7 With serrated knife, diagonally cut 8 cm slice from 1 end of cake. On to diagonal side of slice, spread small amount of Chocolate Cream Icing. Firmly press iced side of slice to cake, about halfway down side.

8 Cover cake with remaining Chocolate Cream Icing. With small knife or fork, mark icing to resemble bark. Keep refrigerated until ready to serve.

CHOCOLATE CREAM ICING

Using this luscious icing or its variations is an easy way to dress up any cake.

Into medium microwave-safe bowl, pour *175 ml double or whipping cream*. Heat on High (100% power) for 2–4 minutes, until small bubbles form round edge. Add *350 g chopped bittersweet chocolate*; stir until melted; add *1 teaspoon vanilla essence*. Cover and refrigerate.

With mixer at medium speed, beat chocolate mixture until fluffy and thick enough to spread. Makes enough to ice 1 sandwich cake. 2,254 cals.

Orange Chocolate Cream Icing: prepare icing (above), adding *1 tablespoon grated orange zest* with the vanilla.

Almond Chocolate Cream Icing: prepare icing (above), substituting *1 teaspoon almond essence* for the vanilla.

Rum Chocolate Cream Icing: prepare icing (above), substituting *1 teaspoon rum or rum essence* for the vanilla.

Special Cakes

CHOCOLATE LEAVES

Makes about 20 leaves. 431 cals. Low in sodium. Good source of iron. Begin 40 minutes ahead.

75 g plain chocolate chips

1. You will need about 20 real leaves (rose, lemon, ivy or geranium). Rinse leaves and pat thoroughly dry.
2. In 500 ml microwave-safe measuring jug, place chocolate. Heat on High (100% power) for 1¹⁄₂ (1:30)–2 minutes, until melted, stirring once. Remove from oven; stir until smooth. With small pastry brush, brush melted chocolate on to underside of leaves. Refrigerate for about 15 minutes, or until set. With cool hands, carefully peel leaves from set chocolate.

CHOCOLATE ROUNDS

Makes about 12 × 5 cm rounds. 33 cals each. Low in sodium. Begin 25 minutes ahead.

50 g plain chocolate
15 g white vegetable fat

1. Line baking sheet with non-stick baking parchment. In 500 ml microwave-safe measuring jug, place chocolate and shortening. Heat on High (100% power) for 1¹⁄₂ (1:30) minutes, or until melted, stirring once. Remove from oven; stir until smooth.
2. On to lined baking sheet, drop teaspoonfuls of hot chocolate mixture. Spread out slightly with back of spoon. Refrigerate for about 15 minutes, or until set. Lift off with palette knife.

CHOCOLATE CURLS

Makes enough curls to decorate top of 21.5 cm cake. 144 cals. Low in sodium. Begin 15 minutes ahead.

25 g plain chocolate, in a block piece

1. In small microwave-safe bowl, place chocolate. Heat on High (100% power) for 15 seconds at a time, just until beginning to soften.
2. Using vegetable peeler or cheese slicer, draw along wide surface of chocolate to form large curls. For short curls, draw along narrow side of chocolate. To avoid breaking, use cocktail stick to pick up and place curls on cakes and desserts.

APRICOT CREAM ROULADE

Colour Index page 101. 14 servings. 428 cals per serving. Begin 3 hours ahead or early in day.

175 g butter or margarine, softened
175 g caster sugar
3 eggs, separated
1 teaspoon almond essence
Yellow food colouring (optional)
175 g self-raising flour
¹⁄₂ teaspoon baking powder
3–4 tablespoons milk
Icing sugar
1 × 340 g jar apricot jam
500 ml double or whipping cream

1. Line bottom of 31 × 23 cm microwave-safe baking dish or tray with layer of non-stick baking parchment.
2. In large mixing bowl, with mixer at low speed, beat butter and 150 g sugar until light and fluffy, occasionally scraping bowl. Into butter mixture, beat egg yolks, ¹⁄₂ teaspoon almond essence and, if you like, 1–2 drops food colouring. Stir in flour and baking powder alternately with milk.
3. In medium mixing bowl, with mixer at high speed, beat egg whites until soft peaks form. Gradually sprinkle in remaining caster sugar, beating well after each addition, and beat until sugar completely dissolves and whites stand in stiff, glossy peaks.
4. With rubber spatula or whisk, gently fold beaten egg whites into cake mixture until blended.
5. Spoon mixture into prepared dish or tray. With palette knife, evenly spread batter and smooth surface. Elevate on microwave-safe trivet or rack, or on ramekins turned upside down. Cook on High (100% power) for 6–8 minutes, until cake springs back when lightly touched with finger, rotating dish or tray halfway through cooking.
6. Meanwhile, evenly sift icing sugar on to clean tea towel. When cake is done, immediately invert on to towel; remove parchment paper. Starting at 1 short end, roll cake with towel, Swiss roll fashion. Cool completely, seam side down, on rack.
7. In medium microwave-safe bowl, place apricot jam. Heat on High for 2–3 minutes, until warm, stirring twice. Over mixing bowl, set fine sieve. Pour warm apricot jam through sieve and press with back of spoon.
8. Carefully unroll cooled cake; spread evenly with sieved jam. Starting at same short end, roll up cake without towel. Place cake, seam side down, on serving platter.
9. In medium bowl, place cream, 4 tablespoons icing sugar and remaining almond essence. Whip until soft peaks form.
10. Spoon whipped cream into piping bag fitted with medium rosette tube. Pipe on to cake in decorative fashion. Keep refrigerated until ready to serve.

CHOCOLATE MOUSSE BOMBE

Colour Index page 101. 10 servings. 601 cals per serving. Good source of calcium, iron. Begin early in day.

1 × 500 g packet American chocolate fudge cake mix	500 ml double or whipping cream Cocoa
250 ml water	
60 ml corn oil	
3 eggs	
6 × 68 g containers chocolate mousse	

1. Grease 2 litre microwave-safe bowl. Line bottom of bowl with 7.5 cm circle of non-stick baking parchment.
2. In large mixing bowl, with mixer at low speed, beat cake mix, water, oil and eggs until blended, constantly scraping bowl. Increase speed to medium; beat for 2 minutes, occasionally scraping bowl. Spoon into prepared bowl; smooth surface.
3. Elevate bowl on microwave-safe trivet or rack, or on ramekin turned upside down. Cook on High (100% power) for 9–12 minutes, until cake springs back when lightly touched with finger, rotating bowl halfway through cooking.
4. On heatproof surface, allow cake to stand in bowl for 10 minutes. Cover and allow to cool completely on rack.
5. With serrated knife, cut out centre of cake, leaving 4 cm shell. Reserve removed cake centre. Spoon chocolate mousse into centre of shell. Cut reserved cake into small chunks and press on to surface of mousse. Invert on to serving platter. Carefully remove bowl to unmould cake. Cover and refrigerate until chilled.
6. In medium mixing bowl, whip cream until soft peaks form. Spoon cream into piping bag fitted with medium rosette tube. Pipe rosettes over surface of cake. Dust with cocoa. Keep refrigerated until ready to serve.

Decorating the Bombe

With rosette tube, pipe rows of rosettes to cover surface of cake.

With fine sieve, lightly dust cocoa over cream rosettes.

MARBLED CHOCOLATE RING

Colour Index page 101. 16 servings. 294 cals per serving. Begin early in day.

This rich cake has a delicious cream cheese filling. If you like, for a special decorative effect, dust finished cake with sifted icing sugar and pipe whipped cream round bottom.

Ingredients for 16 servings		Microwave cookware
225 g cream cheese, softened	250 ml water	2.5 litre decorative ring mould
65 g caster sugar	60 ml corn oil	Trivet, rack or ramekin
4 eggs	Chocolate Glaze (page 358)	
½ teaspoon vanilla essence		
1 × 500 g packet American devil's food cake mix		

1 Grease ring mould. In small bowl, with mixer at low speed, beat cream cheese until smooth. Add sugar, 1 egg and vanilla; beat until well blended.

2 In large mixing bowl, with mixer at low speed, beat cake mix, water, oil and remaining eggs until blended, constantly scraping bowl. Increase speed to medium; beat for 2 minutes, occasionally scraping bowl. Spoon one-third of mixture into prepared mould.

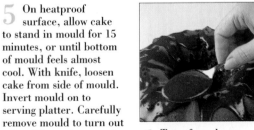

3 With tablespoon, drop spoonfuls of cream cheese mixture in a ring on to cake mixture, taking care not to let cream cheese mixture touch side of mould. Carefully cover cream cheese mixture with remaining cake mixture.

4 Elevate mould on trivet or rack, or on ramekin turned upside down. Cook mixture on High (100% power) for 10–15 minutes, until cake springs back when lightly touched with finger, rotating mould halfway through cooking.

5 On heatproof surface, allow cake to stand in mould for 15 minutes, or until bottom of mould feels almost cool. With knife, loosen cake from side of mould. Invert mould on to serving platter. Carefully remove mould to turn out cake. Allow cake to cool completely. Meanwhile, make Chocolate Glaze.

6 Transfer cake to serving platter. With spoon, drizzle glaze over cooled cake.

Tray Bakes and Brownies

Tray bakes adapt beautifully to microwave cooking, turning out moist, chewy and tempting. So too do brownies, one of America's favourite sweet snacks, which get their name from the dark brown chocolate used in their making. The American fudge brownie mix used in some of these recipes works perfectly in the microwave oven, and is widely available in large supermarkets.

RICH NUT-TOPPED BROWNIES

Colour Index page 101. 191 cals each. Low in sodium. Begin early in day.

Ingredients for 24 brownies		Microwave cookware
115 g butter or margarine	1 teaspoon vanilla essence	30 × 20 cm baking dish 2 litre glass jug or bowl Trivet, rack or ramekins
115 g plain chocolate	1/2 teaspoon salt	
400 g caster sugar	125 g plain chocolate chips	
4 eggs	50 g shelled walnuts, chopped	
95 g plain flour		

1 Grease baking dish and line bottom of dish with non-stick baking parchment.

2 In glass jug or bowl, place butter or margarine and chocolate. Heat on High (100% power) for 1½ (1:30)–2 minutes, until melted, stirring once. Remove from oven; stir until smooth.

3 To chocolate mixture, add sugar and eggs; beat until well blended. Stir in flour, vanilla and salt until smooth. Spoon into baking dish; smooth top. Sprinkle over chocolate chips and walnuts.

4 Elevate baking dish on trivet or rack, or on ramekins turned upside down. Cook on High (100% power) for 5–6 minutes, just until beginning to set (do not overbake), rotating dish halfway through cooking.

5 On heatproof surface, allow brownie mixture to stand in dish for 5 minutes. Cover and refrigerate until well chilled.

6 To serve: cut firm, chilled brownies into 24 squares with sharp knife. If not using immediately, store in airtight container.

BUTTERSCOTCH SQUARES

Colour Index page 101. Makes 24. 134 cals each. Low in sodium. Begin early in day.

115 g butter or margarine, softened	1 teaspoon vanilla essence
165 g light brown sugar	1 egg
140 g plain flour	75 g desiccated coconut
1 teaspoon baking powder	75 g shelled pecan nuts or walnuts
1/4 teaspoon salt	75 g plain chocolate chips

1. Grease 30 × 20 cm microwave-safe baking dish; line bottom of dish with non-stick baking parchment.
2. In large mixing bowl, with mixer at low speed, beat butter or margarine and sugar until blended. Add flour, baking powder, salt, vanilla, egg, 50 g coconut and 25 g walnuts; beat until well blended, constantly scraping bowl. Spoon mixture into prepared baking dish; smooth surface. Over top of mixture, sprinkle remaining coconut, pecans or walnuts and chocolate chips.
3. Elevate dish on microwave-safe trivet or rack, or on ramekins turned upside down. Cook on High (100% power) for 5–6 minutes, just until beginning to set (do not overbake), rotating dish halfway through cooking. On heatproof surface, allow mixture to stand in dish for 5 minutes. Cover and refrigerate until well chilled.
4. Cut into 24 squares; store chilled squares in airtight container.

NO-BAKE MINT CHOCOLATE SQUARES

Colour Index page 101. Makes 24. 233 cals each. Low in sodium. Begin 2½ hours ahead.

175 g mint-flavoured chocolates (not cream-filled)	185 g shelled walnuts, chopped
175 g plain chocolate chips	1 × 400 g can sweetened condensed milk
60 g butter or margarine	1 teaspoon vanilla essence
120 g digestive biscuits, finely crushed	

1. Grease and flour 30 × 20 cm baking dish.
2. In 1 litre microwave-safe measuring jug, place mint chocolates, chocolate chips and butter or margarine. Heat on High (100% power) for 2–3 minutes, until melted, stirring once. Stir until smooth.
3. In large mixing bowl, combine crushed biscuits and walnuts. Stir in condensed milk, vanilla and chocolate mixture until blended. Spoon into prepared dish; smooth surface. Leave at room temperature for about 2 hours, or until firm.
4. Cut into 24 squares; store in airtight container.

Tray Bakes and Shortbread

CHOCOLATE AND MARSHMALLOW TRIANGLES

Colour Index page 102. Makes 16. 344 cals each. Good source of iron. Begin 2½ hours ahead

1 × 610 g packet American fudge brownie mix	100 g shelled walnuts, chopped
80 ml water	50 g miniature marshmallows
80 ml corn oil	175 g plain chocolate chips
2 eggs, lightly beaten	

1. Grease 2 shallow 21.5 cm microwave-safe pie dishes; line bottoms with greaseproof paper. In large mixing bowl, beat dry fudge brownie mix, water, oil and eggs until blended. Spoon mixture into prepared dishes; smooth surface.
2. In medium mixing bowl, combine walnuts, marshmallows and chocolate chips. Sprinkle mixture evenly over cake mixture.
3. Elevate 1 pie dish on microwave-safe trivet or rack, or on ramekin turned upside down. Cook on High (100% power) for 5–7 minutes, until top puffs slightly and marshmallows begin to melt, rotating dish halfway through cooking. Allow to cool completely in dish on rack. Meanwhile, repeat with remaining mixture in second dish.
4. When cool, cut each round into 8 wedges; store in airtight container.

CREAM CHEESE BROWNIES

Colour Index page 102. Makes 16. 296 cals each. Begin 2½ hours ahead.

225 g cream cheese	1 × 610 g packet American fudge brownie mix
3 tablespoons caster sugar	80 ml water
½ teaspoon almond essence	80 ml corn oil
3 eggs	

1. Grease 2 shallow 21.5 cm microwave-safe pie dishes; line bottoms with greaseproof paper. In medium microwave-safe bowl, place cream cheese. Heat on Medium (50% power) for 1–2 minutes, until softened. Add sugar, almond essence and 1 egg and stir until smooth; set aside.
2. In large mixing bowl, beat dry fudge brownie mix, water, oil and remaining eggs until blended. Spoon mixture into prepared dishes; smooth surface. Drop cream cheese mixture by spoonfuls on top of cake mixture. With knife, cut through 2 mixtures to obtain marbled effect.
3. Elevate 1 dish on microwave-safe trivet or rack, or on ramekin turned upside down. Cook on High (100% power) for 5–7 minutes, until top puffs slightly and is almost dry, rotating dish halfway through cooking. Allow to cool completely in dish on rack. Meanwhile, repeat with remaining mixture in second pie dish.
4. When cool, cut each round into 8 wedges; store in airtight container.

ALMOND SHORTBREAD

Colour Index page 102. 177 cals each. Begin 1½ hours ahead or early in day.

Almond Shortbread is a classic made special by the addition of toasted sliced almonds. Shortbread dough can be very delicate and somewhat difficult to handle, but cooking it in the microwave makes the finished biscuit beautifully light. As an alternative to the almond flavouring, substitute ¼ teaspoon ground ginger for the ½ teaspoon almond essence, and decorate the top of the shortbread with thin slivers of crystallised ginger to emphasise the flavour.

Ingredients for 8 wedges		Microwave cookware
115 g butter or margarine, softened	½ teaspoon vanilla essence	Shallow 21.5 cm pie dish
40 g icing sugar, sifted	½ teaspoon almond essence	Trivet, rack or ramekin
140 g plain flour	¼ teaspoon salt	
½ teaspoon baking powder	Flaked almonds, toasted, for decoration	

1 Grease pie dish; line bottom with non-stick baking parchment. In large mixing bowl, with mixer at low speed, beat butter or margarine and sugar until light and fluffy.

2 To butter and sugar mixture, add flour, baking powder, vanilla and almond essences and salt. With mixer at low speed, beat until ingredients are well blended, constantly scraping bowl. With fingers, gently and evenly press dough into prepared pie dish.

3 With fork, prick dough all over in decorative pattern. With knife, mark dough into 8 wedges.

4 Into dough, press toasted flaked almonds in decorative pattern. Elevate pie dish on trivet or rack, or on ramekin turned upside down.

5 Cook shortbread on Medium (50% power) for 7–8 minutes, until puffed and set, rotating dish halfway through cooking. Allow shortbread to stand in dish on heatproof surface for 5 minutes.

6 With sharp knife, cut shortbread into wedges along knife marks; allow to cool completely in dish. Remove and store in airtight container.

Creative Biscuits

Delicate biscuits are perfect with after-dinner coffee. For a change, substitute the same quantity of grated lemon zest for the grated orange zest in the recipe for Coconut Rounds (below). Store soft and crisp biscuits in separate containers with tight-fitting covers for maximum freshness.

COCONUT ROUNDS

Colour Index page 102. 44 cals each. Low in sodium. Begin 1½ hours ahead.

Ingredients for 30 biscuits		Microwave cookware
50 g desiccated coconut 2 tablespoons plain flour 50 g caster sugar 1 tablespoon grated orange zest	¼ teaspoon vanilla essence 2 egg whites 60 g plain butter or margarine 75 g plain chocolate	Shallow 21.5 cm pie dish 500 ml measuring jug 30 cm round platter Trivet, rack or ramekins Small bowl

1 In pie dish, place coconut. Heat on High (100% power) for 3–4 minutes, until coconut is lightly toasted, stirring occasionally. In food processor with knife blade attached or in blender, process toasted coconut until finely ground.

2 To coconut, add flour, sugar, orange zest, vanilla and egg whites. Process until blended. In measuring jug, place butter or margarine. Heat, covered with kitchen paper, on High for 45 seconds–1 minute, until melted.

3 Into coconut mixture in food processor or blender, with motor running, pour hot butter or margarine in thin, steady stream. Process until blended.

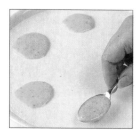

4 On to lightly greased platter, drop 6 teaspoonfuls mixture, at least 5 cm apart, in a ring. Elevate on trivet or rack, or on ramekins turned upside down. Cook on Medium-High (70% power) for 3–4 minutes, until biscuits begin to brown lightly, rotating platter halfway through cooking. Allow to stand for 1–2 minutes.

5 With fish slice, transfer biscuits to rack. Allow to cool completely. Meanwhile, repeat with remaining mixture. (If you like, only use some of the mixture, then cover and refrigerate remainder for up to 5 days.) In small bowl, place chocolate. Heat on High for 2–3 minutes, until melted, stirring once. Remove from oven; stir until smooth.

6 Over each cooled biscuit, drizzle melted chocolate. Allow to cool completely. Store in airtight container.

LEMON TUILES

Colour Index page 102. Makes 30. 43 cals each. Low in sodium. Begin 1½ hours ahead.

100 g caster sugar 35 g plain flour 2 tablespoons cornflour ½ teaspoon grated lemon zest	½ teaspoon almond essence 2 egg whites 60 g butter or margarine 50 g flaked almonds

1. Grease flat 30 cm round microwave-safe platter. In food processor with knife blade attached or in blender, process sugar and next 5 ingredients until blended.
2. In 500 ml microwave-safe measuring jug, place butter or margarine. Heat, covered with kitchen paper, on High (100% power) for 45 seconds–1 minute, until melted. Into mixture in food processor or blender, with motor running, pour hot butter or margarine in thin, steady stream. Process until blended.
3. On to greased platter, drop 6 teaspoonfuls mixture, at least 5 cm apart, in a ring. Sprinkle with almonds. Elevate on microwave-safe trivet or rack, or on ramekins turned upside down. Cook on Medium-High (70% power) for 3–4 minutes, until biscuits begin to brown lightly, rotating platter halfway through cooking. Allow to stand for 2 minutes.
4. With fish slice, transfer biscuits to rack. Or, if you like, quickly remove each biscuit and roll round rolling pin for characteristic 'roof tile' shape. Allow to cool completely. Meanwhile, repeat with remaining mixture. Store in airtight container.

VIENNESE MELTAWAYS

Colour Index page 103. Makes 36. 51 cals each. Low in sodium. Begin 1½ hours ahead.

115 g butter or margarine Icing sugar 140 g plain flour	60 g blanched almonds, freshly ground 1 teaspoon almond essence

1. Grease 30 cm round microwave-safe platter; line with greaseproof paper. In medium microwave-safe bowl, place butter or margarine. Heat, covered with kitchen paper, on Medium (50% power) for 45 seconds, or just until softened; do not melt. Add 30 g icing sugar, flour, ground almonds and almond essence; stir until blended.
2. Shape dough, 1 teaspoonful at a time, into 2.5 cm balls. Place on platter in a ring, 2.5 cm apart. Elevate on microwave-safe trivet or rack, or on ramekins turned upside down. Cook on Medium for 4–5 minutes, until dry and firm, rotating platter once. Allow to stand on platter for 2 minutes.
3. With slice, transfer biscuits to rack. Allow to cool completely. Meanwhile, repeat with remaining dough. Store in airtight container. Dust with icing sugar just before serving.

FLORENTINES

Colour Index page 102. Makes 24. 111 cals each. Low in sodium. Begin 2¹/₂ hours ahead.

60 g butter or margarine	45 g plain flour
100 g caster sugar	65 g diced mixed
125 ml double or	candied peel
whipping cream	30 g flaked almonds
2 tablespoons honey	115 g plain chocolate

1. Grease 30 cm flat round microwave-safe platter. In 1 litre microwave-safe measuring jug, place butter or margarine, sugar, cream and honey. Heat on High (100% power) for 4 minutes, or until butter or margarine is melted, stirring once. Stir in flour until blended. Fold in candied peel and almonds.

2. On to platter, drop 6 teaspoonfuls mixture, at least 5 cm apart, in a ring. Elevate on microwave-safe trivet or rack, or on ramekins turned upside down. Cook on Medium-High (70% power) for 2–4 minutes, until biscuits begin to brown lightly, rotating platter halfway through cooking.

3. With 6 cm round biscuit cutter, trim uneven edges off biscuits. Allow to stand for 1–2 minutes, until slightly firm. With fish slice, transfer biscuits to rack. Allow to cool completely. Meanwhile, repeat with remaining mixture.

4. In small microwave-safe bowl, place chocolate. Heat on High for 2–3 minutes, until melted, stirring once. Remove from oven; stir until smooth. Spread smooth side of cooled biscuits with melted chocolate. If you like, with fork, make a design in chocolate. Allow to cool completely. Store in airtight container.

MAPLE SNAPS

Colour Index page 103. Makes 24. 49 cals each. Low in sodium. Begin 1¹/₂ hours ahead.

60 g butter or margarine	45 g plain flour
4 tablespoons maple	30 g shelled walnuts,
syrup	finely chopped
4 tablespoons golden	
syrup	

1. Grease 30 cm round microwave-safe platter. In 1 litre microwave-safe measuring jug, place butter or margarine, maple syrup and golden syrup. Heat on High (100% power) for 4 minutes, or until butter or margarine is melted, stirring once. Fold in remaining ingredients.

2. On to platter, drop 6 teaspoonfuls mixture, at least 5 cm apart, in a ring. Elevate on microwave-safe trivet or rack, or on ramekins turned upside down. Cook on Medium-High (70% power) for 2–4 minutes, until biscuits are golden, rotating platter halfway through cooking.

3. Allow biscuits to stand for 1–2 minutes until slightly firm. With fish slice, transfer biscuits to rack. Allow to cool completely. Meanwhile, repeat with remaining mixture. Store cooled biscuits in airtight container.

MEXICAN WEDDING BISCUITS

Colour Index page 102. 80 cals each. Low in sodium. Begin early in day.

Make an unusual and attractive addition to your baking repertoire with these Mexican Wedding Biscuits, made light and delicate in the microwave. Chilling helps make dough easier to handle. For an alternative, striking effect, decorate half of the biscuits with icing sugar and half with cocoa powder.

Ingredients for 24 biscuits		Microwave cookware
115 g butter or margarine	¹/₂ teaspoon vanilla essence	Flat 30 cm round platter
175 g plain flour	40 g shelled walnuts, finely chopped	Medium bowl
90 g icing sugar, sifted		Trivet, rack or ramekins

1 Grease platter; line with non-stick baking parchment. In medium bowl, place butter or margarine. Heat on Medium (50% power) for 45 seconds, or until softened; do not melt.

2 To softened butter or margarine, add flour, 30 g icing sugar, vanilla essence and chopped walnuts; stir until blended. Shape dough into ball; flatten slightly. Wrap in cling film and refrigerate for about 1 hour, or until dough is firm. On lightly floured surface, with floured rolling pin, roll out chilled dough 5 mm thick. With crescent-shaped biscuit cutter, cut out as many biscuits as possible. Reroll trimmings and cut again.

3 On platter lined with greaseproof paper, place biscuits, at least 5 mm apart, in a ring and in centre. Elevate platter on trivet or rack, or on ramekins turned upside down.

4 Cook biscuits on Medium (50% power) for 4–5 minutes, until biscuits are firm and look dry, rotating platter halfway through cooking. Allow to stand for 2 minutes.

5 With fish slice, transfer biscuits to rack. Allow to cool completely. Meanwhile, repeat with remaining biscuits.

6 Sift remaining icing sugar over cooled biscuits to coat completely. Store in airtight container.

Cake Decorations

There are many cake decorations, confections and colourings available to make microwave cakes, biscuits, pastries and desserts look even prettier. Choose from hard and soft sweets, as well as glacé and crystallised fruits and chocolate decorations.

These sweets (above) are commercial products made from boiled hard sugar tinted with food colourings. They range from pretty little flower heads to larger shapes such as teddy bears and clowns, which can be used as instant decorations

Diamond Jellies: soft and chewy sugar decorations

Marzipan Fruits: tinted almond paste shaped to resemble fruits

Dragees: shiny, smooth-coated, hard-sugar balls

Glacé Cherries: candied cherries coated with sugar glaze

Glacé fruits and other sugar-based decorations make ideal finishing touches for cakes and biscuits. Glacé fruits can also be used as ingredients in cakes and sweets

Angelica: candied stalk of the herb

Orange and Lemon Jelly Sweets: 'fruit slices' made of sugar and gelatine

Rainbow Sugar Crystals: small refined sugar crystals coloured with vegetable dyes

Candles: small decorative candles with a variety of patterns; used for celebration cakes

Chocolate Milk Flake: can be used in pieces or crumbled

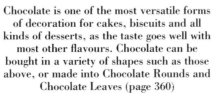

Chocolate Vermicelli: tiny tube-shaped decorations

Chocolate Flakes: plain chocolate and milk chocolate pieces

Chocolate is one of the most versatile forms of decoration for cakes, biscuits and all kinds of desserts, as the taste goes well with most other flavours. Chocolate can be bought in a variety of shapes such as those above, or made into Chocolate Rounds and Chocolate Leaves (page 360)

Chocolate Leaves: small, commercially made chocolate decorations

Chocolate Curls: homemade Chocolate Curls (page 360)

Chocolate Biscuits

CARAMEL PECAN BARS

Colour Index page 103. 168 cals per bar. Low in sodium. Begin 2 hours ahead.

Ingredients for 24 bars		Microwave cookware
115 g butter or margarine	110 g shelled pecan nut halves	1 litre measuring jug
220 g light brown sugar	6 tablespoons double or whipping cream	250 ml glass jug or bowl
105 g plain flour	6 tablespoons golden syrup	
1/4 teaspoon salt	100 g plain chocolate, broken into pieces	
1 teaspoon vanilla essence		

1 Grease bottom and sides of 20 cm square baking dish; line bottom with non-stick baking parchment. Preheat conventional oven to 180 °C (350 °F, gas 4).

2 In large bowl, with mixer at medium speed, beat 60 g butter or margarine until creamy. Add 75 g brown sugar, all of the flour and salt, and 1/2 teaspoon vanilla essence; beat until smooth, constantly scraping bowl. Pat dough evenly into prepared baking dish.

3 Over dough, evenly arrange pecans. Bake conventionally for 20–25 minutes, until pecans are toasted and dough is golden.

4 Meanwhile, in 1 litre measuring jug, combine remaining brown sugar, butter or margarine and vanilla. Stir in cream and golden syrup. Cook on High (100% power) for 6–8 minutes, until Soft Ball Stage is reached (see Cold Water Test, page 369), stirring twice.

5 Over biscuit layer in baking dish, pour caramel mixture. Allow caramel to cool completely in dish on rack. In 250 ml jug or bowl, place plain chocolate. Heat on High for 2–3 minutes, until melted, stirring once. Remove from oven; stir until smooth.

6 Over cooled caramel layer, drizzle melted chocolate. When set, cut into 24 bars. Store in airtight container.

FRUIT AND NUT BARS

Colour Index page 102. Makes 16. 226 cals each. Low in sodium. Begin 1 1/4 hours ahead.

140 g blanched almonds
125 g shelled walnuts
130 g dried apricots
145 g seedless raisins
180 g stoned prunes
175 g plain chocolate chips

1. Line bottom of 20 cm square baking dish with foil. In food processor with knife blade attached or in blender, process almonds and walnuts until finely chopped; spoon into mixing bowl. Process apricots, raisins and prunes into very small pieces (do not purée); add to chopped nuts. Press evenly into prepared dish.
2. In small microwave-safe bowl, place chocolate chips. Heat on High (100% power) for 2–3 minutes, until melted, stirring once. Remove from oven; stir until smooth. With rubber spatula, spread melted chocolate over fruit and nut mixture. Cover and refrigerate until firm.
3. Cut fruit and nut mixture into 16 bars. Store in airtight container.

CHOCOLATE CHIP CRISPIES

Colour Index page 103. Makes 30. 69 cals each. Low in sodium. Begin 1 1/2 hours ahead.

125 g shelled walnuts
110 g brown sugar
1/4 teaspoon ground cinnamon
2 egg whites
1/2 teaspoon vanilla essence
60 g butter or margarine
175 g plain chocolate chips

1. Grease 30 cm round microwave-safe platter.
2. In food processor with knife blade attached or in blender, process 60 g walnuts until coarsely chopped; remove. Process remaining walnuts until ground. Add brown sugar, cinnamon, egg whites and vanilla essence; process until smooth.
3. In 500 ml microwave-safe measuring jug, place butter or margarine. Heat, covered with kitchen paper, on High (100% power) for 45 seconds–1 minute, until melted. Into walnut mixture in food processor or blender, with motor running, pour hot butter or margarine in thin, steady stream; process until blended.
4. On to platter, drop 6 teaspoonfuls mixture, at least 5 cm apart, in a ring. Sprinkle each biscuit with chocolate chips and chopped walnuts. Elevate on microwave-safe trivet or rack, or on ramekins turned upside down. Cook on Medium-High (70% power) for 3–4 minutes, until biscuits begin to brown lightly, rotating platter halfway through cooking. Allow to stand for 1–2 minutes.
5. Transfer biscuits to rack. Allow to cool completely. Meanwhile, repeat with remaining mixture. Allow to cool completely. Store in airtight container.

Hard Sweets

VANILLA-WALNUT DROPS

Colour Index page 104. Makes 42. 64 cals each. Low in sodium. Begin 1½ hours ahead.

220 g light brown sugar
200 g caster sugar
80 g golden syrup
60 ml water
125 g shelled walnuts, chopped

15 g butter or margarine
1 teaspoon vanilla essence

1. Lightly grease baking sheets; line with grease-proof paper.

2. In large microwave-safe bowl, combine brown sugar, caster sugar, golden syrup and water. Cook on High (100% power) for 7½ (7:30)–8 minutes, without stirring, until Soft Ball Stage is reached (see Cold Water Test, below).

3. To syrup, add chopped walnuts, butter or margarine and vanilla essence; stir until well combined. Allow to stand for 2 minutes.

4. On to prepared baking sheets, drop teaspoonfuls of mixture. Allow to cool on rack for about 1 hour, or until set. Store in airtight container.

COLD WATER TEST

This Cold Water Test is a simple way to measure the temperature of a sugar mixture. Fill measuring jug with very cold water. With clean spoon, drop ½ teaspoon hot sugar syrup into water. Allow to stand for 1 minute, then test firmness with your fingers.

Soft Ball Stage

Small amount of syrup dropped into cold water forms soft ball that flattens between forefinger and thumb when removed.

Hard Crack Stage

Small amount of syrup dropped into cold water separates into hard, brittle threads.

MINT IMPERIALS

Colour Index page 103. 70 cals each. Low in sodium. Begin early in day.

Washing up is so much easier when you cook the sugar syrup for Mint Imperials in the microwave. Use different food colourings for a pretty effect.

Ingredients for 36 mints		Microwave cookware
600 g caster sugar 3 tablespoons golden syrup Water 1 teaspoon peppermint essence	Food colouring (optional) Melted chocolate (optional)	Large bowl

1 In large bowl, place sugar, golden syrup and 175 ml water. Cook on High (100% power) for 7–8 minutes, until sugar completely dissolves, stirring twice.

2 Continue to cook fondant on High for 5–6 minutes, until Soft Ball Stage is reached (see Cold Water Test, left). Do not stir.

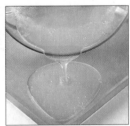

3 Without scraping side of bowl, pour fondant into 38.5 × 26 cm Swiss roll tin. Place tin on rack and allow fondant mixture to cool until temperature is 50 °C (120 °F).

4 With wide, stiff metal fish slice, pastry scraper, or clean, wide paint scraper, push mixture to one end of tin, fold over, then spread out to 5 mm thickness. Repeat pushing, folding and spreading until fondant turns white and clay-like. Knead mixture to form ball. If not ready to use immediately, store fondant in airtight container for up to 1 week.

5 When ready to use, lightly grease baking sheets; line with greaseproof paper. Crumble fondant into cleaned large bowl; add peppermint essence, 2 drops food colouring, if using, and 2 teaspoons water. Heat on High for 1½ (1:30) minutes, or until softened, stirring once. Remove from oven; stir until smooth.

6 Working quickly, drop teaspoonfuls of mixture on to prepared baking sheets. (If fondant becomes too hard and thick, add few drops water and heat on High for 20–30 seconds.) If you like, dip into melted chocolate when mints are firm. Store in airtight container.

Hard and Soft Sweets

PEANUT BRITTLE

Colour Index page 103. 142 cals per 25 g serving.
Begin 1¼ hours ahead.

Peanut Brittle is one of the simplest and most delicious sweets to
make conventionally because of the all-in-one preparation and
cooking process. Using your microwave oven makes it even
quicker and easier! Be sure to grease your baking sheet well
before pouring the peanut and caramel mixture on to it; this will
help lifting and breaking it into pieces for serving.

Ingredients for 450 g brittle		Microwave cookware

200 g caster sugar
165 g golden syrup
60 ml water
¼ teaspoon salt
145 g shelled roasted
  peanuts
	30 g butter or margarine
	1 teaspoon bicarbonate
	  of soda
		2 litre measuring jug

1 With pastry brush,
generously oil large
baking sheet.

2 In measuring jug,
place sugar; add
golden syrup, water and
salt. Stir until well
blended.

3 Cook syrup mixture
on High (100%
power) for 12–15
minutes, without stirring,
until Hard Crack Stage is
reached (see Cold Water
Test, page 369), just until
caramel begins to turn
light golden. Watch
carefully since caramel
burns easily and
continues to cook and
darken when removed
from the oven.

4 To caramel mixture
in jug, add peanuts,
butter or margarine and
bicarbonate of soda. Stir
well until peanuts are
evenly coated.
Immediately pour peanut
mixture on to prepared
baking sheet.

5 With 2 forks, quickly
lift and stretch
peanut mixture into
35 × 30 cm rectangle.
Allow to cool on rack
until firm.

6 With hands, break
cold brittle into small
pieces. Store in airtight
container.

BUTTER CARAMELS

Colour Index page 104. Makes 64. 45 cals each.
Low in sodium. Begin 1½ hours ahead.

350 ml double or
  whipping cream
200 g caster sugar
165 g golden syrup
	60 g butter
	1 teaspoon vanilla
	  essence

1. Lightly grease 20 cm square baking dish.
2. In 2 litre microwave-safe measuring jug, combine cream, sugar and golden syrup. Cook syrup
mixture on High (100% power) for 15–20 minutes, without stirring, until Soft Ball Stage is
reached (see Cold Water Test, page 369).
3. Into mixture, stir butter and vanilla essence.
Pour caramel mixture immediately into prepared
baking dish; smooth surface. Allow to cool completely in baking dish on rack until firm.
4. Invert baking dish on to cutting board.
Remove baking dish to unmould. With sharp
knife, cut caramel into 2.5 cm squares. Wrap
each square in cellophane or cling film. Store in
airtight container.

CHOCOLATE CHERRY CUPS

Colour Index page 104. Makes 36. 68 cals each.
Low in sodium. Begin 1½ hours ahead.

175 g plain chocolate,
  broken into pieces
30 g white vegetable fat
150 g icing sugar
2 tablespoons orange-
  flavour liqueur
	2 teaspoons golden
	  syrup
	2 × 275 g jars
	  maraschino cherries
	  with stalks, well
	  drained

1. On baking sheet, arrange 36 fluted paper petit
four cases. In medium microwave-safe bowl, place
chocolate and vegetable fat. Heat on High (100%
power) for 1½ (1:30) minutes, or until melted,
stirring once. Remove from oven; stir until
smooth.
2. With small pastry brush, coat inside of each
petit four case with chocolate mixture. Refrigerate for about 30 minutes, or until set.
3. When chocolate is set, carefully remove paper
petit four cases, handling them as little as possible
so that chocolate cups keep their shape.
4. In small bowl, combine icing sugar, orange-
flavour liqueur and golden syrup until smooth.
Spoon 1 teaspoonful filling into each chocolate
cup; top each with 1 cherry. Cover and refrigerate until ready to serve.

Chocolates

SUPER-EASY TRUFFLES

Colour Index page 104. Makes 30. 59 cals each. Low in sodium. Begin 1½ hours ahead.

225 g plain chocolate
60 g butter or margarine
60 ml double or
  whipping cream
¼ teaspoon almond
  essence

1. Arrange 30 foil cases on baking sheet. In medium microwave-safe bowl, place chocolate and butter or margarine. Heat on High (100% power) for 1½ (1:30)–2 minutes, until melted, stirring once. Remove from oven; stir until smooth.
2. Into melted chocolate mixture, stir cream and almond essence until evenly blended. Set bowl over pan of iced water. With whisk, beat mixture until soft peaks form.
3. Spoon truffle mixture into piping bag fitted with medium rosette tube; pipe into cases. Refrigerate for about 1 hour, or until truffles are set.

CHOCOLATE MALLOW FUDGE

Colour Index page 103. Makes 36. 111 cals each. Low in sodium. Begin 1¼ hours ahead.

300 g caster sugar
1 × 120 ml can
  evaporated milk
60 g butter or margarine
115 g marshmallows,
  chopped
125 g shelled walnuts,
  chopped
175 g plain chocolate
  chips
50 g bittersweet
  chocolate, chopped

1. Lightly grease 20 cm square baking dish.
2. In 2 litre microwave-safe glass bowl, combine sugar, evaporated milk and butter or margarine. Cook sugar mixture on High (100% power) for 8–9 minutes, stirring after 3 minutes, until Soft Ball Stage is reached (see Cold Water Test, page 369).
3. To mixture, add marshmallows, walnuts, plain chocolate chips and chopped bittersweet chocolate. Stir until marshmallows and chocolate melt. Spread fudge into prepared baking dish; smooth surface.
4. On rack, allow fudge to cool completely in dish until firm; cut into 36 pieces. Store cooled fudge in airtight container.

Chocolate-based sweets cook easily in the microwave and can be stored in the refrigerator for as long as you like. Adding water to the caramel in the fudge slices (below) makes it much easier to handle and spread, while the sweetened condensed milk added to the chocolate makes the fudge rich and creamy.

CHOCOLATE AND CHERRY FUDGE SLICES

Colour Index page 104. 97 cals each. Low in sodium. Begin 3 hours ahead or early in day.

Ingredients for 36 slices		Microwave cookware
175 g plain chocolate chips, or plain chocolate, chopped 120 ml sweetened condensed milk 60 g icing sugar 1½ teaspoons vanilla essence	1 × 275 g jar maraschino cherries, drained 200 g caramels 1 tablespoon water 125 g shelled walnuts, chopped	Medium bowl Shallow 21.5 cm pie dish

1 In medium bowl, combine chocolate pieces and sweetened condensed milk. Heat on High (100% power) for 1½ (1:30) minutes, or until chocolate melts, stirring halfway through cooking. Add icing sugar and vanilla essence; stir until smooth and well blended.

2 On square piece of foil, with palette knife, spread half of fudge mixture to make 15 cm square. On another piece of foil, repeat with remaining mixture. Freeze fudge for about 5 minutes, or until easy to handle. With kitchen paper, pat cherries dry.

3 On each fudge square, arrange cherries in single line, about 1 cm from one edge.

4 Starting at edge with cherries, loosen fudge from foil and roll up Swiss roll fashion. Press to seal join. Wrap roll in greaseproof paper; refrigerate for 1 hour, or until set. In pie dish, place caramels and water. Heat on High for 1½ (1:30)–2 minutes, stirring halfway through cooking. Remove from oven; stir until smooth.

5 Working quickly, with palette knife, spread half of caramel mixture over 1 fudge roll; coat with half of chopped walnuts. Reheat caramel mixture remaining in pie dish on High for 30 seconds; spread over remaining fudge roll.

6 Coat roll with remaining chopped walnuts. Refrigerate both rolls for about 1 hour, or until set. Cut each roll into 18 slices.

It's so quick and easy to make popcorn in the microwave now that microwave popcorn is readily available. Always follow the manufacturer's instructions on the packet; never 'pop' corn in your microwave using any bag other than the one provided with the packet – it could catch fire. You can also use your microwave to refresh stale popcorn: place 25–30 g in large microwave-safe bowl and heat on High (100% power) for 45 seconds–1 minute, until warm, tossing popcorn after 30 seconds.

POPCORN BALLS

6 servings. 248 cals per serving. Low in sodium. Good source of iron. Begin 25 minutes ahead.

35 g popped corn
115 g glacé cherries, cut in half
250 ml golden syrup
1¹/₂ teaspoons white vinegar
1 teaspoon vanilla essence
Salt (optional)

1. With pastry brush, oil large bowl. In bowl, mix popped corn with cherries.
2. In 2 litre microwave-safe glass bowl, heat golden syrup and vinegar on High (100% power) for 10–12 minutes, without stirring, until small amount of syrup mixture dropped into very cold water forms hard but pliable ball. Stir in vanilla essence. If you like, season with salt.
3. Quickly pour hot syrup over popcorn mixture, tossing kernels. With greased hands, shape mixture into 7.5 cm balls, using as little pressure as possible, so balls will not be too compact.

Making the Popcorn Balls

With pastry brush, lightly brush inside of large bowl with oil.

Over popcorn mixture, pour hot syrup; toss to coat kernels.

With greased hands, scoop up handfuls of popcorn mixture; shape into balls.

MAKING POPCORN CHRISTMAS ORNAMENTS

Let Popcorn Balls harden overnight. Wrap length of ribbon round each ball; tie bow on top. Fold 20 cm lengths of very narrow ribbon in half; gently thread folded end under knot of bow. Take loose ends through loop to close. Attach balls to Christmas tree by tying narrow ribbon round branches.

Chewy Sweets

COCONUT HAYSTACKS

Colour Index page 104. Makes 20. 72 cals each. Begin 1¹/₄ hours ahead.

95 g desiccated coconut

225 g bittersweet chocolate

1. Line baking sheets with greaseproof paper. In shallow 21.5 cm microwave-safe pie dish, place coconut. Heat on High (100% power) for 3–4 minutes, until coconut is lightly toasted, stirring occasionally.
2. In medium microwave-safe bowl, place bittersweet chocolate. Heat on High (100% power) for 2–4 minutes, until chocolate melts, stirring once. To melted chocolate, add toasted coconut; stir until smooth.
3. On to prepared baking sheet, drop teaspoonfuls of coconut mixture, mounding them slightly to resemble haystacks.
4. Allow sweets to cool completely, until firm. Store in airtight container.

PISTACHIO BITES

Colour Index page 104. Makes 32. 73 cals each. Low in sodium. Begin 3 hours ahead.

350 g white chocolate, chopped
80 ml double or whipping cream
15 g butter or margarine

³/₄ teaspoon vanilla essence
Green food colouring
2 tablespoons finely chopped pistachios

1. Line bottom and sides of a 21.5 × 5 cm loaf tin with foil. In medium microwave-safe bowl, place white chocolate. Heat on High (100% power) for 3–4 minutes, until melted, stirring once. Remove from oven; stir until smooth.
2. To melted white chocolate, add cream and butter or margarine; stir until smooth. Transfer half of white chocolate mixture to mixing bowl; set aside.
3. To white chocolate mixture remaining in bowl, add vanilla essence and few drops green food colouring. Evenly spread green mixture in prepared loaf tin. Refrigerate.
4. To reserved white mixture, add chopped pistachios; stir until blended. Evenly spread pistachio mixture over green layer in loaf tin. Refrigerate for about 2 hours, or until set.
5. Invert tin on to cutting board. Remove loaf tin to unmould; remove foil. Cut layered chocolate mixture in half lengthways; cut each strip into 16 pieces. Cover and refrigerate until ready to serve.

Preserves
and Sauces

PRESERVES · CONDIMENTS · CHUTNEYS · SAUCES
GRAVIES · SWEET DESSERT SAUCES

Preserves and Sauces

Small amounts of preserves and relishes to keep on hand at home or to give as presents can be quickly cooked in the microwave. It is therefore possible to take advantage of seasonal bounty from the garden, market or farm without spending long hours over a hot stove. Quantities of up to 1 litre are easy to prepare, requiring little stirring, and with no danger of scorching. However, it is important to stir according to recipe instructions, in order to redistribute the sugar in the mixture so that it cooks evenly.

Jars which will hold 500 ml are a convenient size for storing your preserves in the refrigerator, but they must be sterilised first. This cannot be done in the microwave; jars and lids must be covered in water, boiled on top of the stove for at least 10 minutes, then kept hot. Add the preserves and relishes directly to the hot, sterilised jars and, according to recipe instructions, remember to leave a 5 mm space between the preserves and the top of the jar. You can store preserves and relishes in the refrigerator for up to 3 weeks if you keep them tightly covered.

This chapter also contains a wide variety of savoury and sweet sauces. Always use a large enough container to prevent sauces from boiling over; ideally, the container should have the capacity to hold twice the volume of the sauce. Be certain to stir when indicated to prevent lumping, especially if sauces are flour-based. Most sauces cook on High (100% power), but delicate egg-based sauces such as Hollandaise, Béarnaise and custard turn out more smooth and even when cooked on Medium (50% power); the lower temperature prevents boiling, which would result in curdling.

Dessert sauces are especially quick and easy to make in the microwave, and they make delicious toppings for ice cream and desserts. As well as traditional chocolate, fudge, Melba and butterscotch sauces, there are also popular and simple fruit-based sauces, such as orange, cherry and peach.

FRESH FRUIT FLAVOURS

Preserves are quick and easy to make in the microwave, so if you store away a few jars as fruits ripen, you will always have a selection of favourite flavours on hand.

Accompany a croissant or breakfast roll with a fruit preserve such as (left to right) Fresh Strawberry Jam (page 375), Blackberry Spread (page 376) and Apricot/Pineapple Spread (page 375).

Preserves

FRESH STRAWBERRY JAM

Colour Index page 108. Makes about 1 litre.
45 cals per tablespoon. Low in cholesterol, fat,
sodium. Begin 1 day ahead.

600 g strawberries	*75 ml bottled liquid fruit*
700 g preserving sugar	*pectin*
2 tablespoons lemon	
juice	

1. Sterilise four 250 ml jars and lids conventionally by placing in enough water to cover and boiling for 10 minutes; keep hot.
2. In 2 litre microwave-safe glass bowl, with potato masher or slotted spoon, thoroughly crush strawberries.
3. Into crushed strawberries, stir sugar and lemon juice. Cook, covered, on High (100% power) for 7–10 minutes, until mixture boils and thickens slightly, stirring occasionally. With spoon, skim foam from surface of strawberry mixture; stir in pectin.
4. Into hot sterilised jars, immediately ladle hot strawberry mixture, to within 5 mm of tops. Cover with lids. Store in refrigerator for up to 3 weeks.

APRICOT/PINEAPPLE SPREAD

Colour Index page 107. Makes about 500 ml. 36 cals per tablespoon. Low in cholesterol, fat, sodium. Begin 55 minutes ahead.

350 ml water	*1 × 225 g can crushed*
225 g dried apricot	*pineapple in natural*
halves	*juice*
50 g preserving sugar	

1. Sterilise two 250 ml jars and lids conventionally by placing in enough water to cover and boiling for 10 minutes; keep hot.
2. Into 2 litre microwave-safe glass bowl, pour water; add apricots, sugar and crushed pineapple with juice. Cook on High (100% power) for 15–20 minutes, until apricots are very tender, stirring occasionally.
3. Into large bowl, press fruit mixture through food mill or sieve to make smooth.
4. Into hot sterilised jars, immediately ladle hot fruit mixture to within 5 mm of tops. Cover with lids. Store in refrigerator for up to 3 weeks.

PEACH SPREAD: prepare Apricot/Pineapple Spread (above), substituting *225 g dried peach halves* for the dried apricots and *175 ml orange juice* for the crushed pineapple and juice. Makes about 500 ml. 30 cals per tablespoon.

The microwave is ideal for making small amounts of jam and other preserves to share with family and friends when fruits are in season. It is much quicker and easier than the bulk jam-making of days gone by. Pick fruit when it is just ripe, then, using the microwave, simply make up a jar or two. If necessary, use fruit that is slightly under-, rather than overripe, because early fruit contains more of the pectin necessary for setting.

PEACH PRESERVE

Colour Index page 108. 37 cals per tablespoon. Low in cholesterol, fat, sodium. Begin 1 day ahead.

Ingredients for 1 litre	Microwave cookware
6 large peaches (about 1.4 kg) *500 g preserving sugar* *60 ml lemon juice*	2 litre glass measuring jug or bowl

1 Sterilise four 250 ml jars and lids conventionally by placing in enough water to cover and boiling for 10 minutes; keep hot. With small, sharp knife, peel peaches. Cut each peach lengthways in half and twist apart. With small spoon, remove stones; discard. Thinly slice peaches.

2 In glass jug or bowl, combine peach slices, sugar and lemon juice.

3 Cook peach mixture, covered, on High (100% power), for 5 minutes, or until mixture boils. Uncover; stir. Cook on High for 20–30 minutes longer, stirring occasionally, until syrup thickens and fruit is translucent.

4 Remove jug or bowl from microwave. On heatproof surface, with spoon, carefully skim foam from surface of hot peach mixture.

5 Into hot sterilised jars, immediately ladle hot peach mixture, to within 5 mm of tops.

6 Cover jars with lids. Store in refrigerator for up to 3 weeks.

Preserves

HOT PEPPER JELLY

Colour Index page 108. 38 cals per tablespoon. Low in cholesterol, fat, sodium. Begin 1 day ahead.

Hot Pepper Jelly makes a great accompaniment to ham or any cold roast meat or poultry. In this recipe, sweet red peppers are used, with the added zest of a red-hot chilli pepper to create a clear jelly with a jewel-like colour. If you like, you can use green peppers and flavour them with a fresh green chilli.

Ingredients for 500 ml		Microwave cookware
2 large red peppers *1 large hot red fresh* *chilli* *80 ml white vinegar* *300 g preserving sugar* *75 ml bottled liquid* *fruit pectin*	*1–2 drops red food* *colouring (optional)*	2 litre glass measuring jug or bowl

1 Sterilise two 250 ml jars and lids conventionally by placing in enough water to cover and boiling for 10 minutes; keep hot.

2 On cutting board, with sharp knife, finely chop red peppers and chilli. Over glass jug or bowl, set fine sieve. Transfer peppers and chilli to sieve.

3 With spoon, press peppers and chilli in sieve until liquid drains into glass jug or bowl, making about 120 ml juice. Discard chopped peppers and chilli.

4 To pepper and chilli juice in glass jug or bowl, add white vinegar and preserving sugar; stir well to combine. Cook, covered, on High (100% power) for 8–10 minutes, until mixture boils, stirring twice.

5 Into juice mixture, stir pectin. If you like, add red food colouring. Cook on High for 5 minutes, stirring halfway through cooking. With spoon, skim foam from surface of juice mixture.

6 Into hot sterilised jars, immediately ladle hot juice mixture, to within 5 mm of tops. Cover with lids. Store in refrigerator for up to 3 weeks.

BLACKBERRY SPREAD

Colour Index page 108. Makes 1 litre. 38 cals per tablespoon. Low in cholesterol, fat, sodium. Begin 1 day ahead.

575 g blackberries
 2 cooking apples,
 peeled, cored and cut
 into quarters
 500 g preserving sugar

75 ml bottled liquid fruit
 pectin
 2 tablespoons lemon
 juice

1. Sterilise four 250 ml jars and lids conventionally by placing in enough water to cover and boiling for 10 minutes; keep hot.
2. In 2 litre microwave-safe bowl, combine blackberries, apples and sugar. Cook on High (100% power) for 10–12 minutes, until apples are softened and sugar dissolves, stirring twice.
3. Into mixing bowl, press fruit mixture through food mill or sieve to make smooth. Pour mixture back into microwave-safe bowl. Cook on High for 8–10 minutes, until mixture thickens slightly, stirring occasionally. With spoon, skim foam from surface of blackberry mixture; stir in pectin and lemon juice.
4. Into hot sterilised jars, immediately ladle hot blackberry mixture, to within 5 mm of tops. Cover with lids. Store in refrigerator for up to 3 weeks.

MINT JELLY

Colour Index page 107. Makes 1 litre. 45 cals per tablespoon. Low in cholesterol, fat, sodium. Begin 1 day ahead.

350 ml apple juice
 120 ml cider vinegar
 50 g fresh mint leaves,
 chopped
 700 g sugar

75 ml bottled liquid fruit
 pectin
 1–2 drops green food
 colouring (optional)

1. Sterilise four 250 ml jars and lids conventionally by placing in enough water to cover and boiling for 10 minutes; keep hot.
2. Into 2 litre microwave-safe jug, pour apple juice and vinegar; add chopped mint. Cook, covered, on High (100% power) for 8–10 minutes, until mixture boils, stirring twice.
3. Over mixing bowl, set sieve. Pour mint mixture through sieve; discard chopped mint. Pour liquid back into microwave-safe jug. If necessary, add enough water to make 425 ml liquid. Stir in sugar. Cook, covered, on High for 8–10 minutes, until mixture boils, stirring twice.
4. Into mint-flavoured mixture, stir pectin. If you like, add green food colouring. Cook on High for 4 minutes, stirring halfway through cooking. With spoon, skim foam from surface of mixture.
5. Into hot sterilised jars, immediately ladle hot mint-flavoured mixture, to within 5 mm of tops. Cover with lids. Store in refrigerator for up to 3 weeks.

Condiments

CRANBERRY CHESTNUT RELISH

Colour Index page 108. Makes 1 litre. 48 cals per tablespoon. Begin 1 day ahead.

350 g fresh cranberries, or frozen cranberries, defrosted	*120 ml water*
	80 ml cider vinegar
	1 teaspoon dry mustard
350 g pickling onions, peeled	*¼ teaspoon ground cinnamon*
70 g sultanas	*1 × 275 g jar marrons*
440 g light brown sugar	*(chestnuts) in syrup, drained*

1. Sterilise four 250 ml jars and lids conventionally by placing in enough water to cover and boiling for 10 minutes; keep hot.
2. In 3 litre microwave-safe casserole, combine cranberries, onions, sultanas, brown sugar, water, vinegar, mustard and cinnamon. Cook, covered, on High (100% power) for 10 minutes. Uncover; stir. Cook on High for 15 minutes longer, or until mixture thickens, stirring occasionally. Stir in chestnuts.
3. Into hot sterilised jars, immediately ladle hot cranberry mixture to within 5 mm of tops. Cover with lids. Store in refrigerator for up to 3 weeks.

SWEETCORN RELISH

Colour Index page 107. Makes about 1 litre. 13 cals per tablespoon. Low in cholesterol, fat, sodium. Begin 1 day ahead.

4 corn-on-the-cob, husked, or 1 × 450 g can sweetcorn kernels, drained	*1 small tomato, diced*
	1 small onion, diced
	250 ml cider vinegar
	100 g caster sugar
1 small green pepper, diced	*¼ teaspoon celery seeds*
	¼ teaspoon dry mustard
1 small red pepper, diced	*¼ teaspoon turmeric*

1. Sterilise four 250 ml jars and lids conventionally by placing in enough water to cover and boiling for 10 minutes; keep hot.
2. If using fresh corn-on-the-cob, with sharp knife, cut kernels from cobs.
3. In 2 litre microwave-safe casserole, combine sweetcorn, green and red peppers, tomato, onion, vinegar, sugar, celery seeds, mustard and turmeric. Cook, covered, on High (100% power) for 5–7 minutes, until mixture boils. Uncover; stir. Cook on High for 10–15 minutes longer, until vegetables are tender-crisp, stirring occasionally.
4. Into hot sterilised jars, immediately ladle hot sweetcorn mixture, to within 5 mm of tops. Cover with lids. Store in refrigerator for up to 3 weeks.

The microwave is ideal for making small, easily stored quantities of relish in a fraction of the time it takes to make them conventionally. Combine cranberries and chestnuts for an unusual accompaniment to Christmas lunch, or serve your hamburgers with relish made from summer sweetcorn. Or, try spicy Tomato Ketchup (below) – it's easier than you think!

TOMATO KETCHUP

Colour Index page 107. 29 cals per tablespoon. Low in cholesterol, fat, sodium. Begin 1 day ahead.

Ingredients for 750 ml		Microwave cookware
900 g ripe tomatoes, cut into quarters	*¼ teaspoon celery seeds*	2 large bowls
300 g preserving sugar	*¼ teaspoon ground cloves*	
250 ml cider vinegar	*Pinch of cayenne pepper*	
1 teaspoon dry mustard	*1 tablespoon cornflour dissolved in 2 tablespoons cold water*	
½ teaspoon ground cinnamon		

1 Sterilise three 250 ml jars and lids conventionally by placing in enough water to cover, and boiling for 10 minutes; keep hot.

2 In 1 large bowl, place tomato quarters, sugar, cider vinegar, dry mustard, ground cinnamon, celery seeds, ground cloves and cayenne pepper; stir to combine.

3 Cook, covered, on High (100% power) for 20 minutes, or until slightly thickened, stirring occasionally. In food processor with knife blade attached or in blender, process mixture.

4 Over another large bowl, set fine sieve. Press tomato mixture through sieve to remove seeds; discard seeds.

5 Into tomato mixture in bowl, stir dissolved cornflour until blended. Cook on High for 8–10 minutes, until ketchup boils and thickens, stirring occasionally.

6 Into hot sterilised jars, immediately ladle hot ketchup to within 5 mm of tops. Cover with lids. Store in refrigerator for up to 3 weeks.

Chutneys

Cooking chutneys in the microwave makes quick work of a job that used to take hours – and it won't leave strong smells in your kitchen. Try a delicious, traditional chutney such as Apple and Onion Chutney (right), or an unusual combination of fruit as in Curried Melon Chutney (below right). Both add contrast and texture to cold meats, cheese and rice dishes.

GREEN TOMATO CHUTNEY

Colour Index page 108. 21 cals per tablespoon. Low in cholesterol, fat. Begin 1 day ahead.

Ingredients for 1 litre		Microwave cookware
450 g green tomatoes, cut into quarters	250 g preserving sugar	Large bowl
500 ml cider vinegar	1 tablespoon mustard seeds	
2 green peppers, cut into quarters	1 tablespoon celery seeds	
2 red peppers, cut into quarters	³/₄ teaspoon ground allspice	
1 large onion	¹/₄ teaspoon ground cinnamon	

1 Sterilise four 250 ml jars and lids conventionally by placing in enough water to cover and boiling for 10 minutes; keep hot.

2 In food processor with knife blade attached or in blender, process tomatoes and 250 ml vinegar until tomatoes are roughly chopped. Transfer tomato mixture to large bowl. Process green and red peppers and onion until roughly chopped.

3 To tomato mixture in bowl, add chopped peppers and onion; stir to combine. Cook, covered, on High (100% power) for 10 minutes, or until softened; stir once. Uncover; drain off liquid and discard.

4 To vegetable mixture, add sugar, mustard and celery seeds, ground allspice and ground cinnamon; stir to combine.

5 Cook vegetable mixture, covered, on High for 10–15 minutes, until sugar dissolves and vegetables are tender, stirring twice.

6 Into hot sterilised jars, immediately ladle hot vegetable mixture to within 5 mm of tops. Cover with lids. Store in refrigerator for up to 3 weeks.

APPLE AND ONION CHUTNEY

Colour Index page 108. Makes about 1 litre. 27 cals per tablespoon. Low in cholesterol, fat, sodium. Begin 1 day ahead.

2 large cooking apples, peeled, cored and diced
2 onions, diced
1 medium green or red pepper, diced
1 garlic clove, crushed
150 g preserving sugar
175 ml white vinegar
120 ml water
350 g stoned prunes, cut into quarters
1 tablespoon finely chopped peeled root ginger
2 tablespoons mustard seeds
¹/₂ teaspoon dried hot red pepper flakes

1. Sterilise four 250 ml jars and lids conventionally by placing in enough water to cover and boiling for 10 minutes; keep hot.
2. In large microwave-safe bowl, place apples and next 6 ingredients. Cook, covered, on High (100% power) for 10 minutes, or until mixture boils. Uncover; stir. Cook on High for 10 minutes longer, or until vegetables are tender, stirring occasionally.
3. Into chutney mixture, stir prunes, root ginger, mustard seeds and red pepper flakes. Cook on High for 10–15 minutes, until mixture thickens and becomes slightly syrupy, stirring often.
4. Into hot sterilised jars, immediately ladle hot chutney to within 5 mm of tops. Cover with lids. Store in refrigerator for up to 3 weeks.

CURRIED MELON CHUTNEY

Colour Index page 108. Makes about 1 litre. 30 cals per tablespoon. Low in cholesterol, fat. Begin 1 day ahead.

4 garlic cloves, crushed
3 onions, cut into 2.5 cm chunks
2 tomatoes, cut into 2.5 cm chunks
1 rock, charentais or ogen melon, peeled, seeded and cut into 2.5 cm chunks
330 g light brown sugar
175 ml cider vinegar
70 g sultanas
1 tablespoon curry powder
1 tablespoon mustard seeds
2 tablespoons cornflour dissolved in 3 tablespoons cold water

1. Sterilise four 250 ml jars and lids conventionally by placing in enough water to cover and boiling for 10 minutes; keep hot.
2. In large microwave-safe bowl, combine garlic and next 8 ingredients. Cook, covered, on High (100% power) for 10 minutes, stirring twice. Uncover; stir. Cook on High for 10–15 minutes longer, until vegetables are tender, stirring occasionally.
3. Into vegetable mixture, stir dissolved cornflour until blended. Cook on High for 3–5 minutes, until mixture thickens, stirring twice.
4. Into hot sterilised jars, immediately spoon hot chutney, to within 5 mm of tops. Cover with lids. Store in refrigerator for up to 3 weeks.

Sauces

BARBECUE SAUCE

Colour Index page 106. Makes about 250 ml. 32 cals per tablespoon. Low in cholesterol, fat. Begin 25 minutes ahead.

1 onion, diced
1 garlic clove, crushed
2 tablespoons olive or
  vegetable oil
1 fresh green chilli,
  seeded and finely
  chopped
150 ml tomato ketchup
2 tablespoons cider
  vinegar
¼ teaspoon dry mustard

1. In 1 litre microwave-safe measuring jug, combine onion, garlic and olive or vegetable oil. Cook, covered with kitchen paper, on High (100% power) for 2–3 minutes, until onion softens slightly, stirring twice.
2. Into onion mixture, stir chopped chilli, ketchup, vinegar and mustard until well blended. Cook, covered, on High for 3–5 minutes, until sauce thickens, stirring occasionally. Allow to stand, covered, on heatproof surface for 10 minutes until flavours blend. Spoon sauce into serving bowl. Serve hot.

HOT CHILLI SAUCE: prepare Barbecue Sauce (above), adding **1 tablespoon chilli powder** and **1 tablespoon Worcestershire sauce** with mustard.

SATAY SAUCE

Colour Index page 106. Makes about 80 ml. 40 cals per tablespoon. Low in cholesterol. Begin 10 minutes ahead.

2 garlic cloves, crushed
1 red pepper, diced
130 g crunchy peanut
  butter
Chicken Stock (page
  125) or stock from a
  cube
1 tablespoon finely
  chopped peeled root
  ginger
1 tablespoon soy sauce
1 tablespoon cider
  vinegar
¼ teaspoon sesame oil
  (optional)
Coriander sprigs to
  garnish

1. In 500 ml microwave-safe measuring jug, combine garlic, red pepper, peanut butter, 120 ml stock, root ginger, soy sauce and vinegar. If you like, stir in sesame oil. Cook on High (100% power) for 1–2 minutes, until hot, stirring halfway through cooking.
2. If necessary, add few additional drops stock to thin sauce to desired consistency. Spoon into serving bowl; garnish with coriander sprigs. Serve warm.

These microwave sauces are all based on traditional recipes, but are much quicker to prepare, some taking only 5 minutes! Time is also saved on washing up, since most sauces, like the Cranberry Sauce (below), require only a single microwave-safe measuring jug or bowl. For easy and safe pouring, a jug is the best choice, but remember to use oven gloves as the handle may be hot.

CRANBERRY SAUCE

Colour Index page 107. 25 cals per tablespoon. Low in cholesterol, fat, sodium. Begin 35 minutes ahead.

Ingredients for 425 ml		Microwave cookware
175 g fresh cranberries	*120 ml orange juice*	2 litre measuring jug
135 g preserving sugar	*80 ml port*	or bowl

1 Inspect cranberries; remove any stalks and discard any shrivelled, soft or imperfect fruit. In colander, rinse fruit under cold running water.

2 In measuring jug or bowl, combine cranberries, sugar, orange juice and port. Stir to mix. Cook, covered, on High (100% power) for 5–7 minutes, until cranberries pop and sugar dissolves, stirring occasionally. Uncover sauce; stir.

3 Cook sauce on High for 3–5 minutes longer, until sauce coats back of spoon, stirring occasionally.

4 Into serving bowl, pour hot sauce; serve warm.

5 If you like, make Moulded Cranberry Sauce: rinse 500 ml loaf dish or mould; pour in warm sauce. Cover and refrigerate for 2–3 hours or overnight, until firm and well chilled.

6 Loosen mixture from sides of dish or mould with knife. Invert on to serving platter. Carefully remove dish or mould. Cut into slices and serve chilled.

Sauces and Gravies

Making gravy often creates a last-minute rush in the kitchen, but with the microwave you can prepare perfect Giblet Gravy (below) hours ahead. Cook, cover, and refrigerate gravy ahead of time, then reheat to serve with roast turkey or chicken. Brown Gravy (below right) goes beautifully with creamy mashed potatoes.

GIBLET GRAVY

Colour Index page 107. 8 cals per tablespoon. Good source of vitamin A, riboflavin, niacin, iron. Begin 40 minutes ahead.

Ingredients for 1 litre		Microwave cookware
500 ml Chicken Stock (page 125) or stock from a cube Giblets and neck of 1 chicken or turkey 2 garlic cloves 1 small onion, sliced 1 carrot, sliced	1 celery stick, sliced 1/2 bay leaf 30 g butter or margarine 2 tablespoons plain flour 1 teaspoon gravy browning Salt and pepper to taste	2 litre measuring jug or bowl Medium bowl

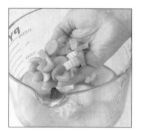

1 In measuring jug or bowl, combine stock and next 6 ingredients. Cook covered, on High (100% power) for 15–20 minutes, until giblets are tender, stirring occasionally.

2 With slotted spoon, remove giblets and neck from stock. Transfer to cutting board.

3 Over bowl, set sieve. Pour stock through sieve to remove vegetables and seasonings; discard.

4 On cutting board, with sharp knife, finely chop giblets. Cut off meat from neck. Set chopped giblets and meat aside.

5 In medium bowl, place butter or margarine. Heat, covered with kitchen paper, on High for 45 seconds, or until melted. Stir in flour until blended. Cook on High for 45 seconds, stirring once. Gradually stir in stock. Cook on High for 3–5 minutes, until gravy thickens and is smooth, stirring twice.

6 To gravy, add reserved giblets and meat and gravy browning. Heat on High for 1 minute, or until giblets and meat are hot. Season with salt and pepper; serve hot.

TOMATO SAUCE

Colour Index page 107. Makes about 600 ml. 11 cals per tablespoon. Low in cholesterol. Begin 45 minutes ahead.

2 garlic cloves, crushed
1 spring onion, sliced
2 tablespoons olive or vegetable oil
6 ripe tomatoes, cut into quarters
4 tablespoons chopped parsley
1 teaspoon red wine vinegar
3/4 teaspoon caster sugar
1/2 teaspoon dried basil
Pinch of pepper
2 tablespoons tomato purée

1. In 2 litre microwave-safe glass bowl, combine garlic, onion and oil. Cook on High (100% power) for 1–2 minutes, until spring onion softens. Stir in tomatoes, parsley, vinegar, sugar, basil and pepper. Cook, covered, on High for 10–12 minutes, until mixture thickens, stirring occasionally.
2. In food processor with knife blade attached or in blender, process tomato mixture until smooth. Over large bowl, set sieve. Press tomato mixture through sieve to remove seeds and skins; discard.
3. To glass microwave-safe bowl, return tomato mixture. Stir in tomato purée. Cook on High for 10–12 minutes, until flavours blend and sauce thickens slightly, stirring occasionally. Serve warm or cover and refrigerate to serve chilled later.

BROWN GRAVY

Colour Index page 106. Makes about 500 ml. 13 cals per tablespoon. Low in cholesterol, fat. Begin 20 minutes ahead.

2 tablespoons meat dripping, or 30 g butter or margarine, melted
1/2 small carrot, diced
1/2 celery stick, diced
1/2 small onion, diced
2 tablespoons plain flour
500 ml Chicken or Beef Stock (page 125) or stock from a cube
1/2 bay leaf
1/2 teaspoon gravy browning (optional)
Salt and pepper to taste

1. In 2 litre microwave-safe glass bowl, place dripping, or butter or margarine. Stir in diced carrot, celery and onion. Cook on High for 2 1/2 (2:30)–3 minutes, until vegetables are tender but still crisp, stirring twice.
2. Into vegetable mixture, stir flour until blended. Gradually stir in stock. Add bay leaf. Cook on High for 6–8 minutes, until gravy boils and thickens, stirring occasionally.
3. Over medium microwave-safe bowl, set sieve. Pour gravy through sieve to remove vegetables and bay leaf; discard. If you like, add gravy browning. Season with salt and pepper. Heat on High for 2 minutes, until gravy is hot. Serve hot.

HOLLANDAISE SAUCE

Colour Index page 106. Makes about 250 ml. 59 cals per tablespoon. Begin 20 minutes ahead.

115 g butter or margarine	*Salt and cayenne pepper to taste*
2 egg yolks	
1 tablespoon lemon or lime juice	

1. In 500 ml microwave-safe measuring jug, place butter or margarine. Heat, covered with kitchen paper, on High (100% power) for 1¹/₂–2 minutes, until melted.
2. In small microwave-safe bowl, with whisk, beat egg yolks, lemon or lime juice, salt and cayenne pepper until smooth.
3. Into egg yolk mixture in bowl, gradually pour hot butter or margarine in thin, steady stream, beating constantly until butter or margarine is completely incorporated.
4. Cook sauce on Medium (50% power) for 30 seconds–1 minute, until slightly thickened, beating every 15 seconds. Do not boil or sauce will curdle. Keep warm over hot (not boiling) water, or in vacuum flask, until ready to serve.

BÉARNAISE SAUCE

Colour Index page 106. Makes about 250 ml. 85 cals per tablespoon. Low in sodium. Begin 20 minutes ahead.

60 ml white wine vinegar	*¹/₄ teaspoon pepper*
¹/₂ spring onion, finely chopped (1 tablespoon)	*175 g butter or margarine*
1¹/₂ teaspoons dried tarragon	*2 egg yolks*
	1 tablespoon chopped parsley

1. Into small microwave-safe bowl, pour vinegar; add spring onion, tarragon and pepper. Cook on High (100% power) for 2–4 minutes, until vinegar is reduced to about 1 tablespoon. Set aside.
2. In 500 ml microwave-safe measuring jug, place butter or margarine. Heat, covered with kitchen paper, on High for 2¹/₄ (2:15) minutes, or until melted.
3. In medium microwave-safe bowl, with whisk, beat egg yolks until smooth. Into beaten egg yolks, gradually pour hot butter or margarine in thin, steady stream, beating constantly until butter or margarine is completely incorporated.
4. Cook sauce on Medium (50% power) for 30 seconds–1 minute, until slightly thickened, beating every 15 seconds. Do not boil or sauce will curdle. Into sauce, stir spring onion mixture and chopped parsley. Keep warm over hot (not boiling) water, or in vacuum flask, until ready to serve.

BASIC WHITE SAUCE

Makes 500 ml. 17 cals per tablespoon. Begin 15 minutes ahead.

60 g butter or margarine	
35 g plain flour	
500 ml milk	
Salt, pepper and grated nutmeg to taste	

1. In 2 litre microwave-safe glass bowl, place butter or margarine. Heat, covered with kitchen paper, on High (100% power) for 45 seconds–1 minute, until melted.
2. Into melted butter or margarine, stir flour until smooth and blended. Cook on High for 45 seconds–1 minute, stirring once. Into flour mixture, gradually stir milk. Cook on High for 3–5 minutes, until sauce thickens and is smooth, stirring twice.
3. Season sauce with salt, pepper and nutmeg. Serve immediately.

PARSLEY AND LEMON SAUCE: prepare Basic White Sauce (above). Stir in *1 teaspoon grated lemon zest, 2 tablespoons lemon juice* and *1 tablespoon chopped parsley*. 17 cals per tablespoon.

CHEESE SAUCE: prepare Basic White Sauce (above). Stir in *25 g grated cheese* until melted. 54 cals per tablespoon.

MUSHROOM SAUCE
In this variation of Basic White Sauce, sliced mushrooms are lightly sautéed in butter or margarine before sauce is thickened and enriched with cream and sherry. It is delicious with grilled steaks and hamburgers.

Makes 500 ml. 23 cals per tablespoon. Begin 25 minutes ahead.

30 g butter or margarine	
225 g mushrooms, thinly sliced	
1 tablespoon plain flour	
300 ml half cream	
1 tablespoon dry sherry	
2 tablespoons soured cream	
Salt and pepper to taste	
2 tablespoons chopped parsley	

1. In 2 litre microwave-safe glass bowl, place butter or margarine. Heat, covered with kitchen paper, on High (100% power) for 45 seconds, or until melted.
2. To melted butter or margarine, add sliced mushrooms; stir to coat. Cook on High for 5–6 minutes, until mushrooms soften, stirring occasionally. Stir in flour until blended.
3. Into mushroom mixture, gradually stir half cream and sherry until blended. Cook on High for 5–7 minutes, until mixture thickens, stirring occasionally.
4. Into mushroom mixture, stir soured cream until well blended. Season with salt and pepper. Stir in chopped parsley.

Brandied
Strawberry
Sauce

Custard
Sauce

Peach
Sauce

Hot
Fruit Sauce

Chocolate
Sauce

Butterscotch
Sauce

HOT FRUIT SAUCE

Colour Index page 105. Makes 1 litre. Low in cholesterol, sodium. Good source of vitamin A, vitamin C, iron. Begin 10 minutes ahead.

3 nectarines, stoned
  and chopped
3 large plums, stoned
  and chopped
100 g sugar
120 ml orange juice

1. In 2 litre microwave-safe glass bowl, combine chopped nectarines and plums, sugar and orange juice.
2. Cook on High (100% power) for 3–5 minutes, until tender, stirring twice. Serve warm, with ice cream.

BRANDIED STRAWBERRY SAUCE

Colour Index page 105. Make 600 ml. 35 cals per tablespoon. Low in cholesterol, fat, sodium. Good source of riboflavin, vitamin C, calcium, iron. Begin 10 minutes ahead.

850 g frozen
  strawberries, sliced
  and defrosted
1 tablespoon
  cornflour dissolved
  in 1 tablespoon cold
  water
150 g redcurrant jelly
60 ml brandy

1. Drain strawberries; set aside, reserving 120 ml juice. Into juice, stir dissolved cornflour.
2. In 2 litre microwave-safe glass bowl, place redcurrant jelly. Heat on High (100% power) for 30 seconds–1 minute, until melted; stir once. Stir in dissolved cornflour; cook on High for 1–2 minutes, until slightly thickened. Stir in reserved strawberries and brandy. Serve warm with crêpes, or chilled with ice cream or rice pudding.

CHOCOLATE SAUCE

Colour Index page 105. Makes about 750 ml. 54 cals per tablespoon. Good source of vitamin A, riboflavin, calcium, iron.
Begin 10 minutes ahead.

250 ml double or
  whipping cream
250 g caster sugar
115 g plain chocolate,
  chopped
30 g butter or
  margarine
1 teaspoon vanilla
  essence

1. Into 2 litre microwave-safe glass bowl, pour cream; add sugar, chocolate and butter or margarine. Cook on High (100% power) for 8–9 minutes, until chocolate melts and mixture boils, stirring occasionally.
2. Into chocolate mixture, stir vanilla essence until smooth. Serve sauce warm, with banana splits or sundaes.

BUTTERSCOTCH SAUCE

Colour Index page 106. Makes 250 ml. 76 cals per tablespoon. Begin 10 minutes ahead.

220 g light brown
  sugar
60 ml half cream
2 tablespons golden
  syrup
30 g butter or
  margarine

1. In 2 litre microwave-safe glass bowl, combine all ingredients.
2. Cook mixture on High (100% power) for 5 minutes, or until sugar dissolves and sauce boils, stirring twice. Serve warm with ice cream.

CUSTARD SAUCE

Colour Index page 105. Makes about 300 ml. 27 cals per tablespoon. Begin 15 minutes ahead.

250 ml half cream
2 tablespoons caster
  sugar
2 egg yolks
1/2 teaspoon vanilla
  essence

1. Into 1 litre microwave-safe measuring jug, pour cream; add sugar. Cook on High (100% power) for 3 minutes, until boiling; stir twice.
2. In mixing bowl, whisk yolks slightly. Stir small amount cream mixture into beaten egg yolks. Slowly pour egg mixture back into remaining cream, beating rapidly.
3. Cook mixture on Medium (50% power) for 3–4 minutes, until sauce thickens slightly, beating twice. Do not boil or sauce will curdle. Stir in vanilla essence. Serve warm.

PEACH SAUCE

Colour Index page 105. Makes 250 ml. 17 cals per tablespoon. Low in cholesterol, fat, sodium. Good source of vitamin C. Begin 10 minutes ahead.

275 g canned peaches
  in natural juice,
  drained
1/4 teaspoon almond
  essence
Pinch of grated
  nutmeg

1. In food processor with knife blade attached, process peaches, almond essence and nutmeg until smooth.
2. Transfer peach mixture to 1 litre microwave-safe measuring jug. Heat on High (100% power) for 1–2 minutes, until hot, stirring twice. Serve warm, with ice cream or fruit.

Cherry Sauce

Brandy Butter

Orange Sauce

Blackcurrant Sauce

Fudge Sauce

Melba Sauce

ORANGE SAUCE

Colour Index page 105. Makes 600 ml. 10 cals per tablespoon. Low in cholesterol, fat, sodium. Begin 10 minutes ahead.

500 ml water
65 g caster sugar
1 tablespoon grated orange zest
120 ml orange-flavour liqueur

1. Into 1 litre microwave-safe measuring jug, pour water; add sugar and orange zest. Cook on High (100% power) for 4–5 minutes, until sugar dissolves and mixture boils; stir twice.
2. Into orange mixture, stir orange-flavour liqueur until blended. Serve warm, with fresh fruit or ice cream.

CHERRY SAUCE

Colour Index page 106. Makes 500 ml. 15 cals per tablespoon. Low in cholesterol, sodium. Begin 5 minutes ahead.

450 g sweet cherries, stoned
50 g caster sugar
1 tablespoon water
1/4 teaspoon almond essence

1. In 2 litre microwave-safe glass bowl, combine cherries, sugar and water.
2. Cook cherry mixture on High for 2–3 minutes, until sugar dissolves and mixture boils; stirring twice. Stir in almond essence. Serve warm, with crêpes, waffles or ice cream.

BLACKCURRANT SAUCE

Colour Index page 105. Makes about 250 ml. 26 cals per tablespoon. Low in cholesterol, fat, sodium. Good source of vitamin C. Begin 20 minutes ahead.

275 g frozen blackcurrants
90 g caster sugar
1/4 teaspoon ground cinnamon
Pinch of grated nutmeg
Pinch of grated lemon zest
1 teaspoon lemon juice

1. In 2 litre microwave-safe glass bowl, combine blackcurrants, sugar, cinnamon, nutmeg and lemon zest. Cook, covered, on High (100% power) for 5 minutes, or until sugar dissolves and blackcurrants defrost. Uncover; stir. Cook on High for 3–4 minutes longer, until sauce thickens slightly.
2. Into blackcurrant mixture, stir lemon juice. Serve warm, with poached or fresh fruit or ice cream.

FUDGE SAUCE

Colour Index page 105. Makes 300 ml. 76 cals per tablespoon. Begin 10 minutes ahead.

150 g caster sugar
45 g cocoa powder
120 ml double or whipping cream
60 g butter or margarine
1 teaspoon vanilla essence

1. In 2 litre microwave-safe glass bowl, combine sugar, cocoa and cream. Cook on High (100% power) for 2–3 minutes, until sugar dissolves and mixture boils; stirring twice.
2. To mixture, add butter or margarine. Cook on High for 2–4 minutes, until butter or margarine melts and mixture thickens slightly, stirring occasionally. Stir in vanilla essence. Serve warm with ice cream.

BRANDY BUTTER

Colour Index page 106. Makes about 150 ml. 73 cals per tablespoon. Good source of vitamin A. Begin 5 minutes ahead.

45 g butter
120 g icing sugar
1/2 teaspoon vannilla essence

1. In 250 ml microwave-safe glass jug, place butter. Heat on High (100% power) for 5–10 seconds, until softened.
2. Into butter, gradually beat sugar until creamy. Stir in vanilla essence. Serve with Christmas pudding and mince pies.

MELBA SAUCE

Colour Index page 105. Makes 250 ml. 33 cals per tablespoon. Low in cholesterol, fat, sodium. Begin 15 minutes ahead.

275 g frozen raspberries
4 tablespoons redcurrant jelly
2 tablespoons water
4 teaspoons cornflour dissolved in 1 tablespoon cold water

1. In 2 litre microwave-safe glass bowl, place frozen raspberries, redcurrant jelly and water. Heat on High (100% power) for 5–6 minutes, until raspberries defrost.
2. Into raspberry mixture, stir dissolved cornflour. Cook on High (100% power) for 3–4 minutes, until mixture boils and thickens; stir twice. Press mixture through fine sieve to remove seeds: discard. Serve warm, with poached fruit or ice cream.

COOKWARE

What can I use to keep butter or margarine and bacon from spattering when I cook them in the microwave?

Foods that tend to spatter during microwaving should be covered with absorbent kitchen paper, which soaks up any fat but also allows microwaves to penetrate and cook the food. Lightly moisten kitchen paper to cook food such as poultry, fish and vegetables; wrap in the kitchen paper, then 'steam' in the microwave.

I have been told that some kitchen paper is unsafe for microwave use. Is this true and, if so, which sort is it?

It is true that kitchen paper made from recycled paper is unsuitable for use in the microwave oven because it contains impurities, such as small amounts of metal, that may cause blue sparks (arcing).

Look for plain white kitchen paper that contains all natural fibres and no artificial colours – some manufacturers state on the packet whether their paper is safe for microwave use or not.

How can I be sure that my china bowl will not break during cooking before I actually use it in the microwave?

Place the bowl in the microwave beside a glass measuring jug containing 250 ml cold water. Heat on High (100% power) for 1 minute. If the bowl remains cool and the water in the jug is warm, the bowl is microwave-safe. If the bowl is hot, it has absorbed too much microwave energy for efficient cooking and should not be used.

Can I use plastic containers, measuring jugs and bowls in the microwave?

Avoid using plastic containers, jugs and bowls, etc to microwave anything with a high fat or sugar content. For other foods, the safest plastic cookware to use is the specially formulated type labelled 'microwave-safe'.

Dishwasher-safe plastic containers can be used for brief reheating in the microwave. Plastic containers that hold shop-bought, ready-prepared food are generally considered to be unsafe because they may break or melt.

Which cookware is best used for microwaving desserts?

Desserts that have a high sugar or fat content reach very high temperatures during the cooking process therefore they should always be cooked in microwave-safe glass measuring jugs or bowls, not plastic cookware.

Which cookware is recommended for microwaving sauces and gravies?

A microwave-safe glass measuring jug is convenient, and it saves on washing up. Always use a jug that is able to hold twice the volume of the sauce or gravy to be cooked in it.

TECHNIQUES

How can I prevent chocolate from overcooking when I melt it in the microwave?

Melting chocolate in the microwave is almost risk-free. However, when chocolate is melted in the microwave, it retains its shape and you may not realise it is ready. When the chocolate loses its dull look and becomes shiny, that's your clue it is done; remove from oven and stir until smooth.

Why do my cakes overcook when done in the microwave?

If you remove cakes from the microwave when they *look* done, they will be overcooked and will become hard on standing. Cakes should look moist when removed from the microwave; they will spring back when lightly touched with a finger.

Standing time is necessary to complete the cooking process: after standing time, the cake will pull away from the sides of the pan and a skewer inserted into the centre will come out clean.

Why do my vegetables sometimes have dark spots on them when cooked in the microwave?

Salt may be the culprit. If you use salt, add it to vegetables after cooking, or dissolve it in the cooking liquid or sauce.

When I microwave eggs, I find the yolks are always tougher than they should be. How can I prevent this?

 Egg yolks contain more fat than egg whites, therefore they attract more microwave energy and cook faster. To avoid overcooking the yolk while waiting for the white to be done, you must remove the eggs before the whites are completely set and let stand for the time recommended in the recipe; this allows the white to finish cooking outside the microwave. Don't forget to gently prick yolks with a cocktail stick before cooking. This permits the steam to escape and prevents the egg from exploding during cooking.

 When I scramble eggs in the microwave, I find the edges too set and hard while the centre is still liquid. Why does this happen and how can I prevent it?

 Microwaves penetrate food to a depth of about 4 cm, thereby cooking the food nearest the edges of the dish first. To prevent this, push the cooked part at the edges towards the centre of the dish before it is set completely, allowing the uncooked eggs to flow to the edges. Remove from oven while still moist. Eggs will complete cooking during standing time.

 I find that after heating water in the microwave, it boils over when I add instant coffee, tea or dry soup mix. How can I prevent this?

 Be sure to stir the water *before* heating it. This incorporates air into the liquid, which will prevent boiling over from happening once cooking has started.

 How can I keep gravy from becoming lumpy, and the edge of the gravy from becoming too thick?

 Stir gravies and sauces frequently with a whisk or fork to obtain a smooth consistency throughout.

 Why am I advised not to deep-fry food in the microwave?

This potentially hazardous procedure is not recommended because the temperature of the cooking oil can climb rapidly in the microwave and the oil can suddenly burst into flames. In addition, microwave-safe cookware may not be able to withstand the intense heat and has been known to crack or explode.

 My food seems to cool more quickly when it has been cooked in the microwave. Why?

 In the microwave, only the food gets hot from the cooking process – any warmth you feel in the dish has been transferred from the food. This is the opposite of what happens in a conventional oven, where the cooking heats up the dish first, then the food, and the hot dish keeps food warmer longer after it is removed from the oven.

To help keep microwaved foods warm, heat food that has been stored in the refrigerator an extra minute or so to give the cooking vessel time to warm. Cover foods while reheating or cooking to hold in warmth. At the table, wrap a covered dish in a pretty towel or quilted casserole holder, or keep warm on a warming tray.

 How can I keep microwaved foods warm without retaining steam? I find crumb-coated chicken dishes get soggy if I use a cover.

 Casserole lids and cling film hold in steam, which may make certain foods limp, such as breads, cakes, or anything with a crumb coating. To prevent this, cover these foods with greaseproof or kitchen paper, which holds in heat but not steam.

 How can I make poultry, meat and fish look as if it has been conventionally cooked?

 Make a sauce to rub on food before the start of cooking: in a glass measuring jug, place enough butter or margarine to coat the food. Heat, covered with kitchen paper, on High (100% power) until butter or margarine melts. Stir in gravy browning, teriyaki, soy or Worcestershire sauces. For a zestier flavour, mix in mustard or tomato ketchup.

To glaze poultry and give it a lovely golden colour, brush it with marmalade, honey or apricot jam during cooking.

You can also brush meat, poultry or fish with butter or margarine, beaten egg, milk or water, then coat with breadcrumbs, crushed cornflakes, herbs, grated cheese or onion soup mix. There are also specially formulated coating mixes with seasonings to complement the taste of meat, poultry or fish.

How can I make breads, cakes, biscuits and pastry cooked in the microwave look as if they have been conventionally baked?

 For a baked appearance, choose recipes that call for brown sugar, black treacle or molasses; alternatively, you can add ground allspice, cinnamon or nutmeg to cake mixtures, or add a few drops of yellow food colouring or gravy browning. Try substituting wholemeal flour for part of the plain flour in tea breads and scones. For an attractive coating to conceal an underdone appearance, evenly sprinkle ground or chopped nuts or wheat germ on to inside of greased cake or loaf dish before adding mixture or dough.

Toppings that add texture and flavour include sugar, chopped nuts, ground cinnamon and toasted coconut.

 When I make caramel in the microwave, I frequently find it burns. How can I prevent this?

 Microwave the mixture just until the sugar is golden; it will continue to cook during its standing time outside the oven, and a deeper colour will develop. A microwave-safe glass measuring jug should always be used. Its handle makes pouring easier, and the special glass can withstand the high cooking temperature of sugar.

 How do you convert conventional recipes for use in the microwave?

 Not all recipes can be converted for microwave cooking, but in general the following rules should be applied: keep serving numbers small – up to eight at the most; reduce liquids, fat and seasoning; use microwave-safe cookware; cut cooking time down to a quarter or a half of the conventional recipe time.

 What foods should be pierced before being cooked in the microwave and why?

 Any food enclosed in a skin or membrane should be pierced to release steam and prevent the food from bursting during cooking. Pierce with a fork whole vegetables with skins, such as potatoes, tomatoes and peppers. Use a cocktail stick for anything with a delicate membrane, such as egg yolks or liver. Sausage casings should also be pierced with a fork or slashed diagonally with a knife.

 Why do some microwave cookery books give a range of timings for recipes?

 This is because of variations in microwave wattage, cookware and density of food. Cook for the shorter time, check to see if food is done, then cook for the longer time if necessary.

 My microwave has a different wattage from that used in most microwave recipes. How do I adjust the timing to give good results?

 If a recipe has been developed in a 600-watt oven, reduce the timing by 10 seconds per minute if you have a 700-watt oven and increase it by 15 seconds per minute if you have a 500-watt oven. This is a very general guide, so check the food frequently to prevent it from overcooking.

 I am instructed to rotate certain foods in the microwave. Why is this?

 In general, rotate foods that cannot be stirred, such as lasagne and bread pudding. Get to know your oven's personality (cooking pattern) by observing how food cooks – for example, food may cook more quickly on one side than the other; if this happens, rotate the dish for more even cooking. Other foods that must be rotated in their dishes include fish that may be too delicate to move, and a cake mixture that has to set. Rotate the dish in one direction only and keep track by marking the cookware with a dot. Place the dish in the microwave with the dot at the oven back. When a quarter turn is specified in the recipe, turn the dish so that the dot is at oven side; for a half turn, rotate the dish so that dot is at the oven front.

 How can I be sure that the microwave has heated shop-bought 'cook-chill' foods thoroughly?

 To ensure that food is piping hot and thoroughly heated through, it is important to follow packet instructions to the letter. Most important is to know the wattage output of your oven and to realise that if your oven has a low wattage output the food will take longer to reach its required temperature than in one with a higher wattage oven. It is also very important to stir, rotate, turn or rearrange food during heating in the microwave, if this is instructed, so that the food is heated properly *throughout*. Microwave ovens have 'cold' spots, so it is important that food is not left to stay in the same position for the total cooking time.

My microwave retains the smell of any strongly spiced dishes I cook, such as curry or chilli con carne. How can I prevent this?

 Be certain to wipe oven clean after each use with a damp cloth. Use a mild detergent when needed. For a quick oven refresher, pour 125 ml water into a 1 litre microwave-safe measuring jug or bowl. Add one of the following fresheners: 2 slices fresh lemon, orange or lime, 1 tablespoon lemon juice, $\frac{1}{4}$ teaspoon ground cinnamon, 8 whole cloves with 8 whole allspice berries. Heat on High (100% power) for 1–2 minutes, or until water boils. Your oven will smell really fresh and clean.

To make your whole kitchen smell wonderfully fresh, try this oven pot-pourri: into 1 litre microwave-safe measuring jug, pour 250 ml warm water; add 2 teaspoons mixed spice or a few thyme sprigs. Heat on High (100% power) for 3 minutes.

DEFROSTING AND REHEATING

 Since the microwave is so useful for reheating food, why am I advised not to reheat egg dishes?

 Most leftovers, such as meat and pasta dishes, reheat very well in the microwave, but delicate egg dishes will overcook if reheated.

The same principle applies when trying to reheat cheese dishes in the microwave; the cheese toughens and becomes stringy.

 Is it a good idea to use the microwave for defrosting food from the freezer?

 Yes. Follow the instructions that come with your oven. In general, most small items can be defrosted by placing them in the microwave for a few seconds on High (100% power). Larger items are best defrosted, covered, on Medium-Low (30% power) or Defrost power level for several minutes at a time, then allowed to stand. They are briefly microwaved again, allowed to stand, and so on until defrosted. This standing time is very important when defrosting larger items because it allows the temperature to equalise throughout the food. Do not microwave until the centre defrosts because the outer edges will start to cook; delicate parts of chicken and fish may have to be shielded with smooth strips of foil. Melted ice should be drained off at intervals. Food should be cooked immediately after defrosting in the microwave.

 How can I tell when an individual dinner reheated in the microwave is ready to serve?

 Allow about 2 minutes for 1 dinner plate of food. Heat, covered, on Medium-High (70% power). Remove from the microwave and feel the centre bottom of the plate. If it is warm, the food is ready to serve; if cool, cook, covered, 1 minute more.

 When I reheat dinners, the centre sometimes stays cold. How can I ensure even reheating?.

 If the food at the edge of the plate is hot while food at the centre is not, cut out a doughnut-shaped piece of foil to place over the food, making sure that the foil is smooth and at least 2.5 cm away from the oven walls. The centre will become hot while the edges will be shielded from microwaves.

Another solution, especially when reheating different types of food, is to arrange denser foods (eg potatoes), which take longer to heat through, at the edge of the plate, while leaving more delicate foods (eg fish) in the centre.

 What size container should I use for defrosting and cooking frozen food?

 Always use a dish that fits the food as closely as possible so that the edges of the food do not melt, spread out over the bottom of a large dish, and burn before the centre of the food is hot. Cover while defrosting to retain heat.

 My family loves hamburgers, so I often make them up in bulk and freeze them. How can I use my microwave for speedier defrosting?

 Freeze the hamburgers with sheets of greaseproof or waxed paper between them. Defrost on Medium-Low (30% power) or Defrost power level; discard the paper as soon as possible, separate the still partially frozen hamburgers, and place in a single layer on a microwave-safe rack set in a baking dish. Using a rack prevents the hamburgers from stewing in their own juices, which could cause the surfaces to start cooking.

 When I reheat baking goods such as rolls or hamburger buns, they become dry. Am I doing something wrong?

 You are overcooking them. Baked goods should be *just* warmed through; otherwise they become dry and tough. Most breads reheat successfully in the microwave if they are wrapped in kitchen paper to absorb moisture. Heat rolls, hamburger buns and bagels on High (100% power) for 10–15 seconds.

The Index

Page numbers in *italics* indicate recipes with step-by-step illustrations

Q

R

Cookery Notes

The recipes in this book are given in metric measurements only. The following charts are a useful guide to converting measures from metric to imperial, if you prefer to use imperial measurements. Do not mix both measures in any one recipe, as they are not interchangeable.

WEIGHT

25 g	1 oz	175 g	6 oz
50 g	2 oz	200 g	7 oz
60 g	2½ oz	225 g	8 oz
75 g	3 oz	250 g	9 oz
100 g	3½ oz	275 g	10 oz
115 g	4 oz	350 g	12 oz
150 g	5 oz	450 g	1 lb

VOLUME

150 ml	5 fl oz (¼ pint)	450 ml	15 fl oz (¾ pint)
200 ml	7 fl oz (⅓ pint)	500 ml	16 fl oz
250 ml	9 fl oz	600 ml	20 fl oz (1 pint)
300 ml	10 fl oz (½ pint)	1 litre	1¾ pints
400 ml	14 fl oz		

All spoon measures used in this book are level unless otherwise indicated and sets of special spoon measures are widely available for accurate measuring: 5 ml = 1 teaspoon; 10 ml = 2 teaspoons; 15 ml = 1 tablespoon.

NUTRITIONAL INFORMATION

Serving portions at the beginning of each recipe are based on the recommended daily amount (RDA) for a healthy, balanced diet. Beneficial nutritional information only is given with each recipe, based on the criteria in the table below, and is not intended for people on special diets. For example, if a recipe is low in sodium but high in cholesterol, only the fact that it is low in sodium will be mentioned.

FAT	2 g or less
CHOLESTEROL	30 mg or less
SODIUM	140 mg or less
FIBRE	3 g or more
VITAMIN C	30 mg or more
VITAMIN A	125 mcg or more

THIAMINE	0.38 mg or more
RIBOFLAVIN	0.43 mg or more
NIACIN	5 mg or more
CALCIUM	100 mg or more
IRON	1.8 mg or more